Tales of Dionysus

Noël-Nicholas Coypel, "The Abduction of Europa" (1727), Philadelphia Museum of Art. Acquired with the kind assistance of John Cadwalader, Jr., through the gift of Mr. and Mrs. Orville Bullitt (by exchange), the Edith H. Bell Fund, and other Museum funds, 1978, 1978-160-1.

Tales of Dionysus

THE *DIONYSIACA* OF NONNUS OF PANOPOLIS

A Group Translation

William Levitan and Stanley Lombardo, Editors

UNIVERSITY OF MICHIGAN PRESS
ANN ARBOR

Published in the United States of America by the
University of Michigan Press
Manufactured in the United States of America
Printed on acid-free paper
First published August 2022

A CIP catalog record for this book is available from the British Library.
Library of Congress Cataloging-in-Publication data has been applied for.

ISBN 978-0-472-13311-6 (hardcover : alk. paper)
ISBN 978-0-472-03896-1 (paper : alk. paper)
ISBN 978-0-472-22036-6 (e-book)

For

Douglass Parker

ΠΟΙΚΙΛΟΝ ΥΜΝΟΝ ΑΡΑΣΣΟΜΕΝ

Contents

Editors' Preface

William Levitan and Stanley Lombardo

We have two aims in mind for this book. The first is to allow readers of English greater access to one of the most extraordinary poems of the Greek literary tradition, the *Dionysiaca* of Nonnus of Panopolis, or as we have rendered the title, *Tales of Dionysus*. The second is to offer a sense of the wide spectrum of possibilities open to the contemporary practice of classical translation. For both we have called upon a set of forty-two translators, a large and diverse group to take on a long and variegated poem.

By any measure, *Tales of Dionysus* is a formidable work. It is by far the longest poem surviving from the classical world, a massive mythological epic stretching to over twenty thousand lines written in the tradition of Homer. In some obvious ways the poem takes its ancestry very much to heart. Nonnus speaks of himself as a son of Homer; he invokes Homer's Muse, uses Homer's verse, Homer's language, his narrative turns and motifs, as if thoroughly at ease in the permanence of the epic world. But *Tales of Dionysus* is also the *last* ancient epic to follow a Homeric model, composed so late in fact that, as Gordon Braden has pointed out ("Nonnos' Typhoon," p. 851), it stands as close in time to the European Renaissance as it does to archaic Greece, and the Homeric Muses, daughters of ancient Memory, are not the only spirits presiding over this poem. At the outset Nonnus also enlists the sea god Proteus, mythical paradigm of endless change, as his "partner and pattern"; "polymorph Proteus," he calls him, "muffled in multifold forms." Flux, not permanence, is the watchword of this poem. Like Proteus certainly, but also like Dionysus with his own fluidity of forms, names, and divine incarnations, like Zeus with his plural disguises for the sake of amorous intrigue, and like the several many-headed, many-armed monsters who inhabit its many pages, the poem itself is continually shifting shape. Out of its formal epic frame spills a tumult of ancient literary types: tragedy, elegy, didactic, panegyric, pastoral idyll, and the novel are all parts of this gigantic enterprise, each genre and its ancient instances coming to the fore one after the other after the other. A son of Homer to be sure, Nonnus is no less a child of Euripides, Hesiod, Callimachus, Theocritus, Longus, and Ovid, among many others. His poem is unabashedly fulsome; unabashedly extreme; unfailingly energetic; at times majestic; at times burlesque; a poem of relentless variety, boundary transgression, and a potential riot of forms. It winds through hundreds of narratives large and small, many of them digressions with only little point, many transparently the same story retold in slightly different form, with different genre features, with a different tone, or with (sometimes) different actors—a kaleidoscope of a poem, continually recombining elements in continually shifting patterns.

It was in part a practical decision to approach this enormous poem through the vehicle of a group translation, although we also saw how apt a way it was to render, even if perhaps to amplify, the poem's protean nature. But as the project developed, we came to appreciate more fully just how provocative this poem can be of diverse translations of a very special stamp. Unlike some standard authors who have attracted translation in anthology form—Dante, Ovid, and Horace all come to mind—Nonnus has only the scantiest tradition of English translation behind him. In the nineteenth century, Thomas Peacock, Elizabeth Barrett Browning, and Charles Abraham Elton each published a few verse snippets of the poem almost as if in passing; in the mid-twentieth century, W. H. D. Rouse published a version of the whole for the Loeb Classical Library in the accurate prose that characterizes the series—and that is all that has ever seen print. This means that the translators in this volume came to the poem as pioneers ready to rethink what translation is and what it can look like. Some chose to take up variants of established modes of classical translation and make those modes their own, self-conscious about the tradition in which they themselves read and write—a very Nonnian position in itself. Some took their cue from Nonnus' verbal overreach, his extremity, wordplay, or arch literary sensibility and wrote up their own versions of that. Some found the violence and bloodthirstiness of Nonnus' narrative to be the inescapable point, what comes at the tail-end of a male heroic tradition. For some, Nonnus' distance in time was something to overcome; for others, difference was something to preserve as lying at the core of all translation. And a few who, as readers, found Nonnus to be less than congenial nonetheless found, as translators, that his poetry forced their hand. *Something* must be done with such a poet. In the pages that follow, forty-two translators offer examples of what that something can be. Toward the end of the book, under the heading "On Translating Nonnus," a cross-section of these translators discuss their reasons why.

The translators brought together for this project come from a range of backgrounds, with different experiences and different potential relationships to the text of Nonnus' poem. This is by design. There are professional Hellenists and academics from non-classical fields; there are poets with deep experience and established reputations as translators, and poets whose work has primarily been in other genres. There is a wide geographical spread and a wide generational spread. Some of the translators have come to the poem through the mediation of Rouse's version. Most have chosen their own books to render. All have determined their own approaches to the poem, to translation, and to poetic form. This also is by design. As editors, we did not seek a unison of voices, or even a harmony, for that matter. We initiated the project, we managed its many steps, we were available for consultation, but we did not orchestrate it, at least not in the sense of seeking to bring all its parts into some kind of concordant whole. The stress has always been on the soloist, on the choices each translator has made, and we have done what we could to encourage each writer's distinctive tones. Long and tangled as it is, Nonnus' poem has a continuous narrative arc; for a convenient sketch, we refer readers to the "Summary of the Poem" printed below. But the individual books of this translation are best understood as individual poetic works, each connected to the others, certainly, but each with its own ambitions and its own sense of decorum.

Our project also has a personal dimension. Toward the end of the 1960s, the late Douglass Parker—extraordinary translator, teacher, performer, and exemplar—encountered Nonnus for the first time and took up the cause with a vengeance, offering innovative courses on the *Dionysiaca* both at his base at the University of Texas and, for a term in 1982, at Dartmouth. One of the products of his enthusiasm was a verse translation of the poem's first 696 lines that he circulated among his students, colleagues, and friends. It looked—and sounded—like little else in the world. In fits and starts over the next decades, Parker kept returning to the piece, mostly to adjust its appearance on the page as the computer replaced the Selectric as his instrument of choice, but the translation has not appeared in print before now. A good number of the contributors to this volume trace their academic lineage through Douglass Parker, including the two of us, and we feel the connection deeply. We never saw the project, though, in terms of piety, that is, as duly completing a task that Doug himself may have started, but more as inviting all to gather for some boisterous conversation with a cherished friend whose voice has kept us company for over fifty years. In this spirit, then, the editors offer the book to the memory of that friend.

Acknowledgments

This book is nothing if not the work of a crowd, and we owe our gratitude to colleagues and friends, individuals and institutions for pitching in to help make it possible. First and foremost, we thank the book's two score translators for their art and industry, their stoic patience, and their resilient sense of humor. We thank Stott Parker for permission to print his father's translations of Nonnus for the first time. We thank Walter Michener for his essential work on the "Summary of the Poem"; and Walter again, along with Charlie Boyles, Bethany Christiansen, and John Gronbeck-Tedesco for their contributions to the "Glossary of Proper Names." The skilled and heroic labor of Alison Parker lies behind the "Suggestions for Further Reading," and we are gratefully in her debt. We thank Debra Nails for lending her extensive intellectual, technical, and editorial talents to each page of our work. We are grateful to the staff of the University of Michigan Press and in particular to Ellen Bauerle for the support she gave the project in its tentative, early stages, and to our Production Editor, Mary Hashman, who saved our bacon on more than one occasion. Our frontispiece, Noël-Nicholas Coypel's "The Abduction of Europa," is reproduced with the permission of the Philadelphia Museum of Art. The original of our cover art-work, "The Triumph of Bacchus," the painter Dosso Dossi's unsettling take on European expansionism *circa* 1514, resides in the collection of the Chhatrapati Shivaji Maharaj Vastu Sangrahalaya in Mumbai, India; we thank Anne Shaw and Mike Shaw for putting us on its trail. We owe the title *Tales of Dionysus* to its use in the doctoral dissertation of our old friend and colleague, Jack Winkler, and we gladly acknowledge the borrowing, as we imagine how pleased he himself would have been by the project.

Introduction

Gordon Braden

What you have in your hands (or on your tablet) is a new English translation, by various hands, of one of the strangest and least known monuments in Western literature, an astonishingly intact forty-eight-book Greek epic (the *Iliad* and the *Odyssey* are each twenty-four books, Vergil's *Aeneid* a mere twelve) on the life of the god Dionysus—Dionysus Mainomenos, the "mad god," Homer called him—that is the longest, last, and least accountable epic poem of a tradition in which epic held pride of place. It was the classical epic to end all classical epics—which, as it happens, it did. At 20,426 lines, it is, if the truth be told, an almost impossible read. It seems longer than that, with a sprawling, repetitive, digressive, often confusing narrative, relentlessly violent (some very weird battle scenes and ugly sexual assaults take up well more than half of it), written in a highly mannered mutation of Homer's language and style that comes across as tightly ordered and insanely unruly at the same time. Just to put it that way is to suggest what might fascinate someone about the poem: this telling of the story of Dionysus is itself a Bacchic rout, as told by a participant caught up in the frenzy. After living with the poem for five decades, I am still not sure what to make of it, not sure whether it is any kind of artistic success or even what that would mean in a case like this, but it got its hooks into me and hasn't let go. I am not alone, as I found out when I was approached (in an outdoor Greek theater in Lynchburg, Virginia, an incongruity on which I've had occasion to meditate) about being part of the current project, which is an attempt to share that experience with readers who may at this point have no idea what is waiting for them.

The only solid bit of biographical information that we have about Nonnus, from an adjective regularly accompanying his name, is that he was from a city near the southern rim of the Roman empire now known as Akhmim but in his own time as Panopolis, "Pan's City." It is a fair-sized outpost on a bend in the Nile some four hundred miles upriver from Alexandria (Cairo, an Arab foundation, was not to exist for several more centuries). The invocation to the *Dionysiaca* and an epigram putatively by Nonnus in the Greek Anthology both suggest that he composed his epic in Alexandria, and in view of the considerable, if often chaotic, book-learning represented in his poetry, it is entirely likely that he had the assistance of the Roman world's greatest library. Various kinds of evidence indicate a literary *floruit* in the fifth century AD, possibly as late as 470. That is an unexpected time to be composing a monumental epic on the life of a pagan deity; late in the previous century, Theodosius I had completed the establishment of Nicene Christianity as the official religion of the empire, forbidden pagan cultic ceremonial, and silenced the Delphic oracle. At least two Christian churchmen possibly of the right time, more or less—a bishop and an abbot—were called Nonnus (maybe a nickname, something like "uncle"), and our author could conceivably have been one of them. The historical odds are certainly strong that our poet was some kind of Christian. It accordingly both is and is not a surprise that Nonnus' name has also been consistently attached to a verse paraphrase (*metabolê*), in almost exactly the same strange style as the *Dionysiaca*, of the Gospel according to John. That attribution has sometimes been disputed but is now accepted, and it locates Nonnus astride the great cultural division of his time, though without giving us any clear indication of what to make of that. An immense amount of inconclusive scholarship has gone into trying to sort things out: for instance, establishing the chronology of the two works as being written sequentially either by a pagan who converted or by a Christian who, like the emperor Julian a century earlier, turned apostate. These arguments have proved no more secure than theories that Nonnus was engaged in some syncretic project of unifying the two religious dispensations, or subtly critiquing one of those dispensations under the cover of serving it. All we can say with assurance is that as classical Greek poetry Nonnus' two big poems share the same literary space, and for a poet with a strong sense of style that may be all that needs saying.

The only definite context we can establish for the *Dionysiaca* is a corpus of poetry written in a very similar style: brief epics on events at the end and the beginning of the Trojan war by, respectively, Triphiodorus (third century) and Colluthus (fifth century); a brief epic on Hero and Leander by Musaeus (undatable, fifth or sixth century?); epigrams and an extended description of Hagia

Sophia by Paul the Silentiary (sixth century); some fragmentary ceremonial and panegyric poetry by Dioscorus of Aphrodito (sixth century); a few other texts. Beyond the works themselves and the names of the authors we have almost no circumstantial information here. (Musaeus is also the name of a mythic friend of the original Orpheus, so that may be some kind of *nom de plume.*) It used to be conventional to speak of a "school of Nonnus"; things now look too spread out for that, though Egyptian connections do seem to be at work (Triphiodorus is said to have been from Panopolis, and Colluthus and Dioscorus from other cities in the Egyptian Thebaid). The clearest marker of this poetic brotherhood is their observance of a newly restrictive set of rules for the dactylic hexameter, resembling the Hellenistic practice of Callimachus but tighter. These rules make the meter notably more dactylic, and give a propulsive, emphatic bass line to a new brand of epic diction, heavy with polysyllabic adjectives (some of them apparently compounded on the spot) and unexpected verbs. Here from the *Dionysiaca* is the suicide of the defeated general Orontes, an action traditionally seen as noble and somber: αὐτοφόνῳ βαρύποτμος ἐπεσκίρτησε σιδήρῳ. The flair of this, like most of Nonnus' stylistic signatures, defies transfer into English; an attempt to copy it directly yields leaden translationese. As literally as I can manage: "heavy-fated he leapt / skipped / danced onto his self-slaying sword." The same root verb, without the prefix, is later used to describe the death throes of a speared dolphin. I can't think of any way in English to reproduce the effect of having the line bookended by the sword and its modifier, or that of having four Greek words exactly fill out the long line of the hexameter. (Four-word hexameters are not alien to Homer, but they are a much more common flourish for Nonnus, who brings off three of them in the opening invocation of his epic.) At the general's death, an opulent blanket of adjectives swirls about a sudden balletic shriek of energy. By this point in the poem, the reader is used to moments like that. The disorienting symbiosis of elaboration and vehemence is part of the poet's own bardic self-characterization: *poikilon hymnon arassô*, I bang out a multiform anthem—there using a verb that Pindar uses for what the fire-breathing oxen of Colchis do to the ground with their hooves.

The violence of Nonnus' diction blends readily with the violence of most of the poem's action. The central episode is the mad god's bloody conquest of India, which starts in Book 13 and doesn't end until Book 40 (with a six-year pause between Books 24 and 25). This war is flanked by a tumultuous battle between Zeus and the polymorphous giant Typhon in the first two books and a gigantomachy that Hera raises up against Dionysus in the last; there is also a brief civil war among the Olympians in Book 36. The battle scenes throughout are brutal, lengthy, and fantastical:

> With their goat-hooves the Pans tore up the bodies
> of their enemy. One Pan pierced a fleeing enemy
> warrior on his horns, pitched him flying
> over the peaks, head over heels.
> Crops were scythed, and with the crops, enemy
> heads rolled down for Dionysus, the blades
> dripping with a blood libation drunk by the victors.
> A goat-footed Pan laced a man's hands
> behind his neck and then ramrodded him
> in the gut with his sharp horn.
> Another man was smashed between the eyes
> as he ran to cudgel yet another Pan.

Catherine Anderson's translation of a passage in Book 17 sounds like the storyboard for a CGI set piece in some superhero movie; over its longer stretches, Nonnus' epic does sometimes come across as a dark-winged anticipation of that art form. In and around the battles are the attempted rapes, some of them successful and some of them not. Four of the former are committed by the god himself. One of the latter involves a freshly slain woman warrior and comes right up to the edge of necrophilia. Cases where the rapist is defeated can themselves be gaudily violent and perfect for CGI: twice a female warrior in the god's army fends off an assault when a snake appears between her breasts and wraps itself around her suddenly terrified attacker.

Nonnian Greek, however, inflects its characteristic tensions even into the poem's quiet scenes, such as Cadmus' visit in Book 3 to the gardens of Electra to meet his bride-to-be Harmonia. There, two rivulets "thundered gently 'round the Laurel's Roots, / Like Phoebus played for Daphne on the Lute." The Greek verb behind "thundered gently" is *epebombee*, boomed or roared out—as if in miniaturized imitation of Dionysus Bromius, the roaring god. The reference to Apollo and Daphne continues a string of erotic intimations as a light breeze stirs the crowded, flourishing garden: male palms pledge their love to female palms, the myrtle of Aphrodite intimidates the laurel that shied away from her divine lover, and the hyacinth stirs poignant memories of another love of Apollo's. The last of those prompts a touchstone line that can be taken as a kind of aesthetic and even philosophical manifesto: ἄστατον ὄμμα τίταινε πόθων ἀκόρητος Ἀπόλλων. More or less: Apollo, insatiable with desire, strains / stretches his restless eye. In the translation you will be reading below, "Apollo seethed / With longing." Nonnus' verb, a slightly fancified epic reduplication of a shorter one, is used by Homer for a horse pulling a chariot, oxen pulling a plow, a man stretching out his arms to carry something; it would be a good verb to use for isometric exercises. After Homer and Hesiod, it all but disappears from Greek literature until Nonnus makes it one of his favorite, indeed obsessively favorite verbs, used in a wide range of contexts. Less than a hundred lines later it describes the way Cadmus reaches out to serve himself at Electra's table (he does have reason for feeling a bit tense about how lunch is going). Applied to Apollo's eye, the verb suggests fierce intentness manifested in rapid small movements as the god scans the garden seeking the object of his desire. The movements are endless and the desire insatiable. The two adjectives, *astatos* (unstable) and *akorêtos* (unsatisfied), are also among Nonnus' favored terms, and together, like the towers of a suspension bridge, they give the line its profile; this is the sort of thing the contemporary Italian scholar Enrico Livrea has in mind when (in his critical edition of chapter 2 of the *Metabolê* [2000], p. 100) he calls adjectives the "loadbearing structure" (*la struttura portante*) of Nonnus' style. Even the gentle shining of the sun on a peaceful garden testifies to a universe taut with ceaseless agitation.

The poem is densely but playfully self-conscious about its own literary past. Epic conventions are conspicuously observed, specific Homeric passages quoted or imitated. It's likely that if the records of classical Greek literature, especially post-Homeric epic, weren't so tattered, the catalogue of evocations of Nonnus' predecessors would be even longer. Some scholars think it should include nods to Ovid's *Metamorphoses*, which would be an unparalleled instance of Latin influence on Greek literature (that library at Alexandria did have a lot of books). Homage can be especially gamesome with some of Homer's signature phrases. The beautiful nymph Nicaea is a new rosy-fingered dawn, handsome Cadmus has a rosy-fingered palm, the goddess of persuasion is hailed as rosy-fingered Peitho. We hear of a wine-dark grape cluster, wine-dark ivy, a wine-dark victory, and more than once of wine-dark Bacchus (the wine-dark wine god). The famously onomatopoetic *polyphloisboios*, which

Homer applies repeatedly to the much-resounding sea, gets even more of a workout, being applied to, among other things, life, battle, anxious thoughts, and Thetis' house under the ocean; a calm sea is, on the other hand, *aphloisboios.*

At the other end of the scale, the sheer scope of the *Dionysiaca* outdoes that of previous epics. Its action is set before the time of the Homeric epics; that in itself is not unprecedented—Hesiod tells of these times in his *Theogony*, and a papyrus fragment from the first century AD appears to be from an epic about Dionysus—but the prophetic reach of Nonnus' poem also encompasses the rest of ancient history the way the Old Testament has been said to prefigure the New. The Trojan war is still in the future, but the poem already knows about Achilles. The invasion of India is the template for what will be the climax of Alexander the Great's legendary career. The Romans are foreseen, and their establishment of universal empire and the rule of law and, the poem's vision exceeding even that of the *Aeneid*, the empire's shift of power and authority eastward with (skipping over any reference to Constantinople) the establishment of the law school at Beirut (Beroë), known in the empire as the "Mother of Laws" and a major player in Justinian's consolidation of the Roman legal code. We hear about this from Nonnus immediately after the conclusion of the Indian war, when the epic poet turns to an encomium of Beirut, not just the oldest city in the world, twin sister of Time, the site where (not many people know this) Aphrodite first emerged from the sea before transiting to Cyprus, but also *Dikês pedon, astu themistôn*, the Land of Justice and City of Laws (the list goes on), and also home to the eponymous nymph Beroë, who was born to Oceanus and Tethys (or actually it was Aphrodite and Adonis), and whose beauty made both Dionysus and Poseidon fall in love with her and fight a great contest which is about to take two more books in the telling . . . by which point, and for far from the first time in reading and trying to think about the *Dionysiaca*, it has all started to seem—what's the word?—goofy. Is this some kind of joke? And if so, what kind?

History did have a specific joke to make, and sooner than Nonnus could have expected: the timeless glory of the Beirut law school, pinnacle of classical civilization, was summarily ended by an earthquake and a tsunami in 551. The main plot line of the *Dionysiaca*, though, anticipates no such reproof; it is unapologetically triumphalist, the story of its hero's struggle to transcend his hybrid identity as the son of a god and a mortal to join the ranks of the Olympians. Thanks among other things to the hostility of Hera, who plays a role like that of Poseidon in the *Odyssey* and Juno in the *Aeneid*, Dionysus encounters his reversals (including an ill-starred first birth as Zagreus) but ultimately succeeds. This struggle takes place in a cosmos with an ongoing history of brutal generational conflict. Zeus' overthrow of his own father Cronus is a vivid recent memory, and the insurgency of Typhon in the first two books threatens to repeat the kind of celestial regime change that both Zeus and his father had shown could be brought about. Typhon spends time in Book 1 imagining what his new order might be like, but his revolutionary ambitions collapse into the chaos that becomes the poem's usual weather. Chaos, as Lord Baelish is happy to observe in *Game of Thrones*, is a ladder; Dionysus himself has no thought of challenging the Olympian order as such but simply wants his place in it.

That ambition sharply distinguishes his epic from its most important predecessors, whose principal characters are mortal human beings who remain mortal and have no serious expectation of being anything else. The tragedy of that limitation is powerfully felt and gives those poems their emotional depth. The Homeric poems take place in a world obsessed with memorialization but effectively without history; the message of Achilles' iconic shield toward the end of the *Iliad* is that human life will never be different from what it is now. The *Aeneid* looks forward to a time when Rome will change the rules of human history and bring warfare to an end, but the poem itself is suffused with a deep and even subversive feel for the mortal cost of that prospective achievement, the *lacrimae rerum* never wiped away by the triumph. The epic struggle in the *Dionysiaca*, by contrast, is one of individualistic ambition, and one in which mortality is left heartlessly behind. Dionysus does so at the head of an immense army, composed not only of conventional Homeric warriors, catalogued in the classic Homeric manner, but also of great cohorts of Bassarids, Corybants, satyrs, Pans (as in Panopolis; Nonnus seems to think of them as large satyrs), sileni (essentially old satyrs, though more human in their physiognomy), dryads, centaurs, cyclopes, panthers, and other assorted animals, all contributing to the fight in their own vigorously described ways. (Satyrs, Nonnus does admit, aren't of much military use, being short on discipline and courage, but they do make a colorful and festive addition to the war effort.) Yet Dionysus himself is alone at the head of it all; he has no beloved Patroclus, no faithful Achates, certainly no Penelope. His military career is punctuated by his intense but always transient desire for a series of young virgins, some of whom elude him (Beroë, as it happens, is one of these; she marries Poseidon). Most of them don't. Late in the poem he successively marries two of them, Ariadne and Pallene (the latter after first killing her evil father), but doesn't stay with either. Ariadne is turned to stone by Perseus, but her angry spirit later makes clear that she feels that Dionysus has deserted her, just like Theseus. The god is sad she feels this way and does at the end take her crown with him to Olympus as a memento. Nicaea and Aura he rapes after they have passed out from wine. Aura as a result gives birth to twins and in derangement and despair kills one of them and then commits suicide; Dionysus has the surviving child passed on to Nicaea to raise. We are at this point almost done. The ending does seem rushed, but there is some appropriateness to that; five quick lines report the god's final apotheosis as he ascends, unaccompanied by any earthly companions, to his father's heaven and successfully completes the divestiture of his humanity. At Zeus' table, we are told, he exchanges wine for nectar as his drink of choice.

The thing is, the wine which no longer interests him is his main legacy as far as mortals are concerned, the main difference he makes in their lives. The great Indian campaign against opponents regularly characterized as dark-skinned (*aithopes* as in Ethiopian, *kyaneoi* as in cyanotic; we get a brief glimpse of Dionysus shaking his golden hair against his snowy cheeks) makes the poem into antiquity's uncanny prophetic epic about European imperialism. Actually establishing an empire, though, shows no signs of being anywhere on Dionysus' mind. The stated motivation for the invasion is perfunctory, and after the death of the Indian king Deriades India and its people abruptly disappear from the poem, nothing said about annexation or colonization—but then Dionysus never shows interest in worldly governance of any kind. He's not the type. The permanent difference that he makes in life down here is his discovery and proselytizing of wine, a previously unknown kind of sweetness with previously unknown powers. The immediate contrast is with honey, which does not make you drunk and also soon becomes cloying. Wine, once you start, brings no *koros*, satiety; you can go on drinking forever, or at least until you drop. Dionysus' discovery of this astonishing improvement, in Books 11–12, follows from his first experience in love, his total infatuation with a beautiful young boy (with an adorable little tail) named Ampelos, who is killed while bull riding and metamorphoses after death into a grapevine; *ampelos* then becomes the Greek word for such a plant. Dionysus realizes wine's power as a palliative for the grim fact of mortality, and makes something of a crusade, alongside and sometimes inside his military campaign (on more than one occasion Dionysus turns rivers into wine and gets his enemies helplessly drunk), of encouraging its spread throughout the world. The great scene comes in Books 18–19, when Dionysus discovers that one of his earliest followers, the Assyrian prince Staphylos (the Greek word for "grape-cluster"), has died and left his wife Methê (intoxication) and son Botrys (another word for "grape-cluster") in unconsolable grief. The god-in-training knows just what they need and introduces them to wine and before long they are feeling no pain. The funeral turns into a party, and the widow discovers that she no longer cares that her husband is dead, or for that matter her father, and it would not even grieve her if she lost her son, and makes an extraordinary declaration: "I'll take Bacchus for husband, for father, for son." She has found her savior, and he is a trinity.

Is this some kind of joke? We suddenly feel at the crossroads where the two vectors of Nonnus' literary output meet, to baffling effect. The Christian doctrine of the Trinity is part of the Nicene creed, promulgated in 325; the concept of the third person as husband fits with Matthew 1.18, where Mary is "found with child of the Holy Ghost." The whole scene at Staphylos' palace, once you stop to notice, has obvious affinities with the scene at the house of Lazarus in Bethany; Nonnus comes to that story as a matter of course in his *Metabolê* of John. Does the linguistic continuity between Staphylos the man and *staphylos* the grape-cluster that brings joy to the man's bereaved family count as a resurrection to complete the parallel? It could be some transmigratory form of resurrection, or a metaphor or allegory of resurrection (standards there would be less exacting), though it could also, since the final blessedness is unconscious stupor while the staff clean up around you, be a parody, even a mockery of resurrection. It is hard to escape the sense that some kind of web is being strung, or stringing itself, between Nonnus' two texts. The rivers Dionysus turns into wine could constitute weaponized transubstantiation; in the second chapter of John is the wedding at Cana, where Jesus introduces just that miracle, and some of Nonnus' Dionysiac vocabulary slips right into place in the *Metabolê* (the wineless table is *abakheutoios*, un-Bacchic). Later Jesus will tell his disciples, "I am the true vine" (John 15.1), where the Greek word is *ampelos*; Nonnus enhances this to "I am *zoês ampelos*, the grapevine of life." What has become perhaps the most quoted line in the *Dionysiaca*, spoken by one of the Fates when Dionysus' grief for Ampelos leads to the creation of wine, has an almost shockingly Christian sound to it: "Lord Bacchus wept and washed away the tears of humankind / with his own." This echoes Jesus' famous response to hearing of Lazarus' death, "Jesus wept" (John 11.35); it comes even closer to a line in a fourth-century commentary on John by one of the early church fathers, Cyril of Alexandria, which if Nonnus was a churchman it would have made sense for him to consult when composing the *Metabolê*: "the Lord weeps so that he may relieve our tears." These intimated parallels between Christ and Dionysus are stubbornly hard to add up. Assimilating Dionysus to Christ snags on the details of Nonnus' portrayal of the former. Assimilating Christ to Nonnus' Dionysus yields something like the mordant twentieth-century affirmation of William Carlos Williams in the poem he entitles "Io Baccho!":

> God created alcohol to release
> and engulf us. Shall I
> say it is the only evidence of God
> in this environment? (*Collected Later Poems* [1963], p. 135)

The pagan/Christian grid, however, may not be the ideal framework for reading Nonnus' epic. One extraordinary document offers a look at how unpredictable and unaccountable the spiritual mix in late antiquity could be even after the institutional triumph of Christianity. A hagiography, extant in Syriac and Greek, by a deacon who calls himself Jacob tells the story of how his bishop, named as it happens Nonnus, summoned to a council of bishops in Antioch, reacted to his first meeting with the woman who became St. Pelagia. In an idle moment the churchmen were sitting in front of their lodging when a wealthy local courtesan came by:

> in front of her was a great throng of her servants and she herself was decked out with gold ornaments, pearls, and all sort of precious stones, resplendent in luxurious and expensive clothes. On her hands and feet she wore armbands, silks, and anklets decorated with all sorts of pearls, while around her neck were necklaces and strings of pendants and pearls. Her beauty stunned those who beheld her, captivating them in their desire for her. . . . As this prostitute passed in front of us, the scent of her perfumes and the reek of her cosmetics hit everyone in the vicinity. The bishops as they sat there were amazed at her and her clothes, as well as the splendor of her cortege, and the fact that she went by with her head uncovered, with a scarf thrown round her shoulders in a shameless fashion, as though she were a man; indeed in her haughty impudence her garb was not very different from a man's, apart from her makeup, and the fact that her skin was as dazzling as snow. To put it briefly, her appearance incited everyone who set eyes on her to fall in love with her. (*Holy Women of the Syrian Orient*, trans. Sebastian P. Brock and Susan Ashbrook Harvey [1987], pp. 42–43)

The other bishops "averted their eyes from her, as though she was some sinful object," but bishop Nonnus has a very different reaction; he "observed her carefully in his mind, filled with wonder. Once she had passed in front of them, he turned away his face, placed his head between his knees, and wept with great feeling, so much so that his lap was filled with tears." It seemed as if he couldn't stop; the hair shirt that he always wore under his episcopal garb got soaked.

The outcome is of course foretold; it comes with the *genre*. The woman will be converted and renounce her sinful life and become a Christian saint (and, interestingly, take to wearing men's clothing). But to get there we have to pass through Nonnus' reaction to the sight of her in her full profane splendor, a reaction so overwhelming that it is a while before he can do anything but weep. If the account stopped here, we would have the scenario for a potential poem by Constantine Cavafy, a companion maybe to "The God Abandons Antony." In that never-written poem, the pious churchman's weeping for the sinfulness of the woman's beauty would also be weeping for what he knows will be his role in depriving her of it. (Indeed later, as St. Pelagia, "her astounding beauty had all faded away, her laughing and bright face . . . had become ugly, her pretty eyes had become hollow and cavernous as the result of much fasting and the keeping of vigils" [p. 60].) When the bishop in Jacob's story finds his voice again, his explanation is different from either of those. He has, he says, been awed and humbled by the example of her virtuoso self-cultivation: "What a reproach to us, seeing that we have not taken pains to make ourselves pleasing to God nearly as much as this prostitute we saw passing in front of us has taken pains to please men"—and he ends with a startling declaration: "maybe we should even go and become the pupils of this lascivious woman." There is much to be learned from her artistry: "I imagine she must have spent many hours in her boudoir putting on her eye-black, making herself up and dressing in her finery; she will have looked at her face in the mirror with the greatest attention, making sure there is not the slightest speck of dirt on it" (p. 44). Attempts have been made to identify this Nonnus with the fifth-century Nonnus who was bishop of Edessa (in what is now Turkey), and also with the fifth-century poet, though dates don't align perfectly. The deacon tells us that his bishop hailed from the Egyptian Thebaid, though he also tells us that "he had no secular education" (p. 47), which the poet clearly did. Whether this Nonnus is our Nonnus or not, he demonstrates the possibility at his still volatile moment in cultural history of, at least for individuals, a response that cuts impulsively and recklessly across some stern lines of demarcation. The bishop's devout Christianity does not make him, as do the other bishops in Antioch and as becomes a *cliché* for centuries of medieval and early modern churchmen, reflexively avert his eyes from the astonishing spectacle of this woman's carefully crafted beauty. Nor does he disown his admiring response to this miracle that as he admits is not of God's making but of her own.

Terms keep coming up in Jacob's account that are also woven deeply into the text of the *Dionysiaca*, as they have been in almost everyone's discussion of it: astonishment, amazement, wonder, miracle. We meet them all over the place. When Dionysus comes upon the abandoned Ariadne, the sight makes him mix love with wonder and speak with an astonished voice; *mega thauma*, great wonder, recurs as an interjection throughout the poem like a music cue. Such words are unmistakably the poem's aesthetic, signals for an effect that the poet relentlessly seeks out, one with affinities to what comes to be called the sublime, but more tumultuous. It is there in the poem's way of beginning *in medias res*: not in this case in the middle of the hero's narrative (there is no flashback structure, and Dionysus will not be born until Book 8—no one familiar with English literature can keep from thinking of *Tristram Shandy*) but with the bizarre tableau of Europa (what does she have to do with any of this?) freshly abducted, clinging to the back of a huge bull that by plying his legs the way a hummingbird flaps its wings can scud across the open water without even getting wet, like a hovercraft. That spectacle occupies almost a hundred lines. The first character we hear from is an unnamed Achaean sailor who takes a gander at what's going on and (gobsmacked as it were) cries out, "Eyes, what is this wonder?"—the start of an extended speech in which he tries, with unavailing ingenuity, to answer his own question. Has Zeus invented sea-going land? Is the moon goddess Selene riding a bull? Is the sea nymph Thetis driving a chariot on a watery racetrack? And so on, for thirty-two lines, with no real conclusion. At which point the Achaean sailor is out of this saga; he is conjured into existence solely to register amazement. The endless intoxicated narrative that begins this way exists to generate wonders, unpredictable and inexplicable reconfigurations of the bits and pieces of over a millennium of epic poetry, in a world hungry for miracles.

More on that shortly.

This massive poem's survival essentially intact is itself something of a wonder. That survival appears to have depended on a single manuscript, copied out in Constantinople in 1280 and in 1427 exfiltrated to Italy as the Byzantine empire entered its last decades. Ultimately the manuscript came to repose in Florence in a library designed by Michelangelo while the last scenes of the Italian Renaissance played out around it. (It is still there.) Important humanists (Angelo Poliziano, Marc-Antoine Muret) read the poem and left brief but enthusiastic comments about it. Copies were made, and one of these probably provided the text for an edition from the Plantin press in Antwerp in 1569, the poem's debut in print. A Latin translation by Einhard Lubin was printed at Hanau in 1605, and another edition there five years later offered a revised Greek text, Lubin's Latin, and extensive scholarly and critical commentary by a new circle of scholars (Petrus Cunaeus, Joseph Scaliger, Daniel Heinsius). The first vernacular translation, into French, was published in Paris in 1625. Nonnus' epic, by this point, had its place on the Western European literary map. That place, however, stayed small. After the initial excitement of the humanists, the novelty of reaching land's end of the classical canon wore off and comparisons with Homer became better informed, more acute, and more censorious. Heinsius confessed to a youthful enthusiasm for Nonnus, but had been set right by Scaliger and Cunaeus; he now saw the *Dionysiaca* as more a chaos than a poem, a judgment with which even fans find it hard to argue. Scorn among professional classicists became, at least in the anglophone world, a long-running tradition. The Loeb edition comes with an introduction by H. J. Rose so contemptuous of Nonnus and the poem ("a faded and overcrowded tapestry, moving a little now and then as the breath of his sickly and unwholesome fancy stirs it") that you wonder why he undertook the assignment. Perhaps several colleagues had already begged off.

Things were somewhat different in the literary and art worlds, whose citizens, despite their reputation for snobbery, tend to be less interested in judging or ranking what they read than in what they can make of it. Seldom if ever a school text, the *Dionysiaca* did keep finding its way over the centuries to writers and painters who thought it worth reading or at least consulting. The documentable record of this is discontinuous but once started keeps going. Even before the poem saw print, Ronsard expanded a characteristic conceit from the *Dionysiaca* (the personified Seasons were feeling sad and pointless before the introduction of viticulture) into the climax of his hymn to Autumn ("Bacchus woos and marries Autumn and ends her melancholy with the joy of wine"). When Milton's devils, faced with free time in hell, "with vast Typhoean rage more fell / Rend up both rocks and hills, and ride the air / In whirlwind," close scrutiny of possible sources establishes that the reference has to be to the first two books of Nonnus' epic. Goethe became interested in Nonnus after reading the German-language study that a Russian scholar published in St. Petersburg. Thomas Love Peacock was an enthusiast, recommending the poet to friends (leading to Nonnus' cameo appearance in Percy Shelley's "Defence of Poetry") and quoting him in several novels; the quotations in *The Misfortunes of Elphin* (1829) cast Seithenyn ap Seithyn, the legendary alcoholic warrior of Arthurian Wales, as an avatar of Dionysus. Passages from the *Dionysiaca* were translated by Elizabeth Barrett Browning into rhymed English pentameters, and by Marguerite Yourcenar into intermittently rhymed French alexandrines; Simone Weil took an interest in Nonnus. The German avant-gardist Stefan George, in a eulogy for his friend Stéphane Mallarmé in 1898, rapturously remembered their devotion to the "tormented and subjugated style" of late classical poetry, and especially "how the hard-born verses of the hot-blooded Egyptian, which hum and hurry along like Maenads, filled us with more delight than those of old Homer." Cavafy, in a poem he did write (in the first months of World War I), imagined a group of fugitive Byzantines meeting quietly under assumed names in what was by then Arab Alexandria: "The other day we read some lines by Nonnos: / what imagery, what rhythm, what diction and harmony! / All enthusiasm, how we admired the Panopolitan" ("Exiles," trans. Edmund Keeley and Philip Sherrard). The sound of those unmistakable hexameters brought comfort in dark times.

As reception history, this one has no particular arc to it; it is mostly an array of interesting anecdotes. The most ambitious attempt at an exception made an impression in its own time, but proved something of a stillbirth. In the early seventeenth century, the trendsetting Italian baroque poet Giambattista Marino discovered the *Dionysiaca* through Lubin's Latin translation while already at work on what was supposed to be a brief telling, under a thousand lines, of the story of Venus and Adonis, itself tracing back to less than a hundred lines in Ovid's *Metamorphoses*. Nonnus' inspiration and guidance helped make Marino's *L'Adone* one of the monsters of European literature, at 40,984 lines almost exactly twice as long as the *Dionysiaca*. The larger stage—more like an arena—generously accommodates the shameless opulence and intricacy of the verbal manner already being called Marinismo. The poem circulated in manuscript and was famous even before its publication in Paris in 1623, accompanied by a lengthy essay by the young Jean Chapelain (later to be one of France's most influential literary critics, here making his first appearance in print) in which he praises Marino's poem for its very Nonnian qualities of *la diversité* and *le merveille*, copiousness and wonder. Marino would have had no trouble recognizing Nonnus as a soulmate, and probably have been grateful to find classical authority for his own literary instincts. The poem was scandalous (the Catholic church almost immediately placed the printed book on its Index) and an international sensation, easily outselling the Shakespeare Folio that appeared the same year. It is now of course almost forgotten.

Still, just when you think that's all there is to it, something turns up—in this case a long unnoticed treatment by a French rococo painter of what that Achaean sailor sees in the epic's opening scene. It is perhaps the most assured artistic response from any of Nonnus' readers to his work, and deserves to hang at the entry to the present book. Early on the *Dionysiaca* joined the library of sources drawn upon by painters for scenes from antiquity, and its mark has been detected in mythological paintings of Nicholas Poussin and Claude Lorrain. Recently Robert Shorrock, a scholar who has spent much of his career with Nonnus, has been able to demonstrate that the second of two versions of the abduction of Europa by Noël-Nicolas Coypel is a deliberate rendering of the scene as Nonnus presents it—and, the more you take it in, a surprisingly insightful and resonant one. ("*Ut poesis pictura*. Nonnus' Europa Episode as Poetry and Painting," in *Nonnus of Panopolis in Context II*, ed. Herbert Bannert and Nicole Kröll [2018], pp. 374–92.) Coypel's first painting on the subject (1722) was based more conventionally on Ovid, but the second (1727, currently in the Philadelphia Museum of Art) matches both in specifics—Shorrock calls it "a perfect pictorial mirror of the textual Nonnus"—and in general spirit the suddenly, festively busy crowd scene that Nonnus conjures up out on the water. In places, it even goes Nonnus one better. The frightened girl on a bull is of course there, but also the sea god Poseidon himself, his wife Amphitrite (not actually at the scene in Nonnus but mentioned in passing), his son Triton (blowing on a conch as if for a wedding procession), the wind god Boreas up above (attracting Europa's attention with his own pneumatic assault), the lesser sea god Nereus and assorted nereids (several of them literalizing what is only a simile in the Greek by riding or trying to ride dolphins), even a river god (Enipeus, his identification requiring a bit of detective work), and cupids all over the place, up in the air, frolicking in the water. Coypel doesn't get everything; he passes on the uncanny water-walking of Nonnus' bull—this one is realistically (if that's the word) paddling away chest-deep in the ocean—and doesn't find a place for Athena, who Nonnus tells us blushed at what's going on. And Coypel also omits that anonymous Achaean sailor—but as Shorrock points out, that omission has the effect, very possibly deliberate, of putting the viewer in that character's place. And if you think about it, a decidedly WTF look on the bull's face (Shorrock's term is "perplexed") reflects back the viewer's own likely response to this aquatic mythological barnyard: the lustful king of the gods is as addled by all this as we are. Coypel's snapshot readies us for the rest of the poem.

Which, as it happens, is where I come in. I first encountered the *Dionysiaca* a half century ago when I was a graduate student in classics at the University of Texas and signed up, almost on a whim, for a seminar on the *Dionysiaca* taught by the late Douglass Parker, whom I knew mainly through his inventive translations of Aristophanes. At that point I had never even heard of the poem; the lure Parker offered in fishing for students who might otherwise wander off after Euripides or Horace was precisely the disorientation of this opening tableau. Parker called it "the best attested rape in classical antiquity," but epitomized it in the speech of the Achaean sailor as a tumble of inventive detail with no center. A hundred lines of ingenious speculation get us only from "What's that?" to "I don't know." That opening followed us through the semester, inflecting everything. Parker's question to the class, over and over again, was "What *is* this thing?" And his characteristic way of trying to answer such a hopeless question was translation, trying to find or create a manner in English, a style of addled vehemence, that might make poetic sense of what was so clamorously going on in the Greek. Below, with Book 1 and the first part of Book 2, you can read his answer, as far as he got, animated by his intimation (which he passed on to me and others) that this unintended last hurrah of classical pagan literature (*iakhe phônên!*) is indeed some kind of joke—not necessarily the kind that makes you laugh (though it's always good when that happens) but the kind that makes your jaw drop, and sometimes stay there for a while. Like the artful prostitute in front of the bishop, it might also make you weep, though it does help if you've had enough to drink. The suspicion that the poem is somehow funny (James Joyce always insisted that *Ulysses* was funny) surfaces frequently in what over the last fifty years has become a substantial body of respectful commentary on Nonnus' epic, though scholars usually then hurry on to something easier to discuss and decide. But of course discussing such tricky topics is one of the things that translation does, through its search for what Milton called answerable style. The rest of what you have here is the much belated completion of Parker's brave enterprise of mimetic homage.

With these origins, and with an epic whose poet begins by summoning Proteus, the god of changeability, as his dance partner, it seems right that there will then come many different answers from forty-two different translators, all pursuing their trade in their own ways according to their own very diverse rules and resources; some of them discuss their experience in a section at the end of this book. Reading the poem straight through, you should expect a sudden change when Parker's contribution ends in Book 2; that is, as they say, not a bug but a feature, and only the first of many such mood swings. The hope is for a refraction of this crazed literary leviathan into as many versions of what on earth it might be as the abilities of the translators will allow. Something of a Bacchic rout, in other words. Readers unequipped or disinclined to tackle the poem in Greek are invited to enjoy what's on offer here and then perhaps try to imagine as best they can the strange original that somehow provoked it all. Welcome to the party.

Summary of the Poem

Book One: The Rape of Europa / Typhon Runs Amok / Cadmus the Piper

Not only the Muse, but Proteus must aid the poet, who will twang his lyre to a diversity of songs. Zeus in the form of a bull speeds across the seas toward Crete with the abducted Europa on his back. An Achaean sailor expresses amazement at the sight, and Europa guesses where all this is leading. Cadmus appears, following the traces of Europa, his sister. Zeus unwisely caches his celestial weapons in a cavern, where the polycephalous monster Typhon finds them. Emboldened, Typhon begins to wreak havoc in the cosmos, overwhelming various powers of earth and heavens. Arrived in Crete, the bull, observed by angry Hera, ravishes Europa, whom he marries to the king of Crete. Zeus, back on the job, conspires with Cadmus and Pan to defeat Typhon. Cadmus, disguised as a shepherd and playing the pipes, enchants Typhon, whom he tricks into returning Zeus' stolen sinews.

Book Two: The War with Typhon

With Typhon distracted, Zeus steals back his thunderbolts; discovering the theft, the monster lays waste earth and heavens. Amid the devastation, two dryads bewail their fates. Night falls and while Typhon sleeps, Victory visits wakeful Zeus to warn that the heavenly order is breaking down. At dawn, Typhon boasts of his ambition to replace Zeus as lord of the cosmos, then the battle resumes, as Typhon hurls pieces of the earth's crust, and Zeus retaliates with thunderbolts. Eventually, Zeus' assault lays the monster full-length on the Earth (his mother), and Zeus exults. The Earth violently manifests her grief, but Nature, Helios, and the Moon working together soon heal both terrestrial and celestial wounds. As reward for his help, Zeus promises to make Cadmus the son-in-law of Ares and Aphrodite. With order restored to the cosmos, the other gods return to celebrate on Olympus.

Book Three: Cadmus Finds His Reward

Cadmus' ship lands on the Thracian coast. Awakened the next morning by the din of dancing Corybants, Cadmus sets out walking. An attendant of Aphrodite, Peitho (Persuasion) in mortal guise, guides him into the city, hidden in mist. A crow mocks his timidity and urges boldness. Emathion, ruler of this land, welcomes and admires the handsome stranger, who nonetheless remains reserved at the feast, amid frenzied music and dancing Corybants. To Emathion's mother, Electra, Cadmus relates his lineage, including the story of Io. Electra recounts her own sorrows, separated as she is from her sisters, the Pleiades. Zeus dispatches Hermes to effect the union of Cadmus with Electra's stepdaughter, Harmonia, born of the illicit union of Ares and Aphrodite. (Electra's other son, Dardanus, has emigrated and founded Troy.) Taking Electra aside, Hermes urges that Harmonia be given to Cadmus without dowry as reward for his recent service to Zeus.

Book Four: Harmonia Comes Around / The Dragon's Teeth

Harmonia is appalled at the thought of marrying an empty-handed stranger, but Aphrodite visits in mortal guise and in feigned envy waxes rapturous on Cadmus' charms. Harmonia's reluctance becomes enthusiasm, and after loving farewells to her home, she departs with Cadmus. Selene, the Moon, rebukes Aphrodite for duping her own daughter, then warns Harmonia of sorrows to come. The Delphic oracle tells Cadmus to abandon the search for Europa and instead found a city named Thebes on the spot where "the unerring prophetic cow" comes to a halt. Cadmus follows a cow through landscapes associated with various myths. When the animal sinks down, Cadmus prepares to sacrifice it, but the closest source of water is guarded by a dragon, which kills many of Cadmus' men before wrapping him in its coils. Things are looking dire when Athena appears, encourages Cadmus, and tells him to sow the dragon's teeth after killing it. This performed, armored giants spring from the furrow ready for battle. Cadmus kills many; the remainder turn upon one another.

Book Five: Wedding Gifts / Aristaeus / Actaeon / Reminiscences of Zagreus

After bloodily subjugating neighboring peoples, Cadmus lays out and builds the seven-gated city of Thebes. Cadmus and Harmonia celebrate their marriage, and the Olympians shower them with gifts. That of Hephaestus is a necklace with an elaborate snake motif—it will bring ruin to later generations. The ill-fated daughters Autonoë, Ino, Agavê, and Semele are born, followed by a son, Polydorus. Autonoë marries rustic culture-hero Aristaeus, whose many gifts to mankind will include hunting lore, beekeeping, olive oil. Their son Actaeon, after gazing on Artemis bathing, is transformed into a stag and ripped to pieces by his own hounds. Agavê gives birth to Pentheus (later to face a hideous punishment for resisting the worship of Dionysus). Sister Ino marries future homicidal maniac Athamas. Sister Semele is reserved for a "more dazzling union," for Zeus plans to sire a replacement for Zagreus, the short-lived son born of his union with Persephone.

Book Six: More about Zagreus / Zeus' Cosmic Rage

In a narrative of past events, we learn that all the male gods desire Persephone. Her anxious mother, Demeter, consults the prophet-god Astraeus, who casts Persephone's horoscope. Appalled by the result, Demeter hides Persephone in a cave, but Zeus visits her in the form of a dragon. The resulting child, Zagreus, has Zeus-like powers, but jealous Hera incites the Titans to cut him to pieces, which they do, though only after he passes through a lightning series of bodily transformations. In his rage, Zeus scorches the earth, then in pity releases a cosmic flood, described at length, while various mythological figures and geographical features hail one another among the waves. Finally Poseidon carves a drain, the waters subside, the earth dries, and men rebuild their cities better than before.

Book Seven: Zeus and Semele

Man's life is but suffering. Father Eternity begs Zeus to give men the gift of the nectar of the gods, which would make the human condition bearable. Zeus proposes a different but similar solution and briefly sketches Dionysus' coming birth, deeds, and destiny. Eros has individually etched arrows, one for each of Zeus' mortal conquests. He chooses the one with Semele's name. In Thebes, Semele has a prophetic dream. After Tiresias interprets it for her, she travels in a mule-cart with her maidens to a temple of Zeus, where she sacrifices a bull, then bathes in the river Asopos to wash off the sacrificial blood. Emerging naked from the water, she is spied by Zeus just as the arrow of Eros enters his heart. A passing naiad exclaims on Semele's beauty. Inflamed with passion, Zeus wills night to fall, then leaps down from heaven to ravish Semele in her chamber.

Book Eight: Gestation and Incineration

Dionysus in her womb, Semele plaits her hair with ivy, frenetically roams the mountains, dances to the sound of panpipes. Envy, disguised as Ares, visits Athena and Hera to fan the flames of jealousy of Semele and provoke resentment of the arriviste god she will bear. Hera flies to Crete and borrows from Deceit a girdle, which allows her to assume the form of Semele's elderly nurse. The seeming crone visits Semele's bedchamber and natters on, wondering which of the gods that might have been her visitor. If Zeus, surely he would have come with "lustful thunder?" Returning to heaven, Hera begs her husband's neglected weapons (thunder, lightning) to avenge her. Semele, now indignant that Zeus has not honored her as he had her predecessors, demands a visit in his true form. Reluctantly, Zeus grants her wish; dying, Semele has the satisfaction of a happy end "in that she gave birth as she died." Hermes whisks the preterm infant to Zeus, and Semele is raised to the sky.

Book Nine: Infancy and Youth of Dionysus / Aunt Ino / Grandmother Rhea

Zeus sews Dionysus into his thigh until it is time for him to be "born," after which Hermes takes the child to a series of caregivers: first the Daughters of

Lamos, river nymphs who care for him well until spiteful Hera drives them mad. Hermes then brings him to the home of Semele's sister Ino, who is nursing her own child, Melicertes. While in Ino's loving care, little Dionysus is also tended by the handmaid Mystis, who invents the future rituals of the god: rattle, cymbals, thyrsus, vipers, ivy, dancing. When Hera discovers this refuge as well, Hermes again whisks Dionysus away, this time to Phrygia and the care of Rhea, mother of Zeus. Under Rhea's loving tutelage and amid the racket of dancing proto-Dionysian Corybants, young Dionysus flourishes, mastering or slaying all manner of beasts. In heaven, proud mother Semele triumphantly taunts Hera. Meanwhile, Ino, maddened with grief at the disappearance of her foster-son, flees her home and rampages through the region of Delphi until Apollo soothes her. Reason recovered, she establishes the rites of Dionysus at Delphi. Back at Thebes, Mystis grieves and Athamas takes a new wife, Themisto, who bears him sons whom she will kill.

Book Ten: Madness of Athamas / Ino Leaps / Dionysus and Ampelos

Athamas is driven to madness, which lasts for four years, during which he kills his older son, taking him for a stag, then starts to boil little Melicertes. Ino returns home unexpectedly, seizes the child, and flees to the edge of the sea with Athamas in pursuit. She bitterly reproaches Zeus for his ingratitude but remembers also her own attempt to kill the children of Athamas' first wife. Melicertes in her arms, Ino leaps into the sea and becomes a nereid, while Semele in the heavens jeers. Meanwhile, back in Lydia, young Dionysus frolics with his satyr playmates and moons about for the comely satyr youth Ampelos, taking care that Ampelos always emerges victor in their boyish sports.

Book Eleven: Ampelos Rides a Bull / Dionysus Inconsolable

Dionysus urges a swimming contest, allowing Ampelos to win. Overconfident, Ampelos begins to dress and behave like Dionysus, even sporting with bears, lions, and tigers. Dionysus sees a dragon kill a fawn: a portent of Ampelos' death. To please Hera, Atê (Delusion), disguised as a playmate, encourages Ampelos' dissatisfaction: did not the favorites of other gods receive higher honors?

Were Ampelos to ride a bull, Dionysus would finally realize his worth. A beautiful bull appears, which the boy bedecks with flowers, then mounts. Unwisely, he taunts Selene, the moon, who sends a gadfly. The bull stampedes, then, ignoring the boy's pleas throws him to the ground and gores him mortally. Dionysus, heartbroken, laments. Eros in the shape of an old Silenus gives advice: such grief is only cured by new love. He tells the story of Calamos and Carpos. The four Seasons, described in detail, travel to visit Helios, their father.

Book Twelve: In the House of Helios / Dionysus Finds His Calling

The Seasons arrive at the mansion of Helios, and Autumn, who alone of the sisters has no privilege, asks her father when winecraft will come to the world and under whose tutelage. Helios indicates the Tablets of Harmonia displayed on the wall. Among many other prophecies, appears this one: Dionysus will be the god of grape and wine. Meanwhile in Phrygia, the grief of bereaved Dionysus continues. One of the Fates offers comfort: Ampelos will be transformed into the vine, and Dionysus is to spread his worship to the four corners of the earth. Ampelos becomes a grapevine, his friend Cissos, ivy. Squeezing the grapes, Dionysus makes the first wine and exults drunkenly and at length. Nonnus also relates an alternative origin story for wine, this one involving Pan.

Book Thirteen: The Mission to India Explained / The Mustering of Hosts

Zeus gives Dionysus his charge: conquer India and its impious king Deriades, teach all nations the cult of the vine, and by great deeds earn a place in heaven. Rhea summons forces for the war, and there follows a lengthy description of the various centaurs, satyrs, cyclopes, and peoples who rally to the Bacchic standard. Aristaeus had hoped that the honey he had discovered would find the favor that wine has acquired, but presents himself as commanded. Further tales of Cadmus and Harmonia in Lydia. More troops arrive.

Book Fourteen: More Mustering / First Engagement

Marshaling of the hosts continues: cyclopes, Pans, satyrs, centaurs, including those descended from the daughters of Lamos (the first nurses of Dionysus). Anecdotes of their earlier care of the god: Hera punished them by turning them into a particularly ugly species of centaur. The war begins. Dionysus sends heralds (accompanied by Pan) to announce to the Indians that they must fight or flee, but Hera in disguise emboldens the Indian monarch, and the heralds are contemptuously driven away. The two armies engage. The maenads exercise with snakes and ivy and tear animals apart. Dionysus turns the Astacid lake into wine. An Indian noble stops to drink.

Book Fifteen: The Indians' First Taste of Wine / Nicaea and Hymnus

Unaccustomed to wine, the Indians become drunk and unruly, mistaking animals for foes before falling into drunken slumber. Dionysus' troops bind them and haul them away. The virgin huntress Nicaea spurns the advances of the lovesick herdsman Hymnus, whom she eventually slays, angering other nymphs, various gods, and especially Eros.

Book Sixteen: Nicaea Undone

As Nicaea bathes, Eros sends an arrow into the heart of Dionysus. The god's blandishments leave the huntress cold: even if she wanted a god for a lover, it would not be one weaponless and "womanish." Dionysus, aided by Pan's dog, pursues her through the forested mountains. An ashtree-spirit points out that when Zeus wants a woman, he takes her. Nicaea, unknowing, drinks of the wine-waters, sees double, falls asleep. Dionysus rapes her in her sleep, observed by at least one satyr, who mocks Pan, who has never consummated his own desires. Pan laments that his friend Dionysus, not he, has the gift of the grape. Nicaea, awakened, curses the wine-waters, bewails her fate, makes futile attempts at suicide and vengeance, and bears a female child, Teletê.

Book Seventeen: Exploits and Death of Orontes

The wars resume. The god rewards the hospitable shepherd, Brongus, with vine-craft. A second battle with the Indians, who, forewarned this time, avoid drunkenness. Orontes, godson of Deriades, kills centaurs and puts the satyrs to flight before engaging Dionysus in single combat. After toying with him, the god splits Orontes' breastplate with the tap of a vine-cluster. With a defiant apostrophe to Helios, Orontes falls upon his own sword. The battle continues; steel weapons and armor are useless against the ivy and vines of the maenads and satyrs. The Indian commander Astraëis flees, the battle ends, and Aristaeus heals the wounded. One of the Indian chiefs, Blemys, submits to Dionysus, who sends him off to settle Ethiopia.

Book Eighteen: Staphylos Throws a Party

An Assyrian king, Staphylos, invites Dionysus to his palace, first relating three tales in which hospitality goes horribly wrong. The god is entertained riotously by his new disciples: feasting, dancing, rivers of wine. Much drunken dancing by the god's charioteer, Maron, and the host family, including Staphylos' son, Botrys, and his wife, Methê. All stagger off to bed. Dionysus awakes from a prophetic nightmare and prepares to sally forth to battle. First he must listen to long stories from Staphylos. Dionysus sends a messenger to Deriades: submit or be destroyed. Sending the message apparently takes the entire day, so the god returns to the palace of Staphylos only to discover his host has died.

Book Nineteen: Funeral Games of Staphylos

Botrys and Methê are grief-stricken, but wine quickly sets things right, and a series of entertaining contests begins. First, two lyre-players compete, then two dancers: Maron the charioteer and Silenus. The latter's dance tells the story of the struggle for favor between two beverages: honey-water and wine. Silenus at the end collapses and turns into a river, forfeiting the contest: Maron claims first prize.

Book Twenty: Hera's Ruse / Lycurgus Drives Dionysus into the Sea

The games concluded and Methê and Botrys consoled, all feast, then seek their beds. Discord in the shape of Rhea visits Dionysus in a dream, taunting him for carousing with battles yet to fight. The god leaps up and girds for war, as do Methê and Botrys. The army enters Arabia, land of the bandit/butcher Lycurgus. At the bidding of Hera, Iris in the guise of Ares visits Lycurgus with the gift of a poleaxe, urging the slaughter of the Bacchic forces. Then, in the guise of Hermes, she visits Dionysus, assuring him he will be a welcome guest at the home of wine-loving Lycurgus. Unarmed and expecting revelry, the god and entourage approach Lycurgus' abode, only to be ferociously set upon, while Hera thunders above. Dionysus, unprepared and believing himself attacked by Zeus himself, flees into the sea. There Nereus welcomes and comforts him, while Lycurgus rages impotently at the water's edge.

Book Twenty-One: Lycurgus versus Maenads / Dionysus Under the Waves

Lycurgus returns to pursue the routed Bassarids and struggles to capture the nymph Ambrosia, until she becomes a vine and binds him with her leafy tendrils. The other Bacchantes fling themselves upon him in fury. In the midst of an earthquake brought by Poseidon, madness seizes the local populace, who dismember and devour their own children. Lycurgus struggles in vain against his viny fetters, defiant of the celestial forces arrayed against him, until Hera frees him. One day he will become immortal, but for now Zeus punishes his presumption by sending him off as a blind wanderer. Dionysus tarries among the kindly sea nymphs and is reunited with his aunt Ino and foster-brother Melicertes. Meanwhile there is no joy among maenads, satyrs, Pans: their god is in the sea. Deriades mocks Dionysus' herald and sends him away with an insolent challenge. The herald returns to find all rejoicing: Dionysus has re-emerged from the waves and instantly makes battle plans. Deriades waits in ambush.

Book Twenty-Two: Maneuvers / Battle by the River Hydaspes

As the Dionysian hosts enter India, all of nature joyously celebrates the god: woodlands ring, trees sing, wild beasts cavort. The Indians, observing this, would flee but for Hera's intervention. A Hamadryad warns of the Indian ambush, and with Zeus' aid the army safely (and soberly) passes the night. In the morning, the armies clash ferociously. Oeagrus and Aeacus lead the slaughter of the Indians, till the river Hydaspes runs red; in the crimson water, a naiad begs for an end to the butchery

Book Twenty-Three: Rout of the Indians / Raging Waters

Aeacus and Dionysus continue the slaughter of the Indians in the river, until the sight of the heaped corpses drives one Indian warrior to suicide. A dying Indian in the water reproaches Hydaspes for drowning his own people. Of the Indian army, only the commander Thureus is spared to carry the tale to Deriades. Now Dionysus' troops undertake the crossing of the river, variously and according to their station and species, but the angry river hurls itself on the god and his minions, calling on other waterways for aid. Satyrs, Bacchantes, and Pans succumb to the raging waves until Dionysus kindles a fennel stalk at the sun and throws it into the waves, setting ablaze waters, fish, mud. At this, the river Oceanus enters the fray, issuing dire threats of cosmic upheaval against Zeus and his upstart son.

Book Twenty-Four: Across the River and into the Hills

With a thunderclap, Zeus instantly reasserts his authority. A contrite and garrulous Hydaspes begs for forgiveness, and Dionysus withdraws the flames. At this moment Deriades sends his troops to attack Dionysus' followers as they ascend the far bank of the river, but various Olympian gods and assorted immortals swoop in and ferry their favorites to safety. Bacchus in the vanguard, the rest of the army crosses the river and ascends into the mountains, where they resume the usual Bacchic pursuits. News of the rout reaches Deriades, who postpones further battle; the Indian city mourns its losses. In the forests, the jubilant Dionysian hosts feast, as Leucus the harper sings of the battle of

Zeus with his father Cronus, then of Aphrodite's calamitous attempt to rival Athena at the loom.

Book Twenty-Five: Armor from Heaven

A pause to consider how the feats of Dionysus surpass those of such other sons of Zeus as Perseus, Minos, Heracles. Alas that Homer wasted his talents on Troy; Nonnus will do his best to sing the more worthy theme of Bacchus. As the Indians cower in their city, where the air smells prophetically of wine, in the mountains Dionysus despairs at the stalemate. The self-castrated Attis arrives from Rhea, bearing divine armor for Bacchus and as well as a prophecy: the war will be won in the seventh year. All marvel at the Hephaestus-wrought shield, decorated with scenes of the heavens, of the founding of Thebes, of wine-steward Ganymede, and of the serpent-story of Tylon, Moria, and Damasen.

Book Twenty-Six: Gathering of the Indian Hosts

In the form of Orontes, Athena visits dreaming Deriades and rebukes him for inaction. In the morning, the Indian king orders the mustering of his armies. A lengthy recounting of the names and qualities of the doughty peoples responding to the summons, with divers ethnological, genealogical, and geographical observations. Highlights include the tale of Tectaphus and his daughter, some ornithological notes, the tale of Aretus and his mute sons, and disquisitions on the elephant and on the Ethiopians who wear horses' heads into battle. We learn the ancestry of Deriades, who, in the crowded and excited city, feasts his generals on the eve of battle.

Book Twenty-Seven: Haranguing the Troops / The Gods Choose Sides

As the morning of battle dawns, Deriades addresses the armies, heaping scorn on Dionysus and mocking his ragtag forces. The Indian forces march onto the plain of the Indus, ready for battle. Dionysus, meanwhile, having divided his troops into four parts, addresses them in a similar vein. And on Olympus, Zeus urges Apollo, Athena, and Hephaestus to intervene in support of Dionysus, and though they hurry off to do this, Hera, Ares, and Demeter depart to support the Indians.

Book Twenty-Eight: Slaughter on the Plain

Dionysus' motley hordes clash with Deriades' forces beside the Indus, with gory slaughter among both foot soldiers and cavalry. Exploits and deaths of Phaleneus, Dexiochus, and Clytius. Exploits of Corymbasus. Strange deaths in battle. A series of cyclopes hurl about bits of landscape, wreaking havoc, and Corybants, ever dancing, display their skill and valor.

Book Twenty-Nine: Hymn to Hymenaeus

Deriades rallies his flagging troops, while Dionysus hovers near valiant Hymenaeus, his beloved. The arrow of Indian Melaneus, meant for Dionysus, strikes Hymenaeus in the thigh. The god, after much lamenting, heals the wound and both return to battle, Dionysus sticking to his lover like a shadow. Aristaeus, the Cabiri, and the Corybants distinguish themselves in battle. Rampaging Bacchantes fall in the thick of battle, but the god heals each before pressing the assault. Rhea's messenger exploits the jealousy of Ares, an Indian ally, to send him on a fool's errand.

Book Thirty: Battlefield Exploits

Shaken, the Indian hero Morrheus points out to Deriades that leafy twigs are defeating steel and that Dionysus appears invulnerable; the Indian monarch is unmoved. Morrheus nearly slays Hephaestus' sons Eurymedon and Alcman, but their father intervenes. Morrheus fights on; Tectaphus meets his end. Morrheus slays Phlogius and numberless women. Deriades, rendered all the more terrifying by Hera, frightens Dionysus into retreating into the hills, but Athena shames him into returning to the battlefield, where his prodigious exploits soon put the Indians to flight.

Book Thirty-One: Hera Sets a Trap

Hera first visits Persephone, from whom she borrows the Fury Megaera, then visits Iris, whom she dispatches in search of the god Sleep, whose mission it will be to take Zeus out of action and gain respite for the Indians. From Aphrodite she borrows the sexually irresistible cestus belt.

Book Thirty-Two: The Trap Closes / The Raving God / Rout of the Bacchic Forces

Adorned, perfumed, and cestus-clad, Hera calls on her consort. Zeus rediscovers the pleasures of the conjugal bed, then succumbs to Sleep. Megaera drives Dionysus mad and torments him with visions. The god rampages through the mountains, slaughtering beasts and attacking satyrs and Bacchantes, who flee in panic. With Dionysus sidelined, the momentum of battle shifts, and Deriades, Ares (in the form of Modaeus), and Morrheus inflict enormous carnage and rout the forces of Bacchus—Pans, satyrs, Bacchantes, Corybants, human heroes, and even cyclopes take to their heels.

Book Thirty-Three: Morrheus Smitten

One of the Charities glimpses mad, wretched Dionysus wandering the forest and observes the satyrs and maenads fleeing the Indian onslaught. Back in heaven, heartsick, she reveals her woes to Aphrodite, who sends for her son, Eros. Found gaming, the god of love speeds to his mother, who dispatches him to the Indian war, his target the Indian Morrheus. Eros' dart unsuits for war the Indian hero, who, listless and lovesick, pursues the craftily seductive maenad Chalcomedê. Night fallen and the battle paused, Morrheus renounces both war and his native land, declaring himself henceforth a follower of the Dionysian rites. As Morrheus roams the sleeping city, mad with frustrated desire, Chalcomedê, fearful of a forced consummation, considers leaping into the sea. Thetis reassures her.

Book Thirty-Four: Love-Agonies of Morrheus

Morrheus wanders the night, aflame with conflicting desires. After confiding in Hyssacus, he returns home, falls into a slumber, and dreams that Chalcomedê returns his love. In the morning the Indian hosts confidently take the field, while the demoralized forces of the still-absent Dionysus sullenly prepare for battle. Morrheus slays many and captures eleven maidens, whom he delivers to his father-in law Deriades as belated bride price. The captured women are driven within the city and variously and horribly executed. Chalcomedê shows herself at the head of the Dionysian army, then flees with Morrheus in pursuit. Some of the routed maenads disperse to the four winds and return to being normal women, while Deriades drives the remainder inside the city walls to be butchered.

Book Thirty-Five: Slaughter of the Maenads / Morrheus Bitten

As the Indian women and old men watch from atop the walls, Deriades and his soldiers cut the trapped Bassarids to pieces. An Indian soldier struggles with the passion aroused by the maiden he has just murdered, and the wives and widows of the Indian heroes join the slaughter. Chalcomedê appears outside the walls; as hoped, Morrheus pursues her, and as she runs she encourages him to cast aside arms and armor and to bathe in preparation for their nuptials; he complies. Emerging from the sea freshly washed, he eagerly seizes her, only to be bitten by a serpent kept in her breast. At this moment, Hermes craftily sneaks the surviving Bassarids outside the city. Zeus awakens, furious at the trick played; at his command a chastened Hera lifts the madness of Dionysus. The god addresses his troops.

Book Thirty-Six: Olympians at War / The Battle on the Plain Resumes

On Olympus, the partisans of Dionysus battle those of Deriades until Hermes imposes peace. In India, the opposing armies return to the battlefield with renewed ferocity and widespread carnage. The giant Colletes slays prodigiously until brought down by a Bacchant's stone. Shapeshifting Dionysus throws himself on Deriades in myriad forms—fire, water, lion, foliage—but the Indian king fights on until immobilized with vines. After feigning submission, the moment he is freed Deriades returns to the attack. Years pass in stalemate. The Arabian Rhadamanes finish building a fleet ordered years ago; Dionysus dispatches Lycus to command it. Faced with this new threat, Deriades summons his allies, and Morrheus rallies them with a bloodthirsty oration. Dionysus and Deriades agree to a truce: the dead must be buried with honor.

Book Thirty-Seven: Funeral Games of Opheltes

The Indians pause to bury their dead, and the Bacchic forces do likewise, Dionysus overseeing an immense pyre laid for Opheltes. Countless livestock are sacrificed, as well as a dozen Indian warriors. When the flames have done their work, Dionysus lays out a course for chariots. Actaeon's father Aristaeus leads him aside for detailed last-minute advice on the charioteer's art, but Erechtheus wins anyway, after a breakneck race rife with taunts and treachery. Next, Melisseus knocks down Eurymedon in boxing; in wrestling, Aristaeus grapples unsuccessfully with Aeacus; Erechtheus outruns Ocythoös in the footrace; the Cyclops Halimedes hurls the weight farthest; Hymenaeus wins the archery contest, his arrow plucking a pigeon from the sky. Aeacus wins the javelin fight.

Book Thirty-Eight: Portents and Prophecies / The Tale of Phaëthon

Following an eclipse and other portents, the seer Idmon prophesies victory; Hermes visits Dionysus to confirm. This is not the first time the course of the sun has been perturbed: Hermes relates the tale of Helios' son, Phaëthon, who insists on driving the Sun's chariot across the sky. Helios reluctantly assents, after a lengthy disquisition on celestial mechanics and the details of the route. The inexperienced driver careers wildly across the heavens, disrupting the cosmos till Zeus strikes him down with a thunderbolt and restores order to heaven and earth.

Book Thirty-Nine: The Battle at Sea

As the Rhadamanes' fleet approaches India, Deriades raises a fleet of his own. Speaking to his men, he insolently belittles Dionysus' claim to divinity. Dionysus addresses his own forces, boasting of his many connections among sea-folk. As the Arabian fleet surrounds the Indian ships, Aeacus prays to Zeus and Erechtheus to Boreas, begging the wind to favor their fleet and bedevil that of Deriades. The rival fleets clash till corpses clog the choppy waters, while the Cyclopes rain missiles on the Indians. Dionysus wounds Morrheus, who repairs to the city to be healed by Brahmanic incantations. Wounded Indians in the water sink and drown, though wounded partisans of Dionysus float. Erechtheus' fireship sets Deriades' fleet ablaze, the Indians abandon the waters, and Deriades takes to his heels.

Book Forty: Death of Deriades / Sightseeing in Tyre / Brunch with Heracles

Athena disguised as Morrheus upbraids Deriades for his cowardice. The Indian king, shamed, returns to the battlefield only to be put to flight by Dionysus and is then slain at the river Hydaspes. The Indian War is ended. Deriades' wife and daughters lament the loss of husbands and father, and Morrheus' wife, Chirobië, reflects on the bitter fruits of her husband's passion for Chalcomedê. After the obsequies of the fallen, the Bacchic hosts celebrate their victory, parcel out the spoils, and depart for their homes. Dionysus, with a company of satyrs and maenads, passes through Arabia and Assyria before sightseeing in Tyre and visiting the former house of Cadmus. In the temple of Tyre's tutelary god, he loquaciously apostrophizes Heracles, who appears, lays a feast, and spins a yarn that explains both the invention of sailing and the founding of the city before detailing the history of the city's famous fountains.

Book Forty-one: Beirut, Jewel of Phoenicia / Aphrodite's Ambition for Her Daughter

Freshly born of the waves, Aphrodite makes first landfall at ancient Beirut. The eponymous Beroë, a nymph, is born of Aphrodite's union with Adonis. Eager that her daughter be tutelary deity of a city of distinction, Aphrodite visits Harmonia in heaven and consults the oracular tablets: Beirut will be famed for the study of Roman law. The goddess asks Eros to use his arrows on Dionysus and Poseidon.

Book Forty-Two: Vine God and Earthshaker Woo in Vain

Dionysus moves through the forests, anxiously trailing Beroë. Unable to win her interest, he pours his heart out to Pan, who counsels duplicity, but neither a rustic guise nor his revealed godhead makes an impression. Poseidon's blandishments, too, are unsuccessful. Aphrodite proposes a contest, with Beroë the victor's prize, provided both contenders agree to favor her namesake city thereafter.

Book Forty-Three: Thyrsus versus Trident

Dionysus and Poseidon array and harangue their forces. The armies clash. A parade of undersea celebrities, including Triton, Nereus, and Proteus, wreak havoc among the Bacchic hosts, but frenzied Bassarids, satyrs, and sileni retaliate in kind, until Zeus, touched by the prayer of a nereid, halts the hostilities, awarding battle and prize to Poseidon. Cheery sounds of underwater nuptials reach the ears of Dionysus as he sadly departs, and the marriage alliance with the Earthshaker assures Beirut's prosperity. Eros consoles Dionysus with news of amorous adventures yet in store, and the god briefly visits Rhea in Phrygia before crossing into Europe to further spread the cult of the grape.

Book Forty-Four: Pentheus Recalcitrant

Dionysus returns to his birthplace of Thebes, where his cousin, impious King Pentheus, defies the god and bars him from the city, despite ominous portents and the enthusiasm of the populace. Pentheus' mother, Agavê, recalls a horrifying prophetic dream, which the seer Tiresias understood but forbore to interpret. Pentheus mocks Dionysus' claim to divinity, while styling himself an equal of the Olympians. The angered vine god asks for and receives the aid of the moon goddess: a Fury rises from Tartarus to prepare the site of Pentheus' imminent destruction. Under cover of darkness, Dionysus slips into the palace and tricks his aunt Autonoë into believing that her son Actaeon is not dead after all but is joyously roaming the mountainsides with Artemis.

Book Forty-Five: Thebes in Chaos / The Enchanted Pirate Ship / The Palace in Flames

In demented Bacchic frenzy, Agavê, Autonoë, and other women of Thebes rush into the hills. Within the walls even snowy-haired Cadmus and Tiresias perform Bacchic rites, disgusting Pentheus, who upbraids them. Tiresias responds with cautionary tales: the ill-advised abduction of Dionysus by Tyrsenian pirates and the equally unsuccessful attack by the Sicilian Giant Alpus. Unimpressed, Pentheus dispatches his soldiers to capture the god, who tricks both soldiers and king into mistaking a bull for Dionysus. Pentheus' dungeons cannot hold the Bassarids, who run amok in the hills, performing prodigies and tearing animals to pieces. Dionysus, enraged to encounter resistance, rocks the foundations of Thebes and engulfs the palace in flames.

Book Forty-Six: Pentheus the Maenad

Pentheus heaps scorn on Dionysus' Olympian pretentions, but the god persuades him to disguise himself as a woman and witness the Bacchic rites in person. Before the astonished gaze of the Thebans, Pentheus, seeing double and in full maenad regalia, dances out of the city and up into the hills, where the god places him in a tree overlooking the dancing-grounds. Agavê spots him and, believing him a lion, with mad strength uproots the tree. The maenads rip Pentheus to pieces, and Agavê, brandishing her son's head, runs proudly to Cadmus, who laments the fates of his five children. Dionysus restores to Agavê her reason. Agavê and Autonoë bewail the cruel deaths of their respective sons. Dionysus consoles them with an elixir before departing with his entourage for Athens.

Book Forty-Seven: The Murder of Icarius / Ariadne / The Achaean Resistance / Brother Perseus

In Attica, mankind and nature rejoice at the god's imminent arrival. The kindly Athenian gardener Icarius welcomes Dionysus and learns the art of winemaking. Icarius hosts a party of his countrymen, who, unaccustomed to wine, believe themselves poisoned and brutally murder him. Icarius' bloody shade brings the dire news to his daughter, Erigone, who hangs herself. Zeus transforms father, daughter, and faithful dog into constellations. Dionysus departs for Naxos, where he finds Ariadne sleeping, unaware that Theseus has sailed without her. Awakening, Ariadne berates the treacherous winds and faithless Theseus. Utterly charmed, Dionysus reveals himself and quickly convinces her of her good fortune. Their nuptials celebrated, Dionysus resumes his tour of Greece. Meeting resistance in Achaea, the angry god makes mad the women, who butcher their own children. An Achaean disparagingly compares Dionysus with local hero Perseus, who, urged on by Hera, enters the fray, accompanied by many Argive heroes. Hermes intervenes and makes peace between half-brothers Dionysus and Perseus, though Ariadne is among the casualties, turned to stone by Medusa's head.

Book Forty-Eight: Attack of the Giants / Wrestling Pallene / Another Virgin Huntress

Arriving in Thrace from Argos, Dionysus is attacked by the Giants but makes short work of them. Not only must Pallene's prospective suitors wrestle her, but her father murders every one. Dionysus pins her, wins her, and slays the father. Then on to Phrygia, where Aura, a virgin huntress, after a dream featuring Eros, Aphrodite, and Adonis, speaks imprudently to Artemis. The goddess, furious, turns to Nemesis for retribution. This leads to Dionysus being love-mad and desperate for Aura. The ghost of Ariadne appears, rebuking his inconstancy. The god, assisted by the Seasons, prepares a tempting fountain of wine-mixed elixir for the parched huntress, who falls for the stratagem and is quickly asleep. Dionysus binds, ravishes, releases. Aura awakes; understanding dawns; she rampages through the countryside seeking and inflicting death. In labor, she receives multiple visits from Artemis and Nicaea, who gloat and commiserate respectively, before giving birth to twins, one of whom she succeeds in killing before remorseful Artemis spirits the surviving twin away to Dionysus. The god entrusts the babe to Nicaea and ascends to a seat in heaven, exchanging wine for nectar.

The Poem

Book 1

Douglass Parker

ONE has light-bearing Zeus
Putting a nymph to sad use.
The sky-striking fists of Typhoon
Drag down darkness at noon.

SING,
O
MUSE:

Cronides' go-between gutting the pallet in blaze
Thunderbolt's orgasm birthing in strain at the coupling flash
Sheet Lightning, *Semele*'s chambermaid, strewing her bride-bed

&
SING:

Twyborn *Bacchus*' blessed event:
Unfinished foetus
of mother unmidwifed, scooped still damp from the embers by *Zeus*—
whose gingerly fingers slot his thigh to a he-man womb,
a uterine device which double-casts him, matripaternal,
to bring the baby to term in terms of his prior confinement:
From forehead gravid with swollen bolus by temple spermatick,
Zeus fired unconceived, unconceivable *Athena* glinting in full kit.

MUSES:

Here with my spear of fennel
thrum and thrimble the cymbals;
stuff my fist with the thyrsus of *Bacchus*, my bel canto's burden . . .
Not Solo:
As I impinge on the ensemble, nip next door
to *Pharos* and find me my partner and pattern—polymorph *Proteus*
muffled in multifold forms: I thumb a multiform anthem.

Let *Proteus* sneak in as snake and score a spiral spoor:
I'll render the score hung up by my Hero's cissoid shillelagh,
rendering brigades of *Giants*, hispid with viperoid bangs.

Let *Proteus* bristle his mane in a shaggy upsweep:
I'll hooray *Bacchus* balanced on *Rhea*'s stubbly elbow,
depleting her titanic teat in deceit, lactation of lions.

Let *Proteus* project himself in cyclonic bound from his pads
and, poised in air, baroquely refurbish his form to a leopard's:
I'll hosanna *Zeus*' issue who flindered the Indian race,
caused their elephants into the ground with leopard-drawn droshkies.

Let him mutate his mode to facsimile boar:
I'll hymn *Thyonê*'s
scion poleaxed by the sex appeal of pigsticking *Aura*,
Cybele's daughter, mother of lategotten *Bacchus* the thirdmost.
Let *Proteus* dissolve to aqua falsa:
I'll sing *Dionysus*'
plunge to the pleats of the sea when *Lycurgus* waved his crest.
Or let him switch to tree and swish in an ersatz rustle:
I'll tell the tale of sprinter *Icarius*, whose feet competed,
flat soles drubbing vinefruit to slush in the dybbuk winetub.

MAENADS:

Here with my spear of fennel
Off with my drabble
of everyday togs
And drape my shoulders with the dotted dash
of dappled fawnskin, fresh with the essence of vintage nectar,
drawn tight over my heaving chest

[*Old* Homer *and one*
of his principal nymphs, Eidothea, *can fend with the strong rank reek*
of sealskin bespoke for Menelaus' *foray into* basse couture.]
Fetch me the hallelujah timbrels
Reach me the loudbooming goatskin
But hold the twintoned hautboys of soulsweet strain, and check them
out to another

[*I refuse to pique my Apollo, who disowns*
the naughty notes from the breathed-on reed—ever since he shamed
the impious pipes of Marsyas, *husked that hubristic herdsman,*
and hung the pared-off hide on a tree to bulge in the breeze.]

. . . .

Take it, **Muse**, from the top—

from Cadmus, the Roving Researcher:

Lang syne on the sands at *Sidon* did *Zeus* the bull, horns high,
low from his counterfeit larynx, a bogus mating moooo
and shake to a stink of sweetness when *Eros* wrestled a woman
into position. Locking his hands in the curl of a twin-pronged
band 'round her belly, the godlet heave-ho'ed. Beside him, the bull
who strides the sea depressed the hump of his crest to mattress
the virgin's mounting and slithered meek and oblique to his knees;
then fretting the strings of his slackened back into tautness, he raised

Europa up, and scudded away over walkable water,
his upborned hood in silence scoring the sea with the tiniest
tippytoe traces. Aloft above the main, the maiden
pulsed in a spasm of terror, but held her course on bullback,
high and dry.

To a casual glance, identity doubtful:
Mayhap *Thetis*, or else *Galatea*, if not *Amphitrite*
[the girl who goes to bed with *Earthquake*]—say, *Aphrodite*
bestriding the back of a *Triton*.
And bluetressed *Earthquake* gaped
at the slewfoot cruise. Bemused by *Zeus*' seducer's mooo,
Triton disconced his conch and blew a fugal toot
to the tune *Here Comes the Bride*. *Nereus* noticed the horny
stranger aswim; his phthisic finger stirred fright with funk,
tracing the attractive *tourist*'s track for his daughter *Doris*.
On high, the virgin traveled steerage, light freight which barely
dampened her ox's dewlap. Atwitter at the soaring yaws
of her sloshy excursion, she clutched at the cuckoldy rudder.

Desire crewed.

Boreas, flustered with lust, twitched in libidinous bluster,
slyly bellied her shift away from her body, the better
to whistle in lurking amaze on her brace of budlet breasts.

AS WHEN:

Up from the ocean's basement a nimble nereid
bobs, bestraddles a dolphin, and slaps at the jellied flood
from her sinusoid chairlift, flapping her hand in a dewy pastiche
of the breaststroke, the while her watery wayfarer fairs through water
halfseen, humpbacked, his airy passenger arid of brine,
lightly limning his route with the splay-tined fork of his flukes . . .

SO:

The bull carried cargo, with tensing, tautening rumples.

And Cowboy *Cupid* laid on, lambasted the subjugant neck
with his mother's ensorcelled cincture, hefted his bow to shoulder
like a drover's crook, raddled *Hera*'s hardbreathing helpmeet
with the rod of *Cypris* and drave him to damp *Poseidonian* pasture.

And bluish blushed the virgin cheek of motherless *Pallas*,
aghast to gaze at her purebred daddy bridled by bride.

But on *Zeus* course, scissored the surge in a saturate gouge,
his hot not damped by the wet of salacious sea, which once
pregnant in submarine womb from skysown furrow, outsquirted
the foamy, amorous, glamorous goddess damp on a clamshell.

And so, steerswoman for the hush-hush transit of *Taurus*, our virgin
shipped as pilot and payload.
A peregrine boatswain from *Achaea*
goggled at the pumping knees of the trumped-up hugger-mugger lugger
[no meeker vessel], and screamed a statement, somewhat as follows:

"*Now,* there *is something you don't see every day:*
what's ahoy?
A bovine agronomist taking the waters, plowing the sounding
deep to raise a crop in the sea unabounding? Strange.
Has Zeus *decreed the dredging of dry land? Is a road being mapped*
for a line of waterlogged wagons?
A hodgepodge passage, *this.*
Has Lady Moon *removed from the wild blue yonder to take*
the tour by single bull through the wild blue hither? Has Thetis
deserted the depths for the reins, to jockey in a soggy sweepstakes?

Something's fishy.
Perhaps it's the Sea-Bull *or* Ox-Ray, *that haunts*
*these waters [*Cephaloptera Giorna; *carnivore; staggering bulk]* . . .

but no. The image is wrong; this is garden-variety bull.
And if that's a nereid *cowgirl goading her eccentric steer*
to unharnessed riptide ambles, she's damnably out of costume,
swathed in that prissy pelisse:
A nereid's *normally nude.*

A tufted hairdo?
Perhaps it's Demeter *who harrows the wheat,*
cultivating comber, scratching the briny's spine with an ox-hoof.
If so, up top, Poseidon! *Bloom, and be transplanted!*
You've had your surfeit of surf; your sea-legs are lost—and now,
luffing at sandstorms, beach your pedestrian barge and trudge
to gouge Demeter's *groove.*

—Hey, Barnacle Bull!
You've gone straight off the charts! Nereus *curries no cattle;*
Proteus *prods no plow;* Glaucus *futters no parsnips.*
No marshes here, no meadows to fill the billows. This,
I say, is the SEA!
Barren, uncropped, and cropless. Its toilers
are sailors. They harrow no harbors, prefer the tiller's slice
to the ironshod split. Earthquake's *minions sow no furrows.*
Ruminate, please, and respect the peculiar traits of the seafoam.
A gloss:

Fruit: kelp.
Seed: spume.
Rube: gob.
Rut: wake.
Share: ship.

But—putting your aqueous humor aside—why, pray, are you carrying
on with that virgin? Do bull's libidos itch to snatch women?
Don't tell me Poseidon's *at it again, re-raping in mufti?*
*Rivergod's horns—*same tired disguise*—to shame the shape*
of Bos Domesticus?
Shame, Poseidon!
Plotting another

ploy for The Lays of Ancient Greece, *with* Tyro *still warm?*
It was only a day ago you forced her freshwater loveseat,
aping the mucky Enipeus, *dissolving in bogus gurgles!*"

In such a fashion, a passing *Hellenic* sea dog expressed
his shock and amazement.

Meanwhile, back at the bull,
our maiden, scenting a stable union, ripped her coiffure
and broke into plaintive yawp:

"O Waters *who bear no oars,*
O Beaches *who know no speech, proclaim my plea to the bull*
[presuming, of course, that cattle communicate feasibly!]:
BULL,
TAKE PITY AND SPARE THIS VIRGIN!
O Shores, *inform my daddy*
his darling Europa's *abroad, an emigrant holding a seat*
on a bull who swims, who abducts, who now—I imagine—rapes.
O Breezes *who wheeze about me, deliver my mother my bridecurls.*
O Boreas, *god of the North Wind, who snatched a bride from* Athens,
waft me aloft on your wings . . .

Oh, no, Voice, STOP!
Better let sleeping winds lit. This bull's an old goat, but Boreas
might just—oh, dear—be a wolf!"

And these, the heartrending peals
of the girls as she wrung her bad ferry's withers, spurred and sped
Cadmus' travels. He stepped from land to land, bulldogging
the ceaselessly unsparing spoor of the ox-turned-groom.
At length
he came to the bloody pit pockmarking the erstwhile site
of the far-ranging *Arima* range, those mounds snapped loose from their roots
to bruise *Olympus*' shockproof postern, what time the *Gods*
took chicken-heart wing over *Nile* (that utter stranger to weather),
matching in fabricant flutter safe birdlife, tactless, intact,

flailing bizarrely an *outré* wake through the blast of heaven,
flogging the welkin through seven ringing zones.

—The cause?

Zeus (son of *Cronus*), the ever-moved mover, all in a sweat
to breach the bed of *Plouto* (daughter of *Cronus*) and beget
Tantalus (frantic felon who'ld burgle celestial goblets),
had stowed his *Luftwaffen*, locked his lightning deep in the marrow
of the living rock. Confined, claustrophobic, the thunderbolts coughed
smoke and smutted the cliff's chalk cheeks. Darkly, a spark
rose from a firebarbed arrow, enchafed a springsource . . .
and down
the *Mygdonian* flume the torrid torrents boiled and moiled
to debouch in reboant boom.

At this, from *Cilicia*, the monster

TYPHOON!

[a.k.a. *Typho*, *Typhœus*, and *Typhon*; a thoroughly bad hat]
returned with his hundred bestial heads the nod of his mother
Earth, extended his twice a hundred hands, and rifled
the *Thunderer*'s weathergod arsenal, weapons of fire and snow.
He rallied the ranks of his throats from their usual guttural rumble
to blend their animal howls in a deafening zoo's diapason.
He sprouted snakes, which slicked across his *Leopards'* chops,
licked at his *Lion*'s bush thatches, looped the crumpled
horns of his *Bulls* with flick-flack helical twists of their tails.
From tapertongued chins, the toxin that darts with death at a distance
dripped and swirled, combining in fatal form with *Boar*spit.
Locking *Zeus*' simmering missiles away in a rocky pocket,
the monster stretched straight up. An airborne scramble—and heaven
bloomed sudden hands. Massed metacarpals formed into fists
and assaulted the vault.

—There's one! Down by the skydome's shank,
pulling *Little Bear*'s tail!

—Up there! *Callisto*'s relaxed
on the *Zodiac*'s axle, but one's got her by the short hairs, pitches
Big Bear from her perch!
—Another's aiming its knocks at the *Oxherd*:
it batters *Boötes*!
—Alas for *Lucifer*, Star of the Morning . . .
mugged!
—And down at the turnaround rim of the sky, the vain
and plaintive swish of a whip:
With *Dawn* abducted, and *Taurus*
penned in her path, the stunted *Season*, trapped out of time,
dismounts for a breather.
Light wriggles through a scaly fringe
of corkscrew curls, glow fused to gloom. My Lady *Moon*
seeks daywork, rises to share the shining with My Lord *Sun*.
No rest for the busy colossus: About-face, quickstep, *HARCH!*
On parade from North to South, he quits one pole for a post
at the other. A longhand snatch secures him *The Man With The Jug*
as a switch to flail a shower of hail from *Capricorn*'s back.
Fishing in troubled heavens, he hooks the finned twins *Pisces*
and chucks them back in the sea. *Aries* he rams and leaves sheepish,
unsnaps that fastener star that clips the heavenly band
in place, that plugs the day to the dark in the unshorted circuit
of its blazing springtime boarder.
Erected to cloudy estate
on back-dragging feet, *Typhoon* arrays his multi-armed forces,
dispatches his spraddled bands of hands on a widespread front,
and blankets the sky's unclouded silver blaze with his blitz—
the sidewinding ranks of snakes.
—There goes one now! It shoots
on a line through the *Zodiac*'s rim *en grand jeté* to the spine
of *Draco* [the resident *Serpent* of heaven], and hisses a warwhoop.
A hoopsnake bounces to *Cepheus*' daughter, twirling itself
in a loop precisely the size of the maiden's starstudded bracelets;
bending skewed in a band beneath her bonds, it bundles
Andromeda Bound in a double bind.
—*Cerastes cornutus*,

horny as ever when like meets like, encircles a spike
of its *Doppelhörner*, the *Bull*, hangs down in a spiral athwart
the bovine brow to mimic and madden with jaws agape
the *Hyades* [winsome quintet disposed as the spit-and-image
of *Moon* when she wears *her* horns].
—Clutches of vipers,
banded together in venomous cummerbunds, are belting
Boötes!
—Another, espying *Olympus*' second *Serpent*,
essays a mighty leap: It loops the anguiferous wrist
of *The Handler of Snakes*, then leaps ahead, neck bent
and belly coiled, to slither and shake in a bonnie braiding,
a new coronet to crown *Ariadne*'s existing *Tiara*.
No shortage of arms: A stretch, and *Typhoon* flaps *West Wind*'s belt,
wags *East Wind*'s wing, with a simultaneous twist and turn
in either direction to touch both ends of the world at once.
He follows the *Star of the Morning*'s dejection with *Star of the Evening*'s,
and leaves the far-west crests of the *Atlas* very depressed.

HOW OFTEN IT HAPPENS:

He angles in *Ocean*'s kelpy cleavage, hooks onto *Poseidon*'s
rig, and flicks it up from the deep to lie on the dry.
He tangles a hand in the pickled mane of a stabled stallion,
fishes it out of its submarine stall, and flings the displaced
mustang away, an airborne missile—its target, *Olympus*.
A Palpable Hit! The Sun's two-seater shudders on impact;
its team strains along its gloomy-go-round with many a whinny.

HOW OFTEN IT HAPPENS:

He snatches an ox who only a moment ago was relaxing
its limbs by a back-country plowtree; in the cattle-rattling grip
of his threatening forearm, he frets the creature to mawkish moos,
then launches it straight at its hornbearing double, the crescent *Moon*,

and punctuates her career with a full stop. He screeches through heaven
in mad cadenza, dispensing the vicious drip-drop-drip
of a viperoid hiss, then snaffles her bridle in deadly downbeat
to cut off her white-strapped bulls at the yoke in sudden Grand Pause.

But *Luna*, true spawn of *Titans*, throws in no towel at his onslaught:
Battling the *Giant* head to heads and antler to antlers,
she racks up many a notch to score the glistening arc
of her bullish horns.

Then hark! A moo from *My Lady Moon*'s oxen,
glowing and lowing on high in amaze at the cavernous chasm
of *Typhoon*'s gullet!

No deference found in the *Seasons*; they outfit
their starry brigades. The heavenly *Orbits*, ranked and arrayed
to the round for the fray by the *Zodiac*'s muster, burn hot for combat.
New-spangled battalions sparkle in crazy gavotte through heaven
to the tune of their fires' wild hiss, a stellar assemblage amassed
from *North*,
from *West Wind*'s back,
from the edge of *East*,
from the crook
of *South Wind*'s elbow.

Like a single heavenly body, the *Fixed Stars*
[that imperturbably static crew] desert their stations
and amble away to greet their vagabond fellows, united
in *NOISE*.
The hubbub flusters the *Axis*, the pole that pierces
the void of heaven stiff through its middle; it squeaks and moans.
Orion the Hunter, fixing his gaze on the wild-beast show,
lugs out his claymore; the blazing machete's *Tanagran* blade
glints and sparks as its bearer prepares his mettle for battle.
At his heels, the *Major Canis*, sensing the coming of dog-days,

sparkles and thirsts as his starry throat boils over and erupts
in ardent barking. Forsaking his usual prey—the *Rabbit*—
between his teeth he vomits forth a jet of steam
on *Typhoon*'s zoo.
Reboant, the welkin resounds.
Rebooming
in turn to the seven circles of heaven, from an equal number
of throats there ululates forth a seven-mouthed wail for war
[the *Pleiades*' contribution]. The *Planets* [again a seven]
increase the foofaraw's swell with a balancing banging and clanging.

One glimpse of the *Giant*'s ophidian form, and *The Handler*
Of Snakes blushed forth into blaze. One shake of his venom-proof hands
removed the clutches of bottle-green *Serpents* who nursed at his flames
and molded their mottled mass to a lopsided missile of mischief
he then fired off. Around his fires, the hurricanes howled,
as viperine shafts went twanging aslant and unbalanced the air
into madness.

Now *Capricorn*'s buddy [bold enough to befriend a being
half goat and half fish] *The Archer* snaps a shot. Inside
the *Wagon*'s circle, the *Serpent* [you know, he's bright in the middle,
and portioned out—half to the *Little Bear*, half to the *Great*]
flailed a sparkling gouge in the sky with his heavenly tail;
the *Virgin*'s next-door neighbor *Boötes* [he drives the *Wagon*
and shares its route] shook in spasmodic seesaw the crook
in his flashing hand.
Close by the knee of the *Kneeler* [or *Idol*,
as you prefer] and over against its companion *Swan*,
the starry *Lyre* sounded a prophecy:

Zeus Will Win.

So much for the sky.

Typhoon pounced down on *Corycius*' peak
and tweaked it viciously, squashed the flux of *Cydnus* River

(a neighbor of his in *Cilicia*), and, pinching between two fingers,
rammed it through downtown *Tarsus*.
Off shot a volley of crags
to batter the deep's battalions, marking a shift in operations:
Ordnance: Clifftops.
Objective: To Paddle the Sea.

The *Monster*
lumbered his way through the combers on saltsoaked soles. Above,
in the buff, his crupper was dry: the billows broke at mid-thigh
in pounding resounding. His snakes slithered down for a dip, hissing
assault from gullets bespattered with spume and venting their venom
in marine melée.
Picture *Typhoon*:
Stockstill in midocean,
his feet's flat plats aroot in the depths of its weedy bed,
awash with fish. His belly, massaged by clouds, holds close
intercourse with air. And, up at his summit, the *Giant*'s *Airlions*
flaunt their manes and roarrr. Down deep, the *Sealion* shudders
and skulks in his slimy crevasse.
The vasty deep was congested:
Leviathan legions, behemoth brigades overspilled the abyss. . . .
And everywhere

GIANT!

He glutted the sea till he strained its seams
with his earthborn bulk and overbulked earth, his ungirt girth
outflanking the banks.
A bleat from the *Seals*.
The *Dolphins* dove
in purposive panic to hiding.
Only the *Octopus* stuck:
Slick and shifty, knotting his supple twists in a netted
coil of collage on his usual rock, his tentacles tracing
a parodic boulder.

Nothing There Was That Did Not Tremble.

[*Especially so the* Lamprey: *Lost in her lust for serpents,*
she quivered and spent in mad nymphomaniac joy at the impious
hiss of the Snakes—*so MANY! —in submarine war with heaven.*]

The high seas soared. Pyramiding, the main piled up to keep
Olympus company. Streaming, it forded the sky until
that arid bird of the upper air, who never knows water,
noticed the ocean next door and took an overdue bath.
Typhoon reached over and ripped up an island, a flange from the land
that edges the briny. Cupping this improvised trident in the palm
of a fathomless hand, he wound up, whirled it around, and let
the whole mass fly in an inside outshoot. To support the onslaught,
his hands took arms, moved in on the stars, and sortied forth
to *Olympus*' haughty headland.
Slipping the bounds of sea
and the bountiful seat of earth, the pseudo-*Zeus* shaped his grip
to the thunderbolt's blazing barbs. But *Cronion*'s kit of equipment
was massy, a weight which scarce the concerted grabs of *Typhoon*'s
two hundred hands could manage, flat out and straining. [True *Zeus*
was used to hefting the load with the flip of a knuckle.]
The plugugly
tugged.
Nothing.
No nimbus gathered.
The thunder rubbed at
his bonedry arms and emitted a muffled *pffft*, a *sotto*
voce plop to a clapless echo. Air shriveled, and only
one weazened wisp of dew dropped down in a withered snowflake.
The lightning fizzled and flickered, a frail fire, flaming
in fitfully flashy abashment like smoke from a greasy grid.
The bolts, embarrassed, sensed the clumsy touch of a tyro;
their masculine splendor shrank to a soft and sissified shimmer,
repeatedly slide with spontaneous jerks from the numberless thumbs.
The firebrands mourned the loss of their normal heavenly guidance
and glided off course.

AS WHEN:

A man with a horsewhip [unknown
to the horse, and horsemanship strange to him] artlessly flogs
and flogs again with no success at a stubborn, bit-spitting
stallion. The animal flouts him, instinct sensing his driver's
sham from the bogus handling.
It shies in frenzy, checks;
raises its bentknee forelegs, flails, paws madly ahead,
jerks its neck aloft till the bulky mane that spraddles
along its spine flaps broadcast down over both its shoulders.

SO:

The *Giant* tried hand after hand, in moil and toil
to uprear the runaway flash of a bolt that would not stay put.

Now, Rover *Cadmus* was paying his call at the *Arima Mountains* . . .

Meanwhile, over in *Crete*, the aquatic bull inclined
his neck and delivered his virgin, unspotted, unsoaked, on the strand
below *Mt. Dicte*.
But *Hera*—who always has eyes for cattle—
saw *Cronides* quiver in lechery's spasms. Demented with envy,
she compressed and exploded her pique into speech with a highpitched
cackle:

"Phoebus, *dear,* do *give your father some moral*
support. Let's not have a rustic catching and hitching the great god
Zeus *to the earth-shaking plow.*
On the other hand, why not?
Yes, lace him up in the traces! I have a few words that a bull
can certainly follow:
'Hut, you rotter! Haw for the harrow
and Gee for the Girls!'
—But Phoebus, *dear, although you're a famous*

bowman, you do *have another title:* God of Pastures.
Go down and earn it. Heed me, and herd your father. A stray
is always fair game. Take the Lady Moon*: A woman drover*
like her just might stick Cronides *under the yoke in her rush*
to visit the shepherd Endymion*'s bed, and tattoo* Zeus*' back*
with the swish and the slash of her lash!
—Hey, milord Zeus*!*
Poor Io—
so sad she had to miss you like this, you ox, *when you were*
her lover and she was a simple crumplehorned cow. What might
have been that fling's sweet issue—a precocious calf, as horny
as daddy!
And do *be careful of* Hermes. *Nice lad, of course,*
but still, by trade, a compulsive cattle-thief. I'm afraid
—your being a bull, and all—the boy might rustle his father,
and have to give Phoebus (your *son, remember) another harp*
to pay for the raper raped!
—But what can I do? Pen him up?
If only Argus *were still alive, and peeking from every*
pore with those shining eyes. Oh, he'd ride herd for Hera,
haul Zeus *off to a godforsaken pasture, and jab*
and beat those cheating ribs with a crook!"
And so spoke *Hera*.

—The ebullient son of *Cronus*, however, demuzzled and slipped on
a stripling's shape, then gyred around the chaste young thing
in a giddy chase. A tentative touch of her ankle, her knee,
and now he became the very first to loosen the band
that bound her bosom, to squeeze in assumed confusion the swelling
round of her firm, proud breast, to kiss her lips on the tips,
to fold back the long-preserved and holy girdle
from unwed maidenhood, to crop the fresh first-fruits of love.

Her womb soon swelled and tossed, plump with gestating twins . . .
and *Zeus* her mate turned over his gravid bride and her blessed
travail to *Asterion*, King of *Crete*, a husband rich
and famous enough for any girl.

The freshwater starstudded *Bull*
of *Olympus* mounted the sky to shine by *Auriga*'s shin.
in *Spring* he rises, keeping his back [which dotes on dew]
to the *Sun*, whose track he squats athwart. Observe him halfsunk
in the *Ocean*, pointing his right hoof out to *Orion*. At evening
he speeds his pace on the rim and outstrips *Auriga*, who rises
to share his race.
Thus did he gain his place in the sky.

BUT:

TYPHOON'S *TENURE OF* ZEUS' *MUNITIONS WAS NOT TO CONTINUE . . .*

Collecting the little *Lovegod*—and bidding him bring his bow—
Cronides quitted the dizzy zenith to encounter Relentless *Cadmus*,
the Roving Researcher, tramping the mountains. The trio concocted
a complex congame, sewing a shroud for *Typhoon* from the deadly
thread on the spindle of *Fate*. And goatnibbled *Pan* put in
for a share, and supplied Omnipotent *Zeus* with appropriate props:
cattle and sheep and goats and goats and goats, He plaited
wattles, strung them in spiral swaths to fashion a cabin,
and moored it fast to the ground. In mufti not to be fathomed,
he draped the shape of *Cadmus* with timetested rustic vestments,
and, turning him out in this bogus livery, turned him into
a synthetic shepherd. To pilot *Typhoon* in his race to erasure,
he handed canny *Cadmus* his own beguiling *pan-pipes*.

Zeus, then assembling the humbug herdsman and the winged driver
of procreant lust, imparted his single overall plan:

"Please, Cadmus, *pipe for life! Then heaven's climate will clear.*
But hold back only a bit, and Olympus *loses its skin.*
At present, Typhoon *is equipped with the weapons I use in the sky;*
all I have left is the aegis—and tell me, what possible good
can a goatskin cape do me in a fight when he's stolen my thunder?

I'm frankly afraid of becoming a butt: Titanic *titters*
from old daddy Cronus. . . *and I root in terror to think of the highborn*
scorn of my stiffnecked opponent, Iapetus.
But most of all
I shudder at Greece, *forever enceinte with the cheapest in fiction:*
No doubt some Achaean *will set up a shout of* 'Raingod Typhoon'—
or 'Typhoon *Who Rules On High*'—*or* '*Lord God* Typhoon *In*
The Highest'—
and roll my name in the mud.
Just play the good shepherd, Cadmus,
till morning blushes again, and rescue The Shepherd Of All.
Pipe up a tune to addle the wits, to keep me from hearing
the echoing yawp of 'Typhoon *Who Accumulates Nubilous Clumps*'
or the singlestick drumming thunder of one more brummagem Zeus.
His fighting with lightning, his battling with bolts has simply got
to stop. O great-great grandson [through Io, Inachus' *daughter],*
display your pedigree now! Your pipes are pure panacea:
Spellbind the mind of Typhoon *with a tricky tune and turn*
a profit with music!

I offer a brace of blessings, bounty
unstinting for all your trouble. By my unilateral action
[1] lead Harmony *back to the world;*
[2] lead Harmony *off to wed.*

—*And now for you, O* Eros, *first sower of fertile wedlock:*
The merest bend of your bow, and the world is no longer vagrant.
If you, as you shepherd life through love, are The Source of All,
then loose just one last shaft and preserve The Sum of Things!
Fit yourself out in your fire for Typhoon *and summon back*
my blazing bolts to my hand. No one is not your victim—
so burn this *victim to ashes. Let fly your enchanted shaft*
to bag a prey which Zeus *himself could not bring down!*
And may his wits twitch madly for Cadmus' *entrancing strains*
as much as ever I did for Europa's *imperial lay.*"

He spoke, and mounted aloft in the shape of a highhorned bull
[from which occurrence, of course, we derive the name *Bull Mountain.*]

—Meanwhile, his back in repose on the bole of an oak in the wooded
pasture, *Cadmus* twisted his reeds into fine adjustment,
tuned to a pitch of deceit. [But his clothes were authentic enough:
genuine cowherd, the best.] Then, swelling his cheeks to impel
the caressing breath, he dispatched an ensnaring air to light
on *Typhoon*'s right ear.

The *Giant*, a friend of the fine arts, jumped
to his snaky soles at the sound of this ravishing rondo. The flaming
hardware of Zeus he deposited low in a handy cave,
entrusting its care to his mother, *Earth*. Then off he glided
to track down, note by delectable note, the pipes' seductive
theme which seemed to live right next door.

And *Cadmus* saw him
reach the hedge.

This rather rattled the human, who hid
in a rocky niche. However, our *Monster*, his heads held high—
way high—perceived him skulking, and tried, with unvoiced becks
and nods, to call him. [*Typhoon* did *not* perceive the hook
behind the shrillness, the web of doom.] He peered the shepherd
full in the eye, selected a right hand, stretched it out,
and then, from his human face [the one in the very middle;
ruddy as blood], he laughed and cracked the stillness with bombast:

"Hey, goatherd, why this terror? Why hide your eyes with your hand, kid?
Do I resemble the sort of monster that flushes out mortals
after he's bagged a Zeus, *or follows up purloined lightning*
with poaching whistles? Oh, show some sense—there's no connection
between his bolts from the blue and those stiff stalks that you blow.
Don't worry. That instrument's yours; you keep it. Typhoon*'s got one*
of his own: the Olympian *organ, plays by itself.*

—But Zeus?
Sitting in silence, no cloud to call his own, and twiddling
his thunderless thumbs, completely deprived of his natural noise—

now, there's a god who could use your outfit. Give your reeds
to him; they should make quite a bang.

—Those reeds, they're nothing.
To string them along with other reeds and swing them around—
that's not my style. I'm more for clouds. I roll them up
in a bundle with other clouds, and then let fly . . . and right
on the beat, a fortissimo boom with echoes all over they sky.

—Look, what do you say to a friendly game? Intone a tune
on your reeds; I'll render a crash on my thunder. Inflate your cheeks
until they bust in plumpness, and make your embouchure push;
but Boreas blasts for me—my bolts rebound at the beat
of his breath.

—Cowherd, why not give me your pipes? For a price:
When I take over the sceptre from Zeus, and sit in the saddle
heaven's throne, come along. Desert this earth for the sky.
I'll settle you and your pipes in heaven . . . and even your flock,
if you want: I refuse to break up a man and his herd. I'll give
your goats a special spot on Capricorn's back; a family
matter.
Or maybe down where Auriga drives his rig:
He shoves that splendid She-Goat along in the sky with a flick
of his shining wrist.
Your cows, now . . . well, there's the Bull. A little
damp, but he's got broad shoulders. If I make them stars, they'd rise
right there . . . or down by the turnaround rim, where the dew falls thick.
That's where Lady Moon's calves are mooing: windy, of course,
but a really vital sound.
Your hut? You won't need that.
And forage? Bushes are out. Combine your flock with the Kids
that live in the sky [it's a flashy group]. I'll make them a stall.
a perfect match for the Asses' Manger, just as shiny
and right next door.

If you turn star, you can stop cow-punching;
you can see we have Boötes. *I'll give you a starstudded staff;*
try driving Callisto's Wagon.

Ever herd bear?

—Shepherd,
you are in luck! Typhoon, *the son of heaven, extends you*
a place at his table. Today, your tunes are earthbound; tomorrow,
Olympus *rocks!*

And play for pay:
Your face in lights,
your very own spot in Heaven's Dress Circle. I can fix it.
But why play those pretty pipes a capella? *The sky has a* Harp—
I'll arrange duets.

—Perhaps you'd like to get married? Leave it
to me: There's Athena . . .
A shade too holy? Don't like gray eyes?
Take Leto, *then . . .*
Or Aphrodite?
Well, Artemis?
Charis?
Hebe, *maybe?*
But please, no request to bed Hera; *she's mine.*

—Might be you've got a brother who follows the horses, good man
with a team? The Sun's *got a four-horse outfit, and these are really*
firebreathers! Let him drive them.

—Seeing as you're a goatherd . . .
Zeus *has a goatskin cape, the* Aegis. *You want it? It's yours,*
my treat. He'll wear no armor when I reside on Olympus;
that way, less worry.
Athena *can keep her gear. No female's*

worth the bother. What could she do?
—Hey, shepherd,
MUSIC!
A march:
The 'HAIL-TO-THE-VICTOR-TYPHOON'-tune.
A hymn to Me, the New, Legitimate Lord of Olympus,
bearing the sceptre of Zeus,
wearing his thunderbolt robes!"

He spoke, his words provoking a few terse notes from *Nemesis'*
pen.

And *Cadmus knew*: This clodpole son of the soil,
smitten in mind by the exquisite sting of the rapturous reeds,
sped by the suture of *Fate*, has willingly tripped the trap.
He suppressed a smile and keened his reply in a cunning shout:

"I'm glad you enjoyed that piece from my pipes, but it's really nothing.
My proper instrument's seven-string harp. So how would you like me
to thrum you a victory anthem on that *when you own the throne?*
I competed with Phoebus *once, and, for all his heaven-made plectrums,*
ran rings around that god with my very own harp. But he's
an extremely bad sport: to keep his defeated son happy, his father
Zeus *had to launch a bolt and burn up my sweet-toned strings.*
Now they're nothing but dust.

But there is *a set of strings*
somewhere, with perfect body and tension—old sinews of Zeus*'.*
If I can find those hamstrings, I swear I will pluck a refrain
to fascinate forests, to mesmerize mountains, to temper the temper
of savage beasts. I'll stop the very river of Ocean
[old as the Earth, and set in his ways*], I'll make him reverse*
the course he wreathes around Earth*'s edge and double his flood*
back on himself without leaving his bed. I'll stay the stars,
make planets pause, stop Sun, *and freeze my* Lady Moon*'s axle.*

One small request: When you smite Zeus *and the other gods*
with your fiery shaft, please spare Apollo the Archer; *just him.*
And then, when Typhoon *sits down at table to banquet,* Phoebus
and I will compete. We'll find out who beats whom, when the theme
is 'TYPHOON IN ALL HIS GREATNESS'!
And please: Don't murder the Muses.
They move divinely, sing beautifully, too. They're just the group
to weave a soprano descant in concord with your manly bass
when your humble shepherd or Phoebus *leads the ensemble in dance."*

He spoke.

The *Monster*, glassy-eyed, nodded and quivered his curls.
Each single hairstrand vomited viperous venom and sprinkled
the hillpeaks. He coursed to his cave at a bound, reached in and lifted,
extracted the sinews of *Zeus*, and presented canny *Cadmus*
with a princely potlatch.

[Said hamstrings, of course, had come unstrung—
sad loss—when *Zeus* was engaging *Typhoon* in lust for battle.]

The shifty shepherd tendered thanks for the gift that would keep on
giving. He fondled the tendons with care, as befits prospective
harpstrings, and cached them away in a rocky niche, expressly
for use by *Zeus the Giant-Killer*.
In purposeful pucker,
he tipped his lips to his pipes and breathed the slightest of sighs,
squeezing the reeds to slits and sneaking the notes into being,
musing a delicate strain:

harmony...

Typhoon, however,
pricked up ear after ear to hear it, but knew it not:
To this charmed and ecstatic *Monster*, the spurious shepherd beside him
was piping impending confusion and rout to the deathless *Gods* . . .

but *Cadmus,* in fact, was lauding in song the triumph of *Zeus*
and crooning the doom of *Typhoon* to *Typhoon* as he sat hard by.

Æsthetics swelled into Œstrus.

AS:

An elegant, delicate youth,
gone mad with passion, thrills in thrall to love's fond wound
at the side of a virgin his age, with many an amorous glance,
now at the silvery grace and captivating curve of her face,
now at a wanton ringlet escaped from her hairs' lush plenty,
and now at a rosepetal hand, or feasts his gaze on the blushing
round of her breast so lusciously pressed by her bodice, or stares
at her neck slipping in and out of bareness;

& AS:

he joys to send
his eye aroving over and over her lovely surface
in blind survey which knows no surfeit, and vows he never
will leave his maiden . . .

SO:

to the dulcet sweetness of *Cadmus,*
all consciousness, reason, and sense were yielded up by *Typhoon.*

Book 2

Douglass Parker

In TWO, Typhoon ambles high,
Battling his way through the sky.
Fulgurant Zeus cannonades,
Olympus, in triumph, parades.

So...

SITTING TIGHT in his site by the spinney's pasturing shank
and whiffling his lips in undulant flux and reflux on the pipetips,
our make-believe gaucho exhaled—Cadmus, Agenor's scion.
But Zeus now, Cronus' scion, unseen and signless, in silence
inserted himself in the grotto and once again armed his hands
with their old, familiar fire. A mist masked Cadmus, and kept
his rock under wraps:
Once detecting the cheatin' art
of the underhand thunder thief, Typhoon might revise his mind
and butcher that part-time shepherd.
For now, however, the Monster,
twitching bewitched at Art's sweet spur, was lusting to listen
to more and more of that irresistible beat.

AS WHEN:

Ein Schiffer im kleinen Schiffe gives ear to the rich Melodei
Ach! how gewaltigt! and Ach! how verschmitzt! by a Siren gesungen:
At the yank of the Liebeslieds glamor, he races in premature traction
to self-willed

Kismet.

No more for him the slashed wave's splash,
no more the swathed sea's froth, no more the combed blue's foam
from oars unwaved and unwaving. Netted by Fate's falsetto,
he drifts rejoicing, the rudder erased, the Pleiades' sevenfold
warning effaced, the circular track of the Bear forgot—
and thinks [if he thinks at all] all nautical lore a lie.

SO:

The vibrant Giant, thrummed to a pitch of desire by the breath
of the tune in its cunning craft, embraced the pipes' sweet shaft,
his guide on the road to ruin.

But Hark! A Hush!
Around
the euphonious herdsman the shadowy turban of cloud swirled closer.
It muffled the breath-on reed and cut the Harmony short . . .

At a bound, the Monster resumed his abiding craze for combat
and tore to the grotto's bottom. Berserk with frenzied panic,
he rummaged and groped for windwalking thunder, for graspless lightning.
He probed with a toe, he scoured with a sole in footloose search
for the scintillant spark of the purloined bolt . . .
But when he got there,
the cavern was bare.

And then too late did he wot the plot,
Cronides' wily devices, the artful dodges of Cadmus.
Munitioned with scarps and crags, he aimed a leap at Olympus.
Trailing a rococo spoor from his foot's reptilian sole,

he spat a venomous jet from the depths of his picador throat.
Raining cascades from the toxic locks of his high-held heads,
the Giant begat a swell and surge in the rocky arroyos.
At his gallop, Earth's foundations sank; the base beneath
the hollows of roughridged Taurus exploded in crashes, and made
Pamphylia's nearby hills go prancing in terrified shimmy.
Earth's chasms gave booms abysmal. The headlands shivered and shook
by the shore. The inmost recesses writhed. The coast receded
and slipped away as the sand dissolved at the earthquaking pulse
and throb of his feet.

No fields, no fauna, no thing there was
he left unhurt.

Carnivorous Bears made meal for his molars,
ground in the grisly jaws of Typhoon's ursine personas.
The tawny frames of Lions, hair and all, were a main dish
gulped down in one by the counterpart maws of his leonine heads.
A cold collation of earth-fattened Snakes made dainty nosh
for viperoid gorge.

The Birds of heaven, faring on high
through air untrodden, discovered a sudden neighbor—a throat—
and furnished him dinner.

The handy Eagle, his dish of choice
(on the menu as *Oiseau de Zeus*), he devoured with jovial gusto . . .
and devoured the Ox at the plough, extending no whit of pity
to see its withers scored with bloody track of the traces.

With on postprandial swig, he left the rivers dust,
and roughly rousted the naiad brigades from their unmade beds.

Envision a naiad:

This child of the depths now plods along
a pedestrian stream through walkable water, her limbs unmoistened,

unshod her feet . . . and comes to a stop:

The onetime Nymph
of the Damp Directions now flails and stamps her maidenly soles
at the thirsty path of the river . . . and sticks fast, knees impacted
high and dry in the prisoning mud.

An aging Shepherd
took one horrified look at the wildly eclectic visage
of the maddened Monster, discarded his Syrinx, and hobbled away
at speed.

A Goatherd viewed the widespread bands of hands
and threw up his own, to the breezes entrusting his fluttery flute.
And the Laboring Plowboy?

Now no more did he shroud the seed
with soil, and now no more did he broadcast backhand the grain
on the new-scored ground, and now no more—since the managing spasm
of Typhoon's hand had already gouged—did he gouge the glebe
with the earthshaking share . . .

But despaired, and broke up his team.

Sprayed with the Monster's salvos, the ground split wide, denuding
the hollows beneath, and lancing their watery arteries. Up
from the opened abyss the nethermost channels bubbled and gushed
from the Earth's uncumbered nipples.

Crags were hurled on high,
drop from the air in rocky torrents, parching the waters,
expunging the sea. [This earthy bombardment sowed itself
and rooted to shape the underpinning of newborn islands.]

Trees—foundations and all—were fulcrumed forth from the Earth
to droop their callow fruit in the dirt; the fresh-leaved garden
was flattened and seared; the rosespeckled meadow dwindled to tinder;

and even the Western Wind spun dizzy and dumb at the blows
rained up by the waterless fronds of cypresses whirling in place.

And oh! what a day for dirges:
A Whimper, *molto con lamento*,
indulged in by Phoebus, keening more keenly for Hyacinth's havoc,
weaving a wail more mournful for far-off Amyclae's debacle,
than ever he did for Daphne's laurel felled at his feet.
A Plaint from Pan the Great in pain and pity for Pitys,
his sharply declining pine whom he, Pan, set to repotting.
A woeful Moan, as Our Lady Grey-Eyes, struck with recall of
her Olive beloved, broke into bawl at its shivered bole,
at the dole of its indwelling Attic nymph who once delivered
to her, its mistress, the city of Athens. A Threnody, throbbed
by the Peri of Paphos turned tears, Aphrodite, who melted in blubber
when her windflower rolled in the dust, spelling doom for her darling Adonis,
when her bed of roses, shaved bald, shed its buds to encrust with dust,
and slashed at her soft coiffure in compassion. A Bleat from Demeter,
earth-mother diffused in demented lament at the unfinished finish
of half-grown wheat, postponing forever the Harvest Feast.
Inconsolate Sobs from the tree nymphs, at one and the same
crash-rend-rip
evicted *from* and de-siblinged *of* their ravaged cottages
and non-identical twins, mute bark of departed shades.
One madly disturbed Hamadryad sprang nude from her truncated laurel,
her bushy companion since birth, while out of a lonesome pine
striding forth in flight, another virgin materialized
beside her neighbor and let down her hair, deciduous Nymph
that she was, as follows:

"Hamadryad delaurelled, in defoliate fear
of deflowering, join me in journey; here, worse is yet to come:
Left alone, you might see Phoebus;
gone alone, I might scan Pan.

O Woodsman, Woodsman, spare these trees! Touch not with your axe
a single bough of the blighted bush that was hapless Daphne.

O Shipwright, shape no wrong!
Shiver no timbers!
Sever
no thankless planks from my frightened Pine for the flanks of a freighter
that someday may surge the swells of Aphrodite, Our Lady of Foam,
and ruffle her ripples!

O Woodsman, grant me the coup de grace:
Strike not my c-cone, but aim me your axe at m-mid-trunk,
and chop my b-breast with the virginal bronze of s-spouseless Athena,
and send me still chaste (better dead than w-wed!) to Hades—
like Pitys and Daphne, forever green with respect to Eros."

Such was the speech of the pine nymph.

Finished, she plucked a few leaves
and devised an ersatz brassiere—oh, modest nymph that she was!—
with whose fresh-picked enshrouding she veiled the globes of her breasts,
the while she crossed her legs, and riveted thigh to thigh.

Such depression attracted the eye of her neighbor,
who shrieked out
in comforting tones:

"I know what you mean. Congenital virgins
like us are gifted at birth with unchastity's check: prim, prime
paranoia. Especially I, of Daphne's stemma, now hotly
traced, like Daphne's self, on the run. The question is, Whither?
Try crawling beneath a crag?

Well, no:
The lightning flung
at the mountains flang at Olympus burned them to bits. And besides,
these hills are the haunts of your Pan, whose lechery record is creepy!
He'd caper at me in the very same way he goateed at Pitys
(now, as you point out, a pine tree) or Syrinx (a roulade of reeds
and wax) . . . I'd wane to nix at his sex attacks, become ex-,

or shrink to a trace like Echo, a hill-ranging last retort,
where never is heard a spontaneous word, and nothing besides.
So, NO. No more do I dwell in blossom and leaf below
the timberline. The strange device for me: **EXCELSIOR***!*
Away aloft on the mountains; their peaks are still above water,
their slopes are the happy hunting grounds of Artemis, Virgin
Deluxe . . . and yet, consider Callisto: Zeus made up
as Artemis, Virgin DeCeit, slipped under Callisto's sheets,
and shrank her chastity's maiden defence to a bare minimum . . .

I guess I'll try full fathom five: What coupling could single
me out underwater?

—But hold: God Earthquake races along
the briny's bottom to grab Asteriё's. A-bubble with lust.
I better try air. With wings, now—oh, to have wings!—
I'd lightly skim over the airways, and wend my route on the roads
where goes each wind that blows—

but maybe the lightest wings
can supply only slightest safety:
Typhoon can clutch at the clouds
with his ladderless highsoaring hands . . . and that would give me pause.
But I can, should he force me into lawless and shameless embrace,

metamorphose!

I'll hide as a bird among birds . . . Yes! Oh, to be fair Philomela!
That's it!
I'll flit as the swallow, a smallë fowlë makynge
melodyë of the Rose's Romaunce, hearautinge the flow're-fleck'd dewe,
eke dere to Zephirus in thatte Aprillë, whan that I voyce
my lyrick notes and chatter, sprinting in wingèd dance
thither and back to my nest on the roof, whilst sister Procne
in sadness and suffering—you, sweet nightingale Procne, may warble
your woe in melancholy mode for Itys your son, and I
will moan and rasp at my . . . rape!

O great god Zeus, I pray you,

keep me unswallowed, no bird—or else the vile King Tereus,
annoyed at his avian state, will fly me down . . .
like Typhoon.

The Air, the Peaks, the Deeps—no one of these affords
a place to run, much less to rest. Beneath and below
the Earth is my refuge . . .

Ain't No Hidin' Place Down Deah:

The lampreys
and vipers that crowd this ogre's soles are invading the caves
that pock the underworld, spew venom wherever they squirm.

I'd really prefer to turn to water, a country fountain
as Comaetho did, when, in the first flush of her flowing, she joined with
her
fa-
ther
Cyd-
nussss . . .
actually, though, I'd rather not follow
the legend from source to debouchment . . . that would involve diluting
my virgin aqua purissima with the geysers of virginly, er, lust.

But what recourse have I left? Do I mate with the Monster TYPHOON
and bear it a manifold multiform otherly alien Monster,
taking after—no doubt—its daddy?
On balance, NO. Let's see:

I could stick to family trees, and shift from one to another,
maintaining a stemma that keeps its taxonomy free from any
and all suspicion of unladylike behavior. One danger:

I daren't slip into a myrrh-tree, bedaubing myself with the sticky
residue of Myrrha's incestuous passion.

No, here's my desire:
May I please become one of the Heliades, the poplars crowded
beside the banks of the plaintive Po? In diligent grief
I will shed from my orbs a positive stream of amber tears
and spread my leafy clusters to mingle and clutch in sorrow
and sadness with those of the poplar next door—the while, of course,
I lament, not Phaëthon their brother, but my longed-for chastity lost
in lament's maneuvers . . .
I'm sorry, laurel, I didn't mean it!
I could never climb into another trunk after being yours.

Then what?

Niobe turned to stone; I can do that too!
Be a stone with a groan, the object of pity to passing pilgrims . . .
But why should I pick as a pattern a rock with an acid tongue?
Forgive me, Leto. Wipe out forever the name that wars
with gods. It's not for a nymph who loathes fertility."

Book 2, continued

William Levitan

she spoke   and the sun bent west and set
night leapt skyward from the earth   a sudden cone
stretching to unimaginable height
cloaking the upper air   the deathless gods
wandered along the Cloudless Nile
while Zeus   son of Cronus   awaited dawn
seated on the solemn brow of the Bull

night
        around Olympus and the seven rings
of planets   sentries kept their posts
and sounded their nightly calls somewhat as men
call from high towers   the watchcry of the stars
in many tongues   echoed through space
from outmost Saturn to the inmost
circuit of the moon
                                        the Horae   Seasons
metronomes of the sky   handmaids of the sun
had secured their guard over the upper air
with a ring of clouds like city walls
the stars had barred the gates   no sound of fifes
and shawms   no tumult of soldiers   only
the airy whistle of breezes through the night

the Oxherd kept guard   the Serpent   the Bear
sleepless against a night attack
the Morning Star kept watch in the east
the Evening Star in the west   the Archer
kept the south gate   Cepheus the north

and watchfires everywhere   the blaze of stars
the lamp of the unsleeping moon
did the work of torches   lights spun
in furious whorls about Olympus
incising the air with flame   acrobatic
lightning twisted   tumbled   wheeled   danced
ripped   through the clouds in fantastic displays
a comet trailed long dreadlocks of light
meteors   warpartners of Zeus
shot lines of fire that spanned the sky
like rafters across a ceiling
and storm's companion   rainbow
plaited its many colors in an arc
opposite the radiant sun   twining
pale green with indigo   violet with rose

then Nike who is Victory   came to Zeus
in the guise of Leto   and spoke sharp words
to her father   full of twists and turns

think of your children Zeus   look to their safety
I could not bear to see virgin Athena
bound to Typhon's bed   do not permit
the unmothered   to know motherhood herself
no   you must fight   muster your clouds again
rainlord   retrieve your thunderbolt   it is time
even now   the pillars of the world
are being shaken   under Typhon's hands
the union of its four elements dissolves
Deo has disowned the harvest   Hebe
the cup   Ares the spear   Hermes the staff

Apollo has renounced his lyre taken
swan's form winged away his feathered arrows
left scattered on the ground Aphrodite
who sees to couplings has wandered off
distracted and the world goes without seed
the cords of settled harmony have slipped
as Eros who adorns the bride who masters all
and is unmastered bold Eros has fled in panic
and Hephaestus has left Lemnos limping
I even pity Hera despite her hatred
for me I could not bear to see your father
Cronus return to sit among the stars
or see the Titans lords of Olympus again
though I myself am called a Titan
I say the rule belongs to you my lord
and to your children take your thunderbolt
defend our daughter Artemis the chaste
how could I bear to keep her for a suitor
who offers only violence as a bride price
how will I call upon the Midwife
when the Midwife herself is in labor

she spoke and Sleep led all of breathing nature
to its rest alone Zeus son of Cronus
remained awake while Typhon sprawled heavy
vast and slow upon the bed of Earth his mother
and she opened wide her folds for him
her hollows sinkholes grinning chasm
and his snake heads sank deep into the ground

at daybreak all the mouths and all the throats
of Typhon of the many arms bawled out
their challenge to Zeus and that dread noise
carried to the far rim of the earth where Ocean
rolls in his fixed bed endlessly circling
the established quadrants of the world
the air rang with the echo incoherent

jagged sound   raucous   indiscriminate
as the monster assumed   his panoply of forms
howls hisses bellows brays grunts shrieks
the roaring of lions the gibbering of apes
the gaping rasp of leopards yap of dogs
and in the center   a single head
on a single neck   cried with a human voice

now let my hands   lay waste the house of Zeus
now let them shake   the world's foundation
and with it the generation of gods
let them shatter   the fastenings of Olympus
drag down the pillar of the sky   let Atlas
throw off his burden   Atlas my brother
for I will never let a son of Earth
be bowed under compulsion of the heavens
let Atlas join the fight   let him break off
mountains   launch them against the sphere of stars
he once carried on his shoulders   let the Seasons
run in panic   pallid handmaids of the sun
fleeing a rain of mountains in the sky
let all separate elements be confounded
let earth mix with air   water with fire
let Olympus and the sea be one

the four winds   I will compel as slaves
day and night   I will commingle with a single hand
Ocean will overwhelm Olympus
rising high   he will swamp the stars
and the Bear who never sets   will be drenched
the Great Wain will be hauled through the sea

now let my bulls bellow   now let them shake
the equatorial circle of the sky
let them break with their own notched horns
the horns of the fiery Bull   their like in form
and let the cattle of the moon   abandon

their usual pastures in fear
of the heavythroated bellow of my heads
my bears will face down the Bear of Olympus
my lions will drive the Lion from the sky
the Serpent will shudder at my serpents

and there is nothing that Zeus can do

he has only lightning   my weapons
are the ordnance of Earth   tsunamis   mesas
archipelagos   massifs   escarpments
fjords   cataracts   and inundations
in which his lightning will drown
                                        and then
I will set Iapetus free   chain Poseidon
in his place   I will unbind Prometheus
send a new and hungrier eagle
to tear at Hephaestus' liver instead
I will take on the twin forms
of Iphimedeia's sons   seal Hermes up
in a brazen jar the grifter god
he freed Ares from prison   he will know
the same prison himself   I will strip
the manslayer of his armor
and I will make him crawl
Artemis will be forced to Orion's bed
Leto will spread her pallet for Tityus
Pallas will be carried off and joined
to Ephialtes   married at long last
o let me see it all   Ares a slave
Athena a mother
                              Zeus son of Cronus
will heft the spinning mass of heaven
onto his own shoulders   the load of Atlas
and there he will stand   biting back his rancor
at my wedding   as I take his Hera
for my bride   his lightning will supply

my marriage torches   the blazing sun itself
will light my chamber   constellations
will provide my nuptial lamps   the Moon
and Aphrodite   will prepare my bed
the Seasons   will erect a lovebower
for me   as they once did for Zeus
and Artemis   the Graces   Aphrodite
Leto   Athena   Hebe   all will draw
water for the bridegroom's bath
from his kindred Ocean   and at the banquet
Apollo will sing of Typhon   not of Zeus

I only claim ancestral rights
for Uranus the Sky is my brother
a second son of Earth
and the sky which I will rule   where I will dwell
is in my mother's gift
my brother Cronus   god who swallowed gods
I will lift from the abyss   restore to light
a partner in my work   the ancient Titans
and earthborn Cyclopes   I will raise aloft
and settle under one celestial roof
I will have more and better weapons forged
for my two hundred hands   new thunderbolts
of new and hotter fire   and I will build
a new and greater heaven   an eighth sphere
higher   broader   brighter than the rest
with new and brighter stars   no less than that
will be adequate for Typhon
then   to supplant the swarms of children
fathered by Zeus   I will beget
a new generation of gods
each with a hundred heads   a hundred necks

Zeus heard these boasts   and laughed

then Eris Strife led Typhon into battle
and Nike who is Victory led Zeus

and they waged war

not for a herd of cattle or flock of sheep
not for a lovely woman's face
or some inconsequential town
but for lordship of the upper air
the throne and scepter of Zeus

Zeus took up a position among the clouds
whipped them until they thundered and rang
with the song of Enyo sacker of cities
then he fit the clouds around him as a breastplate

the monster's bullheads trumpeted back
of their own accord a deep booming
swollen sound that rumbled through Olympus
his intermingled serpents hissed and skirled
like warpipes in shrill accompaniment
and he fortified his station on the earth
piling cliff against cliff crag against crag
ridge on top of ridge until he raised
a circling wall of landforms fitted tight
like an army echeloned for battle
canyons leaned on canyons bluffs on bluffs
one neckland supported another
and valleys climbed on valleys into the air
great alps were Typhon's helmets and his heads
were encased in their steep places
the monster when he fought had just one body
but many necks and many arms
on that one body and the spearsharp claws
and teeth of lions and the plumes of serpents
that overmount the stars
now Typhon ripped

great trees from the earth   balled them in his hands
and hurled them at the son of Cronus   Zeus
easily burnt them to dust   with a single spark
of lightning   ancient elms   white poplars   firs
enormous planetrees   baobabs   sequoias
cypresses   all uprooted   burnt to dust
earth's crust split   gaped open

every quarter of the world was shaken
the four winds   warpartners of Zeus
raised funnels of black ash into the air
they swelled the waves   they beat the sea
and all Sicily quaked   between Pachynus
and Pelorus   the slopes of Etna
shook and roared   the rocks of Lilybaeum
in the west   howled in prophetic dread
and in the north   the nymph of Athos   wailed
the woods of Macedonia   cried aloud
and in the east   the aromatic trees
of Assyrian Lebanon   toppled and crashed

new shots from Typhon   some went wide
and veered across the circuit of the moon
others were blown aside by winds
stray thunderbolts of Zeus   fell into the sea
Nereus the ancient   fetched them out
and brought them to the strait
of the northern waters called Cronian
where he offered them as dedications
to the god
                    now Zeus marshaled
the grim sons of Ares   Panic and Fear
guardians of the upper air
Panic he invested with his lightning   Fear
with his thunder   and Typhon was afraid
then Nike who is Victory   raised her shield
and held it before Zeus   and Enyo shouted

and Ares doubled her call   and Zeus son of Cronus
who bears the aegis   breasts the hurricane
stormed down from the clouds
riding the chariot of Time   whose horses
are the four winds   now he attacked with lightning
now with thunder   now with dense falls
of flintsharp ice   heavy hail   pelting
the monster's heads   slicing off his hands
as if with knives   one amputated hand
tumbled in the dirt   rolled   but kept its grip
on the hilltop it had seized as weapon
even as it fell   the hand fought on
alone   selfwilled   it flung its missile
berserk   in its hatred of Olympus

Zeus brandished his thunderbolt
and Typhon of the many arms   raced
to the cataracts of earth   the mountain torrents
swollen streams   he laced his many fingers
cupped his palms   and with a prodigious hoist
yanked   massive chunks of water from the floods
cascading down the heights
and flung them   at the lightning of Zeus
the fire of the upper air burned brighter
for all the icy water   and the water
touched by the brilliant flame
boiled and steamed   dried away to nothing
Typhon had meant to drown the lightning
in this water   fool   he did not know
that lightning has its birth in those same clouds
that also bring forth rain
                                        still he fought on
cutting riverbeds from their banks   uprooting
headlands   crags   stone outcroppings
to hurl at Zeus   but each of these
Zeus turned aside   or dodged   or batted back
to Typhon like a ball   or burned to ash

or shivered   with his lightning
so Enyo
wargoddess   sacker of cities
held the two in balance   Zeus and Typhon
and the upper air crashed and rolled like the sea
and lightning danced like bacchants in the sky
as firebarbed arrows   hurtled downward
the thunderbolts of Zeus

For a dryish exhalation of the earth, akin to smoke, had already risen up from the underground cavities where it is formed, become compressed within a cloud and stifled, as it were, in the cloud's tight places, producing considerable heat. This friction-heated cloud now rumbled, as the flame confined within labored to escape along some inner path. The flame, of course, cannot go upward since the upper layers of cloud are thick with condensed moisture and prevent escape in that direction. But the lower layers are dry and rarified; hence, lightning takes this route and flashes downward. And so, just as sparks are born from rubbing stone on stone, male flint against the female pyrite, fire aloft is engendered by friction inside dense and murky clouds. Now as you know, a thinner, lighter exhalation gives rise to winds, but there is another vapor of the earth, a moist exhalation, drawn up by the sun from the waters high into the air, where it thickens and becomes a veil of clouds. Then, mixing with the thinner exhalation of which winds are made, it dissolves into a fall of rain, thus returning to its original state as water. Such then is the character of lightning, of thunder, and of clouds.

the next bolt   cut through Typhon's rank of lions
skewering them with fire   a spinning flame
flew at his screaming heads and necks
one blast   seared his many hands   another
scorched his shoulders and his horde of serpents
a longmaned comet   singed his hair   Typhon
was ablaze   his flesh   his hair   his serpents'
venom   dried in their throats   their hissing stopped
by heat   his many eyes   shriveled   to cinders

Zeus then unleashed a squall of freezing rain
that slashed Typhon's skin   rimed his cheeks
wherever he turned   the monster met constraint
dawnward   fires stoked by a dire east wind
northward   bitter gales and snow
to the south   the hot together with the wet
to the west   Enyo's cracking tempests
Zephyrus and Notus   pyrebright mist
so fire followed frost which followed fire
and when the rainlord   loosed his storms again
their ice was balm to Typhon's blistered limbs

dry Earth was also battered   bruised
mother of Typhon   mother of Titans
she saw the spikes of ice in one son's flesh
and begged another   Helios the Sun
to melt the flintsharp hail of Zeus
with a red hot ray
she too was warmed and thawed   but when she saw
the burns on Typhon's tribe of hands
she called on winter storms to cool
the withering heat that overmastered him

Earth lifted her veil of forests with a hand
watched Typhon's faces shrivel   his heads smoke
and she grieved   the Earthborn's knees gave way
as heavy   he went down   drunk with the fire
of the lightning   stricken with a weapon
not of steel   he lay supine   upon the Earth
his mother   his limbs   snaking in her dust
his lungs   belching flames   into the air

Zeus thundered his victory   and jeered

impervious to lightning I see Typhon
what a fine   brave   friend to Cronus you are
what a stupendous son of Earth

what sweet revenge   for all the Titans suffer
how long now before you take your seat
in the unreachable regions of the upper air
before you claim   the throne of Olympus
the staff and robe of Zeus
                                        you fraud
you bogus potentate   you tinsel shah

go on   restore the Titans   all of them
Eurynome   Astraeus   Ophion
Cronus   release Prometheus from his chains
strip Zeus of his lightning   rip Poseidon
from the sea   they are both helpless now
and they are both your slaves   Zeus with a torch
at your marriage feast to Hera   writhing
with jealousy and wrath   the Earthshaker
with no trident   but a cup by your table
in case your throats get dry
                                          yes   all the gods
serve you now Typhon   Ares   Apollo
Hermes son of Maia   your messenger
will rush the Titans news of your success
and shout your triumph to the sky
Hephaestus   now will craft his treasures solely
at your command   a necklace for your bride
perhaps   or sandals for her feet   or a second throne
in gold for her   your goldthroned Hera
the earthborn Cyclopes   will forge your weapons
and Eros   the bewitcher   the deceiver
who conned your mind with hope   you will bind
with a golden chain   along with golden
Aphrodite   and you will force Ares
governor of iron   to chains of bronze

with all this power Typhon   tell me
how could you not stand   the feeble fire
of the smallest lightning bolt Zeus has

how could all those ears recoil
from one tiny clap of thunder
when did you become so delicate
Typhon   where are all your weapons
your little houndheads   your yawning lions
where is the booming rumble in your throats
that shook the ground   your serpents that spat poison
your bulls   your boars   your bears   where are the hands
that used to fling whole continents to the sky

yield to the sons of heaven   son of Earth
for with one hand of my own   I overpowered
two hundred hands of yours

and now let Sicily
swallow this monster whole   bury him deep
under broad   heavy hills   griming the hair
of his hundred heads   with thick Sicilian muck

yet   for all your arrogance   your blasphemy
your fatuous assaults   I will raise
a monument to you   and your presumption
a cenotaph   marked with the words

Typhon
Earthborn   who struck the upper air with stones
but the upper air consumed him   with its fire

so Zeus mocked the son of plowland Earth
and Bull Mountain in Cilicia
bellowed the god's victory
the river Cydnus   danced in bacchic joy
as it flowed past Tarsus   its ancient twin

but Earth herself   lay broken   bereft
stone mantle torn   exposed to winds
that beat her breasts and sheared away a forest
as a mourning lock   her tresses fell
as in a month of autumn   she gouged gullies

in her cheeks   wailed   wept   swollen rivers
that crashed down echoing mountainsides
while Typhon's thrashing arms and legs
stirred storms that swamped ships
even in safe harbors   swept across
fields   where crops grew tall
and smothered them with dust

then Nature
housekeeper of the world
who mends its fabric   renews its substance
closed up the fissures in the broken land
set cliffs and canyons in their former beds
and bound them again within the framework
that cannot be undone   the harmony
that will not be untuned   among the stars
confusion yielded   as Helios the Sun
restored the Lion to his proper place
beside the Virgin   and Selene the Moon
led the Crab back into position
across from Capricorn   and fixed him there

at last   mindful of Cadmus   Zeus son of Cronus
dispelled the cloud that covered him   and spoke

Cadmus   my virtuoso   you have secured
the gates of Olympus   with your pipes
now   with the Lyre of heaven   I myself
will celebrate your marriage   you will be
son-in-law   to Ares and Aphrodite
the gods   will be your wedding guests   and I
their king   will enter your house   what more
could any mortal want

let me advise you though
son of Agenor
take care not to anger the god   at Dirce stream
Ares   resentful of his dragon's slaughter
but at night   with your eye upon

the Serpent aloft   and holding in your hand
a fragment of sweet-smelling serpentine
make sacrifice to Ophiuchus
to him who holds the Serpent
and burn on the altar fire   the antlers
of a great Illyrian stag
and so may you escape the bitterness
spun out as your apportioned fate   if indeed
the Fates   are ever open to persuasion

no longer think   of your father's anger
no longer fear   for your brothers
wandering far   but alive and safe   Cepheus
has made his way   to the southern realms
of Ethiopia   among people who will be called
Cephenes   Thasos has sailed to Thasos
and Cilix reigns as king over Cilicians
under the snowy heights of the Bull
Phineus has come to the coasts of Thrace
where I will make him great with wealth
drawn from Thracian mines
and he will marry Cleopatra   daughter
of Orithyia and the chill North Wind
your own future   will be no less than your brothers'
you will rule over Cadmeans   bequeathing
your name to your people
                                        but for the present
give up this endless circling after the bull
your sister   has been married to the king
of Cretan Ida   Asterion of Dicte
all further revelation   I leave to Phoebus
at the navel of the earth   so off with you now
to Delphi
                    he spoke and sent
Cadmus son of Agenor on his way
then he turned his chariot toward the wheeling stars
with Nike who is Victory at his side

to drive her father's team
and so
Zeus son of Cronus   returned to the upper air
and the Horae   Seasons   opened the gates
to receive him   wreathing the sky
with garlands for his sake
the gods travelled homeward
in their accustomed guise
when they crossed into Olympus
they took on fleeting   new personas
Athena now unarmed   in party robes
Ares   as festive Comus
and Nike who is Victory   as Song

then Themis   who abides in law   set out
the spoils stripped from the fallen monster
and she hung them high in the forecourt of Olympus
grim notices   for Earth to contemplate

Book 3

Joseph Harrington[1]

In which brave Cadmus' Ship wanders the Sea;
Electra offers Hospitality.

The Fight was finished by the Winter's end,
That Time the girded Hunter doth ascend;
When no more doth the Bull his Footsteps chill
Beneath the circling Sea, but riseth still;
Nor in the northern Region of the Bear
Do feet then pass unsodden o'er the Mere;
No more the Massagetean Istrus plows
With wooden Wheels in place of wooden Prows
With which to cross the River with his Brood.
For Lo! Zephýrus brings the Blossoms Food—
That Herald of the brimming season, Spring—
When Swallows in the heavens 'gin to sing

1. I have interpolated, into "my" Book 3, translations of the more "decorative" passages by a certain Scilly Cobber, an English poet of little renown who "flourished" in early eighteenth-century London. Of him a waggish contemporary wrote, "For Cobber as a *Poet* was so *bad* / He didn't even make the *Dunciad*." Be that as it may, Cobber must be given credit as the first English writer to attempt a translation of the *Dionysiaca*. "Pope has cornered the Homer market," Cobber complained in a letter to a friend. "Do you know any epics nobody's done?" To which the friend replied, "Well, there's Nonnus, I guess, but . . ." How far Cobber got is not known, as only these fragments remain; the

That early waketh mortals from their Sleep,
When laughing Buds unfurl'd, begin to peep.
Spring bathéd every Vein in such Liqueur
That all Life laugheth through the Springtime Flow'r.
  Eftsoons when Darkness rosy-fingered Dawn
Had cleft, didst Cadmus come, walking along
The Path from pointy Peaks of Taurus' Heights
Unto the saffron Vales Cilíciïte.
'Twas now the Time for Ships to slip their Reins,
And Cadmus itched to ride the stormy Main.
The Masts did lift their Heads into the Air
As Breezes promised Passage passing Fair.
  But soon the fickle Waves began to prance
And stop't the tumbling Dolphin in her Dance—
The Forestays hummed as all the Hawsers hissed
And Sails responded to the tempest's Kiss.
Th'intrepid Ship the restless Flood displaced
And raced the Waves and Swells across that Space;
The Keel gallumph'd o'er Billows with a Splash
And broke the Ocean's Backbone with a Crash.

Then ten circling dawns after the vernal turning,
Zeus glided across glassy seas.
But when his prow parted the Trojan Hellespont,
gales pushed him backward on the swelling sea-road,
past berserking Scamander's mouth, past
Samothrace's isle, thence to shores of Sithonia,
virgin Harmonia's safe waiting-place.

---

rest tragically served as tinder for kindling, and other household needs. It is the present author's hope Scilly Cobber has been derived from various letters, diaries, government records, scrapbooks, coal bills, memos, grocery lists, and unflattering reviews. Cobber was born in the parish of St. Malfund's (this the same St. Malfund's that figured so prominently in the Conquest), son of a parson (Barry) and a squire's daughter (Pertie). Pertie's family, the Wagstaffs, had once been hereditary doorkeepers for the Earl of Scumford, a fact of which the family was inordinately proud. The marriage was an unhappy one, as Pertie came to the conclusion that she had "married down"; money problems continu-

Thither inspired breezes escorted them shoreward,
Rhea-guided. The crew rejoicing spied
the Samothracian torch and finally furled sails.
Oar-tips wrinkled the samite-smooth bay;
they beached hull in harbor; stones held hawsers;
anchors gripped bottom; and men leapt ashore.
When sun set, they spread bed-rolls.
After evening meal, their eyes fell shut,
and wandering sand-man stole upon them then.

Dawn rose upon the fiery wings of Eurus,
dispelled lapis twilight, glanced along Phrygian
Ida's peaks, showing herself as she panned
the harbor and revealed the purple waves beyond.
Then Cypris cloaked the sea in calm no sail
could cross, keeping Cadmus for Harmonia.
Already gulls disturbed the calm with cries; already
helmeted bands of desert-dwelling Corybants
thumped their shields in Cretan dance and, frenzied, leapt,
whirled, rivals' louder thudding iron on hide;
double pipes played double time to rhyme
the bounding steps. Trees hummed, rocks drummed,
spirited branches swayed along, and dryads sang.
Even bears joined the dance, padding, reeling,
face to face. Lions joined in: their roars
mimicked triumphant cries of priests of Cabiri,
maniacally sage. The shrilling single pipes
(those the horn-polisher contrived in Cronus' days)
played in praise of Hecate, goddess of dogs.

---

ally beset the couple, whose household eventually grew to fourteen children, seventeen cats, and a basset hound (who was apparently rather fatalistic). At one point, Pertie was tempted to decamp with a band of "gypsies," but forbore; she later earned quite handsome royalties on her book *Why I Did Not Decamp with a Band of Gypsies (And Why You Shouldn't Either)*, enough to maintain a separate establishment in London, far from the parsonage. Barry, a native of Cornwall, was dead-set on his son's entering the ministry, but Scilly was intent upon the writing life and made his way to live with his mother in London. Shortly thereafter Barry, disillusioned and penniless, apparently gave up the

The Corybants' noisy clamor then woke Cadmus;
the Sidonian sailors slept no more, as the leathery thump
thumping raised them from the clattering pebbly shingle,
and they trudged away from their wave-washed bed.
Cadmus left them there to tend the ship while he
sauntered out to find the city and Harmonia's house.
As he neared the walls, where he saw some women treading
and treading in a vast pit of dirty clothes,
Peitho, Lady of the Spousal Chamber, stopped him.
You would have thought she was a mortal woman then,
a housemaid, cradling to her bosom a silver jug
filled with sweet spring water, like the customary
groom's bath, a life-giving nuptial plunge.
Peitho cloaked Cadmus in invisibility,
erased his form from head to toe, and led
the way to the glittering palace, by command of Aphrodite.

Then this crow, perched in lacy shade
cast by silvery olive leaves, starts squawking,
inspired to clack its beak and loudly chastise
the youth for his dallying walk to his bride to be.
It flaps its wings, caws, and castigates him thus:
"So the Bachelor's a virgin! Or is he just a kid?
Eros is fast—he'll ghost slow grooms!
(Sorry, Peitho—Aphrodite's in a hurry, so
get a move on!) Hot Eros beckons, bro,
so why are you dragging your heels? Some Adonis you are!
You wouldn't know what to do with the babes of Byblos.

---

ministry and decamped with a band of Roma people, as a juggler. When Scilly arrived at the capital at the age of thirteen, he was apprenticed as a printer's "devil," a title he took quite literally. Like the young Benjamin Franklin, he began leaving unsigned essays and poems on his boss's desk. Unlike Franklin, Cobber's were never published; rather, his boss responded by saying, "Scilly! Boy! Din' I tell you never to do this agin?!" But the young Cobber persisted. The printer's office was quite dreary: small windows that were never cleaned but were shaded by the soot of London coal stoves; rack upon rack of dead-looking lead type; rickety tables; a tobacco-spattered floor; and the large, unwieldy

Dude, you don't even know where Byblos is, *do you?*
And you grew up near there—near
the Graces—and Assyrian Cytherea?—the one
with the dance? And *an Athena who's actually totally hot.*
Seriously, Cadmus, Peitho's no Artemis—her name
means 'Persuasion,' dude! And has she found
a bachelorette for you! So forget about your sister
and all that bull—Harmonia's a sure thing,
but you gotta act fast. Oh—and her mom will love *you:*
you're husband material—and Harmonia will love you
even more (heh heh). She's Aphrodite's
daughter, dude—no, I'm serious! All you
gotta do is hand her the rose. And thank me,
Bro Crow, the love bird, heh heh.
(Actually, thank Aphrodite—I'm working for her.
But Athena's my real boss.)"
And with these words,
the noisy crow became a silent watchful crow.

Cadmus slipped along the winding way, 'til
the towers and pillars of the guest-loving royal court
peeked above the hills; Peitho pointed to it,
silently signing the words in her mind, mutely displaying
a painted palace glittering like the shining stars;
whereupon Peitho rose into the sky—
and then she was a He—with winged feet—a different guide
to fly ahead along the king's highway.

---

press itself. Those who worked in the shop, like the others in Grub Street, were typically at least mildly intoxicated, so that collisions were not uncommon: types would get mixed or lost, so that "important" would become "impotent," for instance, or "careful" became "covfefe." Scilly thrived in this atmosphere, and there were so many printshops at that time that even his poems could find their way into print. When he was seventeen, Mars Quoin & Sons published portions of *To Thalia, from Her Shepherd Love; Being an Epico-Pastoral in Four Parts; Interesting Tale of Intrigue and Lust; No Politics* (1718). The rest, sadly, has been lost. It has been suggested by Tudd (1974) that the tale in *To Thalia*

Then Cadmus conn'd the House with great Amaze,
The Masterpiece Hephaestus didst upraise
As Gift for young Electra, when a Bride.
There the many Ornaments he spied,
The which th'industrious god from Lemnos brought,
For to bedeck the Palace newly wrought,
With well-formed brazen Portico before
The Pillars framing massive double Doors
That led into a Vestibule whose Walls
Bore wondrous Carvings, covered overall
By cupola'd Dome to serve as Roof, withal.
The Palace Walls within, of Cément made,
Were covered o'er with Stones, which were inlaid.
Before the House a walléd Orchard bore
Much toothsome Fruit within its Acres four.
The amorous Palm, his Branches spreading wide
Did plight his Troth to Female by his Side;
The sibling pear Trees whispered in the Breeze
That made their pendulous Fruit stroke olive Trees;
Springtime Zephyrs made the Myrtle wave,
Saluting virginal Laurels, ever grave;
While wafting perfumed Morning did caress
The verdant little Leaves of Cypresses.
The juicy Pomegranate and the Fig,
Grew red and purple on adjacent Twigs;
And Apple plumped 'gainst rosy Apple Cheek.
Thus did the Gardens flourish through the Weeks.
Apollo's mournful Flower blossomed there:

---

represents Cobber's own attempts to woo and win the favors of one Adelaide Whipsnipe, a farmer's daughter who lived near St. Malfund's. Each morning, pretty Adelaide would sally forth, poking the kine, driving them to pasture on the upper field. Young Cobber would contrive to be "accidentally" in her way, reading a small volume of what looked like poetry. A neighbor once recalled a loud, young female voice yelling, "Wha? *You* agin?! Bloody 'ell! Sod off, you!" Whether or not this affair formed the *materia poetica* for *To Thalia*, the extended similes of, for instance, "a whale to the seven planets," or the "beloved's nonpareil white skin" to polar bears' fur, were undoubtedly Cobber's own.

It traced a single Word amidst its fair
And placid Blue. And when Zephyrus breathed
The flow'ry Garden through, Apollo seethed
With longing for his ever-youthful Love;
And when the Wind assailed it from Above,
He quailed for fear the Quoit would rebound,
And jealous Gusts would knock the Flower down—
If you believe the Tale the Poets tell
(That Phoebus bawled when Hyacinthus fell
And writhed about all bloodied in the Dust;
That tearless Eyes let many a Teardrop pass,
which on the Plant embossed its own "Alas!").
Hard by this shady Garden gushed a Spring,
Dividing into Channel, following
Two separate Paths. From one the People drank;
The Other was cut up along its Bank
To flow in Furrows to the thirsty Shoots.
These thundered gently 'round the Laurel's Roots,
Like Phoebus played for Daphne on the Lute. }
Within, a Troop of golden Boys stood
With Lamps, so that the Guests could see their Food.
Without, two Rows of golden Doggies stayed
That snarled, as though to keep the Guests at bay;
But when familiar Persons turned the Latch,
They'd roll right o'er to have their Tummies scratched.
(For these automatonic Canines were
And if they knew you not, they would not stir.)
With friendly Barks they now did Cadmus hail
And wagged their little artificial Tails.

(Adelaide's father was a notorious drunkard whose wife had died of dropsy some years earlier; he was accounted a very poor farmer because, instead of herding cows and planting crops, he kept adding to his stone house. Indeed, sometimes it seemed as though his only object in taking his plough out to the fields was to find new rocks. Old Whipsnipe became known as the "Rock Farmer" over pints at the local tavern, and patrons would bait him when he came around: "'Ow's the price fer a bushel o' rocks, Whipsnipe?"—followed by peals of laughter. The old farmer would scowl, spit, walk past, and return to his construction project. The house began to take on the bizarre ap-

The Gardens, Sculptures, glinting inlaid Walls,
The Paintings and the grandeur of the Hall:
All this to see did Cadmus move his Face
And was impressed by the palatial Place.

Meanwhile, Emathion left the marketplace,
exchanged royal judgment seat for saddleback,
and pointed his courser's arching neck towards home.
This man was King of Samothrace, seat of Ares,
by virtue of his mother, Electra's royal line.

The reins of sovereignty were passed from Dardanus,
his brother, who left his native soil to settle
in the Troad, to harrow dust of Ida's sides,
and to plat Dardania, fortress city
named for him. He drank confluent water of Rhesus
and the seven streams, and left Emathion
the monarchy and scepter of the Cabiri.
This Dardanus, brother of Emathion,
Zeus begot, and Justice nursed. The Seasons all
raised the baby (this in days when they brought Zeus'
scepter, the Robe of Time, and Olympus' staff
up to Electra's hall, to prophesy
the coming of the everlasting Pax Romana).
But when the lad, in bloom of youth, went forth,
an irrevocable oracle of Zeus ordained
a third great deluge deep to drown the world
(this after the Ogygian flood had covered Thessalian rocks
and Delphi's cloudy heights with snow-cooled flow;

---

pearance of a termite hill or lava flow—something formed by nature, not by man. The original cottage had been given an upper floor, a wing supported by piles, a long hallway without a room at the end. It is not known how Adelaide felt about the floorplan.) Be that as it may, young Cobber continued to support himself by his meager salary; his love life was rather meager as well, given that he was living with his mother. His mother, however, had become a rather successful authoress. After her sensational debut, she published a sequel, *What to Do If Your Husband Decamps with a Band of Gypsies*, in addition to a popular manual of household management, *Girl! Wash Your Slop-Bucket!* Her

and after all the earth and all its people died
in a second exterminating, globe-girdling torrent,
when only Deucalion and Pyrrha bobbed about,
lodged in a little hollow boat, their only home,
wafting over mountain tops, atop the seas.)
At this third storm, when rains from Zeus covered
Mounts Athos and Itamos, Dardanus fled,
cleaving the sea-road to ancient Ida's peaks.

His brother Emathion, ruler of snowy Sithonia,
rode from the clamorous marketplace, arrived at court,
dismounted, and stood amazed: the handsome hero's mien
combined manly beauty with the natural grace of youth.
His form telegraphed his noble birth to the prince,
whose intuition silently heralded the news;
he regaled his guest with welcoming honors,
bounteous fare, and Electra's hospitable toil.
Cadmus wanted for nothing, yet looked at his shoes through the meal,
hid his anxious face from servers and hostess alike,
meekly served himself and barely touched the feast.
As they feasted, Corybantic reeds
breathed their tunes in turn, players' fingers danced
the riddled run of the pipes, hands in time with feet;
brassy cymbals crashed in time with reeds and drums;
the seven-string lyre twanged beneath the quill.
When Cadmus had enough of the reveling flutes and the food,
he moved nearer the queen, who peppered him with questions.
He brushed aside his fevered sea-wanderings

fame included a bit of fortune, enough for the down payment on a handsome Queen-Anne townhouse; Scilly occupied the garret, per his request (in a diary he wrote, "Blimey! Living in a garret in London, getting a poem published—I'm a real writer now!"). Indeed, after the publication of the excerpt of *To Thalia*, other publishers tried to discover the author (it had been published under the pen-name "Farcecalian"—apparently, "Pharsalian" was meant). This was not a hard task, as Quoin, his boss, had lost a not-insignificant amount of funds on the venture and had vowed never to publish anything by the young Cobber again. Into his early twenties, the aspiring author was

to speak of his illustrious lineage, and words
poured from his lips like a fountain's ceaseless flow.
"Mistress Nymph, why ask me of my blood and origin?
When I think of offspring of mortals, I think of leaves:
some the wild wind of autumn scatters wide;
spring brings forth others a tender green.
Thus the ephemeral generations of men:
one travels on the road of life 'til death
calls a halt; one thrives, then must away.
Thus time cycles *back* upon itself;
thus gray age metamorphoses to youth.
    But I will tell you of my noble lineage.
In Argos, Hera's city, famous for horses—
situated like the navel of the Peloponnese—
lived Inachus, who gave his name to the land about.
He was a temple-keeper, foremost hierophant,
the patron goddess's voice in Her awful rites.
In reverence of Hera, he refused his beautiful daughter,
Io, to the Lord of gods, Leader of the stars.

Then Io, her face and form transmogrified,
was herded out among the kine to feed;
Hera sent sleepless Argos, spotted with eyes,
to watch the horned bride of Zeus, Whom no one
may watch and live. The eyes spooked Io;
but the gadfly goaded her to the bone; she fled,
her hoofs skimming across the Ionian Sea
as far as Egypt, where, when the air heats up

---

mostly employed writing what was uncharitably termed "filler." These were mostly witty (sometimes bawdy) apothegms and epigrams, some of which strike the modern reader as less than comprehensible; for instance, "Whenever *One* is *Done*, and *Two* are *Dressed*, / The *Dunning-Man* will find a *Willingnesse*." It was at this time that Cobber also attempted a versification of the Book of Leviticus, but nothing ever came of it. Sometime between his twenty-second and twenty-fourth year, Cobber befriended a youth by the name of Sapson (first name unknown), a dram-drinker and visitor of houses of ill-repute. Sapson, a gentleman, would rove up and down the streets of the capital, having

and the waters rise, folk are in the Nile;
there she was transmuted from miraculous cow
to goddess of abundant crops, an Egyptian Demeter
who fills the breezes with sweet fragrances.

She bore Epaphus (named "Toucher," for Zeus, whose
horny hands had fondled the udder of Inachus' child),
god-begot Epaphus, father of his country, Libya.
Thither Poseidon flowed (and after Memphis, walked),
to find Epaphus' daughter, who bore the god a son,
Belus, the Zeus of Libya, my family's progenitor;
His voice is heard through all the thirsty sands,
that father of sons: Phineus and Phoenix went abroad;
while Agenor, my father, hopped from town to town,
Memphis, Thebes, Assyria—a wandering life;
Aegyptus, father of a flock of short-lived sons;
Danaus, whose daughters slew them in their wedding beds,

painting their bridal chambers red with husbands' blood
with swords slipped them by their father's wiles,
like Enyo, who bedded then beheaded naked unarmed Ares.
But Hypermnestra brushed aside her good father's
bad command, kept her hand undefiled by gore
and kept her wedding vows.

Ah, but our sister,
Europa, was carried away by a wild renegade bull—
if it really was a bull . . . if bulls really desire
human girls . . . But Agenor sent my brothers and me

---

no particular fixed abode of his own, admiring the stone cornices, neoclassical columns, and brightly-liveried servants in the better parts of town, and revel in the blackguard oaths, drunken brawls, and indecent enticements of the worse. Naturally, such *flânerie* appealed to a rather undisciplined and hot-headed youth, and so Cobber lost most of what little he could save—not by his taking part in Sapson's dissipations, but rather by loaning Sapson the money to gamble, drink, etc., thereby vicariously participating in them. It is not known whether Cobber attempted to translate the immortal Panopolitan in order to raise funds (the allowance from his mother was most inadequate) or to cel-

to track our sister and the bull—that bastard,
that pirate—rapist!—who abducted her
and carried her, airborne, over a glassy sea . . .
Anyway . . . that is the journey that brought me here."

Thus Cadmus told his tale in the cloistered hall,
eloquently describing how his father threatened
the brothers, if they came back empty-handed;
how the pseudo-bull, ravisher of the maid,
overflew Tyre; no news of maid,
no news of bull.

To this, Electra returned
words of consolation:
"My dear guest,
let memories of sister, country, and father
disappear in amnesiac Lethean deeps!
This is how the life of mortal man flows:
it's always something. We, mortals born,
serve Necessity and the sister Fates:
I am a queen—but don't I know!

Was I not born one of the Pleiades,
seven sisters, carried under our mother's heart,
she seven times calling Eileithyia
to ease the pains of multiple births?
I know! For my father's house is far away—
neither my sister Sterope nor Maia nor Celaeno

---

ebrate the wine-god out of sheer *joie de vivre* and *raison d'être*; the latter is more probable, as the demand for translations of Nonnus in the period seems to have been rather small. In any event, 1731 is the date on the portions of the manuscript of *DIONYSIACA, or, The Most Interesting Adventures of the New God Dionysus, by NONNUS, Told in Forty-Eight Books, From the Abduction of Europa to the Installation of Dionysus in Olympus; A New Translation by the Author of* To Thalia, *&c.* that remain to us. When asked about his plans, Cobber would often respond, "I'm working on Nonnus? *The Dionysiaca*? It's twenty thousand, four hundred and twenty-six lines, you know." Which would elicit

to sit beside the fire; no sister Taÿgetê
nor nephew Lacedaemon to bounce, or rock at my breast;
Alcyone's house is not nearby; nor do I hear
Merope speak a cheerful word. But most of all,
I miss my son—the blooming youth has left my home—
just as downy whiskers sprouted on his chin, he left,
and left me to lament—my Dardanus went abroad
into the bosom of the Idaian land. He sacrificed
his unshorn locks to Phrygian Simois, drank
the waters of the River Thymbrius, far from home.
While far away, by broiling Libya, my father,
Atlas, shoulders blistering and bowed, upholds
the seven-zoned vault of the starry firmament.
Nonetheless, I hold fast to hope
that the promises of Zeus will come to pass and I
and my sisters shall ascend from earth to live as stars,
as a constellation, together in the heavens' dome.

Lay aside your sorrows and follow your fate,
whose thread has rolled through wandering ways,
and welcome Hope, who foreruns things to come.
If you spring from the line begun by Io,
if Poseidon's blood in Libya strengthened your own,
endure in exile the iron fetters of necessity;
live among strangers, like my son Dardanus;
make your home in foreign lands, as did your father
Agenor and your uncle Danaus.

---

exclamations such as "Good God, boy!" or "O, my—well, that should keep you busy for quite some time." (We know this from his mother, Pertie, who kept one of the most meticulously detailed diaries of the early Georgian period. From her we know when well-to-do London homes had coal delivered, who was walking up her street on June 7, 1739, and the day Alexander Pope came to her salon [he apparently realized he had mistaken the address of the salon he was actually going to and left in short order]). Pertie's salons were the toast of the second- and third-string London literary establishment. Usually, Scilly would descend from his garret, dressed in clothes his mother had bought

For another man, also one of the divine stock
Zeus seeded and Io brought forth, Byzas,
also drank the seven-headed waters of the Nile,
also carried his home on his back like a snail and moved—
to live along the Bosporus (over whose waters
sped the Inachian cow) and shine a light to all
who lived about, after he challenged another
strong-necked, maddening bull."
So she spoke,
lulling the anxious thoughts of the son of Agenor.
But Zeus had sent his mercurial messenger,
Maia's son, to wing his way to Electra's house,
to bind Cadmus harmoniously to Harmonia,
illicit immigrant from heaven, born of lustful
Ares' adulterous union with Hephaestus' wife.
Aphrodite did not nurse her infant daughter,
the evidence of her mother's secrecy and shame,
but down from Olympus bore the babe in arms
to fostering Electra, whose own newborn, Emathion,
was fed from her swollen breasts; she took the unloved child,
and gave her equal rights: a nursling daughter
the left breast suckled, and nursling son, the right.

Just as the shaggy savage Lioness
To twin Cubs doth her milky Dew express
Thorough twin Teats so each may drink its fill,
And grooms their tender Pelts with equal Skill,
So did Electra then with loving Breast

---

him. Indeed, at one salon he turned bright crimson when a young naval officer, eyeing his outfit, asked him if his mother had *dressed* him. As it transpired, the officer was a recruiter. He invited Cobber to join the Navy, since it was clear he had few prospects, but the latter hesitated. When the naval officer disclosed that he had a press gang outside, waiting to round up all service-age men present at the salon, Cobber relented and enlisted. He shipped out in 1732 on the HMS *Cronian*, bound for Gibraltar and thence, the eastern Mediterranean. The captain's initial log entries indicate that he thought they might swing by France to fight the French for a bit or harry a few Barbary pirates. None-

The Boy and Girl full equally caress,
And raised them both with equal nurt'ring Care:
Upon her Knee she sat the Girl so fair,
And on th'other the manly Boy did sit
(When Mother let her Knickers out a bit);
Or, singing Lullabies with Mother's Charm,
She lulled them each to Sleep on either Arm,
An Elbow Pillow and a Knee for Bed,
And softly fanned the little sleepy Heads
With garment Hems, so as to keep them cool,
And thus did quench the Waves of Heat so cruel.

As the wise queen was tête-à-tête with Cadmus, a youth
silently slipped into the house, unapprehended:
locks of loose uncovered hair framed his face;
downy whiskers ran along his rosy cheeks.
This was Hermes, caduceus-bearing herald,
nearing the rich table as the feast neared its end.
But he was wrapped in a glamor of invisibility:
Emathion didn't see him, nor Harmonia,
nor Cadmus, nor the corps of liveried footmen.
Only devout Electra saw, and understood
the god's subtle embroidered speech in the language of men;
she startled, as He led her to the corner of the hall
to reveal the secrets he bore:
"Hail, Electra,
Blessed art thou amongst women, my mother's sister,
bedmate of Zeus! And blessed is the fruit of thy womb:

---

theless, all we know for sure is that the ship made ports of call at Sidon and Samothrace. It is not clear why the vessel followed this itinerary. It has been speculated that it was some kind of intelligence mission to the Ottoman Empire, though the presence of Cobber on board makes that theory highly unlikely. However, from Scilly's own journal, we do know that at Sidon he met—who of all people—but his father! The elder Cobber had been sold into bondage by his erstwhile friends, escaped in the Levant, and had survived by juggling and selling conch fritters on the street. Ah, the waterfalls of tears that were shed at that long-yearned-for meeting! Words could not express the tumult in Scilly's

lordship of the earth will be your children's—
this has Cronus' son ordained, this your dower!
You will twinkle in the sky with my mother Maia
and your five other sisters, tracking Helios,
and rising with the moon. I, Hermes, your kin,
am your children's friend and the gods' winged envoy.
Your Lover, Guardian of Guests, sent me,
on behalf of your own god-fearing visitor.
Now yield once more to Cronian Zeus:
Let Harmonia leave with Cadmus as his bride,
without asking dowry. Grant to Zeus and the gods
this one gracious gift: for when distress assailed
the Blessed Ones, this stranger saved them all—with music.
This man aided your immortal Lover—opened
the way to freedom for Olympus! Let not
the girl persuade you with a chorus of filial moans,
but in submission to the Cronion, to Ares and Cytherea,
give her up to Cadmus as his future wife."

---

breast (he said) upon meeting his sire, whose hair had turned entirely white in the intervening years. They embraced one another, and Scilly told his story: his failure with Adelaide, his arrival in London, attempts at authordom, enlistment and wandering sea voyage. Barry lamented his own fate, a lonely old man living amongst foreigners, selling the flesh of dead shellfish! Moreover, it transpired that one of the Cobbers' daughters, Scilly's sister Eudora, had been kidnapped by the infamous pirate Jesús "El Toro" Guzman, the Terror of the Spanish main!

Book 4

Judith Roitman

In which Cadmus (with Harmonia) sails the ocean's heath
and, after some adventures, sows the dragon's teeth.

Hermes spoke. He grabbed his wand and left,
fragile wings spreading out, shoes beating like oars, like wind.
    Electra had no choice. She had to listen to him, to Hermes
the son of Zeus. To Hermes the *employee* of Zeus.
    So she beckoned Harmonia, Ares' unmarried daughter.
extending her hand palms down (Asian fashion).
    Harmonia noticed Electra's strange look, Electra's
strange cheeks. Trouble was coming for sure.
    But Harmonia was a good girl and jumped up,
following her (step) mother. Electra unbolted seven bolts.
Electra unsealed many seals. Electra crossed the doorstone
of her bedroom, knees knocking in their anxiety, in their fear—
what will happen to Harmonia? Her white hand grabbed Harmonia's rosy arm—
think of Hera and her daughter Hebe [the bride of Heracles].
    In fear and anxiety Electra crossed the gorgeous room
in her gorgeous red shoes. Sullen Harmonia sat on a gorgeous chair.
Electra sat on a silver stool. She told Harmonia
what Cronion said. She told Harmonia everything that Hermes
had told her.
    Harmonia couldn't believe it. Her own mother

wanted her to marry this wandering, unstable,
homeless wretch, this unwanted houseguest—
this *stranger*. She didn't care what plans
that damn cattle-drover Hermes
egged on by his father
had for her. She'd rather marry a nice local boy.
A nice local boy who had, you know, a *house* to live in.
What use are wedding gifts if you're married
to a homeless bum?
Grabbing her step-mother's hand
with her own sorrowing one
crying hysterically, she burst out
"Mother, how could you do this to me, your daughter?
You want me to marry that asshole? What gift
will this sailor give me? What kind of bride-price—
a ship's hawser? I never imagined you were
raising me, nurturing me, loving me,
taking me in when I was cast out by my immortal
immoral mother—just so I could marry
a panhandling drifter. You nursed me!
I have suitors, lots of suitors,
wonderful suitors, local suitors, the best suitors,
boys we know—why should I be tied to
this naked broke foreign derelict who is
running away from his own father? What kind
of excuse do you have for this? That he helped
your husband Cronion? Well if he was such
an Olympic hero, why didn't Zeus give him
an Olympian gift? Why didn't Hera betroth
her daughter Hebe to *him*? Zeus doesn't need Cadmus.
may Zeus forgive me—Hermes lied. You expect me
to believe that Zeus neglected Ares the god of war
and called in a mortal to help him? Zeus is the master
of earth and sky!
"Here's another thing that doesn't make sense—
Zeus threw the Titans in the pit, and then
asked Cadmus kill just one? Unbelievable! Listen to me:

My grandfather Zeus married his sister Hera.
My father Ares married his sister Aphrodite.
Sisters fucking brothers—usually that sounds disgusting,
but right now it sounds good to me.
A lot better than sending me off with a douche-bag
whose daddy kicked him out."
    As Harmonia spoke, Electra wiped the tears from
her daughter's face, distraught because (a) she felt sorry
for Harmonia, but (b) Zeus had threatened her whole family.
    At which point Aphrodite [Harmonia's
birth mother!] tricked them all by putting on the love robe
of Persuasion [= the goddess Peitho], cinching it
with the cestus -belt [look it up—not the video game]—itself
a love potion—and came into Harmonia's perfumed room,
disguised as Peisinoë, a local girl, pretending to be in love with Cadmus,
suffering from love-sickness, with only a hint of color
in her pale face. She chased the servants away
and when she was alone with Harmonia sat next to her
and lied.
    "You are *so* lucky! You've got such a gorgeous
houseguest. What a guy! And he wants *you*! You are
the luckiest girl I know. He is *so* sexy,
he's got to be great in bed, and you're
the woman to land him.
I bet he comes from Assyria! That's
where the sexy men come from—Adonis,
for example, from Libanos. Aphrodite dances there,
how sexy can you get?
Wait! I'm wrong! Cadmus is so gorgeous
his parents must be gods! His father
must be Zeus! and he's too modest
to tell us. I bet I know where he comes from!
I bet Cadmus is Cadmilos!
And we sing hymns to Cadmilos
because he's really Hermes!
Oooh, Hermes has disguised himself
as Cadmus! Or maybe he's some other god.
Oooh, maybe he's Apollo!

"Apollo! Wowsers! you are *so* lucky.
You're are even luckier than your mother
when it comes to Olympian desire,
Olympian marriage. Amazing! Smart-ass Zeus
bedded Electra in secret, but
Apollo woos you in broad daylight!
You are *so* lucky! I wish Apollo
wanted to marry *me!* I wouldn't say no.
Nope, not me. Remember what happened to
Daphne? I wouldn't say no to Apollo. I wouldn't
even think of saying no. Not like you,
Harmonia. I would leave my inheritance
I would leave my house and my parents
(and I *really* love my parents)—I would go anywhere
to marry Apollo. A long time ago
I went with our father into the oracle's
house, and I saw the Pythian image of Apollo—
and that's your guy, that's the so-called drifter
guesting in your house, he's the spitting image
of that statue.

"Oh, I know what you'll say:
but Phoebus Apollo has a shiny gold crown!
Girl, take a look—Cadmus is gold all over!
I'll trade you all my slaves for him. I'll give you
all my money. I'll give you royal robes, my father's house, my parents,
my waiting-women—just let me marry this Cadmus, please?

"Why are you shaking, girl?
In springtime you love sailing across
the narrow strait—fa la la such fun!—but me,
I'd cross the ocean in winter with Cadmus!
Don't be scared by crashing ocean waves—
Aphrodite, daughter of the sea, will keep love's cargo
safe. Girl, if you have Cadmus, you don't need
Olympus' throne! I don't want
rubies, I don't want pearls, I don't want
the gold tree of the Hesperides, I don't want
Phaëthon's sisters amber tears. I just want
to fuck this guy for one night.

"Your father is Ares,
your mother is Aphrodite, and she's found you
a marriage every bit as good as theirs.
Cadmus is like a flower—spring blooms
naturally in him. I've seen
his rosy fingers, his glance
like honey. His sexy cheeks are rosy red.
His feet shine, dark where the sun hits,
white where sandals protect them.
His arms are white like lilies. And I won't
say anything about his hair, or Phoebus
might get jealous. When he moves
his eyes are like the full moon shining.
When he shakes his hair and bends his neck
it's like the Morning Star. I won't mention his lips,
but his mouth persuades, like the ferry of love,
and his speech is like honey. Girl, the Graces
are in charge of his whole body.
If I were to talk about his hands and fingers
I'd have to say that milk isn't white enough.
"I am *so* unhappy! I need you to be
my friend. But if I touch this boy's right hand
and stroke his tunic, that would be good medicine
for my secret sickness. I might see his bare neck.
I might pretend to be unconscious and just happen
to press a finger in the right place—I'd die happy
if only he'd slip a hand between my breasts, touch
my boobs, kiss me even with closed lips
brushing up against me—and if I could
hold him in my arms I'd willingly enter
Acheron's River of Pain. I'd be ecstatic
in the middle of the laments of the dead,
the erasures of Lethe. I'd tell all the dead
of my fate and, even as Persephone pitied me,
she'd be jealous. I would teach all those women
who died of unrequited love how to kiss
as Cadmus taught me how to kiss.

I would make all the dead jealous! even in
their bitterness at their doom.
"Are you scared? I'll go with you,
I'll be your companion. Don't be so stubborn!
Marry him already. And I'll be your maid,
I'll be his maid, I'll be the maid to both of you—
But I've said too much. I'm afraid you'll get
angry and jealous over your bed even though
you're trying to hide it—even Hera, the great goddess,
queen of the heavens, is jealous of Zeus' bogus
wives on earth. She was angry with Europa.
She tormented wandering Io. She didn't even
spare goddesses—her son Ares persecuted Leto
when she was giving birth. But, listen,
if you're not jealous, give me medicine
for my desire. Give me Cadmus for one dawn—
I beg you!—and for one night. If you can't
let me do this, then kill me yourself,
give me relief from carrying this desire always
night and day, feeding on my heart's secret,
this huge insatiable fire!"
That did it. Harmonia completely flipped.
Suddenly she wanted Cadmus. She was desperate
to marry him, to travel with him. She was ruled
by desire, a walking contradiction—
the old trope of being carried off
by a sexy stranger; the old trope of never wanting to leave
home. Her heart split in two. And then desire won.
"How did this happen? What changed my heart?
I will never see my home of Samothrace again! I will never see
my brother Emathion again! I will never see my family again!
I will never see the grottoes of the Cabiri and Corybantian
cliffs! I will never see the torches of my mother and her friends
in night ceremonies for Hecate! Farewell, maidenhood!
I will wed sweet Cadmus.
"Don't be shocked, Artemis—I'm going to cross
the blue swell of salt water. If someone tells me

that the ocean depths are pitiless—I don't care about angry
giant surging waves—if Cadmus and I drown together,
my mother's sea will receive us both.
[Beware the fallacy of literary romance!] I follow my lover,
invoking all goddesses who wedded theirs.
If Cadmus carries me off to the sunrise
I'll remember how Orion loved Eos, the goddess of Dawn,
and how Eos also loved Cephalus.
If Cadmus carries me off to the sunset,
I'll remember Selene, the moon goddess,
who loved the shepherd Endymion of Latmus."

So Harmonia rambled on, unable to stop
talking, her mind wandering. There was no way
to restrain her. Her mind was consumed
by insatiable desire. Her face was wet with grief
as she kissed Electra's hand, eyes, feet, head, breast.
She kissed everything in sight, even her brother Emathion's eyes
although she knew this was wrong. She embraced
her handmaids. She caressed the carved doors
around her bed. She caressed the walls of her room.
She caressed every lifeless object in her room,
finally picking up and kissing the dust of her country's soil.

And then—everything happened so fast—
Electra took Harmonia's hand and took her to Cadmus—
the gods witnessed this!—without even a dowry—as if he deserved her—
wiping Harmonia's tears from her face. It was by then
early morning, and Cadmus took Harmonia
together with an old woman servant
and another servant—gift of the queen, leaving
the house, walking through the city to the sea.

The moon goddess Selene was pissed. When she saw
Harmonia following the stranger Cadmus along the cliffs
above the sea, her anger boiled up, she could scarcely
contain it. She confronted Aphrodite (a.k.a. Cypris) sarcastically:

"So you can't even keep yourself from attacking your
children, Cypris! You shoot your lousy love arrows at your own
daughter! You gave birth to her! And you can't even feel

any sympathy for her. Who the hell can you care about,
when you drag your own child into this kind of madness?
Well if she's going to wander, you'd better wander too.
Tell your mother that Phaëthon mocks you and
that I, Selene, call shame upon you. Oh, Harmonia,
entering on your love-tormented exile, forget about me
and my bridegroom Endymion. Take good care of your
homeless husband Cadmus. Be prepared to suffer
the kind of suffering I've endured, and when you can't take
any more of love's anxiety, remember that you are not alone—
I was also wounded by love."

While Selene was venting, Cadmus rushed his crew along the shore.
[Things were moving fast.] He
- released the ship's hawsers
- shook out the sail in the spring breeze
- guided the boat across the swell
- fastened the two ropes to a pin
- braced the sheets like a Phoenician

—he knew what he was doing!
His family taught him well.

He stayed by the steering oar,
keeping Harmonia—his Harmonia now!—
close on the high deck
still untouched.
He saw passengers he didn't know
coming on board
looking at him and at Harmonia.

One of them spoke the way you'd speak
if you saw a couple of movie stars
and couldn't shut up about it
but had the sense to keep your voice down.

"That sailor looks like the god Eros!
And why not?

Didn't Aphrodite have a sailor son?
But this sailor's got no wings.
He's got no bow and arrow. He's got no torch
the way Eros does.
Still, this boat is Sidonian.
Maybe that's Ares sitting up there on the high deck
stealing Aphrodite from Thrace to Libanos.
Be kind, Aphrodite!
Let the seas be calm, without storms, without waves!"

That's what the passenger said, stalking
Harmonia in his peripheral vision.

And that's how Cadmus ended his voyage to Greece
inspiration stinging his mind like a gadfly
Zeus' words ringing in his ears
driving him on.
His job was to give new gifts to all the Greeks
to make them forget what Danaus had brought—
irrigation and all its troubles. Yes Danaus
brought water and life. Yes Danaus

- dug the ground with bronze pickaxes
- flooded the gaping canals
- slaked the city of Argos' thirst
- made the dust wet for people to walk in
- summoned a stream from the deep caves

But that's it. And nobody is happy
that it took a foreigner to find their water.

But Cadmus—they'd remember him! He brought together

- voice and thought.
- tools that echoed speech and song—
  vowels! consonants!
  co-existing in harmony [pun intended]
- how to speak in silence

[I.e.,: the alphabet, therefore reading and writing]
And how could he do this?

• he was Phoenician [where this stuff was invented]
• he'd lived in Egypt [which had a serious literature]
• his father Agenor had lived in Memphis [no, not Tennessee]
    and founded hundred-gated Thebes [in Egypt]
    before reigning in Phoenicia.
What else did Cadmus do?
• he absorbed sacred books connected straight to the gods
    [you don't get holier than that]
• he copied the self-same sacred holy books—
    scratching their scratches right to left [Phoenician, remember?]
    letters curving when curved, straight when straight
• he demonstrated the Euian secrets
    of Osiris the wanderer [Osiris = Egyptian version of Dionysus]
    learned their nightly mystic arts.
    declaimed their magic hymns in a wild secret language—alleluia!
Even as a boy
• he learned inscriptions
    deeply carved into the walls
    of temples filled with statues
And as a man
• he thought deeply of the heavens
    measuring bright star paths—too many to count!
    learning the sun's course
    measuring the earth,
• he used his hands to calculate the
    necessary
    intricate
    calculations [a kind of human abacus technique]
• he understood the moon,
    coming back and back again
    changing her shape
    turn and return,
    her three circles:
        new moon
        half-moon
        full moon
    her splendor expanding and contracting

at the sun's male surface
born and born again
from no mother
as her father's self-generated fire
lit and lit and lit the moon again
and again.

[No bum, this Cadmus! He had every possible PhD!]

He wasted no time, setting out for Achaian cities
and once he got there abandoned the boat.
Cadmus, Harmonia, and a swarm of companions
left the sea and travelled over land
in carriages pulled by horses
and wagons filled with their possessions
traveling to the oracles and their sanctuaries.

He reached Delphi.
He went to the oracle at the earth's midpoint,
never-silent Pytho's oracle
and the oracle himself spoke to him
in words you actually could understand
[no priestess speaking in tongues; no
mansplaining priest]:

"Cadmus, you travel around and around
wandering all over the place.
What do you think you're doing?
You seek a bull without a mother;
you seek a bull no mortal can find.
Forget about Assyria! Find
a real cow to guide your mission;
stop looking for a bull from Olympus.
You think you'll find Europa's bridegroom?
You think you can control Zeus when he's a bull?
Is that what you're looking for?
No one can control him.

He has no pasture he hangs out in
no meadow to graze in.
He responds to no prod, obeys no whip.
He submits to Aphrodite's harness
not the plow's yoke.
His neck strains for Love alone
not Demeter's harvest.
Stop missing your Tyrian father.
Live among foreigners.
Found a city.
Name it after Thebes
your Egyptian home.
Make this new Thebes your home.
Do it wherever this cow—this *correct* prognosticating cow—
sinks and rests her foot
under its heavy knee."

So Pytho's oracle—
the voice of Apollo himself—
spoke
silencing the tripods' wild voice.
The ridges of Parnassus quaked at his voice.
Castalia [the nymph of the waters of Delphi]
sent the stream bubbling—inspired bubbles—an oracular stream.

The god spoke and Cadmus listened.
He saw a cow near the temple. He stalked her.
His men followed him, good servants that they were,
walking slowly, keeping pace
with the slow hoof-beats
of the unerring prophetic
cow.
[And so the search begins]

The first place Cadmus noticed from the road
was conspicuous and sacred:
the place where Apollo tracked down the dragon/snake

that tormented his mother when she was pregnant, the python
with nine circling coils—this is where Apollo killed it
and stopped its poison. [i.e., the dragon/snake/python
to whom Delphi is dedicated].

Then Cadmus left Parnassus and moved on to Daulis,
which is where Philomela,
raped by her sister's husband Tereus,
her tongue torn out by her rapist—
a "wedding" with no dancing,
shunned by Hera, queen of marriage—
created a dress whose pattern encoded her rape.
Voiceless Echo echoed Philomela's groans as her
hymen's blood mingled with that of her
severed tongue. [There is more,
much more, to this story. Look it up.]

He saw the city and the nearby Panopeus woods
where Tityus assaulted the goddess Leto and grabbed
her sacred robe. [Apollo killed him before he got too far;
in death, vultures eat his liver in perpetuity.]

He passed through Tanagra, and moving from
Coroneia to Haliartus came close to Thespiae,
the deep ravines of Plataeae, and Aonia in Boeotia.
This is where, when the giant Orion assaulted
the virgin goddess Artemis, seizing her by the skirt of her tunic,
the horrific Scorpion sent by Earth/Gaea crawled slowly
towards him and pierced his heel with a freezing fatal sting.

While crossing Chaeroneia, the cow's hoof
became white from walking through silvery dust,
following the winding rocky path,
trying to shake the dust off. The oracular cow's hoof
gave way. She sank to the ground—
The prophecy fulfilled, what could Cadmus do
but prepare to sacrifice the cow beside an altar

smoking with incense, near the rill
of spring water to cleanse his ministering hands
[the river Dirce],
pure water to pour over the sacrifice—
there were no vineyards yet, no delicate
ripening grapes to marvel at.

They stopped there, beside the river Dirce,
a river protected by dragons [they should
have known better]. Cadmus froze in shock
as a giant dragon/serpent with a
speckled back appeared—
Ares' child [believe it or not]—
coiled around the spring,
attacking Cadmus' companions—
- biting one under the chest with flashing jaws
- destroying another with a bloody bite
- tearing out the liver of one who dared to fight—
  disordered hair slipped out of the man's helmet and
  tumbled down his neck.

The snake
- leaped above another man, scaring him to death
- slithered up another's face to bite his eye with incurable venom—
  in death the man's gleaming eye grew dark
- caught another by the foot, trapping it in his jaws,
  tearing it with his teeth, spitting out green foam
  on the man's body, now frozen from the poison
  as if it were made of steel.

Another man panted as the jaws
bit his skull and his brains' membranes
exploded from his head
while a stream of melted brain fluid
poured out of the drenched nostrils.

This done, the dragon instantaneously
coiled around Cadmus' legs,
binding him in lethal bonds. Cadmus

strained to raise his body above the snake's, and grabbed
his oxhide shield. But his legs were trapped
by the snake's spiral coils.
He was exhausted by the serpent's weight—
too heavy to bear!—but dragged himself upright
until the serpent dragged him to the ground and opened
its terrifying mouth. The monster glared,
and its bloody mouth stretched wide,
exposing its raw, hungry throat. Turning sideways
it curved its neck backwards into its hood,
stretching high above its victim.

Cadmus was exhausted.
But Athena approached, flaring her goddess cape
embroidered with the snaky-haired head of the Gorgon—
what could be more appropriate!—and she cried out
to the paralyzed man:

"Cadmus, you supported Zeus in battle
when he slayed that Giant! Are you afraid when you see
only one snake? Cronion trusted you in battle,
bringing down Typhon, Typhon who had head after head
after head and each head a snake! Stop shaking
at every hiss of this creature.
I tell you: go on! I tell you
that that hotshot god Ares won't save
this murderous snake guarding Ares'
murderous river. When you kill
this creature, take its terrifying teeth,
sow the ground with them and reap
its harvest of warrior giants born only of the earth,
to fight and destroy each other. Leave only five of them
alive; this crop of sown teeth will sprout, becoming glorious fruit
for the future city of Thebes."

That's how Athena got through to
freaked-out Cadmus. Then she flew through the air

with her feet like the wind until she got back
to Zeus' house.

Cadmus, inspired by her words,
standing on the dry earth
lifted a smooth round stone—a hard stone missile—
and threw it straight, smashing through
the dragon's head. Then he drew a knife
from his thigh and cut the monster's neck.
The hood fell away from the body,
but the tail still moved in the dust,
uncoiling itself again and again until it
stopped. The dragon stretched out on the ground,
completely dead. Ares, furious, angry,
leaned over the corpse shouting curses
at Cadmus—that's why Cadmus
in extreme old age would end up
a serpent in Illyria [Harmonia too,
the two living forever—not bad
for a curse].

But that came much later. Now Cadmus
gathered the dragon's teeth in his helmet,
a grim harvest of death. Then he took
the humped plow of Athena from her temple there
and plowed a furrow in the bright earth,
and sowed the poisonous teeth in long lines
to breed battle. From these teeth
a crop of gigantic men sprouted:
- one shot straight up with head held high,
  shaking his breast-plates of mail;
- one's head leaned forward, stretching a horrifying
  shoulder as the earth opened;
- another came out of the ground as far as his navel
  bending forward;
- and another rose up out of the ground
  half-finished, his shield made from the earth;

- another shook a plume as he rose,
  while his chest was still under the earth—
  while still rising slowly from the earth
  he started fighting against suddenly fearless—
  although unarmed—Cadmus.
  Who could believe that Eileithyia, the goddess of childbirth
  had armed this dragon-tooth spawn even before
  he was fully born from the earth!
- not to mention the clumsy one who threw his spear and missed;
- or the one who easily pulled his whole body out
  but left his toes stuck in the ground.

Cadmus, undistracted,
remembered Athena's instructions.
He mowed down the giants as they sprung up
one after another. He
- struck one with a spear in the breast
- beheaded another
- tore another—who had not risen past the stomach—with a stone.

Rivers of blood flowed from the giants: Ares himself
slipped in the gore, his body stained red,
the robe of Nike [the goddess of victory] was stained
with purple blood as she watched the battle.
Yet another giant tried to fight, and Cadmus ran his sword
through the oxhide shield and pierced through the
hip joint to the small of the back. The slaughter continued.
As Cadmus hacked the giants their blood
bubbled out from the earth.

Then, still following Athena's advice, he lifted
a stone high over the giants' heads. Now they were
drunk with lust for Enyo, sister of Ares, goddess of war
and destruction. They went at each other furiously,
hacking away at each other until
they found death and burial in the dust.
One fought with another, over and over. Their shields'
surfaces were saturated with blood

as they died. That field's crop was cut down
by their knives, knives whose purpose
was for brother to murder brother, multitudes of brothers
murdering brothers.

Book 5

Rob Turner

Scope out the fifth, with dogs on Actaeon,
Not born a fawn, but morphed to one and torn.

So Cadmus squashed those born of snake's teeth,
Reaping flesh, more gore for Ares.
After the red harvest he lowered himself
Into the stream of Dirce. And then: more blood,
A Delphian cow, to be slit on Athena's altar.
Here, there, on both horns he scattered barley,
Taking the Assyrian blade from his thigh, trimming
Her top hairs. Theoclymenus grasped a horn,
Twisting her throat for Thyestes' hungry axe—
And the stone of Oncaean Athena was spattered.

She fell, and the work began: iron slid into ribs,
Dividing the body piecemeal, rolling back the hide.
Laying aside his bright robe on the earth,
Cadmus joined the labor, slicing thighs
And sandwiching them between pieces of fat.
These were skewered with copper and grilled,
Hovering, glowing, over embers. Then lifted—
Still warm—and laid on the grass in a row,
Down there among the flowers. Assyrian incense
Whirled, up through the air. Sacrifice made,

Feasting began. Cadmus offered up an equal share
For all, and the men were sated with meat.

Slaying dragons was not enough for Cadmus.
After the snake, and the wild giants of the earth,
He smashed the Ectenes, and then the Aonians
(More babbling corpses for Ares) and the Temmicessi.
Calling for warriors, he was joined by all sorts,
Along with unholy Eris and Enyo, swollen with gore.

War roared:
Bows bent, spears swerved, helmets hammered,
Arrows whirred, and shields shivered—struck
On the center-spot as stone split ox-skin.
Blood, more blood: it streams through the pasture,
As half-dead bodies eat dust. And with the red din
Fading, clamorous Cadmus founded Thebes.

Work began again, dividing the land piecemeal,
Scraping out roads with saw-toothed ox-ploughs.
Streets were drawn up, intersecting the four winds,
And the city shone with Tyrian art.
One after another, workers cut into striped rock,
Burrowing under the forested hills of Boeotia,
Dwarfed by the peaks of Helicon and Cithaeron.
Temples were raised for gods, homes for men,
All spinning in a cosmic artist's plan:
Seven urban zones for the seven spheres of heaven.
Only the walls were left for a future craftsman:
Amphion, with his stone-raising lyre.

And the seven gates were named for seven spheres:
First: Athena's Oncaean portal (facing the evening sky),
Cadmus named for the moon, hearing honking cattle
In its horned shape. The second he called
Hermes, for the moon's neighbor. Honoring
Electra (the sun's daughter), he gave the fourth—

The gate facing the dawn—to Helios himself.
The fifth was for Ares, the third for Aphrodite,
With the sun slicing between them.
The sixth was a blazing image of Zeus,
Metalwork shimmering with skill, and the last
Was named for Cronus, the seventh planet.

Such was the sacred seat of Cadmus:
Thebes (named for the city in Egypt),
An earthly realm equal to Olympus.

A pause.
Then girls whirled up for Harmonia's wedding,
Crying out the name of Cadmus' bride.
As Aphrodite, her mother, decked the chamber,
Her father Ares danced:
Bare, without shield, gentle and tamed,
He slid an unclad arm around the Paphian,
And used his war-trumpet to blast of love.
Unhelmeted, free of gore, the god's locks flowed.
Joining this sweet dance of Eros
Apollo came, hymning Harmonia
On a seven-toned harp, beside the nine Muses.
Sacred Polyhymnia raised her dancer's palms
And she drew: an outline of sound in the air,
Speaking with just
fingers
and moving eyes—
As Nike skidded away in her sandals.
Cheering loudly for Cadmus, champion of Zeus,
She sent a song around his bridal chamber
Before fluttering back to the dance,
Humbled by the wings of Eros.

Burning torches spat light all over the earth,
A false dawn in the evening.
Clear voices through the chamber

A cluster of happy dancers raved;
Hermes had left his wand at home,
So forget about sleep. Thebes became Olympus
For one night only, filled with dancing gods:
Cadmus and Zeus shared a table.
Up in the stars, Draco rose, near the Plow.
This was an omen: Cadmus and Harmonia
Were doomed to turn to snakes,
Shriveling down, one day, and losing human form.
Now, though: wedding gifts! The gods heaped up
Presents for Cadmus: Zeus brought good fortune;
Poseidon, honoring Hera (Harmonia's grandmother)
Brought the riches of the sea;
  Hermes—1 staff;
  Ares—1 spear;
  Apollo—1 bow;
  Hephaestus—1 gold band (for Harmonia's brow);
  Hera—1 studded throne (only a little duller than her own);
And Aphrodite, seeking to please Ares, brought
1 pale necklace, and clasped it round Harmonia's throat.

This had been a gift from her own husband,
Hephaestus, marking their first glimpse of Eros.
He thought she would bear him a limping son,
A broken copy of a broken father,
But instead he saw a fluttering infant—
Eros, shining like Hermes. And so he forged *this*:

A spangled coiling serpent,
Two-headed: an amphisbaena.
Poison drips from both mouths
As it slithers along—
Head and head glide
Ahead of a trembling back.
The dappled necklace curls
On itself, over its own

Rippling trail.
Two necks,
Covered with scales, a plait
Of snakes meeting at one navel.
A shimmering spine-spiral,
Jaws belching up with a hiss.
Where the mouths meet
(The beginning and the end)
A golden eagle cuts the air.
Between scales
It shines with four fastenings:
The first is yellow jasper,
The second pale moonstone,
Fading and waxing
With the liquid light of the moon,
Milk from the fire of Helios.
The third is topaz,
The same stone that gleams
Through the Erythraean Sea,
And fourth: Indian agate,
Spitting more wet light.
The snakes' mouths
Clasp the eagle from either side—
In their eyes, rubies throw out
Javelins of light, burning
Like red lamps.
Among the other stones
A pale sea shines
(Emerald and foamy crystal)
As white brine grows black.
Counterfeit sea creatures
Flock in gold, shepherding
Invisible bodies.
Dolphins flick fake tails,
Under multi-colored birds.
And you can almost hear
The windy thud of their wings—

Such was the necklace that Aphrodite
Fastened around her girl's neck.

Yoked, Harmonia would carry
So many in her womb, bringing forth
One after another. Again and again
She delivered. First: Autonoë sprang
Out of her busy womb, following
Nine full circles of the moon.
Then Ino, who would—in turn—bear
Two babies to Athamas. Third:
Agavê, who'd marry some snake-tooth giant,
And bear him a son. Then the fourth,
Like Zeus' Graces, lovely Semele,
All alone with her untouched beauty.
Late in the day, Harmonia
Finally made Cadmus rejoice: a little boy,
Polydorus, youngest of all.
He would be a morning star to Thebes,
Until lawless Pentheus stole the scepter—
Time would bring all this to pass.

Now: labor for Cadmus. Dividing four daughters,
One after another, between four husbands.
First to bring gifts was Aristaeus—
Son of Apollo and the huntress Cyrene—
He claimed Autonoë. Cadmus consented,
Giving his girl to a man skilled
In feeding many. Aristaeus was smart,
He knew things, and could cool the dogstar
With holy breezes. To the wedding feast
He brought oxen, goats, and flocks
Down from the mountains. A long line
Of porters bearing huge jars of oil,
(More marriage gifts), and skillful bees
Lurking in intricate combs.

Aristaeus! What a trailblazer.
He worked out how to hunt young deer,
Driving dogs (and their miraculous noses)
Up dizzying mountain paths.
He threw together net traps, and crept alone
Onto sandflats at dawn searching for tracks.
And that's not all: he invented boots
Custom-built for keeping up with dogs,
And taught others to wear short tunics
(Ideal for speed, and for showing off thighs).
And if that's not enough, there's more:
Aristaeus built the fiddly hive, with cells,
A rental home for wandering bees
Who wobble across the meadow
From blossom to blossom, sucking
Dew from the tastiest tips with their beelips.
He took fine linen cloth, and wrapped himself
All the way up—from toenails to head-hair—
To blunt their stings. And (just in case)
He also used smoke: waving a torch
To threaten the little ones,
Smashing a pair of copper plates
To drown out their bumbling babble.
Until—at last!—cutting off the wax veil,
He stole their dripping treasure.

And not just honey: also the dew
That spurts from a plump olive when it's pressed
Under a stone. From the shade of groves
He led men out to marshes and meadows,
Teaching them to toil from dawn to dusk.
When sheep were slow—hooves skittering off piste—
He'd find a goat to lead the way . . .
And, wait, he's musical, too!
The first to play Pan's tune on the mountain.
I already told you about him lulling the dogstar:
He raised a holy fire to Zeus,

Poured buckets of ox -blood on, and honey,
Filling cups with sweet potion.
Soon Zeus (his grandfather) heard him, and
Sent a blast of healing wind
To combat the fiery heat of Sirius.
We should all be grateful to Aristaeus, even today,
When Etesian winds come from Zeus,
Cooling the earth and ripening vines.

So much for Aristaeus, whom Eros led
To the wedding. Thebes was gripped
With the sacrifice of oxen, and the straight streets
Thronged with dancers. By the bridal chamber
Citizens spun, women sang
And Aonian pipes took up the tune.

Soon, from Aristaeus and Autonoë's bed—
Up sprang Actaeon. He lived for the mountains
(The blood of Apollo pumped through him)
And ended up, like his dad, stalking Artemis.
Cursed boy, grandson of Cyrene!
Mountain bears couldn't get away from him,
Lionesses glaring over their cubs didn't faze him,
And he snatched panthers from the air, mid-leap.
Even Pan's eyes saucered in amazement,
Watching him dart past running deer.
But, you guessed it: light feet and fancy arrows
Weren't enough. The Fates swallowed him
(*Not born a fawn, but morphed to one and torn*)
When he came home, panting, from the Indian War.

Now, here's the story: Actaeon curled into a tree,
Above the wayless woods, and gazed
Upon the body—all of it—of Artemis.
He devoured the goddess, picking
Over naked flesh . . . until, from a way off
(Eyeing him as he eyed another)

A naiad spotted him, and screamed.
Alert to our wild boy, Artemis
Snatched up her dress and hunter's belt,
Covered her privates, and slid
Her dripping limbs into the stream
Sinking
          little by little
                    until all was hidden.

But Actaeon! Your shape . . . it's not *human* . . .
Four feet, cloven hooves?
And that long face! Your legs are so *thin*,
And, oh, now—two long, pointed antlers
Sweep around your forehead.
A borrowed body!
A hairy hide beset with speckled spots:
There's nothing left of Actaeon but a brain.

On quick hooves he crashed into the woods
A hunter quivering in fear of hunters.
The dogs didn't know him: at a nod
From Artemis they were sicced into a rage,
Snapping jaws at the false fawn.
In a frenzy they shredded his new body—
The mind still moving within—
Torn little by little into scraps of pain.
Until, with human feeling, he bellowed:

"TIRESIAS . . . you never felt like this . . .
You saw the tits of Athena and lived . . .
Didn't get torn, lose your form,
Feel horns break your forehead.
You lost your eyes, but lived!
(And—soon enough—grew
Fresh eyes of prophecy.)
Artemis is worse than Athena!
She could have dished up pain like yours,

Or swapped my brain along with my body,
Instead of trapping me here, in this.
Animals don't fear death: I do! My tears
Gather in the eyes of a beast.
And—my dogs—you're wilder, too.
You never tore at a lion like this . . .

"Sing out! Hills, beasts, sing.
Mountain, tell my mother . . .
With pebble tears, tell my father.
I'm eaten by my own: I fed them, my murderers.
Why not a lion, a panther, bears?
Any of them could have ripped apart
This new body. Why my own dogs?
They didn't know me,
Didn't know my voice . . ."

Half dead he gurgled—words unheard,
All scrambled into braying noise.

Soon Rumor flew down the hills to Autonoë,
Crying of foul play, of dogs tearing her son
(Leaving out the shapeshifting)
Until she too was torn with grief.
She pulled her hair out in clumps, ripped her dress,
Clawed her cheeks with reddening nails.
Blood ran over exposed breasts,
A horrid memory of feeding a lost son,
As her tears soaked her. Actaeon's dogs
Slunk back from the mountain, their strange eyes
(Filled with impossible tears) backing up the news.
Seeing their mourning, Autonoë moaned,
Cadmus cut his grey hair. Harmonia, too,
Wailed aloud: the house shook with pain.

Hunting for the dead, Autonoë left Aristaeus,
And picked about among scattered remains.

There Actaeon lay, but his mother's eyes
Couldn't see, finding a mottled fawn,
Not a man. She left the bones
Abandoned on the ground—ignoring them—
Seeking a human corpse. Don't blame her.
Autonoë wanted her child: his face
Couldn't have hidden this misshapen jawbone,
Fingering these horns didn't call back his forehead . . .
These skinny legs, these bony hooves,
They couldn't have worn his flesh, his sandals.
Don't blame her. She just couldn't place his eyes
Onto this shape (his chin had just started to fluff!)
Here in the dirt. Autonoë wandered on,
Into the woods, without shoes, robe loose,
Winding her way back from the mountains.
At last she fell into bed with Aristaeus,
And both lay haunted by sickly dreams—
Dark feathers moving over flickering eyes.

Now, a cold spirit hunched by a downcast man.
A dull fawn, eyes glinting with human tears,
Muttering a human sound:

"O, father. You know nothing.
Wake. Look at my looks.
Touch my horns. Wake.
Kiss the beast, born in her womb.
Autonoë's autograph . . . See . . .
Actaeon's echo . . . listen to this tongue.
These hooves, your boy's fingers.
His head, this. These horns,
His brow. Look at my fine fur coat.
I'm your son, left to rot by Apollo.
Moan for your boy, left up in the mountains:
Cover me with dust, even so changed,
Don't leave me unburied, unsung.

"O, father. If you'd kept me safe,
Far from the hills . . . I'd not have hungered
For the archer, never seen her godly form:
I'd have loved some human. But I fled them
And hunted a goddess. She raged and I became
A feast for dogs. The hills have eyes—
If you don't believe them, ask the nymphs.
Ask the trees, ask the beasts (like me!),
Ask the herdsmen. But, please, one thing:
Forgive my dogs, they knew not what they did.
Take pity on those that killed your son,
Don't blame them. They trusted their eyes:
What kind of dog would spare a stag?
After, they scampered round the hills,
Searching for me—the man they'd killed . . .
It's strange, but: tears flowed from their eyes,
They pawed fondly at the abandoned nets,
Weeping like men over my grave.
Don't kill them: they saw this hide
Not my face. They snapped their jaws,
And howled to the hills:

'Our Actaeon's been snatched!
Rocks! Tell us where he's gone!
Nymphs! Naiads! Tell us!'

Until the hills answered:

'The deerhunter's hunting himself!
Actaeon's taken on a new form:
A fawn with a mind . . .
The hunter hunted: the hunter's blood
Shed by man-hunting Artemis!'

And the goddess laughed at the dogs:

'Down, boys! Stop your whining:
Why seek what's in your bellies?
Actaeon? You scoffed him, here's the scraps!
Nothing left now but the bones.'

"O, father, you're confused. Let me clear it up,
Let me put the story back in order . . .
I was out there hunting among olive trees,
When like a coward I climbed those holy branches
To gaze upon the flesh of Artemis.
A double crime: clambering into Athena's tree
And seeing the body of another goddess.
With that one act I riled them both.
But, ah, Artemis! She was *glistening* . . .
Wet *all over* with the sweat of the hunt.
Leaving her usual prey, she bathed,
Splashing rays of light up into my eyes.
It was like the full moon, a flash on the water:
Beams bending with the ocean in the evening.

"And then, the naiads saw me, and screamed.
Loxo and Upis, calling upstream to Hecaërge.
Darkness veiled me like a wave,
And I fell from the tree to the dust, where I changed:
My human form was swept with fur,
The pack sprang upon me . . .
You know the rest: no need to hurt you again.
No need to make you groan in your sleep.
But you passed by my tree, passed the remains
Of Actaeon. You strolled on by the bones of a fawn,
Scattered, torn and forgotten on the ground.
There's another sign of my death lying there:
Near that cursed tree you'll find my quiver and bow,
Unless Artemis morphed them, too.

"O, father! Otos didn't turn into a fawn!
Dogs didn't feast on Orion!
Why couldn't I be killed by a scorpion's sting?

I know I was a fool, mind spun with horny talk,
Boasts of how Apollo had entered Cyrene
And fathered you, my father . . . I thought, well,
I thought I could bring Apollo's sister, Artemis
Into the family. I dreamed of Dawn taking Orion,
How Selene took Endymion, Deo took Iasion,
And I thought: I'll take *her*.
Anyway, I beg you: bury this bastard shape.
Don't leave me as a toy for other dogs!
Put me into the earth, and set
My bow and arrow beside my cairn:
Grant that one last wish to the dead.
No, wait, no bow and arrow!
(Artemis is keen enough on those.)
Here's a better idea: find an artist,
A bright one, who can carve my form,
Capture my counterfeit body from neck to hoof—
Leave just the face as human.
But don't write my story down: travelers
Couldn't bear to read the tale."

So spoke the shadowy fawn, and vanished.
Aristaeus leapt up, shaking away sleep
From his eyes. He woke his wife, haunted,
And told her of his deformed vision,
Recounting the words of the strange beast.
With dry eyes, Autonoë drifted back to the woods,
Sadly tracing the path to that fated tree.
And there they were: a quiver and a bow.
She gathered up the strange remains from the earth,
Fondling a sweet horn in her palm
And kissing the lips of a rotten fawn.
Groaning, the mother buried her son's corpse,
Silently cutting into the cairn the words
That Actaeon had uttered to her dreaming husband.

As Autonoë's home rang with grief,
Her sisters' bulged with new life.

First, Agavê bore a son to Echion the giant:
They called the boy Pentheus, his name echoing
The pent-up sorrow of his cousin's death.
Next (moving in after he'd left Nephelê),
Ino entered the chambers of Athamas.
She bore unlucky Learchus, and Melicertes,
Before turning immortal and moving into the sea.
She was to be a submarine nurse for Dionysus.
(And *that's* how our hero found himself
Sharing his milk with mer-boys . . .)

Semele's union would be more dazzling.
Zeus wanted a new Dionysus,
A horned copy of a long-lost original:
Doomed Zagreus, who he missed so madly.
Zagreus—the *first* Dionysus—was born
To Persephone, on a bed of scales.
Held in the dark below by gloomy Hades,
She'd been approached by Zeus, on the sly,
Coiled into a false form, a grinning dragon
Twisting himself up in lusty spirals,
And stripping away her virgin's core.

Here's how it unfolded:
The hulking Olympians were after her,
A pack of suitors for an unmarried girl.
They brought so many gifts:
    Hermes—1 staff;
    Apollo—1 well-tuned harp;
    Ares—1 spear, 1 breastplate, and & 1 shield;
    And Hephaestus—1 multi-colored necklace.
(*Poor Hephaestus, hobbling from his furnace!*
He'd broken up with Aphrodite,
After shaming her in front of the others.
The smith had caught her in bed with Ares—
On a hint from Apollo—and snared the pair,
Scooped into a gigantic spider's web,
Naked Ares bound with Aphrodite . . .)

But, no surprise: Zeus was the keenest of all.
His eagle eye took one look at her shape,
And flashed, hungry for Persephone.
A storm boomed in his chest, a fire roared:
Lit by this tiny spark, Zeus became a slave.

For days the girl would sit—all alone—
Cheering herself with a copper mirror,
Turning back and forth a copy of her own face.
She smiled at the shadow, an unreal form
Reminding herself that she was *real*:
Persephone gazing upon Persephone.
And then, one day, haloed by steam,
She left her loom at high noon,
Wiping sweat from her gleaming face.
Undressing
                she slid
                        into a bath,
Floating there in dim, cooling water.
Her threads were still fixed to the loom.
Zeus saw the whole thing.
He devoured Persephone, picking
Over naked flesh . . . The thrill was stronger
Than the throb he'd felt for Aphrodite,
That time he'd spent his foam on the earth!
(In case you're wondering: that horny Cypriot soil,
Spattered with hot seed, is where centaurs grow . . .)
O, Zeus! Master of the Universe!
Charioteer of heaven, yoked by lust—
No thunder, no lightning can wage war
With the soft machines of Aphrodite.
So: he bolted from Hera's house,
Quit Dione's bed, dumped Demeter,
Fled lawful Themis, and left Leto,
All of him burning for Persephone.

Book 6

Brian Walters

The one where Zeus drowns all the earth
to honor great Zagreus.

Zeus wasn't unique in his lusting—
all who dwelt on Olympus
felt the same bolt flash thru
and began advancing on Deo's
lovely daughter.

O, how the radiance on Deo's face drained!

Anguish gnashed
her bursting heart, and hair crashed
in headlong trainwrecks
against her shoulders,
as she trembled for her girl.
Tears flooded careworn cheeks.
She wanted to scream out
in the teeth of unchecked wooing,
and scarce believed Love's flame
could kindle so many frantic epistrophes—

Rivalry. Heartache. Longing.

All appalled the abundant mother,
but especially the idea of lame
Hephaestus, hobbling
and limping to her daughter's bed.

* * *

She sped on perfect feet to the home
of the prophet-god Astraeus,
her grape-cluster hair tossing violently,
unbraided in the fitful winds.

* * *

The Morning Star heralded her coming,
and ancient Astraeus rose.

He'd been tracing dark geometries
in the blackened dust—
A square enclosed
in the circuit of a circle,
and inside both
a triangle with equal angles, equal sides.

Now he set aside his compass
and hurried Demeter across the hall.

The Evening Star sat her near his father,
as sibling winds greeted her
with cups of ready nectar
which Deo first refused, being drunk
enough already on Persephone's woes.
(Parents often tremble so for an only child.)
But Astraeus' tongue was honey,
and tho unwilling, Deo soon gave way
to his soothing pleas.

Then the ancient god prepared a feast
to ease the anguish from her mind.

The winds all played their father's servers.
Eurus dipped and distributed nectar
from mixing bowls,
as Notus made the rounds
with washing-water,
and Boreas spread ambrosia atop the bar.
As androgyne Zephyr coaxed
sweet music from new green reeds,
the Morning Star spun wreathes
of fragrant morning glories
dusted with halos of radiant dew.
Last of all, the Evening Star,
brandished torches and led the dance—
for he knows best the intricate footwork
of newlywedded Love.

After the feast, once the goddess
had had her fill of dancing,
she cast aside the pain
that stung her soul
and placed a hand upon the knees
of ancient Astraeus
and touched his beard
in a gesture of supplication
and wove the tale
of her daughter's suitors,
pleading for a soothing oracle.
Prophecy often softens care
and holds out hope to troubled minds.

Ancient Astraeus did not refuse.

First, he mused on the girl's birthday,
noting the moment of her birth

down to the second
and every last detail of the season.

Then, with a twist of hand,
he traced the circuit of her days,
measuring and enumerating
their steady count upon his fingers.

A servant fetched an orrery—
its swirling orb a mirror
of the dome of heaven,
a mechanical clockwork echo
of the revolving universe—
and set it before the ancient seer.

He spun it on its pivot,
floating his gaze along the Zodiac's curve,
noting the positions
here, then there, of planets
and unwavering stars.
The pole spun.
The heavens whirled.
Fictive constellations flickered.

Divine Astraeus took everything in.

The curve of the full Moon's course.
The opposing angle of the Sun.
The shadow leeching across from Earth
entirely obscuring the Moon.

Forewarned of wedded rivals,
he kept a special watch
for Ares, and found the god-adulterer
bedded down with the Evening Star.
The parents' piece of heaven

he found near Virgo's brightest stalk.
Stormy Zeus circled beside.

After noting everything,
the god tucked his whirling orrery
in its spacious box,
where its face rotates forever,
before unleashing an oracular backwash
of prophetic sound:

"Beware, O loving mother,
the Moon's bright rays grown faded
beneath a blackened sky.
Beware her wan and vanishing light.
Guard against the thief
who seeks to ravage your virgin Persephone,
if Fate can be persuaded.
Prior to marriage, a bedmate comes
folded in secret falsehoods,
half-beast in form and ungodly cunning—
this much I see from other stars.
Yet I proclaim you supremely blessed!
For you will be revered
throughout the fourfold universe
for bringing up grain from fallow soil,
so Virgo's glowing stalk portends."

Saying this, he lulled his voice to sleep.

And sickle-bearing Demeter,
hearing omens tempered bad with good,
groaned and smiled in turn.
Then sped away thru the upper air.

* * *

She entered her home with a heavy step.

Around her dragons' defiant necks,
she fastened a bent yoke-strap
and slid a jagged bit between their teeth,
then whisked her girl away
beneath a haze of thick black cloud.

Boreas roared at her passing,
but she lashed him back with her whip,
and flexed her raging drakes,
which darted like chargers across the winds
and over the Libyan brine.

Near Dicte, she heard the crashing song
where Cretans dance in helmets
and bash spearpoints on oxhide shields.

On she raced in search for the perfect cave.

At last, she landed on Sicily's shore,
where Adriatic currents
curve and wash Pelorian cliffs
near Drepana's sickle-shaped bay.
Beside the place
where Anapus bathes Cyane
and pours cool waters around his bride,
she found a towering grotto,
whose mouth was a crown of stalactites
resembling a loom
that local nymphs tended.

Entering the cavern
the goddess stashed her daughter
deep inside its limestone hall,
unfastened the dragons
from her car

and hid them
as guards at posts beside the door.
She left her old nurse, Calligeneia,
with baskets and implements for spinning,
and her chariot, too,
with the nymphs as guards
inside their wayside cave.

Then she cut barefoot
through the heavens and flew away.

* * *

At first, the girl carded fleece
with bristling comb
and packed the distaff with wool,
twisting the dancing spindle
to spin thin yarn.
Fixing the warp's strands,
she ran them round the beam,
forth and back and forth
on roving feet.
With rod and bobbin
she wove, and sweetly hymned
her cousin Athena.

But o, young Persephone,
there's no escaping your destiny!

* * *

And now—in the form of a dragon
with coils that radiated desire.
Zeus came
and prowled the bleak corners
of the cavern where the maiden slept.

Shaking his regal mane
he lulled to slumber
the serpents placed beside the door.

He licked the girl
with a flickering tongue,
and her womb began to swell
and from this union

great Zagreus was born—

the babe with horns
who ascended
the throne of Zeus unaided
and brandished his fulgent thunderbolts
in newborn hands.

Tho' not for long.

For Titans smudged their faces
(inflamed by Hera's deathless rage)
with obscuring chalk
and murdered the child
with a blade forged in deepest Tartarus
as he marveled at his reflection
in the echo of a mirror.
They butchered his limbs
with Titan steel.

Yet even this life's end
merely reset the beginnings
for reborn Dionysus.

One after another after another
his shapes rapidly changed:

He was Zeus, young
and cunning, and shaking his aegis;
He was ancient Cronus,
assailing with rain;
A young babe
for whom figure itself
was a hallucination;
A frenzied boy
with a beard first bristling
in early bloom;
He was a massive lion,
roaring from an angry throat
and raising its neck, thick-
sheltered with mane,
as he lashed both flanks
with his tail;
An unbreakable stallion,
nickering shrilly
and rejecting the bit
from his foaming jaws;
Now, a great horned serpent,
he hissed with a lightning-tongue
that slashed round the head
of his Titan attacker;
Now, a striped tiger;
Now, a lowing bull,
he gored his murderers
with savage horns.

Thus, he fought and clawed
for life 'til raging Hera
(his bitch stepmother)
screamed a jealous yell
that rattled the gates of Olympus
and shattered all of heaven.

Then, the spirited boy
collapsed,
and his killers eagerly dismembered
the bull-formed Dionysus.

* * *

Father Zeus, by the smiting
of this Dionysus, first learned
the treachery of a mirror's reflection.

He sealed the slayers of horned Zagreus
in Tartarus' prison,
then he unleashed his anger
with punishing fires
against the Titans' mother—
Earth.

Trees burned
as the world's hair caught flame.

The East was reduced to embers.
Bactria crackled in an inferno
of blazing thunderbolts
as Assyrian waves ignited India's mountains
and boiled the Caspian Sea
and the Red Sea sparked bonfires
that almost scorched Arabian Nereus.

In the West,
wherever Zephyr stepped,
half-burnt oceans burst
like geysers and violent fumaroles.

Even the frozen North
bubbled and burned.

Even the distant South,
under snowy Capricorn.

* * *

Now Father Ocean poured rivers of tears
as libations from watery eyes.

Zeus calmed his anger
at the sight of wretched Earth.

He pitied the world
and wished to rinse away
the ashes from her wounds.
He covered the sky with clouds
and readied a deluge.

Cosmic trumpets blared with thunder,
and the planets took
their places among the stars.

The Sun guided his chariot
over the Lion's back,
as the three-faced Moon
transversed the eight-leg Crab.
Aphrodite abandoned the Ram
and moved to her springtime home
beside the Bull, where Ares
leered and Scorpio promised
to carry forth the Plow.
Zeus bestrode the heavenly Fish,
Moon to right in trine,
as Cronus was bathed in icy light,
and Hermes hovered,
like a judge administering justice,
at Virgo's side.

The floodgates of sevenfold heaven
opened wide
and Zeus unleashed his rain.

Mountain torrents thundered
beyond their banks,
loudly flooding gulfs,
as Ocean's daughter-lakes
filled their basins to bursting,
and fountains jetted
sprays of water
to the skies.

Cliffs were drenched.
Dry hilltops were drowned.
Sea levels rose
forcing nereids to change abodes
with mountain nymphs.

Wretched Echo swam
with untrained arms.
She'd once avoided Pan,
but now feared pursuit by Poseidon.

Sea lions splashed in the very caves
where lions had once lain.
Boars met face-to-face
with dolphins.
Beasts and fish commingled
in mountain streams,
as squids prowled towering summits
hunting rabbits,
and dripping
scale-tailed Tritons
haunted wooded dells,
and traded in conch shell chariots
to sail the winds.

Even Nereus
took to the hills
and abandoned the sea
(passing Pan underwater on the way)
and made his home in the flooded cave
that Echo once called her own.

* * *

Now the wretched dead
were buried
beneath the waves.

Bloated corpses bobbed
like corks and logs
carried on swollen tides.

Here a lion choked,
here a boar swallowed
open-throat
the whole torrential flood
that poured
over every mountain face.

Now all streams
and rivers and lakes
and rains and seas combined,
and the Four Winds blew
as one
in a single unceasing inundation.

* * *

When Poseidon
saw everything drowning
from the depths
in Zeus' world-shaking deluge

he threw aside his trident
in a fit of rage—

How could even a giant fork
compete with such terrifying waves?

An entire army of nereids swam
atop the flood.

Thetis cruised the waters
on the arm of a bearded Triton
while Agavê plowed
on fishback
thru the open air
and Doris was carried
on the neck
of an exiled dolphin.

A whale from the deepest sea
flopped in the hills
and searched for a lion's cave.

* * *

Then, Pan saw Galatea
beside a nearby rock and exclaimed:

"Where are you going, Galatea?
To the mountains instead of the sea?
Perhaps you're seeking
a love song from Polyphemus?
By Aphrodite, don't keep it from me,
if you've seen my Echo
among the raging swells.
Does she swim like you?
Does my Echo sail like Thetis
astride a dolphin across the waves?

I'm afraid: this flood has scared her.
I'm afraid: she's been dragged down.

O, wretched thing,
so restless and aimless!
Now my maiden of the rocks
is made a mistress of the sea!

Why not, Galatea,
abandon your dull Polyphemus?
Climb upon my shoulders,
if you want, and I will save you.
This flood is nothing to me.
If I want, I can scale the heavens
on my goat-like feet."

And Galatea replied:

"Dear Pan,
your Echo doesn't swim—
Go and bear her thru the waves.
And don't bother to ask
where I go today.
For Zeus has found for me
a higher purpose.

And forget about the Cyclops.

Tho his song is sweet,
I'm done for good with Sicily's sea.
For this flood, it terrifies me,
and I couldn't care less
for Polyphemus."

So she spoke, and soon was gone.

* * *

But the uncontainable tide raged on.

Every city and every nation
was now a flood.
Every corner of the world
was drenched.
Not a single hilltop remained—
Not the heights of Ossa,
nor the summit of lofty Pelion.

The seas encircling Sicily
clashed beneath its triple peaks.
Tyrrhenian breakers screamed
and lashed their fury
on Adriatic cliffs
that painted the heavens
with a briny spray.

Phaëthon's radiant reins
grew faded and soft,
and the Moon's light dimmed
in low orbit
as her cattle were quenched
under rising waves.

Rainwater mixed its mist
amid the legions of the stars
and whitened the Milky Way.

* * *

Even the seven-mouthed Nile,
while coursing wild, met Alpheus.
He wished to move through thirsty soil
and kiss his bride.

Alpheus had lost his way
and was churning in sadness.
That is, until Pyramus slid by
and Alpheus suddenly cried:

"O, Nile, what ought I do
about missing Arethusa?
O, Pyramus, where are you rushing,
and where is your Thisbe?

Euphrates has been lucky
to not have known Love's spurs!

But I am pierced by jealousy—
and afraid.

What if Zeus has had his way
with Arethusa?
No doubt, he's also had
your Thisbe in his bed.
Yet, seeing you, Pyramus,
consoles me.

Zeus' rains don't rouse us
more than bolts
flung by foam-born Aphrodite.

As a lover, now, I track Arethusa!
Take my lead
and find your Thisbe.

But you will say
that everything shakes
that heaven threatens
that seas rage
that skies are unsailable
and sealed in a frothy spray—

But I am not afraid!
My heart holds something
amazing.

The burning earth,
the boiling rivers,
the flaming sea—
all have been swept clean
by the hurricane of rainy Zeus.

Yet one fire is yet unquenched:
the fire of Love in Alpheus!

And even if floods overwhelm me,
if I suffer from the flame,
one small medicine
still lessens my pain—

That Adonis, too, wanders
and breaks the heart of Aphrodite."

His speech had not yet finished
when fear overtook his voice.

* * *

Then, Deucalion crossed
the surging flood and sailed
thru untouched regions
of the outer-darkened sky.

No canvass propelled
nor harbor held his bark
as it stirred its solo course
and plowed a furrow
atop the raging swell.

* * *

Now, the cosmos
had almost collapsed into chaos,
and Father Time
was about to erase and fray
entire generations
of unborn men,
when mighty Zeus
commanded Poseidon
to strike the earth
with his world-breaking trident
and split the peaks
of Thessaly
down the middle
and gouge a trench
for the water to drain down.

Now, the Earth
was unburdened
of the towering flood
and stood revealed again.
Now, streams
were gulped down
by deep caverns
and cliffs were laid bare.
Now, the sun's thirsty rays
drank the surface dry.

And where water had evaporated,
mud grew harder as before.

And cities were rebuilt
better on better stones,
where palaces were raised,
and streets laid out
for later ages of all mankind.

And Nature laughed again,
as the air was stirred
by wings of birds on the wind.

Book 7

Christian Teresi

The seventh sings of the ancient prayer of Eternity—
And Semele, the desires of Zeus, and their secret intimacy.

Already the ever-flowing trees flower again
And sow the fertile plow-marks with seeds.
Untilled work of Eros waiting for the ploughman—
And growth takes root from the furrows' offspring.
And earth and fire fuse, and air entwines with water
That shapes existence with its quadruple union.

But mortality was measured through shades of sorrow
Starting with suffering and endless worry.
And Eternity showed Zeus the misery of mortals
Who were unfamiliar with happiness in their lifetime.
Zeus had not yet found his threads for creation
That allowed Dionysus to surge from his charged thigh
Giving humanity the respite of the open field
Where the sweet smell of grape vines clung to the air
And drown the meadows in honeyed intoxications.
The Seasons were joyless daughters entwining months
With routine variations on mundane meadows.
Without Dionysus' music their dance was half-hearted.
They did not know how solitary and graceless they turned
Dancing about in circles in a whirlwind of feet shuffling
With nodding platitudes, fumbled words, and no songs.

So, Eternity spread his ever-flowing hair across the knees
Of existence—his polychrome strands knew generations—
Suppliant to Zeus over whom his beard fell, and gave
His prayers—stretched and drawn to the ground, his head
Pressed down, his back fell bowed fully to his neck.
And kneeling without end, hands spread out
The Old Shepherd of life spoke clearly.

"Zeus, my lord, witness the natural order of sorrow and pain—
The truth of the whole world goes mad with conflict
That reaps grave concerns and quickly extinguished lives.
We accepted the remnants, after the mortal world went forth
Dowsed and you drowned its colonies in a colossal tempest,
Climates of blustering waves, and seas sputtering near rage.
Celebrate the brevity of existence that is their destiny.
Heavenly Pilot, no longer refuse them fortune before pain
Or I will let loose the cables binding life to land.
Let another of your kinsmen hold fast the suffering
And toil in the pity of humanity's woeful inheritance.
To trust into existence the burden that withers youth
And slows life's pace to a slumped and listless bow
Bent shaking in fear: walking foot then cane then foot.
The heavy-kneed gravity acquainting one with old age.
Trust into being a destiny that softens this knowledge
To the young groom mid-dance with his lover
And liberates the life-bearing cables of their union.
See the truth of this loving wedding with my clarity
Accompanied by songs and flutes to please Athena.
Besides, what advantage is the dissolution of love
When already melodic chords echo and ascend.
The instruments in ecstasy—two in one truth—
Since Eros will stop a dance of ephemeral passion
If he finds a wedding without burning desire.
But the toils of life speak of the knowledge—
The remedy of hope preserved from heaven,
And the debt of the lid pulled from Pandora's jar
That contaminated lives with the stench of disease.

But from Prometheus we were born of despair
When he mourned for the wretched form of man
And gave them fire to bless and delight their minds.
If he was a thief with the gift of compassion
He would have poured nectar to soothe their troubles
And repair the wild uncertainties of their breathing.
You see with downcast eyes no joy in your festivals—
Without wine the offering is a vagrant of empty air."

Know the mark of eternal wisdom that draws silence.
This knowing turned endlessly before almighty Zeus.
His heart took the reins unbound by the swelling counsel
Fruitful in his head and whirling by his eager desire.
Then Zeus, whose divine discourse resonated
Across the celestial expanse, spoke by elucidated decree.
"My Eternal Creator, clansmen, and self-sown shepherd,
Do not resent their misfortune since humanity's truth
Ripens or fades with nature just like the moon.
Nectar is for Gods, but I will give mankind a defense for grief
Whose taste flows sweetly, but it is more suitable
For drinking and speaking and existing on earth.
I order yesterday's grief to find a new dawn in this child
That I will deliver from myself as a father that endures the pangs
Of childbirth in a way that saves others from agony.
Yesterday, at my command, grain was removed from chaff
And the fruit of the earth was cut by the reaper's iron teeth.
I am the harvester who delivers the fruit of my fields
And now bestows my dear child, Dionysus, to remedy
Grief with the fragrant juice of the late summer grape.
My child frees them from sorrow with his bountiful fruit
That softens death as I proudly keep a close watch
While the grapevine is flushed with the liquid of wine
That heralds cheer from pastures to the wooden vats where
Talon-like feet grasp and squeeze the growing season.
Then wine's disciples intensely shout in joyous revelry
Shaking wild tresses across legions of frenzied shoulders.
Their hearts are full goblets toasting Dionysus' mysteries.

I honor him with melodic cries of my own. For his resolve
Will lead the battle to protect humans against Indian hordes.
And as reward these trials will elevate him to where stars
Monitor the earthborn—and their battle-heavy exhaustion
Flashes below from the nimble grace of my heaven.
His hair will grow entwined with incarnadine-laden vines
To crown his head turning around with creeping verdures.
He will possess this youthful sign of a serpent-like coronet.
His name and fortune will be honored by the living now—
Vineyard-rich Dionysus, said as if Golden-footed Hermes,
Bellicose Ares, Marksman Apollo. His name too will never die."

The patriarch spoke and the Fates agreed with his words.
The Seasons quickly saw the harmony and knew this was
A noble omen. Their dialogue finished, Eternity and Zeus
Parted carrying the truth of their assembly homeward.

Now the art of Eros, the self-taught inciter of life,
Battered the melancholy signals of firstborn Chaos.
His quiver held divine arrows that changed loneliness
Into longing desire to encourage terrestrial unions.
These fire-fed gifts for Zeus disseminated life—
Twelve arrows engraved in golden words prescribing
How his heart will be pierced by love's affliction.
One holy arrow makes Zeus yearn for a heifer-eyed Io.
One marks him a rapacious bull seducing Europa.
One satisfies his cupidity for the nymph Pluto.
One brings Zeus as a golden rain bedfellow to Danaë.
One allows Semele to burst aflame as a bridal song.
One brings the Heavenly King as an eagle taking Aegina.
One morphs him into a satyr that rapes Antiope.
One makes his mind a swan swooning over nude Leda.
One spurs Zeus as a horse to run around adoring Dia.
One disguises him as Alcmene's husband for three nights.
One brings Zeus tenderly to Laodamia's bedchamber.
And one lays with Olympias in her dream of serpents.
One by one, Eros looked over and felt along each,

But chose the lone inflamed arrow that could find Semele
And nocked its fiery feathers to his bowstring
As a sprout of ivy creeped around the point—
The seedling of the god clothed and crowned in vines—
And dips the arrow in a fount of nectar to temper its aim—
So when the sweet harvest arrives, Dionysus is exalted.

Eros easily fluttered along to Zeus' house
While Semele was outside in the rosy daybreak.
Her silver whip flew and cracked over the city
As she drove her mules up a dusty hilltop
Well-worn and rutted by frequent wagon wheels.
She strained to keep sleep out of her tired eyes
And her thoughts and soul wandered to a vision
Spoken by prophesy of dappled green leaves
Vined with hope around her house. Of a garden
Pregnant, heavy with the weight of nascent grapes
Nourished and bathed by the fertile rain of Zeus.
Suddenly, divine flames were cast downward
And upturned the garden, but left its fruit whole.
Then in revelation a bird longingly descended
And took the wanting unripe fruit to deliver
To the fatherly bosom of Zeus, who reached out
And handstitched it inside his thigh. The fruit gestated
And emerged bellowing as a bull-horned infant
Completed over his groin and perfect with his parts.
Semele knew she was the lightning-stricken garden.
She leapt from her bed trembling, and told her father
About the wreaths of green leaves clouded in light
And the flames and fruit that birthed the horned man.
King Cadmus listened, then summoned seer Tiresias.
Cadmus told him about Semele's burning dream,
And with authority he received prophecy
That sent Cadmus' daughter to the temple of Athena
To sacrifice to the deity of hurtled thunderbolts
A fine and noble bull whose large appearance
Evoked the horned man of the razed harvest vines.

Semele walked out from the city to sanctify the altar
Of the Lord of Lightning. She stood by her sacrifice,
Its blood in service spattering across her chest
And hair that was saturated by rivulets of stunning red.
The gushing bull unsparingly soaked her clothes.
She then raced down through the meadow grasses
And waded into the Asopos River where she was born
To wash her mottled dress in the water's current.
The gore and stains lifted from the billowing cloth.

Semele watched the Asopos' waters flow.
As she bathed, the Furies flew overhead laughing
And recalled Zeus who delivered destiny
With flashes and strikes of doubtless thunderbolts.
Semele busily washed her naked body with joy
And swam through the swift water floating—
Her dry head deftly raised above the surface.
She rode—the waterline lapping at her hair ends,
Her wetted breast buoyed on the river flow.
She kicked her feet propelling over the water.
Attendants set her clothes on the eastern shore
That later honored Dionysus, Warder Off of Evils.
She took to the breeze without the fear of dreams.
Unaware of divine aid that flows among all things—
The farsighted Seasons carried her into this current.

Here the omniscient eye of Zeus' found her
From his eminent perch. His limitless vision
Charged Eros' bow-sight to where she stood.
The archer readied his stand and stared eagerly.
His skills were unrivaled with feathered arrows
And the string of the bow was drawn confidently
Then let whistle through the air its shrewd art.
Zeus watched the lesser god with approval—
Spying the arrow arc like a shooting star
And it arrived piping the passionate joy of union
Into his heart and then turned suddenly pulsating

To where the point swerved to graze his thigh
Foretelling the birth from this son of a Titan.
Restless, Zeus looked for what drew his need.
Stimulated and secured to the girl he longed for—
He leapt at the sight of Semele on the river bank
Unsure if he again found his desire in Europa
And would labor back to her Phoenician splendor.
For the girl had a similar face and silhouette
And the natural radiance of Europa's family.

Devious Zeus transformed his appearance
And let his desire shape him into a darting eagle.
From high above the Asopos River he soared
Portending his airborne union to Aegina.
Eagle-eyed, he looked over the girl's shape in measure.
Wanting her near, he left the air for the riverbank.
He found and studied her fair-haired naked body
For he could no longer behold her only from afar.
Close at hand, he wished her whole body his wife.
His vast power was everywhere and without bounds,
Yet her eyes baited him with their ornamentation.
He knew the truth only when near the unmarried girl.

Framed by her healthy color, the dim river reddened.
The water became a lovely meadow coursing
With lightening's grace seducing the young bride.
A bare nymph called out wondrously remembering—
"When Cronus commanded a birth in Cypriot seas;
Tossing his father's castrated genitals into the foam
Causing a spontaneous form in the brackish tide
Where young Aphrodite self-delivered in the surge.
Would this river command a birth like the open sea
And in waves swell an unaided childbed to breed—
Begetting another Cypris-like yield from the river?
Have the Muses chose these home-waters
And leapt from the neighboring Mount Helicon
Forsaking the honeyed fount carved by Pegasus' hoof

Or the Olmeius whose stream is bent by its own flow?
I spy a silver-footed virgin dwelling about my waters
Persuaded to walk upon the bed of Mount Latmos
Into a marriage like the eternal shepherd, Endymion,
Who washed his body in a deluge of moonlight—
Since Selene, indifferent to the Asopos, is brightened
For the delighted shepherd by bathing daily in the ocean.
Her body is as white as the snows of heaven.
With an aching mark, Selene shows on Semele
Whose mule stands harnessed to the cart's silver wheels
On the riverbank subjugated to the broad yoke strap
While Selene's moonlight rides above pulled by oxen.
For the maiden might be mistaken for a goddess
Whose gleaming eyes sparkle as the source of silver;
Such a sight caught elderly Tiresias in his feud
With Athena who blinded him for watching her bathe.
The girl charms any envy with her godlike body.
She is proud of her earthly burden of a womb.
She is worthy to come to Zeus' heavenly bed."

From under the rushing water the voice testified.
Zeus was shaken with stinging flames of longing
When he gazed at the rosy hands of the girl swimming.
Restless, his vision wandered about her appearance.
Transfixed, he stared upon her blushing face—
Transfixed at her big coruscating eyes and long hair
Flickering in the breeze. Her hair fell from her head
Leaving bare her neck that he watched ardently.
He knowingly cast his sight over her naked breasts;
Exposed, they were fortified with everlasting passion
And youthful skin hiding her sex that he left overlooked.
The secret mysteries of her sex made him avert his eyes.
Zeus carefully abandoned his lordly elevation
To join Semele awash in her own enchantment.
And he felt the full sweetness of her inborn spark.
He knew he was defeated by the struck arrow—
The small flames of Eros truer than his thunderbolt.

Not the deluge of flashing storms he created
Nor lightening could protect him from the conquering
Calm whose peaceful fire erupted like a great flame.
Cherubic petite Eros now turned to confront
The shield of Zeus stitched in quarrel with affection.
The echo of his thundering din was enslaved
To the spurred excitement and longing Semele incited.
He was amazed to find cherished wonder so near.

Zeus reluctantly returned to his celestial sphere
And reverted back to his supreme nature,
But swore to lay in Semele's bed nightly.
He looked to the west awaiting the warm Evening Star.
He cursed the long daylight preventing eventide
And spoke about the torments of desire, crying out—
"Tell me, unhurried Night, when will daylight sink?
Lift your burnt-out torch and lead Zeus to his desire.
Let your dark beacon wander to foretell Dionysus.
Let jealous Helios hurry his languorous self—
Honor my unbearable yearning, my desire for Semele.
Helios, you harass me, yet you have known lovesickness.
Why do you spare your sluggish horses the whip?
I know a way to make you sink by accident or force,
And if I choose, I will conceal morning in fog
And cover your light to show you distorted in darkness
In order to urge and make this romance happen.
Stars will shine at midday to guide my passion,
And the Evening Star will rise and cause to wane
The lagging Morning Star unless my favor is found.
For I yearn to do pleasurable things all night
And immediately start to enjoy Semele nocturnally.
Selene, I command you, yoke your bright chariot
Whose shine makes gardens grow and reproduce.
Prophesy speaks of the plant-zealot Dionysus' birth.
Climb and rise over the rooftop of lovely Semele.
Give light to my longing with the star of Aphrodite.
Lengthen your sweet darkness for my waiting maid."

Confident in his commands, Zeus finished speaking,
At his urging, sunlight rushed from earth, springing
An immense cone of cloudlike darkness to traverse all
With plunging gloom that vanquished the waning day.
Star-bright, Zeus piloted the infinite sky above the house
Into Semele's bridal chamber without any footsteps.
At once, he leapt over the whole distance between them.
He crossed the whole sky instantly to arrive at Thebes.
He flashed through her rooftop like a thought on wings
And beneath his laurel crown they rejoiced in his embrace.

With welcoming hand, Zeus lifted and held Semele
In her bed with the bellowing voice of a bull
And the form of human limbs with a horned head
In an imitation of ox-headed Dionysus—
Then he changed to look like a shaggy-headed lion—
Then a leopard that fathered a son who just as boldly
Was a charioteer, a constellation-driven predator.
With perfect vision he sowed his movements.
As the groom, he bound his hair with vines.
The wine-colored ivy twisted about his mane
In the glory of Dionysus like a slowly coiling snake
Whose tongue playfully licked Semele's rosy throat.
Gentle lips slid down to her trembling breast
And circled them as they were held in a girdle.
He hummed a bridal hymn as serene as bees forming
To merrily pour honey instead of a viper's poison.

Zeus in wedlock lingered joyfully as if drunk
And in a wailing love cry implanted his son.
Mouth touched mouth maddened by tender desire,
And Semele grew from her inamorato's nectar
So she would bear a son who herald the kindly harvest.
To signal the coming relief, Zeus cradled grape bunches
And braced his laden forearm with fire-bringing fennel.
He raised a pinecone-crowned scepter covered with ivy.
Overcome by infatuation, he wore a fawnskin

And its speckled hues shook over his pleasure.
All the earth laughed, and self-budding leaves
Wrapped their garden around the marriage bed.
The walls blossomed, teeming like a dewy meadow.
From the bed, Zeus swelled and climaxed from within
And let the cloudless sky thunderclap all around
Forecasting the night-ritual beating drums of Dionysus.
Between bedsheets he held beloved Semele and spoke
Consoling the young girl with the hope of his release.

"My darling, I am your heavenly groom, Zeus.
Lift your head to rejoice this assured union
That offers a child mightier than mortal offspring.
In contrast, my passion for Danaë does not compare.
Your aunt was seduced by my bullied desire,
But you outshone Europa who when glorified in bed
Went back to Crete. You, Semele, will go to Olympus.
You will sail beside me starlike in the vault of heaven.
And when anyone says that Zeus ferried honor
To Cretan underlings, they will recall divine Dionysus.
Your sisters will only bear flawed human children.
One is felled, killed by his young dogs. One is born
Cursed—destined to be die from his own father's arrow.
And one is murdered by his own raging-mad mother.
You deliver an immortal son, and you too are immortal.
Happiness is yours, pure woman, bring forth joy—
A son conceived for mortals and immortals to forget worry."

Book 8

Frederick Ahl

Eighth comes a mythical whirl: the ferocious envy of Hera,
Semele's marriage cremation, and Zeus, now cast as a killer.

That said, the god strode up to Olympus. His mind, though, continued
Drifting back from within those loftiest halls to his new bride's
Thebes: spurred outward by lust, not drawn to the brilliance of Ether.
Semele's house was the Heaven that Cronus' son really yearned for:
Cadmus' handmaids replaced Zeus' strict-paced Hours (and made pastries).

Pricked by an out-spurted sperm during Zeus' marital cloudburst,
Semele's womb began swelling tight over oceans of movement.
Her heart's joy in arranging such wreaths as delight Dionysus
Presaged his birth. Into already flower-bedecked tresses she plaited
Self-coiling ivy. When coiffed as for ritual kill, she resembled
Foxy Bassarid seers who made "ivy" their term for the seasonal
Cravings expectant girls undergo before labor and birth-pains.

Were she to hear (though now pumped plump by her god-fathered foetus!)
Some wizened shepherd limberly trill honeyed tunes on his reedpipes
(Notes re-intoned by a neighborly Echo, a lover of woods' winds),
Out of her bedroom she'd sweep, barely frocked, in delirious frenzy.
Were she to hear hills shrill to the rasp of a double-yoked oboe,
Up she would leap, self-spurred, unshod, from her palace's soaring
Roof, trekking on, mounted now on a desolate saddle of bushland.

And, if the cymbals clanged, she'd whirl to her feet in an arching
Whipped throw, spiraling lateral leaps, shaping ovals of footfalls.
Should she hear long-horned moans bellowed out by a bullock with eyes closed,
She'd mimic cattle calls, bellowing back full-throated responses.

Often, in necks of the woodland pasture, her rendingly frenzied
Voice sang along with Pan's limned song, as his counterpoint Echo,
Ringing back pastoral tones from the rasping horn double oboe,
Coaching her footfall to dance. Then the unborn boy, fully sentient,
Tucked away deep in her womb, kicked his heels up, and pranced with his mother,
Mimicked her oboe obsession, proclaimed his musicianship self-taught,
Sounded, inchoate in being, his personal uterine echo.
That's how this intellectual embryo, herald of gladness,
Grew in the mass of her male-child womb. And around this prospective
Young god, the Hours, maids to Cronus' child, made a Crown in the heavens.

JEALOUSY cast evil eye both on Skylord Zeus in his bedroom,
And upon pregnant Semele's god-fathered anguish of birthing,
Fixing his heartlessly ill-willed gaze upon still foetal Bacchus.
JEALOUSY, self-absorbed, self-fanged by his venomous toxins,
Crafted a scheme with his wits (and his eyes that could target advantage).

Minting a counterfeit shape for himself, he dressed up as Ares,
Tricked out with theater props. He fashioned a seemingly gore-stained,
Much gouged oxhide shield, daubed crimson with artily spattered
Plant pigment. Fingers, steeped in convincingly counterfeit ochre,
Showed red, suggestive of foemen slaughtered. His hands he dyed crimson,
Purpled with Tyrian blood—but from mollusks, not actual humans.
Out of his mouth he blared clangorous blasts, as a many-lipped monster's
Menacing jaws scream terror, so voiced as to shatter mere humans
Yet either sound as sweet as a mind-stealing song to Athena's
Hearing, or, like a whip, boost rage in the envious Hera.

JEALOUSY, priming both for a fight, spins words very shrewdly:

"Hera! You'd better produce a new Zeus, a sky resident hubby
Substitute. Semele's eagled yours off; and, to keep her embedded,
He's traded Heaven's seven orbiting planets for seven-gated Theban
Floorspace for sexual romps. There he pleasures himself with an earthborn
Girl, not you, squeezed tight in his arms. And she's already pregnant.
Where's all our momma's maternal aggression gone? You mean Hera's
Warrior rage lacks balls to stand up against Semele's nuptials?
Why can't your pitiless horsefly's sting prick now? The assaulted
Girl's not yet cowed, herded by waves. No Argus the cowpoke
Keeps, thanks to myriad, seed-strewn eyes, the most recently burgled
Victim of Cronus' rapist son under sleepless surveillance.

"What is Olympian life for me now? I'll abandon my father's
Heavenly estates. I'll walk upon earth, set up house in my sovereign
Thrace, where I'll never again have to watch my distressed mother's anguish
Or see that bridal-suite burglar, Zeus. For if *he* breaks and enters
My sovereign land, hot to needle his juice into any Bistonian
Girl, he'll learn how tough Ares is when enraged. With my sovereign
Titan-demolishing blade, death-dealing and towering upright,
I'll chase him clean out of Thrace, this woman-obsessed son of Cronus.
I'll have him charged with abducting a minor, with kidnap and child-rape,
I, self-appointed counsel, redeeming my birth-bed's distinction.
He, through his sexual throes, has stuffed our star-spangled Ether
So full of earthling bimbos that it's just a gossipy mortal
Suburb now. So, Ether, farewell! I'd try Circumpolar
Heights, but their axial tilt leaves Callisto circling Olympus—
And there's her polar cluster that bears shaggy Arcas (her son)'s name.
Pleiades' Seven Star Drive I loathe. I'm enraged that Electra
Stars, oh so flashily, up on Olympus along with Selene.
Hera! Why passive now? You gave Leto's Apollo, when womb-wrapped,
Constant pain, but you don't foment trouble to wrack Dionysus.

"YOU, birth's head-section hacker for third-born Athena, HEPHAESTUS!
Zeus will be surrogate self-birthing wife for his counterfeit wife's son:
Pains for yet one more birth! but now from his masculine femur!
None of your ox-axe chops needed this time!
  YOU TOO ATHENA!

Trim back your boasts about birth-mark scars carved into your forehead!
Birthing by cranial section, once state of the art, Dionysus
Renders old hat! Though seeded in earth-grown rootstock, a hybrid,
Grafting will make him a selfling! He'll be like Athena, though he'll trump
Pallas' brag of her motherlessness. I feel that my being's diminished:
Mortals, like scholars, now sum it all up in their simplistic clichés:
'Ares got Quarrels from Zeus as his realm; Dionysus: the Good Life.'

"Leaving the starways, then, to Cronides' counterfeit birthlings,
I'll play the drifter and wander away from my heavenly orbit.
Better that ice-dense Danube host its authorized ruler
Than that I stay on to watch that well-groomed immigrant cowboy,
Now inner-circle Olympian, Ganymede, serve Zeus his claret,
Leaving the truly Olympian Hebe's chalice unsampled.
I'm to watch Bacchus and Semele ranked as 'Olympian Residents'?
Watch Ariadne's earth-launched Crown rise up into stardom,
Partnering Helios' prancing course that mothers the morning?
Thrace is for me! There I'll see no Monster, no sickle of Perseus,
No Andromeda statue, no eye of the Gorgon Medusa.
All of these Cronus' son, would, in due course, install on Olympus."

These words scrambled the rational thinking of self-birthed Athena,
Gave keener edge to the wrath of deeply envious Hera.

JEALOUSY rose in a flash; then, zig-zagging off upon crooked knees,
Cut oblique vapor trails through air. Human eyes and perceptions
Registered him as smoke; but he'd helmeted up for deception,
Setting his artful, demonical mind in pursuit of pure evil.

Zeus' enraged bedmate didn't take a break either. For Hera
Leaped up and sped on her way, like a hurricane slipping on sandals,
Into the infinite astral fire of the sky's constellations,
Off for astoundingly numerous down-town tours of the cities,
All in the hope that she'd find what she sought: self-serving DECEPTION.

From high above Cretan Dicte's peak, Zeus' Corybant-guarded
Birthplace, she spotted the Amnīsós with its childbirthing waters.

There, bride with mountain bride, DECEPTION met up with the goddess.
She loved to hang out at Zeus' trumped up burial chamber,
Thrilled with the Cretans, beguiling masters of falsification.
Round her chest ran a Cretan bra, puffing breasts out like quinces.
In it, there lies all wizardry mortal artists can fashion,
In it, yes, all kinds of highly skilled thievery; in it, seductive
Rhetoric, many-masked fraudulence; in it, each Sworn Word
Lies, set to fly out and race with the cloud-spawned gales of DECEPTION.

Hera, then, softened up fraudster DECEPTION with fraudulent patter;
Hers is an intricate mind when it comes to controlling her partner.

"Hi there, you fraud-minded goddess, you masterful trickster and tracker!
Hermes himself couldn't out-wheedle *you* with his wit-stealing smooth talk!
Hand me that polychrome bra Rhea once strapped onto her torso
Just to befuddle her husband. I won't be importing for Cronus'
Son what *she* brought Cronus: a rock kid that looked . . . rather rocky.
I won't now outmatch my bed-partner's crime with a stone fake,
I've been kicked *out* of my bed by an earth girl! And, mad that it's *her* bed,
Wild Ares now refuses to use his own heavenly penthouse!
What's gained by being immortal? Some death-doomed nobody female
Owns my spouse—though Leto, a goddess, lacked talons to hold him.
Rainy Zeus didn't come into Danaë's bedroom for seconds!
That bride soon came to regret her exchange of a steel-sealed palace
Prison for gold-bought marriage, for Love on the unbridled, briny
High seas, incessantly humped by the shifting winds on her gale-powered
Honeymoon cruise, clammed tight in her own bridal chest with her trousseau!
After he put in at Crete, our Olympian bull was done sailing,
Nevermore spotted Europa's sheets, whereas water-dipped Io,
Purpled by stable-fly stings, sailed on, Nile-rigged upon cow horns.
Leto, a goddess herself, got no free carriage in marriage;
She, while shipping the load in her belly and ceaselessly spinning,
Gazed as the foothills danced upon islands ceaselessly wandering,
Gazed at the nonstop surge of the never welcoming seaways,
Barely discerning the olive branch marker where she would deliver.
She had to bear it alone. Her bedmate did nothing for Leto.

But to slip under the covers with this one short-lived and death-doomed
Girl, he has sworn off the heavenly bed of his own sister, Hera.
I'm afraid Cronus' son, whom the world calls my husband and sibling,
Might, to show thanks to the woman he bedded, drive *me* out of heaven,
Might end up crowning Semele queen of his private Olympus.
If you're more thankful to Zeus, son of Cronus, less thankful to Hera—
And you won't lend me your Cretan bra, so ultra-seductive,
So I can get that wandering son of mine back to Olympus,
I'll make my way to the outermost rim of encircling Ocean,
Leaving the bright skies behind. Thanks to his honeymoon with a mortal.
I'll share a fireside with Tethys, primordial mother of waters!
Next stop, Harmonia's House; then I'll stay nearby with Ophion.

"You, for your part, should respect Zeus' bride. She's the mother of mothers,
Help me out! Give me that brassiere to wear to entice the wild Ares,
Now self-exiled, to relocate back to his heavenly penthouse."

This said, the goddess responded with words suggesting obedience:

"Mother of Ényalius, first bride of Zeus enthroned in his Great Hall,
Yes, I'll give you my bra. Should you demand anything further,
Further persuasion's unneeded. You share Zeus' rule and his power.
Take this leather support! Strap the cups on tight round your bosom!
You could make Ares rise to the sky, and if that's what you wanted,
Charm Zeus out of his mind—Ocean too, in his angry remoteness,
If you control him. Zeus rules from above, he'll abandon his earth-born
Darlings. He'll rise to the sky on his own. No, you won't have to call him.
Our frilly lingerie's lure will arouse him to tack round this headland.
My stuff outclasses my Paphian rival's frilly seductions."

This said, fraud on her mind, the spirit fled, wafted by breezes,
Powered on an aerial path by the thrust of her wing-furnished sandals.

Leaving the Cave of the Dancing Shields on precipitous Dicte—
Inner delivery room and birthplace of Childbirth (the goddess)—
Hera, already focused on fraud, asthmatic with envy,
Entered Semele's honeymoon chamber. She fashioned her outward

Form to resemble an older and oh, so beautifully spoken,
Woman who loved kids. Her model here was the nurturing nanny
Agenor hired and gave land to—he even arranged for her marriage,
As would a father. In thanks, she repaid all his kindness by nursing
Cadmus, an infant as yet, at her very own breasts, and by nestling
New-born Europa in smooth cupped palms and cradling forearms.

Hera, on entering the house, let this outer façade mask her inner
Rage against Semele, Cypris too, and, of course, Dionysus,
Yet to see daylight. And she, not wanting her own eyes to settle
There, where the bridals were recently proofed, turned to face the opposing
Wall, so she'd not have to cope with the actual fact of Zeus and his love nest.

Then Peisiánassa, Semele's 'Royal Advisor,' of Tyrian
Rootstock, settled her comfily in on the dazzling and high raised
Throne. Thelxinóë, 'Beguiler of Minds,' rearranged rugs and carpets.
Weaving her plots right next to the girl now, the Goddess discovered
How much pregnancy pain she'd endured with the foetus maturing.
Yet the moon marked as her month for delivery had not arisen!
Greenishly wan cheeks and, upon limbs once blushingly wine-red,
Greenish skin told loud of a womb unsealed. Lying Hera's
Fake body shivered with fraudulent shudders as she sat beside her:
Quivering old woman's neck slumped down towards earth upon shoulders
Curved like a hunchback's, burdened as if by labor and suffering.

Finding a pretext was hard. And she groaned as she started her story,
Blotted a beautifully crafted tear from her face-masking make-up,
Framed epic fraud with a soothing voice that seduces the senses:

"Tell me what brings pallor to ma'am's cheeks, my dear royal princess?
Where is your fabled beauty? Whose envy wilts your appearance,
Dulls down the sparklingly red regal glow of your usual blushes,
Who's swapped your roseate bloom for Adonis' swift-dying windflowers?
Why downcast, eyes flooded with tears? Perhaps you've been hearing
All that disgusting stuff people now shout aloud, and in public?
Damn women and their murderous mouths, those inventors of evil!

"Who tore your underclothes off? Tell me! Don't keep it a secret!
Which of the gods raped you? Who took your virginity from you?

"If it was Ares who snuck in unseen and played bridegroom with my girl,
Sleeping with Semele, quite unafraid he'd affront Aphrodite,
Make him grope, when he comes to your bed, for the spear that's his wedding
Present! Your mother remembers her father's firmness in combat!
If Hermes, speedy when sandaled, once saddled you down at an orgy
Then said 'No!' to his darling Peithó, thanks to Semele's beauty,
He should present you his magic rod to announce he's your rapist!
Or trick you out—and how pretty you'd look—in his own golden sandals,
Giving a premium gift in return for a premium service.
Then you'd be gold-sandaled too, just like Zeus' bed-partner Hera!

"If it was handsome Apollo who came out of heaven to wed you,
Passion for Semele robbing his mind of its memory of Daphne,
Let him dance nobly towards you, no tricks, no disguise, through the breezes
Riding his chariot drawn by swans (never mute, always singing).
Tangible proof that he's been in your bed. For the moment he sees it,
Cadmus will know that it's Phoebus' actual heavenly *kithara*,
Which he'd seen played at a banquet, voicing its chords and arpeggios
Right at his table, when, human with god, he married Harmonia.

"If it was girl-mad, dark-blue-bearded Poseidon who raped you,
Fancying *you* over tragedy's Dark Horse, Wise Melanippe,
Then make him plant his trident's prong at the entrance to Cadmus'
Theater, thus doing you, and your wedding, in public and granting
Status to match that of Dirce, whose serpentine hair fountains water.
Lion-breeding Lerna's serpentine water too, down in Argos,
Where he set up a memorial stone for his mate, Amymónê:
That place still shows the name of the bride—and the trident.

"Why though, am I referring to you as the Earthquaker's bedmate?
What proof have you that your bed's guest was really Poseidon?
That Enipeús who assaulted Tyró was no fresh-water lover:
Once in her arms, his fake foam frothed out spuriously saline.

"But any push you may make for Cronus' son as your husband
Will need support. Have him enter your bed to the wild thrill of thunder,
Head crowned with lightning crests for your wedding! Then people will comment:
'Hera and Semele both get bridal thunderbolt send-offs!'
Prone to envy as Zeus' wife is, she's not going to harm you!
Ares, your granddad on your mother's side, would never permit it!
Semele, though, hasn't fared so well as Europa. Zeus hoisted
Her on his back in his horny state as a love-stricken bovine;
Then, without dampening his hooves in the swell, began *running* on water.
Some honeymoon yacht *he* made! What an astonishing tableau:
'Girl holding reins steers reigning holder of heavenly power.'

"Semele fares less well than Danaë over whose bosom
Raining Zeus cascaded torrents of gold from the rooftop,
Infinite, swirling streams from a girl-maddened, oncoming blizzard.
Yet, the most blessèd bride wasn't asking for gold as her present;
Her wedding gift was her husband's whole being.
Let's both have a silent
Moment now. We don't want your father Cadmus to hear us."

This said, she went from the house, left the bride with a still harbored grievance,
Now augmented by envy of Hera's incomparable wedding,
And by complaints against Zeus. When she herself journeyed homeward,
Hera, on entering Ether saw, on the floor, by the heavenly
Throne, not Zeus, but the ordnance he hurls, which, in friendly and flattering
Words, she began to address now as if it could actually hear her:

"THUNDER, has my Cloudgathering Zeus abandoned you also?
Who's now seized you away, leaving your proper brandisher naked?
THUNDER, you're plundered. And Typhoon's not responsible this time!
You share your suffering with Hera, my helper! He's dressed for a wedding,
Our rainy Zeus! He has no use for either of *us*. We're rejected!
Earth gets no blankets of snow these days; there *are* no more stormy
Downpours. Drought now ranges at large over what were our farmland's

Furrows, withering crops. And farmers have taken to calling
Zeus, once 'Cloudy with Black Storms,' Clear Zeus, 'Utterly Cloud-Free.'

"LIGHTNINGS, burst out appeals to Cronus' son with your fiery
Voices. And you, dear THUNDERBOLTS, crackle your claps
at the girl-mad
Zeus, be avengers of Hera's deeply envious anguish!
COME YE TO SEMELE'S WEDDING! And let her be granted the bridal
Send-off she's begged for: the blazing fires that will be her assassins!"

So belled Hera's pain on the anvil of Zeus' insensate
Ordnance. Her inner god swelled wrathful on oceans of envy.

Semele's heart, shackled now by her sense by new and personal grievance,
Lusted for lightning now, kept begging her bedmate for blazing
Cherubs to serve her as bridesmaids. Her tone was direct and acerbic.
Hera's bed was the model she wanted; with pillows of fire:

"Since riches flooded your courtship, Danaë, do me, Europa's
Horney spouse, this favor! I saw you, but only so vaguely.
Much as I'd see a dream . . . I'm embarrassed to call you
Semele's partner. You honored Cadmus less than Acrisius,
Rainy Zeus! I'd loved to have seen a wedding that golden!
Perseus' mother made her grab first, though, and beat me to that prize.
And I'd have loved it if you, as a trail-blazer bull, had been shipping
Me overseas on y'alls' broad backs, and Polýdorus, my kin,
Cadmus style, would have then set out to track down the stray bride's
Rustler, the bull who was wrangling me: Zeus fathered by Cronus.
Recycled bovine or climatological weddings don't suit me!
No merely matching honors for me, no earthling betrothals!
Leave Europa her bull, let Danaë relish her rain shower!

"*I* envy only Hera's marital rites! If you honor
Me, you'll cook *me* up a wedding with heavenly, cosmical blazes.
Spark an erotic flash in the bridling clouds, let your lightning,
Gift as reward for my love, dazzle nonbelieving Agavê!
Terrorize self-assured Autonóë so she'll hear, from up close,

My escorting Bridal Loves peal thunderous percussion:
Symbolic, self-proclamation of Marriage whose banns weren't published!
Let me enfold in my arms your beloved fire, let your lightning's
Fondling caresses enrapture the very core of my being!
Let me take conjugal flames from *your own bed*. Every new bride's
Marital rites demand fiery consummation as send-off!

"Or perhaps you don't think *I* rate a thunderbolt wedding,
Even though *I'm* born of Ares' blood and *your own* Aphrodite's?
Semele's worthless, then! Oh, how quickly my marriage's bright fires
Die down to household lamplight! The bride who's empowered to fondle
Your bolts now, and to stroke their fire into flashes, is Hera!
Bridegroom, discharging bolts thrills you! You adopt your divine form
When you're astride Hera's mattress, aglow with marital lightning,
Blazing down on your bride in her multiply radiant chamber,
You're Fiery Zeus! But to Semele, you come as bull or as serpent.
Hera can harken to resonant, baritone Loves on Olympus;
Semele just gets an earful of counterfeit bellows that issue
Out of the indistinct shadowy shape of a totally fake bull!
Zeus musters neither a sound nor a cloud when he's visiting my bed.
He's just the 'Cloudgath'rer' when mixing juices with mule-stubborn Hera.
My father—your Cadmus—skulks off into corners, avoiding
Verbal abuse for his daughter's dreadful sex life, and shunning
Personal contacts, ashamed to be seen by the locals. The townsfolk
All hurl insults at you and your covert affairs, but their harshest
Blame is for Semele, thief of a lawful wife's stolen husband.
My fine present from you is the slander of gossipy women!
My own staff, like a tragic chorus, blame *me*, and I fear,
More than the rest, the unstoppable mouth of my personal nursemaid!

"Wasn't it Cadmus, recall, I beseech, whose wearing of sinews
Got you your sparkling bolts back and doomed their thief, cunning Typhoon?
Get them out *now* for my father! Display them to Cadmus. He's so old!
He begs, and *you* owe *him*, clear *proof* that I was your bedmate!
I haven't seen a face on Zeus I could clearly remember.
I've noticed no scintillatingly radiant eyes, and no shimmering
Face, no bearded chin whose whiskers are flashes of lightning.

I've never seen your Olympian forms, but I'm fully expecting
Panther or lion. I've seen no trace of god as my husband.
I'm giving birth to a god, but envisaging you as a mortal!
And I myself have learned of another flame wedding: Helios
Once forced himself on Clyménê—made bride in the fieriest bridal."

That's how she scripted her own epic doom. This bride of a single
Hour was hoping she'd be Hera's equal, looked forward to marriage
Where lightning twinkled gently in skies amid whispers of thunder.

Hearing this, Father Zeus blamed restrictions that Nature imposes.
Pity for Semele's premature death, and his knowledge that Hera,
Bitter and cunning with rage, was implacably hostile to Bacchus,
Prompt Zeus to bid Hermes rescue his new son when lightning cremated
Semele, "Sacrifice Girl," as some later called her: "Thyonê."

Father Zeus spelled the whole narrative out to the mule-stubborn young girl:

"Dear woman: envious Hera's mind used fraud to deceive you.
Do you, a mortal woman, imagine that lightning is gentle?
Hang in for just a bit longer, while you're giving birth to my boy-child!
Don't demand now those fires that will kill you before your delivery!
I wasn't reaching for lightning when I ravaged Danaë's hymen,
There were no thunderous booms, no lightning bolts at Europa's
Bridal festivities . . . yet, like you, this bride was Phoenician.
Io, my cowed girl mate, saw no flashes. Only you, death-doomed
Mortal, demand what Leto, a goddess, had never requested."

He'd said his epic say, and felt no urge to challenge restriction
Nature imposes. So Zeus, flashing thunderbolts, sped from the blazing
Sky's lap, as he, though unwillingly, honored his bride's supplications.
Dancing in zig-zags to Semele's side, he entered as husband:

Lightning Gath'rer Zeus! His sad hands drooped as he wielded
Wedding torches that sparked with the lightning that blasts away weddings.
Thunderbolts started to lantern the room, Ismenós began shimm'ring,
Fiery with vaporous smoke. Thebes glowed with its dazzling fires.

Semele gazed at her blazing assassins. Undaunted, her neck held
Splendid stiff, she spoke thus, in a voice high-minded and haughty:

“I don’t want some tinkling harp, I don’t need an oboe.
I’ve Zeus’ thunder now blowing every reed of my Loves’ pipes,
And, for my oboe’s rhythm, the beat of Olympic percussion;
Lightning from heaven is the brand for my consummations. I see no
Value in routine torches. To my mind, ‘torches’ means lightning!
I’m Zeus’ spouse. Our Agavê is one of Echion’s *belongings*,
Or Autonóë I’ll call, I guess, Aristaeus’ woman,
I’m not the wife who gave birth to his son, the soon dead Actaeon,
Woodsman turned ruminant, savaged by hounds that made hunter the
hunted.
Even Inó is Nephélê’s *replacement*. I *share* Zeus with Hera!

“No simple yoke-lute for me! No! *I* have a whole constellation!
Heavenly Lyra sing star hymns at Semele’s wedding!”

Epic, exultant words! For she wanted to grasp, with her own hands,
Lightning’s destructive force and to brave deadly thunderbolt’s discharge
Into her palms, in relentless defiance of Nature’s restrictions.
Marriage brought Semele death. In this ritual, Nature wrought vengeance:
Her wedding chamber served her as both crematorium *and* tomb.
Conjugal panting of thunderbolts and arcing fires of delivery
Instantly burned the bride’s being to ash. Zeus too was relentless.
Yet lightning did serve as midwife; the thunderbolts *were* Divine Childbirth.
Heaven’s fire was now relenting. It helped while Bacchus was hurtling
Our from his mothers’ flaming womb, as her consummated
Marriage was shriveled and withered by sparking flashes that killed her.
Thunderbolts’ panting relented. They’d soon set to bathing the infant
Born prematurely but, nonetheless, quite unharmed by delivery.
Semele, who had herself watched the course of her fiery destruction,
Perished with joy, knowing she’d given birth. So, in this single compound,
Passion, Childbirth, and Vengeance too could be witness together.
Hermes transported the infant, brought half way to term and with limbs
washed
Clean with the sky’s fire, up to his father to finish maturing.

Zeus redirected the thought of profoundly envious Hera,
Tempered the savage and massive power she'd unleashed in resentment.
Semele, although cremated, he resurrected and transferred
Up to the starry vault as "Mother of Bacchus" and housed her
In among inmost Olympians, given "Hera's Family" status:
"Born from Harmonia, sired out of Aphrodite by Ares."
Once she had bathed her renewed skin and cleansed it in sparkling fire
Semele gained an indestructible life on Olympus,
Freed from Cadmus, deadly earth crops, Autonoë, Agavê.
She found she sat next to Artemis now and conversed with Athena,
Honored as bride and welcomed at one high table she shared with
Zeus and with Hermes and Ares and Cythera's Aphrodite.

Book 9

Anne Shaw

In the ninth, Hermes and Mystis come to light,
Along with Lamos' daughters and Ino in flight.

Zeus may have been the father of Dionysus,
but the womb of his mother, Semele,
was in flames. Thunder was acting as midwife,
but Dionysus was still not complete. And so . . .
Zeus had to sew him into his thigh, and had to wait
for the flash of Selene, the moon, as the signal
the fetus was finished. Cronus' own son
became his own midwife and had to cut the threads
in his pregnant thigh, which itself
was not designed for this kind of labor.
His premature child had to go from womb to womb,
except the one womb was feminine and the next one
was masculine. But happily, the Hours,
whose job it is to tend babies, crowned the infant's head
with ivy and flowers and even writhing snakes
(markers of things to come). His head already
had horns on it, bull-like as he was.

Hermes was ready to hand at Dragon's Hill where, despite
the inauspicious name, births take place.
Hermes, acting appropriately as the son of Maia

(nursemaid in chief, as her name shows), scooped him up
as he flew through the air. He gave Dionysus another name,
Lyaeus or Loosener, because he had, in a way, delivered
both himself and his father, who had been limping along
with his heavy thigh. Dionysus was the baby's name,
because Dio has something to do with a god, and -nysus,
as every Sicilian knows, means "limping."
Even Zeus got a new name, because he was
newly delivered, and his thigh turned out to be
a good place for childbirth, even though no one really knows
what "Eiraphiotes" means. But, there you are.

After all these new names, Hermes, his brother, still
carrying the baby, who still had his horns on
and was quite happy, handed him over to some river nymphs.
They were the daughters of Lamos, another child of Zeus,
who had yet another name, the Vine Planter.
The nymphs gently nursed the baby, who, wideawake and happy,
kicked his legs and looked at the sky. He laughed at the stars, all
new to him, not knowing they were his father's.

But his father's wife, who knows how to bear a grudge,
Hera, looking at the child was maddened with rage
and, in turn, drove Lamos' daughters mad
with the same whip of furious resentment that goaded her.
Instead of the kindly nurses they were by nature,
they became raving, foaming, fiends, tearing their hair
and their saffron dresses. They attacked women in the house,
murdered strangers at the crossroads, and were on the point of
dismembering baby Bacchus (a.k.a. Dionysus),
had not Hermes flown in in the nick of time
and nicked the baby, taking him to Ino, who had just had
her own baby, Melicertes, a honey of a child.
She was nursing him, still an infant in her arms, holding him with
loving hands, her full breasts gushing out their dewy milk.

Hermes, with friendly words from his divine mouth,
softened her up, saying:
"Lady, take a new son
and put him to your breast—your sister Semele's son.
The flash of lightning and the thunderbolt's sparks
may have killed her but not him. So, here he is.
But you must keep him in the dark, in case Phaëthon
spies him by day, or Selene by moonlight.
If they did, spiteful Hera, no longer Homer's flattering
'ox-eyed' Hera, would see him, and be able to hit
the bull's eye now, because she could hear the little bull-god playing.
He is your own sister's son. You have to take him.
Zeus"—(says Hermes, calling him Cronion, and we remember
that Zeus is the son of crooked counseling Cronus,
so labeled by Homer, but probably not in Ino's mind
at the moment)—"will certainly make it up to you.
After all, you are blessed to be one of Cadmus' daughters."

He reminds her of her equally lucky sisters, starting with Semele
and her brilliant ending; then there's Autonoë, fortunate enough
to be the mother of Actaeon, killed by his own hounds;
and don't forget Agavê, equally blessed in killing her own son,
Pentheus. Cithaeron will hide them both in their graves.

"But you will be the luckiest of them all. After all,
you'll be in the SEA, as a sea nymph. Enough already
with Cadmus, you will be called the daughter
of Nereus, the Old Man of the Sea, and be known as
the White Goddess, Leucothea. As the White Goddess,
with your (at that point) immortal son, Melicertes,
you will rule the calm seas, next in importance
only to the winds and their god, Aeolus.
The merchant sailor will trust you and will worship Poseidon
(for once not the usual "Earthshaker")
along with Melicertes, worshipped together at one altar.
(Your name, White Goddess, suggests whitecapped waves,
which may not quite go with calm seas and prosperous voyages,

but let that pass.) And your son will get a new name, of course,
and no longer be called Melicertes, but Palaemon,
an ancient name of honor, and he'll be lucky enough
to drive the chariot of blue-haired Poseidon."

And immediately Hermes made himself scarce.
And, Ino, of course, did not disobey.
She took the motherless boy, Bacchus, lovingly in her arms,
and nursed him with her own son Melicertes/Palaemon.
Mystis, her maidservant, whom her father Cadmus had brought
from Sidon, when she was still a girl with lovely hair,
looked after him, too. But although she kept him in the dark,
as she had been told to do, the light from his shining face
could not be dimmed, and even the walls of the darkened house shone.
All night, Ino sat near the two babies as they played:
Melicertes, not too steadily making for her breast
or crawling towards Bacchus (with yet another name, Bromius,
because he was already rambunctious and noisy),
who was babbling "Euoi," later to be the Bacchants' cry.

Mystis stayed awake tending Bacchus (with still another name,
Lyaeus, because in his birth he loosened both himself and Zeus).
Later there was an additional meaning of Lyaeus:
the wine that loosens people from care.
Mystis was the one who led the Mysteries
for the initiates who, like her, stayed awake through the night
with all the tools of the Bacchants' trade: the tambourines,
the cymbals, the torches, the shout of "Euoi."
She first wreathed her hair with ivy and the vine;
she made the thyrsus, a staff twined with ivy
and tipped with iron, which she covered with leaves
so it wouldn't scratch Dionysus. And she covered her breasts
with bronze bowls and girdled her waist with fawn skins.
She even taught the little Dionysus while he was playing
near the holy chest, which was bursting with sacred objects
all pregnant with meaning, to use them as toys.
And it was Mystis who first twined snakes together
to make a double-braided belt for herself.

But it didn't matter that Mystis took care of Bacchus hidden
in the innermost nook of this strange house.
Hera, with her all-seeing animal eyes saw him.
By the Styx, by its late but sure avenging waters, she swore
to deluge Ino's house with a flood of evils.
Once more she was on the point of doing away with Zeus' son,
but, would you believe, Hermes grabbed him
and took him to Cybele's wooded ridge.
Not to be outdone by the quick Hermes, Hera ran from the sky
as fast as she could, but he outdid her. Not only that,
but he put on the shape of Phanes, the eternal, boundless,
firstborn of the gods. And Hera did not realize this,
didn't see through the wiles of the false face,
shining and teaching the torches to burn bright (as his name shows).
In reverence for the first-born of the gods,
she bowed down before the lying sheen,
so Hermes, with his quicker step, could pass over the mountain ridge
ahead of her, cradling the little horned boy in his arms.
He gave him to the mother of Zeus, to Rhea,
nurse of lions, the mother of the best of children.

He said: "Goddess, receive the new son of your own Zeus.
After fighting the Indians on earth, he will ascend
to the region of the stars: a great favor to grudging Hera!
It just won't do for Ino to be the nurse of a child
whom the son of Cronus birthed with his own labors.
The nurse maid of Dionysus should be
Zeus' own mother, his own grandmother!"

So, to the mother who cares for her children, he
handed over Bacchus, who would grow up again
(because he was actually Zagreus, an early victim of the Titans,
now identified with Dionysus). And Hermes (once more Hermes
and no longer looking like Phanes), quickly flew off to the sky,
letting the wind fill his wings as he went.

Rhea looked after the boy, and while he was still a youth, she
set him on a chariot with ravening lions.

Meanwhile the Corybantes, in the house that had taken in a god,
raced around with their child-minding dancing and clashing swords,
and made their shields crash with noisy iron—
all to hide the child Dionysus as he grew up.

When he was nine, he started hunting, and was quick as a hare,
no, even quicker. He tracked the strong young deer,
and with boyish hands, he laid the dappled fawn on his neck.
He lifted and stretched out on his shoulders tiger cubs
that he had dragged from their mother, to show his mother, Rhea.
He pulled by their feet frightening lions, while they were still alive,
as gifts for the mother goddess, for her to yoke to her chariot.
Rhea watched the feats of the young boy
with amazed laughter, and his father, Zeus Cronion, took delight
when he saw Bacchus—now "Yobacchus!"—driving grim lions.

When just a child, Bacchus called upon as Euios, wore
rough, hairy tunics, and covered his shoulders with
the dappled colors of a deerskin. In this way
he mimicked the spangled star-studded sky.
On Phrygia's plain he drove lynxes to his stables
and yoked spotted leopards to his chariot,
as if honoring the appearance of his father's domain.
And often, standing on immortal Rhea's chariot
and holding in his soft little hand the bridle's reins,
he pulled back his team of impetuous lions.
With high-ruling Zeus' boldness in mind, he stretched out
his hand to the maddened she-bear's mouth,
bringing his fearless, still youthful, fingers
to her terrible jaws. The wild animal just stood there,
and humbly and gently entrusted her mouth to the young Dionysus,
—also aptly called the loosener—
and kissed Bacchus' fingers with rough affection.

And so he grew up beside cliff-loving Rhea,
still just a youth who was raised on a mountain.
Amongst those rocky cliffs, Pans, with their shaggy goat legs,
encircled the son of Semele (who was also called Thyonê,

and once an actual burning sacrifice), as he was beating the ground.
They were crying "Euoi Bacchus," while their hircine hooves
rattled on the rocks in their spinning dance.

And Semele on Olympus, although with the whiff
of thunder still about her, proudly lifted her neck
and spoke in exultation:
"Hera, you are done for.
Semele's son is simply better. Zeus himself bore my son,
and he carried the child in his pseudo-womb.
Necessity changed his very nature.
Bacchus is just stronger than your war-crying son
Ares-Enyalius. Zeus only fathered Ares,
he didn't bring him to birth in his thigh.

"Thebes, my son's birthplace, has eclipsed the glory
of old Delos and Ortygia, with its bunch of quails,
even if it was the birthplace of Apollo.
When divine Leto was hunted, she had the baby
Apollo in secret. Leto was the one who gave birth to
Phoebus Apollo—Cronion Zeus was not in labor for him.
Maia was the one who had Hermes, not her spouse, Zeus.
But his father gave birth to my son, right there in public.

"Surprise, surprise, to see Dionysus
in the loving arms of your own mother, Rhea,
the housekeeper of the eternal cosmos,
the very beginning of the gods, everyone's mother.
She nursed Dionysus (even then called boisterous Bromius).
She even offered baby Bacchus her breast,
the breast that Zeus with all the big ideas sucked.
Did any child of go through labor
for a son of yours? Did any Rhea, mother of the gods,
bring up your Ares? Rhea, i.e., Cybele of the mountains,
who is said to be your mother, gave birth to Zeus and nursed
both Zeus and Bacchus at the selfsame breast!
She lifted and held both of them, begetter and begotten.
And, passing on to another child of yours,

Hephaestus didn't even HAVE a father,
so he can't rival a child of mine. I alone am Semele!
Hera, you, on your own, self-generating him,
made a mess of it. He limps along on flimsy legs
that don't even match, hiding his mother's birthing of him—
an incomplete child and not even finished off.
Maia wasn't like Semele, either. Maia's son, Hermes
(remember him disguised as Phanes?), always tricky,
helmeted like Ares, tricked you, Hera
(irony of ironies) until he sucked the milk
from your breasts, so even you couldn't turn on him.

"Give up, Hera. I, Semele, am the only one
to have a husband who both labored in childbirth
and was father of the very same child.
I'm Semele: most beloved because of my son.
Our Dionysus won't need any trickery
to come to the dancing place of the stars,
to live in the upper air of his father.
He will come there on his own behalf
because he was nursed at the breast of the goddess who
nourishes gods, Rhea. He doesn't need your milk,
Hera, because he has been nursed by a nobler breast."

Semele said all these things, triumphant in the sky.
Hera, still spiteful because Semele was out of reach,
still resenting Dionysus as he grew up,
and consort of Zeus as she was, out of the blue,
fell heavily on the house of Athamas.
She terrified Ino into flight. Ino, Semele's sister,
had lovingly cared for Dionysus after Hermes
rescued him from Lamos' daughters, who, in their turn,
had been driven mad by Hera for looking after the baby.
Now it was doomed Ino's turn for punishment.
She fled from the house, barefoot, bounding over the rough hills,
trying to track down the hidden Dionysus.
Ranging wildly, the woman went from hill to hill,

until she came to the ravine of the Pytho at Delphi.
She barely made it to the lair where the dragon had been
(that would be before he was killed by Apollo),
gazing wildly about, unstoppable. She tore her clothes,
visible token of her grief, and raced on, naked, wild.
A shepherd heard her deranged wailing,
"oimoi" (that would be "woe's me"), and trembled.
There was a snake, the Python, that coiled around
the divine tripod at Delphi, the seat of prophecy.
Ino even seized this, often using it as a wreath
on her dirty, unkempt hair, making the snake
a ribbon for her tresses tossed about her helpless face.

She drove away the young girls serving the temple.
There was no libation offered, no one sacrificing,
no man of Delphi dancing to honor the god.
Instead, women were whipped with plaited ivy,
which tore their skin. A hunter, seeing Ino
as she ranged over the mountain, fled,
leaving his traps set out on stakes. A goatherd drove his goats
under a cleft of the high-crested rock,
and an old plowman, driving his yoke of sweating oxen,
shuddered as he saw Ino leaping wildly above him.

Even the Pythia herself, in the midst of prophecy, gagging
on the otherworldly vapor and hearing
an echo from below ground, ran into the hills,
the sacred wreath on her head shaking as she ran.
In terror of maddened Ino, she stayed in the Delphic cave
deep within the shoulders of the cliff.

But all-seeing Apollo saw Ino driven through
the twists and turns of the forest. Pitying her,
he came quickly in human form to the grove where she hid.
Barely touching her with his hands,
he wreathed her head with wise laurel, and laid
sweet sleep upon her, anointing her skin with ambrosia,

moistening her maddened limbs with soothing drops.
She stayed in the woods of Parnassus a long time,
until the fourth dawn. And then, by the sacred navel of
the earth, Phoebus' own place of prophecy,
she founded dances for Bacchus (when he was still a child).
The Corycian Bacchants, from Mount Parnassus,
led their secret rites at night with pine torches and clouds of incense,
and plucking drugs with holy hands, healed the woman's madness.

Meanwhile Athamas called his servants to search for Ino.
The women, wandering the hills in zigzag journeys,
sought any trace of their lost mistress. It was useless.
The women wailed and tore their cheeks and breasts
until they bled; they ululated through the city,
and the royal house, wracked with grief, howled.
Mystis, knowing so much of rites and mysteries,
suffered the yoke of necessity. She felt a double grief:
Ino still wandering, still plagued with troubles, and Dionysus
(seized earlier by Hermes to save him from Hera), lost.
Very different was the reaction of Ino's husband, Athamas.
Why should he mourn her? He had two children
(Phrixus and Helle) by his first wife, Nephelê,
and after the disappearance of Ino, he threw off her love,
and made for the soft, enveloping bed of buxom Themisto.
When he played with his and Ino's son, Melicertes,
tossing him in the air as he babbled for daddy,
he even offered his own breast to the little boy,
to make him forget his longing for the mother who bore him.

Themisto had two soldier sons from her bedding with Athamas,
Schoeneus and Leucon, who were to be guardians
against the war goddess. And these were only her first two children.
Then came twins, Porphyrion and Ptoios, both darlings
and warders-off of evil. These two boys Themisto herself
later killed, as if they were a stepmother's, thinking them to be
the twin progeny of Ino, who bore glorious children.

Book 10

Michael Shaw

In the tenth, see Athamas go mad and Ino run
Into the sea with Melicertes, her newborn son.

And so Themisto became a crazed pedicide.
Athamas, the boys' father, implicated in crime
because he harbored Themisto, the offspring destroyer,
Athamas, driven by Pan's maddening scourge,
charged into the innocent fleece-bearing herd
and whipped the poor flocks as if they were servants.
He lifted one up, who he thought was his wife—
in fact, it was a ewe, with nursing twins—
and bound her hairy feet with a double knot.
Then he loosened the belt around his waist
and whipped the bound body of the ersatz Ino,
not knowing the shape was fake. In his ears,
the lash of Cronian Pan throbbed.

Often he leapt from his seat, disturbed,
driven by dragons' breath in his terrified ears.
Or he would bend his curved bow, and shoot
at a fantasy target in the empty air.
Next he saw the snakey shape of the goddess of Tartarus,
and he stumbled, afraid of the polychrome specter;
he spewed white foam, sign of a madman;

and he stared about, with drunken, spinning eyes
veined with blood from chaotic urges.
The feeble brain spun, unhinged in his head.
A third of his soul was lost, the stable
impulses damped in his insane mind.
His glances danced in dizzy whirls,
a man driven by Bacchus. His hair wandered,
shaken around the back of his unkempt head.
His mouth muttered; his lips wobbled;
senseless words came out, mere strange sounds.
The Eumenidean wind-storm drowned human cares
and his tongue was thick with a fanatic timbre.

He turned his head and caught a glimpse
of the strange bastard shape of Megara, the invisible.
Driven by mania, Athamas lurches
as he tries to grab the whip -snake from the hand
of the grim goddess of mental collapse.
Baring his blade in the face of the Erinys
he intended to clip Tisiphone's serpent curls,
but suddenly, with a shout, he heads for a wall,
where he caught a glimpse of a deceptive shadow
that resembled Artemis, and seeing the specter,
floored by a phantasm, he longed for the hunt.

Ino, tear-drenched, returned to this house
after four years away, and was struck by the sight
of her husband demented and Themisto with sons,
a double dose of pain. After so long an absence,
her husband did not know who she was.
But having a sudden lust for hunting deer,
he rushed to the peaks with his boots awhirl,
where his son seemed to him to be a beast with horns.
He bent his bow and lurched at Learchus,
who he thought was an antlered stag,
a four-legged beast. Learchus fled;

he ran for his life, quick knees flashing.
With lunatic hands, Athamas notched his shaft,
and the father stopped his son with a pedicidal shot.
He sliced off the agnostic head with a knife,
the head of a stag, so it seemed. He patted it,
the top of the bloodstained cheek, and laughed,
massaging it like meat; then he ran with demented leaps,
while Learchus' body still shuddered, unburied,
and sought out his mother, his eyes whirling.
No servant ventured near. On rapid heel,
he wandered through the seven-chambered house,
calling for the son he had just killed.
He saw Melicertes in the hall, newly arrived.
He put a steaming pot on the hearth,
and there dunked the toddler. The fire blazed up,
and the murder pot bubbled with humid burps.

"Papa," his child screamed out. But no servant
could help. Ino, his mother, tornadoed in,
grabbed him from the pot, what little was left,
and ran with the footwind, in aimless leaps.
She sliced the dust of Leucos' plain,
which is her eponym now, Leucothea.
Then from the hall, addled Athamas fanned his windy knees,
and chased Ino in vain, the swifter mountain runner.
When the crackpot spouse caught up to her,
making crooked track with unstable feet,
the poor woman planted her heel in sea wash,
and raised a wailing moan over her groaning child,
and blamed Cronus-Son and his lackey, Maia's child:

"Big-Sky-Flasher, you paid me well for nursing Bacchus.
Gaze on this parboiled child, a playmate for Lyaeus.
If you want, put an end to the mother and the child
with your merciless bolt—the child I nursed in my bosom,
as I nursed Dionysus son of god, your son.

"My child—Necessity rules—where can we flee?
No mountain will receive you, let's escape to the sea!
No Cithaeron can hide you in hidden hollow.
What mortal pities you? Surely not your father!
It's the sword or the sea, since Necessity rules;
better death in the sea than death by the sword.

"What causes this pain that floods your mother?
I know it is Nephelê who sends me the Furies,
to die in the sea, where virgin Helle fell.
I hear Phrixus flew to the Colchian land,
the airborne pilot of the ram that snatched him.
Phrixus still lives abroad. If only
my son might fly on the golden-fleeced ram,
my son, Melicertes, a fugitive exile!
Poseidon may save you, pitying Ino
as once he did Phoebus, the host of Glaucus!
I fear that I will see you dead,
gasping from the bloody knife of your father,
like Learchus, unburied, a body without a grave,
and with no one near to mourn your death.
Hurry, flee maniac Athamas. Don't watch
your filicide father kill your mother as well.
Take me too, Ocean, farewell to Earth,
and Nereus, take Ino as once you took the chest
in which Danaë sailed, with hospitable hand,
and save Melicertes, as once you did Perseus.
I've suffered enough for my transgressions.
Cronion unseeded our family line,
because I unseeded the earth's fertile fields
to root out Athamas' crop of bastards
like some kind of stepmother, and Hera hates me,
the real stepmother of neonatal Dionysus."

Thus she spoke, and she leapt aptinto the sea
with fearful feet, deftly diving with her son.
The dark-haired god embraced Leucothea,

who now shares his hearth with watery divines,
and so she aids sailors who are lost, a nereid
who governs unwavering calm on the sea.

Cronus-Son pointed her out to Lyaeus' mother,
because, thanks to Bromius, she was a goddess,
and she gleefully hurled bitter words at her sea sister:

"You have the sea, Ino; Semele has Olympus.
Bow down to me! I had an immortal spouse,
Cronus-Son, who planted the seed of my line,
who took my place, in the pain of the birthing.
But you were wed to an earthly partner,
Athamas, the destroyer of all of your line.
Your child's lot is the sea, but my child
will come to Zeus' aerie, to dwell in the sky.
Dionysus celestial tops marine Melicertes."

And so the sky bride Semele baulked,
and mocked Ino, her oceanic sister.

At that time:
                    Dionysus in the Lydian latitude,
twirling the Evian instruments of Rhea Cybele,
grew into fulness as he desired.
Fleeing the flail of Helios at zenith,
he bathed his body, splashing gently
in a Maeonian river. Pactolus splashed back—
it gave pleasure to Lyaeus—and poured gold-bearing water
onto purple sand, and golden fish rolled in the rich water.

Satyrs also played, raising their heels,
and poured into the river, diving headlong.
One of them swam, rowing with his hands,
headlong in the swell, his rush leaving a wake;
with feet stretched back, he split the rich current,
while another dove deep to undersea dwellings,

hunting the varicolored fish at the bottom,
stretching a blind hand toward swimming schools,
and then left the depth and offered fish to Bacchus
purpled with slime of the ore-rich river.
And vagrant Silenus mocked the satyr,
bent over, and grabbed his feet with his hands,
and cannonballed into the flow, head down,
into the deep, and muddied his hair
as he fixed his two feet in the glittering ooze,
searching for the pebbled wealth of the river.
And another, against the current, stood still
and showed his back to the air, with his shoulder left dry,
his hips damp in the deep. Another bared his ears
and whirled hairy thighs in the marmoreal flow,
and twirled his tail and lashed the flood.

And the god, head erect, spreading his chest,
rowed with his hands and split the golden calm.
The banks, untouched by wave, spit out spontaneous roses,
and the lily bloomed, and the seasons crowned the banks,
while Bacchus bathed, and in the gleaming surge
the uncombed locks of his dark hair reddened.

Once, while hunting in a shadowy, secret wood
he was warmed by a roseate young companion.
For Ampelos, a lad, had grown up gamboling
on Phrygian ridges, a young sprout of the Erotes.
There was no delicate down on his red-flushed chin
to mark the smoothed circles of his snowy cheek,
the gilded flower of youth. His twining hair,
pushed back, ran over his silver shoulders,
uncombed, roiled by the whistling breeze,
lifted by its sighs. When the hair was blown back,
the middle of his neck appeared, laid bare, on high,

and the gleam, unshrouded, struck like the shine
of Selene splitting a soggy cloud and beaming through it.

His speech, honey-breathed, escaped his rosy mouth,
and from his limbs, all of spring shone forth.
At his silver foot's approach, the meadow blushed roses.
If he turned his eyes, with their bright bovine circles,
Selene, the full moon, seemed to blaze.

Dionysus took him as companion in his luxurious play.
He questioned him, wonder in his voice,
but disguised as a mortal—this weaver of wiles.

"What father begat you? What divine womb gave you birth?
Which of the graces bore you?
What lovely Apollo was your sire?
Speak friend, do not hide your race. If you come
as another Eros, without wings or bow, or quiver,
which of the immortals lay with Aphrodite?
And yet I would fear to call your mother Cypris,
since then Ares or Hephaestus would be your father.
But if you came from heaven, and are the one they call Hermes,
show me your light wings and your spirit sandals.
Why do have your uncut hair on your neck?
Surely you aren't Phoebus, here without lyre or bow,
the unbarbered one who shakes his curls unbound?
If I am of Cronus' line and you are earthly,
having the short-lived blood of cow-horned satyrs,
be king with me, a god with a mortal.
Your Uranian looks won't shame my Olympian blood.
But why do I call you one from a short-lived tribe?
I know your blood, even if you try to hide it.
Selene slept with Helios and gave you birth,
the very image of graceful Narcissus. For ethereal
is the shape you bear, spitting image of hornéd Selene."

That is what he said. The youth rejoiced at his words
so pleased that he surpassed his agemates in beauty,
in his more splendid figure.
If the boy plucked a tune

in some mountain copse, Bacchus was pleased to hear it.
If the boy stayed away, his face was unsmiling.
If a satyr, frolicking at a feast at his table,
struck the drums with his hands, shaking them round with a rattle,
and the boy was out, following a deer-shooting chase,
he rejected the doubled sound, with the boy not there.
If ever, by the blossomed flow of Pactolus
he tarried, to get sweeter water to bring to his king,
Bacchus was lashed with woe for want of the boy.
If he ever boldly played the flute of Libustian Echo,
feebly tweeting with inflated cheeks,
Bacchus thought he heard the Mygdonian flutist,
the son of Hyagnis, who lost his skin to Apollo,
fingering the double pipe of Athena.
When he shared a single table with the youth,
he drank in whatever the boy was saying,
and his face fell when he came to a stop.
And when Ampelos would pirouette with prancing feet,
carried away by the love of the dance,
and joined hands as he danced with a playful satyr
pointing one foot and then the other,
Bacchus, observing, was spun in envious care.
And if he joined the sileni, or with some boy
his age, went along in a hunt for deer,
Dionysus restrained him, jealous lest someone
shot with a similar shaft, a slave of Eros,
should win the heart of the naive hunter,
and steal away the sweet child from Lyaeus,
some adolescent like the boy, delighting his agemate.
And when he raised his thyrsus to hold off a mad bear,
or he shot at a lioness with his high-powered rod,
Bacchus turned his eyes toward the west, worried,
lest Zephyr's lethal breeze should blow it back,
just as once a bitter breeze killed an ephebe,
reversing the discus shot of Hyacinthus.
He feared lest Cronus-Son, as a lust-winged erotic bird,
unforeseen, too fast to catch, should appear above Tmolus

and pluck the child in the air with gentle talon,
just as once he nabbed the Trojan cup-holder.
He feared the sea king as well, a failed erotic,
after what he did to the Tantalid in his golden cart,
lest he might grab Ampelos, this oversexed Earthshaker,
driving his war car down the skyway road.
And he had a sweet dream once, on his bed of dreams,
in which he spoke dear words to the youth's image,
seeing a shadowy form, a mimetic shape.
If his love-sick gaze took in some deformity,
this was a pleasing thing to love-struck Dionysus,
dearer than the whole body of the youth. If the tail
straightened and joined at his waist hung slack,
this was sweeter than sweet honey to Bacchus.
And the filthy hair of an untended head?
Even this pleased the sight of the god madly in love.
He loved to be with him by day; he hated night
when it came, when he no longer heard the boy,
but with his ears bewitched took in the familiar sound,
as he slept in the cave of Rhea, whose child is almighty.

Once a satyr saw the boy and, charmed by his divine shape,
spoke *sotto voce* of his hidden love:

"Much beloved Persuasion, manager of the human heart,
may this lovely boy be kind to me alone!
If I had him to play with, as Bacchus does, I'd have no need
to be translated to dwell in the sky, nor do I wish
to be a god, no light for mortals no Phaëthon for me,
nor do I want nectar; ambrosia means nothing.
If Ampelos loves, let Cronus-Son hate me."

Thus the satyr, consumed with erotic venom,
spoke to himself, envy in his voice.
But Evios
transfixed by the sweet youth's spur, smiled as he said
to his father Cronion, himself a loser in love:

"Do me this favor! I'm in love, Phrygian Zeus!
Rhea, my nurse then and now, told me as a child,
how you gave lightning to Zagreus, the earlier Dionysus,
still babbling "'papa,'" gave him your fiery lance,
and the thunder stick, and the celestial monsoon.
And this baby was a second pluvial Zeus!
Now, I do not ask for heavenly fire and storm;
no cloud, no thunder clap for me. If you want to,
give the spark of lightning to fiery Hephaestus.
Let Ares have clouds for his breastplate cover,
give Hermes the sudden Jovian cloudburst,
and let Apollo wield his begetter's lightning.
What a fine thing for me, to wield the minor Semelean bolt!
Matricidal thunderbolts just don't turn me on.
I'm a true Maeonian, what good is heaven to Dionysus?
The beauty of my satyr is more loved than Olympus.
Speak up, Father! Don't hide. Swear it by your boyfriend.
There was a time on the slopes of Ida, when spread-eagled,
you lifted him to heaven with a softened snatch of claw.
Did the cowboy have such beauty, the one who joins you
at the heavenly table with his barnyard aroma?
Zeus, be gracious, with your wingspread supreme;
don't tell me about your Trojan cup-holding steward!
Bearing the gleam of a more shining face,
lovely Ampelos puts your boy Ganymede in the shade—
The Tmolian beats the Idaean! There are troops
of other lovely demigods, you can have them all,
for all I care; but save this one child for Lyaeus."

Lashed by the whirl of lust, that is what he said,

And not so much did Apollo delight, herding his heifers
within the shaggy Magnesian wood
and pierced by the sweetness of a child Eros bore,
as much as Bacchus delighted his heart in play with a boy.

Both sported together within a wood,
sometimes tossing a thyrsus on a sun-baked plain,
sometimes wandering over the rocks,
hunting the mountain dwelling cubs of lions.
And sometimes, alone on a deserted bank
cavorting in the sands of a pebbled river,
the two of them wrestled, a playful contest.

No tripod prize for them, and not for victory
was a flowered cauldron laid by, no grazing horses;
for them the twin voiced flute of the soprano Erotes.
Struggle was loved by both; in the ground between
stood lunatic love, a winged Hermes as umpire,
weaving narcissus with hyacinth, a wreath of wanting.

Both athletes of Eros came to the center
and, twisting palms over their backs like a garland,
compressing the mutual knot of hands at the waist,
and squeezing their ribs with a forearmed yoke-pull,
each lifted the other's body off the ground
in turn with their hands. Bacchus reached Olympus
during this sweet wrestling; he got a double
erotic thrill, lifted and lifting in turn.
The boy, rolling his hand around the Bacchic wrist,
pressing a double bind with hands conjoined,
compressed the joined fingers in a double knot,
as he squeezed the right hand of a willing Dionysus.
Then Bacchus, circling the youth's waist with his hands,
and pushing the boy's body with eroticized palms,
lifted Ampelos high. But Evios, laughing sweetly,
was struck behind the knee by the young friend's soft foot,
and Bacchus with a deliberate roll stretched out in the dust,
and the youth with naked belly lay on top. And he happily
stretched out, spread this way and that, and lay on earth
pushing back the sweet burden with his paunch. His taut,
raised foot he planted in the sand,
and turned and raised his back, but he revealed

only sparing *virtù*, and with the firm palm
of a restrained hand, he shook off the erotic burden.
Twisting his torso, the expert youth leapt on the opposing back
aslant his ribs, and above his flanks fitting
one foot in the back of his knee, one foot by his ankle,
he cinched the mid-belly with a double bond,
scissoring the ribs, and with his knee he twisted his foot
straight and elevated. They both rolled in the dirt then,
and the sweat flowed, both clearly spent.

And so Bacchus the unconquerable was conquered,
having mimicked his athletic parent Zeus at Olympia,
and was willing to be beaten, just as the great one, Zeus,
took a fall wrestling, bending a voluntary knee to Heracles.
So the friendly bout ended. The happy hand
of the boy raised the prize, a double flute.
The youngster wiped sweat off his limbs in the stream,
and he sponged off the sodden dust. From the bathed
and sweat-drenched skin, the blaze of love broke out.

After the mighty-muscled victory, Bacchus,
along with the kid, did not end his play
but established a wind-swift match of flying feet.
In order to bring swift suitors to the love-game,
he set out as first prize the tools of Rhea Cybele,
brass cymbals and spotted skins of fawns;
and as second prize, the costume of Pan,
sweet breathing syrinx, and a resounding drumhead
rimmed with bronze. He then set out for third prize
some glittering sand given up by the river.
Then Bromius, measuring the ground for the stade,
marked the two limits of a competitive track,
setting up a ten-palm-high finish line for the course,
a tall wooden signpost set in the ground.
And he planted a thyrsus in the ground to mark the turn.
Then he challenged his satyrs to strive for the win.
When dance-loving Lyaeus shouted the command,

Leneus swift as the breeze got the jump, and on his tail
Cissos the prancer and Ampelos the charmer.
They were strung out in a line, faithful to the swift heel
of a foot straight on the track. And Cissos
floated with a whirlwind rush of feet.
Leneus hotly breathed down his back,
And ran fast as breezes, clear second to the leader,
so near, that he struck the dust as it fell
into the track of the feet of the leader.

And the measure between the two was like
the distance between the rod and the chest
of a girl weaving, so close but not touching.

Ampelos was in third. And Dionysus was watching,
melting with jealousy, as he turned and saw
the two prize athletes running in front,
fearing they might win, and Ampelos finish last.
But the god gave him aid, breathing might into him,
and made the boy run swifter than whirling dust devils.
The first of the two front runners reached the bank,
but there his knees flailed in the muddy slush—
Cissos it was—he slipped, and fell in the sandy slurry,
and then Leneus' rushing knees slowed, and he fell
when he reined back his feet. The would-be champions
were left behind and Ampelos grabbed the prize.

The silenian elders echoed the "Euoi,"
amazed at the young man's win. The youth, his hair luxuriant,
took first; Leneus took second, full of envy,
for he knew the jealous trick of Lyaeus,
and his lust. And Cissos sheepishly glanced at his friends
as he stretched out his hand for third and last prize.

Book 11

Darwin Michener-Rutledge

In the Eleventh see the alluring Ampelos
Carried off by a murderous, rampaging bull.

The games were done.

The beautiful boy exulted in his victory,
skipping winding circles,
circles around his companion Bacchus,
and caught him up in an embrace with his pale arms.
When YoBacchus saw him celebrating
his double conquest, he said to him tenderly:

"Come on now, dear boy, after winning
that swimming race, and that wrestling bout
on dry land, let's have a third match!
Swim against me, your comrade, your friend,
and see if you can come out victorious!
You beat me once, Ampelos, wrestling
on the sandy shore. Now see if you can be
nimbler than Lyaeus here in the river!
Leave the frivolous satyrs to their frolicking,
and match up with me in a third contest.
If you prevail both on land and in water,

I will crown your lovely tresses twice,
a double garland for a second victory
over the invincible Dionysus!

This stream is as lovely as you, it befits
your beauty, and its glimmering reflection
will create a double Ampelos cutting through
the sun-flecked water with cupped golden hands.
As you surge through the Pactolus' water
its droplets will embellish your bare skin.
Phaëthon shoots rosy rays down to Oceanus:
grant this river Olympian glory by doing the same
and lending your radiance to the Pactolus. You will seem
to rise from the waves like the Morning Star!
Both of you shine like stars, this metallic red river
and your glorious limbs, so let it hold you
close in its depths where the silt matches your skin.
Let the river blend beauties, so I may say to the satyrs,
'How did rose come to rose? How did ruddy skin
and gleaming water fuse into one radiance?'
If only the Eridanus were here also, my love,
where the fast-falling tears of the Heliades converge:
then I could wash you in gold and amber . . .
But, since I live so far from that western river,
I will go to the nearby city of Alybe
for precious white water from the Guedes' stream,
so that when you climb dripping from the Pactolus
I can make you glisten with its silvery current.
Leave the wide Hermus, which has no golden waves,
for others to swim in, for the satyrs.
A golden youth should have golden water."

As soon as he finished, he dove into the water.
Ampelos, rising from the ground, jumped in too,
and off they went! What a time they had, criss-crossing
from one point to another through the rich river.

The god, gaining a lead with ease,
pushed on through the water, breasting the currents.
Kicking hard with his feet and stroking with his arms
he etched the stream's serene, opulent surface.
At times he would let the boy's course run close to his own,
then he would shoot past him, taking care though
to keep Ampelos close behind. Sometimes he would pause
to tread water, moving his hands in circles,
as if the waves wearied him, and then of a sudden
flutter-kicking Dionysus let his opponent win.

Ampelos left the river and went into a wooded copse,
his head held high, proud of his victory.
He crowned himself with a wreath of snakes,
very much like Lyaeus' own serpentine headdress.
Having often seen Bromius in a dappled tunic,
he mimicked this with a spotted chiton,
pulled purple boots onto his delicate feet,
and across one shoulder threw a speckled robe.
Whenever he saw YoBacchus driving
his leopard-drawn chariot up in the hills
he would make a spectacle of himself
cavorting with wild things. Riding a bear
he would tug at the fur of the grizzled creature,
or flick a bristling-maned lion with a whip,
or ride freestyle on a tiger for the sheer fun of it.

Dionysus would warn him from time to time,
his words kind (and prophetic), his voice full of pity
as he reprimanded the boy:

"Where are you off to, my dear boy?
Why do you like the woods so much?
Stay close to me in the hunt—hunt with Dionysus!
When I am at the table, eat along with me,
party with me when I rouse the satyrs to revelry!

No need to tremble at the mountain lion's jaws,
fear only the horns of the merciless bull."

So he warned bold Ampelos with deep affection.
The boy heard the god's words with his ears,
but all he could think about was play.

Then an ominous vision appeared to lovesick Dionysus,
announcing that Ampelos would not live much longer:
a scaly, horned dragon arose from the rocks
with a tender fawn clinging to his back. The dragon
slouched across the steps of an altar, then hurled
the poor creature upon it, tumbling along, gored
by the dragon's terrible horn. As the fawn shrieked
its vagrant soul escaped into the air.
A slow stream of blood turned the altar-stone crimson
flowing out like wine (prelude to the coming libation).

When Euius saw the low-bellied bandit and the fawn,
he knew that a horned beast would slaughter
his carefree darling. He moaned but laughed it off,
his mind uncertain and divided. His heart split into halves:
he choked on a sob for his ill-fated beloved,
then giggled for the sweet wine. Nonetheless,
he went with his enchanting boy to the mountains,
up to the flats where they were accustomed to hunt.
Bacchus still delighted to gaze at him; lovers never tire of looking.

Often, as they sat together at the table, the boy would play
an awkward tune, fumbling the notes of the reeds.
Young Bacchus would leap about and clap his hands.
Even when the melody faltered, he cried out with joy
as though the song were perfect, and pressed his soft lips
to the singer's own, kissing him sweetly for the music.
And he swore with the ardor of youth that, by Zeus,
no sweet-tongued Pan or golden-voiced Apollo
had ever sung so mellifluous a melody.

But death-dealing and delusive Atê
saw the impetuous boy wandering off from Lyaeus
as they hunted on the mountainside.
Assuming the form of one of his friends,
she coaxed Ampelos and deceived him,
all to please Dionysus' stepmother.

"Brave boy, your friend is called Dionysus for nothing!
What honors have you received as his companion?
You do not drive his divine, panther-pulled chariot.
That rig has been given to Maron, and now
its ruling whip and ornate reins are in his hands!
What such gift have you received from your god?
The Pans have their flutes, their resounding pipes,
the satyrs have rattling drums from your own Dionysus,
the Bassarids of the mountains ride on his lions' backs.
What token have you received equal to your love, you,
beloved not at all by leopard-driving Dionysus?
How often has Atymnius been seen piercing the air
with the chariot of Phoebus? And Abaris
also flew, perched upon Apollo's winged arrow.
Even Ganymede got to sky-ride an eagle,
a metamorphosed Zeus, father of your own Lyaeus.
Bacchus never made himself a lovebird to carry you,
lifting your body with the gentlest talons!
That Trojan wine-pourer has one-upped you,
and the court of Zeus is now his own home!
But see here, my boy, if you still want a chariot
don't take a jittery colt out on the road
rather a thunder-hooved horse that goes galloping
in a whirlwind of speed and flings off the driver!
Glaucus' horses bucked him to the ground in a mad frenzy,
just as swift-winged Pegasus threw Bellerophon
and sent him hurtling from the sky, despite his being
a child of Zeus and the bloodrun of Poseidon.
Come along to the herd, this way, with its shrill-piping
drovers and docile cattle. Get on one of the bulls!

I will make you a spectacular wild-bull rider.
Your taurine king Dionysus will admire you so greatly
when he sees you with a beast between your legs!
There is nothing to fear. Europa did this as a young girl,
grasping the horns tightly, and she didn't need any reins."

This overture persuaded Ampelos, and the goddess
flew off, up into the open air.
And there he was,
a lone bull, careening down from the cliffside!
His parted lips revealed a dark tongue
that hung over his wet jaws: he was thirsty.
He drank deep, then stood there staring at the boy
as if he knew him, as if the boy were his own master.
He did not tilt his horns sideways in welcome,
but as the imposing bull belched up water over
and over through his maw, a spray of droplets
showered on the boy, foretelling the future:
for oxen still trudge round and round capstans
endlessly, pumping water that irrigates the vines.

As the boy stood at the bull's brow,
fearlessly petting the curved horns with his hand,
he smarted with an almost erotic desire
for the animal and felt a deep impulse
to mount and ride this bull from the mountains.
He pulled up long shoots of pliant reeds
from a lush meadow and braided them into a whip;
then he bent and twined some withered,
sharper twigs into bundles to fashion
a makeshift bridle. He decorated the bull
with fresh dewy leaves, wreathed him with roses,
decked his brow with lilies and daffodils,
and circled his neck with purple anemone.
Then he scooped up handfuls of golden clay
from the river nearby and gilded the horns.
He laid a spotted hide on the animal's back,

climbed on up, and with his pretend whip
switched his mount as if it were a pony.
Then he called out, boasting to the bull-faced moon:

"O, Selene! Bless me, horned cattle driver!
I'm both of those! I have horns and I'm driving your bull!"

Bold words from the satyr-boy to the moon.

Selene's pale face shone with jealousy
and her eyes cast moonlight through the night air
down to Ampelos, sitting astride the murderous beast.
She dispatched a gadfly, a cattle tormentor,
and the bull, stung all over by its sharp bite,
galloped off like a horse through the trackless hills.
While the animal, tormented by the stings,
carried his rider over the perilous mountain tops,
the boy, fearing his doom, cried out mournfully:

"That's enough for now, Bull! Stop! You can run again
tomorrow! Don't kill me on these high, barren cliffs
or anywhere that Bacchus would never discover my death!
Forgive me for gilding your horns, Bull,
and do not envy the love I give to Bacchus!
But if you must kill me to spite Dionysus,
if you have no mercy for your unhappy rider
because I'm young, and am Lyaeus' best friend,
at least take me back to the satyrs and finish me off there,
so that when I am dead, tears will mingle with my ashes.
Dear bull, I'm begging you! It will be at least some comfort
if Dionysus, who never cries, mourns my death.
If you are a traitor to me, who have horns just like yours,
at least learn to talk so you can tell Lyaeus I'm dead.
O Bull, enemy to both Demeter and Dionysus,
when one of them grieves, so does the other!"

That was what the rosy boy cried in his misery,
so close to Hades now. The enraged bull leapt up
to the trackless peaks of the mountain and there
flung the boy headfirst from his back.
He fell on his skull and rolled into a mangled heap,
his neck breaking with a sharp snap.
And then the beast
rammed him into the dirt again and again,
pinning him down with the sharp tip of his horn
until there he lay, a headless corpse,
milky pale upon the darkened earth,
both ground and boy stained with gore.

One of the satyrs caught a glimpse
of beautiful Ampelos as he lay in the dust,
and brought the terrible news to Bacchus.

Hearing this, the god ran swifter than the wind;
even Hercules didn't run as fast, when the nymphs
had covered delicate Hylas with their nefarious waters,
to be a carefully kept bridegroom for a rapacious water sprite,
as Bacchus ran when he bounded over the mountain.

He wailed when he saw his boy lying on the ground,
still so beautiful, and as if he were still alive.

He took a fawnskin to clothe the unbreathing body,
draping it across his love's cold chest and shoulders,
and put boots on his feet. He laid roses and lilies
upon the corpse, and crowned his hair with
short-lived anemone flowers, for one taken from life
too violently and too soon. He put a thyrsus
in the boy's hand, shrouded him with his own purple robe,
and from his own soft curls he cut a lock of hair
and placed it on the body as a token, a last, sad gift.

He gathered ambrosia from his mother Rhea,
and poured it over the wounds, (and because of this
grapes were imbued with fragrant ambrosia
when Ampelos later changed into his new form.)

No pallor came to dull the boy's rosy cheeks as he lay
cold upon the ground, and when the gentle breezes blew,
strands of his golden curls brushed across his youthful face.

He was a dazzling sight, even in death.

Gathering around the body,
the sileni wept and the Bacchae wailed,
and all the while his beauty never left him.
Instead, he lay with a gentle smile across his face,
as if his honey-sweet voice still sprang from his muted lips.

Dionysus, who had never mourned, was now wracked with sobs.
His smile long vanished, he cried out,

"O Fates! Stop your spinning! Drop your spiteful yarn!
Are even bulls as covetous of boys as the very breezes?
What Zephyr has attacked Apollo and now me?
Phoebus Atymnius is a lucky bastard, taking his boy's
sweet name, and now in mourning that youth
he can drag him up from the earth in blooms
bearing his name, and carve 'sorrow' into every iris leaf.

"What do I have? What garland can I wear?
What flower can murmur comfort to me in this grief?
You died too young, but I will avenge you! I'll drag
that rogue bull back and slaughter him on your grave!
I won't go after him with an ax, no, many bulls die like that,
but a shattered skull would be too kind for him.
I will tear open his heinous guts with my own horns,
just the way he butchered you with his.
O, the Earthshaker is lucky too! His lover was a Phrygian boy,

from near my own lover's home, and Zeus took him away
to his golden house on high Olympus, and made it his home.
And when he wanted to race, Zeus lent him his own
unfailing chariot to honor Hippodameia's wedding.
All I've ever had was this boy who has died too soon.
My sweet Ampelos never knew the joys of marriage,
never prepared my chariot for his journey to the bridal chamber.
No, he died leaving only grief, insurmountable grief,
for Dionysus the ungrieving.
You are dead, but there is still persuasion on your tongue,
my dearest, it hangs there upon your breathless lips.
Your cheeks are still flushed, your eyes are bright with mirth,
your arms and hands are fair, still fair as snow. O, even
your curls move in the whistling wind. Death holds you gently;
every loveliness remains . . . But love is lost to me!
Why did you ever get on that vengeful bull?
If you were swept up with a passion for whirlwind horses,
why didn't you tell me? I would have brought you a chariot from Ida,
and horses too, from that ancient celestial breed of Tros!
I could have stolen Ganymede away from this country,
who also came from Ida and is nearly as beautiful as you,
but Zeus saved him from such massacring bulls
and flew away with him in his gentle talons, up to the sky!
If you wanted to hunt the wild beasts of these mountains,
"Why didn't you tell me that you needed a chariot?
You could have taken mine without peril, you could have
held my Rhea's untouchable reins and whipped a team
of tame dragons without so much as wobbling!
You no longer sing sweetly with satyrs over wine,
or order the boisterous Bassarids' song.
You can no longer pursue the chase with me while we hunt!

"Damn it! Death is never kind, and accepts no gems or jewels
as ransom for a corpse, or I would buy Ampelos back his life.

"Alas, Hades is relentless. If he permitted,
I would steal the trees from the bank of the Eridanus

and lay their gleaming amber at his feet.
I would bring him glittering Erythraean rocks from the Indies,
and all rich Alybe's smooth silver. For my dead boy,
I would give away every last current of Pactolus' gold."

So he lamented his perished beloved,
and looking upon him again as he lay in the dust,
Dionysus cried again to Zeus in a desperate howl:
"Father Zeus! If you love me, if you have ever known
the anguish of love, give Ampelos back his voice, just for an hour,
just so he could speak to me one last time and say,

'Why do you mourn me, Dionysus? Mourning can't wake me.
I still have ears, but they do not hear you calling.
I still have eyes, but I do not see you wracked with grief.
Dionysus, my always happy one, cry no tears for me.
Come now, leave your mourning; the naiads may grieve
by that fatal spring, but Narcissus doesn't hear them,
and Phaëthon is ignorant of the Heliades' wretched pain.'

"Father, why couldn't you have made me mortal?
Then I could be frolicking with my boy, even in Hades,
and I would not have to leave my darling Ampelos
to slip away into Lethe alone.
Apollo was so lucky with the boy he loved,
for now Apollo is called Hyacinthian.
If only I were called Ampeloian in the same way!
How long will you sleep, my dearest love?
Are you done with your dancing? Aren't you going
to the river today to fill your pitcher?
It's time for your dance in the woodland glades again . . .
If you are angry with your lovesick Dionysus, my darling,
speak to the sileni so I can hear what you wish to say.
If a lion killed you I will destroy every one, yes,
all that dwell upon Tmolus' slopes, I will not even pity
my Rhea's team of lions, I will kill them too
if they were your killers with their gristly jaws.

If a leopard destroyed you, O my love blossom,
I will abandon my band of leopards.
There are countless other savage beasts.
Artemis, queen of wild things, drives an antlered
chariot pulled by stags, so I will wear a fawnskin
and hitch my chariot to a team of fawns!
If you were killed by any of those ruthless boars,
I will gather them all for slaughter, and leave not one
for the Archeress. If it was an arrogant bull,
then I will wipe out their entire bloodline,
every last one, with my sharp-tipped thyrsus."

And so he lamented again and again.

Then Eros came and stood near him, taking the form
of a shaggy silenus gripping a thyrsus, and leaning
on a fennel stalk like an old man's trusted staff,
a dappled fawn skin draped over his shoulders.
He spoke comforting words to the moaning Bacchus:

"Light another love with the embers of this one,
leave this pain for another youth, and forget the dead.
New love is always the remedy for old love,
since time cannot destroy love, though it can conceal all.
If you need an anodyne for your grief,
pursue a better boy: affection can stifle affection.
Hyacinthus shook Zephyrus, but when he died
that amorous Wind found young Cyparissos
to console him for losing the Amyclaian boy.
Ask a horticulturist if you want:
when a gardener sees a flower lying in the dust
he plants a new seed to comfort himself for his loss.

"Listen, I'll tell you an old story.

"There was a rapturous boy, surpassing all his agemates,
who lived near the banks of the branching Maeandrus,

He was tall, fine-featured, fleet-footed,
with long straight hair and no fuzz on his chin.
Upon both cheeks there was an inborn grace
that flickered across his face and modest eyes,
and beauty darted from his eyelids like arrows.
His complexion was pale as milk blended with rose.
He was called Calamos, *Reed*, by his father Maeandrus,
who lurked deep in the folds of Earth with his water,
flowing through those depths and pulling his twisting stream
up towards the light, crawling unseen over slanted paths
beneath the Earth's surface, except where he leaps up
all of a sudden to raise his neck above ground.

"That was Calamos, swift and beautiful.

"The rosy-armed boy was fond of a charming agemate,
Carpos, *Fruit*, who possessed more beauty
than any mortal man. If he had lived in a bygone age,
he would have been the bridegroom of Eos, Dawn,
shining lovelier than Cephalus, handsomer than Orion,
outdoing them all with his roseate glow.
Deo would not have held Iasion as her husband
in her fruitful arms, or Selene, Endymion. No,
this most beautiful youth would soon have wed them both,
one husband for two goddesses, and taken the couch
of golden-haired, bountiful Demeter,
and had the jealous Moon beside him as well.

"Such was Carpos, Calamos' cherished friend,
a flower of the Loves in all his beauty.
Both the same age, the two played together
on the banks of that meandering river,
where they had laid a racecourse, out and back.
Calamos, who could run like the wind,
set an elm tree as the starting point and finish,
and an olive at the turn. And they were off,
running neck and neck along the riverbank,

but the nimble Calamos, all too willing
to let Carpos win, fell intentionally in the final sprint.
Afterwards, the two of them bathed and played together.
Then they had a second race, this time in the water,
which would see Calamos swim slowly with the current,
allowing Carpos to pull ahead as he himself
just paddled along, in second place at Carpos' ankles
while he watched the bare back of the boy ahead.

"The race had begun at a starting point in the water.
The game was to see who could beat the other
swimming out and back as they pulled themselves
first around one turning point, and then another
on the opposite side before coming back.
The water was flowing with them at the start;
Calamos stayed close to his friend as they swam,
watching his rosy fingers and restraining his own hand
as he pulled himself along through the water.
When he was in the lead, he checked his speed
and allowed his young friend to catch up,
the boy stormily beating the water with his strokes
and lifting his head up above the water.
Just as Carpos was about to leave the river
and gain the shore, winning this race
as he had won the one on land, a blast of wind
beat against his face and drove the waves
into his open mouth, mercilessly drowning
the tender boy. Calamos escaped the the invidious wind
and climbed the nearest bank without his friend.
Unable to see him or get any answer to his cries,
he called out in a lament full of love:

"'Speak to me, you naiads!
What wind has swept my Carpos away?
Grant me a final grace, I pray you,
leave my father's deadly waters, go to another stream,
drink not of the river that has murdered Carpos!

No, my father did not kill that boy. It was the West Wind,
who has held a grudge against Calamos
second only to his grudge against Phoebus,
that has destroyed my Carpos. No doubt he desired him
and so struck him with a gale out of jealousy!
My star has sunk beneath the surface and has not risen,
my Morning Star will never shine again!
Carpos is drowned in the river, so why should I need light?
O speak to me, naiads!
Who has extinguished the light of my love?
How long you linger, O my beloved
Why are you so fond of the water?
Have you found a better companion down there
and thrown poor Calamos' love to the winds
so you can stay stay below with him?
If a nymph, one of the naiads, has fallen in love with you
and carried you off, tell me and I will battle them all!
If you want a married life, if you want to wed my sister,
tell me and I will build you a bedroom in the depths!
Have you swum past me, Carpos, beyond our familiar shore?
I am hoarse from shouting, but you haven't heard my calls.
If Notus came onto you, or bold Eurus, let him dance off
alone, without a partner, brash enemy of love!
If Boreas did you in, I will go see his wife Orithyia.
If the waves overwhelmed you without pity for your beauty,
if my father swept you off in a merciless flood,
let him receive his own son into those murderous waters,
and conceal Calamos beside dead Carpos.
Wherever Carpos went off and died, I will fall headfirst
and drink Acheron's water to quench my searing love.'

"Thus Calamos, tears streaming from his eyes.
Then, to honor his dead friend, he sheared off
with gloomy steel a long-cherished lock of hair,
and holding it out to his father Maeandrus
he spoke his last words:
'Accept first

this lock of hair, and then my own body,
for I cannot stand to face tomorrow's dawn
without Carpos. The two of us shared one life.
We both felt the same burning love on earth,
so let there be one watery fate for us both,
the two of us together in the same stream.
Build here on the banks of this river, O naiads,
one empty barrow for us both, and on the tombstone
engrave these lines in sorrowful letters:

I entomb Carpos and Calamos, who loved each other
And were killed by the pitiless water long ago.

Cut a small lock of your own hair for Calamos,
your dying brother, so cursed in his love,
but for Carpos cut off every last strand.'

"Saying these things, Calamos plunged into the stream
and sank, drowning in the son-slaying water
of a father loath. Then Calamos bestowed
his form on the reeds, which took his name as well,
and Carpos flourished as the fruit of the earth."

So impetuous Eros comforted Dionysus
with kindly words to lighten his grief.
But Bacchus' heart was lashed yet again
with sorrow for his boy's untimely death.

Then came the rose-cheeked Seasons,
daughters of the yearly, coursing Light,
their storm-footed father, making their swift way
to the house of Helios.
                    Winter wore a veil like snow,
casting her face in shadow, but for a gentle gleam of light
that came as though through dark clouds.
Upon her feet were frigid hailstone shoes,
her braids were bound up about her moist head,

held fast across her brow with a diadem of raindrops
and a garland of evergreen pine,
and her frosty breast was rimed with snow.

Then came their soft sister, Spring,
her lips puffed with breath of the sweet West Wind,
a seraphic solace to mortal men,
and her hair tied back from her windy face
with a dewy diadem, and all the while
she laughed like a flower in bloom.
In her wake she left behind the scent
of wild roses opening at dawn
as she wove this way and that in a merry dance
for springtime Adonis and for Cytherea,

Harvesting Summer came with her sisters,
holding in her right hand a ripe ear of wheat,
grains clustered at the top, and in her left hand
a sharpened sickle, foretelling the harvest.
The gentle maiden was wrapt in diaphanous linen
that revealed the mysteries of her white thighs
as she moved through the dance; and when
Phaëthon cast down heat upon her face,
her cheeks grew damp with beads of sweat.

The last one, leading the dance for a good plowing,
was crowned with an olive wreath
about her sparse temples, which dripped
with the waters of the seven-mouthed Nile
upon her withered body, but the ends of her hair
were sparse and dry. This was Autumn, pining away,
tearing down leaves from the trees
and casting them into the howling wind.
There were no vine branches yet to wind around
the nymph's neck with her tangles of golden curls;
her mouth was not yet stained purple

with Maronian vintage from the winepress;
her ivy had not yet run wild with reaching tendrils.

But then the fated time was upon them, bringing
the Seasons running together to the house of Helios.

Book 12

John L. Gronbeck-Tedesco

Delight in the twelfth! Here Ampelos becomes flower, vine,
then fruit, plucked, crushed, fermented into fine wine.

The Seasons sailed from the vast verge of the western oceans
to the bright-sky home of their father, sun god Helios,
the life-giver. Western Hesperus, the bright Evening Star,
leaped high to meet them. Moon goddess Selene, the lustrous
one—she now rising new again, with starlight beyond her,
also greeted the four busy dancing sisters. Just then,
that young-blooded, sky prancing, light-bearing charioteer,
golden-skinned Helios, returned ready for what came next.

The ladies stopped at the sight of their father radiant
but now ready to settle in for the night after his
daytime journey across the sky. Then, gleaming Phosphorus,
finished with his morning-star rounds, put away the steamy
tack and silver-drenched whip. In an amiable sea current,
he wet-brushed the prancing fire-grazed, sweat-slick horses. And then,
the hours, Time's spawn and servants of Helios, presented themselves.

Autumn stood tall and spoke to her father, gesturing with
her long crook:

"My sisters bear fruit: vegetables, grass and
clover, while I stay barren. Please, give me something wondrous
to birth—something not yet of the known world but still to come."

Helios chuckled, pointing to the prophetic tablets
gathered by Harmonia from the agile fingers of
Phanes Firstborn, the Revealer. Then, Hyperion
summarized the work of that illustrious illustrator.

The inscriptions went straight to the heart of the matter:
"The third tablet, dark-stained, well-formed and specific tells how,
where and when the marvelous grapes, new to nature, shall come.
The fourth names the purple-robed god of the vines and pictures
Ganymedes pouring that wonderful stuff given by
the grapes, to be named 'wine' always forever."

But to begin at the beginning.
Sunshine's daughter danced to the prophetic wall. The first tablet
told tales from before time mattered: all that the mutilated
serpent Ophion seeded into the ground tooth by tooth,
fresh from his gore-smeared gums. Next, the crimes of Cronus: how he
castrated his lust-driven father, whose bloody seed spilled
into the Venus-birthing ocean, how infant-eating
Cronus was tricked by his clever wife-sister Rhea
with a stone that saved last-born Zeus from his jaws and rebirthed
her children from the vomit of their stone-gagged father.

Stormy Autumn landed—*en pointe*—before the second fine
tablet in the sunny cloister. There chiseled deep: how once
upon a time the first human burst from a pine without
father or mother; how Zeus the thunder maker drowned all
cities in the world, leaving only Deucalion high
and dry in his chest near the pallid moon.

The third tablet predicted the course of the world written in
letters ablaze in Phoenician reds no less. And here
the glaring prophesies:
"Argus, herdsman, grim, will be turned

into a bird bright-eyed. And, Harpalyce son-butcher
father-fucker will sprout feathers storm-chaser swift. And,
Philomela, bustling weaver, who sewed upon a robe
the story of how her tongue was torn from her mouth, will fly
after her own swallow-sweet calls. Niobe, though in stone,
will always mourn her progeny. And, next to her, Pyrrhus
adamant in lust for Rhea must stand stone-hard, pallorous,
still. Thisby and Pyramus will be two torrents of want
always separate. Smilax and Crocus, never happy,
will turn floral for love. And, Atalanta, the virgin
runner, slowed into marriage by the Paphian apples,
will tumble into madness, morph into a lioness by
will of Artemis, goddess of wombs, sister to Apollo."

Autumn wind-dancer, restive and urgent, two-stepped to where
blazing Hyperion marked the oracles: Here, Leo
shines. There, Virgo holds torrents of blossoms stickled pink, white,
green—born in the promised vineyards.

Autumn stopped to look again to see again deep into
the scripted stone:
"Youthful Cissos will sault high to become
soaring ivy that will wrap Calamos' reed—straight but pliant—
to keep it strong enough for the heavy weave of the mild
new verdure. Ampelos will be transfigured, his goatish
body becoming the fruit of the vineyard: beautiful
with lovely locks of purple,"
Then ever-searching Fall with her hope-filled eyes finds across
the near wall streaked with radiant prophecies even more.
Etched into time eternal, Ganymedes—beneficent—
pours forever Ampelos' benediction into gold.
Thrilled to her core, Fall luminates when her eyes seal upon
these words for the ivy-lavished Lyaeus:
"Zeus vouchsafes
prophecies to Phoebus, queathes roses to Aphrodite,
gifts Athena with olives, commits corn to Demeter.
Ah, but the generous vine belongs to Dionysus."

Thus Zeus' promise, etched in bold dark strokes
—and a whole lot more.
Virginal Autumn, enthralled by the holy tablets streaks east
into the light again with her season-sisters behind
Phaëthon's swift coursers to the ever-moving confluence of
currents in the deep sea where eastern waters run dark blue.

Destroyed, Dionysus could not gladden his heart, emptied—
beaten up by the deep-rooted dark rhythms of lament
for love of Ampelos. Hermes dried his coursing currents
before the face of this grief-struck god. Love and pity
stanch the wave-maker's pulsing waters. Saffron Pactolus
ceased his bustling golden flow—he near human in his
empathic sorrow. Likewise Phrygian Sangarius,
deep source of fountains, quit pumping to honor the dead boy.
Niobe, the daughter of Tantalus, still in mourning,
doubled her tears for Dionysus. The fir, the pine, the
Phoebus-laurel, Athena's olive: all shuddered with grief
in the grieving wind. Dionysus, the god of laughter,
mourned, implacable, still bound by the cuffs the Fates had sewn.

Then, Atropos:
"Get a grip. Your lover lives.
Your grief dissolves the tight knots of destiny. Ampelos
hunkered down on the sunny side will not cross Acheron's
bitter boundary. Dead yet still alive he will become
a terrific nectar, beyond others. By my will I
will it. Believe it, O' god. This world shall bless his life with
feasts and celebrations, with dance and harmony, with kicks
and fills of Dorian drumming, in Phrygian tunes,
in the fine cabarets of Marathon and Ismenus.
The Muses shall belt songs of triumph and praise
to Ampelos. Listen, Bacchus, uncoil your crown of snakes! Let
vines of the vineyard circle your brow and ears. Jealous
Phoebus sulks, stuck with only a limp Iris, forever.
You and Ampelos foment the ecstatic drink, body
of love and comfort too—heaven-come-to-earth, you know,

and there's more.
Against the Amyclaian boy's lust for blood
from sharp bronze, your goat-boy lusts for the juicy torrent
of reverie and delight. You are like a country of grapes
and vines more excellent than a country of that precious
metal. Wine is better than buttery gold—and how!—just
as the water of the Pactolus is better than what flows
in the Eurotas. Ampelos, think of it this way: once,
you were to Dionysus as death was to grief. Now you
are to Dionysus as wine is to delight. And, wine
is to you as blessings are to Dionysus. Know this.
Lord Bacchus wept and washed away the tears of humankind
with his own."
So spoke fateful Atropos and vanished.

Then, an avalanche of miracles tumbled upon Bacchus.
Ampelos broke the soil as a coiling plant. He flowered.
His belly morphed into a supple stalk; his long fingers
into high-reaching vines; toes into sinking roots; his thick
curls now heavy-clusters of grapes; his once fawn-umber skin
now the color of the bloom. From head to neck to shoulders
to elbow: all grapes, and the land around him, heaped high
and wide with the newborn, unknown fruit.

Cissos, young and playful, launched himself from a lofty tree;
shapeshifted midair into ivy and circled the fresh
orchard with tough vine-knots to hold against troubles that travel
on the ground.

Dionysus, renewed, free now from grief, shaded his head
with this gift as Ampelos ripened red the grapes in his
resurrected body, and his lover-god gathered them
like kisses. Dionysus, new to grapes, used his hands and
time to press juice into wine. Quick into his ox horn the new
swirling, purple body of Ampelos flowed, and the passionate
vine-god sucked him to the dregs—heady in his mouth—and ate
his lover's fruity load—the tart ginger skin full of new tastes.

Then in the gasp and grasp of delight:
"O god, O god, my Ampelos, your body! You are Zeus'
vessel. I taste his very life in yours—the thunder
maker. Apollo decked in laurel and iris cannot
feed or nourish, neither . . . nor. Demeter's stiff-tall corn cannot
incarnate a god. But you, you are food and drink for gods
and mortals too.

The sacred juice is the reason—must be, best guess—why stone-
willed Persephone saved a satyr from Styx, why Lethe
would not drown you, why blazing Tisiphone refused to
cremate you. Destiny, hard-bitten, single minded,
relentless, came all unhinged and heart-full gooey when she
tasted what flowed from your body. Earth unworthy demurred.
No tomb for you. Hades, gone all soft and merciful, had to pass."

More from Dionysus:
"My father fathered by Cronus made
you anew for me. Your naked body a torrent of golds
or reds. No longer mortal, now you are divine wine. I
am still made for vengeance though. I will smear the grapes, your new
body, onto the moonbeam feet of your pale destroyer,
The scent will curse Selena: she will bear you in silver
sandals and vaunt you in all of her light-lit steps; so you
always precede the sovereign of darkness. Wherever
she goes, all will smell the taste of you first, no matter her
night-time footwork, and they will know that you are eternal.

"Figs, apples go tasteless behind the teeth. The taste of your
body keeps on, quick and deep into the throat, heart, brain, soul.
Believe it: roses, lilies, iris, grass, leaves, herbs—fruits and
flowers—all sucked into the taste of your body. Call it
terroir, mon pote. And, you engross all, Archer and Ares
come always wreathed in grief and blood. I cum sucking rapture
from your body in delight. I cum gauzed in beauty. I
cum soaked in grace. Ampelos, you engross me too! Pallas
Demeter and their paltry gifts—olives and corn—cannot

enchant. Myrtle, fragrant, bright on the breeze? Tart pears, biting
but sweet? These cannot do what I and my ample vines of bold
wine can: wash bitter grief from hearts and minds, shrive the weight,
the unbearable pain, from the shoulders of memory, kindle
laughter, ignite the dance, flame the dancers to ecstasy.

"Wash. Shrive. Kindle. Ignite. Flame. Olive oil hot lubes the flesh.
So what? My vines do better. They lave the sorrow of an
infant's death and a mother's grief and a father's anguish.
Ampelos, I take you in joy, in rapture; you alive
in death alive. Living! All flora bow. Your desirous
body entwines palm, apple, and fig—all florid verdure.
Phaëthon's blistering threats cool from the breeze of your faithful
trees, and steamy Sirius brings wet summer gusts to warm
your rich red load before the busy hands of Autumn bring
you off, jetting fruit under joyful dancing feet—purple."

So, Dionysus claimed again his purpose, restored nature's
throbbing pulse—he the god of ravishment, of juicy jizm,
of glistening life-pumping pearls, of ecstatic joyance.

This, then, is the story told of how the wine vine was named
for young Ampelos. But there is another and older
tale spun by those who sing verses about the endless past.

Long ago, Ichor the fruit-maker fell from Olympus,
and in the rocks where his body had landed sprang new vines
that grew wild and free. Not yet named, the fresh plants mingled deep
into other verdure, growing fruit lush and tight-skinned with juice.
Unintended and untended, the vines spread far and fast
with lugs of grapes bobbing and swinging as they darkened into
shades of red.

Here, some were dappled with spots white as surf.
There, some shone with a wondrous golden glow.
Others hung with black backs shining over
their red bellies. All thrived and mingled with
older flora.

A shadowy mist fogged the wonderful fruit loading it
with juice. The knotted growth invaded the tops of nearby
pines crowning them in swags of grapes. Pan laughed
when tree branches, pushed by the Boreal wind, pierced the grapes,
soaking their leaves in wine. A snake wound around a tree, sucked
the potent potion of the new fruit, dyeing its jowls
with a ruby drool.

The hill-leaping god wondered when he saw the snake wet
with wine slither into the deep hollow of a nearby
rock. When he spotted the juice of the plump-bellied grapes
Bacchus remembered the prophesies spoken by Rhea
once upon a time.

He struck a pick hard into stone to carve a deep chamber;
then shaped the sides until he had fashioned a smooth wine
press. Quickly, he turned his thyrsus into a sharp sickle
and harvested the new fruit of the vine.

His posse of satyrs went to work: some
gathered, while others heaped the vines into
baskets. While others stripped leaves, some picked
the new fruit.

Bacchus piled and layered the grapes in the sculpted hollow,
until the chamber was full; then, sounded the Doric strain
as he danced upon them. His hoof-stomping chorus of goat boys
followed his lead,

shaking their manes of hair wildly,
tightening their fawn skins,
flattening the fruit,
trilling the cry, "Euoi! Euoi!"
dancing and sounding the anthem of Bacchus.

Wine ejaculated into the rock reservoir; filled
the basin up to its bright, rock-rimmed edges. The satyrs

ladled Ampelos' wad-spunk deluge with ox horns, for cups
did not yet exist; so "Holy Wine Horn" is still the name
given a chalice of wine.

New to wine and sloshed way beyond mindless,
the goat boys went mad. One lost the rhythm
of the dance, reeling "bass ackwards."
Another, possessed by the relentless
booming drum, somersaulted up a tree.
One more soaked his hairy body until
it turned bright pink.

Things turned ugly:
Satyrs exposed boners, schlongs with minds
of their own. One hunted a nymph ready to chase her up
a tree. Bacchus saved him from a fatal fall, and her he
saved from violent lust. Another plunged after a naiad
swimming naked, but she dove deep just in time to escape.

Dionysus, armed by Rhea with a magic pendant
to keep him sober, could not save all from the ravenous
lust ignited by the wine and dancing. A satyr caught
by drum-driven passion assaulted one bound to Bacchus
by vows of chastity. His war mate, crazed by drink, seized
an unwilling virgin, tore off her clothes and raped her from behind.
Another pulled a bacchant maiden as she lit a torch
for her order's ritual of dance. Even though unnerved
by his sacrilege, he could not keep his fingers from her
adolescent breasts.

Thus, the first feast of Dionysus.
After the revels and the slumber of the denouement,
proud Dionysus arose, swanked in his glorious fruit.
He entered the home of his stepmother, goddess Rhea.
Later he assigned to the women of Maeonia
the festive liturgy of the grape vines to celebrate
the yearly resurrection of glorious Ampelos.

Book 13

Mike Lala

In the thirteenth book,
I'll show you the swarm of heroes.

Zeus sent Iris to the halls of Rhea
to tell Dionysus to drive out the Indians
from Asia with his thyrsus, to sweep
the horned river child, King Deriades,
into the sea, and to teach the other world,
the unjust—the wide world—his wakeful
sacred dances and his favorite thing, to drink.

Iris rowed with winds' wings, entering
the echoes of lions' den noiselessly,
pressing pantone finger to magenta lips
pliantly, spine curving slave-like
from an l to r, or even c, as Rhea
stuck her foot out, waiting to be kissed.
Rhea told her Corybants
to serve the prismed rainbow girl
a bowl atop her table, pulling back her foot.
Dizzily, she chugged a gulp, slammed it down,
and spoke like Zeus to Dionysus, thundering,
"Daddy charges you with orders.

"Sweep Bhārat of blasphemies
raise your thyrsus for Olympus' glory;
the Horae will not swing the gates
out toward you till you do.
The messenger of flocks only entered
once he shut ol' Argus' twinkling eyes
and freed red Ares from his wooden prison.
Apollo killed the serpent first,
Daddy roped the Titans fast.
See, even he did not ascend
before the knot was tight.
The never-will-not-be blue court
among the stars is earned by sweat.
He hid them down in Tartarus,
and so you must bind yours."

With Zeus' message sung she left
on air that, feathered, pulsed her home,
so mother Rhea sent a living dance named Pyrrhicus
with tambourine to mold a swarm
of soldiers under Bacchus' charge,
searching all the villages
of Europe and the far-flung east,
gathering the heroes' flock in Lydia to bleat.

These well-bred killers—furry satyrs,
Centaur ichor, donkey-bottomed sileni,
and the maenads' squadron—
do I sing them all, Corybantes?
Not even if my mouth, ten trumpets,
pursed their tongues
would time enough
exist to sing the whole host
Bacchus gathered, so I'll prune.

With Homer's help, that name which means
the model tongue, its single mouth,

the harbor sailors call out to
on hairs of blue with breath gone black
to save them from a starving, slurping sea,
I'll name their chiefs.

Actaeon, the first to hear the call to arms
and swiftly leave the seven gates,
for family ties with Bacchus drew him on.
Boeotian infantry surged up like water
out from Theban walls and Onchestus
(Poseidon's sanctuary,
which the chariots run near);
Peteon; Ocalae; Erythrae; Arne in vines,
so pleased with Dionysus; and Midea's men,
from the famous seaside towns
of Eilesion and Scolon; salty Thisbe
(Aphrodite's harbor—that girl loves the sea);
the homes of Schoenus, green Eleon, and lakeside Copae
with its perfect soil and the eels; mossy Medeon;
smooth-and-lengthened-pastured Hyle's holders
(gave us Tychius the tanner);
hell's prophet's threshing floors
they named for Amphiaraus and his chariot.
Too Thespiae, slanted Plataeae, snow-wet Haliartus
at the base of Helicon, across a streamlet from the slope.
Anthedon out toward the ocean,
Glaucus and its deathless fisher swimming,
stormy Ascra—home of Hesiod the farmer and his poem,
holy Graea's fortress, Mycalessus with its grassy
plains whose name reminds the reader
of Euryale's growl. From the dreamy dirt of Nysa, too,
and the city named for Coronus—
All these towns sent men to follow Actaeon;
their noses whoofed the victory his father's father,
storied seer, had sneezed.

The next Boeotian regiment
closed in behind Hymenaeus, whose baby face
and wispy locks made Bacchus fall in love.
Behind him followed Phoenix,
the white-haired chief like Laocoön
who manned the Argo, Jason's vessel,
sailing with Meleagrus to the Colchians.
Just like he—his friend—Hymenaeus,
at peak of youth and crowned by locks,
never knicked by sword or knife—
he waged the war.

His phalanx followed: brilliant shields.
They came from fortress Aspledon
and Minyas' city Orchomenus,
famous for the Charities,
who groove, but never part.
They also came from Hyria,
which welcomed gods and took its name
from Hyrius, adoptive father
of Orion, born not from a girl,
or bed, or boy, but three gods' pissing
in a dried-out hide, which step-dad buried,
then dug up, finding baby boy.

The place the Greeks hid, jagged Aulis,
Artemis' stone mountain altars,
where Agamemnon torched the doe
young Iphigeneia was meant to be
and doubled Artemis in jealous rage
as breathing in smoked venison,
she whisked the girl away to face the sea.
Odysseus meant her to be Achilles' wife
before the war, hence Aulis took a broker's name
for her who never wed. That lodestar called above
the Argive ships and rescued Agamemnon,
while the girl flew off to Taurus,

learning nasty ways—first you boil,
then you carve, then you eat the men you find—
but in the end, inside the shrine,
she saved Orestes' life.

These Boeotians joined Dionysus
to march against the Indians,
a swarm of fighters off to war,
too many men to count.
They were joined by men from Phocis—
Sybil's rock nearby—frontier Cyparissos'
holders and the pass near Hyampolis,
which takes its name from the sow
unbowed to Tritogeneia's soft splendor.
Pytho and its cliffside gardens,
Crisa, Daulis, Panopeus, from whose rock
Prometheus made all up through Olympus.
Even Bacchus and his brother Phoebus, on Parnassus.
As these gathered—as the Delphic rock leaked vapors
into Sybil, as her voice spoke that of Zeus,
the tripod in self-reference, whispered "Priestess,"
and Castalia sprung forth
into the mouths of poets, always slurping,
sagelike in their babble—more assembled.

Corybants commanded the Euboean ranks,
stretching drum skins, bearing shields
as they did, encircling baby Bacchus.
Those who found their future leader's
infant horns wrapped up in purple
on the rocks where Ino poured him,
leaving him a charge of young
Corymbos' mother, Mystis.
From the storied island,
Prymneus and Mimas swaying;
Acmon sweating, lumberjacking;
Damneus; and Ocythoös, his shield on his back.

Melisseus with helmet gleaming
next to brother Idaeus—
their blasphemed father Socus
sent them with five siblings
and their mama Combê packing.
They ran away to Cnossus' plains,
then Phrygia, expatriates until King Cecrops
ended wicked Socus.
They then left salt-sea Marathon
and turned back to their countrymen,
living on the soil that the Curetes sprouted from.
That tribe's life sounds out of pipes
and clanging swords; their hearts beat toward
dancing in formation, in a circle, with their shields.

Augmented by Abantes'
thick-browed young men from Eretria,
Styra, Cerinthus, the far-strung rock of Carystus
alongside barren Dion, the always-roaring beach
at Geraestus, and Styx, the fort at Cotylia
little village there at Sirus, stretched-out Marmarion,
and the ancient village of Aegê,
these were joined by boys of Chalcis, city of Ellopians,
whose combed-back hair both flowed and parted
as they all marched forward.
This whole, one nation,
was coalesced by seven captains, undivided,
whose one purpose signified itself atop the altar
which, lit beneath the constellations,
led them by the sun's ecliptic,
marking their campaign against
the planets' correspondence.

Erechtheus drummed up the Cecropides,
gourmand as he was of bloodlust,
he whose blood descended from the babe
that nuzzled Pallas' chest

in the flickering of her unwed bedroom,
she whose eyes glowed, turned down toward him,
of Hephaestus, he who grew from cum swift Justice
wiped from thigh, a friend of Siphnus.
He who led the men of fecund Oenoë;
those of near Hymettus, buzzing with the bees on wind
that blew to wooded Marathon, which sent men, too;
Eleusis; those from Athens' harbor;
seaside Brauron, empty crib of Iphigeneia;
and Thoricos; aswarm Aphidna,
those of Eleusinia, land of loving mother Deo
and the baskets of her fruit.
These were sons of Triptolemus,
who, way back, drove Deo's freight of corn
by whipping serpents' backs.
They came with those from Acharnae,
its many fathers multiplying steel to their sons,
who strapped it on and joined the fray
from Attica, who raised up silver swords and spears
as next to them, the wealthy men of Athens
brushed their helmets, pushing forward.
So throughout old Phaleron
footsteps of the thousands stood up hair
beneath girls' brooches
sounding out a chorus as they hummed.

Eagle-boy Aeacus left his home too, thirsty,
son of Zeus and river-daughter—you, Aegina—
whom Zeus raped on drunken Oenone.
Here to help his brother, Bacchus,
Aeacus called the Myrmidons to perfect order
like he was of the colony he begged for company.
Zeus simply snapped and from the clay
those formicidae twitched alive;
their six feet slipped together into two;
they stood and spoke.
Aeacus' captain's shield's bright inscriptions

told his story:
False Zeus in flight to take his mum
in lustful claws, and nearby,
his mother's father dead, on fire,
on the shield's rim. And by his body riverside,
pale and limp, she seems to say,
with tear-soaked eyes turned from Zeus,
"My bridegift's no more dad?"

Crete of many languages came out under Asterius,
second cousin of Semele and Cadmus,
a dandy, strong but cute.
His mom was Phaestian Androgeneia
who slipped her girdle off for Minos.
She bore him in Cydonia, the son of the island's king.
So for his father's pride and kin
he brought a hundred towns' boys out
beneath his shining beauty
to the wine-drunk face of war.
Scattered across the wide-ranged island,
spurred to fight by handsome Asterius,
soldiers of Cnossus, Lyctus, Miletus coalesced
and joined the masses.
Rich men from Gortyn's hills and Rhytion,
fruitful Lycastus, Nodaian Zeus, Boebe's
homes and hills surrounding Cisamus and bright Cytaeus.
That was he, a son of Crete;
the star of Ares shone on him
with light that looked like victory
entombed in molten beams.
Later on, post-victory,
he'd long for what he'd traveled
from a Scythian plot.
Instead of for Dicte—Zeus' birthplace—
he was homesick for exile.
He left old Minos and Androgeneia,
turned away from the shining peak of Ida,

and joined the Colchians, who kill their guests,
and gave them his own namesake.
He taught them things I can't describe,
left his childhood, and the river of Amnisus;
drinking the water of Phasis with modest lips,
he'd never go home.

Then beekeeper Aristaeus showed up tardy,
solo, last Hellenic hero,
head held high in vanity from his glacé hives.
He licked their honey from a wound
he gave himself—in hubris—through
a bed he made before the gods
from challenging the vinter.
Some might say his pride was sapped.
The Olympians judged a tasting test.
Between the vine and hex-pocked hives,
wine won, hands down, the contest.
The falling gods can't drink enough,
so Bacchus poured it through the night
while Aristaeus' honey languished in a glass like amber.
Zeus pronounced his fascination,
but could only drink a cup.
Those bees made art, but art is not
a trouble-killing brew.
This goes years back. Aristaeus' grudge was stuck
to everything he touched. He'd give it up
before he moved to starred Meropis.
He hadn't brought Zeus' winds there yet,
nor had he curbed the dry seasons' fire.
He hadn't stood armed in Sirius' eye,
beating back its flames. Right now,
the cool wind toked him on
as he speared the heat
with his smoldering throat.
He still lived there in his childhood home
of Arcadian Parrhasia.

A scabby crew of that land's vagrants,
eating acorns, wandered forward
those who owned Lasion, the clearings of Lycaeus,
rocky Stymphalus and well-known Rhipe,
Stratia and Mantinea, Enispe and forested Parrhasia,
where you can find the unwalked patch
where Rhea bore Zeus via Cronus.
They also came from Pheneus,
Orchomenus full of sheep,
where the people love to dance—those joyful Apidaneans.
There were also some from Arcadia,
the realm of Callisto and Zeus' son.
Arcas' father poked him in the stars and called him by Boōtes.
He rained down hail with their lances,
pointing hounds who howled up to their city's namesake
in the night and, in the day, bit men.
Winged Aristaeus led them, son of Cyrene and Phoebus,
who stole her away from Pelion to Libya, to mate.
Apollo left his laurel tree,
bent down from the firmament,
and with his two immortal hands,
lashed the young man's quiver.

Sicily sent men along: Achates and his company:
a throng of shield-backed island scruffs
from Cillyrii, Elymi, and the ring around the Palici
those of Lake Catana's nearby city, near the Sirens,
whom the muse named Terpsichore
floated down by Acheloös' surges.
Those who held Camarina,
where the untamed river Hipparis
unleashes its bellowing torrent.
They came from holy Hybla's citadel,
on Aetna's outskirts,
where Typhon's bed melts rock
and boils fire to the surface.
Thick-browed Peloro's dotted houses

and Cape Pachynus sent men
to join with Syracuse, where Alpheus landed, garlanded,
and damn proud of it, bringing fire unextinguished,
drawing water unmixed with the sea.
Finally, Faunus left that salt rock,
caped and three black peaked like he, who,
brushing sulphur through receding hair
was born to witch-nymph Circe
in the arms of Cronion Bathypelagic,
who lived among the rocky trenches
of her shadowed home.

The Libyans came eastward,
out of cloudy cities Cadmus wandered,
blown about on conflicted winds
with a girl he never touched.
His love's sweet name, Harmonia,
whose mention echoed earthly beauty,
became a dumb war's scapenanny
if only by boys' gossip.
Libyan soldiers called her Charis,
though she grew to be more exquisite,
so in a way the Graces' mound
took its name from her.
Then the Maurusians from the desert
all went wild, so they said,
lusting after Charis' looks and
channeling it toward thiefdom.
But Cadmus stood up, palmed Athena's spear,
and, with Zeus, sent them packing,
calling on Cytherea and Ares, for his wife.
She stood behind his shield at Lake Tritonian
and flush with lust,
rode him to a song by Hesperides,
under apples. They ran the fruit leaves
through each other's hair;
the lake's lips lapped the air;

you should have seen her see him see her—
Aphrodite's lever.
Her granddad Atlas startled upward
to a harp-stringed wedding song
and kicked the spinning firmament
with arched foot, singing "Harmony."
Cadmus raised a hundred towns
in memory of that first night,
each with walls enclosing towers
stood up firm, in stone. With these thoughts,
and with his song, came men who lived
within the clay he hardened back in Libya,
to join Enyo's front lines:
those who lived where the Moon was born,
and near the horned god Zeus Ammon—
his prophesies take the form of rams
with three voluted horns.
They also came from the dusty plains
near Chremetes' river, Cinyps' water,
Auschisae and Bacales, those warring, western climes.

Crataegonus brought thousands from
his hundred cities—that lost son of Achiroë,
daughter of Chremetes and dumb Psyllus,
brought to be beside his river.
Notus burnt his dad's crop to a crisp,
so Psyllus drummed up one slick fleet,
staffed the boats with metalheads,
and savored upwinds of sweet vengeance.
But on the way to Aeolus,
those upwinds turned to ruin.
They thrashed his ships in southern blasts
from bow to stern, then broke the masts,
casting off his shipmates
before handing the depths him.

Then from Samothrace came
the shieldmen of bearded prince Emathion,
whose leaden knee and snowy hair
prevented his own coming.
Their arms and legs were Titan-esque,
they held the island Myrmex,
the flowered peak of Saoce,
the acreage of Teumerius,
and Phesiades' glades and clearings.
These latter places' rocks were ringed
with Corybants worshipping
Perseïs, who lived in holy Zerynthus
and stayed beneath the shade.
Still others came from the dappled wall
of the land surrounding Brontion
and a place I've only heard of, near the sea,
called Atrapiti. They came together, loyal to
their brother Bacchus and the clan,
for home was where Zeus, Cytherea, and Ares
granted Cadmus, divine ally, the love of her
who, from the sea and sky, without a price,
made him one of them, in tune,
Harmony, her name.

As the heroes swarmed in front
of Bacchus' long and pointed thyrsus,
Electra's star rose with her sisters' voices,
calling *Victory* for her brother,
sending waves of twinkling bravery
down the spines of all the men
who stood to lose their lives for him
and for their fathers' glory.
Ogyrus, B-list war god, started marching first—
head high, back straight—
his long hair fell to taught, round cheeks.
Beneath, his shoulder blades edged in like razors.
Throat like stone, a tower to the heavens

(that's how close he thought he'd gotten),
he swore a song in cyclic rumination
to his ego, singing *genocide, genocide,*
death to all India, if by my spear
alone an oath—no chance of their escape.

Ares' boy Oeagrus left Pimplea and the plains around it,
cutting through to join the men who served his father's theme.
He left his baby Orpheus on Calliope's stirring knees
suckling milk up from her stream, barely of this world.
Litrus proudly marched the Cyprians
alongside thin-haired Lapethus: their weapons flowed
from slat-lashed Spheceia, the circle rock,
and Cyprus, welcome to the gods,
where Uranus spilt his cum
and raised the Paphian from its foam,
and to that barbed island swam a creature
more intelligent than most.
Nereus carved the island's borders
in the outline of the dolphin who
played horse to Aphrodite,
who sung sweetly, on its back.
Hylates sent men too, alongside those of Sestus,
Tamasus and Tembrus, Erythrae,
woody-mountained Panacrus, and Soloi.
Lapethus, the town named later
for the one who led them into war
and fell in it, leaving only his name
for its citizens to bear.
Craggy Cinyrus' namesake came too;
those from star-flecked Urania,
whose men were brilliant, like the heavens;
Crapaseia surrounded by the ocean;
Paphos, with its harbor,
where the dolphin finally let Love off,
near the river Setrachus, where Cypris bathed Adonis,
and then wrapped him in the softest cloak.

Finally, the ancient town that Teucer,
from Salamis, named Salamis.
We flee our fathers, just to build a home.

Then came forth the Lydians,
streaming in, in elegance—
from pebbled Cimpsus and Itone;
wide-plained Torebius,
farm-rich Sardis, old as morning light,
and from the land of Bacchus
where he mixed the wine for Rhea's cup
and named the city Cerassae—
high-peaked Oanus, the stream of Hermus,
muddy water sparkling in Metallon,
and scorched Statali,
where Typhoeus burnt his neighbors and the mountains
till the priest burned incense,
sharpened holy words like arrows,
leaving Zeus' temple wrapped in smoke,
but still unarmed.
His words an iron shackle,
bolts of lightning crackling, tongue of spears,
he bent a trembling Typhon to his will
with one "Stand up."
And thus the giant Earthson shook,
not at Zeus, but at the priest
whose bolted words unfurled from his tongue
in magic trains. Typhon stumbled,
pierced by phrasis,
burnt and run-through with the spear of flames,
but knowing now the searing lick
of a well-honed mind.
His twisting feet held firm to Earth,
braced against concrete force,
but maimed by points
that, bloodless, leave no mark and no sign.

But these are all ancient men,
in an ancient time, that is lost to time.
Armed by Stabnius and Stamnus,
this new generation, dancing
here and now, toward the Indian war—
so much so you'd think their captain'd rather dance
than fight—this new generation
found their lock-step's thunder under
a Mygdonian lyre's melody,
which mimicked combat's clamor,
with the trumpets' bells,
and the Berecynthian flutes,
whistling thin through two fat pipes
beside the calfskins sounding, two-palm struck.

The Phrygians fanned out beside
the ruckus of the these Lydians:
those with plots in Boudeia
and tree-thick Temeneia, famous land
of country shadows. They also came
from Dresia and Obrimus (whose waters join
Maeandrus'), Doias' earth,
the shimmering roofs of Celaenae,
where a Gorgon's image slithered,
à la Perseus, beheader.
The cities on the Sangarius, too, sent boys
alongside the Elespids, who were
led by a Dircean captain
from Aonia's darkest corners
named Priasus.
He fled when Zeus soaked Phrygia
to treetop level, swimming out
from flooded house above the hedgerows
swaying on the hilltops.
He swam and swam, then walked, then sailed,
looking back across the sea.
Now Priasus' memories appeared to bluely waver.

He missed his favorite brook,
so Zeus upon the heavens
stopped the flooding rains
and drained them down from Sipylus
as Poseidon swept the water
out to the sea.
The cliffs drained off above the surf,
and, with regret, and joy,
and thanks to Zeus
who saved his pious neck,
he doubled back to hold his father.

Grey old man Asterius
had marched beside another group,
but young Miletus blooming mannish
lined up under Bacchus next to a boy.
That Caunus led the Carians—
long before his lust for his sister
made him sing a song about Hera.
Don't you know the tune?
The one in which Zeus lay supine
beneath her, squirming brightly.
The one with Latmian shepherds, never sleeping;
Endymion, the groom of Selene.
For now, his sister Byblis tweened
and loved her independence.
Her body flesh and not yet water,
Caunus was still unfled, undefiled.
He proudly marched the warriors
of Mycale 'round Maeandrus
which flows below after wandering above,
like everyone, like us.

To number this swarm would take forever.
They came. They marched as one.
And the halls of Cybele and the streets of Amphaxitis
shook beneath their sum.

Book 14

Michael B. Lippman

Pay attention to the events within Book 14:
Rhea will arm the entire divine host against Indian Ares.

Swift-sandaled Rhea, beside their mountain manger
Bound round about each lion's flowing mane.
Once bridled, she lifted them up along the windy way.
Flanks buffeted by breezes, Rhea beat time with her sandal,
Assembling the divine ranks for Dionysus, the Loosener.
Light as a feather or thought, she crossed the seat of heaven
Southward, northward, toward Sunset and Dawn's bed.
To both rivers and oaks she spread her sole message,
Summoning forest ranks, nymphs from water and tree.
The divine offspring obeyed Cybele's child's call.
They gathered from all over. Then to the Lydian land,
On unerring flightpath, airborne Rhea touched down.
Once back, at nighttime she lifted the mystical torch,
Warming the upper atmosphere for fiery Mygdon.

Now that we've covered heroic allies of the mortals,
Inspire me, O Muses, about the army of the gods.

First, from fire-jagged craggy Lemnos, beside the mystical torch
The rising report from Samothrace rallied Hephaestus' two sons,
The Cabiri, whose native name came from their mother, Cabiro.

She bore them both before to the heavenly blacksmith.
Alcon and Eurymedon, divine helpers of the hearth.

From Crete gathered together the Idaean Fist.
Fierce fighters all, citizens of the craggy spring,
The full troop of Earthborn Corybantes, whose race
Once upon a time burst forth from the earth for Rhea.
With shield-bearing beats, they had swaddled baby Zeus,
A newly born babe, besides the birthing boulder.
They danced and clanged and crashed, an all-deceptive bash.
They Bacched and rolled but still controlled. By beaten bronze
Their thunderous sound drowned out and overshadowed
The puerile cries of Cronus' son from Cronus' ears.
Yelling and shouting they sure pulled a fast one.
Leaping Pyrrichus and shield-bearing Idaeus led as
Captains of the whirling Corybants. Along with them
Cnossian Corybas, named for the city, armed the clever clan.

From the sunken sea-depths also gathered together
A troop of envious Telchines, eyes toward the Indian War.
Brandishing in his massive grip a gargantuan spear
Came Lycus the Wolf. Scelmis followed the Conquerer
Damnamenes, guiding his father Poseidon's sea chariot.
Beyond Tlepolemus' land came these manic marines,
Seafaring nomad gods, exiles against their will.
Once upon a time from their paternal land,
Three Sun's sons had driven the Telchines away.
Sons named Thrinax the Trident, Macares the Blessed,
And shining Auges the Sunbeam. Thus the Telechines, chased
From their cradle, with deeply jealous hands, drew Stygian water
Using it to make the gardens of fruitful Rhodes barren.
So the Telchines irrigated fields with the waters of Hell.

Next came the double formed Centaur tribe: the gentle ones.
Chiron attended Pholus, whose appearance was more horse-like.
Chiron was different: untamed and unbridled, but bearded.

Phalanxes of Cyclopes flooded forth, battle-lust upon them.
In unarmored arms they held headlands for hurling,
Stony spears, with their shields from cliff faces.
A look-out point helmet, ridged and fjordified, sat atop
Their forehead's peak. Sicilian sparks acted as fiery arrows.
Eye on the prize, they kindled fires and stoked hearths.
With firebrands in hands, the fighters armed themselves.
Brontes and Steropes, Euryalus and Elatreus,
Arges, Trachius, and arrogant Halimedes.
Only one was left behind from battle—but such a one!
Polyphemus the cloud-close, the Earthshaker's son!
Eros of the watery ways had kept him back at home.
A different Eros, more seductive than war. Once he'd laid eye
On Galatea, spied in murky depths, he howled to the nearby sea
A virginal ballad with pan-pipe accompaniment, aching for a bride.

Speaking of pan-pipes—there also was a pandemic of Pans
Peak-dwellers and neighbors, from their wilding father.
Every one of them was named Pan. So came the Pan panoply.
Shaggy-haired goat's form blended with human shape,
Quite horny bastards, mutts to the last one.
The Pans numbered twelve, led on by their horns,
Born from a single Pan, their primal peak-dwelling pater.
They dubbed one Grimy Pan, as his appearance would testify.
Another one was Shiny Pan, named because he was so clean.
Goatboy Pan's name suited him, since habitually in goat flocks
His passions drove him to keep massaging out their breast milk.
Another one was called Pansy Pan, for him a portentous name
With his abundant beard's overgrowth and such luxuriant locks.
Savage Pan was armed alongside his sidekick Brutish Pan.
While Fearsome Pan strode near shaggy-shanked Sheepish Pan.
Ol' Grey Pan accompanied Blondie Pan; the body of the former
Colored as the grey sea; his fur was salt and pepper,
His eye piss and vinegar. But Blondie was blond,
A horny fellow nicknamed in his panoramic land.
Bold Lazy Pan with snow-white hair slowly brought up the rear.
There were two other Pans too, whom Hermes begat,

After he mingled in "special" friendship with twin nymphs.
The one Hermes begat after he inclined toward the bed
Of god-filled Sosê the mountain nymph. Her child came via divine voice:
Hunter Pan, always wrapped up in the beast-butchering thrill of the hunt.
The other Pan, Pastor Pan, sure loved his sheep pastures.
Born when Hermes crossed the field nymph Penelope's bed,
Where Hermes had skillfully plied his shepherd pan-pipe.
Grazer Pan, savage and insatiable, came as part of the Pan Parade.

Twin-formed old man Silenus grasped his thyrsus-stalk staff
Helmet erect on his horny head, Mother Nature's son.
He led forth his three kids: a whooping war-party.
Astraeus was armed, Maron marched, Leneus loped along.
This club gladly uplifted the arms of their mountain-man papa
Supporting his aged burden. Even the sluggish carcass
Of a strength-depleted elder is invigorated by Bacchic infusions.
Even for the very, very aged, who were once the busy
Progenitors of the entire lusty race of salacious satyrs.
The leaders organized these horny satyrs for battle:
Shepherd of the satyrs, Party-Meister, Hyperhorny,
And Hillbilly, while Redneck aroused horny Glenn.
Gemon came fully armed, as did Wolf in satyr's clothing. Phereus followed
Dogging the heels of his rocking, rustic inebriated joke of a father.
Mountain-man Lamis marched alongside Wooly-Bully,
Scirtus meanwhile bounded alongside Oestrus buzzing round.
Lycus howling for war accompanied peaceful Pherespondus.
Then came Pronomus, whose special quality jutted forth.
These last three Hermes fathered after he snagged in clandestine marriage
A fine woman, Dorus' daughter. Thus they were all offspring of Zeus' family
And primal seed of the Greek clan. For from this one forefather, Dorus
Had sprouted the Achaean family tree of the Dorian people.
Dionysus the Wrangler entrusted to them a gift and staff
Of the heavenly herald, their creative procreator.
The entire satyr party courageously stood by
Perpetually plastered, always equipped, cups at the ready.
They boasted that from battle's din they alone always survived.
With the fight far away, they were lions; when at hand, rabbits.

Peerless dancers, always standing far beyond the rest,
Whenever it came to drawing fine wine from the krater.
Still, a few were born warlike by nature, and bold Ares
Taught them of the manifold sorrow of battle
Plus how to command a phalanx. When Dionysus the Loosener
Called them to arms, some covered themselves with
Untanned oxhides, while others were fortified with hairy lionskins
Still others wrapped around them fierce veils of leopardskin
While others strapped on breastplates of well-woven grapeskin.
Some girded onto their chests an intricately woven chiton,
Decorated with stars balanced by long-horned deer.
Around their own foreheads, upon their temples
Two well-sharpened horns extended out from the crown.
On every pointy-head a bald patch sprouted
At the tip near their googly eyes, while both ears
Flapped about upright, tousled and tossed by the wind
Snapping about like sails round their wooly chins
So the satyrs advanced with equine galloping. Erect,
Behind their backs, curved from their waists, flowed . . . their tails.

Next of the multiformed came the second shaggy Centaur clan
The fierce horny Pherans, the ones whom Hera gave
An external shape of horn-bearing men. Before, with human form
They were children of the water-born naiads,
The naiads called the Hyades, Lamus' riverside family.
These not-yet-centaurs had once nursed Zeus' fertile offspring,
Bacchus, still gasping, untimely ripped from his thigh C-section.
So they were the healing nursemaids for Dionysus still unseen.
Not yet having their later weird form. So in the shadowy hall,
The men often cradled the lad in their arms, as he howled:
"Papa! Papa!" to the heavens, wherein lay Zeus' home,
His son's paternal seat. Though still a child, he was a wise lad.
No way would he have been the same as another newborn kid.
He lived a stable life in hiding there. As his locks grew long,
His body changed. Awkward bleatings poured from his tricksy teeth,
As he enacted a faked hoofbeat with goaty footsteps.
Or by wearing deceptive dress, Dionysus played the woman's part.

With his clothes and yellow veil, he pretended to be a young girl—
A sexy one. Thus jealous Hera's mind was sent awanderin'.
Through mimicking lips he managed womanly sounds
And had tightly bound round his locks a fragrant veil
While wearing an elaborately decorative dress.
Across his chest he bound the straight curve of his breast
He put on a training bra and other such girly stuff.
Finally, he tied on his waist a purple circle girdle.
The trick came to naught when Hera up on high caught on.
Her all-seeing eye, rolling about, saw through it all.
She spied with her little eye the shape-shifting shape
Of Dionysus the Loosener and grew angry with his guards.
From Thessalian Sorrow she took deceptive flowers
Pouring sleep upon the bewitched guards' heads
After Hera trickled over them the drugged cask's contents.
She daubed the enchanted delicate ointment upon
The tip of each man's face, transforming their former form.
Long ears appeared on their newly-made figures,
A horsey tail gushed straight forth from their loins,
Lashing their shaggy-chested packhorse hips,
A horned oxhide blasted from their temples.
Their eyes grew wide on their longhorned faces.
Tangled locks sprouted forth from their heads.
Snaggle-toothed jaws protruded from their chins.
Naturally chestnut hair grew from their loins to their toes
Abundantly flowing from their now wooly necks.
Now, their leaders arranged the twelve in battle formation.
Spargeus, Dancer Gleneus and odd-shaped Ceteus too,
The sprinting viniculturist who came with Eurybius
Petraeus accompanied Riphonus, with Boozer Aesacus
Beside Orthaon, lined up together. Next to them
Amphithemis and Faunus galloped in time as one.
Finally, accompanying well-horned Phanes, went Nomion.

Then came yet another multiformed centaur clan, from Cyprus.
Where Cypris used to blow through like gentle breezes
As she dodged the tracks of her desirous father, lest

She lay eyes upon her parent trying for a forbidden bedfellow.
Father Zeus, however, withdrew from his attempts,
Allowing Aphodite, soft and swift, to stay unattained and untouched.
Spurned Zeus then spilled seed on the ground instead of Cypris' bed,
Pouring forth from his childmaking tool a sexy storm.
Mother Earth then received her grandson's bridal shower.
And that's how this oddly formed horny clan popped out.

Alongside these troops, the Bacchae ran together in a mass,
Dashing ahead. Some hailed from rugged Maeonia,
Others from the hillside beyond the steep peaks of Sypylus.
The Oreads: tunic-trailing mountain nymphs of manly spirit,
Berserkers with well-thyrsused warriors, they charged ahead.
In the whirling racecourse of time, as the years kept on turning
These women would live and live almost eternally.
Some dwelt near the cliffs, guardians of the sheep pastures.
Others left their wooded groves and wild forest ridge.
They were the Meliae, ash-tree nymphs, same age as trees,
All in one group then drove on towards the brawl.
Some beat bronze drums, Cybelian Rhea's instrument.
Others tossed thick locks, leafy with winding ivy.
Yet others wore snaky crowns of flowering wreaths.
Every hand brandished a sharpened thyrsus.
Next came the Lydian maenads, rushing fearlessly
On towards the Indian brawl. Then the Bassarid party
Mighter in warcraft advanced. All Dionysus' nurses gathered
Together: radiant Callichorê, Eupetalê, and Ionê,
Calycê and laughing Bryusa, partners of the Seasons,
Plus Silenê and Rhodê and Ocynoë and Ereutho,
Acretê and Methê and the partners of Harpê,
Rosy Oenanthê and silver-footed Lycastê, Stesichorê
And Prothoë all followed along. Last one to rally was
Old merry Trygië, with her belly full of wine.

Each one led their own separate army for Bacchus.
But fire-breathing Dionysus was the first in command.
Brilliant, flashing, and fabulous. He danced into battle

Holding no shield, no furious spear, no sword on shoulder.
He wore no dogskin helmet on his flowing locks,
Nor bronze covering on his unhurt head. Instead,
He bound his hair up in a dragon-hide covering,
Such a manly wreath encircled his head. And instead of
An elaborate fabricated greave, to the top of his thigh
He wore silvery woven reeds above purple booties,
Slinging a fuzzy fawnskin all round his chest.
His breastplate was speckled and emblazoned with stars.
A golden belt encircled around his sides.
He held a horn of sweet wine plugged with a cork,
Made of pure gold, well wrought. When the craving came
Wine would flow out the horn in a lovely stream for him.
Light in his right hand he bore a thyrsus as a goad
Circled with wine-dark ivy. On the tippiest top
It was covered with bronze strips, pointed and sharp!

At that moment, Dionysus was within the Corybantian courtyard,
Then he entered the well-built golden abode of warlike Enyo,
Abandoning the gentle garden of Rhea, who delights in the dance.
So he departed Maeonia. Along with the mountain-haunting Bacchae,
The troops double-timed forward for their divine lord of wine.
Some were the steersmen for the swift speeding transport,
They grafted animal-men, wine, and supplies upon Bacchus' ship.
Though many of the mixed-breeds marched on foot in rows.
On their own backs they bore amphoras of more divine wine.
On the long-suffering backs of their sluggish mules they packed
Purple carpets and speckled fawnskins. The party went prepared!
Others, proud sommeliers, brandished their golden cups
And bore forth silver mixing bowls, weaponry for the table.
The Corybants buzzed around near fearsome picnic baskets
Having wrapped their necks with massive leopards' cloaks.
They trusted their lions with ivy-wrapped halters—no bites!
'Cause they bound their mouths tight with restraining bits.
One of the centaurs, who came with a shaggy, bristly beard,
Voluntarily and unbidden stretched his neck under the yoke.

Meanwhile the majority of satyrs were craving sweet wine.
One horny half-man sent Dionysus upward and then whinnied
To his horse, telling him to drive the god with his shoulders.

Well-born Dionysus leaned upon the chariot's railing
Along the Sangarius stream, round the Phrygian gulf
'Til he arrived at the suffering rock that once was stony Niobe
The weeping stone, having detected the Indian troops, filled
With strife for the Loosener, cried out again with mortal voice:

"Do not attempt to fight against divinity, you stupid Indians!
Don't oppose Zeus' child! Or else Bacchus will put an end to
Stone-hearted ones threatening War, as well as he will you!
Just like Apollo, he might strike a blow on those wailers,
Equal to my stony form! And do not even gaze
Upon the flowing river named from Indian Orontes,
The crashing, smashing, splashing son-in-law of Deriades.
Rhea, when wroth, has more power than archer Artemis.
You must avoid Bacchus, the brother of Apollo! I feel pity
For foreign tears pouring down over the Indian dead."

Silence shut down the stone again after she cried out such things.
The wine god strode around the coastline of the Phrygian cliffs
In Ascania, where all the citizens thronged him in a mass,
All those whom Io-Bacchus had gifted with his sweet fruit.
They were accepting of his rites and embraced his choruses,
Reaching out for blessings from unconquerable Dionysus
Wishing for the calm that comes with bloodless peace.
Such was the horny Bacching army, with whom the Bacchae
Had armed so as to be battle ready. Meanwhile heaven
Dispatched all through the night divine signs for the
Loosener wide awake: firerunning, streaming, shooting stars.
Along with rumbling thunder. After, the fiery evidence was
Read by Rhea, who foretold the end: an Indian-slaying victory.

Come daybreak, the god strode towards the battle.
Driving against the dark-skinned people's hubris,

All to throw off the yoke from the Lydian slavish neck,
And loosen Phrygian native and Ascanian citizen from
Wicked bondage. So then he sent two heralds of battle,
To announce his ultimatum. They must flee or fight.
As they set off, he assigned to them a goat-feeding Pan
Who bore over his entire chest a shadowy, mighty beard.

Swift-sandaled Hera, as she spotted the outline of Indian
Curly-haired Melane, ordered Astraëis, the spear shaking
Leader of men, not to just capture the wine-dark thyrsus.
Nor should the bleating of booze-loving satyrs be spared.
Rather, they should wage implacable war against Dionysus.
So she spoke persuasively to the Indian leader thus:

"A man cowering before a weak feminine line-up is indeed a sweetie.
Get to battle, Astraëis! And you too, Celaneus, strap it on!
Grab hold of your bronze weapon for ivy-crowned Dionysus.
Don't make a thyrsus out to be some spear. But, Celaneus,
You remain focused on furious Deriades, who might actually kill you
Because you keep dodging an unarmed, worthless woman."

So speaking she won them over. The goddess then rose to the sky,
A wicked stepmother plotting evil for Dionysus the battle-ready.

Then the heralds of Bromius departed. Nearby appeared
Astraëis, armed and arrogant, threatening cruelty to come.
He grew enraged at the ox-horned satyrs and pursued the Pans
Throroughly dishonoring the heralds of gentle Dionysus.
They returned back, fleeing on fearful feet and hooves,
Whipping around fugitive footprints to rabble-rousing Dionysus.

Bacchus armed his host against the ranks of Indian opposition.
He did not forget Enyo, the gloomy dark lady of war.
Swift Astraëis, on the other side, boldly jumped
To arm the entire Indian host. He whipped them up into
A warlike frenzy as he stood beside the churning current
Of Lake Astacis, braced for the assault of wine god Dionysus.

At the same time in each opposing side of the double armies
The respective leaders marshalled each rank on both sides.
With a screech, the dark-skinned Indians marched to battle,
Just as Thracian cranes do during that time they flee
Winter's lash and the flood of rainstorms from on high.
Squadrons of cranes dive-bomb the heads of the Pygmies
Around the channels of Tethys. With their pointed beaks
They prey upon the powerless blood of the worthless clan.
Pressing hard *en masse* like storm clouds beyond Ocean's crest.
On the other side the soldiers were Bacched up for a war-cry,
Steadfast wartime attendants for brawl-stirring Dionysus.
The phalanxes of the Bassarids were streaming forward
One wilding wrapped her head with a snaky chain,
Another had crowned her hair with fragrant ivy.
Yet another was armed with a bronze-tipped thyrsus.
Her sting would drive one mad. Another around her neck
Let the curls of her long hair fly loosely and unfettered.
One maenad went bare-headed, and around both her shoulders
Her unplaited braids blew about wildly in the wind.
Another brandished a tambourine with bronze castanets
Tossing her curling locks whirling round her head.
Another, ecstatic from her leap of madness, strapped on
Cymbals that crashed the shrill echo of battles in her hands
As she rattled round the deep resounding oxhide sounds.
Thyrsuses were spears. Covered over with carvings
Like shafts from a vineyard each had a bronze tipped point.
Another was eager for the laurel-winning battle to begin.
She draped around her neck chains of flesh-eating snakes.
Still another wore upon her breast a dappled cloak made
From leopard skin. Another to protect her flesh wore
Merely a tunic of spotted hides of hillside-loving fawns.
And she bound round her head a sheer veil made of deer.
Yet another carried a lion cub. Its furry lioness mother
Entrusted her own cub to nurse at a human breast.
One wore a serpentine belt, thrice coiled insidiously upon
Her welcoming waist, its jaw open by the side of her thigh.
To her it hissed quite gently and kept a sleepless vigilance
Over the dreamlike, wine-loving maiden's maidenhood.

Yet another went barefoot, her arches sandal-less.
She strode over brambles and sharp-quilled thorns
With unfeeling feet and her footsteps trod upon prickly pears
Another one darted forward on a long-legged camel.
She had braided its curved neck with a thyrsus sickle
And headlong with blind feet she flew down the path
Carried, half visible through the galloping gait.
The frenzied camel's bulky trunk carried her along
Its hooves beating the sunken ground along the slippery ridge.
As it bounded about its belly was scraped down in the dust.
Still another cowgirl tracked her way into the forest hillside
Clutching in her hands the invincible hide of a frenzied bull
She had sawed through its neck with her taloned nails
And ripped the bull's invulnerable skin off for her veil.
Yet another was entirely covered with entrails. So much so that
One could only recognize her as a bare headed, barefooted girl
From higher up, as she leapt about the rocky cliff's edge.
She didn't shudder at the sheer inaccessible heights.
The jagged hillside's claws didn't pierce her bare feet.

Here and there, beside the mouth of Astacis harbor
Many Indian tribes trembled before the Curetian sword.
The warriors circled the enemy phalanxes, battle-ready,
With their clashing armor. The rhythm of the shield-bearers'
Chorus matched the spiraling pounding of their feet.
With his shaggy palm Leneus lifted his crested helmet
Cut from the mountain peaks and strapped it atop his head,
Hurling his barbed spearpoint amidst the enemy ranks.
A Bassarid follower of Bacchus howled and hurled
A vine-twined javelin's point. Among the dark-skinned clan
The feminine thyrsus rammed through many men's heads.
One brave man was chopped in two by the bloody point
Of Eupetalê's weapon. For she sent her ivy thresher
With its grapeloving edge, driving through the enemy sword.
Stesichorê grape-rich sprung into the battle, slaying her way
Hunting the enemy with her rank-breaking instrument
Whirling doubled-up bronze cymbals that crashed like thunder.

The battle clash was colossal on both sides. The pan-pipe wailed,
The battle-stirring pan-pipe, that is. Enyo's aulos rung out while
The Bassarids howled aloud. Once battle commenced
A darkened haze rumbled with crashing thunderclaps
From Zeus, prophesying a thundering victory for Dionysus.
Swarms of attackers fell upon each other. All land turned
Red from gore, as if thirstily guzzling water. Astracis' mouth,
Bloodsoaked, choked as the harbor overflowed with Indian carnage.

In his playful heart, the god felt pity for his enemies.
So he poured down on them, in floods, a gift of drink.
He altered the form of the icy clear stream-water,
So the river gushed sweeping floods of flowing honey.
These flows made people drunk. With streams transformed
The breezes blew fragrant with freshly poured wine
And the riverbanks turned purple. One brave Indian took a drink
His jaw dropped in astonishment and he cried out the following:

"I saw the stranger and his suspicious drink. Not foamy white
Goat's milk was this! Nor was it dark the way water is.
Nor was its appearance like prismatic beehives' nectar
Honey from the pasture dripping in the sweet comb.
No! This captivates the mind as it delights in its delectable smell.
Any man, made thirsty from unrelenting heat and humidity,
Once he cups a miniscule mouthful of water in his palms
Immediately brushes off the whirlwind of fierce thirst.
The water satiates more sweetly than honey. But wow!
What a wonder! Oh, I wish I was drinking it again right now!
This draft is sweeter and men will never want it to end!
Hey girl, grab me a pitcher and bring it on over here
My Trojan cupbearer, attendant of the holiest of vessels!
So that by drawing up a serving of this river honey flows
Ganymede might fill to the brim all of Zeus' wine bowls!
Come on, friends, grab a taste of the honey-dripping river.
Whoa! I realize I can see patterns in the sky! All because it
Flows so freely! They call it Zeus' pick, Olympian nectar.
Now the naiads gush forth from underworld streams!"

Book 15

John L. Gronbeck-Tedesco

In the fifteenth I sing the ruddy muscle-armed killer,
Nicaea, nymph of the naiads, eager
to purge heat from her sex-fevered lover.

While the fierce Indian warrior spoke, his comrades bound
their chariots close to the ceaseless river now flooded
with new amber honey—sweet, then sweeter with each new taste.
One shunted the wine to his mouth with a greedy hand.
Another drank Bacchus' potion
at the river's near bank. One more, with his hands on the sandy
bottom, did pushups, filling
his mouth on the way down and
swallowing on the way up.
Most were content with the traditional cups carved and smoothed
or ladles made of potshards. The generous river
kept on giving while the enemy kept on drinking.

Krunked, libated, pished, schnokered, quadled, poonted, right-rack-ripped,
shellacked, blasted, hammered—drunk:
the whole wine-basted brood saw rock, rill and river in twos,
doubling their pleasure and venom.

One of the mind-numbed posse—made for the herd and hauled
out a bull, which he took for the double-horned god, Bacchus.

Another ripped a dark, iron-spined sickle through the neck
of the sure-footed mountain goat believing it was Pan.

Delusions piled up: someone slaughtered a brood of cattle
thinking them hoof-footed satyrs.
Another hacked through a line of deer, convinced the dark blood
came from a phalanx of Bacchae.

Neither was the spring-greening flora saved from the blood binge
One of the burnt-skinned gang sliced through misty dark foliage,
shredding the shaking branches of entwined leaves mistaken
for the crown of Dionysus; then, he scythed the hoarse blade
through new growth looking for the blood of satyrs in the pulp
of what spring had blessed just now into new, fresh pulsing life.

One in a blood-soaked war squadron went maenad-mad; grabbed up
a drum he thought a war spear;
banged out a deep double beat on the dark skins at both ends.
A comrade dipped and circled
en developpé, prancing to shrieking notes blown off key
on the Mygdonian pipes.
Sotted, another vaulted—*grand jeté*—into a tree
where he sucked bitter olives,
imagining the taste of fine Maroneian wine.
Others, wrapped in armor, brains gone wild on mind-throbbing wine,
orgied themselves still shelled
in bronze, dancing like Corybants, *sissonné* to rhythms
banged on shields by hand or bronze.
With eyes on the muse—priestess of the choral orgies—
someone stumbled *en glissade*,
yawing drunk to dance like the satyrs. Another gentled
by music into a *piqué* turn
added a *relevé*, quiver of arrows strewn in the wind.

A chief of the lust-driven Indians
grabbed the flying hair of a child virgin,
ripped off her belt and pinned her to the ground.

But she unleashed a viper from her breasts
that lunged to his neck, fastened tight to his throat
and sent the warrior gasping as he ran.

Just then, sleep went to work putting droop-browed
Indians out for the night—all of them
made willing by wine and blunderous dance.
One snored mightily on his battered back,
blasting alcoholic gas through nose hair.
Another conked his blotted head against
a rock, then mumbled his drunken visions
stretching his fingers to rub his temples.
Someone else, all wellied up, lay balanced
on a ledge: bare butt down, thighs up and hands
gripping bruised knees. A guy, half-cut ploughed, shoved
his head between his wrists and drooled amber
all over himself. Some slack-assed bibbler
passed out, lay on his side coiled like a snake.

India's finest, now shit faced: each now
blended into the inhospitable woods:

some . . .	others . . .
blotto under an elm,	corpsic in an oak tree,
bent against a laurel,	comatose on elm leaves,
giggling in the tickle-toe river,	throbbing with a migraine,
groaning tuned to the wind,	chattering like chipmunks.

Now, Bacchus seeing his foes senseless, laughed hugely and said.
"Tie up these sons of India, but do them no new harm.
They shall bow enslaved to me to labor for my Rhea
and her friends, who raise and shake the fennel-scented thyrsus,
purple in my honor. Strip the army of silver latched
shin-guards. Replace them with buskins; knock off their feather-topped
helmets and crown them with my own ivy. So much for all
their slaughter-bound war cries and saber rattling. Lift your voices
in Euian song to grapeful Dionysus."

The satyrs got busy.

One . . .
wound a snake around a
prisoner's throat then dragged
him by a venomous
rope made of more vipers.

Another . . .
grabbed his man by the beard
and yanked him to slavery.

Another . . .
took shook his slave by a
curly swag of dark hair.

One . . .
bound an unconscious
enemy wrists-to-neck.

Old Maron—priest of Apollo at Ismarus—lurched low
beneath the load of a dormant Indian. His war-mate
dumped one more into a chariot to sleep with lounging
leopards. A chorus of victors, all raucous and cheery,
shackled fast an enemy to the neck of an elephant.
Many were tied to their shield handles, hands cuffed behind.

A Bassarid sent an enemy into slavery tied
to her shepherd's crook. Iron-man Poseidon, ocean god,
bench-pressed a man cased in bronze armor high and held him there.

A mountain Bacchant pilfered a black elephant
from its drunk owner. Nuptial Hymenaeus
stole a golden shield and lifted it high up,
while Bacchus looked upon him with a smoldering
gaze as the young warrior gleamed in brilliance
the way Diomedes sparkled when he swapped bronze
for the golden armor of Glaucus on Troy's bloody shores.
The Bacchant army continued their sport, bloodless
robbery, while prisoners slept in wine-deep bliss.

There was a Bacchant girl of the desolate wood, a new
ally to the Astacian nymphs, gorgeous Nicaea
chaste follower of Artemis, so a stranger to love
and to Cytherean Aphrodite.

Nicaea ignored the company of scented women,
hunted in the rocks and combed the steep slopes after fresh game.
This new local Artemis strung a bow not a distaff.
Her fingers were not for the loom but for the wide woven
net to capture prey. A mountain-climber, chaste Nicaea,
Athena of the slopes and peaks,
staked the meshes for hunting among the stone-sided hills.
Ignoring easy prey, she lamented the dangerous beasts left
by Artemis who used worthless deer to pull her carriage.

Nicaea trained lions to the bridle with a whip, speared
charging bears, felled dangerous carnivores with her bow,
refused fine perfumes and preferred clear moving water
to alcoholic potions.

Midwife to the cats of prey, she cared for pregnant leopards,
lay near she-lions postpartum that would lick her body
sweetly and purr through genteel lips; he-lions mistook her
for Artemis and bowed down low.

Now, living in those woods there was a drover, straight, tall, muscular and strong—
more so than other young men. And his name was Hymnus. He raised prize-winning
beef near the places where Nicaea hunted. He worked his stock hard
with a staff, but when he saw that nymph, he fell insanely in love and spoke to his cattle

"For that girl, I'd bear the brunt.
Anything she wants is what I want."

Hymnus then
forgot about his job. He let calves and heifers wander far into trouble
or get lost while he searched and found sight through trees of the girl's seductive eyes.
Just then, ever-clever Eros sent a breeze to lift her thin hunting smock
and unveil everything from her ankles and lush thighs to the promise

of her hips—everything. The sight of her naked body drove Hymnus
into a convulsive passion blown fierce by her hair flying high, leaving
her neck bare to his imagination. The young man stalked her where she hunted,
touching her arrows and tracing her recurve with his fingers when she put
them aside, obsessed with the sight of her deft hand and jealous to the bone
of the lance she gripped so forcefully. He should have known better than to love
a vestal, and his soul told him

"she would be hard to bear
with no love to share."

But he was out of his mind. Damn fool wanted her to throw him a life-line.

Out of sight, he watched her while she drew the bowstring, saw it catch on her horn
and move it down and around to bare her breasts.

"I gotta have that woman.
Don't care she's a mystery,
she's gotta walk with me,
because love just spins me, spins me around
until I'm fallin' and looking up from the ground."

Often Hymnus chased her into the moonlit night seeing that her gleaming skin
held more light than the skin of Hera or Selena. He locked on the girl
and studied how she moved: how she drew the arrow against the bear, how she
yoked the lion with her bare arms, how she cleansed herself of sweat in a brook
at the end of a day, almost showing her body under her dress where
the wind would shake and lift it to her navel and show the untouched flower
of her chastity. Hymnus prayed for more wind and rejected
the voice that told him

"Nicaea has you in a cold state of mind.
You're in a place
That's too hard to bear.
I hope I'm wrong,
but life isn't fair,
and I'm sayin' for you, boy, there
might be no song."

He saw Nicaea in full thrall of the chase. Too callow to think first, he called out jealously:
"By the gods, I wish I was an arrow
or a quiver; or a thick, black-oak spear
rubbed ready by oil from your agile palm;
or the shining gut of that recurve bow
that moves low past those delicious breasts!
Girl, I know you know all about the rest.
Your sacred forest has become my shroud.
Now, I wander here like a single cloud.
Cytherea, mercy on my desire!
I can be no threat to your holy plan.
Hell, I don't know the island Thrinacia
I do not tend the sun god's sacred herd.
I am the low-born son of a low-born
father who knew nothing of where Ares
bedded Aphrodite. Aren't they just fables?
Look, your secrets, if they are secrets,
are safe with me, because I am all too
human, so no one would listen."

Then again to Nicaea thus:
"Don't forsake me, O my darlin', because
I am a cattle man. Girl, pound me with
hot studded kisses. Come stir my desire.
Many like me roll and swell on lusty,
noble mattresses.

Take Tithonus, for instance, he was seized
by morning-Eos to heat her chilly body.
Remember Ganymede, Zeus' sommelier.
Once a drop-dead handsome goatherd, he was
kidnapped to adorn the god's dinner parties
and satisfy his friends.

Please—I'm on my knees—help me, join my herd.
Be a new and brighter moon and I your
Endymion. No need for the spear; take
hold of my staff. Please be my destiny.
Let everyone know you are my heart and I
am your bone."

This is what the poor boy said, his knees bleeding from kneeling in passionate frenzy. But he wasn't done. One day, he stole all of Nicaea's gear: spear, bow and arrows too. Mindless now, he took one, kissed it and put the point against his heart. Then spoke these words to himself.

"Come on, grove of Paphian Aphrodite,
sing out for sex. Remember the old days
when the passionate coupling of Pyrrha
and Deucalion made life come back strong
after the flood. Talk sense now to this cruel
celibate. Daphne, speak through your laurel
leaves. If Nicaea had lived long ago,
she would have taught lusty Apollo how
to treat a woman with the respect I
have shown her, and you still would be flush full
of flesh and blood."

When he vented his pain in a wedding tune on his pipes,
she mocked him.

"Your version of Aphrodite's marriage tune
is a joke. It didn't work for Pan when he
tried it on Echo. Same thing happened when

Phoebus Apollo used it on sweet swift Daphne.
The louder he played, the deeper she dashed
into the laurel forest because he,
a fool like you, didn't take no for an answer."

Then, Nicaea got serious; threatened Hymnus with her spear,
but he did not get the message. Out of his mind with love,
and refusing to believe Nicaea had no room for
him in her soul, he dared her,

"Go 'head. Murder me the sooner the better.
A quick death would stop this pain at the core
of my heart. Relief. But please, not the spear
to the neck. Follow Cypris' lead: put an arrow
through my heart, which is already wounded,
in the name of Paphian Aphrodite.
No, wait.

If it's the only way I can
pleasure you, I'll take on the second too;
May earth preserve both wounds: the heart by love,
the throat by a spear.

Better yet, use that recurve. Your hand sexes
the arrows. The string bares your succulent
nipples. Yes, use the whole damned quiver-full.
The fiery arrows of love bleed my heart.
Yours arouse me but soothe me too.

After I'm dead, do me just one favor.
Don't cremate me. Love has inflamed me enough.
Sprinkle dust on my tomb; so people will
say you pitied your victim.

If you don't
mind, please don't let my pipes, flute or crook

lie around on my grave. Post your spear above my
tomb, drenched in my clotted blood.
                                                  One more thing,
I promise this is the last. In tribute
to passion, place daffodils on my tomb
to honor Narcissus; saffron's good
too; so is bind-weed,
and, come spring, plant blue
anemone. It dies young, so all will
know that my years were few,
and if you have
any feelings at all for me, shed some
tears—just enough to moisten your cheeks,
and, put these words on my headstone:

      Here lies Hymnus, the oxherd,
   Killed by Nicaea who wouldn't share his bed.
But she did perform his last rights after he was dead."

Nicaea went mad. She tore open her quiver; drew back
the recurve until both ends bent round and drove an arrow
deep into his throat—while he was talking. Then, more than someone
wept for the shepherd.
                                    The mountain nymph, the one from deep spring
waters, was enraged to tears by Nicaea. Barefoot she
swam, driven by the current of the river Rhyndacus,
lamenting loudly. Naiads mourned too.

Niobe, although turned to stone by the murder
of her children, opened into tears. Abarbarea,
young and devoted to chastity, unleashed her anger
at Nicaea. Far off upon the shores of Didymus,
even the Astacides piled their grief upon her. These
daughters of Helios wept more bitterly than for
the murder of their blundering brother, Phaëthon. Eros,
shocked by heartless Nicaea, threw down his bow and vowed
to drag her before Dionysus.

Rhea Dindymis, borne by lions, mother of Zeus,
keened for Hymnus, and so too did Echo.
All cried from pity.
The oaks in the Paphian grove shouted as one:

"What did that poor, dumb kid do?
How did he offend you?
How severe was his trespass?
Aphrodite, show her no mercy!
And you too, high Artemis!"

All nature sounded this lament:

"Strong and handsome but, alas, too young to be wise,
Hymnus was murdered by the naiad Nicaea."

Adrasteia, mother of cold steel retribution charged
Nicaea with the murder of Hymnus and vented her
bitter sorrow on insolent Eros. Filled with grief, she
repeated the refrain:

"Strong and handsome but, alas, too young to be wise,
Hymnus was murdered by the naiad Nicaea."

His animals—
cows, calves, and bulls—wept for their caretaker with grief that seemed
to speak:

"Our herd master has come to bloody death.
His looks and confidence did him no good,
for a gorgeous girl has murdered him.
Instead of pity for his passionate
love, she smeared her bronze armor with his blood."

She would not heed the bark offered as prayer by the wolf
for this life gone dark, and ignored the howls for mercy by
elm and slim pine. Lion and bear mourned outright.

The four strong winds carried the forlorn melody everywhere,

> "Strong and handsome but, alas, too young to be wise,
> Hymnus was murdered by the naiad Nicaea."

Phoebus and Pan both were deep-struck by grief in the wake
of Nicaea's sin. Cry, Cypris! Groan, Nemesis, and go
avenge the dead boy's youth! Even Artemis, stranger to
love, could not hide her pity for Hymnus, a man whose love
was illicit to one plighted by vows to Astacia's
grove. Pastures, streams and woods have been stripped of their holiness,
right order turned to dust. Blind murder destroys what the gods
have balanced. And again and forever:

> "Strong and handsome but, alas, too young to be wise,
> Hymnus was murdered by the naiad Nicaea."

Book 16

Rachel Hadas

In Book 16, the slumbering Nicaea is my song,
The bride of Dionysus, god who never sleeps for long.

The mournful shepherd's murder was avenged, and in this fashion:
Drawing his bow, bold Eros chose an arrow full of passion,
And aimed at Dionysus as the god sat by a stream,
Little suspecting such a missile could be shot at him.
Nicaea the swift nymph, exhausted, having hunted all
Day long, and sweaty after chasing up hill and down dale,
Was bathing her bare body in a mountain stream. And so
Far-shooting Eros, wasting not a moment, drew his bow.
Barbed, and gleaming at its tip, the arrow he released
Flew to its target, buried in the god's love-maddened breast.
When Dionysus spied the girl rinsing each naked limb,
The fiery sweetness of that arrow wholly maddened him.
Wherever nymph Nicaea ran as she pursued the hare,
The lovelorn god trailed after her, following her here and there.
Gazing at the little curls that trembled in the wind
As she moved past him, staring at the splendor of her skin,
Her shining neck revealed in glimpses when a lock of hair
Was brushed aside and like the moon her glowing flesh was bare.
Satyrs and Bacchants now to him meant nothing any more;
But turning toward Olympus, he let out a lovesick roar:

"Whichever dewy road she hunts on, I will hunt there too,
Wherever her quiver and arrows are, wherever her splendid bow,
I will be there! And on whatever lucky ground are spread
Covers perfumed by innocence to make her virgin bed.
Hunting with her, I'll help with all the tasks she has to do;
And when she shoots her prey, a fawn, then I will shoot one too.
If like an angry Amazon she should find fault with me,
Spewing a load of honeyed threats as is a woman's way,
Then I shall touch the angry virgin's knee, a light caress,
And as a suppliant approach her frowning loveliness.
But I will bring no branch of olive, for the olive tree
Is sacred to Athena, stern in her virginity.
Instead of bitter olive I shall offer to my sweet
A bunch of grapes, wine-dark and honeyed, as my suppliant's fruit.
If the armed virgin is resistant, may she not thrust her spear
Into my flesh or aim one of her deadly arrows there,
But may she rather gently tap my body with her bow,
A soothing touch so sweet to me I'd welcome such a blow.
And even, if she wishes, with her tender hands she may
Undo my braids, pull out my hair—I'll let her have her way.
I won't resist the maiden; rather, I'll pretend to be
Angry, and press the rosy little hand that squeezes me
In my hooked fingers, as a way to soothe the malady
Of love I suffer. I, a god, am now a virgin's prey!
Forgive me, Isle of Cerne, for the birth of a new dawn;
Flawless Nicaea shines in heaven like a younger moon.
In my desire how I'd love to take on many guises;
Only respect for father Zeus discourages disguises.
As a bull I'd love to swim across the Tyrian Sea,
Shielding Nicaea from the waters as she rides on me;
I'd play the part Europa's bridegroom played, and I would shake
My back so my sweet passenger would be alarmed, and take
My horn in her white hand. Or I'd dance, winged, through the air,
With my love perched upon my back and riding safely there,
Like Zeus with Aegina. And a child of ours, combining these
Forms—bird, star, eagle—would attend on love's festivities.
One thing I will not do is wield a thunderbolt to slay

Nicaea's father—such a bride price is too high to pay,
And I don't want to anger her. No, rather let me be
A bird with gorgeous plumage, because I know that she,
My huntress queen, prefers her arrows thickly feathered too.
Or even better if like Danaë's suitor I could flow,
A shower of gold. On my beloved as she slumbered there,
Myself both spouse and wedding gift, and pour my dew on her;
For golden in her loveliness, Nicaea ought to be
Matched with a bedmate of pure gold as beautiful as she."

These were the words the lovestruck Bacchus in his fervor cried.
Then one day, strolling in a fragrant meadow, the god spied
The hues of his beloved in the flowers everywhere,
Whereupon he raised his voice and shouted to the air:

"Nicaea, now I see you! You have lent these flowers your guise,
And given them your beauty. In this rose I recognize
Your rosy cheeks. The rose that blooms in you will never die;
For growing in your garden I see the anemone,
Pink and perennial. Your arms are lilies, snowy white;
Your flowing hair is hyacinthine, dark and rich as night.
Oh, let me hunt beside you! And if you will allow,
I'll be your beast of burden, bearing stakes and boots and bow—
And yes, the arrows of desire I will carry too.
To help you in your hunting would be my greatest joy;
My attendant satyrs mean nothing now to me.
Apollo hunting in the woods hoisted Cyrene's snare;
Why shouldn't I do this for you? What joy if I could bear
You on my shoulders, sweet Nicaea! Not that I compete
With Zeus, whose passenger Europa never wet her feet.
That maiden clinging to his back, my father made his way
Across the waves, at once a bull and creature of the sea.
Why, rosy virgin, do you choose the woodlands when you stray?
Your tender limbs will be exposed to the rough ground that way.
I beg you, let me wait on you when it is time to rest.
I'll strew your bed with leopard skins; and on that dappled nest
The tawny, furry lion skin I like to wear I'll spread.

How sweetly you will slumber, snuggling in this rustic bed!
The velvet pelts of my own fawns I'll lay upon this heap;
Cuddled beneath it you will sleep a Dionysian sleep.
And finally, to top it off, I'll raise a leather tent
Of skins taken from my satyrs' deer. And if your mind is bent
On hunting dogs, I'll offer you my comrade Pan's—he breeds
Hounds. Or else Apollo's pack of dogs may meet your needs,
Or Aristaeus—he has hounds and hunting gear also.
His nets and stakes and boots would be the perfect gift for you,
Since he takes pleasure in green pastures but loves hunting too.

But if you fear the thirsty season with its scorching heat,
Then tender little shoots of vines above your bed I'll set,
So that sweet breezes scented with intoxicating grapes
Will waft above you as you lie beneath these living drapes.
Elusive girl, be careful of your tanned and lovestruck face—
The sun might wither all your beauty with its glaring rays,
The wind might ruffle those sleek curls so tidy on your head—
So come and sleep beside me in a flower-petalled bed.
And having rested, you and I will revel; celebrate
The elemental forces ranged in a divine quartet:
Apollo, Zephyr, Aphrodite, Dionysus—me!
All of us gods, so all possessed of immortality.
And take my Indian captives if you want them by your side
As your attendants. But they are too dark to serve my bride.
Does radiant Dawn mingle with Night in his black veil?
Instead, my youthful huntress, for your sake I will call
Sixty dancing handmaidens to come and join with all
The dancers who surround you, entourage as numerous
As Ocean's daughters or the maidens of the Archeress.
So Artemis, though queen of hunting, cannot rival you.
The Graces of Orchomenus on you I will bestow;
They are my daughters. All I wish is that your hard heart may
Melt with desire. When you are tired from hunting the whole day,
Lie down with me! Be Artemis as long as you're abroad
Among the rocks; but oh, be Aphrodite in our bed.
If I accompany you hunting, how can that be bad?

But if, aspiring Amazon, you itch for something more,
Then come with me to battle! Come to the Indian war,
Where first you'll play the role of Pallas on the battlefield
And then Persuasion when, strife ended, the opponents yield.
To slay a fawn, here, take my thyrsus for the fatal blow,
And with your own hands you may decorate my chariot too.
And yoke together leopards, lions; let them pull the cart
Your hands will first have beautified, oh huntress of my heart."

As he pursued the mountain maiden, that is what he said.
And then he shouted "Wait for Bacchus! Let us go to bed!"

Raising her voice in turn, the virgin, angry, now let loose
Wild words at him: "Go find some other victim to seduce!
If Artemis or Athena can be drawn into your lures
And wed you, then and only then will Nicaea be yours;
I'm bosom friends with both of them. But if you can't persuade
Athena to be your wife (and she's eternally a maid—
No marriage and no children for Athena!) and if you
Fail to charm the archer goddess Artemis also,
Leave me alone! Do not pursue me! Let me never see
You lay a finger on my bow or quiver! Or else I
Will conquer you, will bring you down, as I've already done
With the shepherd Hymnus. You're a god, invulnerable one,
But I will wound you! If you can't be hurt with steel or lance,
Then I will emulate the deed of Iphimedeia's sons
And tie you up with iron chains exactly as they did
To Ares, or in a brass vessel I will keep you hid
And guard you in that prison till twelve moons will have gone by
And till your passion for me will have finally blown away.
And keep your woman-groping fingers off my quiver! Know
You wield the thyrsus, but I am the mistress of my bow.
I hunt along with Artemis, the wild crags are my place,
I aim my shafts at boars and lions. So go away and chase
Fawns with Aphrodite. Your bed I will refuse,
Even if you share the bloodline of your father Zeus.
If I did wed a god, he'd never be a god like you—

Soft-haired, unarmed, emotional, and altogether too
Womanish. No, the archer god or war god bold as brass—
One of them might share my bed and be my glorious spouse.
One might charm me with his bow, the other's sword would woo
Me—but to wed a god is something I would never do.
To be in Zeus' family has no appeal for me;
So, Bacchus, find some other girl more likely to agree
To be your bride. Why hurry? For in this race victory
Will not be yours. Apollo pursued Daphne; even he
Failed to catch her; Hephaestus failed to catch Athena. Do
Not run a race you're bound to lose. Why rush? And look: your shoe
Is wrong among these rocks. I'm wearing boots—you can't catch me!"

And having said this, she sped off and left him there. But he
Ran after her up hills, down valleys, and before him ran
The wise and faithful hunting dog given him once by Pan—
Pan the horned god, the dog-breeder, when Bacchus used to roam
And hunt among the cliffs he loved. The god now spoke to him,
His canine friend who followed him and knew his every mood,
With loving words, as if he thought the creature understood:

"Oh wandering dog, why do you run so faithfully with me
When Pan, whom you are worthy of, desires your company?
I try to track the maiden down and you track her with me,
As if you had been trained to pity love's anxiety.
Go seek the girl, and let me climb these hills, disconsolate
And solitary; only you have pity on my state,
And, more a person than a dog, you track her footsteps through
Hills and valleys; where she wanders, there you wander too.
Work for your master! And your toil I promise to repay:
Like Sirius the Dog Star, I will set you in the sky,
Beside the other dog star. That way, shining down on earth,
You too will nurse the grapes to ripeness and bring them to birth.
Your home will be in heaven; you will be the third dog star,
Coursing through the spangled skies beside the running Hare.
Now turn your eyes from heaven, if it's lawful, toward the hill
Of Cybele. And the modest girl—she's running from me still—

Reproach her this way: Why would a mere mortal want to flee
From an immortal in pursuit of her—a god like me?
Adonis too, and Cytherea, are worthy, both, of blame;
Scold them—and Echo, mountain nymph, who copies every name
As she flits through the hills. Don't let her make my maiden shun
Marriage more than she does already. Oh, and rustic Pan
Keep him away, or he may seize the maiden and subdue her
And force her into coupling with him; he's a brutal wooer.
So if you spot her, come to me, and either make no sound
Or meaningfully bark to let me know that she is found.
You will be love's messenger! Some other dog can sniff
Out boars and lions, tracking them along a rocky cliff.
My dear friend Pan, I call you blessed. And see why this is so:
Your pack of hounds tracks down love and desire as they go.
Oh Fortune, many-formed, and toying with our mortal race,
Mistress of dogs, mistress of men, controlling all our fates,
Be kind to us—and even to this poor wandering hound you see,
Who serves both Pan and also lovestruck Dionysus—me!
Rocks, trees, please tell her even dogs take pity when I moan;
Only she, the Amazon, still has a heart of stone.
For there are dogs as wise and understanding as mankind;
Zeus has denied them human speech, but not a human mind."

It happened that an ancient ash tree, standing there nearby,
Heard the lovesick Dionysus uttering this cry,
And now through her thick foliage she addressed him scornfully:

"Other hunters bring their dogs to serve the Archeress,
But clearly, Dionysus, Aphrodite's your mistress.
How sweet that it's a tender virgin you are frightened of—
The bold god Bacchus now the humble suppliant of love,
Beseeching the defenseless maiden with those hands that slew
The Indians! Charming speeches weren't your father's way to woo
And lead a girl whom he'd persuaded toward the marriage bed.
No suppliant to Semele, he made love to her instead.
And how he caught Ixion's wife—you know the tale, of course,
His winsome whinny, since the divine bridegroom was a horse.

And in the game of love he also fooled Antiope—
The laughing satyr, the false husband, all that trickery."

The dryad, having mocked the god, slipped back into her tree.
But Dionysus ardently pursued the maiden; he
Was passionate from head to toe, his feet were wild with love.
The speedy-sandaled Amazon raced onward, high above,
On mountain paths that hid her footsteps from him as she ran.
But now the girl was thirsty, her lips baked dry by the sun
Fiercely blazing overhead. And being unaware
That lovestruck Dionysus uses liquor as a snare,
And spying the amber waters of the river loved by men
Who drink, she gulped from that sweet stream where Indians had been.
Then Bacchically tipsy, and with her mind askew,
She reveled, tossing back her head, and saw the world as two.
Perceiving an expanse of lake, she thought she saw its twin,
And, dizzy, saw a double hill instead of only one,
Till, stumbling in the dust, she fell; and winged Sleep, beside
Her, overtook the maiden, soon to be a slumbering bride.

Seeing her asleep there, Eros pointed the girl out
To Bacchus (Eros pitied Hymnus). Nemesis at the sight
Laughed. And wily Dionysus, wearing silent shoes,
Tiptoed toward consummation, making not the slightest noise;
Approached the girl and, moving slowly, gently, carefully
Untied the belt whose knot protected her virginity
So deftly that she never woke. Whereupon Mother Earth
Opened up her fragrant lap in a sweet burst like birth
For Dionysus' sake. Grape leaves tangled up together
Around the vine poles that held up the bridal couch's cover,
So that the marriage bed became a trellised arbor whose
Purple clusters hung and swayed in Aphrodite's breeze,
Covering the bridal pair, while drunken ivy clung
And twined around the fruitful vines that over the lovers hung.
Strange ceremony—like a marriage dreamed in someone's sleep;
The maiden lost her maidenhead and never once woke up,
Sleep was Eros' groomsman, as far as she could tell,
Attendant of the ceremonials under wine's sweet spell.

And gently blowing here and there, each echoing little breeze
Wove hymns to love among the branches of the forest trees;
And to the windborne music of the mountain wedding song
Modest Echo made reply and carried it along—
Echo, the voice that follows Pan. Flutes shrilled to dancing feet:

"Hymen! Hymenaeus! Blessings on this marriage rite!"

But then the soul of the slain shepherd, windblown, wandering,
Addressed the sleeping, dreaming girl in words that bore a sting:

"Lovers, oh happy bride, have their avenging furies too;
Rejecting Hymnus, you chose Bacchus as the groom for you.
But in the marriage sweepstakes, girl, your judgment is askew;
You kill the one who loves you, while the one whom you pursue
Will never marry. Hymnus loved you; he sleeps with the dead.
A different sleep, a deep sweet sleep, cost you your maidenhead.
You only laughed when you beheld the dying shepherd's blood;
That laughter turned to groaning at your bleeding maidenhood.

The lovelorn shepherd, weeping, spoke; and hard to catch as air
Or mist or smoke, proceeded to the court of Tartarus (where
So many go) still full of envy for the wine god, whose
Intoxicating trickery had won him a fair spouse.
And Pan, the music master, now piped a wedding tune
On his shrill reed, but hid his secret envy deep within
His heart, as to the ill-matched pair he sang of blame and blight.
A lusty satyr in a grove spied the forbidden sight
With greedy wonder—Dionysus and his bride in bed!—
And was inspired to make a speech, and this is what he said:

"O horned Pan, still solitary, chasing down desire,
It's Echo you pursue—but will you ever marry her?
And could you manage such a trick to gain your marriage bed—
A virgin wedding? Better till the soil instead
Of herding, Pan. Put down your shepherd's crook and leave your flocks
Of sheep, and leave your oxen wandering among the rocks;

Shepherds are useless. Better far for you to plant a vine;
For vines yield grapes, and grapes yield love's enchanting wedding wine."

He's hardly spoken when the goatherd god wailed in reply:

"I wish my father had taught that craft of bridal wine to me!
I wish that I, like Bacchus, could be master of the grape
That dizzies minds, for then I could have lulled Echo to sleep,

The wandering nymph who drives me wild, and had my way with her.
No, goodbye, pasture; goodbye, spring. I water my sheep here
While Dionysus lures reluctant virgins to his stream;
They drink of it and then, intoxicated, marry him.
His plant's an aphrodisiac. Goat's milk, sheep's milk? No more!
You cannot make a virgin marry, nor can you lull desire.
Eros and Aphrodite! I am tortured; woe is me!
Syrinx fled Pan's courtship, left him solitary; she
Now chants "Euoi!" for Dionysus' marriage willingly.
And to the sound of Syrinx as she pipes her wedding tune,
Echo responds as usual with music of her own.
Oh shepherd Dionysus who herd mortals with your spell,
You're blessed! You're happy! You won over the unwilling girl
With wine, love's helper, to assist you in your nuptial."

Such were the words that mournful Pan in his frustration said,
Envious of Dionysus, who'd attained his marriage bed.
And having in that rustic bed satisfied all his lust,
Stealthily the god got up. The girl, now waking, cursed
The river that had drugged her. She was furious at all three—
Sleep, Aphrodite, Bacchus—for even as her tears flowed, she
Could still hear snatches of the wedding song the dryads played,
And see the herald of the god's desire, the marriage bed.
That couch, with vine leaves shaded and with piles of fawnskin strewn,
Betrayed both the god's passion and its consummation.
But when she saw her maiden zone was moist with love's own dew,
She tore her cheeks and struck her thighs and cried,
"Ah, woe is me!

Cursed be the drunken stream that took my maidenhood away!
Lulled by love's sleep, I've lost forever my virginity!
That rascal Bacchus, vagabond, stole my virginity!
Oh nymphs and hamadryads, which of you should be the first—
And love and sleep and guile and wine, all worthy to be cursed—
You all have stolen my maidenhood. And I'm abandoned too
By Artemis, whom I have served faithfully. And Echo—
Why did she never warn me? And why, whispering in my ear
About this plot too low for Dionysus to hear,
Why did not the pine tree and the laurel say 'Beware!
Don't drink that water! For a god has worked his magic there.'"

Those were her words. Her tears ran down, her mind raced to and fro:
Should she thrust a sword into her throat, or should she go
To some high cliff, leap from its summit, fall into the dust?
Should she destroy that fateful stream, that river full of lust?
But no; the waters had already cleansed themselves, and ran
Pure and clear, no longer vinous, Dionysian.
Next she implored Artemis and the Cronides to fill
The nymphs' cave up with dirt and dust, to choke them with dry soil.
Often she strained her eyes toward the mountains; might she see
The tracks of Dionysus staggering unsteadily
And unsuspecting? Might she then manage to draw her bow—
A mortal woman shoot the god who makes the grapevines grew?
And even stronger was her wish to burn, destroy, uproot
The vines that twined on the bridal bed. Or when she had a sight
Of Bacchus; footprints on the hills, she shot into the air
A storm of arrows; raised her spear and hurled it here and there,
Hoping to strike the body of the god. But all in vain—
She threw and threw but missed the mark; she never wounded him.
Angrily she reproached the river; she would never taste
Its wily waters ever again, no matter how great her thirst!
She swore henceforth to keep her eyes wide open all night long
And never let sweet sleep approach the hills she roamed among.
The dogs that should have kept close watch but that had failed to guard
The girl, she blamed for failing to fend off the lustful god.
She looped a noose around her neck and tried to stop her breath,

Hoping to avoid her girlfriends' mockery—with death.
Regretfully she left the ancient forest where beasts roam
And would not face the Archeress, she was so full of shame
At having lost her maidenhood. And full of Bacchus' seed,
That dew divine, her womb grew heavy; it was time to breed.
After nine months had cycled in the rhythm of the moon,
The fertile seasons served as midwives when her child was born.

And thus from Bromius' coupling a divine daughter came,
Lover of celebrations, and Teletê was her name,
Her mother's choice: "Initiation" and "Festivity."
This girl like the god her father danced the nights away,
And always revels and loud music were her greatest joy.
And Dionysus built a city, Nicaea, of fine stone,
Beside the drunkards' lake whose waters were as strong as wine,
Both to commemorate the nymph he had deflowered, and for
The victory he himself had won fighting the Indian war.

Book 17

Catherine Anderson

In the seventeenth book, I celebrate
the first fruits of war and how the honey-trickled river
waters turn to wine.

Amazed to wake bearing no wounds of war,
Dionysus watches the lax Warriors of the River Indus
as they sleep the sleep of the drunk
and conquered. He lets the Amazon girl
and the trick he played in wine-brimmed
passion fall to forgetfulness.

Dionysus then lifts his pinecone
spear, not against the winds but rushing forward
to meet the challenge of Deriades.
His face radiant, this son of Zeus gathers
the caravan surrounding his Lydian chariot.
Above the pine cone spears of his warriors arced
in formation our god is ringed in light.

> *Like another heaven, his beauty*
> *so bright all else is cast in shadow.*
> *Like the sun god Helios, he shines*
> *among the scattered stars.*

A time of war without the arms of war:
According to plan, Dionysus carries no sword,
no deadly ashwood spear.
For bronze he carries the ivy plant,
a weapon to wield through Asian cities
as he drives the chariot of the goddess Cybele.
He threads grapevines under the shadow
of this ivy, brother to the vine that bears
the red juice of Maronian fruit
whipping drunkenness down the coast.

Meanwhile, the whole company of Bacchi
swells with confidence after their victory.
Silenus in his madness clutches his arms
around the full armor of a sleeping
Warrior of the River Indus
to carry him off as prisoner.
A Bacchant woman dances drunk,
feet bouncing in fury as she
clangs a pair of cymbals that ripples
above the head of another sleeping soldier.
She ropes his neck and drags him
away like bounty.

From city to city our god travels until
he comes to a rainy country full of wealth
where rivers streak silver through the rocks.
Traveling with his footmen and horned satyrs,
Dionysus meets Brongus, a highland shepherd
who lives in a hut carved from quarried
boulders shaping the landscape.
In welcome the enchanted Brongus
milks a goat and pours the snowy
drink in a rough-hewn cup to serve.
Brongus then brings a fleecy sheep
from his fold as a sacrifice to the god.
"No, no, spare your sheep" says Dionysus

and raises his hands to halt the shepherd.
Instead Brongus brings plump autumn olives
swimming in brine, fresh cheese carried in baskets,
a simple shepherd's meal with no meat.

Laughing, the god accepts the humble meal
with gratitude, thinking of a meatless table
set for the goddess Cybele of the uplands.
Dionysus' eyes fall on the stone doors of the courtyard—
the rugged walls, the cambered roofs and he thinks
of the work it took to make a dwelling here
among unending cliffs and rocks and hills.

After the dinner, Brongus takes up his pipes
to play the sweet tunes of Pan, touching his fingers
to Athena's double aulos in honor of the god.
Dionysus, delighted with the music and the food,
mixes freshly pressed wine into a bowl and offers it,
"Old man, take this gift brought down
from heaven and forget your snowy
goat's milk. Wine is what makes men
happy and brings comfort to their sorrows!"

Brongus accepts the gracious gift, the fruit of
fine new grapes. Before leaving, Dionysus speaks
of his love of the vineyard and offers to teach
Brongus how to cultivate his own grapes—
to layer the slips of plants over the fertilizing pits,
and shape the top of flowering shoots of an old
vine so new grapes may grow—

an interlude in the midst of war,
this moment in which a god shows kindness
to a shepherd who lives at the ridge
of the wild forest.

Old Brongus forgotten, Dionysus' talk soon turns
to battle against the Warriors of the River Indus,
now high in the mountains.
Dionysus bids the horned satyrs to rush upland
at full speed as they join the wild Bacchants.

Angry and shaking his thyrsus spear,
the blood-craving god picks up the war trumpet
and blasts it over the ears of his soldiers who
listen to the thundering sound the way men
guzzle wine to full intoxication.

Now enraged, they're ready to follow
their leader to war against a people
whose only offense is worship
of different gods,
none of them named Bacchus.

As Dionysus chases war against the Indus soldiers,
Astraëis rushes to find Orontes and deliver
his sorrowful report: "You'll be enraged,
so let me tell you quickly: Our men were conquered
by the weaponless Dionysus who drenched
them in the soporific waters of wine,
rendering them incoherent, malleable, defeated.
A strange battle, with Dionysus standing frightened
among his satyrs wielding no sword, slewing no arrows!
Bacchus instead held up a huge oxhorn and in its hollow,
the crimson drug of defeat.
He lifted it above the silvery river, pouring
its potion into the waters, turning them red, sweet,
wine-washed. Our brothers, thirsty from the rage
of battle drank and drank until they went mad."

The soldier pauses to catch his breath
as Orontes listens, growing more furious
by the minute and thinking only of revenge.

"They danced, they laughed joyfully, and then they fell
into the deepest sleep, collapsed on their leather shields.
All over the earth their bodies were piled like stones
to be picked up by Dionysus and his weak, armless forces.
What deception! I know you're furious to hear this story.
Our men were enslaved by Dionysus and his satyrs.
That is the truth. I escaped, not touching my lips
to those waters. Watch out for the power of wine!
We must be aware of any more tricks coming from
The deceitful Dionysus!"

What wounded most was the mockery
his soldiers were made by Dionysus.
Orontes lost no time rushing
to the battlefield to continue the fight.

Along the mountains, Ares was arming
the Indus Warriors, preparing for a second conflict.
The Dionysian women, known for their madness
and crazed love of wine, met the armed
and marching Bacchi up the winding glens
of Taurus. And there they saw the centaurs,
needing no arrows and swords as they hurled
large splintered rocks to cut the bewildered
faces of the Indus Warriors.

What ensued was crazed, maddened warfare
of blood and evisceration:
the Pans skipped over the peaks, reaching
the people Dionysus inspired them to hate.

With their goat-hooves the Pans tore up the bodies
of their enemy. One Pan pierced a fleeing enemy
warrior on his horns, pitched him flying
over the peaks, head over heels.
Crops were scythed, and with the crops, enemy
heads rolled down for Dionysus, the blades

dripping with a blood libation drunk by the victors.
A goat-footed Pan laced a man's hands
behind his neck and then ramrodded him
in the gut with his sharp horn.
Another man was smashed between the eyes
as he ran to cudgel yet another Pan.

What could the leader of the Indus Army do
but cry out to the sky
bent over the battlefield?

"Fight the deceitful Dionysus in the open!

"Fight him on the battlefield where you can keep
your eyes on him! He's weak, unarmed but very wily.
And use extreme caution: never, never
drink his yellow wine.
It's poison! Once you drink it,
you'll fall into a mad, cruel sleep you'll
never recover from, like our brothers
who were slain by the blade of Lyaeus
as they lay sleeping!
I dare Dionysus to stand up to me in battle!
I dare him to fight me in the open field!"

But is it wise to dare Dionysus?
Doesn't the Warrior leader realize where
this will lead?

"When he tries to slice me with his wispy grape leaves,
I'll come back with my flashing bronze!
And when I raise my spear, what will
he do? Hit me with weeds? Ha!
Look at his long, flowing locks of hair, more
like a sister than a man of war,
swinging those braids the way women do!

Ha! You scare me, Dionysus, using the same weapon
as your beautiful Bassarids, the women you hide behind!
Come on, Dionysus, fight me."

Orontes then dashes into the ranks of his enemy,
both men and women, and makes
a gruesome war harvest of their bodies.
The often brave Eurymedon, and Alcon,
and even Astraeus, chief of the Satyrs,
leap away in fright. Deriades' angry son-in-law
rushes in, lifts up giant boulders and lets
them fly at the leaping centaurs, using
the same weapon of rocks as the centaurs
threw not long ago at the Indus army.
He crushes the shaggy forehead of the centaur Hylaeus
with a huge stone, breaking the headpiece
made of chalk that covers his face.
Hylaeus falls like a white cinder on the ground,
his human arms flailing as he dies.
And then the hairy chest of another centaur
is jabbed with a double-bladed ax
as his tormentor carves away the
curved horn from his bull's head.
The centaur tumbles in misery,
his ears raising the dust as he falls.
In a last wild effort the centaur prances
around in circles—enraged,
tortured, a monster mortally
struck in the skull and roaring in pain.
And Helice, now struck, writhes on the ground,
the wind lifting her robe as she frantically
tries to pull it over her wounds.

The god bellows as loud as an army
of nine thousand men when he realizes victory
might cede to the enemy.

Orontes, a mortal human, challenges Bacchus
with his spear and strikes him on top
of his large bull's head, but the effort is useless.
The head of the god is shaped like the ox-eyed
Moon, with divine horns that cannot be shattered.
Bacchus, in return, throws his wine-dark
thyrsus toward the broad shoulders
of Orontes, but misses!
Orontes, not realizing the god's aim
was off-kilter on purpose, breaks into laughter:
"You, Bacchus, with your team
of girls: Come out and fight a real warrior,
come see what an ancient father of the River Jhelum
has produced in a warrior son like me!
I'm armed, remember, and the drug of wine
won't save your weak girly fighters this time.
I'll capture your crazy women, and snatch your sileni
from battle to become servants for my king.
And your satyrs I will swiftly seize and kill
as they beg for mercy beneath my spear!"

Bacchus becomes even more furious
on hearing this mortal defiance.
He lightly taps Orontes' breastplate
with his vine cluster, not scratching
his body, not touching his flesh, merely
brushing it softly until the breastplate
protecting the mortal warrior shatters,
the pieces falling to the ground with a clang:
Orontes stripped naked.
Helpless, the mortal steps back and turns
to the eastern sky, uttering his last words—
"Helios, as you ride your chariot pouring light
on the plowed land below, listen as I announce
that now we are conquered, the Indian people
are slaves. I will soon give up and destroy
myself in shame. Let this be known:

We were felled by a light bunch of leaves,
wine and a thyrsus. I bring as witness all
the gods of my people. Farewell!"

Orontes then draws his sword and falls upon it.
He rolls down, deep into the river
and in sinking, offers it his name.

Did this last act silence the Lord Bacchus?
Did this brutal suicide bring him closer
to feeling the mortality of humans?
Does he now understand the irony of a warrior
who never drank the honeyed wine waters,
but still dies, swept into the course of rivers, destined
to drink the fatal stream of Acheron?

Bacchus rages at the corpse of Orontes like an ignorant ass.

The body jets down the swollen whirlpool lands
on the river bank—cold, bloated and stiff.
The nymphs bury the body and sing
their lamentations under a large golden laurel.
They carve a commemoration in its trunk,
noting the Indian leader who insulted Bacchus,
and then killed himself, his corpse riding
the waters beneath the tree.

The Warriors of the Indus River gather again,
and the Bacchant women join to oppose them.
Bacchus' army throws poisoned garlands, slaying
the bronze-clad Warriors of the Indus.

Twigs sliced their open armor, and Death
returns again—sharp, stealthy, mean.

The Bacchi, servants of the so-called unwarlike
Dionysus, stand like rocks, unscathed

by ax blunts and whirling
two-edged swords.

Their foes are ordinary men killed by leaves.

The useless shafts of the Warriors stick
in the branching trees, battering the firs and pines.
In an attempt to avoid the eyes of Apollo,
Phoebus' laurel, struck by these arrows,
hides under its thick leaves as a cloud
of feathers comes flying,

A Bacchant woman with no shield
or sword shakes a rattle and a warrior falls.
As drums beat, the Indus soldiers dance;
when the cymbals strike, another warrior
of the Indus River pleads for mercy.
The sharp ivy leaves continue their pricking,
slicing rampage, splitting armor
and breast plate, breaking bones and heads.
Bacchus wins, the Indus River warriors, defeated.
Astraëis, watching the war favor Lyaeus,
decides early to run away and save himself.

The war is over when Aristaeus, chief of the satyrs,
clomps goat-footed over the fields,
and with his human fingers
spreads herbal unguents on the wounds
of the Bassarids, healing them by the art of Phoebus.
He wipes the blood and gore away,
and of the Bacchants who weep, he spreads
herbs to quiet their open wounds.
The war is over when he draws the sharp point
of an arrow, discharging
the blood drop by drop.
The war is over when he mixes honey
with fresh flowers and then pours

Bacchus' painkilling wine
into the tinctures and over the wounds.
The war is over when he makes men whole
by reciting ribald, healing verses—
outrageous ones, taught by Phoebus.

But when does war truly end, wounds
healed, men and women recovered?

The mended Bassarids sweep the battlefield
of the captive warriors. In the background,
the defeated fighters drive their elephants
through the Taurus Mountains
to the mansion of Deriades in the Indian region.

All the time Pan bellows loudly in victory, as the satyrs
surround him in drunken celebration.

Only when Blemys, chief of the Indians to the south,
bearing an olive branch and bending his knee
before Dionysus does the god offer protection—
really isolation—
lifting him over the earth, away from Deriades
now dwelling in the land of the Arabs,
between sea and land.
The humble Blemys passes through the mouth
of the seven streamed Nile to become
the king of the Ethiopians.
A land of endless harvests welcomes him
where he will be remembered in name
for generations.

The battlefield is empty for now,
the first fruits of war harvested, the rivers
running in honey-trickled wine.

Book 18

Tessa Cavagnero

Now for the eighteenth book, where Staphylos and Botrys call
Thyonê's mountain-ranging son to their festivities.

Already winged Rumor, many-mouthed,
was flying, visiting Assyrian cities one by one
to spread the news of vine-crowned Dionysus, his bold war
against the Indians, his crops of brightly colored grapes.
So Staphylos, the king of the Assyrians, heard tales
of unarmed hordes of satyrs celebrating sacred rites
in honor of the vine, and wished to see the god himself.
He rushed his lofty wind-swift chariot along, and brought
his son, Botrys, to meet with Dionysus as he came.
When unshorn Botrys saw him drawing near, his chariot
bedecked with silver wheels and pulled by teams of panthers yoked
with lions, gleaming-reined, he reined his father's horses in,
and Staphylos, the sceptered king, leapt down from where he sat
and gazed on Dionysus' panthers, halted in their tracks.

With shaky knees the king knelt on the ground,
and offered up an olive branch with one god-fearing hand.
With friendly words he welcomed Dionysus to his land:

"By Zeus, your father, god of suppliants,
by Semele, who bore you: Do not overlook my son.

Yes, I have heard the tale of Lycaon, how he received
your father and the other gods: he slaughtered Nyctimus,
his son, with his own hands, and served him up to Zeus the Lord
of All, when they broke bread together on Arcadia's plain,
and Zeus was none the wiser. On the peaks of Sipylus,
or so they say, King Tantalus received your father, too,
and killed his own son, Pelops, setting him before the gods.
The son of Cronus fit the body back together, limb
by limb, but Deo had consumed one shoulder at the feast.
This he replaced with ornamented, well-carved ivory,
and resurrected Tantalus' mutilated son.
But why, O Dionysus, do I speak of Lycaon,
who slew his son to feed the blessed ones, and Tantalus,
sky-wanderer and twisted charlatan, the cunning thief
who stole cups full of nectar and ambrosia from the gods?
Macello hosted Zeus and Phoebus at the same table

[*There is a short lacuna in the text here.*]

when the Earthshaker fragmented the Isle of Rhodes
with his trident and drowned all the Phlegyans
except for those two women, in the sea's depths..
You, follow the example of your father, god of guests;
come with me to my hall, and stay until the morning light;
bestow this gift upon us both, the father and the son."

His speech convinced the god. And on he went,
believing his house blessed, with Dionysus right behind.
And daring Botrys lifted up the horse whip, beating out
a winding path along the Taurus Mountains' rugged edge,
and drove his father's chariot into Assyrian lands,
escorting Dionysus. Meanwhile Maron, Bromius'
chauffeur, who never spared the whip, took up the golden reins
of the Mygdonian chariot, the straps placed on the necks
of panthers, and with unforgiving lash he spurred the beasts
and started up the storm-swift car. Out front, a chorus line
of satyrs started up a jig, and frolicked to and fro

around the mountain-ranging chariot of Bromius.
And here and there a crowd of blossom-loving Bacchants ran—
although their path was harsh, their feet were swift, and gracefully,
with nimble steps, they traveled steep, uneven folds of stone.
They rattled castanets and rhythmically stomped their feet,
and in their madness made the rocky ridges of the path
seem effortless. And Pans, from high on their accustomed cliffs,
joined in the dance and stomped the dust with finely shodden feet,
traversing crags as yet untrodden, passing by the peaks.

And as they neared, the royal hall appeared
before them in the distance, glittering, ornately built
with multicolored stone; then Botrys with his flowing locks
leapt from his father's car and ran inside on hurried feet,
since he was in the lead; and carefully, with great finesse,
prepared a varied feast to grace the table of the king.

While Botrys organized the revelry
for Bromius, King Staphylos the ever-prosperous
was showing off his hall to Bacchus, with its stone-paved floor
and lovely craftsmanship. The walls were streaming brilliant beams
as luminous as sunlight or the moon's reflecting face:

Silvery metal glinted on the walls,
and rubies spit out bright electric sparks
to dazzle watching eyes; the house surpassed
itself with blushing Ethiopian stone,
and sapphire verged on wine-dark amethyst.
Pale agate shone with smoky radiance,
the dappled serpentine was flecked with scales,
and emeralds were glittering with green light.
The gilded wooden ceiling-beams were laid
across a hundred column-tops, and spread
with rich red thatch; mosaics blanketed
the gleaming floor with tiles of precious stone;
the massive doors were beautifully carved
from wood that looked like new-sawn ivory.

Such things the ancient scepter-bearing king
showed Bacchus. Hardly able to support himself, the king
took Dionysus by the hand; the god went wandering
with slow, admiring step throughout the hall, and cast his eyes
around him, marveling at all the gleaming ornaments
and at his gracious host's star-spangled, gold-encrusted hall.

And Staphylos gave orders to his slaves
and his attendants, urging them to slaughter flocks of sheep
and herds of fattened bulls for ox-horned Dionysus' crowd.
The house slaves rushed to carry out his orders, under threat
of discipline, each in their turn, and many laborers
applied their talents to the feast; they butchered bulls and ranks
of robust, grazing sheep. There was a dance. Throughout the hall
accomplished lyrists played, and aromatic breezes blew,
and wafted up and down the city's pleasant-smelling streets.
Free-flowing streams of wine intoxicated the whole house.
There was a clattering of cymbals, pan-pipes whistling
melodious across the table, and a clamoring
of double flutes, two-headed drums of oxhide thundering
in double rhythm in the hall; and following the feast,
the din of rattles. In their midst, wine-heavy Maron danced:
unable to contain himself, he wandered here and there,
and whirled insanely, borne along on trembling feet; his legs
went swinging back and forth, and kicked up, perpendicular
to the floor. His arms were slung across two satyrs' shoulders, and
they lifted him between them; he was weightless, moved along
by others' feet; his skin was glossy with a golden sheen,
and scarlet light cascaded from his gleaming countenance,
the very likeness of Selene with her reflecting horns.
In his left hand he clutched a wineskin newly flayed and full
of customary wine, its neck secured with sturdy straps,
and in his right he held a cup; the Bacchae circled round
the old man as he skipped along on other dancers' feet.
His head was nodding, always on the verge of falling down
but never falling. The attendants, and the house slaves too,
were reeling drunkenly and raving, frenzied, in the dance,
since this was the first time they'd tasted such exquisite wine.

And even Staphylos' noble wife,
Queen Methê, was inebriated with the Bacchic brew.
She skipped around the wine-filled mixing bowl Lyaeus brought,
and drowsily she asked the Bacchae for another drink;
she whirled her lolling head from side to side, and whipped her hair
across her shoulder with unsteady tossing of her head,
reversing course from time to time, her sandals slippery,
and every time she seemed about to tumble to the ground,
a Bacchant took her by the hand and set her right again.
King Staphylos had gotten drunk, and Botrys, with his cup
of wine, became intoxicated, and his cheeks grew red,
and with his father Staphylos' assistance, he—a boy
just old enough to grow a beard—bound up his flowing locks
with unaccustomed ivy, braiding it into a crown,
and alternating footsteps, whirling, hopping right to left,
he danced a spiral pattern with enthusiastic feet.
And Staphylos himself was prancing on cavorting feet,
and running round and round on his swift path with crooked steps,
he draped his arm across his dancing partner, Botrys' neck.
Unable to stand still, he sang the praises of the wine
that chorus-weaving Dionysus brought; from side to side
he shook his tumbling curls onto his shoulders. Methê danced,
her forearms resting on her husband's shoulders and her son's,
supported between Staphylos and Botrys: Ah, to see
the triply-twined delight, the family in their woven dance!

And Pithos, old but active, shook his white
hair in the wind, completely filled up to the teeth with sweet
cascading wine, and turning circles, reeling drunkenly.
His yellow facial hair was growing white, deluged with foam
that flowed down from his gargling gullet in sweet rivulets.

They drank all day, and in the evening, once
their cups were drained, a shadowy blackness covered all the land,
descending from above; the aether showed its darker face;
the insubstantial stars were shimmering with gauzy light.
Then Phaëthon's chariot sank beneath the shadowy horizon

with the remains of Eos' light still fading from the sky;
and silent Night unfurled herself across the darkening air,
enveloping the firmament in her celestial cloak.
And after they had drunk the kraters dry and polished off
the banquet, Botrys, Staphylos, and Dionysus, god
of wine, departed one by one for richly covered beds,
accepted Hypnos' gift of sleep, and lost themselves in dreams.

When Daybreak, Eos' stealthy messenger,
pierced through the lightening fog with rosy rays and morning came,
then long-haired Dionysus vaulted out of bed, abuzz
with hope of victory; for in the night he had cut down
the Indian people with his ivy-decorated wand,
with battle-fervor's lifelike image leading him along.
And bellowing he shook the clash of satyrs off, the thud
of javelins, the battle roaring loudly in his sleep;
he waved the warlike dream aside, but in his heart he nursed
a dreadful terror of the threatening vision coming true.
For he had seen a prophecy of things to come, a scene
of battle with Lycurgus: how an irrepressible
and valiant lion leapt out from a crag with raging maw
at Bacchus, who was dancing in the grove and had no sword
to hand, and drove him off in fear toward the ocean's edge;
he wrapped himself in waves and fled the terrifying beast.
And he had seen another horror, too: a lion chased
the thyrsus-bearing women, doggedly, with jaws agape,
and tore at them with bloody talons, slicing them to bits;
initiates let Bacchic implements fall from their hands
into the dust, and cymbals lay inert upon the earth.
One Bacchant turned around and tightly bound the lion's jaws
with rope, and wound restraints made out of vines around its head,
and tied a tether fit for strangling round the lion's neck.
The throng of women sprinted, crowding on each other's heels,
toward the monster, and they sliced its shaggy paws with thorns.
And with great difficulty, Artemis revived him, twined
among the spiral grape-vines, and from the celestial void
a bolt of fiery lightning struck the beast square in the face,
transforming him into a sightless, circling wanderer.

Such was the vision Dionysus saw;
and hurtling out of bed he donned a starry yellow robe
upon his chest, bespattered with the blood of Indians,
and bound his tresses up with intertwining snakeskin bands.
He fastened crimson buskins on his feet, and in his hand
he lifted up the thyrsus, Enyo's blossom-heavy spear,
and called to an attendant satyr. And Lord Botrys heard
the call, divinely sweet and echoing, from Bacchus' mouth
and woke, and donned his tunic; sleeping Pithos

[*There is a half-line lacuna in the text here.*]

and Methê heard his voice;
laboriously she raised up her head, weighed down with wine,
and, sluggish, drifted off again; at dawn, the queen was still
asleep, enjoying a delightful nap with resting eyes.
Late in the day, with hesitating steps, she left her bed.

Grape-loving Staphylos accompanied
Lyaeus to the road, and showered him with friendly gifts
while he rushed off: a golden amphora with silver cups,
from which he always used to drink the milk of dairy goats,
and many-colored robes, which Persian Arachne wove
with insubstantial thread beside the Tigris River's flood.
The ever-prosperous king addressed these words to Bromius:

"O Dionysus, fight, and prove yourself
a worthy son of Zeus; show that you bear his bloodline, for
when he was still a boy, just nearing manhood, he beat back
the earthborn Titans from Olympus. Hurry, now, to war—
you must destroy the haughty race of earthborn Indians.
There is a story, I remember, which my grandfather,
Assyrian Belus, the protector of our city, told
my father. And now I, in turn, will pass it down to you:
how Cronus, splattered still with ichor, lifted up the blade
he used to castrate Uranus while he was hastening
to Gaea's bed to consummate the marriage once again.

"Broad-bearded Cronus, as commander of
the Titan host, attacked your father, fanning Enyo's flame.
He hurled his icy bolts down on the head of Cronion,
bombarding him with frozen, slippery missiles, and he sent
the sharp-tipped bolts cascading from the heavens, thick as hail.
But Zeus was armed with fire, surpassing even Helios;
he melted Cronus' frozen rain with scintillating heat.
So do not fear the elephants, or hesitate to drive
your ravenous lions into battle with the Indians;
your father, king of heaven, struck the mighty Campê down
with thunderbolts, though she was monstrous and multiformed.
From snaky tendrils she was belching poison from afar,
and countless reptiles seethed around her convoluted, coiled
and ever-shifting form and simmered with destructive rage,
while fifty bestial heads were flourishing around her throat.
Some took the form of lions, and they roared, resembling
the unintelligible Sphinx's face, with bristling manes,
and some, with tusks like wild boars, were foaming at the mouth;
thus Campê rivaled Scylla in her form, surrounded by
a single-minded multitude of crowding canine maws.
And in the midst of the amalgamation, there appeared
a maiden's body, long hair made from poison-spitting snakes;
her lofty torso was encased in scales, sea serpent-like,
unearthly, from her chest down to the creases of her thighs.
The fingernails of her wide-spreading hands were curving in
upon themselves, like a crook-taloned sea-bird's crosswise claws,
and from her shoulder blades, down over her unyielding back,
a spiral scorpion crept along the ridges of her spine,
and reared up, bearing icy venom in its razor tail.
So Campê, with her jumbled and contorted form, arose
and took flight, spiraling into the air, across the lands,
across the ocean's depths, with shadowy wings fluttering
in unison. The Tartarean nymph whipped up the winds
with pitch-black feathers, churning up a hurricane; her eyes
discharged a roving flame that left a far-flung trail of sparks.

"But Zeus, your father, lord of heaven, killed
the beast, defeated Cronus' serpentine monstrosity.
You, follow the example of your father, that I may
address you as Destroyer of the Earthborn, just like Zeus,
demolishing the scions of the earthborn Indians.
Your current enemy is similar to his: for Zeus
laid low the long-limbed Indus, Cronus' massive champion
of battle, ancient and majestic, sprung straight from the fields,
from whom the race of Indians can trace their heritage.
His nemesis was Indus, and Deriades is yours.

"Take after Ares, too, since he himself
cast down Echidna's mighty son, who battled with the gods.
The creature, spitting out the venom he inherited
from hideous Echidna, had two bodies fused as one,
and shook the spiral of his mother's spine deep in the grove.
Enormous and obedient to Cronus, whispering war
with every step of his deceitful feet, he warded off
the thunderbolt and raised his hands before his chest to fight
your father, Zeus. And on his aerial path he crowned himself
with clouds arranged in rows upon his lofty crested head.
He laid hold of the birds that wandered in his unkempt hair
and feasted on them, gullet yawning wide, his usual meal.
Such was the shining paragon your brother Ares slew.
I would not call you Ares' inferior, for you
could rival Zeus' brood, excelling with your bloody wand
as much as Ares fighting with a spear. You will achieve
success to equal Phoebus. And another son of Zeus,
another monster-slayer, I have hosted in my hall:
for recently the well-winged Perseus came to my house,
with Cydnus, Corycion's radiant neighbor, left behind,
and told me how he marked the boundaries of a city of
Cilician settlers, newly founded, named for his swift foot.
He held Medusa's massive head, the Gorgon who could not
be looked upon, but you bring with you grapes, the vineyard's fruit
that brings men pleasure and allows us to forget our grief.

Perseus slew a monster near the Erythraean Sea,
and you laid low the race of Erythraean Indians.
So kill Deriades, just as you killed Orontes, worse
than any monster in the ocean. Perseus rescued sad
Andromeda, and you must save the starry Virgin, whom
the unjust Indians abducted, cruelly, on a whim,
that I may offer up one sacrifice to Perseus
the Gorgon-slayer, and to Bacchus, scourge of Indians."

Thus speaking, Bromius' gracious host,
the frail old king, turned back toward his hall; and Bromius
was moved to tears, rejoicing at the king's uplifting speech,
and brandishing his thyrsus, he was struck with madness, ears
bewitched by tales of battles, hearing of his father's war.
He envied Cronides and wished to vie with him; he hoped
a third and greater victory would follow on the heels
of his two battles with the Indians. He called upon
the son of Iphthime the messenger of heaven, wise
and wind-like Pherespondus, greeting him with friendly words:

"O son of Hermaon, O courier
beloved by me, convey these words to proud Deriades:
'Your Majesty, accept Lyaeus' gifts without a fight,
or emulate Orontes and make war on Bromius.'"

He finished speaking, and the courier
with his swift-sandaled feet advanced from land to land
toward the Eastern plains, his father's scepter in his hand.
The god, astride his golden chariot, held harvest grapes
before him as a joyful sign; he passed from town to town
on ever-dancing feet, and handed out his blooming vines
to rustics, filling up the countryside with blossoming grapes.

But while the roving wine-dark chariot
traversed the soil of Syria near fiery Eurus' wing,
a peaceful death took Staphylos; and in the royal hall

the house slaves ripped the garments they were wearing into rags,
the king's attendants started up a mourning cry and bruised
their breasts with beating hands, and women singing threnodies
scratched bloody furrows in their cheeks with mournful fingernails.

Too late did Dionysus turn his car,
bedecked with vines, around and come again to Botrys' hall,
remembering his feast with tender-hearted Staphylos.
But when he noticed Pithos' countenance downcast with grief,
the god divined the fate of Staphylos with silent skill,
all on his own, and calling Methê to his side, he spoke:

"Lady, what suffering has changed your looks?
I see your light diminished, though I left you radiant;
who snuffed out your unutterable loveliness? Your cheeks,
once bright with drunkenness, no longer glow with inner fire.
And you, old man, do not conceal your reasons; tell me why
you shed these tears: who cut your flowing locks, O bearded one,
what man defaced your venerable head and tore your robes?
And you, O son of my dear Staphylos, whom Methê, fond
of wine, gave birth: why have you shorn your head completely bald,
or did some act of malice rob you of your curly hair?
No longer do your locks cascade, perfumed with Tyrian oils
and left unbraided, over your resplendent shoulders; now
your cheeks, which once were flushed with Bacchic revelry,
no longer seem to shoot out rosy sparks. Why do you wear
bedraggled garments streaked with poured-on dust? Your royal robes
of Tyrian purple never looked so grim to me before;
I hardly recognize you, with your beauty tarnished so.
And where has scepter-bearing Staphylos departed to?
I want to know: who stole your father, even for an hour?
But no, I recognize your pain, although you try to hide;
I do not need an explanation; even without words
the very sight of you makes obvious your suffering.
I recognize your misery, although you try to hide;
Your tears are evidence of your bereavement, and your robes,

disheveled, testify to my dear Staphlyos' fate.
But this catastrophe has snatched away my joy, for I
had hoped, after my battle with the Indians was done,
to raise an evening torch with Staphylos, and celebrate
the wedding night of Botrys, my companion, by his side."

Book 19

Sheila H. Murnaghan

In Book 19, Bacchus honors the grave of King Staphylos,
setting up a diverting contest, with a bowl of fine wine as the prize.

Those words pierced the boy with fresh darts of grief.
Silently mourning, he pressed his lips shut
and gave way to tears. At long last his mother,
Queen Methê the Tipsy, spoke to the god.

"The tireless friend of your nocturnal dances,
Staphylos, Lord of the Grape Cluster, sleeps,
Staphylos snatched by the Underworld's winds,
and I've been afflicted by double despair:
you'd gone away and my husband grew sick.
I suffered a twofold pang of longing,
with Staphylos failing and you gone away.
Bacchus, my friend! Quick hand me a cup
filled to the brim with your bubbling brew
so your pain-numbing wine can quiet my pain.
Lord Dionysus, with your joyful shout!
Show me that cup and I'll shed no more tears."

He pitied her troubles and set to work mixing,
then gave to the boy and his downhearted mother
cupfuls of cheering, care-banishing wine.

Tipsy Queen Methê and Botrys the Wine Pip
drank it all down and silenced their groans.
In thrall to Lord Bacchus, she spoke again.

"You've come to me Bacchus, my savior, my light!
Dionysus is here and my sorrow has left.
You've come to me Bacchus, my savior, my light!
Your healing potion has dried up my tears.
I'll not mourn my husband, I'll not mourn my father.
I'll give up young Wine Pip, if that's what you want.
I'll take Bacchus for husband, for father, for son.
I'll go to your house, if that's what you want.
I'll be a maenad, if that's what you want.
I'll lift up your wand and your succulent fruit.
I'll touch my lips to the winemaker's flute.
Don't leave me a widow doubly bereaved,
with Staphylos dead and the wine god gone.
Teach Wine Pip, your squire, your dances and rites—
your Indian battles, if that's what you want.
I so long to see him up there on the winepress
laughing, and trampling the fruit of your vines.
Think of Wine Jug, his grandpa; do not let this boy
still be unschooled in your rites and your potions."

Lord Bacchus gave an encouraging smile
then spoke in response to the bibulous Queen:

"O Lady, your gifts are like Aphrodite's!
You bring men good cheer and awaken their love.
Come sit at the feast beside Lyaeus.
Put on a garland like Aphrodite's,
a circlet of flowers and bunches of grapes,
that is certain to make proud Victory jealous.
Beside golden Hebe, you'll pour out the wine.
You will rise up on high beside Lyaeus,
helping to fill the revelers' goblets.
The buzz brought by wine will be called after you,

Methê the Tipsy. My care-soothing fruit
I will dub Wine Pip, and clusters of grapes
bursting with juice will bear Staphylos' name.
If Methê is absent, I won't start the feast.
If Methê is absent, I won't start the dance."

Then Lord Dionysus, dispeller of grief,
established a contest at Staphylos' tomb,
to chase away grief and honor the Tippler.
He set out two prizes, a goat and a bull,
and called on all masters of Pierian song
to join in the games. With mellifluous words
he stirred up those lyrical virtuosos.

"Now for a proper Athenian revel!
The winner takes home the glistening bull;
the shaggy goat is the loser's reward."

As soon as he spoke, two singers leapt out:
Oeagrus first, from bitter cold Thrace,
clutching his lyre with its dangling pick,
and challenging him, Erechtheus of Athens.
The two contestants stepped into the ring
and brandished their lyres. There were circlets of laurel
entwined in their hair; their robes were hitched up.
Running practiced fingers across the strings,
they plucked each in order, tightening the pegs
so the pitch would not rise too high or too sharp,
but still not fall slack in a womanish way.
By lot it fell out that Erectheus of Athens
was the first to compete. He took up his lyre
and gave them a local Athenian song:

Once in Athena's holy city, King Celeus welcomed life-giving Demeter,
joined by his son and Metaneira, his august wife.
In return, Demeter taught them to bring forth the nourishing grain:
Triptolemus rode on a cart filled with sheaves and threw out the seed.

When Celeus died, Demeter took her place by his newly built tomb;
the fruitful goddess lamented her host without shedding a tear,
and speaking heart-soothing words, she quenched the deep grief
that had seized Triptolemus and Metaneira, his august wife.
In just this way, the sceptered Assyrian King welcomed Lord Dionysus;
In return for the rich bounty of Staphylos' hospitable table
Bacchus gave plentiful gifts and the sweet fruit of the grapevine.
And when Staphylos, King of the Tipplers, had died, Lord Dionysus
banished the grief of his mournful son, Prince Botrys the Wine Pip,
and silenced the sobs of his mournful wife, Queen Methê the Tipsy.

When the skillful singer offered this hymn,
everyone, Bacchus included, was charmed:
they admired the well-made Athenian tune.
Then an artful air was produced by Oeagrus,
the Muse's consort and father of Orpheus:
a song of Apollo in just two lines—
a few plain words in the Spartan style:

Apollo brought back Hyacinthus;
Staphylos lives thanks to Dionysus.

In the midst of their revels the people cried out
with unanimous words of full-throated praise
while the satyrs all bellowed in happy approval.
Bacchus leapt from his seat and waved his right hand,
while Wine Pip ran up to him shouting Eu-ee!
and praising the harper's harmonious song.
The god placed a wreath on Oeagrus' head.
The father of Orpheus capered with joy
and accepted the untamed bull as his prize,
while his friends formed a line and danced alongside him.
Meanwhile, deflated by grief and by envy,
the Athenian slunk off with the bearded goat.

Then the long-haired Lord of the Bacchic cry
set out generous prizes for intricate dancing:

A punch bowl designed for the finest of wines,
fashioned from gold and hugely capacious,
full to the brim with a four-year-old vintage,
a masterwork of immortal Hephaestus,
bestowed on the wine god by Aphrodite.
The second prize was not quite so grand:
a solidly crafted and round silver basin,
a guest gift to Bacchus from the king of Alybe,
who lived in a country renowned for rich mines,
where veins of white silver ran through the dark earth.
Encircling its rim was a golden design
of ivy that twined around clusters of grapes.
He placed this before them. Its belly was filled
with a much younger wine, just newly pressed out,
sweet and unmixed—it would only be fair
to offer the loser the most potent brew.
When Dionysus had set out these prizes
he summoned the dancers and laid down the rules.

"The one who excels in skilled pirouettes
and intricate footwork, let him take away
the bowl made of gold and the sweet wine within it.
While someone who totters and falls to the ground
is a second-rate dancer and deserves second prize.
You won't find me thinking the way others do.
For the victor who triumphs with delicate steps
I won't give out prizes like tripods and horses
or breastplates bespattered with Indian blood.
This contest is not about aiming the discus
or running the fastest or throwing a spear.
This is for Staphylos, late lover of dances:
I honor his memory through playful high-stepping.
I won't reward wrestlers with thick bulging muscles;
This is no horse race, no Olympian games,
no trial that's designed to eliminate suitors.
The dance is my goal post, the chorus my track,
the beckoning hands, twirling feet, and swift glances,

the telling expressions and unspoken messages—
that whole dancer's language of gestures and poses."

As soon as he'd spoken, Silenus jumped up,
and the old man Maron slowly rose to his feet.
Maron's eyes were fixed on the gleaming gold bowl,
not for the gold but because it was filled
up to the brim with the finest old vintage.
His lust for that wine brought back his youth;
its heady aroma overcame his gray hair.
At first he tried out some provisional swirls
to make sure he hadn't forgotten the steps
and spoke honeyed words to Staphylos' spirit,
a quite sober speech from his thick shaggy beard.

"I am old Maron, close friend of Lyaeus,
and like Dionysus I don't ever weep.
Mazurkas and jigs are my funeral gifts.
Please welcome my smiles since I don't ever frown.
I am old Maron who never knows sorrow,
the jubilant squire of dry-eyed Dionysus.
I know you've drunk deep from the river of Lethe,
but give me a chance to taste that old vintage
and let the new wine be imbibed by Silenus.
I'll dance for you, Staphylos, as if you were living
since I prefer dancing even to eating.
I'd dance for you living, I'll dance for you dead,
I'll stir up a revel alongside your tomb.
I follow Lord Bacchus, not sober Apollo,
whose sad Cretan dirges are unknown to me,
those weepy laments for his lover Atymnius.
I don't care that Phaëthon crashed the Sun's car
and is mourned by his sisters on the banks of the Po.
I don't mark Hyacinthus' untimely demise
with sad floral tributes as a Spartan would do.
Today, if you're judging the dead beside Minos,
or joining Rhadamanthys at his flowery court,

or just making your way through the groves of Elysium,
please listen to Maron! I can't pour out cups
so I'm making sweet offerings of intelligent speech.
Look kindly on Maron! Let me be the winner,
let me claim the fame, and then I will pour
fine wine on your tomb from glorious cups,
victorious drops from my golden reward."

He spoke, then performed some meandering steps
criss-crossing his feet, first right over left,
and drawing a story with articulate hands.
He sketched out the plot by rolling his eyes
and artfully added significant gestures.
He nodded his head; if he'd had any hair,
he would have tossed that—but in fact he was bald.
He was no Titan, and he did not depict
primordial tales of Titanic achievements:
no doings of Cronus or primeval Phanes
or the age-old offspring of radiant Helios.
He skipped over all that confusing old lore
and painted instead the gods' graceful cupbearer
as he handed a glistening goblet to Zeus
or topped up the punch bowl with heavenly liquor,
unfailing delight for the whole divine chorus.
The sweetness of wine was his one great theme.
At times he mimed Hebe pouring out nectar.
For the satyrs he limned young Ganymede's charms,
then turning to face the onlooking maenads,
gave a silent impression of golden-shoed Hebe.

All this Maron depicted by waving his arms
and rhythmically stamping his dexterous feet
through many long measures of tireless dancing.
Then he stood trembling and carefully watched
to see who'd be the victor, who would go home
with the really big bowl and the much better wine.

Next to compete was goat-horned Silenus,
drafting unspoken signs with his eloquent hands.
The story he told through his dancing was this:
once when the gods were all drinking together
strife was stirred up between lord Dionysus
and a son of Apollo, who was called Aristaeus,
not settled by boxing or running or hurling:
no! cups were the weapons with which they squared off
and two mixing bowls, of which one held old wine,
the other the gift of the herb-loving honeybee.
King Zeus himself was the judge of this contest.
Cups were the weapons, and Eros presided,
taking the place of golden-winged Hermes.
He brought in some ivy and a fresh olive branch,
the ivy for Bacchus, and for Aristaeus
a crown made of olive like the ones at Olympus,
an ornament dear to the goddess Athena.
First Aristaeus mixed honey with milk
and treated the gods to this novel concoction,
passing the cup from one to the other.
At first they lapped up the bubbling liquid,
but after the first taste, the next was too much:
they turned down a third cup, would not touch a fourth.
They complained that the honey was simply too filling.
Then fine-robed Dionysus dipped into his bowl
and filled up two cups; taking one in each hand,
he gave one to King Zeus and the other to Hera.
He filled up a third for his uncle Poseidon,
then served all of the gods one after another.
They all were delighted except for Apollo
who jealously brooded while Bacchus kept smiling.
Their minds were enchanted by cup after cup,
and the more they imbibed the more they were thirsty.
They kept asking for more; it was never enough.
Then the undying gods, with a jubilant shout,
gave Bacchus the prize for his heavenly wine.

And hard-to-get Eros, quite tipsy himself,
put a crown on his head of ivy and grape vines.

When goat-horned Silenus had artfully woven this tale,,
he held his hands still. With his eyes on the sky
he launched himself up with his high-flying shoe,
tapped one leg to the other, then spread them apart,
and landed and bounded from foot to foot.
Then standing upright with his weight on his heels,
he crossed over the floor with swoops and with swirls.
He stood on his right foot and grabbed his left toe;
he bent one of his knees, which he held with both hands;
he kept one leg straight and extended the other.
So Silenus kept flexing his creaky joints.
He stretched his left leg right up to his shoulder,
then reaching around he took hold of the foot
and twisted its sole to the back of his neck.
Quickly performing a nimble back bend
he turned into a hoop, with his face on the outside,
and stuck out his belly up towards the sky,
then twirled and twirled all in one spot.
His head hung down as he spun around,
almost, but never quite, touching the ground.
When he moved on, his foot scraped the earth
as he restlessly roamed with bacchic abandon.

Then all of a sudden his knees gave out.
His head started bobbing and he fell on his back.
And after that, he turned into a river.
His body became a rippling stream,
his forehead a current; his horns were waves
that built to a turbulent crest on his head.
His belly sank down and gave shelter to fish.
As he spread himself out, his hair turned to reeds,
which, when they were shaken by rustling breezes,
sent their shrill whistling across the wide water.

So Maron awarded first prize to himself,
seizing the bowl that brimmed with sweet wine.
The silver vessel that was won by Silenus
he threw into the stream as a form of libation,
which set all its rivulets drunkenly dancing.
That mixing bowl gave its name to those waters
that sprang from bibulous, babbling Silenus.

Then Maron addressed the swift-flowing stream:

"Rest assured, o Silenus, that Maron won't harm you!
I'll call you 'decanter' as I pour in red wine.
Drink up this liquor, insatiable tippler.
Let Bacchus' bowl make your currents run silver.
Whirlpooling Silenus, you still are a dancer!
Your feet trace their circular steps in your eddies.
Your form may be fluid, but you're reveling still.
So be kind to the Bacchants and their wine-giving fruit
and protect the young satyrs who come from your line.
Think well of old Maron, a true connoisseur,
and don't get involved in some fluvial grudge.
Let Maron's grapes grow with the help of your waters;
among all of the rivers, be Bacchus' best friend.
Why did you unwisely compete with your betters?
You make me think of that poor satyr Marsyas,
an arrogant piper who challenged Apollo.
He was tied to a tree and stripped of his skin,
which Apollo then modified into a windbag.
When inflated by breezes, it looked like the satyr,
and gave the impression he couldn't stop playing.
At last out of pity Apollo transformed him
and made him the river that now bears his name.
People still speak of the meandering stream
of wild-haired Marsyas, where the wind in the reeds
makes it sound like he's playing his Phrygian pipes.
Now just like him you've had your shape changed
for daring to challenge a superior rival.

So you can't go on courting a barefooted Bacchant,
that mountain maenad with the loose flowing locks.
For you now it's naiads with their hair in waves.
Don't seek a Lyaean chaplet of snakes,
but be crowned instead with wriggling eels.
Instead of serpents, expect to consort
with the scaly fish that swim in your waters.
You may have parted from Lord Dionysus,
but—lucky you!—you make his grapes grow.
What more could you want, when in Bacchus' place
the rain-god Zeus now nurtures your streams?
Instead of satyrs, you have armies of rivers;
you dance on the Ocean instead of the wine press.
In the watery depths you are still your old self.
It is only right, since you so loved your horns,
that you now have the bull-like form of a river."

So Maron spoke, and everyone marveled,
at the winding channels of streaming Silenus,
at the waters that ebbed and flowed in his image.

Book 20

Andrew W. Barrett

The twentieth concerns the ax of murderous Lycurgus
and Dionysus driven into the fish-rich sea.

The games wound down.
Dionysus, with lovely thyrsus in hand,
passed the evening with the satyrs
in the wealthy home of Botrys.
The wine-drenched Hours reveled
among those taking part in the feast.
After the meal, there was the sound of drums
and the limpid echo of the syrinx.
During the tireless celebration,
servers were pouring wine into goblets
as the diners kept asking for more.

A Baccant leapt into the air
and whirled her cymbals.
The girl loved the dance
and her flowing hair
shimmered in the breeze.

The god of the vine
called the wife of Staphylos,
scraped away the mud

that covered her,
and draped her in a peplos,
the color of wine.

Then he discarded
the mourning robes,
smeared with ash,
of wide-chinned Pithos
and wiped away the dirt
from every inch of his body,
before dressing him once again
in a white chiton.

Botrys' cheeks were no longer damp
with self-flowing tears
and he groaned no more in sorrow.
He opened his fragrant coffers
for Dionysus and glints of light
shot from ornate robes studded with gems.
He selected and donned
the resplendent royal garments
of his father, Staphylos
dyed with the sea's rich purple,
and sat with Dionysus
to take part in the festivities.

As they sat in pleasure,
the evening star rose
and pushed aside
the light of the day
with its joyous dance.

One after the other,
the phalanx of revelers
received the gift sleep
on comfortable beds in the hall.
Pithos, burping fragrant drops

from the sweet wine vat,
took the same bed as Maron.
They exhaled the same breath
and kept one another drunk
the whole night.
Eupetalê, nurse of Dionysus,
kindled a torch and fixed two beds
covered in sea-purple
for Botrys and Dionysus.

In a nearby room,
away from the satyrs
and Dionysus,
The handmaids prepared
a golden bed for the queen.

A dream came to Bacchus:
Eris, nurse of war,
took the form of Rhea,
Goddess who loves the rattle,
and sat in a replica of her lion chariot.
A dream image that panicked Fear
drove in the deceptive form of Attis,
a smooth-skinned man,
in the form of Cybele's driver,
with similar limbs,
who emitted piercing sounds
with a woman's voice.

Frenzied Eris stood at the head
of sleeping Bacchus,
her voice indignant and full of strife:

"Divine Dionysus,
while you sleep,
Deriades calls you to war.
But still you revel here.

Your stepmother, Hera mocks you
When she sees your cowardly Enyo
as you coax your army into the dance.
I am ashamed to appear before Zeus,
I fear Hera and the immortals,
since your deeds are not worthy of Rhea.
I run from Ares, killer of Titans,
a champion of his father,
who lifts his haughty neck,
as he holds his shield,
forever slathered with gore.

"I am even more afraid of your sister,
Pallas Athena with her flashing helmet.
Because she, a self-nurtured child,
without a mother and born
from her royal father's brow,
is a woman who reproaches
lazy Bacchus—a man.
The thyrsus surrendered to the aegis
when heroic Pallas Athena
brandished the aegis,
defended the gates of Olympus,
and scattered the Enyo of the Titans.

"She honored the wise throbbing
of her father's head
but you disfigure the fertile divot
of your father's thigh.

"How Hermes and Apollo laugh—
one lifts two spears,
still smeared with the blood
of the towering sons of Iphimedeia,
while the other holds the staff
that killed the shepherd
of infinite eyes.

"I flee my bright air
to escape being blamed
for cowardly Dionysus.

"The Virgin of the Bow
disparages dancing Dionysus,
lover of mountains,
when she sees him
shunning the liquid thyrsus.
She steers a chariot
of worthless deer,
she kills only swift hares,
she, who walks the mountains
with Rhea of the mountains,
denounces the driver of leopards,
and the leader of lions.

"I disown the home of my son, Zeus.
I fear Leto, still proud, on Olympus.
She shows me the arrow
that defended her bed
and killed the lustful giant, Tityus.

"I suffer twice the pain
when I see Semele grieving
and Maia splendid among the stars.

"You don't seem like a child of Zeus.
You didn't use an arrow
to kill boastful Otos
and towering Ephialtes.
You didn't launch
a swift shaft to fell Tityus,
nor bold, lovesick Orion,
nor Hera's guard,
Argus, the cowherd,
son of the earth,

which always sprouts evil,
who spied on Zeus
as he lay in coitus with cattle.

“Instead, you weave a feast
with Staphylos and Botrys,
inglorious, drunk, singing
without a sword in hand.
You defile the chthonic satyrs,
who also join you
in the bloodless Bacchic dance.
In their cups, the hope
of Ares is drowned.
There may be feasting
after the battle-cry,
and dancing in Staphylos’ halls
after the Indian war.
After victory on the battle-field
let the pan-pipes fill ears once more.
Without toil, you can’t dwell
in the remote aether.
The way of the blessed is not easy.
Virtue, through fixed Olympian decree,
is the only path to the center.
You also suffer every difficulty.
Hera, even though she begrudges you,
still foretells for you the court of Zeus.”

So she spoke, and then flew away.
The god sprang from bed,
the chilling roar of the hostile dream
still pounding in his ears.

Courageous Botrys also awoke,
donned his chiton
of gleaming Sidonian purple,
and slipped snug-fitting

golden sandals over his feet.
He draped a lustrous purple cloak
over his strong shoulders
and fastened it with a brooch.
He cinched around his waist
the exultant belt of his father
and took a scepter.

The satyrs yoked panthers
to a red chariot
at the urgent call of Dionysus.
Sileni gave the cry to war,
and the Bacchae roared,
as they brandished the thyrsus.
The army formed into rows
and marched into the fray
of the Indian war.

The aulos of Enyo sounded
As the general ordered their phalanxes.
One mounted the back of a bear,
with an elegant leap,
and guided it by its mane
as the animal rushed forward.

Another rode a wild bull,
and pinched its flanks
with his dangling feet,
goading the animal's course
by jabbing its shaggy belly with a staff.

Another rode a hairy lion,
grasping its mane instead of a bridle.

Purple Botrys departed
from his father's estate,
and drove his four-horse chariot

alongside Dionysus,
lover of the clustering grape,
while the slaves followed behind.
His mother, Methê, sat
in a mule-cart with silver wheels,
alongside young Phasyleia,
who was dressed in white
and drove the team of mules
with a golden whip.

Pithos, with his wide head, followed
as a servant to Botrys and Dionysus.
He was not uncompensated.
Lord Bacchus took him to Lydia
and set him before a full winepress
to receive in wine jars
the rich harvest of fruit.
And so, the name pithos was given
to the purple hollow of the wine vat,
which stands near the winepress,
to receive the gift of Bacchus,
as a token of venerated Pithos.

If it spoke with a human voice,
it would belch forth
words like these to the satyrs
whenever it heard reveling:

"I am a pithos,
bearing the name
of venerated Pithos of old,
By the wine-press I receive
the sweet trickle
of the cultivated vine.
I was the servant of
Assyrian Staphylos and Botrys.
I was the old nurse,

who reared them
when they were young.
I carry them in my depths
As if they were still living."

But it would be long time
before lord Bacchus brought this to pass.
Now he marched through Tyre and Byblos,
the well-mingled waters
of the fragrant river of Adonis,
Frankincense-trees growing among rocks,
and Cyprian grottos.
He came to Arabia
and under sweet-smelling trees
He marveled at Nysa's rich, green hills
and its lofty city,
a nurse of men, who carry spears.

Lycurgus lived there,
a bloody thirsty man
descended from Ares.
He held the same terrifying
customs as his father.

Raving, unlawful Lycurgus
dragged innocent strangers to their death.
He decapitated men with iron
and crowned his gate with their heads.
He was like Oenomaus and the same age,
Oenomaus, who once locked
his aging, single daughter in his house.
She was ignorant
of married love's pleasures
until Pelops came,
to hold a race to win the bride,
scoring the sea's chariot-path
in the dry four-horse chariot of Poseidon.

That's when cunning Myrtilus
pulled off a deceptive victory
by sliding the wheel over
a fake axle made of wax,
since he was in love
with sad Hippodameia and pitied her.

Nothing came of the race.
Under the fiery chariot of the Sun,
the replica made of wax softened,
the short-lived axle melted
and the wheel shot forth.

Lycurgus was the same kind of man.

At the crossroads,
he often met wanders
with heavy loads,
and had them bound
and dragged to his house
before sacrificing them
to his father, Ares.

They were chopped apart with knives
and their limbs festooned his hostile gates.
Just as a man who has finally returned
from war with his spear still in hand
will mount shields or helmets as trophies,
so too blood-spattered Lycurgus
Strung up the feet and hands
of murdered men upon his gate.

It was complete slaughter.

Moaning strangers were butchered
just like oxen and sheep

before the altar of Zeus,
friend of strangers.

The altars were wet with blood
and red drops speckled
the dust around his door.
The citizens were overpowered,
so they quickly sacrificed
to Lycurgus instead of Zeus.

You did not escape, Dionysus,
the resentment of devious Hera.
Your divinity still had her fuming,
so she sent Iris, her envoy,
on a dubious mission to enchant you,
with a mix of cunning and guile,
and gave her a wicked ox-goad
to gift Lycurgus, son of Dryas,
and ruler of Arabia.

The goddess didn't hesitate.
Trading faces,
she took on the false form of Ares.
She shed her intricately
embroidered saffron robes,
donned a helmet
with a drooping plume,
put on deceptive armor
smeared with blood,
and as the mother
of war's confusion,
her bearded, masculine face
cast hostile, cunning looks.
Then with flowing words,
she mimicked Ares' voice:

"My son,
seed of undefeated Ares,
do you also fear Bassarids
and their dainty threats?
These are not Amazons
from Thermodon,
nor warrior women
from the Caucasus.

"They don't have swift arrows
and they don't launch spears.
They don't have a fierce warhorse,
and they don't carry on their shoulders
the barbarian oxhide crescent shield.
I'm ashamed to call you to the fray
when women call for a war
against unconquerable
Lycurgus.

"Lycurgus,
are you resting as Dionysus arms?
He is mortal, a man miscarried,
and not a sprout of starry seeds.
The myth that he is the son of Zeus
is an invention of the Greeks.
I can't see my way to believing
in Zeus' childbearing abilities.
How could my father
Zeus who rules from above,
birth a female son from his male thigh.
I don't believe in false stories,
myths that say my Zeus,
who shot forth Athena,
gave birth to a mortal man.
My Zeus didn't learn to birth a weak child.

"Take as a witness, your father, Ares.
You know that Athena, daughter of Zeus,
is stronger than Dionysus.

"My son,
you have your own strength,
You don't need your father,
even though he is lord of war.
But if you want, I will arm you
and I will not abandon you in battle.
If you need, you will have a goddess,
Hera, sister and wife of Zeus
She will protect her grandson
From the chaos with a shield."

Ares spoke in this way
and Lycurgus replied with threats for Dionysus:

"In your holy temple
I will plant the thyrsi,
The false spears of the Bacchae.
I will rip those untouched horns
from the heads of the Centaurs
and fashion from them sturdy bows
for Arab archers—as Justice decrees.
I will chop off the sileni's winding tails
and make shaggy whips for flogging horses.

"I will bring these to you after the battle.
But peaceful Bacchus' yellow shoes,
his feminine purple dress,
and the delicate gridle
that pinches his balls,
these I will set aside
for your sister-lover, Aphrodite.
Pleasing gifts for a woman.

"I will bind my slaves
in forced marriage to each row
of girl-crazy Dionysus' followers
and not seek a dowry, proper custom
for those taken by the spear.

"The Arabian fire and its popping sparks
will receive the tender shoots of the vine
and the gentle gifts of Dionysus.

"Let the strong Bassarid,
servant to Dionysus
of the braided dance,
take on an unfamiliar craft,
and trade the hills for a house,
swap the mottled fawnskin
for a cloak that conceals,
and grind corn with a millstone.
Let her cast aside her crowns
and the seasonal fruit, as it is known.
as a compelled slave
of Athena and Aphrodite,
let her learn to combine
two everyday concerns,
with a basket during the day
and a bed at night,
working the loom
instead of Rhea's cymbals.
Let the aged sileni sing 'Euoi!'
at my table groaning with food.
Let them celebrate Ares and Lycurgus
Instead of the familiar Dionysus."

He spoke and the goddess Iris smiled,
her wings a golden shimmer,
as she cut the path of a false hawk.

Lycurgus understood this
to be an omen of victory.
He knew the fast bird,
its beating wings flecked with blood,
could frighten impotent doves.
He knew, because he had a similar dream:
in the forest, a shaggy lion, mid roar,
chased a horned family of swift deer.
He was mindful of this dream
as he prepared for the ecstatic Bacchants,
thinking the Bassarids to be like fawns
that know nothing of war.

So, he felt even more confident.
At Hera's command,
Iris slipped on winged sandals,
took a staff like that of Hermes,
herald of Zeus, and rushed,
as a harbinger, to meet Dionysus.
Wearing a cloak of bronze,
she wove deceitful words
for Bacchus in an urgent voice:

"Brother,
child of Zeus who knows all,
set aside war and celebrate your rites
with Lycurgus, lover of strangers.
Forget the tumult of war,
don't slay friends,
don't run from peace,
be gracious to those are mild.

"Who will conquer a kind man?
Do not summon war
against those who want your mercy,
do not conceal your body
in armor that shines like stars,

do not slip your head
into a high-crested helmet,
do not braid your hair
with a garland of snakes,
drop your bloody thyrsi,
take up your usual staff and a horn
filled to the brim with sweet wine,
and extend Bacchic gifts
to grape-loving Lycurgus.

"Put on a tunic
not stained with blood,
weave a melody
for a peaceful dance,
keep your forces quiet
among the shady trees,
so they don't bring war
to a peaceful king.
Slip your beloved crown
over your hair,
Rejoice as you approach
the open home
of welcoming Lycurgus.
Like a groom,
set forth in a happy mood.

"Save your Indian-killing thyrsi
for disobedient Deriades.
You know Lord Lycurgus
isn't weak in spirit.
He is the son of Ares
and has the blood of Zeus.
During battle,
he displays the innate strength
of his father, Ares
and wouldn't dodge
a fight with your Zeus."

In this way,
he was beguiled by Iris,
who vanished
into the bright air
on her sandals.

Tricked by the goddess,
Dionysus cast aside
his hostile thyrsus,
shook loose his hair
from his plumed helmet
and set aside his glittering shield.
He held, in one bare hand,
a vessel full of red wine,
a sharp horn of the grief-melting grape.
He threaded his unbraided hair
with leaves from the vine and ivy.
By mount Carmel, he left his army
and war-stirring women,
with his lion-drawn chariots.
Unarmed and wearing a delicate robe,
he approached the celebration.
The syrinx piped
a sweet melody for the banquet,
the double-aulos sounded
a welcoming tune,
and the Bassarid shook the Bacchic
tambourines of Dionysus
as he pranced before the gates of Lycurgus.

The fierce lord was enraged
when he heard
the hubbub of the dance,
the melody of the aulos,
the Phrygian echoes,
the breath of the syrinx,
and saw the circular tambourine,
which is struck on both sides.

When he saw the vine god on his porch,
He let out a sardonic laugh
and hurled mocking, pitiless threats
at the charioteer of the Bacchae:

"Do you see the offerings
hung before my palace?
You too, friend, can adorn
my home with your thyrsus,
feet, hands, or bloodied head.
Horned Bacchus,
if you command horny satyrs,
I will thrash all of you like cattle.
with my goad.

"This is my hospitality gift for you:
that gods and mortals may speak
of how Lycurgus' gates were wreathed
with butchered limbs of Dionysus.

"I don't rule the Boeotians,
this is not Thebes,
This is not the home of Semele,
where women birth bastard children
through lightning
or go into labor
because of thunder.
You shake a thyrsus
wrapped in the vine,
I brandish an ox-goad
and will shatter your horns,
before cracking
your cow-face in two."

He spoke and then struck
the nurses of Dionysus
with his goad as he chased them.

Among the women of the dance,
one shook loose Rhea's cymbals
from her palms,
one dropped the drum
from her supple hands,
one flung down a cluster of grapes,
and another tumbled with cups of nectar.
Many cast aside the sweet syrinx
and Athena's breathing reeds
before tripping over each other
in the dust.

Just as when a herdsman
rouses a celebration
near a calm thicket after a storm,
when he sees the joyful hour
of clear Phaëthon
and the nymphs join the dance.

Suddenly, water comes
rolling from the rocks,
and the waves mount
as the river falls
from the mountains.

The herdsman drops his syrinx,
afraid that the ferocious currents
will sweep away the sheep.

So too Lycurgus scattered
the joyful dancers
and drove the Bacchae
into the steep mountains,
their garlands having fallen
from their heads.
Lycurgus clad in bronze,
routed the scattered band of women,

carrying his pointed ox-goad,
an heirloom from Hera,
and warred against
the unequipped Bacchus.

Unbeatable Hera,
the cruel stepmother
unleashed a peal of thunder
that made Dionysus tremble,
as she bore down upon him.

While the goddess prepared,
deep in her jealousy and anger,
the knees of Bacchus shook.

He assumed Zeus
was on Lycurgus' side
when he heard the claps of thunder
echoing through the luminous sky.

He was a traveler
not to be caught
as he ran upon fearful heels
before diving beneath
the Erythraean sea's
shimmering waves.

In the deep, Thetis gathered him
in a warm embrace
and Arabian Nereus
welcomed him with open arms
and soothing, sweet words
as he entered the resonant hall:

"Tell me, Dionysus,
Why so down in the mouth?
You haven't been defeated

by an army of earth-reared Arabs,
a mortal doesn't chase you,
you aren't running away
From a mortal spear.

"But Hera, wife and sister
of Zeus, son of Cronus,
has armed herself up in the sky
and is allied with Lycurgus.
Hera, firm Ares, and the sky of bronze.
Lycurgus, so strong, was the fourth.

"Often your father,
who rules from above,
foremost in the heavens,
has had to yield to Hera.
There will be even more boasts
and offerings for you
when one of the Blessed says
Hera, wife and sister of great Zeus,
raised her hands against
a sober, unarmed Dionysus."

Nereus tried
to calm Dionysus
with such words.
As Dionysus hid
beneath the flashing waves,
Lycurgus, enraged,
screamed at the water:

"I wish my father taught me
the ways of the sea instead of war,
then I would take to fishing,
catch Dionysus,
drag him again to land
from the deep folds of the sea

and make him my servant.
But since I haven't learned the work
of fisherman upon the sea
and don't know the trick
of hunting in the depths
with cleverly woven nets,
You can have
the White Goddess's home,
beneath the waves,
until I remove you
and one of your relatives,
Melicertes, as he's known,
from the sea.

"I have no need for steel
Or an earthbound,
merciless ox-goad.
But I need fishermen to dive deep
in Erythraean brine
and pull Dionysus
From his hidden corner of the sea.

"Fishermen,
hunters Nereus' caves,
don't cast your nets
for creatures of the deep,
but haul up Dionysus in those nets.
Let the White Goddess be caught
with Dionysus and return to land.

"Let courageous Palaemon
come with them to my home
and be my slave with dry limbs,
Abandoning his sea-bred horses
and their Corinthian track,
so he can yoke my chariot
next to a manger upon the earth.

This man will follow Bacchus.
Let there be one house
for both Palaemon and Dionysus."

He furiously provoked
the sea and grey Nereus,
And wished to flog the waters.

But father Zeus shouted
at Lycurgus as he raged.

"Lycurgus,
you are out of your mind.
You confront the winds in vain.
Turn upon your heels
while your eyes still see.
You heard how recently
Tiresias saw Athena naked
by a spring in the mountains?
He didn't lift a wrathful spear,
or make war on the goddess
and still he lost the light
from his eyes."

Zeus, who rules from above,
fired through the air
such words of warning
when he saw the insolent impiety
of Lycurgus.

Book 21

Zachary Puckett

The twenty-first has the Earthshaker's wrath,
Ambrosia's broil, and the Indian ambush.

Yet Dryas' son embraces his lust for battle.
Grabbing his ox-goad, he again rushes into the forest
to pursue the Bassarids. But Zeus from his heavenly realm
gives Ambrosia the strength and courage of a warrior.
Now possessed by Bacchic zeal and swelling with fury,
she picks up a boulder and hurls it at Lycurgus,
striking the sturdy helmet from his head.
He echoes her attack with a larger jagged rock
and aims at the cow-eyed nymph's breast,
but she does not fall, and he raises a bitter shout:

"Ares, master of war and father of mighty Lycurgus,
how can you look upon your son and not be ashamed
as he fights some unarmed woman instead of Lyaeus?
The sea hides Dionysus beneath its waves,
and resists my attack. Have I come here in vain?
Am I supposed to return home empty-handed?"

Having spoken, he throws his firm arms around
Ambrosia's waist. He yearns to carry her off in chains
and drag her from Bromius' company of nursemaids

to his house as a prisoner of war. He prods her back
with his double-edged axe, but she stands firm.
He cannot pull her away, nor crush her head
and dye himself crimson with her blood.
No, saffron-veiled Ambrosia slips from his grasp
and prays to mother Gaea to save her from Lycurgus.
Gaea opens her fruitful bosom and rescues
her dear Ambrosia, Bromius' attendant.
The nymph vanishes. A vine replaces her body,
winding around Lycurgus' neck like a noose.
She now fights not with a thyrsus but with menacing clusters.

Fierce Rhea endows the plant with speech for the nymph,
obliging Dionysus, lord of the cultivated vine,
and enabling Ambrosia to cry out with a living voice:

"Even if I am a plant, I will never flee you in battle.
I will wound your body with shoots. I will coil around you
ceaselessly with leaves, rather than brazen chains,
and I will cling to you as a vine, so that people will say,
'The Bassarids slay killers, even with leaves.'
You should beware the warrior plants;
for vines shoot at enemies and wound with their fruit.
I fought you in life, and I will overcome you in death;
such is the greatness of Dionysus' attendants.
You have heard of the remora, the small fish
that often harasses sailors on the sea,
restrains their cargo ships, and drags them backwards
by the force of their tiny mouths. Behold!
I am your dry land remora. Behold the lithe chain
binding itself to you in battle with grapes and leaves.
Stay here with me. Don't move until the son of Thyonê,
chooses to return from the sea's embrace."

Ambrosia issued these words in her succulent voice
and smothered Lycurgus with leaf and vine.
Yet the savage man, restrained by verdant chains

and relentless leaves, roars defiance at Dionysus,
but lacks the strength to flee; he writhes helplessly
as thin tendrils twist around his neck and chin.
His voice languishes in his constricted throat.
The Bacchae gather around him entwined by the clusters.

But lance-wielding Ares seizes his son's terrible axe,
for he fears that one of Bromius' Bacchants, in a frenzy,
might assault Lycurgus with his own deadly weapon.
Yet he does not free Dryas' son from his bonds,
for he hears the warning of Zeus, rumbling in the distance,
and reluctantly withdraws from his father's lightning.

Polyxo launches herself at the man's head
and tears out his long hair by the roots;
her hands claw at his stomach, seize hold
of his breastplate, and rend it in their rage.
Muses of battle, is it true? Could a woman
truly mangle steel armor with her bare hands!
Cleitê, hair unbound, braids a twisting rope
from long switches. Gigarto, rich with vines,
bruises the body of Lycurgus with a leafy whip,
marking his swollen back with bloody welts.
Crazed Phleio carves into the sole of his foot with long
thorns. Eriphe, a companion of Eiraphiotes
wraps her hands around the man's hairy neck
yearning to fling him onto the ground. Phasyleia,
the leader of the Bacchic chorus, joins the assault
and scores the sides of her enemy with a sharp point.
Theopê, nursemaid to Lyaeus, equips herself
with hide-piercing fennel, and strikes Lycurgus' body.
Bromië, named after Bromius, joins the fray,
and Cisseis, a grape-loving nymph, whips the man with ivy.

But, while Lycurgus is overpowered by belligerent flora,
an even worse calamity appears; for alpine Rhea
has summoned the Earthshaker to arms against Arabia.

Earthshaker, lord of the sea, whose trident splits foundations
and hurls them about with resounding force, has removed the bolt
that locks the winds deep in their hollows.
They carve out vast chasms with their echoing toil
and shake the lands with their buried, scattered gusts.
The trident shakes Arabia's immovable bedrock,
the quaking land topples lofty halls
and the Arabs sway upon Nysa's foundation.
Trees collapse, an elm lies upon the earth,
a laurel now bathes in dust, a pine lies upon a nearby fir.

As the Earthshaker rattles the winds' caverns,
yet another disaster: dragon-haired Megaera
thrashes the women of Nysa who dwell in the forest.
They bellow like cattle at the cracks of her whip,
and begin to murder their children.
One flings her helpless son into the air;
he can only plummet back down to earth.
Another drags her newborn behind,
and abandons her role as mother.
Another butchers her son with frenzied iron,
staining her hands with his blood—a second Agavê.
They hunt their own children, newborns,
and slaughter them with carving knives.

And now Arab herdsmen join the rustic frenzy,
submitting to the insanity of Pan's whip.
Enthralled, they prey upon their children
and devour their sons in their madness.

Nymphs and twisting leaves encircle Lycurgus,
yet he does submit to Lyaeus, nor beg Zeus,
to end the torture. He does not fear the thunder,
but juts his chin and curses the Bassarids.
He senses the lightning rushing at his head,
but he does not yield to Lyaeus or the onslaught.

He stands firm against such assaults, and holds Ares
as his sole protector, contending alone against
Zeus, Poseidon, Rhea, Chthöon, Nereus, and Bacchus.
Still struggling, he spits out a feral shout:

"Light the fire! Burn all these Bacchic leaves in the flames!
Cast the embers into the sea for Dionysus in his underwater lair—
show him our Arabian manliness! Send the charred fruit
to Thetis herself and let her douse the ashes in her bosom.
Remove the apparitions and enchantments of these bonds!
I can spot the deceitful spells of Poseidon and Nereus.
Release me and bring me to the sea. I will equip myself
against the witchdoctor Proteus! Light the torch,
so that I can approach the sea and consume Melicertes,
Bromius' gracious host, in my vengeance!"

As he threatens both Nereus and Dionysus,
Hera descends upon Arabia to rescue
the War God's son struggling in his arboreal battle.
Unsheathing Ares' sword, now hers to use,
she flashes the divine blade to the Bacchae,
and routs the Cybelian warriors.
Severing the leaves of Ambrosia with the sword
she releases Lycurgus from clustered bonds.
She calms the dark-haired Earthshaker, her brother,
then her husband Zeus, and her mother Rhea.
She draws Lycurgus to herself, that he might be counted
among the immortals. The Arabs worship the son of Dryas
like a god, making sacrifices upon a smoking altar,
not wine, the honey-dripping work of Dionysus,
but blood, in honor of Bacchus' foe, Lycurgus.
These things, however, would come to pass later.

Zeus, to prevent others from mimicking Lycurgus
and trying to dishonor blameless Dionysus,
causes Lycurgus to wander in blind madness,
a traveler roaming around an unfamiliar city,

forced to seek a chaperon for his path, or else
stumble over his own feet along a lonely road.

While these events take place on the hills, the nereids
deep within the underwater palace in the Erythraean Sea
honor Dionysus with a maritime feast.
Even Ino, the seaborn foster mother of Dionysus,
has forgotten her jealousy of radiant Semele's bed,
and raises a heroic hymn to Lyaeus the vintner,
while his childhood friend Melicertes serves sweet nectar.

The refugee stays underwater, treating the wide sea,
the palace of the Dark-Haired One, as his home,
and he sprawls out in Thetis' nourishing lap.
He embraces Palaemon, his childhood companion,
as well as the frustrated daughter of Cadmus, Ino,
his noble nurse and sister to his dear mother.
The Mimallon, now that Bacchus is gone,
no longer twirls in dance. She is despondent,
and seeks in silence the tracks of seafaring Lyaeus.
The energetic satyr now carries a gloomy expression,
struggling with newfound sorrow. The Pans run
up and down the thicket, yearning for their wanderer,
seeking word of Dionysus, nowhere to be found.
Silenus retires from the dance and abandons his cymbals.
The Cronian nymph, Macris, exuberant Bacchus' nurse
and driver of his fine-spoked chariot now weeps.
So the downcast wander about, but Scelmis
drives his father's cart from the calm sanctuary of the sea
to declare the return of Dionysus to the grieving.
While Bacchus enjoys his sea-nurtured feast
the wind-swift herald of Bromius, god of vines,
crosses the Caucasus mountains and enters the Indian city
in the shape of bull, having assumed a visage horned
in perfect imitation of a crescent moon.
A mountain goat's hide, clasped around the neck, covers his body,
draped over his right shoulder and hanging to his thighs.

On both sides of his face longs ears hang like a donkey's.
From the small of his back his natural curly tail trails behind.

The dark Indians flood around him with laughter,
as he approaches the chariot where tall Deriades sits.
The leader of men brings his mighty elephants to a halt,
and laughing, mocks the herald with a booming voice:

"Look at the little freaks Dionysus has sent to Deriades!
You pretend to be warriors, but you aren't real men!
You are misfits, trying to be both man and beast,
but you weirdos don't belong with either species."

He speaks, and then strikes his sword against the boss
of his oxhide shield, bordered with rich colors.
The shield resounds with a menacing echo
that sets the tone for a merciless battle.

Astonished by the fearsome king, the swift herald
delivers Bromius' message from open lips:

"Deriades, scepter-holder, Dionysus commands
the Indians to take up the wine of his lighthearted yield,
offer libation to the deathless ones, and thus avoid conflict.
He is ready, if you refuse, to battle until Hydaspes
kneels to the thyrsi of the Bassarids.
You have heard the whole message; I await your reply.
What response shall I return to Dionysus?"

Hearing the message, the king bellows a fierce counter:

"Oh ho ho, what bold words the creature has spoken!
There is no honor in killing an unarmed messenger.
I have heard how much your leader suffers;
word of Bromius' weakness has arrived
and Ganges has heard of Lycurgus' courage.
I know that your king, that baseborn god, fled

and slithered into the depths of the guardian sea.
They call your Bacchus 'fiery' because he was born
from the womb of Thyonê, charred by Zeus.
Water, however, is superior to fire. If he wanted,
my father, Indian Hydaspes, with his roiling streams
could extinguish the fire of Zeus' thunderbolt.

"Turn your course into the land of the Medes
if you want to announce Dionysus' choruses.
Go down to the Bactrian land, where the god Mithras arose,
Persia's Assyrian Phaëthon. Deriades, however,
does not acknowledge the dances of your blessed gods,
nor honors Helios, Zeus, or the ranks of bright stars.
I do not care about Cronus, who devoured his own children
and castrated Uranus, the Sky himself.
Nor do I study the patricidal son of Cronus.
I do not welcome your gifts, nor the fruit you name;
I drink nothing but that of golden Hydaspes;
my spear is my wine, my drink is my shield.
I was not born from the incinerated marriage of Semele
who received a scorching bridal gift in her chamber.
Enyo, bronze-clad and hungry for war, raised me.
I do not care about the blessed children of Zeus;
there are only two gods for me: Earth and Water.

"Tell that to your cowardly Dionysus.
Run while you still can. I won't use my bow
or my spear, yet. Tell your ugly little trolls
and your worthless women to prepare for battle.
Fight Deriades, so that after victory
I can drag you and Dionysus behind me.
But I will not make you an attendant,
because you cannot handle any real work.
But you can fan me at feasts with your oversized ears."

Having said this, he sends him away after
carving a terse message into the tablet:

"Dionysus, arm yourself against Deriades, if you can."

The messenger runs straight for the joyful sileni.
Dionysus has returned from the roaring waves
and mingles with Oreads. Satyrs leap with joy,
Bacchae dance, and Maron, with aged feet,
leads the dance between two Bacchic women,
wrapping his arms around their necks while sweet wine
spouts from his mouth. The Mimallon, hair unbraided,
rattles out the melody of Dionysus' homecoming.

The vine-clad god has cast out his earlier worries,
and now sets his sights on joy, learning everything
from the sea god Proteus, Torone's husband.
He hears how the ground of the inhospitable Arabs shook,
and how blind Lycurgus stumbled over his own feet.
He learns of the lethal madness forced upon shepherds,
how women carved up their own children in the glens,
and how the entire countryside was whirling about.
He hears of the chorus of the ethereal Hyades, and that
Ambrosia has risen from the earth to Olympus,
after equipping herself against unyielding Lycurgus,
a battle of shoots, a vine-laden warfare.

The messenger returned to these celebrants,
safe and long-awaited by exalted Dionysus.
He told of the haughty arrogance of Deriades,
and delivered the tablet that threatened battle.

The bold leader wastes no time; he calls his warriors
into battle after reading the taunting words
that Deriades had scrawled onto the tablet.
He summons the Rhadamans, whom Minos forced
some time ago to roam reluctantly from the isle of Crete
into Arabian territory. He tells them to build ships
to sail with Rhea's wind into battle against the Indians.
He races his chariot to the eastern slope of their land,

shimmering with weapons as if he were Phosphorus.
He circles the Caucasian rock, crossing the crested valleys
and entering the light-bringing border of Eos' land,
traveling towards the sun at its midday peak.

When the sound of thyrsus-filled battle draws near,
and the army of Dionysus echoes in the mountains,
Deriades positions his Indians in close array for ambush,
and sends a lone army to the opposite shore, entrusting
the wily machinations of battle to bronze-armored Ares.
He rows his men across Indian Hydaspes, dividing
the battle cry of Indians between the two armies
stationed on either side of the river, thick with spears.
Thureus stands on the bank that faces Zephyr,
Deriades on the opposite, facing the wings of fiery Eurus.

There is a shady area there, where a forest ranges
wide with dense shoots of all sorts around the ridge.
In that spot there is a grotto, where a wandering arrow
cannot elude the trees in its flight, nor can
the raging sun, bearing down in blazing waves,
slice through the interlaced leaves and brush with its rays,
nor do torrents of rain, sent down from the heavens, plunge
into the bushy woodland and wet the tops of the petals
with rivulets of rainwater from high-shining Zeus.

There in a tall, leafy grove a secret army is hidden,
a confident ambush under the canopy.
The stealthy tread of boots is silent there.
No hidden feet tear through the leafy thicket,
no one fears a faltering step, nor any sound
from murmuring lips, nor pallor on any face.
Each soldier rests his eyes with a confident spirit,
and takes measured sleep on the ground, armed and awaiting
the rhythmic march of the approaching enemy.

Book 22

Richard Jenkyns

Book 22 proclaims the deeds
That Dionysus wrought,
And how the valiant Aeacus
By land and river fought.

Now Bacchus' army on its march had reached
Hydaspes' waters, flowing on pebbly bed.
Their crossing place was where the Indian river
Plunges like Nile its navigable stream
Into the swirling vortex of a hollow.
They heard the song of women—Bassarids,
Sounding their Phrygian revel for Lyaeus
The god-in-darkness, while the hairy satyrs
Danced, and their mysterious cries rang out.
The whole earth laughed, the rocks roared in response,
The naiads wailed with joy, the dancing nymphs
Spiraled above the river's silent stream.
The song they sang was in Sicilian style,
Such as the anthems that the sirens pour
From honeyed throat; the woodland thrilled with it,
The oaks learnt music, resonant as pipes,
The dryads ululated, and a nymph
Peeped from the foliage and joined in the song,
Half seen, half hidden in her wreath of leaves.

The springs, once merely water, now with milk
Grew white as snow, and in the deep ravine
The naiads sported in the frothy streams
And drank the whiteness, while from reddening teat
The rugged rock-face purpled and gushed wine,
Pouring its ferment in ambrosial flow
Over the treeless slopes; the honeybees—
No need of hives—from tunnels made by nature
Dribbled their sugared tribute; downy fruit
Burgeoned on thorny bushes, newly born,
While Pallas' tree, the olive, from its branches
Oozed drops spontaneously, and bathed itself
In oil unpressed by any hand of man.

Hares embraced hounds and joined them in the dance,
Serpents performed a wriggling bacchanal,
Writhing their necks and lowering them to lick
The prints of Dionysus, snake-haired god.
In mutual interchange they issued forth
A gentle hissing from their happy throats.
Wisdom was in the rhythm of their joy;
Fearless of foot and circling the god they tossed
Their spiny backs and interlacing coils.
And tigers playfully bounced round and round
Over the Indian crags, while a great herd
Of mountain-dwelling elephants appeared
And skipped and bounded through the wooded glens.
Next roaming the rocky gorges came the Pans,
Their twinkling hooves speeding on craggy hills
Where foot can hardly tread—a land of shudder,
Where even that light traveler the bird
Might fear to come, which even the lofty eagle
Might shrink from crossing on his beating wings.
A lion shook the mane around his neck,
And danced a polka with the light-foot boar.
Birds squawked in mimicry of human speech,
Aping, imperfectly, the war cry's sound,

And auguring victory in the Indian fight,
Stretching their bright green bodies out and shaking
The feathers of their tails. With equal zeal
The panther leapt and pranced and flew up high,
Taking a bear for partner in the rout.
Artemis held her headlong hounds in check;
She saw the lioness turned mild, in rhythm
Jumping and beating the ground; suffused with shame
She let her bowstring slacken, loath to shoot
Her arrows at the happy animals.

A man was spying on these miracles,
Glancing from high in the thick canopy.
He had parted the leaves so that he could make out
As much as can a warrior peering through
The eyeholes in his helmet, or as when an actor,
Practiced in playing on the tragic stage,
Bawling his words and throwing his voice afar,
Strains to look through the openings in the mask
That falsely bears the likeness of a man.
So the spy hidden in the dusky wood
Watched all these wonders with a furtive glance.
He told the foemen; Thureus trembled,
Blaming both Morrheus and Deriades
For their imprudence, while the Indians
Shook in fear, forgetful of the battle's roar,
And cast the weapons from their frightened hands.
Seeing the wood vibrate with Bacchic force.

Now would the Indian army from the bank
Nearby have plucked the green-grey olive branch,
Token of supplication, and have bowed
Their heads to the all-conquering god,
But Hera, wise in wiles, disguised her form
And cheered the enemy, tricking the Indian lord.
She charged that Bacchus had used magic spells,
Such hymns as the Thessalian women chant

When they invoke the gods, and potions too
Which the enchantress Circe had contrived,
As though he had poisoned that unpoisoned river.
The men were credulous; she warned each one
Against a trap, lest parched with thirst they drank
The waters that would steal their minds away.

Now would the Indians have leapt out
From where they lay in ambush, and have slain
The army as they ate, had not a dryad
Sprung from a bushy hollow; in her hand
She bore a thyrsus, like a bacchanal,
With ivy tangled thick within her hair.
First she exposed the ruse by silent signs,
Then whispered softly in the vine-god's ear:

"Great Dionysus, lord of the clustered grape,
Gardener, master of the swelling fruit,
Your crop lends grace and beauty to the Dryads.
No Bassarid am I, no reveler with Lyaeus;
I seem to lift a thyrsus in my hand,
But it is false; your home in Phrygia
Is not my homeland, neither do I dwell
In Lydia, where the river rolls through wealth.
I am a hamadryad, lovely in leaves,
Here where the enemy soldiers lie in wait.
Forgetting my own country, I will save
Your warriors from death; I will be true
To you and the satyrs; Indian though I am,
I side with Bacchus, not Deriades.
To you I give the favor that I owe,
Because great Zeus your father, lord of rain,
Unfailingly bestows on us his showers,
The pregnant pang, which nourishes the oaks.
Give me your leafage, I will plant it here;
Give me those clusters which dissolve our cares.
But friend, no rashness: do not cross the stream

For fear the Indians crush you in the waters.
Look at the trees; spy in the thickets there
A band of men who watch in ambuscade.
Yet what can these lurking weaklings do to you?
They live no longer than you check your thyrsus.
Now silence, lest the enemy at hand
Hear, or Hydaspes tell his countrymen."

The hamadryad disappeared again,
Swift as the wings of thought, and shifting shape,
She shot in bird form through the tulgey wood,
And flung into the oak that had grown with her,
While Bacchus went among his Bassarids
In silence; yet he dropped into the ear
Of his commanders what the nymph had told,
Nodding and glancing; with unspeaking signs
He got his troops to feed among the trees
Wearing full armor, and explained the wiles
That those wile-weaving Indians had devised:
They must not let their eastern enemy
Fall on them as they fed with armor off.
The men obeyed, and ready for the fray
Consumed the meal in silence, spears on tables.

After this hasty dinner they sped off,
Bearing their shields, and sought the nearby stream,
To sip and let the victuals settle down,
At Dionysus' sapient command,
Lest drink and dark and drowsiness should lay
The army down to sleep; and so the men
Slumped here and there upon the soldier's bed,
Snatching a little slumber on their shields.
And father Zeus stymied the Indians' trick,
Foiling an evening fight with claps of thunder
And all night raining with unending noise.

But when the dawn came on her snowy feet
And split the darkness, gathering morning's light,
Purpling the surface of the soaking rocks,
The enemy, who had sheltered in the wood,
Rousing their courage there, crept to its edge,
Then charged in a mass; Thureus was in command,
Prodigious champion in this Indian war,
Like in his onrush to the giant Typhon,
That Typhon who assailed the thunderbolt.
By cunning Dionysus' guileful plan,
His men pretended fright, though unafraid,
Retreating from the tumult uncompelled,
Until the Indian army left the woods,
Their hiding place, and spilled across the plain.

A Lydian man was clad in costly arms,
Recalling Lycian Glaucus' golden glitter.
This sight proclaimed the nature of his land,
Where the Pactolus glints and sparkles red,
A flow that gleams between the fertile banks.
Facing the dawn he flashed rose-colored light.
Tossing his precious helmet's tawny front.
The Lydian stood conspicuous; on his chest
The ruddy radiance of his corselet shone.
Another of the champions of the god
Had come from Alybe; he too displayed
His country's wealth; the casque upon his head
Was silver, glimmering with the sheen of marble,
Or as the snow-like shimmer of the moon.

Ceaseless in action, Bacchus terrified
The foe; he bared no sword, he shook no spear,
But flew like wind among the foremost ranks,
Wheeling from left to right wing of the battle
He slew the cloud of Indians with his thyrsus,
Long-shadowed like a lance, and cut them down
With wild flowers and ivy rod for spear,

Thureus, though tall and strong, had not the power
To check him, nor any chieftain, nor the army,
But tumbling upon each other they gave way
Here, here, and here to the onrush of the god.

Oeagrus too struck hard the dark host,
Mowing down men in swathes, insatiable,
Reaping the warriors in their glinting helmets,
A golden harvest. As when a storm-filled river
Pours from the cliffs its torrent through the gullies
And floods the plain; nor can the sturdy walls
Around the yards and orchards stem its rush—
Stone bridges' backs are broken by its force,
Many pines go rolling down the hills,
Many tall firs are ripped up by the roots,
And carried headlong by the current's power—
So he drove on and on against the foe
A ceaseless slaughter with Sithonian lance.
Now they wove round him, building with their shields
The tight formation soldiers call a tortoise.
They planted spear by spear; shield linked to shield
Close packed, crest nodded to crest, each soldier
Pressed on his neighbor soldier; horses' hooves
Stirred up the dust and turned the warriors white.

Who was the first Oeagrus of Bistonia
Dispatched and sent to Hades, who the last?
He slew them one by one, feats needing the Muse
Calliope, his wife, to tell the tale.
His swift spear pierced a man above the nipple,
His sword another in the neck; he stabbed
Another raging warrior through the navel
And drew his weapon from the bleeding wound,
The hot guts spilling round the crimsoned steel.
He ran his blade towards another warrior
And slashed his wrist; his hand fell to the ground,
Writhing, convulsing, weltering in blood.

Another's severed hand still gripped his shield,
The fist tight round the dusty strap; his soul
Flew lightly on the wind away, lamenting
The strong young form to which it had been knit.
Oeagrus' ruthless spear then crushed another,
The keen point slicing through the shoulder's top;
His sword then struck the middle of the shield;
The metal clanged, and yet the oxhide held.

The lust of battle stung him into madness:
With practiced hand he spun and whirled his spear
This way and that, by shoulder, neck and flank,
Shaking the lance that darted back and forth,
Till he smashed through the enemy's close packed lines,
Set high upon his horse with tossing mane.
As when chill winter's gloomy season passes,
And sky sloughs off its covering of clouds,
Bright with the clear and radiant light of spring,
So did the hero clear the serried ranks,
Breaking the center, wild with battle's joy,
Uncovering open space where men had stood.

One at the front aimed at a foeman's face,
Slashing the right cheek with remorseless blade.
One hurled a missile high towards the sky;
The whizzing stone flew curving through the air,
Crashing into an adversary's head,
Knocking away his helmet's horsehair crest,
And snapping the strap that went beneath his chin;
Off rolled the helmet, leaving the man's head bare.
It was not men alone who roared; the horses,
Themselves bronze clad, snorted the noise of Strife
Trumpeting War with martial whinnying.
The maiden Echo in the rocky hills
Mimicked the warlike whinnying below,
Her stony voice responsive to the din.

Many a new-killed corpse sprawled on the field
Spitting hot streams of blood; among the dying
Some lay upon their sides and perished so,
One with slit belly rolled upon his wound,
One wriggled in the dust strewn on the ground.
Another had been skewered through the navel,
Another trod the head of one who lay
Convulsing on the earth, another fell
Pierced through the throat, and as he fell he screamed
And kicked his feet up in a dance of doom.
Another lay face down and with mad teeth,
Raging against his slayer, gnawed the soil.
Another's tunic turned from white to crimson,
As the iron head drove deep into his flesh
And the blood spurted like a javelin's flight.
The bows were drawn against another man:
An arrow found his thigh, and dyed it red.

One of the Indians picked his trumpet up
And set it to his lips, sounding the fanfare
To summon the attack, and drag to battle
His cowering craven comrades. They in turn
Answered his call and rushed into the ruck,
Emboldened, clashing once more in the fray,
Shamed that their king should see them unvictorious.

Well-armored men drove Aeacus from his ground
To where they could surround him in a ring,
Encircled and confined; no doughty helmet,
Shield or cuirass availed him in this plight;
But Pallas walled him round, in place of steel,
With her own sire's impenetrable clouds,
Those clouds that quench the thirst of parching fields,
Giving to earth the water that bears life,
When Zeus sends rain—the furrows wed the plow,
The earth grows pregnant and brings forth the sheaves.
The man stood in the midst, full of the god;

His foe stood round; some of them he dispatched
With rapid-thrusting spear, some with scimitar,
Others with jagged stones; the soil grew red with gore
Of Indians killed; the tireless victor's metal
Scattered the field with bodies far and wide.
One man, half dead, was gasping, while another
Thumped with his feet upon the ground, then fell
Down on his back; doom was his comrade now.
Corpse pressed on corpse, tight packed, upon the earth,
Lying as if in rows, their coldness warmed
And reddened by the gush of throats new cut.
And as the ghastly carnage grew and grew,
Earth, dark with streams of blood, and pitying
Her sons, cried with a rocky torrent's voice:

"Offspring of Zeus, bounteous and murderous,
Lord of the fruitful rain and lord alike
Of blood in deluge, all over Greece your showers
Have stirred the fertile tilth, yet across India's fields
You drown the furrows in a flood of gore.
Carrier of sheaves before, now carrier of death,
Whose waters gave the farmers ears of grain,
You reap the Indian army like a crop
Of standing corn; you bring a double gift,
The Sky-God's showers and the War-God's blood."

So spoke the Earth, the source of life, but Zeus
Sounded from the skies: the trumpet of the Lord
And peals of thunder summoned Aeacus
To Indian slaughter. One among the foe
Stretched out his bow at Aeacus and aimed
And shot: the bolt just lightly scraped the flesh,
Grazing the surface of the thigh, no more;
Pallas Athena turned the shaft aside,
And Aeacus fought on; he felt no pain,
Battling unwearied in the Indians' midst:

The arrow's touch was like a fingernail's
That thinly scrapes and merely marks the skin.

One man escaped on foot, plying his legs
Faster and faster, seeking the nearby thicket
Where he had hidden earlier, but Erechtheus
Pursued, his horse's hooves swift as the wind.
Almost he had him—close enough for a soldier
In the front line to poise and hurl his spear,
When the man spun and met him face to face,
On foot, against a horseman. Bending his knee,
He pressed his left leg hard into the ground,
Twisting his body; he lifted his right foot
And stretched it out behind, using his toes
To grip the earth; he bore an Indian shield
Of hide in seven layers, tall as a tower;
His naked sword was sharp; he held the shield
Before his face and bravely met the foe,
Daring to die or hit his man or wound
The horse he rode on; thrusting from the side,
Using the bossy metal on his shield,
He struck the steed above him on the cheek,
Unbalancing its rider, though on foot.
He would have thrown Erechtheus down, had not
That son of motherless Athena's land
Taken a spear and jabbed him through the navel,
Pushing his bloodied body to the ground.
But then he lifted him and sent him flying
In aerial somersault like an acrobat,
Landing head first and tumbling in the dust.
The son of Athens left him gasping there,
And turned his horse to face more enemy.

Oeagrus bent an arrow to his bow,
Pulling the string till wood and metal met,
Then aimed and shot, calling in aid his bride
Calliope, mother of his noble son.

Nine were the long-tipped shafts sped from his bow,
Nine men were killed—a nice arithmetic,
Matching the missiles sent to warriors slain.
One flying arrow split a forehead, one
Engraved the curvature of a hairy chest,
One landed on a flank, one on a belly,
Driving into the middle of the guts.
One pierced a side, one caught a man in flight:
It pinned the sole of his swift-running foot
Nailing it tight, close bonded to the earth.
He poised another shaft, and from his quiver
Shot followed airy shot, rushing as wind,
A whirr of arrows like a shower of rain.
As when a smith beats bronze upon an anvil
With tireless hammer and the roar of fire,
And many sparks leap from the bludgeoned mass,
Glinting and spurting from the tortured metal,
Heating the air—like partners in a dance
Spark follows spark, one close, another jumping
To catch it as it quivers in the air—
So did Oeagrus face the fighting force,
And with his cloud of arrows laid them low.
The center of the line collapsed, and left
Bare open space, just as the crescent moon
Shines with its new made glow from either horn,
The faint light thin but spread from end to end,
And curving round the body's central sphere,
Now visible as merely blank and bare.

Nor did the dauntless Aeacus relax,
Wielding his spear at Dionysus' side.
With Bacchic rage he killed the Indians here
And killed them there; in hot pursuit he chased
The scattering army to the flowing river.
They massed around him, one man amid many,
Striking him with their blades, but he cared nothing
For swords or flying arrows; sweeping fast,

He reaped the iron harvest of black battle,
And fiercely fought them all; some on the banks
His warlike hand laid low, some in the water,
Choking the stream with corpses; white Hydaspes
Reddened and bubbled with the bodies' blood.

One man who fled the champion's wind-swift whirl
Tumbled by choice and dived into the stream,
And many a corpse new slain by thrusting steel
Was borne off by the current's billowing force,
With swollen limbs, staining the river's depth,
So that the naiads washed in crimson waters,
Black but suffused now by the trickling red.
They threw their spears into the stream; unarmed,
They turned to suppliants, one on the bank,
One stretched upon the sand, one on the ground
Kneeling upright, with neck bent in defeat.
But Aeacus shook his head and spurned their pleas,
His wrath unbending, waxing fiercer still.
At Troy Achilles will strike down Lycaon,
A spearman without spear, still begging mercy;
It was not one Lycaon alone that Aeacus
Slaughtered; unnumbered were the enemy,
The weapons fallen from their hands, who rolled
Upon the field; Hydaspes, blood-defiled,
Took many an Asteropaeus to himself.

The god's aid was with Aeacus as he fought:
As fitted Peleus' father, in the river
He slew the warriors who confronted him—
Sodden hostilities, Bellona bathing—
As if foretelling the unfinished battle
Achilles waged within Scamander's stream.
So fought the grandsire; so will the grandson fight.

Unsandaled in the rippling of the flow
A nymph, a naiad, let her head peep out

Above the current, calling, "Cousin of ours,
Kin of the nymphs, whose blood descends from Zeus,
Pity the holy waters of the river
Springing from Zeus alike; your spear has ended
Indians enough; so let your deeds no more
Draw tears of sorrow from the tearless nymphs.
A naiad of the waters was your mother,
Your home, Aegina, was a river's daughter.
Recall whose were the pangs that brought you forth,
And you no longer will pollute the flow.
I go to other waters undefiled,
I seek the sea, where Thetis in the deep
Will welcome me. Now leave the blood-dimmed stream
To Dionysus' and the Fury's care."

Book 23

Anne Carson

I sing Indic Hydaspes crossed,
I sing water and fire at war.

Bloody naiad, bloody water, in she dove!
Aeacus was beating the barbarians down the banks,
while they kept thrashing their arms and legs to mimic swimmers,
making the river a pudding of panic,
flailing away at their fate, but down they went,
fellow upon waterblown fellow afloat on a river-gritty grave.

Not long on the shore of the shield-showered stream
did Aeacus wait in that murdering mob—who
should show up, brutal and brandishing, but Dionysus?
So Aeacus kept pinning and poking and pounding the enemy down,
awful as Ares, with his brother close,
while Dionysus drowned dozens.
Whoever swam by, he sliced through the spine.
Whoever stood up, he waded in and wasted.
For *Dionysus knew water—*
since the day he fled Lycurgus
to Nereus' hydrotherapeutic home.

On this side and that were the Indians trapped by the stream.
One mud-stuck soul half-lunged from the slime

to charge the foe with both hands at once,
aiming a spear at Aeacus, a spear at the god.
Another stood rigid up to his ribs unable to run,
thrysus-thwacked, fouled by his own feet.
There were men submerged to the knee, to the chin, to the chest,
to the shoulder, the face, the top of the head,
with hair seeping red in the water
and lips gulping death—
a last grin left on the wave.

One noble Indian, watching his comrades
speared, stabbed, smitten and split in two,
went wild with rage.
He pulled out his hair,
gnashed his teeth and pointed—mute—at the slaughter pile.
This was a man of barbarian breeding and force.
His model: Orontes.
His choice: suicide.
He bared his sword—meant to slay others—
and brought it close to his own skin.
One final act, one final word, both quick.

"Belly, welcome this blade, our friend.
How shameful if some incongruity kills me,
some Bacchant or satyr—
my father will not be proud!
No! I drive the sword home myself."
And he drove the sword home
as if stabbing a stranger.
Self-slain, like Ajax, except he wasn't mad.

The murdering that day was beyond words,
the Hydaspes a vast, reluctant tomb.
One river victim poured out his voice:
"Father, you drown your own demographic—why?
War as usual, yes,
but the river Araxes doesn't kill its own Medes,

nor Euphrates the Persians, nor Cydnus the Cilicians,
nor the river Tanais send icy rock streams
to flood out the people who live on its banks.
Eridanus won by drowning an enemy (Phaëthon)
not his own citizens—no Gaul, no Celt,

no friendly native: for them,
the river keeps unrolling the silvergold amber they love.
It's true the Iberian Rhine does blot out its own babies,
but the issue is legal:
to discriminate real sons from bastard brats.
But you, you're drowning legitimate offspring here.
Bastardy is not your concern, Hydaspes!
How dare you mingle with other rivers,

with Ocean or Tethys,
sweeping this ghastly gore into them?
Forbear to pollute Poseidon with corpses!
You do more damage than Dionysus in your ruthless roiling."
So speaking he swallowed his last mortal mouthful.
By now the flood was full of weapons.
Swollen bodies floated thick,
a helmet half-under sank slowly, plume up.
Shields sailed like ships and tossed on the waves, straps trailing.
Soaked garments and the weight of his sword dragged many a man down.
Nor did Dionysus call off his attack

'til all those men were killed
and none but Thureus left to bear witness.
Meanwhile Hera was watching the dilaceration of the Indian nation.
She sprang from heaven, inscribing herself on the air as wind,
alighting in Anatolia to launch Indian Hydaspes
against Dionysus.
But now, with the barbarians bending to him,
his cohort were fashioning machines of all kinds

to cross the quiet waves.
The god led them
in his own eccentric vessel—a dryland chariot—
and his panthers wet not so much as a paw.
There went the troops on the waveless water,
one rowing a raft, one steering a skiff, one
stole a boat from some local fishermen, one
lashed logs into a makeshift freighter—
no rudder, no sail, no oars, no helpful Boreas—
using his spear to steer.
And another, who invented sailing on your shield,

channeled across on a fake ship
with his shieldstrap for rope.
Then came the cavalry splashing their way,
horses swimming their feet,
necks just clearing the flood,
riders perched atop high and dry.
And next the footmen, who had no boats.
They blew into skins to inflate them with air

and crossed Hydaspes on personal breezes.
Next Parrhasian Pan planed across on goat's feet
and Lycus guided his father's seahorses
in a four-horse chariot that arrived unwet,
and Scelmis rode smoothly over the stream
alongside his brother Damnameneus,
while another man leapt to the back of a bull
and drove the beast with a cattle prod:
it scored the stream with its hooves.
Paddling on hands and feet came the sileni.
But here old Hydaspes raised a cry,

pouring out
to his water brother
this fountain of threats:
"Dear lazybones brother, how long do you plan to lounge at leisure?

Weaponize your waters!
Deluge Dionysus!
Overwhelm his wayfaring footmen in waves!
This is all a disgrace to you and to me—his soldiers bisect my stream on dry sandals!

You too, Aeolus, do me a favor:
arm your stormwinds against the satyrs.
That horde made a highway of Hydaspes on chariots built for land!
They treat my waters as a bridle path!
Arm your winds against my boatman, Lyaeus,
let the satyrs be dragged under,
the chariots lost,
the riders swept away,
the drivers swallowed up in my flood—
I'll not have this bizarre transportation go unavenged!
His soldiers use me as a sidewalk,

his lions traipse across unwet,
he insults you and me!
I will destroy them!
My stream a highway! Horses neighing at my naiads
and cracking the spines of my fish with their hooves—tell me
why is this happening?
I'm ashamed to socialize with other rivers
when women traipse across me on dry feet.

No Indian has ever dared
scrape my surface with his vehicles,
nor Deriades cut me into furrows
as he squats atop an elephant."
So saying Hydaspes reared his stream up
and brought down his breakers on Bacchus.
Waves stormed.
Water bellowed like trumpets.
The river soared high and came at the satyrs in a gush.
Amid the tumult a Bassarid swam by—she was
beautifully dressed

but shaking the cymbals from her hands
and the sandals from her feet
as water rose to soak her hair.
Another, weighed down by drenched robes and fawnskins,
cast them off:
a rosy nipple sparkled through black water.
A satyr dog-paddled past waggling his wet taut tail.
Old drunk Maron flailing along on aged legs

and lost his wineskin to the stream.
All by itself, alongside his flute,
the syrinx of Pan went sailing and bobbing
and Silenus tossed his hair in rivalry.
Then the river groaned,
dragging up mud and filth to flood the land with its yellow sludge,
and calling Dionysus to water warfare.
Waves boiled high as the clouds,
blasted by wind,
dazzling the air in a deluge that soaked the god.
Not like this did Simois roar into war,

not like this did Camandrus crash upon Achilles,
as when Hydaspes pursued the army of Bacchus.
Then Dionysus cried in fury:
"Why do you assail me, water boy?
Zeus controls rain—I could ask him to dry up your flood!
I'm a son of Zeus, you're just a by-product:
sprung from clouds or something, aren't you?
I am from Zeus himself.

Beware his lightning.
It can generate more than heat!
Soon they'll be calling you Heavy Knee, like Asopus.
Calm your outpour, while I curb my rage.
You're pitting your force against fire.
You couldn't survive a single spark of his lightning bolt.
Or is it your wife's connections you bank on?

Asteriē's kinship with heavenly Hyperion?
But Hyperion's bold son was blasted to bits by my father's flame.
The foreman of fire had to mourn his own skyriding son.
And yet, notice:

he did not start a war over Phaëthon;
he did not raise fire against fire, though he has the jurisdiction.
Now if Ocean is the reason you're acting so confident,
have a thought for Eridanus, your poor burnt brother, struck by Zeus.
Cruel sorrow it was for your oceanic ancestor,
who wears the rim of the world as a belt
and pours out all its sustaining waters,
to see his son go up in flame.

Yet he made no war on Olympus,
nor did he fight fire with flood.
Spare your streams awhile, Hydaspes, lest I see you ablaze."
Deep-booming Hydaspes got angrier than ever at this.
He let flow a tantrum of hightopping torrents
and would have swamped the whole Bacchic crew
except Bacchus stepped in:
from a nearby hedge
he grabbed some fennel—where there's fennel there's fire—
to heat in the sunlight.
The stalk gave a spark that brought forth a flame

that he tossed in the stream.
Then the river ignited, the banks boiled over, smoke rolled up into the air
from lotus and marsh plants as they blazed and baked.
Fire levelled the rushes.
Sooty smoke spiraled upwards
and made the vault of heaven drunk,
blackening all the woods
with a fragrance of reeds razed.

Flame slid into the deeps.
Then fish on fire were burying themselves in mud;

a spark swam down under the water to set the slime boiling;
smoke mixed with steam and rushed from the riverbed channels,
naked naiads came sprinting
out of bedrooms now awash—
one surprisingly dove into the Ganges,
another made loud, roaring Acesines her home on land,
a third went wandering to Persia.
And meanwhile Ocean was bawling threats at Dionysus,
pouring a watery hullabaloo from his throat of fountains

and swamping the shores of the world in a sea of words.
"O Tethys, you who share the bed of Ocean and his age,
who are old as the world,
who nourish all the waters,
source of yourself,
ancient mother,
what shall we do?
Zeus, though he's god of rain, sends fire against my children and me.

Even as he plagued Asopus with a bird,
he launches Bacchus against Hydaspes.
Well, no!
here's my plan:
I'll marshal my waters and make war on the lightning of Zeus!
Drown the sun!
Quench the stars!
Swamp Selene!
Wash the Bear clean from axle to straps!
And send the Dolphin back to my depths where he used to swim—
he'll float in new seas.

I'll drag down Eridanus from strolling the stars
and give him a home with the Celts—
he'll be water again and the sky bare of fire.
And all those fish-shaped stars that swim around heaven,
I'll sweep them down into the sea—from Olympus to me.
Tethys, awake!

Let's drown the stars!
I'd like to see Taurus—who enjoyed quiet sailing

when he left Europa's bed—tossing on wilder waves!
Selene herself may take offense
at me sporting horns and the look of a bull,
bull-shaped driver of bulls that she is.
I'll go high in the sky to see Cepheus drenched
and Boötes soaked to the skin,
as once when Poseidon doused Ares.
I'll submerge the Goat and charm the Waterpourer
with a gift of infinite liquidity.
Tower up, Tethys! And you, O Sea!
Zeus has brought forth a bastard in the shape of a bull

to ruin all rivers and creatures
however blameless they be.
His thyrsus has annihilated Indians,
his taper torched Hydaspes!"
And so,
from deep in its depths,
old Ocean
blustered on.

Book 24

Gordon Braden

In 24, the Indians
express their endless gloom
And Aphrodite does her best
to operate a loom.

I

"My cue to intervene," thought Zeus the Father,
"And stop my kiddo's tantrum." Off he shot
A rumbling thundercloud to calm the water
And dowse mad Dionysus on the spot.
Hera got in there, too, to end the bother
By screaming like a banshee. That was what
Gave wet Hydaspes chance to supplicate
Merciful flaming Bacchus, so: "Please! Wait!

II

"Don't dry me up! These waters come from heaven,
And then water your grapes! Yes, I've been bad,
And, god, you *are* a god; the sign is given
In those bright torches. I just thought I had

To help my son Deriades, yes, even
  If that meant drowning everybody! Mad
Idea just to fight with Dionysus!
I'm guilty, so ashamed! Oh, what a crisis!

III

"I'm boiling up! By Zeus, your father, please
  Stop! Naiads are running away! One's diving
Into my wellhead, and one flees to trees
  To join the hamadryads; one's contriving
To get into the Indus, and one sees
  Her way up to the Caucasus; one's striving
To get to somewhere you have never heard of,
And leave her weepy father with no word of

IV

"Her. Please, oh, please, I beg, don't roast my rushes!
  They use them to make trellises for vines,
To hold them up and make your grapes so luscious.
  And spare those reeds that get turned to all kinds
Of instruments, those hoboys, pan-pipes, such as
  Sing your own mystic songs. Those waving lines
Of fennel in my streams, they are the wands
Your followers now brandish in their hands

V

"To threaten me! The river you just crossed
  Once bathed Zagreus, the first Dionysus.
You look just like him! When his life is lost,
  Zeus eats his heart, and next thing he entices
Your mother, and, well, then out you get tossed!

There's all sorts of connections here! How nice is
That? Only don't incinerate us, please!
Calm down, here, see? I'm begging, on my knees!

VI

"Remember Typhon (from Books One and Two)?
He challenged Zeus. But if, in his defiance,
He'd bent the knee and said that he was through,
I'm sure the big guy would've told his clients,
'We can work with this'—and he'd mean it, too.
I mean, it's not exactly rocket science:
When someone wins, he wins. No hows or whys.
No fireworks, back to work, nobody dies.

VII

Right?" When he finished, Dionysus drew
His torch back, and an icy blast of polar
Air rushed down from the north, and as it blew
It made the burning river rougher, colder,
And put the fire out without much ado,
With honor to Zeus, Bacchus, and the solar
God Helios. They couldn't quench the flames,
They quenched the flames. All glory to their names!

VIII

Meanwhile, that god of war Deriades
Was getting ready for a mighty battle.
He armed his Indians, and had them seize
The riverbank so that the Bacchic rabble
Would have to fight their way up on their knees.
Zeus didn't miss a thing about how bad all

This might turn out for Dionysus, and
Swooped down out of the sky and took his stand

IX

To shield the youngling god. Then all the other
Gods in Olympus took the hint, and leapt
Down there to join the fight. Zeus had a further
Thought then, when he remembered how he'd swept
Across the sky up high to keep a rather
Sweet assignation; he'd become adept
At this, and so, once more an eagle, flew
To snatch his son Aeacus for their crew.

X

Suddenly all the other gods recall
Their favorites and varied offspring; taking
Quick action, they try hard to get them all
Out of harm's way and off to safety, making
Sure as they can their darlings do not fall
In battle. (There's a list here somewhere.) Aching
With care, they whisk away their hamadryads,
And even those cute battle-hardened naiads.

XI

But they regroup, with Dionysus out
In front, driving his car across the river:
He never gets the axle wet. A rout
Of satyrs follows, and then maenads, never
Quite catching up with the Telchines, about
As fast as they come; and behind them ever
Swarming ahead, the rest, thick as can be,
Toward the farther bank. But then they see

XII

An eagle in the sky! waving his wings!
    Clutching Aeacus underneath! For father
Zeus knows a hidden pathway, and he brings
    The troops of Bacchus to it. Up the other
Side they can come, unseen, in secret. Things
    Are different there, a place where they can gather
And dance about the mountains and the trees,
Sleep safely, and do whatever they please.

XIII

Some hunt the deer; some search for dryads or
    Suckle wild lion cubs; one wreathes together
A necklace of venomous serpents. For
    Another, happiness is bounding after
A crazed she-bear, bringing her down; and sure-
    Footed in frenzy like a goat, another
Springs up onto an elephant and rides
The big beast hard, joy bursting her insides.

XIV

The archers take out trees. They shoot away
    At elms, at olive trees, at pines, at fig trees.
But while their revels sound, across the way
    Thureus needs to tell his lord his vict'ry's
Lost. First he wept, not knowing what to say,
    But then: "We hid us there among those thick trees
Along the river bank; up Bacchus rides,
Pipes, drums, and brass then blast out on all sides!

XV

The forest shuddered, oaks cried out, a hill
    Capered and danced! Naiads sang alleluia!
I called our men to arms, summoned their will,
    For all the good that did, 'cause what's that to ya
If you're scared, shaking, just don't care? But still
    They tried, but that god sure knows how to do ya
In. An assault of leaves and fennel stalks
Left acres of dead bodies for the hawks.

XVI

You need to ask the Brahmans about this.
    They'll know if he's a god or not. A battle
Is hopeless in the dark; a gloomy mist
    Is spreading fast. Don't lead your men like cattle
To slaughter out there. You need to resist
    The urge to fight right now; if you don't, that'll
Finish things off right fast. At least just wait
Until it's light again. Don't tempt your fate."

XVII

Deriades agrees. He doesn't want to.
    It's not that he is scared, or feeling weak.
He blames the setting sun for what he can't do,
    And turns his elephant around to seek
The city, and to get to work on Plan Two.
    His army hunkers with him, feeling meek.
Outside the walls victory cries are heard
Of war-mad Dionysus and his horde.

XVIII

Rumors spread through the city of who'd died
And how. The women led the lamentations.
They ripped their clothes and beat their breasts and cried
And tore their cheeks; the bleeding lacerations
Were heart-rending. An old man learned the pride
Of his life, his four sons, all at their stations,
Had all been slaughtered by Aeacus' blade.
A newly married bride now newly made

XIX

A widow rent her veil, tore at her hair.
A pregnant wife now almost into labor
Went mad with sorrow, and in her despair
Cursed at Hydaspes that had been her neighbor
But then had drowned her husband: "I do swear
I will never again do you the favor
Of drinking from the waters which did kill
The father of my unborn child! I will

XX

"Never touch them again. Oh, who will take
Me to his dripping body? I am yearning
To hold him once again, and for his sake
Drown in that river and so end my mourning.
But if I bear a son, what then? I ache
To think of him looking around and turning
To me to ask, 'Where is my father? Show
Me who he is.' And I must tell him, 'No,

XXI

"'I can't.'" So she lamented for a man
Who could not hear her. A young maiden anguished
Over a wedding that now never can
Happen, the young bridegroom brutally vanquished,
Their happiness not even a brief span,
The chamber never decked, the garland languished
That should have crowned his brow, the bridal song
Now never sung, her sorrow deep and long.

XXII

But while the city wept, the forest boasted.
For Bacchus and his crew heifers were killed,
Bulls butchered; flocks of sheep were slain and roasted.
Silenuses and crowds of satyrs milled
About the table with the god that hosted
Their revels; giant cups were filled, and filled
Again, with more wine than you would believe,
From sweeter vintage than you could conceive.

XXIII

A self-taught bard from Lesbos rhapsodized
About the Titans who attacked Olympus
And how Zeus beat them back and tartarized
(A new word there) those who defied his nimbus.
Bearded old Cronus there got satirized
As one big fool. Don't go fucking with Simbas
That run the jungle. "Man, I love your stuff,"
A guy next to him said. "Can't get enough.

XXIV

"Hey, I'm from Cyprus. Could you do the one
About Athena's thing with Aphrodite?
You know, the weaving contest? That one's fun."
So the bard got to work on how the flighty
Goddess of love decided she could run
Wide rings around Athena and her mighty
Shuttle. (How hard could it be?) Down she sat,
Spinning a thread more like a rope. At that

XXV

She worked all day, all night, making a mess,
The woof bursting the warp, hurting her tender
Hands in the process, which made her obsess
Just all the more, going off on a bender
With things she wasn't good at. Less and less
Time for that stuff for which we mortals send her
Those prayers and sacrifices. There was no
More love or marriage, music, all seemed so

XXVI

Dead. When Athena saw what was unfolding,
She seethed and laughed and called the other gods
And raged at Zeus and Aphrodite, scolding
Them both: "Well, dad, you're playing some strange odds
In making reassignments. Sister's holding
The tapestry portfolio and plods
Right to disaster with it, picks a fight
With someone who was armed and armored right

XXVII

“From birth. We’ll see how *that* plays out. I mean,
    Which of your battles did she fight a lick in?
Which Titan did she flatten? But she’s keen
    To poach on my turf, wants to poke a stick in
My eye. Hey, Artemis, have I been seen
    Hunting your game? Do I play obstetrician
To women who once called on Hera?” All
The gods were there by then, hearing her call,

XXVIII

And stared amazed at the celestial bumbler
    And laughed their holy heads off, Hermes more
Than any of them: “Yikes, you ditsy fumbler,
    You got the loom; Athena gets to roar
And strut your sexy underwear. A humbler
    Task is the one you’ve got. As Ares’ whore
You need to make him a new outfit so
You two can get hitched proper. But, you know,

XXIX

“Don’t go embroidering a shield, for what
    Do you want with a shield? [These jokes keep coming
For quite a while; I’m skipping several, but
    If you want you can track them down.] So, summing
All of this up: unhand the threads, and put
    That underwear back on. This thing is bumming
Everyone out. Get back to sex and love
And marriage. That stuff’s yours to take care of.”

XXX

The gods all smile. So Aphrodite blushes,
Puts down her botched-up weaving, and returns
To seeing that the human race (such as
It is) keeps going on. Eros concerns
Himself with all of nature as he rushes
Around the world again; everything yearns
To reproduce, and that's the way it is.
So sang the rhapsode. Around him, the fizz

XXXI

Had gone out of the room. Satiety
Had done its work, and everyone was dropping
Down onto whatever variety
Of bed they found, with streams of wine still slopping
Out of their mouths, a grand society
Of happy dreamers: dreaming still of stopping
The Indians, slicing them up with swords,
Knocking them off their horses, killing hordes

XXXII

Of them with arrows, wounding that big fellow
Deriades—wounding an elephant!
Lions and dogs, great tribes of black and yellow
Leopards patrol the camp so danger can't
Come anywhere near Bacchus; in the mellow
Darkness they keep their watch, while up the slant
Mountainside torches climb, the endless light
Of Bacchants dancing all the blessed night.

Book 25

Alex Dressler

In Book 25, you have
Perseus Agonistes
& Dionysus' masculinity
compared to Hercules'.

1. The second invocation

Muse, make war once more, with wise
noise & with thought's thyrsus. Seven years
has Ares in the East howled battle cries
at Dionysus, on unbended knee. Now rise
the shrill fears of the nestlings, prophecies
of Bacchic war from Indian plane trees,
scared of dragon teeth. I will not sing
the seven years the army stayed within
the walls. No, imitating Homer, I prefer
to celebrate the last year of the war.
I draw a portrait of the battle
equal to my seventh sparrow.
Musically, I mix the fable
with the seven gates

of Thebes. Do you not see how she
dances like a lunatic around me,
how like a nymph who strips her breast
of half her downcast clothes, Thebes remembers Pentheus?
The mountain of Cithaeron stands beside her.
Anxious in old age, beset with shame,
he stretches doleful hand, & he advises
me to go ahead & sing
of anything, anything
except for the accursed bed
of the son who slew
his father as the husband
of the mother who
begot him.

Do I descry Aonian lyres? Say Muses,
say what Amphion now causes
stones to be breathless joggers? I know the noises.
Thebes has been set to music with echoes
from Boeotia, & they thrum
from Pindar's age. So, come
to Zanzibar. We will murder the race of India
again, stirring sweat & woe to ascertain
whether any of the masculine sons of God,
the new or old, has waged a war like Bacchus
has, or whether time has known a
battle such as this before
the Eastern war, which no Bellona
& no Homer saw.

2. The comparison with Perseus

Perseus, first. With knees of speed
& wings which whirred on his feet,
he ran across the sky, & trod the air—

if he *did* fly. Flapping ankles, weird
swimming with empty fans to beat
the air—so what? So, down he cast
his palm. With all the strength of a thief,
he snatched the rolling eye of Phorcys'
watchful child. Cautious to keep
his trenchant tiptoes quiet,
he plowed the serpent ground
of Medusa by herself & pounded
the brood of which she was
in foal, Pegasus,

from out her swollen gut. Soon Parturition mowed
the fertile throat of Gorgon maid,
the first fruit of the hippodrome her throat,
with pangs of birth. Thus, with a wingèd foot,
Perseus raised as a breathless
symbol of his conquest
the reptilian harvest
of the Gorgon mane—
the relic of a broken skull
which dripped
an irrigation of blood
& from its gullet freshly cut
it left a hiss
half finished.

No noise of attack on terra firma
or shout of battle lust accompanied
Perseus as he struggled on the sea.
No sailors swelled with Ares' wild war wind
of battle tatters, & no ruinous rain
of blood empurpled the Old Man of the Sea
at Tripoli; the coughing sea received
no undulating corpses. Perseus simply
flitted on wings as he shuddered

at the shrill snakes of the hair
of raving Stheno,
boasting the hat of Hades, the scimitar
of Pallas Athena,
& Zeus as a father.

Carried aloft on a hurrying sandal,
he was a coward, the conqueror of a little
hollow in Tripoli; he heard
no clarion, only the crying of Euryale;
he never killed a masculine battalion;
he never incinerated a city with a torch
of fire.
    Not like this was the noise of our loud sounder,
Bromius. No trickster, Bacchus foremost
armed himself & never snuck
or laid in wait or made an ambush
on Medusa's watchful eyeball which,
distributed alike from each to each
& weaponless underneath the wing of sleep,
yielded only effeminate one-upmanship.

He sliced the battle lines of those who would destroy him
with a pair of victories in a war on terra firma
& in a hubbub on wet whale roads, which he drenched
with carnage as he watered waves with blood.
He slaughtered a race of foreigners, which empurpled
the daughters of Nereus with a crimson flood.
He buried many a crop of Indians in the earth
with helmets & high crests on chopped off heads,
& many a sailor on the sea he sent to ruin in the depths—
an entourage of Indian corpses, beneath his piercing thyrsus—
because they asked for it. How the noisy warring river
turned its water into a spear & threw
it in aquatic warfare at the Liberator who
never met a conqueror & how the char

of pitch-black pine torch issued in a dripping spark
of Bacchus setting fire to the foreign waters when
the Pakistani river of Hydaspes billowed smoke
& waves of water boiled—*that* I skip, but *you* will talk
about how Perseus killed a monster nursed on salt
& petrified an ocean beast with Gorgon eye. So what?
So, the metamorphosis of Polydectes from a human
form, effected in the view of the wide-awake eye of bleeding Medusa,
spontaneously changed his person into stone of an altogether different
order. The brawny labor of Bacchus, the killer of Indians,
was more than just a Gorgon, more than a sky-high stone that boomed on the main,
& more than Polydectes. With the threshing of his slender
thyrsus for a wrecker, Bacchus the champion thinned
stubble fields of ogres with snakes for a mane.

When he cast his warlike ivy at Porphyrio
& blasted Beelzebub & drove Alcyoneus away
with leaves that blew like spears & when an arrow
of murderous thyrsuses against the two-hundred
hands of the whirling Brood of Land
& against the Sons of the Earth defended Olympus, &
pounded the galactic outer rim even with the mountain
ridges of their heads, & then in submission they bended
knee beneath a lance of ivy & the shrill
foliage hissed as a missile—even still,
the swarm that fell to Zeus' weapon,
the fiery thunderbolt, was nowhere near
the size that fell to the wrecker
of his thyrsus, friends; compare.

Setting his eye on Dionysus,
Helios in the land of sunrises
was aghast at the sweat expended
on killing Indians. On the other side,
in her plunging breast, at Eventide
the Moon saw Perseus in feathers race
& toil with brazen blade.

Well, I proclaim the prize
for prowess goes to Bacchus,
not Perseus. So too, the boast
of Phaëthon, son of the Sun,
goes before the boast
of Selene, the Moon.
The River Inachus

was a witness to them both:
when the weighty Peloponnesian spears
faced the bloodstained fennel stalks
of Bacchus, & when Perseus retreated
from the satyrs' screaming lust for struggle
& he seemed like—no, he yielded
ground to Bromius the Loud,
who bears the thyrsus. All that Perseus
did was toss a spear at helpless
Ariadne. I am not impressed
that a man-at-arms once felled
an unarmed girl in bridal clothes
whose every breath was still
whispering love.

Does Perseus want to brag about
his golden origin in the bed of God?
God came as a rain but he did not
take the mother, Danaë, to heaven; he didn't
glorify his wet & fecund obsession
with the virgin; he considered it illicit.
The other mother Semele came to sit
beside Dionysus, her son with the cluster of grapes.
She touched the table of the blessed gods & of Zeus himself,
but Danaë didn't take a seat on Olympus: no, the maid
was set to sail in Zeus' leaky chest & then condemned
her glory that lasted no longer than
the raincloud that passed above
& robbed her of wedded love.

I know about Andromeda, how she shines
from Olympus but still suffers in heaven. Many times
I suppose she complains even thus with a voice begrudging
Perseus, her husband: "You took me to heaven—so what?
What a beautiful wedding gift Olympus was
to me! Now in asterism, even here, that sea monster
is still harassing me. After fear at sea, on land, & now in the sky,
I am bound by a new hardship, the image of the earlier.
For me, your astral scimitar is useless. Medusa's eye,
now constellated, twinkles in kindness on my behalf
all pointlessly. That monster of the sea
is still harassing me
yet you do not flex a dexterous
feather . . .

"My mother is embarrassed; she harries me;
she complains: 'Cassiopeia herself, even in heaven,
is reduced to skirting the brine & even
as Ursa Major has been awarded an orbit
untouched by dampness & the deep,
she is worrying about the nereids.' She sees
how scared her daughter Andromeda is
& agèd Cepheus is distraught that,
after earth, Leviathan rides
Olympus." Thus, his bride
complains a complaint beset by chains,
many times, beseeching Perseus but
by her bridegroom she remains
protected not.

If Perseus boasts about his stars,
you ought to flex your glance across
the galaxy where the glorious
carrier of the Twisted Snake
is shining as a constellation next
to the Diadem of Ariadne which
is the Sun's own match.

Rising with the Moon herself,
it broadcasts the love of Dionysus, the lover
of diadems. I also know the noisy war
of Minos with a woman
for Bellona, how she waged it
with her waistline
& no leathern

for protection. Aphrodite was donning
a helmet all of a sudden. Persuasion flung
a spear that was made of bronze & turned
into Pallas Athena, a fellow warrior with Minos.
In the din of battle a swarm of Desires,
proponents of married love, cast spears while
Longing who is lovely played the role
of a sacker of cities. Then the blare
of a Cretan horn was announcing war
for the people of Megara & their lord
named Nisus. When Ares' eyes
Shock & Awe accompanying Desires,
though brazen, he feels embarrassed
& stops in his tracks.

3. Concluding allegory

Ares saw Aphrodite & how she waged it with escutcheon
& how the goddess Smitten cast spears. Wearing delicious
attire, Desire took the victory of a tress
from the beautiful soldiers. Scylla already whisked
a lock of wine dark hair from her father's drowsing crown,
& when she mowed a braid from the head of the king,
she sacked the entire city with scissors of iron,
& that was how Minos became a sacker of cities:
with naked physical beauty, no iron aiding his victory,
only longing & desire. When the Liberator donned
a helmet, it was not Longing who softened the darts

of the noisy Indians; Venus did not
don a crest & toss a spear
for the Liberator,

beauty's victor. One cut
was not enough to stop
the noise of war, an object of desire
warding off one love-stung Dionysus.
No lovely deception, no. In the form
of a braid of a King of a different race,
the Indians, & of far flung
battles on the river Hydaspes,
he boasts ever recrudescent
victories. But if you reverence
that Peloponnesian task
of Hercules on Inachus, just
compare each
labor please.

4. Comparison with Hercules

I know the way he pinned the lion
crosswise with his arm & bound
its twisted neck with a sinuous fetter—
death without iron—& I know how
the life-sustaining throat was full of air
just where he bandied it. I am not impressed.
Cyrene too had done no less,
when as a maiden in the leafy
bush, she slew a lion with her hands
all by herself, the male of the species, with
her feminine fetter stiff. When Bacchus was a youth
& playing in the hills, already
a lover of victory, he towed
a deadly

lion by the scruff of its throat,
with just one hand. He squeezed
the lolling beast of twisted neck
& unto Mother Rhea offered it,
while it was still alive. He bound it tight
with strap of dominating bridle by
its servile cheek & chased the savage hides
of terrified lions & sat astride them like
a chariot. The progeny of panthers & the brood
of bears that eat raw flesh did servitude
to Dionysus' infant hand. I know about
the Erymanthian boar, but pigs
& bears in hoards were playthings
for the child Liberator.

So what if Hercules was brave & freed
little Lerna & its snake packed creek
with his "great work"? He burned
the first fruits of the lurking Hydra,
which regenerate themselves & shoot
orchards of bristling dragons. What if
he had exterminated them by himself,
instead of summoning Iolaus to help
strip the freshly sprouted heads in his "great work"?
He plied the cauterizing torch until he threw
the lady snake headlong. I know not what
honor to accord a couple
of people who stirred up
a worthless lizard.

One labor shared by two. But Bacchus who
ululates & bears the thyrsus cut the brood
of serpentine sons of Land himself. He who
ululates commands them all. He is
the champion of Zeus. The dragon world
was growing from every side of them,
over their shoulders, more copious than

they were in Hercules' adventure in
Inachus, whispering shrill
& listless in the vicinity of stars—
& not just Lerna. Iolaus, peace!
You torched the body of the Hydra,
but Hercules, only Hercules, received
the victor's title.

Neither paltry Nemea nor
Lerna did Bacchus, my Champion, restore
to life from throats of thunder, hacking up
regenerating shrubs of dragons. No, he pumped
earth, air, & sea with victories & took
the Southwest Wind, the speedy heel of the North,
& the wing of the East for messengers for his tournaments
of four directions. If a serpent & a lurking Hydra can confer
glory on a person, then these crowned Bacchus' first
birthday. For his coiffure, the Liberator
sported bristling fillets of dragon tresses
from the moment he left behind
his father's parthenogenetic
thigh.

About the golden horn of the "stag,"
I will hold my tongue. I will not disparage
Hercules the Magnificent, the assassin
of one young deer. Remember not the quivering
hind. Such creatures were the itty-bitty trinkets
of any wild maenad, his rushing huntress. Cast aside
the skirmish at Cnossus. I am not impressed
at whatever love-stung bull *he* chased.
He shook a club so big only to break
a little horn. How many times one woman
has done exactly this! How many times a maenad
has made mincemeat
of innumerable herds
with horns of beauty—

insignificant handmaid of Dionysus
with his oxen horns! How many times
when a raving bull was wrangling with sharp horns,
she has drawn it back by its arched horn
& forced the lion-tossing beast to bended
knee! Forget Geryon with triple pointed head.
With his flesh-lacerating ivy has
my darling Dionysus completely destroyed
Alpus who fought with the gods & Alpus who had
one-hundred snakes for hair, & Alpus who laid
hands upon Apollo, then abducted
Selena, the Moon, & with his locks did
scare the choirs
of stars.

The labors of Hercules! Well, he was sired
by Zeus the Immortal who thrice took Alcmene to bed,
which, fruitful & multiplied, is now said
to be the "three-moon bed." His mountain-bred
adventure? Insignificant. The works of Bacchus include
Giants of arms galore, the King of the Indians—no "stag," or
simple cattle driving; no hound or bull or hairy boar,
no gilded produce or listless vagabond of a bird
with insignificant wings with tips unfortified by iron,
no horse that devours immigrants, no trivial
undergarment of Hippolyta, no dung in a barn.
The victory of Dionysus was immense:
the defeat of Deriades & the giant Orontes,
twenty arms in length.

5. To Homer—Invocation complete

Luminous son of the Izmiri river,
imperishable poet of the Greeks,
Your book is time's contemporary.
I wish it peace: Not mine to consign

the song of the war of Troy to memory.
I do not liken Dionysus to Achilles
or Deriades to Hector. Yet your Muse
would have been a better singer
if her song had been the big, magnificent
battle of the giant-tossing Bacchus!
You would have left Achilles' labors
to other singers, had Thetis
not refused you the favor
of that gift.

Breathe upon me with your holy breath
that I may raise my voice & sing. I beg:
Grant me your magniloquence that I may ring
with Ares & assuage the sweat expended
in Dionysus killing Indians. Goddess, send me
into the midst of India once more, & I will wield
my spear of thought & father Homer's shield,
alongside God & crested Bromius
battling mad Deriades & Morrheus.
Let me hear the echo of the flute
of Bacchus & the noise of Homer's shrewd
unending clarion, & I will kill the remainder
of India with the javelin
of my mind.

6. The scene

By the watery small of the forest
on a lonely crag, was Bacchus
sitting in battalion, an inhabitant upon
a precipice in India in a respite from
the war, when Ganges writhed
with pity for her children, & the byways
clanged with the wails of women
addicted to lamentation, & Deriades

writhed in panic, awe, & shame. The doom
of the freshly rotten dead left the city shaken. He knew
it all. He searched with darting eye & wept
at how Hydaspes' look
lost its divine aspect,
babbled black,

& flowed with wine. Disgruntled came
a graybeard. Blind with a dim
fog, he turned his trundling
foot & scattered the sweet-relieving alcoholic
dew on his own closed eyes. When his face quaffed
the dusky drops, his vision unlocked.
Raising his voice, the old man jumped
& danced with feet of joy: the waters
of the empurpled river were a
balm! & thus, he cupped
sheer billows of the purple stuff
& filled his wineskin with
an odorous jet,
& thus he set

fire on the altar of God & for Dionysus who runneth
over. Soon he was beholding
the beams of Phaëthon, long grown
a stranger to him. On the bank,
a boy released his hunting dogs
from service; they got drunk
from lapping the tasty liquid of the empurpled
flood. Armed with a bow,
a mountain nymph accompanied the boy
as he bended back his way
to the city to inform
Deriades that the sweet torrent
of the watercourse
was alcoholic.

Already the vineyard smell spread through the town
& made the byways drunk with warm wet winds:
the prophecy of the victory of the killer of the Indians,
the Liberator. The townsfolk hunkered down
in the towering ramparts, afraid. The guards
girded the fortifications of the high-crested city wall
with oxhide shields. Again & again, Dionysus scolded
Hera from the hills for how she restrained
hostilities, begrudging him the Indians
again; how she counted thirty circuits of the Dawn,
& how the Moon had run ten rounds; still all his hopes
of victory blew out. He spied
his lions in a den of idleness
& like a lion bellowed

in the wilderness; there was no wailing in
his eyes. To Bacchus in such sullenness then came
the sterile herald of Rhea the Sacrosanct,
Attis themself, with voluminous dresses, lashing
a carriage of itinerant lions through the passes
of the Scythian mountains: once they had taken
a knife & bloodied the generative stalk
of the commodious sacrament
of matrimony, their adolescence, & cast
away the unsown swathe of conjugality,
the first fruits of their harvest of masculinity,
with bloodshot, philoprogenitive
drops from a threshing dagger to
their leg.

7. The offer of the shield

With the warm figure they made female,
this is the person who came, driving the carriage
of the Phrygian Mother, to mitigate
the sullenness of the Liberator,

who ran right up in case
Rhea the Conqueror of Worlds
was being escorted there to raise
the war cry of the Indians in person.
Attis brought their untamed carriage
to a halt; they lay the reins on the edge
& shone from the rosy bloom of cheeks
unblemishèd & unto Bacchus
gushed in trilling voice
this speech:

"Dionysus of the clustered grapes,
Son of God & Progeny of Rhea,
speak as I speak & say
when will you slay
the dreadlocked sons of India
& journey home to Lydia?
Not yet has Rhea seen your
blue-black captives.
Not yet beside the
riches-dripping River Pactolus
has she washed your lions of their sweat
from battle in the shadow
of their mountain
den.

Only, you keep rolling
a quiet gyre of battle flowing
year after year. You do not bring
the species of the Indian
lion to the animal-breaking—
yea, even to the god-making—
Mother, as a symbol of success.
So, take you then this armor from Hephaestus
& your own dear deathless
Rhea, armor cast
on the anvil of Lemnos

depicting land & sea
& stars, which are the chorus
of the galaxy."

Not yet had their speech faded,
when the hero Bacchus shouted:
"In but a single day, I'd wipe the Indian capital
completely away! If only the jealousy of stepmotherly
Hera didn't lead me, hungry for victory, astray!
Blatantly battling satyrs, Ares himself makes savage campaigns
as Deriades' champion, & yet I've raged many times
to maim him with this thyrsus! I unleash a bullish attack,
but Saturn's son with clap of thunder draws it back!
If only Zeus would put the noise that rattles the very skies
to rest for just today, then starting tomorrow
I will tie Ares down until I mow
harvests of Indian helmets!"
To Dionysus, Attis trilled:

"As the wielder of this indestructible shield,
which sparkles with the stars, & which was built
in heaven, my dear friend, you need not tremble
at Ares' spleen or Hera's grudge
or whole ranks of blessed gods
or armies bending bows, because
Rhea the Mother of All
is on your side. They will not hurl
darts to hurt Helios, who is the Sun,
or maim Selena, the Moon. For who could blunt
the broadsword of Orion with stiletto
or sting the Plowman in the ether
with earthly arrow?
You might answer:

the father of Deriades, stronger than bulls.
But what could River Hydaspes do
to you when you bring Ocean in your retinue?

Be strong. Make war once more. Do you not know
how Mother Rhea has foretold
how your victory has long since grown
from out this hubbub? The lust for struggle
will not cease until the Seasons
in their fourfold carriages complete
six yearly rounds. The eye of God
& thread of Fate are sound. They nod
on Hera's inclination:
you will raze the Indian nation
in year seven, coming hard

right now." & with this speech,
they handed Bromius the shield.
Thrilled at heart, they took a dip into a meal
of sweet-relieving wine in which their cup
itself rejoiced, & when they quenched their lust
for banqueting, they once more turned the lash
unto their lions' backs & set their off-road carriage
on a course for home in Anatolia. Through the forelands of the valleys
of Azerbaijan, Iraqi highlands, impassable Afghanistan, & crags
of Lebanon, they drove till they reached Izmir, & then they veered
to the palace of Rhea begetter of children of strength,
which is self-contained, divinely made,
& there they hid their lions in their own den
& unto them immortal fodder fed.

Now that Dionysus heard
the Mother's divine inspired word,
in a frenzy from the thyrsus,
he joined the dance of mountain maenads,
tossing to the winds his load
of downcast woes, & in his hand he shook
the escutcheon wrought with art,
the Olympian armament, the canny work
Hephaestus built. Assembled multitudes
began to search the manifold

miracles of Olympian art
with darting eyes, the miracles that sparkled
from the hand of the god,
the shield of many colors
wrought.

8. Images of the shield

Hephaestus wrought earth as a circle in the middle.
Around the land, he built the heavens carved in a sphere
with choirs of stars. He wrought the sea to share
a yoke with land. In the sky, he fashioned
Helios, who is the Sun, hung in suspension
on the golden edge of a carriage of light.
Round & entire, he embossed with white
Selena the Moon in silver element.
All the constellations of the cosmos incandescent,
girded by the swirling galaxy like a garland,
scattered across the seven zones, were the object
of his craftsmanship. By water all untouched,
he fashioned the matching astral wagons which circle the pole
of heaven's carousel.

For shoulder to shoulder, Ursa Major & Ursa Minor
circle a turning post far over ocean depths.
For the head of one Bear always bends as it begins
to sink as much as the other cranes its neck on coming back.
Between the matching wagons, he fashioned the Snake
who almost bridges their disparate shapes in its whirling coils
of stars. For it wiggles its nimble figure like the twisting whirls
of loud Maeander. For that river turns its winding course
in a crisscross path, & the Snake flexes its eye that ever looks
ahead in the direction of the Dipper & girds its figure
with scales of stars, surrounded by the constellations of the Wagons.
For an outstretched star flashes as it spits light from the tip of its tongue.
Next to the lips, it incandesces
light amidst many a fang.

All that was what the canny smithy fashioned in the midst
of the well-wrought shield, & to the delight of the Liberator, shaped
the walls of Thebes, where the heifer led, as the Seven Gates
assembled themselves row after row to the tune of the lyre, & Zethos labored,
lifting stones on burdened shoulders, & his brother Amphion played
the lyre for the founding, raising his voice, & to the sound
the hillside whirled; self-willed, the stones were dancing
as though on the shield the magic were still enchanting.
Even though it was only art, you would have sworn the sportive throbbing
of the stock-still cliffs was shuddering, nimble, bounding. For if you caught
a glimpse of the "man" so carefully wrought with a "lyre" not moving but stopped,
striking exciting chords from unreal strings, you would incline
all ears to hear the tower-building phorminx, with joy in your mind
from the sound of the song that made stones jog.

For beside the sparkling choirs of stars, the well-spun shield presented
a beautiful object of craftsmanship, a Trojan cupbearer in Zeus' court
perfectly wrought by divine art, raised aloft by rapacious talons
presenting, as depicted in paintings, a finely fashioned
eagle with wings which held him in turn. For Zeus looked frightened,
even as he flew through the heavens, lifting the traumatized
child with nails that did not scratch him, for he checked
the strength of his wings which were flapping gently
to keep Ganymede from slipping headlong from the sky & from burial in the deadly
dashing of the sea. For even more was he afraid that the Fates would make
the beautiful youth bequeath his name straightaway to the sea underneath
& rape the Greeks of the honor to come. Reclined
at the heavenly table of gods, the boy was shaped
in the image of one drawing wine.

Presenting a bowl that brimmed with sweet nectar & flowed
of itself, he offered a cup to God as he dined. Next up
was Hera, the image of anger. Expressing the jealousy
of her soul to Pallas Athena, she made a gesture
to Ganymede, child cowherd, sojourner of stars,

& how he served Olympic concoctions of nectar,
bandying goblets belonging by lot to the Goddess
of Youth. For next he fashioned the nurse of Bacchus
Izmir, & the serpent with speckles, & Moria, the heavenly herb
& Breaker the Great, called Damasen, the snake-killing son of the Earth,
& Tylus carved to pieces in doom from a poisonous dart,
whose time in Izmir was short,
who once went for a walk
on the beetling bank

of the Thracian river, which neighbored Gediz, & was
touched on the hand by a snake, which reared its head,
spread its hood, & didn't restrict the gape of its maw,
but sprung at the man, like a whip to the haunch
of a human being; for it shuddered along its length
with a hiss like a treacherous storm, wrapping its back like a wreath
on the flesh of the mortal, dancing about the cheeks
& downy chin, carving furrows on the face
of Tylus with many a fang, spitting the fluid of fate
from poisonous darts. Garlanded on his throat
by the whirls of the tail over shoulders sagging beneath
the weight of the threat, he wore a collar of reptilian death,
the neighbor of Fate; for he fell to the ground dead
like a sprout from the earth.

Sad for the youth, who swooned at the expression of doom, sad & disheveled,
the naiad lamented the death of her neighbor & pulled
the monstrous beast from his neck in order to break it, for many were
the shepherds & travelers whom it felled. Not only Tylus
did it unseasonably kill, but haunting the wilderness, feasting on beasts, it often tore
a tottering tree with the roots themselves with its hinges of festering teeth before
it again brought it up & blew out the chunks of the bristling trunk. For many were
the travelers, spinning in circles, sucked to its maw with insidious gasps
as it guzzled a whole human being in plain sight with a yawp.

Searching with darting eye from afar, Moria the nymph
saw this murderer of her kinsman & shuddered with fear.
Seeing the copious rows of the poisonous darts of its teeth & the intricate
garland of death on the downy chin of Tylus, Moria shrieked
fiercely in the dragon-feeding wilderness.

Then she ran into Breaker, the mountainous son of the Earth,
whom his mother in parthenogenesis bore, complete from birth
with a beard on his cheeks. When he was engendered, Strife was his nurse,
the spear was his mother's milk, his diapers were breastplates, his baths were murders,
as with a big load of grownup limbs, still a child, even a newborn, but stout, he lumbered,
a neighbor of clouds. He wielded a spear the size of himself. At his first appearance, Parturition equipped
the babe in his crib with a warrior's shield. When the plaintive nymph
saw him from the idyllic hill of the forest, with a gesture, she showed him
the monstrous vermin that killed her brother, Tylus, who lay carved up in the dust, panting.
The giant did not ignore her. He forced a tree with the roots themselves from his mother,
the Earth. Facing the snake that ate raw flesh, the monster of a champion
took his position opposite to his serpent Lordship who whirled
into action for battle & hissed his clarion
noise, five acres coiled.

Cinching itself like a shackle about his feet two times around,
whipping its whirling circles around the figure of Breaker, it opened the gates
of its fangs with a frenzied yawp, it shot the flickering missile from its lips, it throbbed
in its eyes, it gasped raw death, it spat sheer fountains of arrows from gushing cheeks
in the Giant's face, vomiting long & furious jets of yellow from its teeth, & then it leaped
over the lofty crest of the giant's head & hurdled straight at him with its earth-
shattering frame. In his unfathomable size, the Giant shook the weight
of the spiny hide of the dragon from his limbs as big as mountains.

Hurling his oaken missile still fringed with foliage,
he sent it shuddering straight from his hand to where the bulge
of the neck is cinched with the spinal cord.
He fixed it, branch & all. Once more, it rooted
itself in the earth where the dragon lay, a coiled
corpse immovable.

All of a sudden, its partner, the female snake, whirling around,
came looking for her meandering mate, homeward bound,
scraping the ground with her weight like a wife when she pines
for her husband who died. Approaching the heights, she shuddered
along her enormous length as she sped to the hills. With her jaws of a lizard,
she plucked the flower of God. From the wilderness on the tips of her lips she brought
the pain-reducing herb & stuffed a balm for doom in the dried nostrils of the horrid
corpse. With a poisonous tooth, she furnished the flower of life to the paralyzed corpse,
which started to shudder, whirling around on itself. One part alone continued
not to breathe; another moved; the half-reanimated corpse was shaking the last,
with a tail that dashed by itself. Its icy gullet caught a second breath.
Bit by bit it began to whistle through the old unclosing throat
& took its former hisses back. It sped
into its ancient pit, & went back home.

Moria took a little of the flower of God, & in the vital nostril of the corpse,
she stuffed the life-producing herb. With pain-assuaging clusters,
the nourishing fodder of the herb enspirited the recrudescent corpse
with enfiguring breath; a second coming of the soul enfigured it.
The icy figure began to take the warmth of salvific flame;
the corpse began to work with vital functions again.
First, it put the right foot flat, & then it set the left foot straight
& began to secure its footing, assuming the image of a person
who just got up from bed & shook the sleep straight from their vision.
The blood flowed back; the fingers of the corpse began to wriggle.
In the course of this resurrection, the rhythm

returned to the form: the power of walking returned
to the feet, the light returned to the eyes,
to the lips returned his voice.

9. The last images

As Cybele, the Mother was carved on the shield
appearing fresh from childbirth & just as when she made
the infant which was not an infant imitate
wriggling on her bosom with arms of art.
As Rhea weaving wiles, she then offered
her unfeeling husband the child of stone,
the cannibal meal that would weigh him down,
& he, the Father with gorging jaws, then swallowed
the stone shape of a human child, gobbled
the false figure of the other god. He struggled
with the burden that he took between his hips
& shaped his Olympian offspring into darts,
which, from his pregnant cheek,
he then heaved forth.

Such were the works of genius versatile
presented in the masterpiece
of the shield of Dionysus,
manufactured on Olympus.
Thunderstruck from looking on it,
one by one, all circled the bearer of the orb,
praising Olympus' fiery forge.

Turning the light of her blazing face
away from them, as they took joy,
day sank into the west. Across the surface
of the earth-dark night began to seep
in silence. Here & there the masses
took some food & on scattered mattresses,
they sank in mountain sleep.

Book 26

Darwin Michener-Rutledge

The twenty-sixth book has Athena in disguise
And the Indian army assembling for war.

As Deriades lay sleeping on his downcast bed, Athena
came near, loyal to her brother Bacchus and intent on soliciting
a second victory for him. She had donned the appearance
of Orontes, mimicking the son-in-law of high-helmed Deriades;
and so, although alarm over the fate of his army's casualties
had torn him from the red haze of war, he was gulled
by the apparition in his false dream as it urged him
to reignite his battle with the wine god:

"You're asleep, Deriades, but I must chastise you:
it is not fit for the princely ruler of a city to doze all night.
A commander governs his sleep. The enemy throngs
about your walls, and you haven't lifted a spear,
deaf to the surging clamor of drums and whistling
pipes, and to the harrowing trumpet that musters the host!
Pity your daughter, Protonoë, a girlish widow grieving
for her husband, and do not leave me unavenged!
Descend upon my butchers while they sleep unarmed.
Look at my chest skewered by a thyrsus!
What a misfortune that brave Lycurgus doesn't live here.

You ought to rule the haughty Arabs! Dionysus was no god
when a mortal hounded him into refuge below the sea!
I have seen Deriades running from battle against women.
Be the fearless lion now, for Dionysus fled
like a fawn in his fawnskin from a mere mortal in armor.
He wasn't the one who destroyed the belligerent Indians.
Your own father who did that. Hydaspes saw your front lines
retreating and he mowed them down! You're unique,
your veins pulse with the celestial blood of your blazing
grandfather, Phaëthon, passed down through his daughter.
Your body's immortal; no sword or spear will ever
bring you down when you attack Lyaeus."

So spoke scheming Athena, and, no longer
in the guise of a dream, she returned to Olympus.

At dawn, Deriades assembled his army,
sending heralds out to all the islands and cities.
Countless storm-footed messengers dispersed
to muster the troops from the many towns
on the eastern frontier, and warriors thirsty for battle
trooped in from all over at their king's command.

The two sons of Eulaeus, AGRAEUS and PHLOGIUS,
those moguls of warfare, were the first in arms,
co-leaders since the recent burial of their father.
With them came all who lived beside the broad waters
of Indian Ombelos in Cyra and Baidion,
and all from turreted, belligerent Rhodoë,
and from craggy Propanisus, and those who occupied
the curving island of the Graeae, too, where children suckle
at manly breasts, filching their drink with pursed lips
from their nursing fathers instead of their mothers.
Some came from steep Sesindion, and men from Gazus
who had fortified their city with linen walls, made it
an unassailable fortress of Ares, constructed of blocks
of plaited thread and with shrewdly spun foundations,

such that no enemy hand bearing battle-ready bronze
had ever broken those ranks of linen-sheathed towers.

Behind them followed the bold warriors of the Dardian
and Prasian armies, and the gold-decked Salangi,
who entertain Wealth himself at their hearths.
They eat dried peas as the staff of life, grinding them
instead of grain with their millstones. Next came
a cavalcade of curly-haired Zabii; their leader was a wise,
god-fearing man, PALTHANOR, who sympathized
with Dionysus and despised Deriades. When the war
was done, Dionysus took him along and placed him
in lyre-built Thebes, a foreign settler, and there
he stayed, beside Dirce, drinking Ismenian water
from the Aonian river, far from his native Hydaspes.

Next came MORRHEUS DIDNASIDES, exulting
in his huge army. His father, Didnasus, sad and old,
was with him, a finely crafted buckler on his aged arm.
Hoary white whiskers shadowed his chin,
heralding his many years. He was still bitter
with sorrow, mourning the undue death of his son, Orontes.
There went Didnasus, tears falling. Behind him marched
Lord Morrheus, ready to slay with his avenging spear
Dionysus' entire army, to fight Bacchus himself,
his brother's murderer, in single combat, intent on wounding
that accursed, as yet unwounded son of Thyonê!
A polyglot brood of Indians came with them:
some who lived in in beautiful Aethra, city of the Sun,
some from the Athene's thickets, from Oryië's swamps,
sweltering Nesaea, Melaenae, and Patalene's delta.
Marching behind them were contingents of Dyssaei
followed by armed masses of hairy-chested Sabiri,
who never cower before Enyo, goddess of war.

Arrayed beside them were the Uatocoetae, "Ear-Sleepers,"
men who sleep pillowed on their long ears. They were marshalled

by PHRINGUS, and ASPETUS, and disdainful DANYCLUS,
who marched together, along with HORSETAIL
and his comrade MORRHEUS, the archer: five brutal commanders,
all of one mind, marshalling the Ear Sleepers.

Another archer, TECTAPHUS, also went to the war.
Once, he had been snatched from death by sucking
the milk from his daughter's breast with hungry lips.
The girl had come up with this ruse to nourish her father
when he was practically dead, a shriveled corpse.
Deriades, the king, had made good a cruel threat,
tying him up in knots of rope and locking him
in a rank, rotting pit to lie there unfed, unwashed,
eroded by hunger, and never to see the sun or the moon.
He lay there in agony, chained underground
his wretched cavern, with nothing to drink, no morsel to chew,
seeing no one but himself, ravaged by hunger
and barely breathing, painfully sucking in the air
between his withered lips, his body fetid with decay.
Prison guards kept watch over him, but they were deceived
by his clever daughter, who had just given birth,
when she stood before them and pleaded with them,
shaking out her dress to show it held no trickery:

"Don't kill me, guards! I don't have anything here,
no food or drink for my father, only tears. My vacant hands
tell you I bring tears alone, and you must allow me that!
If you do not believe me, undo my sash, rip off my veil,
riffle through my dress! If you don't believe me, do it!
Drink would save his life, and I have brought none! Simply
lock me up to be with my father in this pit as well. I am no threat
to you, even if word reaches the king. Who is angry when
one pities a dying man? Who gets angry when a body
is mourned? Who does not pity the dead? I merely come
to shut my father's sinking eyes, so shut me up in there!
Tell me, who begrudges death? Just let us die together,
this one tomb serving for both father and daughter."

She convinced them. The girl darted
into the dungeon, bringing light to her father's gloom.
She felt no fear in that pit, as she let the milk flow
from her salvific breast into her father's mouth.

Deriades was amazed when he heard of Eërië's
filial piety, and he released the father of that clever girl,
and like a shade he left from his dark prison.
Word of the girl's gumption spread rapidly and far,
and the Indian army praised the cunning girl's breast
that had saved her father's life. So this man shone
among the Bolinges like Hesperus, who ushers
the murky gloom that floods in at nightfall
and gleams brightest among the stars.

Towering GINGLON, striding THYRAIEUS,
and cloud-high HIPPALMUS had all armed
the various tribes at the farthest reaches of the earth:
the proud Arachotes and the legions of the neighboring
Dersaei, who bury their battle-fallen men
beneath mounds of earth, leaving the others for carrion.

HABRATHOÖS came with an army of archers
that he had recruited, though he had been slow
to take arms, embarrassed by his newly shorn head.
Deriades, the horned king, had cut off all of his hair
in a fit of mad rage, a brutal insult to an Indian,
and now he resented the overbearing monarch,
nursing a bitter grudge against him. He came
unwilling but compelled to the war, secret rancor
deep in his heart, and hid the shame of his temples
with a high-crested helmet. When battle came,
he joined the fight by daylight, but each nightfall
he sent a trusted servant to Bacchus to reveal
Deriades' next stratagem. In this way he fought in public
for the Indian warlord but in truth for the wine god.
He had recruited the savage Xuthi, the militant Arieni,

the Zoares, and the clan of Eares, along with the Caspirians
and the Arbians: those who guarded the bright
shining stream Hysporus, gilded with its rich, deep
mines of amber, and hold also prominent Arsanië,
where the women are so accomplished at Pallas' loom
that in a single day they can weave an entire chiton.

The Cyraei came alongside them, the distinguished divers.
They know the wave-whipped island coasts and are skilled
in naval battle, but do not use regular seafaring vessels.
They sail in round kayaks made of untanned hide,
which they helm as easily as a shipwright's wooden craft.
They steer their course in these makeshift skins,
the mariner sitting sheltered as he crosses the sea,
etching the waves' backs in his ersatz vessel.
These were commanded by the sons of Tarbelus,
the spearman: THYAMIS and regal HOLCASUS.

A great drove arrived from Arizaneteia,
nourished by the strange tree-honey, where
the trees soak up the fruitful damp of morning dew,
and their leaves swell with amber honey, producing
what the clever bees do working in their hives.
Phaëthon, rising from his morning ocean bath,
sprinkles the fields with the nourishing water from his hair
and waters the fertile earth. This is the honey Arizanteia offers:
Reveling in this, great flocks of birds sail on their wings
and jive above the leaves; or else a winding serpent
writhes along, coiling itself about the sweet tree
in scaly circles, while he licks and sucks down
the leaves' nectar into his greedy maw. In this way snakes drool
the sweet tree sap and spill delicious honey, spitting out
more of the bee's candied syrup than their own bitter venom.
Perched on those honey-exuding branches, the horion bird,
sings as sweetly as an inspired swan;
not striking up a tune harmonizing with Zephyr
or fluttering around with musical whirring wings,

but adeptly warbling a ballad, like a man plucking
the strings for a wedding song as he waits for the bride.
There, the golden-yellow pheasant forecasts the rain
with his clear-toned voice, as the blaze of dawn flashes
in his eyes, performing high aloft in the treetops,
weaving his song in tune to the horion behind him,
a splendor of purple wings. If you heard him singing
his aubade, you might think it was a morning serenade
pouring out from a nightingale's quavering throat.

This was the homeland of the army led by PYLOETES,
Hippalmus' son, along with his brother, BILLAEUS.

The Sibai troops were next, beside the Hydarcans,
along with an army from the city of Carmina, led together
by the sons of Brongus whom Deriades honored:
CYLLARUS and the Indian potent ASTRAËIS.

After them came a muster from the Three Hundred Islands,
scattered close and far, which float where the Indus
endlessly pours out its meandering stream into the delta,
creeping in slow curves through Indian reedbeds
and across the plains to its mouth at the Eastern sea,
after it has cascaded down from its source in the Himalayas,
swollen with summer-brought waters, and growing cubit by cubit
with its own flooding tide as it embraces the rich land
like an aqueous husband, and gladdens with his moist kisses
a thirsty bride, while he takes her into his passionate arms
for a harvesting bridal, from which he begets recurrent streams:
such is the Nile in Egypt, and the Hydaspes in India.
The wandering hippopotamus lives there among the waters,
cutting through the black-pebbled streams with his hooves
just like the denizen of my very own Nile, who cleaves
the summer floods and wanders the depths with his gaping jaws.
He climbs the banks, cracking the woody shoots with his teeth,
and with only his fleshy wet jaw as a sort of sickle
with which to purloin fruit, he steals the wheat harvest,

a reaper of the leafy crops without steel.
Such was the powerful Indian river, like the seven-mouthed Nile,
and these were the warriors who now came together in arms
from the curved island shores and the towns and villages
along the Indus, all led by the gigantic RHIGBASUS.

And no, old ARETUS was not missing when Deriades sounded
the call to war. He was a heavy man, but still wore a fitted
bronze breastplate over his hairy chest and carried
an oxhide shield on his ancient back, slung from a strap
across his bending neck. He armed his summoned troops
together with his five sons, both Lycus and Myrsus,
then Glaucus and Periphas, and Melaneus the youngest.
His helmet covered his curling gray hairs as he stationed himself
on the left flank of his battle line, leaving his sons on the right.
These were men whose lips had been silenced by Nature's
tying their tongues, our instruments of intelligible speech.

It happened this way: a divine prodigy had occurred
at the doors of the bridal chamber, when Aretus
pledged himself to Laobië in the rites of lawful marriage
with sacred dance, joining her in wedlock to bring forth children.
While the bridegroom, having just finished his wedding dance,
was at the marriage altar, busied in sacrificing
to bridal Aphrodite, the hall still resounding with hymns,
a sow, swollen with pregnancy, squealed
in the agony of her labor, an omen of things to come,
and birthed a bizarre, unbelievable litter,
a school of fish that shot out from her womb, sea creatures,
not the life of the land. Rumors telling of the fish-mother sow
flew from mouth to mouth, and people from all over
gathered to stare at the strange land animals
perfectly resembling spawn of the sea.

Aretus consulted a prophet, who foretold
a succession of mute children, as voiceless
as the sow's marine progeny. The seer told him to hide the omen

and curry favor with the guide of quick-witted speech,
governor of tongues: Hermes, the long-winged son of Maia.

Laobië was taken to her bed, and in birth after birth
delivered as many children as the sows' offspring, all of them
as mute as fishes. After the victory, Bacchus took pity
on them and loosened the knots that tied their tongues,
expelling the silence that had plagued them since birth,
and bestowing voices upon them, made whole at last.

These troops were accompanied by shield-bearing warriors
mustered from Pylae and from Eucolla as well,
the territory of belligerent Eos near the East Wind,
and from sacred Goryandis, a fertile land.

After them came armed forces from the far reaches of Oeta,
that sylvan birthplace of the long-lived elephants,
on which nature bestows a lifespan of two hundred years,
and who, rounding so often the century mark, in eternal time,
sometimes even lumber through three hundred years.
They are black from the sole of the foot to the top of the head.
They feed side by side. Large tusks protrude from their long jaws,
two of them, curved like reaper's scythes, sharp and sundering,
and they lumber through the dense woods on long legs.
Their necks are rounded like a camel's, and their capacious backs
can carry a horde of riders, arranged in rows, as they swing
their heavy feet from jointless knees. They have short, curved
necks, the wide foreheads of a snake, and eyes like a pig's.
An elephant is colossal, and as he moves along, the thin ears
near his temples move like fans in the gentlest breath of air.
A skinny little tail whips against his body continually.
Often, in battle, the gargantuan animal swings his tusks and attacks
like a bullheaded beast, striking with whetted sickles
fastened to his natural spears on either side of his mouth.
Often when he has skewered a man, he raises him straight up
to his greedy throat, armor, shield, and all; or else he throws
him down with a pointed tusk, picks up the body as it tumbles,

helpless, in a cloud of dust, and bunts it away to fly through the air.
The sharp swords of his tusks reach down to his feet
as he flings his jaw this way and that with its jagged row of teeth,
aligned between ivory like a cobra's vertebrae.

After the Indian War, Lord Dionysus led these animals
to Caucasian lands along the Amazonian River
and scattered those warrior women while astride
the back of a mountainous elephant. But that came later.
In this battle, when Deriades sent his summons
for war with Lyaeus, it was the chieftain PYLOETES
who answered the call by driving a straight-legged elephant
into the fray. He shared the same belligerent blood
as Marathon, a man most fortunate in his children,
and when he came to the war he was followed
by the neighboring people of a different tongue,
who came from Eristobareia with her crowning battlements.

Tribes from Derbices came to Deriades as well,
as did a vast army of woolly-headed Blemyes,
and many Bactrian tribes, Sacae, and Ethiopians.
These Ethiopians follow a strange and clever custom
in battle: they conceal their true facial features
beneath a mask, the top of a dead horses' head, and so
mingle the dead with the living. In combat, they startle
their unsuspecting foes with these faux heads, and their leader
cries out through two mouths with a misleading sound,
his manly voice emerging as a horse's bray.

These were the forces that answered their king's call.
The entire army was marshaled by that great emperor
of the Indians, born from the union of Hydaspes,
that aqueous lover, and Astris, daughter of the Sun,
(and men whisper that her mother was Ceto the naiad,
daughter of Oceanus) and blessed in her birthing.
Hydaspes slipped into her bower until he flooded it,
and made love to her with a watery embrace.

He had true Titan blood, for he had came from the bed
of primeval Thaumas and his rosy-armed Electra,
that brought forth a river and a messenger of the gods.
Both had an equal speed on their separate paths,
Iris among the immortals and Hydaspes among rivers.

Such was the magnitude of the assembled host.
The city was packed with people. Helmeted bands
surrounded by sweet-faced squires crowded in the circle
of streets that ran all four ways in the city, or gathered
thick at the three-ways, some by the moat, while still others
climbed the height of the walls as the rest lay quietly
on the turrets and slept beside their weapons.
Deriades entertained all the commanders in his hall,
and all ate around the same table as their hospitable king
taking turns in row upon row of seats. They were busy
with feasting throughout the evening until night arrived
on the wing of sleep. Then the army slumbered beneath
their weapons on the eve of battle, and their dreams were
drenched in warfare, fighting shadows shaped like satyrs.

Book 27

Melina McClure

The twenty-seventh: where Zeus strives to find
New allies for war, the celestial kind.

Then, shaking from herself the soft down of unfettering sleep,
Dawn who brings forth war opened wide the gates of the east,
and she crept on tiptoe from her lush bed of light,
so as not to wake Cephalus, still tangled in the sheets.
And thrown into Phaëthon's enveloping arms,
all dark of Ganges was bleached white and blinding,
and little holes like bite marks appeared in the gauze of fog
as the mists resigned to their daily flight, once more
splintered by teeth and shaft of morning light.
And all the hanging fruits in daybreak routine
were busy striving for that high-polished springtime glossy
and they scrubbed their faces red to raw in the dew.

And there was confusion.

Phaëthon, shepherd of the ever-coursing years,
suddenly reined in the clip of his fire-fed horses
at the nearby echoes of Ares' helmet clink clinking,
and he challenged the army to take up the spear
with yellow fiery witness, and cast
into the air one scalding, rose-flush lance.

Crash! Zeus poured out an eerie storm upon the land
and buckets of blood (blood!) fell from heaven as rain,
harbinger of death for the Indians . . .
And the Indian earth's blue-black back, dust-cracked, parched to tears,
blushed to drink raindrops from so mean a downpour, so bloody,
but oh god she needed the moisture
so she swallowed in spite of the shame.
And all around, newly polished iron
reflected the sharp, sharp glint of daylight
and returned to heaven that which it received,
in equipoise to the unflinching glare of Helios.

In all the confusion stood the Indian warriors
dripping, and before them insolent Deriades
set his sharp chin moving and roused the troops with these words:
"My devoted soldiers! Fight with me!
Follow the familiar scent of victory to its source!
I want that cheeky son of Thyonê as my lackey,
the Horned serving the horned,
and I want all his Pans butchered by the iron thresher.
But! If indeed they are a herd of gods
with bodies safe from iron, safe from slaughter,
then I want them collared, I want them
snatched from the hillgrass, on which they leap and they glut,
and forced to shepherd my herds of once wild elephants
so that they may recognize their own captivity
in the tamed and broken eyes of other beasts of burden.
Oh but I must not forget the centaurs—
this zoo is getting crowded, but I'll make room
for the entire Dionysian collections—
Maybe I'll give my daughter some of the vermin,
a hive of bustling ladies-in-waiting, and waiters
to serve meat at the tables of Morrheus.
    "Any man from Phrygia on tour with wine-dark Bacchus
can purge his skin in the rush of Indian river,
disown Sangarius and pledge allegiance to Hydaspes.
Any man from Alybe who follows Dionysus

will be a slave here, and, having sloughed off the waters
of a lesser, silver river, sip the golden Ganges.
Run, Dionysus! Flee Deriades' spear.
Here too is there a boundless sea; may she
be the next to receive you after the swollen flank
of the Arabian main. Our sea, more voluptuous deep,
gags and hiccoughs more violent waters
and she is enough, by far enough
to enfold in brute embrace all the satyrs,
column after column of Bassarids, and Bacchus too.
Here you will not be sheltered by a gentle Nereus,
or an Indian Thetis at her pregnant, haven breast,
for she fears and she blushes before the baritone drawl,
the bursting heave and howl of my ancestral Hydaspes.
"Oh but you will say: In my veins I harbor
the blood of Zeus, Olympic, unspillable!
Well I say that Earth created aether
and etched in our sky the stars, chorus of cosmic bodies.
Yes, yes, heaven birthed you, but this my Earth will bury.
This fertile land gulped down Cronus himself,
who in belated contraception
took his newborn children barely severed from the mother
(before they even turned a living color,
but still blue and wan as an organ)
and bit into them lush and raw with his teeth
as though cooking them might leave an opportunity
for resurrection or maybe remorse.
And he too was born of heaven.
"Of an entire army bold with the spear,
I am the boldest, the very best of Lycurgus
(who also chased your unwarlike warriors).
I'm hardly rattled by your bloodline tumbled down from Zeus,
for I know your mommy Semele's story, penetrated
in turn by all-consuming distrust and consummate fire.
And I need no soliloquy on the flashing lightning
that stood by Zeus' bedside and held his hand,
blotting at sweat and preparing cold compresses;

or about that miracle, cranial birth canal
(what a brow!); or Cronion's thigh, so comely, so manly.
I'm hardly shaken by the thought of Zeus in contractions . . .
I have seen childbirth! My wife has labored so many times
that my knuckles are now squeezed an unfading white.
If he wishes, this Zeus who impregnates himself
can arm girlie Athena, whom they call Victory
as a savior of you 'the very manly,'
and thus having fractured the headland, I might bloody the head
of Pallas on a skin-breaking crag,
or maybe just my trusty spear, and I may shoot arrows
from this lovely, horned bow into the thigh
of Dionysus, lord of the beefy-horned satyrs,
and tether all to sinking shame the happy threesome
of Zeus and Bromius and Pallas.
"But if on their heads they wear fine helmets forged by the one
who takes ginger steps and halts and shudders in limp,
then I too need the rare work of Hephaestus,
so that he can knead copper in ember-rend of hammer
anvil, hammer anvil, and sculpt for Deriades
an abundance of glorious arms.
I'm not afraid of the woman general Athena,
for if she shakes her father's lightning,
with my own father's water I'll douse her out spluttering.
"And cocksure Aeacus, who they say is a sproutling
of heavenly Zeus and a blood brother to Lyaeus,
him I will send dead to that shadow of his father,
father but inverted across horizonal axis,
nether father, Zeus Infernal, Hades.
"Do you hear that thudding to the ground?
Oh that, my friends, is the rosy sound
of all the sons of Zeus who have fallen before now.
Dardanus was of Zeus and he is dead,
and Minos? Also dead, unprotected by Zeus' bull-faced bed.
If Minos lays down the law in Hades,
what harm does it do the Indians
if Aeacus also becomes a judge of the decaying?

If he wants, let him hold sovereignty over corpses
and clutch the scepter to the gaping pit.
 "But do not kill the earthborn Cyclopes,
thrusting whetted spearpoint into the gut or throat of those
who graze the bedrock of heaven with their gangling limbs;
but rather let your bronze drill into their wet rolling eye.
No, do not kill the earthen Cyclopes,
because I will find a use for them too:
kneeling and sweating in an Indian forge,
Brontes will mold for me a deafening war-trumpet
which I will lift to my lips and with blast of mortal breath
shock the air in mimicry of thunder, an earthen Zeus.
And that heaven-sent lightning that shatters night
with deep and downward reaching roots will be rivaled
by the white, new light which Steropes will invent for me,
and like spreading venom or sky-chisel skeletons
my light, my light will crack upwards, upwards
in retaliatory symmetry and rage.
And I will disgrace Him in battle with the satyrs
so that the heart of jealous Cronides be further
carved and cleft to watch Deriades
wrathful wield crash of thunder and whoreson lightning,
and He will flee me as I bloom and flash.
 "I have every right to fill my palms with blaze
and twizzle warp of lightning veins
and set heaven's environs to seething.
My mother's father is keeper of the blazing stars,
Phaëthon (closes his eyes and all he sees is red),
rasping fire-general of all that kindles,
but if I harbor the blood of my father the river,
I will rise against Dionysus with water as weapon,
and turn a dry battle into marshy melee.
I will encircle the Bacchants in the swollen river,
to the height of their ankles, a splash, to their knees,
to the dimples in their thighs, a slosh, a trudge,
to their nipples, panic, up their noses
and over their heads choking choking choking . . .

"Cut down the bodies of the Telchines
with iron threshers and sink them in a neighboring sea,
back to the precinct of their father Poseidon,
and bring back to me the broad, silvery leather
used to yoke their sea-course horses.
Burn with flaming torch Erechtheus slumped under leaden chains,
citizen of Athens and descendent of that other,
famous Erechtheus: the spurned sperm of Hephaestus
jettisoned to earth and allowed a life only
through his adoption by Pallas Athena,
who lay awake in furtive lamplight
holding him to her virgin breast and fighting
creeping starvation from his small body, almost a mother.
She can keep this one hidden away in a box too,
a glinting Indian urn in some empty corner
of her marriageless, childless halls, dark and lonely as pitch.
"Bring to me the Corybants unarmed,
who run about with oxhide shields and know the dance of war.
Let Lemnian Cabiro unveiled scream out
a multiplying grief for her two dead children,
and, having thrown aside his instruments, let Hephaestus
lurk somewhere wiping soot from his eyes
to watch the murderer of his bloodline,
Deriades, sit upon the chariot
and mount the bronze-footed horses of the Cabiri.
"But I want to kill sons of Zeus! I don't blame Morrheus
for killing Aristaeus, hare-hunting son of Phoebus
and master of those wee feisty honeybees,
little but livid and reckless with their lives.
Take your sickles, your double-edged sword, and scythe
through the ripe and supple Bassarids!
May the high-horned son of Zeus
die by the horned son of a river.
May no man blanch to see the enemy riding a lioness
or mounting a she-bear, wild and thrashing with no bridle
but only his knees digging into her brawny haunch!
Do not cower before the maws of his show-beasts;

for what man would flee a leopard or a lion
when he himself marches beside armored elephants?"

With this the king stopped and the Indians
set forth toward the Sturm und Drang of war:
some upon the broad sway of elephants weighed down in iron,
some on horses with gale-force hoofs, hurricane of stomp and champ,
and no gap between these and countless waves of infantry
and their weapons: the point, the shield, the quiver.
One man held aloft the faithful trinity
of shield, bow, and wind-whip arrows, and another held
a brass, beaky sickle as though reaper of war.
And to Indus' mouth they flew in whirlwind cycle of limbs,
braced and tense against the coming onslaught of fatal din . . .

Meanwhile: from behind a thick tangle of woods
Dionysus handed around shields and swords
and lovingly armored his warriors
in sheets of incorruptible, unbreakable leaves
(all the while fidgeting with the thyrsus in his hand).
And naked Dawn was now risen to eye level,
sending squirming sunspots into mortal cornea,
and the Bacchants, squinting too late, stood blinking away
linger brilliances as they were portioned by their lord
into quarters and positioned towards the four winds.
The first quarter occupied thick, woven copse
at the land at the foot of the Bear
(ever in starry arc and cycle),
where rainwater collected in far-forking rivers
runs off from the heights of Caucasus,
and where thrum, thrum Hydaspes leads his swirl out to sea.
He placed the next bunch where Indus with double maws
roams the mountains, winding, inclining towards evenin' clime,
over there in the midlands hemming around Patalene
like a girdle, or like a garland.
The third he placed where the southern lap
of the sea drags noontime in swollen heave,

and the fourth and last he placed all gleaming bronze
at the arched instep of the rising sun,
where Ganges sets out, slipping, whisking about,
and floods the reeds in his sweet-smelling waters.

With his forces now rightly split and well equipped,
Bacchus chose a general for each quadrant hand-picked
and emboldened all his army with a rousing speech:

"Dance here too, my Bassarids, dance here!
Slaughter the barbarous, the bitter tribes
and acquaint your thyrsus with their sword and spear.
You all know my pipe as sunny herald to smörgåsbord,
but now let it become a trumpet of war and sound out
to my satyrs fast-approaching chaos and discord.
May my late summer ripeness, all bright and green,
splinter spears and make iron clatter to the earth.
May my pipe now abandon our nightly dances
and the palate-sweet shadow songs of Echo after dinner,
and call out instead the vengeful hymn of Enyo.
But! If Hydaspes will take a humble knee before me,
never again billow such rancor against me,
then I will be a gracious god. I'll redecorate, revamp
his crystal glass waters into deep plummy wine,
viscid, and girdle up his nape of feral timberland
with leafy vines that flush not dusky green, not dark,
but brilliant green that says to all: sunshine! Lush and supple.
However. If he comes again with relief for his son,
morphing to fill the shell, the imitation, of a man
with bubble bones and cool spume heartstrings of the horned river,
if he comes again as guardian alluvion,
then he'll suffer the gasp! smother of a dam, severance,
and you will tread his back without muddying your feet
and where the horses used to bathe (or cower
from the currents in fear, depending on their temperaments),
hoof will scratch the caking dust of a whilom river
as Hydaspes shivers naked to the sun
and smacks parched lips in prayer to any passing cloud.

"If the warlike Indian people's cowardly leader
is indeed born from Phaëthon's ethereal race,
and in honoring his horned daughter's son
Phaëthon should sic fiery Enyo upon me,
again will I arm my Cronides' briny kinsman
to squelch the fires licking Phaëthon's warlust loin.
I'll go to the island Thrinacia
where roam the flocks and herds of Helios,
sizzling Charioteer, and I will force the daughter
of the fire-yolk sun under the yoke of vile slavery
and push her to her knee looking up at me
lumped in the tent with all the other
war prize girls whose open bodies
are amassed for the sake of a soldier's perks and prick.
"And may Astris wander to the hills
weeping for her Deriades now in leaden chains.
Let her go wandering, if she wishes,
all the way to the land of the Celts
so that she might turn into a poplar
with the Heliads, soft skin hardened to bark,
and cry a tireless coulee of tears.
"Hurry. Take up in your hands the black skin
of our captured Indians and pale the cheeks moonlike
with white streaks of initiate chalk. Entangle that bold one
(you know his name but I'll say it, Deriades) entwined
in windings of vine and clusters of sweet fruit hanging off him,
and soften his bronze-clad shoulders with a fawnskin.
May the Indian king bend a slave's knee
before Bromius after Bromius' victory
and lay bare his body to be uncostumed and redressed:
cold metal corslet swapped for warm, fuzzy pelt,
shiny silver greaves for dark russet buskins.
And after a lifetime learning war, bloody clangor,
let him at last be taught how to dance,
and through the dark night relieve the bodily rhythms,
gyrate, toss his hair, stomp the grapes.
"Bring to windy Tmolus the heads of our dead enemies

signed and pierced by thyrsus witness, vouchers of victory!
From the other side of this war will I bring with me
column after marching column of captive Indian bodies
and I will decorate the Lydian gates
with the horns of raging Deriades."

And as their lord and leader spoke these words,
all were made brave and they looked into each other's eyes nodding
and shaking for a moment . . . until all was hurry,
war-cry, hurry, rally, shout and sing and drums.
And the women responded to the echoing drums
with echoing, rattling clappers clap, clap
and the Phrygian pan-pipes led the army and set the rhythm:
a cacophony somehow somehow in sync.

And conducting all this noise towards the coming battle,
Mydonian fire leapt and splashed on the torch,
reminder to all that Bacchus had a fiery birth,
and the skin of Silenus made waxy by the passing years
reflected the light from his horny forehead
as though from a living, wrinkled mirror;
the wild mane of one hill haunting Bacchant
was held back from her face by a snake
woven all through her hair like a ribbon,
needle-sharp teeth not biting but like
moving bobby pins pulling a curl here, now there,
and forked tongue licking back strays;
and the satyrs' cheeks were white with sacred chalk,
white, white as though disjoined from the body, hovering
phantom faces of soft white calcite,
impermanent but unspeakably depraved.
And under the yoke of one phantom face
was a captive tigress fueled by hunger and pain
who bit at fat stomp stomping ankles and caused a stampede
(elephants sound like people when they scream).
And silvery Maron armed only with spiraling bough
split live Indian bodies with a sapling switch of vine . . .

In the meantime, all the denizens of heaven
ate like cormorants before the throne of Zeus
in golden chairs in the godly court, and Ganymede,
too delectable for the mortal world,
drew nectar from the mixing bowl
(himself a walking confection)
and dripped its ribbons in immortal cups
a viscid sappy: the consistency of loose mucus
but honey amber and the purest sweet.
(For at that time no Achaean war was raging
against the children of Tros as there had been before
when Hebe once more mixed drinks for the blessed
and the immortal Trojan cup boy was kept far at bay
because everyone wanted to shelter him—
so sweet so innocent—from the death of his fatherland.)
And Zeus spoke to the assembly, but specifically
to Apollo and Hephaestus and Athena
and made everyone else feel a little bit neglected:

"Lord of the speaking axle of Pytho,
Master of the bow, Bringer of light, Brother to Bacchus,
remember Parnassus and Dionysus.
Ampelos did not escape your notice,
living for but one day. And you know
the mystic, twin torch fire of both mountain peaks.
Bend your bow for the Bassarids and fight for your brother!
Honor the rock of Parnassus, joint owner,
where a Bacchant lost in revelry dances with eyes closed
and shouts involuntary, urging on her weary limbs
and tending the one common Delphian fire
not only for sleepless Dionysus but also for you!
Remember your Cyrene, dimpled lion-slayer.
Give your grace to both Agreus and Dionysus.
You are the Shepherd; fight for the race of shepherd satyrs!
Don't give Hera the satisfaction of laughing
at her stepsons, you and fleeing Dionysus,
(the humorless, jealous bitch)

(don't tell her that I said that), scurvy spiteful,
evergreen with bile and envy for my dalliances,
ever conniving after all you sweet bastard babies!

"I need not remind you of your own mother's
pains for childbirth, when Leto exhausted did not rest
at all for pregnancy but wandered far, wide, high, low,
waddle-wincing under the double weight of twins,
whip-raw from the sting of forging gods two at a time.
When the flow of Peneus fled your mother, and Dirce rebuffed her,
and Asopus himself graceless, pivoted course on his stiff knee,
and all the waters had fled her, and her own water broke,
only Delos would comfort Leto against the contractions,
and an old palm tree with its spindle-sparse fronds
delivered her and smoothed her hair.

"And you, my brave girl, Pallas, whose mother and father
both are Zeus, defend your brother, commander of your fatherland.
Draw under your wing your people following Dionysus,
don't watch the children of your Marathon perish,
but honor the bough of the Actaean olive-tree
that made you patron. Humor old Icarius,
since one day all the shades of grape,
purple chroma and green the juicy prisms,
will be bestowed upon him by Dionysus.
Remember Triptolemus! Remember Celeus
as he was, and the fields, so novel to be plowed!
Don't dishonor Metanira's baskets of brimming fruit.
For I your fertile father Zeus birthed
Dionysus from my thigh, skin stretched full pregnant
(he tasted grapey when first I kissed his head, even then),
and you I birthed a full woman from my head
without a single ovary of my own.

"You were born with a startling kind of twin, my girl,
as your spear sprung up beside you from just behind my brow.
Raise that spear now and let the aegis feel the sun!
Shake out the dust, rush to save the satyrs,
who wear a layer of goatskin just as you do,
a billy mountain goatskin, but sewn up with their sinew

inseparable. And the god of the wild-tamers, the domesticators,
lord of shepherd's pan-pipe, company to goats on the pasture,
Pan is in need of your aegis.
Long ago he fought against the Titans
and defended my inviolable scepter,
and he was the mountain-crossing herdsman
of my wet-nurse and foster mother, the goat Amalthea.
So save him! Save him, who in the offing I see
at Attica's side frothing for battle: a Mede-killer
and defender of Marathon shaken and chattering.
Shake your aegis and take Lyaeus behind your shield,
your brother in the black goatskin who will protect
your homeland and drive out the Boeotian hegemon.
"And the citizen of Eleutho will sing!
a song of deliverance, honoring Thyonê's son
with cries at the Apaturion,
if Athens strikes up a rushing Phrygian rhythm
after Limnian Bacchus, Eleusian Dionysus.
O fickle Olympian race. What new amazements.
Argive Hera stands with the stranger Deriades,
Attic Athena renounces the Cecropian legions,
and my Thracian Ares, loyal to his mother,
neglects my son Bacchus and the Thracian army
following at Dionysus' heels,
and instead defends this Indian horde! Fickle, fickle.
"But I alone against all will put on my armor
and fight beside Dionysus with my blazing fire
until Bacchus renders this blue-black race to ashes.
And you, Hephaestus, maiden-loving bridegroom
of Gaea (ever-perfecting), do you stand still?
Do you not care for your Marathon,
where the bridal flame burns for the virgin goddess?
I need not tell you about the mystic sparks
of your own ever-shining lamplight.
Remember the lonely box in the young woman's chambers.
In that box was Gaea's boy and in that room
the girl would lean off her bed and open the lid

and offer what she had: a manly breast more muscle than fatty tissue.
Lift your doula of an axe and save Athena's citizens
with the cleaver long ago christened in afterbirth!
Do you stand still, Hephaestus, and will you not save your children?
Take up your usual torch! Shield the Cabiri.
Stretch your eye and see your ancient nymphet,
your Cabiro, loving your sons, blaming you.
The Lemnian Alcimacheia needs your strength."

At this the gods of Olympus sprung from their seats:
Athena and Apollo a helpful duo
and fiery Hephaestus with Triton's daughter.
But Hera consorted with the other undyings
and dragged Ares and thick Hydaspes by the hand,
all ill will in matching zeals for war.
Panic and Fear joined their entourage,
and Demeter too, archrival and foe to Bacchus
since she has the corn and he the grape
and he discovered alcohol first
(disgracing the old pride of Zagreus,
the original Dionysus).

Book 28

Denise Low and Eileen R. Tabios

Cyclops demigods fight the king of India's army.

1. Greeks Parade to Battle

Faunus, grandson of Cronus came from forests.
Aristaeus the Excellent arrived with Zeus' son
Aeacus, who carried his shield from Lemnos.

Demigods drove chariots to battle,
one hitched to panthers, another to lions.
One rode a bull, another the bear of Cybele.

Sileni, followers of Dionysus, marched,
then Bacchant women warriors in deerskins.
A satyr mounted on a lion joined them.

> *Yours is not my war*
> *yet I watch you, sad warriors.*
> *I read your story—*
> *a story become cliché:*
> *mortals dying to please gods.*

2. Soldiers of India Parade to Battle

Enemy Indian soldiers marched with shields,
swords, pikes, and daggers. Their elephants
carried dreaded archers. Earth shook.

Shrill flutes accompanied the war cries of India
as companies of infantry mustered. Garlands
adorned the beautiful men about to die.

Gods never disclose
how flowers become ruthless—
as garlands, they form
the worthless currency
of the poor and powerless.

3. The Fates Shadow the Battle

Blood frenzy possessed all the fighters.
Some men danced, some shouted in anger.
The Fates counted those about to perish.

Some soldiers sounded trumpets and war chants.
Some pounded tambours as loud as earthquakes.
Harps twanged hymns to Ares and Dionysus.

Strains of music mixed with first groans of pain.
Greeks targeted the Indian king and attacked.
He dodged, deflected a spear, and thanked his gods.

Carnage surrounded the regent—Giants
sheared to pieces, Indian fighters beheaded.
The royal elephant, throat slashed, stumbled.

Why depend on fate
which must count before knowing?

Poor warriors who must
believe to rationalize
losing hands, shearing Giants . . .

4. Heroes Fall

One unbelievable sight was a corpse
still standing in place, bristling with arrows,
a flesh statue still poised to throw a lance.

An Athenian lost both arms and said,
"What I want is a third hand to keep fighting."
He rushed into enemy swords and fell.

Horsemen died according to will of the Fates—
some dragged, some thrown, some speared.
Every fighter gambled his life. Many lost.

Manhood when defined
as dying into a stance
"poised to throw a lance"
begets poetry, but who
needs such impotent Beauty?

5. The One-Eyed Giants Join Battle

Many cyclopes, allies and kin of Zeus,
circled the murky battlefield and readied
their torches, lightning, and thunderbolts.

One cyclops, Argilipos, carried firebrands
to find his way to Indian victims. He burnt
countless pike soldiers and swordsmen.

Steropês, Lightning, took molten flame
from Mount Etna to flash and flicker unexpectedly.
He confused the infantry and burnt them to ash.

Brontes, Thunder, sent sky's drum rolls
and pelting rain from clear sky. He raised
a giant iron hammer to smash countless heads.

Sly Zeus. Cruel gods.
Hold Giants to single eyes
to preclude distractions from
gods' predictable desires:
men's deaths for entertainment.

6. The King of India Is Wounded

Brontes broke the Indian ranks and chased
the Indian king Deriades with a sharp crag
torn from rock cliffs. He threw this spear.

The king staggered from the thrust and fell
from his war elephant. His shield and lance
dropped. His guards lifted him to safety.

Justice could be formed
through kings felled in battlefields.
But to be a king
means owning the privilege
of greater warriors at hand.

7. Gods and Demigods Defeat the Indians

Father Zeus laughed at the Giants' thunders
like his own as the cyclopes drove vanquished
men to the sea to bleed and drown, a double death.

The cyclopes terrified the Indian army
with grotesque faces. Each had one eye
as large as the full moon in a night sky.

Halimenes chased the coward Phlogius.
He roared at the mortal Indian with booms
so loud the dozen nearest him were slain.

To kill simply by
roaring—an enviable
skill. Mortals, like Drumpf
(a president in my time),
fail attempts to copy gods.

8. Sounds of Deadly Music

War-cries of the cyclopes resounded to heavens
of Mount Olympus. Battle dancers joined
Bacchant women in feints, quick steps,

ecstatic twirls for Dionysus. Voices
and drums beat rhythms for deft footwork.
The runner Ocythoös sounded his rush of wind.

Giant Mimas wove measured leaps and stamps
into his fighting stance as he slew soldiers.
Their heads were blood sacrifice to Dionysus.

Of course this drunken
god chooses the heads of men,
not hands which wielded
swords for battle. Heads contain
the mouths which, once, imbibed wine.

9. The Armies Create One Chorus of Fate's Song

Melisseus the Bee circled with a deadly sting.
Clanging swords beat terrifying rhythms.
Pyrrhic dances and blades routed the Indians.

Both armies, the victors and the conquered,
swarmed as one host, spiraling the besieged king.
Clamor rose to Zeus as a final victory hymn.

This predictable
cliché of gods demanding
entertainment . . . but
gods first require worship—all
men must bow to Zeus. How sad.

Book 29

Adrienne Atkins

In book twenty-nine Ares pulls from the fight
to try to win back Aphrodite, his bride.

When Hera saw the Indian army being ravaged,
she struck heroic Deriades with a dogged courage.
Bloodlust pressed the frightful king more fiercely,
and he ranged throughout his dark host rank by rank,
railing against his frontline fighters,
drawing deserters back to the fray,
persuading some by encouragement, others by threat.
He grew even bolder and his men rallied, too,
rushing to battle at their king's command.
Morrheus, among them, tore into the army of satyrs:
one minute he was aiming far, bending his bow,
clouding the sky with arrows as he fired on his foes;
the next he was furiously whirling his spear
again and again, striking panic into the horned sileni.

Handsome Hymenaeus sat untouchable
on a Thessalian horse, swinging his sword:
a pale hand among dark men, annihilating them.
He was a blaze of brilliance, like the Morning Star
when it shines bright against a shapeless night.
His enemies scattered; on account of his beauty,

Dionysus had made him a warrior prodigy.
The god was happy to see him excelling in combat;
he wouldn't trade the spear of Hymenaeus
for any other ally, even the lightning of Zeus.
Whenever Hymenaeus rode into the fleeing Indians,
Dionysus whipped his spotted beasts to drive alongside
Hymenaeus' colt; he considered him his boyfriend,
as Atymnius, the son of Zeus, was to Apollo,
and stationed himself nearby at all times, desperate
to appear attractive and brave at once. In the tumult,
he was on cloud nine when fighting beside Hymenaeus.
He only had one worry: Hymenaeus was mortal.
His father was Phlegias rather than Zeus.
So the god also kept close in a fatherly way,
protecting him like a son, in case some archer shot
and hit him. Whenever a missile came close,
Dionysus stretched out his hand to act as a shield.
And when Hymenaeus excelled, the god shouted:

"My love, the way you shoot puts Ares to shame!
You conquered me, the giant slayer,
with your beauty. Conquer Deriades, too,
but with arrows! That sacrilegious idiot.
They'll say you hit two targets with one shot:
Deriades in the flesh, and me in the heart!"

Hearing this, the charming archer battled harder.
It thrilled Dionysus to see Hymenaeus so fired up,
and inspired the god with a fury for war
that shook the whole dark nation to its core:
he was like a hurricane, unsparing in his frenzy,
striking at Indian men relentlessly. Seeing this,
one man addressed Deriades' ally Melaneus:

"You're an archer, where's your bow and arrows?
We've got ladies in little dresses firing on us!
C'mon, shoot an arrow at Dionysus! He's a goner!

Don't buy into the rumor that he's an Olympian.
Don't be afraid of him, ever. His father was mortal,
and died young, too. He's bluffing that he's born from Zeus!
Here's an arrow. Shoot it! If you hit him,
the honors will be endless. Our king has deep pockets.
If he sees Dionysus, the cocky son of Thyonê,
laid out on a pyre, stuck with your arrow . . .
One shot would end this whole mess.
So raise your hands to Water, pray to Mother Earth,
our two gods. Promise sacrifices when you win,
for both of them. Be sincere. Offer a bull
at the altar of Hydaspes, the bull-faced river god,
and let the dark Earth have a dark ram."

These words persuaded Melaneus the archer,
the thought of riches like a stinger to his buzzing mind.
So he quietly pulled off the lid from his quiver.
An arrow poked out; he took it. He pulled the string,
drawing back his practiced hand, and bent the bow
till its arch met the iron arrowhead
and the bloody bowstring stretched beside his ear.
The arrow flew straight, but Zeus intervened;
it swerved from Dionysus toward Hymenaeus,
and struck him in the thigh, soaking it with blood.
But the god had caught sight of the wandering arrow
as it sped overhead on a cold-hearted breeze,
and he slowed it mid-air, as if a woman had shot it,
or as if Melaneus had lost his deadly touch.
Aphrodite, what's more, stripped the barbs off the shaft
in support of her dear brother Dionysus,
and nudged it aside so it wouldn't pierce deep,
as a mother might use the hem of her dress
to brush a stray fly from her sleeping child.

Hymenaeus showed Bacchus his bloody leg
and the nasty wound. He stood very close
and let a precious tear roll down in hopes

that the god would take his hand and rescue him.
He needed a doctor. So Dionysus took his arm
and helped the pale young man onto his chariot.
He drove him away from the roiling battle,
and set him in the grass in the shade of an oak,
but the boy's head drooped. As Apollo once mourned
when his love Hyacinthus was killed by a discus—
but Apollo blamed the jealous North Wind—
so now Dionysus tore at his hair in grief,
and although he never cries, he did for Hymenaeus.
But then Dionysus spotted the arrowhead,
which wasn't fully lodged in the flesh; he was elated.
He touched the wound, the white flesh stained red,
and tenderly pulled out the arrow from his leg.
The poor young man cried, and now Dionysus
grew angry at both Ares and Melaneus.
As he wiped off the sweat from sweet Hymenaeus,
he muttered bitterly under his breath:

"A bull killed my last love, Ampelos.
Now Ares will kill Hymenaeus!
I'd let my whole army die to stop his pain.
Who cares if a Cabirus dies in battle?
When would I ever cry over an injured satyr?
I'd let Silenus fall and the Bassarids scatter
if it meant I didn't have to see him like this.
No offense, Aristaeus, you're a famous archer,
but if you died, what would I care?
You think your honey tops my wine!
I guess it's my fate to always be grieving a boy.
I guess I'll be grieving again, if this one dies.
How did they both get cursed like this?
Off the record, I think Hera is jealous of me
and of this young slayer of dark Indians.
I think she resents him because I love him
so she dressed up Ares like that Indian bastard
and got him to shoot an arrow at Hymenaeus

to throw me off, since I'm so achingly in love.
But I'll get that fake Melaneus
with my spear or my bloodthirsty bow. He'll pay
for what he did to my darling Hymenaeus.
If you die, Hymenaeus, before the war is over,
I'll surrender the fight and give up my thyrsus.
I'll let all my enemies live except one:
your murderer Melaneus. Deriades can live;
he may hate me, but he didn't kill you.
Please, Aphrodite! First it was brave Ampelos,
now another sweet Adonis has been hurt
by bitter Ares. Hurt, right on his pink skin!
Now again it's like Eros himself is bleeding out.
Aphrodite, I need him. Do me a favor.
Go get our brother Apollo, the doctor,
to heal the boy. No, wait! Don't bother him.
Let him sit on Olympus. He might be reminded
of when his own lover Hyacinthus was injured.
Get Paeon instead, if that's okay. Send him here.
He doesn't do passion, he's never been in love.
This wound is one of a kind. Yes, in battle
men get bloodied in the gut, or in the hand
by a sword, or in the side with a spear,
or through the ear. But this one's different
since it's double: it got me, too—in the heart."

That's what Dionysus said, and shuddered
as he glimpsed the wound on sweet Hymenaeus.
But when he wrapped the boy's thigh with grapevine
and touched the wound, the white flesh stained red,
the ivy revived Hymenaeus, with a power like Paeon's!
Then the god sprinkled wine on it, which helped
by having an effect like fig juice on milk:
just as the juice curdles white milk quickly,
so it's ready for a goatherd to press in a mold
when he's making a wheel of cheese for his basket,
so too the young man's wound congealed,

like Apollo had healed it! Now he was back at it,
thanks to the restorative touch of Dionysus.
He drew a deadly arrow, found his distant target,
and bent his bow once again; in vengeance,
he dealt a wound to the archer Melaneus.
Then he charged into battle, striking down bodies
one after another, sticking close to Dionysus;
he trailed him like a shadow, a featureless form
that glides along without a mind of its own,
and follows its owner wherever he goes;
it stands when he stands, sits when he sits,
and joins him at parties, eating with copycat hands;
that's how the young man looked following the god.
Dionysus didn't take it easy in battle; he impaled a man
right through the middle, turning his thyrsus into a spit
and lifting it straight up, so bitter Hera couldn't miss
the Indian man flying high overhead.

Autonoë's husband was fighting there, too,
the archer with three personas: Aristaeus the Champion,
a man like a god; Agreus the Hunter, savvy in battle;
and Nomius the Shepherd, who fights with a staff.
When he held his bow, he resembled his father Apollo,
but his bold swagger came from his mother, Cyrene,
who was also an archer, the daughter of old Hypseus.
Now, in the form of Agreus, he hunted an enemy
like a wild animal and fearlessly took him alive.
Others he killed with a massive rock, a typical method;
he crushed them like he was pressing olives for oil.
He also used his bull-roarer, a bronze plate on a cord
that he swung like a mace, to scatter his daring enemies—
though normally he used it to scatter unruly bees.

Eurymedon and Alcon of Samothrace also raged,
the hotshot sons of the Lemnian nymph Cabiro.
Their father was the forge god Hephaestus,
whose fire sparked and steamed in their eyes.

When they drove their chariot of adamant
their ponies crushed the dust with hooves of brass,
expelling whinnies in creaky blasts.
Hephaestus had crafted these horses specially
to blow deadly fire out through their teeth,
like the two bronze-foot bulls he once made
for the powerful Colchian king Aeëtes,
along with a fiery yoke and plough.
So Eurymedon drove the metallic horses,
steering them with blistering bits in their jaws.
His right hand held a spear forged by his father's hand,
made of wood from Lemnos, his parents' land.
A sword hanging beside his strong thigh flashed
as if fire was coursing the length of the blade;
if even a pebble struck its surface,
the weapon abruptly erupted in sparks.
Alcon, meanwhile, gripped a fire-charred pike
and waved a torch of Hecate, one of their native gods.

The Corybantes from Cretan Mount Dicte fought, too,
shaking their crested helmets amid the chaos,
diving into the melee. They bounded in sync,
their naked swords knocking on their shields
to create a brazen beat. They spun their feet,
inspired by their traditional shield dance,
reveling in the battle. They were mountain herdsmen,
true, but their iron devastated the Indian people,
and whoever heard their oxhide shields thunder
inevitably tumbled face-down in the dust.

One Bassarid woman threw a spear wrapped in blossoms;
in fact, many men who hated Bacchus
were struck down by a woman's thyrsus!
When Leneus, a son of Silenus, used a hairy hand
to snap the peak right off a mountain
and hurl the broken rock crag at his foes,
Bacchant women everywhere raised the war-cry.

They wore ivy and lobbed missiles of vines.
The nurse of Dionysus, Eupetalê the Leafy,
wrote a song for the god and Ares. Fittingly,
she armed herself with leaves, facing iron with ivy.
She decimated the Indian nation using foliage from trees!
Terpsichore the Dancer also waltzed through the fray,
drumming up a deadly panic in the masses
with her hypnotic thyrsus and a pair of crashing cymbals;
even when Heracles scattered the birds from Stymphalia
with a booming bronze rattle, as one of his labors,
he didn't thunder as loud as Terpsichore's war-dance.
Then there was Trygia the Dregs, who was left at the end.
She was frozen with fear and couldn't move her legs!
None of the sileni stayed with her. They left her,
all alone and scared, with no one to protect her.
She begged the hero Maron, but Maron rebuffed her,
thinking she'd slow down the Corybantes and satyrs
when they danced; in fact, he prayed over and over
for the worthless old woman to just get run through.
Also fighting for Bacchus was Calycê the Rosebud,
plus Oenone the Wine Girl, who dashed to the front,
but was sloppy in battle; she'd hit the bottle,
and her soggy hair was waving wildly.

The sounds of suffering were deafening. Furiously,
Indian Astraëis chased Staphylê the Grape Bunch,
Celaeneus chased Calycê. Morrheus charged the sileni
and stuck them with his lance. When the sons of Silenus
—who wasn't born, but rose from Mother Earth herself—
heard Morrheus' war cry, this is what they did:
Astraeus trembled, Maron ran, and Leneus cowered!
Dorocles also petrified sweet Lycastê.

Bacchus helped the women by applying remedies
to their fresh injuries. He rescued Gorgo
when she was disheveled and her foot was hurt
by tying on a bandage of cut vines. Then he used wine

to stop the flow of Eupetalê's numinous blood,
and a charm to lighten Staphylê's bleeding,
and myrtle for Myrto's wounded hand.
He pulled an arrow from Calybe's shoulder
and treated the gash with wine, saving her life.
To relieve the pain in Nyse's wounded face,
he smeared on white gypsum, which is used in his rites.
Although he didn't cry for Lycastê, he still pitied her.

When the god had soothed all the Bassarids' wounds,
his bloodlust surged, and he returned to the fight.
One Bassarid was so inspired by his frenzied leaps
that she went out looking for battles to pick—
all for Dionysus! A flame appeared in her hair,
shining all around her neck, but never burning her.

Then a motley bunch of mighty fighters mobilized,
summoned to battle by the skirl of the war-pipes,
and the sound of Corybantes' beating their shields,
drumming their hands on both sides of the oxhide,
and the crashing cymbals, and the pan flute,
whose danceable tune added sweetness to the racket.
The enemy ranks roared in response.
Arrows flew overhead thick and quick.
Bows twanged. Stones rumbled. Trumpets blared.

The army of Bacchus pushed out to the river Hydaspes,
which was still red with wine from an earlier fight.
Then Bacchus called out from the depths of his throat,
louder than the sound of nine thousand men
all bellowing a war-cry at the same time.
The Indians couldn't take it, and so to escape,
some took to the ruddy river, others to the plain.
Dionysus' army split up to fight on both fronts,
but they were choking from thirst;
the sun was high overhead, and Helios' heat
was the kind that makes travelers tremble.

So the vine god issued a challenge to Deriades,
the Indian king. He spat out this taunting speech:

"You don't scare me. You're born from a river,
but I'm from heaven above; as far below Zeus
as Hydaspes is, that's how far below me you are.
I could rise to the clouds if I wanted!
I could send my arrows to the moon if I wanted!
If you think your father's horns make you great,
then fight me, the ox-horned god—if you can."

At that, the warriors roared and bared their teeth,
and each of Dionysus' allies sought out an adversary.
Gentle Pan used his goat feet to fight,
slicing the archer Melaneus with a sharp hoof
all down his side, tearing open his gut,
as revenge for the damage done to Hymenaeus,
and in support of angst-ridden Dionysus;
the god's eyes were dry, but his sorrow still smoldered.
Then Bacchus himself charged into the melee
and stretched his body upward, towering towards heaven.
He touched the clouds, hands grazing Olympus,
feet planted on earth with his head in the sky.

Eventually the Evening Star appeared above the battle,
forcing a stop to the bloodshed and saving the Indians.

But a devious dream visited Ares as he slept.
Rhea sent it, weaving together clever phantoms
and shadowy shapes that called to the god:

"Ares! Hey Ares! Sweet dreams, sucker.
Sleeping all alone in your armor. As for Aphrodite,
Hephaestus got her back. She's up there in his bed.
He kicked out his second wife Charis—and boy is she sore.
Aphrodite didn't want to return to her previous marriage,
but Eros shot her himself to make her go back

as a favor to his father Hephaestus. But in fact,
it's all Athena's doing, the clever virgin goddess,
and she has Zeus' approval. Hephaestus was after her,
trying to rape her, but he missed and hit the ground.
His son was born from the earth, whom Athena nursed,
but he died, and the tomboy goddess won't nurse another.
Anyway, wake up! Go to the Thracian plain.
Go see Aphrodite at Hephaestus' home on Lemnos.
Go see the gates of Paphos and her shrine on Cyprus,
which her crew of Loves have draped in flowers.
Hear how the women of Byblos sing for her
and her rekindled love for her former husband.
Ares, you lost your Aphrodite. You're savage,
yes, and quick, but slow Hephaestus still outpaced you!
You might as well write their wedding song yourself!
So go to Sicily, where the Cyclopes work the forge.
Hephaestus may be the master craftsman,
but they can give him a run for his money.
Beg them to make you a trap like the ancient one
Hephaestus used to catch you with Aphrodite.
Turn the tables on him and ambush them together!
Catch him stealing your wife, like he caught you!
Bind him in chains alongside Aphrodite!
All the Olympian gods will applaud you
when you nab the man that insulted your bed.
Wake up and get scheming! Wake up!
Get your bride back! What does Deriades matter?
Okay, I'll shut up now, in case the Sun hears."

At that, the vision vanished. Hot-headed Ares
jolted from sleep, caught sight of Dawn's rays,
and flew out of bed. He woke Fear and Terror
to yoke his war chariot, the fast-racing one,
and they obeyed their frantic father. First,
Terror clamped the bits in the horses' mouths
and fastened the harnesses onto their necks.
He yoked them to the chariot and Ares got in.

Then Fear took the reins and off they went,
flying from Byblos in Lebanon to Paphos in Cyprus,
then to the island of Cythera, then back to Cyprus.
But he mostly spied on the island of Lemnos
to scope out the forge of Hephaestus,
jealously searching for signs of the goddess,
seeing if he might spot her at the forge,
where she used to go. He was afraid
that the smoke might conceal her and dirty her face.
Then he took a weapon up to heaven
to confront the gods about his bride,
including Zeus and the Sun, Hephaestus and Athena.

Book 30

Alison R. Parker

Eurymedon sends off Tectaphus just slain
down to the lower house of Hell's constraint.

So Ares stole away to the seven-zoned sky,
love-grudging and horn-mad. But Dionysus,
dancing bravely into the fray, assailed
the bright-faced foe, now taking time to pounce
upon the front fighters with an earthshaking jolt,
now in their midst. And with his hurtling thyrsus,
he reaped first fruits of battle strife so dark,
and raged and rampaged as he hacked away
at the tribes arrayed there in a hostile line.
And Bacchus riled the satyrs all the more for war
against Deriades—for he'd seen the war god gone
from the Indian din. Each satyr strove with each
for pride of place. And in the clustered clash,
Aristaeus gave the raucous front ranks at right
to Dionysus, while he, no bumbler, flew
busily to the bloodshed on stage left.

Morrheus, beholding Bromius' squires
as they fought on the field with leaves and flowery dart,
burst forth in tones of great astonishment
to the crazed and senseless King Deriades:

"What miracle, Deriades, is this?
My warriors hit the dust, and how? They're felled
by thyrsuses and leaves of no account.
The shieldless slay the armed. And Bassarids
don't swerve from axes' blows or those of swords
with double edge; nay, they stand firm, unhurt.
If it's right to say so, sceptered King, you too
should leave your bronze-tipped spear and raise aloft
a thyrsus—wine-red, murderous—because
the foe's hard mettle flashes on the field
with stern bouquets far more than with brute iron.

"I've never seen a struggle of this stamp—
a no-count darting thyrsus bests our darts.
Give me a verdant missile to wave about;
our arrows lose to unwarlike fennel now,
vegetable love. And give me yellow boots;
unbroken greaves are bending down to buskins.
What use is it to wield my shield of bronze?
Mere women win unarmed, and in the battle din
shake cymbals as our warriors sink down,
as helmets yield to garlands, cuirasses to fawnskin.
Often, when facing woundless Dionysus,
I believed I'd rip his blameless flank to bits,
and launched off well-aimed spears. One made its mark,
but made no mark. My dart's sharp-pointed bronze—
unbendable—still bent against Lyaeus."

The bold-faced sovereign smiled and eyed his son-in-law
askance, heralding his wrath with silence now.
Then he growled and thundered forth in arrogant tones:
"Ninny Morrheus, why dread Dionysus so unarmed?
Only an infant fears the satyrs' war of make-believe."
With this undaunted boast he buoyed his daughter's man.

Monster Morrheus took up arms again
to battle against Bromius' foremost men.

He wounded Eurymedon by slashing through
the middle of his groin with blood-soaked spear.
Darting through the thigh, the reveling point
sliced up and flayed the man's well-marbled flesh.
Eurymedon's knee now buckled, and he hit the ground.
But bronze-clad Alcon didn't miss his brother's fall;
raising sword and rounded shield, the champion went straight
to his injured kin, and covered the fighter fully,
building a shield tower over Eurymedon's frame.
Menacing the foe, now here, now there, with whirling spear,
brother defended brother. Straddling the wounded man,
like a lion with his cubs, he roared full-throatedly,
decanting Corybantic cries from his maddened lips.

Morrheus watched. Alcon circled with expert feet,
shield-defender of his fallen Cabirus.
The massive Indian, Typhon's match, was seized
with Bacchic frenzy, and set on them both,
that Cabiro might weep for a brace of slaughtered sons,
cut down in one same day by one iron blade.
He might have delivered an equal end to each—
but straining to force a rough breath from his mouth,
Eurymedon called aloud to his Lemnian sire.

"O Father, fire-breathing master of an arduous art,
return the boon you owe me from the past,
when Deo alone, mistress of the threshing floor,
seized three-peaked Sicily as a prize to mark
first sighting of concealed Persephone.
Deo cast down your gusting bellows of the west,
your wide-mouthed forge and tight-gripped fire tongs.
But champion to my father, I scared her off
in protection of your anvil. Thanks to me,
the air is black, broiled by Sicilian sparks.
Please save your child, laid low by savage Morrheus."

He spoke, and fiery Hephaestus sprang from heaven,
and all around he twisted his flashing fire,
inborn fire leaping in many branches as he twirled
a fiery shoot. The sentient firebrand,
self-winding, twining round Morrheus' neck,
girdled his throat with a fire-warmed chain's constraint,
rolling like a river. His chin's fire-pulsing wreath
ran springing, pulsing down to his very toes,
plaiting a fire-braided noose around the champion's foot.
The steadfast flames flung spangles, dancing coins,
shaking the blazing light onto the ground.

His proud head simmered as his top-notch helmet flared,
and now he might have taken a dying fall,
struck down so brightly by a sparking dart,
had not Hydaspes, Deriades' father, stood guard.
For high above and perched upon a rock,
he watched the combat in a nice disguise,
his bullish form adopting a false mien.

He took the boy back to the toils of life,
pouring on rain that breathed against the heat,
showering cold upon the heated gust
of his fire-blasted face. And he rubbed off
the ashy washings of the crested helm,
then snatching up Morrheus, cloaked his limbs
with lightless fog, and in a purple mist
concealed those limbs again, lest the god,
lame but blaze-bearing, slay him then,
stirring up the kindled Lemnian fire,
death-dealing; lest the child-devoted father,
old man Hydaspes, see another son-in-law
of Deriades—see him dead and done,
and bewail Morrheus' fate, just like Orontes'.

But firebrand-bearing Hephaestus chased away
the warriors, all of them, who stood around

the newly wounded youth,
and lifting him aloft upon his shoulder,
he propped him up against a neighboring oak,
away from the battle bluster, and kept him alive,
sprinkling life-bearing drugs upon his wounded groin.

Morrheus had not forgotten the prior fight.
He was helmeted again, having fled fire-stalker Enyo,
and the lightning-hurling champion, and the smoking spear.
He lit upon the burning man Phlogius,
who was twisting and turning like his father, Strophius,
and killed him—a dancer for leap-loving Dionysus.
At the feasts of tearless Lyaeus, he had whirled
the shifty fingers of his beating hands,
and gesturing Phaëthon's death with thoughtful hand,
he made the feasters pour libations forth
with their unwonted tears. They wailed, bewept
destruction of a fictitious Phaëthon.
Spinning the smoking youth self-rolling down,
he brought a woeful grief to Dionysus,
who feels no grief. Seeing the wretched man
twirling and twitching, spear-shaking Morrheus had to say:

"That was a different dance you plaited near the table,
doing a gleeful herky-jerky by the old wine bowl.
Why do you weave such groaning dance moves in this duel?
But if you're pricked and goated to the choral dance
of Dionysus, ply your mystic rites for Hades.
You don't crave chalk: you carry your face's rounds
self-dipped in dust. And if you wish, go tripping by the side
of dirge-fond Lethe, or let laughless Persephone
glory in your precious song and dance."
He spoke exultingly and ran, ran like the wind—
driving the sileni into flight.

And with his dogged dagger,
shield-shaking Tectaphus was there to meet his foe.

Deriades once bound and hid him down
in a deep smooth-sided hole; nor did he find a way
to escape his deadly doom a second time.
For if he's caught in the yoke of dire constraint,
who can check a man's unfriendly destiny
when Fate, the ruthless dominatrix, bids him die?
No trick could turn up means to rescue Tectaphus from death.
Maddened, he pursued the army of Lyaeus,
slicing and dicing the horny satyrs' playful limbs.
He sheared strife-stirring Pylaeus' throat,
struck the forehead of Onthyrius with merciless blade,
and shattered the broad-breasted wine jug Pithos.
He might have slain another Bacchic horde,
one after one, and yet swift Eurymedon
cast a fast glimpse on him and took him on,
shaking his two-mouthed Corybantic ax
right in his face. He crushed the top of his forehead,
splitting his skull in two. A flute of bloody froth spurted up,
and the champion pitched down on the ground,
drizzling on the dust. As he lay dying, tossing in his pain,
he bemoaned the ancient suffering of the earth-dug pit,
the looming threads now of a younger Fate.
He bellowed in forlorn voice, remembering his daughter's crafty love drink,
death-delaying until now. As he howled and keened, his tears
streamed down in concert with his ruddy gore.

"My mother and my nurse—old before your time—
my darling wily girl, trapped in sad wedlock to me,
why came you not near me when I neared death?
Why didn't you succor me again, you dauntless girl?
And where did your life-giving potion go?

"Do you stay true to your bond while your father lives,
but not when he is dying?
If a trick escorts a man back up from Hell,
look for another, better trick, look for a plan
cunning against death, so after that hollow pit

down in the earth I might escape the gates
of Hell again, even in these wars,
if there's a way back home from the gulf of no return."

He toiled to give a speech like that, and did so barely.
But then his voice no longer did obey.
And viewing her new-wounded dying father
from high in the city walls, she bubbled up in pensive pain,
poured tears in rich profusion. The speaker was
pitiable and forlorn Eërië; her belly churned.
She defiled her curls with dust—askew!—and bared
her bosom to the moon, filleted her frock, and thwacked
her head. Her sire was now past healing, but she screeched
this speech as if he were now listening in.

"My son! You heavy-fated father of a girl
who suckled you! But on this day,
your lips are breathless with your death. What milk,
what life-begetting brew do I bear now
by which I might—me wretched—reunite
you with your soul and carry you back home?
What other succoring mam can I reach out
and feed you with? If only I can cheat
the death gods too. My Father, O my Father,
one honor will I keep intact for you.
I won't abandon you among the dead,
all withered and wasted away.
Be thankful, Father, and may you soon receive
the lively blood from thine own daughter's throat
and suck on it, as you had done before,
with milk from her despondent wrinkling dug.

"Come, all you trusty guards of your Deriades,
and reveal another empty earthly nook
where I can raise a corpse, my dearest father,
back to life. Necrophilia? No, just filial love.
But Hades isn't like those bodyguards.

He won't allow me one last trick, one last good work
to make my beloved father free at last,
free at last from toil and pain.

"I'd long for that same sword in bloodguilt steeped,
that I might be overpowered, heavy in heart,
slip-sliding away by patricidal iron.
You, who clove our father's head in two,
kill Eërië as well after her Tectaphus,
that one might say: "Both papa and his child
were felled headlong. A single saber did it."

She spoke while pouring out too many tears,
and the struggle rose below her double-fold.
And Enyo did double duty with twin armies
by lifting their spirits up, up, and away.

Morrheus used his sword to slay Dasyllius
(Taenarus' son), never one to shed his leather shield
when faced by scary, sneering antagonists.
But the citizen of Amyclae, though unshakable by foes,
felt the Indian shove that weapon through his right jawbone.

Then Morrheus slew the mountain maenad Alcimacheia,
in a single judgment valiant and fair
beyond her peers in age. And she was spawn
of Harpalion, a fine-wine father he.
A brassy gal, she'd even dared to go
into Hera's temple while holding ivy high.
The Argolid goddess so abhorred that plant
as much as she adored her bleeding fruit,
her juicy pet, the ripening pomegranate.

That maiden flogged the exquisite wooden statue
with her wine-faced thyrsus. Sorry—the statue was of bronze.
But she battered it with her grape-clustered shaft,

an insult to Lyaeus' stepmother, now red hot in wrath.
She didn't dodge the frightful bile of Hera wroth—
too bad for Lemnian god-fighter Alcimacheia.
A stranger in strange land, she was laid to rest
far from her own native shore,
and after the war, she didn't see her father again,
not Harpalion, nor Lemnos, her fatherland,
where Jason and Hypsipyle hooked up.
With foreigners she was covered with a mound of dust,
earning a vengeful lot. Poor wretched girl!
She lost her dear Harpalion and was robbed of her Lyaeus.

Her slaughter failed to slake Morrheus' rage—
the maenad Alcimacheia had sported with the gods.
He killed a dweller of the fertile land
of Olympian Elis. The land was near a stream
of the garland-loving River Alpheus.
This victim's name? Codone, a virgin still.

Forgive me, Fates, for what I shall relate.
He pitied not the locks on her withering head,
nor her face's rosy glow beneath the dust.
He threw a pearl away
and passed over the coy maiden's twofold mounds,
those fruits so ripe and curved atop her chest.
No pity yet despite those rounds
plunging up so sweet and firm against her bra.

Did he suffer shame in looking up her thighs' deep slit?
The warrior nipped that beauty in the bud,
and struck out, she pitched over, hit the ground.
Morrheus waved his helmet and pursued
countless maenads with their fine and flirty gowns.
He slew them. Eurypyle, Sterope, and Soë—
he mowed the women down with his short sword.
He slashed Staphylê in twain, and gashed Gigarto,

red in complexion and now yet redder still.
Piercing above Melictaine's rosy teat,
he dyed her purple with his bloody iron.

The green-eyed Telchineës piled on as well.
One held a silver fir—not just a sliver—
one a bushy cherry, root and all;
and one snatched up a rock-hard headland cliff
and shook it all about to make his threats
against the noisy crowd of Indians,
pitching a fastball out with his fearsome arm.

Erratic Hera showed her weighty might
to wear down Dionysus, and bestowed
more force and bravery on überman
Deriades. She gave amazing grace,
a moonlike glow to terrify his foes.
He strutted and showed off—
he was the greatest of them all.
The sturdy adversaries fled the field.

His shield glistened, gleamed, and glittered,
and his helmet sparked and sparkled,
the plumes bursting in air.

Our brave, bold Bacchus trembled at the sight
of Deriades' glossy boss, so luny in the light,
and he flamed out.

Dionysus, wide-eyeing him, was dazed, confused,
and dared not challenge him, for he perceived
Hera's craft in kitting out his foe.
His feet resisted, but he yet recoiled
from the glory of the battle hymn.

Iobacchus withdrew disheartened to a woodland ridge
and allowed the winds to whirl away his battle lust;
he quaked before his stepmother's savage spite.

But Athena came down from the sky; high-ruling Zeus
sent her as messenger to her runaway brother
so shaken by fear of Hera, to change his mind
and drag him again to the shouting and crying of war.
At his back she stood and snatched his tawny hair,
grim goddess manifest to him alone.
Her eyeballs let fly a piercing fiery flash,
and breathing sparks of wisdom on Lyaeus,
she blasted him with a scathing call to arms.

"Where are you fleeing, Dionysus? Why thus choose
dumbstruck flight and not the battle blare?
Where are your thyrsuses? Oh, neutered now?
What of your arrows wrought with fruited vines?
What tale of *you* shall I tell to *my* Cronion?
What rajah matched with you has met his match?
Deriades lives, and Morrheus battles still.
What inborn heavenly valor have you displayed
fit for a sky god's spawn, both son and grandson?
Have you ventured forth to Libya? Have you endured
any such labor as Perseus'? Have you seen
the eye of Gorgon Stheno—petrifying, sure—
or the high-lowing throat of oppressive Euryale?
Or have you viewed Medusa's vipered locks?
Have her serpents' yawning maws run you around?
Semele bore no fighter, but Acrisius' girl
granted my Zeus a worthy son, the Gorgon slayer,
for winged Perseus didn't ditch my scythe,
and he honored Hermes for the boots he gave.
I have a hard-by witness, a sea monster turned to stone.
Ask Cepheus, I bid you, what Perseus' sickle did.
Ask both the East and West. For nereids face
the bedmate of Andromeda with fear and trembling, while
Hesperids sing the man who mowed Medusa down.
Unfluttered Aeacus was far from Bacchus' twin;
he didn't flee Deriades or fear the Indians' howls.
Did the Arab leader scare you yesterday? Again?

I dread to meet with Ares, Lycurgus' rash sire,
who loves to bruit abroad the shameful tales
of . . . his brother? . . . unmanly, war-shy Dionysus.
Our father—yours and mine—was unafraid of carnage
when Titan gods donned arms against Olympus.

"And of the Indian queen—have you carried off Orsiboë?
Nurse Rhea hasn't seen Chirobië serve as your sex slave.
May Zeus forgive my vow, but I won't call you brother
while you flee Deriades and the peaceful Indian race.
Seize your thyrsuses again; recall the joy of battle.
Fight at your army's fore, and you'll observe
full-armed Athena join in flinging spears
with your marshaled Bacchants, and as coup de grâce
raise high the Olympian aegis, so invincible."

Her words breathed higher power into Bromius.
He let go and let god in,
and he fought with spirits bold a second time,
entrusting to Tritogeneia all hope of victory.

Whom first, whom last did Bacchus then bring down
when Athena, avid for the roar of war,
bucked him up and made him brave again?
He slew with ruthless thyrsus a hundred foes,
and the wounds he bestowed on many took many a turn—
he smote with spear, vine tendrils, or branched clusters,
or hurled forth a jagged missile stone.
Those bashed by Bacchic lash grew frenzied, shrill.
His thyrsus punctured Phringus' left shoulder;
the victim fled, though, racing out of reach.
No luck. Mellisseus threw him to the ground
with poleax whetted sharp for felling bulls.

Far-shooting Dionysus, thyrsus-mad,
shook at Egretius his Euian spear
and sprang. The baleful Bacchic spearpoint whirred

and whistled as it darted through the air,
so hot to hit its man. But Egretius got away.
Unfazed, our hero god now thrashed the Bolinges
and frightened into flight the battle-stirring Arachontae.
Wielding wide the wand of unmixed wine, he snuffed out
dire tribes of such spear-bold Salangioi.
The Arienian army was sore afraid,
panicked despite the stalwart shields they wore.

And tracking the front-fighters of Phringus and Egretius,
Euius floored the wild Ear-Sleepers—every one.
And lion-hearted Iobacchus forced
even Lygus from the bloody battle din.
He struck with wine-red thyrsus sly Melanion,
who was shooting the Bassarids with hidden darts.
But Hera, brutal in battle, saved the sprinter without harm,
for he'd often armed himself with such deceit
and attacked the Bacchae with his stealthy raids.
A rock concealed him, or a high-topped tree
hid him behind its leaves as he lobbed forth
missiles the men he shot just didn't see.

The Indians dashed away from the man-killing clash,
aghast and trembling at the manly valor
of their unbeaten archfoe, Dionysus.

Book 31

David Fredrick and Rachel Murray

In this thirty-first book with her honey-sweet talk Hera turns Sleep against the son of Cronus, and against Dionysus turns Persephone.

And so Bacchus wandered the rolling plowland
of Erythraea, his mind stunned with the echoes
of battle, the rumble of Indians a bullroarer hum
as his golden locks shook against the snow of his cheek.

Meanwhile the jealous mind of Hera seethed as she carved
revenge in the sky with the immortal soles of her feet,
seeing the Indian army scattered far and wide,
liked so much ripe grain cut down by those scythes,
the man-slaughtering thyrsi of Lyaeus. Fragments
of twisted iron she saw, all that remained
of Andromeda's chains, washed on the beach
by the Erythraean gulf. An empty stone leaned out
from the sand, crusted with salt, the rough sign
of the Earthshaker, god of the sea. Pinched with grief
she turned her gaze aside from the beaten brass blade
of Perseus, the Gorgon-reaper, hard by the sea.

But already churning his feet and swift knees, ligaments
taut, Perseus was a blur above bone dry Libya, his wings

beating air in time like a swimmer. He had snatched
the wandering eye of the daughter of Phorcis, the one
and only pupil of the sleepless old hag, and through
no man's land slipped into her cave. There by the rock
he threshed a harvest that softly hissed, the tangled
crop of serpentine hair, and reaping the Gorgon's
pregnant throat stained his sickle deep crimson red.
Medusa sat wounded, as in the viper's dew he washed
his palms bathed in blood, and her head had been cut
clean away. From the stump of her neck a double brood
pushed out, the first a child with a golden sword,
and close behind came the second, a winged horse.

Hera was not happy. Her heart gnashed in anger and spite
and she spit up bile against Perseus and Dionysus.
So, why not charm the son of Cronus, bewitch his eyes,
put all that intelligence up to a round of sex, then the soft
down of Sleep after lovemaking so sweet? Zeus like a stone
would lay in slumber, while she weighed down Lyaeus
with a good trick or two. Like an arrow shot she was on her way
to Hades' dark hall, the god of orphans who welcomes us all.
She comes there to Persephone, and she spins her a tale:

"Of all the gods I call you the most blessed, because you dwell
so far from us! Day after day you don't have to see Semele
up there on Olympus, living the immortal life. Quite honestly
I fear that this Dionysus, dropped from the belly of a mortal slut,
will one day grow to elbow out Zagreus and be master of lightning,
thunderbolts hoisted in the grimy hands of this whelp of earth.
Goddess of ripe grain, you have been robbed! Way down yonder
where green acres ripple on the banks of the Nile, your
Demeter, so blessedly fertile, her bosom flourishing with bushels
of grain, is forgotten. They are bringing in the sheaves
to some bastard goddess, some Deo with something
to do with wheat, a cow-girl with horns who gave birth to a bull,
they call her Io, apparently, the daughter of Inachus.

"And Ares, my very own son? The one whom I bore from this
heavenly womb? Inglorious chains held him fettered on earth,
when Ephialtes hid him like so much night soil in a jar of clay.
For him the great sky god, my husband Zeus, was worse
than useless, though he hurried to rescue Semele's brat
when he was swaddled in flames, the premature little bastard.
He plucked Bacchus from the lightning bolt, that drooling runt,
but when Zagreus, heaven's real Dionysus, was shredded
with knives not a finger was lifted. What burns me up more
is the dowry of Semele from Cronus' son: she's a constellation now
in heaven's great vault, while Persephone settles for . . . Tartarus.
A seat up in heaven is saved for Apollo, and Hermes lives up
in heaven, too, while you, my dear, have this house full of gloom.
Exactly why mask up in that serpent's disguise and slither
soft through the folds of your stainless virginity,
if when the loving was finished his only intent
was to snuff out the life you delivered in agony?

"Zeus the great Master reigns on Olympus in a house
full of stars, and allots the salt mist of the sea to his brother,
ocean's master, while the home of your husband is nothing
but soul-sucking darkness. Arm thy Furies against
wine-faced Bacchus, lest I should behold this illegitimate
lump of flesh somehow holding a scepter up on Olympus!
Reverence the wife of Zeus who beseeches you, reverence
Deo, and immaculate Themis who beseeches you, too:
let the Indians catch their breath just a little, as Dionysus
is staggered: let there be vengeance for me in my rage
that Cronus' son gives to Bacchus sweet sips of nectar,
while my Ares drinks deep all the muck and gore of Enyo,
the dread goddess of war. That Athenians raise hymns
to this new Dionysus, that his cult be equal to Eleusinian
Bacchus, that he share in the Mysteries of ancient Iacchus,
that Demeter's basket and the secrets within be dishonored
with his shit-faced rites of spring—none of this can happen!"

As this poet laureate of the embittered held forth, the crocodile tears
welled and flowed down her cheeks, and Persephone's mind ran riot
at this seductive masterpiece of feminine guile. Goddess to goddess
she nodded assent, and bestowed on her the Fury Megaera who would
get the job done for the queen of the gods with her green lizard's eye.

She swept forth then, squall lines swirling around her sandals,
sprang three times and on the fourth came down on the banks
of the Ganges. She displayed to the iron face of Megaera
the heaps of Indian dead, mute testimony to the sweat
of the army and the prowess of Dionysus. As she witnessed
the grim work of Lyaeus concrete in the slaughter
of so many Indians, the grudge of Megaera magnified,
swollen beyond even the wrath of heaven's own Queen.

Hera was delighted. A bitter laugh for the Fury with serpents
for hair and in a lowering voice she broke the silence:

"That's how they do it, these fine young kings of Olympus,
These bastards of Zeus can really throw spears. Zeus mounts
and cranks out one child from Semele, doomed and determined
to destroy all the Indians, so gentle and innocent. They really
should learn, Zeus the Unjust and his sidekick Bacchus,
just how great is the might of Megaera. The shame is cosmic,
when Zeus rules on high with a mind outside the law,
so he has no beef with the Etrurian pirates, who terrorize
Sicily with their thieves' code of honor and their pitiless ships.
Nor does he clean up the impious Dryopes, whose code of living
is their spear in hand. He'd rather slaughter the Indians,
a most spiritual folk, whom all-nurturing Themis brought up
at her breast. The shame is cosmic when his mind is so lawless
that a flesh-and-blood man incinerates Hydaspes, immortal
and flawless, the very own child of the sky god Zeus,
yet burnt to cinders all the same by a flesh-and-blood man."

That said, Hera winged away through the sky, but the Fury in silence
withdrew under Caucasus into a cave's dark instep, shedding

the hideous true coil of her limbs, writhing with snakes,
for the evening-shade outline of Athena's owl. There she remained
until she might learn that great Zeus was in slumber, obedient
to the orders of Hera, her commander-in-chief and immortal queen.

But Hera herself, with her cunning intelligence, came to the shores
of the water of Hesperus, the evening star bathed in sunset rouge
over Libya's dusky Chremetes river, where the back of old Atlas is bent
to bear all the weight of heaven's whirling vault. She sought out
Iris, the wife of Zephyr, the west wind who could not seduce Hyacinthus,
while his rainbow wife bears Zeus' commands, but to him no pot of gold.
Hera had a job for Iris: to carry a message with wing-swift feet
from heaven to Sleep, the morphine god robed in shadow.
So she spoke to Iris, concocting a soothing dose of words:

"Iris, O Iris, golden winged bride of Zephyr, in from the West
he blesses the fields with springtime rain, but you are the mother
of Eros. On storm-cloud sandals ride the wind to the house
where Sleep nods under the late evening sky, or to the isle of Lemnos
caressed by the sea. Once you find him, tell him this and make it clear:
he must charm the charmless eyes of Zeus for just one rosy-fingered day,
time enough for me to bring help to the Indians. This mission
will require a change of outfit. Take on the shape of Night, his mother,
a nightshade corset and a black visage: change your name
and become his darkness. This is just what I do when the situation demands.
I reach back in my closet and perform a makeover
to be just like Themis, or even Aphrodite, or Artemis forever
the athletic virgin. Promise him, promise him the marriage
of Pasithea, whose beauty will drive him to do what I need.
I don't have to teach you that a male in rut will do anything
if he thinks he has hope to get the woman he wants."

No sooner said than Iris took flight, golden wings outstretched
the goddess searched the sky, her glance skipping over the waves
straight to Paphos, Aphrodite's country, then arcing aloft high over Byblus
her eyes came to rest on Lebanon and the banks of Assyrian Adonis,
Aphrodite's lover struck down so young but now his waters are a blessing

for marriages. Thus she chased down the trail, the twisting track
of vagabond Sleep. She found him on the slopes of Orchomenus,
home to the Graces and blessed brides, where Sleep had stayed
his wandering feet to linger again at the doorstep of lovely Pasithea.

Iris paused for a secret metamorphosis, shed her iridescent body
to slip beyond recognition into the indigo form of Night.
In this disguise she drew near to Sleep looking just like his Mother,
and poured out a stream of deception designed to steal his mind.

"My child, my child, how long will Night be a joke to the son of Cronus?
Phaëthon's abuse is not enough, but the first light of Morning is a shaft
to my heart, and Dawn born so early always chases me down.
So Zeus has begotten an inglorious bastard to bring disgrace on my
very own Sleep. This half-breed mortal makes a mockery of me
and you, my son—he's up all night long, kindling torches with flames
from his mystic sparks, making me disappear and doing you wrong
keeping everyone awake. O Sleep, why should you be called
the All Powerful Narcotic, when the mongrel flame of an earthly Lyaeus
has put to flight my nightly celebrations? He washes out the glimmer
of our stars in heaven with his torches' glare. This one phosphorescent
mortal so disfigures me that he all but erases the beams of my Moon,
great though she is. When Dawn breaks early and scorns my Darkness
I wince with shame that I tiptoe around the light of this bastard,
this imposter Phaëthon, whose cheap incandescence makes a day
out of Night. For me, dear son, let your anger be yoked to two outstanding reasons:
the sleepless pricks of those mystic satyrs and their sleepless master, Dionysus.

"Give comfort to your mother in her grave distress, and comfort to Hera:
For just one rosy-fingered day charm the charmless eyes of Zeus,
ruling on high, so she may bring aid to the Indians, whom those satyrs
have routed and whom Bacchus may yet throw into confusion.
Sleep O Sleep why should you be called the All Powerful Narcotic?
Be so kind as to direct your gaze to the seven gates of Thebes.
Do you see the awesome son of Cronus hard at work again on another
all-nighter? Break off this foolishness of Zeus! Amphitryon wears

an iron shirt headed straight into battle far from home and his own
dear bedroom, while in the softest, sweetest nook of his house
Zeus stretches out beside Alcmene, enjoys the bride's lovemaking
neither one satisfied, until the sweet mist of darkness is three moons long.
I'd rather not see Zeus up and at it again for a night now four times
the usual duration. No, my child, you must take up arms against this son
of Cronus, or else he might do it and do it again in the soft cover
of nine long moons. Remember Mnemosyne from that time before?
It's hard to forget how he came beside her for nine nonstop nights,
so intent on it that he would not sleep, the sting of passion so hard
there were children times nine for one uninterrupted honeymoon.

"There is another god winged just like you, brave little Cupid
the All Powerful Erotic, your doublet, Sleep, who overcame Zeus
with his tiny dart. Pity the dark-skinned children of Earth,
the Indians, and give them comfort. They bear the same color
as the Mother who bore you. O dark-winged child protect
these people with their rich dark skins! Do not provoke goddess Earth
whose generation was the same as Chaos, my father. We are all sprung
from that same primal source, all of the gods who dwell on Olympus.
Do not tremble before the son of Cronus, as long as Hera, his wife,
is favorable. Do not tremble before Semele, whose own sky-god
lover burned her alive. Fiery thunderbolts cannot contend with you,
nor the crash of thunder rolling deep from the shattered clouds.
Just shake your wings one time for me, and Zeus will lie senseless
on his level bed, for however much time, Sleep, you command.
I've heard that you long for one of the Graces: if in your heart
the sting is deep to have her in bed—watch out. Do not provoke
Pasithea's mother, the immortal mistress of the marriage yoke,
Hera, goddess of weddings. Since you live near Tethys hard by the rock
of Leucas, shelter Deriades, who is the seed of Indian Hydaspes.
Guard your neighbor truly, for your neighbor Ocean, whose breakers
echo and roar far beyond the coast, is the ancestor of Deriades."

Thus she spoke, and she was persuasive. Just as if he had heard
his true mother's words, Sleep fluttered aloft and swore to charm
the eyes of Zeus the unsleeping until the third sun had run its course:

But Iris, Night's mirage, underscored her request: he should shackle Zeus
in the chains of sleep for the course of just one rosy-fingered day.
And so Sleep remained there, awaiting the blessed dawn of his wedding.

Now Iris had vanished in a blur of wings heading straight back home,
eager to deliver a blameless report to the goddess, her commander-in-chief.

But now Hera split the sky with her storm-cloud heels, weaving together
another crafty snare, how she might draw close to Zeus and flash him
the cestus, the embroidered girdle of mind-numbing desire. So she sought out
Aphrodite, the goddess of Paphos, and she came upon her in Assyria.
She was sitting in solitude above Libanus, as the Graces were out
on the garden paths, bathed in wind song and the fragrance of thyme.
They gathered pastel blossoms there, like the nodding flowers
of earliest spring themselves, the fragrant dancers of Orchomenus.
This one plucked Cilician crocus, the palms of this one were eager for balsam
and shoots of Indian reeds, and the third for petals of sweet-smelling roses.

The visit was unexpected, and Aphrodite surprised. Up she sprang
from her sculpted throne, the daughter of Zeus seeing Zeus' own wife,
and recognizing the clues of deep distress, offered her a perceptive speech:

"O Hera, wife of Zeus, tell me, why are your cheeks so pale? Tell me,
O queen, why are your eyes downcast? Surely Zeus hasn't
magically seduced
a second Danaë, with the gentle drops of a sweet shower of deception?
Surely he hasn't cruised across the waves again, as a roving lustful bull?
Has a second Europa outraged you? Or could it be that another Antiope
is a woman now, though her father said no, in the rough shaggy style
of that faux satyr, Zeus? Or maybe we have a two-trick stallion with a mind
for sex, who has ridden a second Dia, snorting and neighing through his false
horse lips? Surely the torch has not been lit for a second Semele,
that thunderbolt launched and exploding home with Cupid at the helm?
Surely there is no second Io, with the horns of a cow so fair, whose bed
he prances around and mounts with many a lustful bellow? Well,
if you would like, you can surely deputize another ranch-hand spy,

a cowboy Argus tattooed on all sides with piercing eyes that never sleep.
Just tell me what the matter is, and I will help you any way I can."

In response Hera was all over her with a speech less than honest.

"Apparently, O Cyprian goddess, we must yield to mortals our deathless
Olympus. Semele, the mother of Bacchus, sits ensconced up there right now,
and soon, no doubt, Zeus will lead Dionysus into heaven. What home now
is there for Hera? To exactly what place in the universe am I supposed to go?
I shudder to think that I might see Semele as heaven's bastard Queen!
I'm even more terrified that I might see the underworld halls of Iapetus,
that he might put his hands on me and cast me out, just like Cronus,
an exile from Olympus. I am scared to think that he might find even nectar
a taste too common, and transplant up from Mother Earth the 'grapevine,'
if that's the word, so all the blessed gods can toast with cups of cabernet.

"O Justice, O Earth, O Purest Water, I swear on you this cannot happen!
May he never import these invasive shoots into the sky, and make me praise
the sky's grape-clustered trellis in place of the star-clustered vault of heaven.
May I never drink cheap human wine after the fine nectar of Olympus.
I am terrified to my immortal core that I will see that dauntless goddess,
Athena, staggering drunk and all too ready to unload that spear on Ares
or you, Aphrodite. Shots of Dionysus straight can knock you out, and if Enyo
the dread goddess of war should become a little intoxicated,
she might start a fight up there in heaven, set the drunken stars
at each other's throats. Swept away with Bacchus the Olympian gods
would imitate the Corybants, clashing their shields in a savage ecstasy.

"Is the shame not great enough, a divine disgrace, that I must see
that Trojan boy, abducted in his adolescent bloom, become the cupbearer
of Zeus? The youth shames heaven's goddess of youth, who used to pour
those drinks herself, but now this boy with his earthborn hands draws
the sweetest drafts of nectar. My disgrace is plain, and I am done,
headed down to earth below. I'll leave heaven behind to that handsome pair,
Ganymede and Dionysus. I'll leave heaven behind, since after all
it's Semele's new home. Let heaven be a home sweet home for that whole
bastard family, for Perseus as for Dionysus. I'll make my way to my own Argos,

the glorious city of Mycene, and there I'll live, a goddess on earth. My son
and your lover, Ares will follow his wounded mother. Why don't you come?
You share my wrath, so march your way right into Sparta where you belong,
let it welcome Aphrodite in her golden breastplate and Ares in his bronze.

"I know why I'm wedded to such pain. My father's Fury is paying me back
for the hubris of a parent wronged. When Zeus fought his begetter Cronus
Titan-born Hera was no small help, as I leaned hard into the carnage.
So for me it is just wonderful to see Dionysus up there on Olympus,
sitting right next to Cupid and sharing the hearth with Aphrodite herself,
the goddess born from heaven's seed mixed with ocean spray, as he toys
with the aegis between the son of Cronus and his daughter Athena.
So as one goddess to another, help me out, and as the ally of my distress
give me the cestus embroidered with desire, your all-seductive girdle,
for just one rosy-fingered day. I'll catch and bewitch the eyes of Zeus
and after the deed when he falls asleep, I'll bring aid to the Indians.

"I seem to be your mother-in-law times two, since you are the loving bride
of our Hephaestus and our Ares. Grant me a favor late in coming,
since the dark-skinned Indians gave welcome to Erythraean Aphrodite.
Now Dionysus in fury cuts them up, and Zeus himself rages at them,
the woman-crazed, heartless, baby manufacturing god that he is,
and thunderbolts flash, whirl, and crash as he fights beside his Dionysus.
O faithful ally of my distress, give me the cestus! With its singular power
you seduce the universe all in one, yet I am also fit to wear it,
as goddess of the marriage yoke who fights right alongside the Loves."

Book 32

Joseph Harrington

In the thirty-second book are battle scenes,
bedroom scenes, and Bacchus' going nuts.

Scene I. Hera Seduces Zeus

Aphrodite the seductress was persuaded. She fulfilled
Hera's request, eased the cestus from her breasts,
explaining all the while the magic of the band:

"Use this band to aid you in your need.
With it you'll enchant most everything—
channel the desire of Zeus and Helios,
the chorus of stars, the interminable currents of Ocean."

So saying, she dove into the protean sea
around the rocky coast of Assyrian Lebanon;
while Hera headed for Olympus, encircled by wandering stars.
Rapidly she appareled her snow-white form.
Often she tucked a wisp of hair, braiding it
along her head, then daubed the plaits with oils whose scent,
wafting, made the seas, the earth and heavens reel.
She crowned herself with an intricately filigreed coronet

studded with numerous rubies, which, when turned, blazed
with glittering Cyprian fire, doing the work of Eros.
She also sported that aphrodisiac gem
which bears the shining name of the lovestruck Moonstone;
as well as the desire-arousing stone that yearns for iron;
and the Indian gem born on the half-shell, born
like the goddess from the foam; and the sky-blue sapphire,
which Phoebus loves still. Around her hair, Hera
bound that erogenous bloom that Cytherea loves
as much as the anemone or rose, when she's on the verge
of making love with Myrrha's son. Encircling midriff
with the unfamiliar cestus, winding it round and round,
she chose her familiar embroidered cloak
(for it was still spotted with hymeneal blood
to remind her husband of young love, when she came,
a virgin, to meet her brother for their secret tryst).

She cleaned her face, wrapped herself in the cloak,
fastened it with a glittering brooch. Thus bedizened,
she appraised her reflected beauty in the glass, then flew
fast as a bird through the ether, fast as a thought in the mind.

She came within sight of the great god;
he fixed his gaze on her; the cestus, like a lash,
stung him and kindled his lust. His eyes entranced,
the ogling Cronides spoke:
"O my Hera!
What brings you to the realms of dawn? What do you need?
Why do you come? Enraged by vinous Bacchus?
Armed and ready to fight for those supercilious Indians?"

He ceased, and Hera with her many machinations,
pleasant without, seething within, jealously
rejoicing, responded to her spouse deceptively, thus:

"Lord Father Zeus, this is an errand I run for me,
neither for martial Indians nor for Dionysus

the Indian-killer. I went east: to the fiery courts
of Helios I sped. For Eros flies
beside Tethys' waters, drunk with love for Rhodope.
Now he's left off matchmaking!
The fabric of the cosmos is rent, life is useless without
the conjugal bond. So, I told him to return—
for they call me Lady of Marriage, after all,
for I hold in my hands the boon of a healthy birth.
And now, I'm back."
So said Hera to Zeus,
who warmly replied:
"Hera! Dearest Bride—
why bicker? Away with Dionysus the Proud—
let him fell a forest of impious Indians!
But let us to a marriage bed forthwith . . .
Never did I feel such desire for any lover,
as the tingling I feel when I touch this cestus!
Not with Taÿgetê, daughter of Atlas, on whose bed
was begot Prince Lacedaemon of ancient fame,
did I fall so much in love; nor at Lerna
with Niobe, offspring of the primal King Phoroneus;
nor so much with Io, Inachus' ambling cow,
who, on the banks of Nile, carried on the line
engendered by King Epaphus and primal Ceroëssa;
not even my lust for the Paphian, whose lack
caused me to jet my seed in fertile fields,
compares to the delectable desire I feel for you!
Thus you pierce your husband with Cyprian darts,
you, Queen of Conjugality, queen of all that are born!"

Then he conjured up a pleasure dome of golden cloud,
swirling around them and arching into place;
the parti-colored bow of Iris crowned the whole.
A bed materialized for the lovemaking Zeus
and his ivory-armed bride, concealed in their bower.

Within the bonds of gracious marriage they conjoined,
and Gaea diffused her many fragrances, strewing
the bridal bed with beautiful flowers: the crocus from Cilicia,
wrapped about by leaves of morning glory, like lover
embracing his beloved, in floral monogamy.
Thus earth bestrewed Zeus with saffron, & Hera
with purple blooms. Narcissus overgrew
anemone, as silent emblem of the god's eager love.
No immortal spied the Divinities in their retreat,
no nearby nymphs, nor watchful sun,
nor moon's mild eyes spied the deathless bed,
for walls of cloud enclosed it, and Sleep and Love
had clouded the eyes of Zeus, in deep slumber now,
holding his wife in his arms and out like a light.

Scene II. Dionysus Driven Mad

with Zeus asleep
Hera sends   a monstrous agent
:   a Fury   :   armed   to the fangs
     who
roves foothills
          finds Bacchus
                    "the Deliverer"
& buzzes him   damns his eyes
cracks snake whip   shakes her head
snake-hairs hiss   writhe   gape   lunge
toxic gushes   terrify
slather
     splash dead rocks   :   waste waste places

now the god sees   this Fury   :
               now seething   beast-face
hackles   lion snarls   whiskers bristle
opens dark maw   drooling teeth—

come for Dionysus
                    :   his mind   starts wondering
wandering
          wide

when

Artemis sees Bacchus   :   his eyes roll   lips foam:
she hies to help him
                    Hera halts her :
cracking crash like   thunder deafens
flaming shaft smashes   too close   too near
Huntress rears back
frowning   growling—
Hera   wins again—

but
she stops beasts from
tearing the helpless god   limb from
limb   holds back hounds
halters them fast   :   Dionysus' flesh
spared rending   in his frenzy

this Fury   :   this Megaera
in coal-black weeds
fades
          but aims
flash-bangs   poison gas
   & phantasmatic hallucinations
at the Liberator-from-Care
   & that god-damn
crazy-making   snake-whip snaps
                         again & again

Dionysus tortured   aimless   reels
stumbles   woodland paths

pants asthmatically
bangs horns
rock-wall bull-bellows
& Echo
bellows back
no panpipes : a raucous roar
dangerous *dangerous*

Bacchus : soul lost : fleet as storm-
clouds chases both lion & deer & lion
stays away bear
panicked flees : hides in hidden cave
unnerved
by the Deliverer's berserk
flailing
hideous shrieks
while thick snakes sun on stone
harmlessly lick air 'til
he with thyrsus
disembowels them
randomly
butts head loosens boulders
prides
of lions cowering : bloody manes :
all left dead

he pulls trees : weeds
tosses them
roots-up
evicts dryads
pummels bluffs
turns naiads out of rivers : even his
raving maenads spook :
clear out keep clear
of license-giving god :
satyrs gallop away
into the waves hide in

freezing sea : stunned by god's
demented frenzy : keep distance from
roaring lunging frothing form : he
leaves the scene his
mania *rages* *rages*

Scene III. The Rout

Dionysus thus convulsing,
maddened at command of Hera,
could no longer lead his army,
wandered from the field of battle.
King Deriades then assaulted
women warriors, wild Bacchantes—

Like the sea in angry winter,
whipped by winds' erratic tumult,
cleaving air with water-mountains,
crashes down on hapless sailors,
snaps the rigging, tangles canvas,
like a cloak it wraps the sailcloth
round about the swaying mainmast,
skews the yardarm; then the sailors,
driven by their desperation,
drown their hopes in ocean darkness—
So the dauntless Indian hero
stove the hull of Bacchus' army.

Next a scene of crazed disorder,
massacre of weaker forces:
clad in armor, Ares charges,
tireless, whipping up the battle,
morphs into the fierce Modaeus
(bold Deriades' own equal).
Only killing pleased that warrior;
gore, not wine, could slake his thirst;

on his shield, the grim Medusa,
hideous Gorgon hair of serpents.
With the features of Modaeus
stamped upon his visage, Ares,
scowling face and bright escutcheon,
dove into the furious melee,
drove his foemen helter-skelter,
filled his fighters with new courage.
Soon the war-cry of the Indians
rose above the din of battle;
louder than the host of thousands
Ares' roar like thunder pounded.
At his side, the goddess Discord;
Rout and Fear, Deriades serving.

Meanwhile Zeus the Father slumbered;
Dionysus wayward wandered,
left his army panic stricken,
driven into desperate chaos
with Deriades pursuing,
with the godly help of Ares.
Now they move in for the killing,
circling round like hoops of iron,
picking off the surrounded Bacchae.

Tell me now, Homeric Muses,
whom Deriades destroyed
by his spear in open battle!

Thyamis, Opheltes also,
plus Abialus, Telebes,
and Ormenius, Aretus,
Criasus Argasides,
Thronius, also Antheus
born in hilly Lycia,
Moleneus with ashen sapling,
Comarcus in all his power—

so Deriades dispatched them,
leaving heaps of bodies bleeding.
One along the ground extended;
one was swimming through the tempest;
near him drowned another, wounded
by a piercing spearhead
(Nereus buried him in ocean);
one tried running over ridges,
fleeing fate with lightning swiftness;
One tried crawling into bushes,
calling out for Dionysus,
spear in back, his fortune sealing.

Killed by boulder from a giant,
proud Echelus went unburied:
overgrown Morrheus felled him,
Cyprian boy, his body lying,
shaggy hair like fronds outspreading
growing on a severed tree trunk—
he who swung his brand in battle,
downy cheeked, with valor rushing,
'til upon the hip-joint socket
crashed Morrheus' crushing boulder.
Down he went, his body twitching,
holding tight the sacred pine-torch,
curly hair by chance igniting,
burning hair and head to cinders.

Then Morrheus the giant gloated
over brave Echelus' body:
"Boy, how could you be from Cyprus?
You're not scion of Pygmalion,
favored by the Cyprian goddess,
many years on him bestowing:
Where was her beloved Ares
when your fate was fast approaching?
Neither did your Cyprian patron

grant you cycling years unending,
grant you magic getaway car,
you, a muleteer and bumpkin.
Or possibly you *are* from Cyprus—
like Adonis, slain by Ares!"

Then Morrheus propelled his weapon,
skewered the infantry in numbers:
First he nailed the lumbering Bilithus;
Denthis; Erigbolus, dancer—
headless now he dances downward;
Phrygian fighters now are runners,
fleeing far-flung missile falling.
With a rock he slew Sibeus;
Actaeon and the Thebans
scrambled, but he got Eubotes,
Actaeon's friend and comrade,
citizen of Cadmus' city.

With a single voice the screaming
rises from a host surrounded,
driven into nets of Fortune,
by Deriades' destroying
power, total rout befalling—
heaps and rows of dead and dying,
murdered by a single warrior,
steel and blood and dust comingling—
Crimisos and Himaleon,
Phrasius, also Thargelus,
Iaon, Coelon stumbling over
corpses, now are corpses also,
Cyes, too, a bloodied body—
Endless carnage reaping warriors,
steely weapons cleaving torsos
spilled the blood of the invaders,
slaked the thirsty dust of India.

Terror gripped the Bacchic army:
infantry retreated, fearful,
cavalry pulled up their horses,
turned bejeweled bridles, fleeing:
one to hills, a cave for shelter,
one sought refuge in the bushes,
covering himself in leaf-mold;
others hid in caves of lions,
some in caves of bears took shelter,
one across an outcrop hurtled,
then along the hilltops bounded.
One, a Bacchant, slow on tiptoe,
passed a lioness with litter,
wanting not a brave companion,
but a doe as scared as she was,
hiding, in her cervine humor;
then a satyr, bare-hoofed, bounded,
while Deriades pursued him.
Old Silenus scraped the hillside,
rubbing dirt in hair and visage,
then instead of fighting, staggered
off along the trail, secreted,
just outside of range of spearing,
helmeted Morrheus avoiding;
Euios threw away his thyrsus,
let the gusty breezes take it;
Proud Erechtheus was humbled,
slinking off while gazing backward,
shamed at thought of fierce Athena,
warlike patron of his city;
Then Aristaeus retreated,
shoulder wounded by an arrow,
forced to leave the maenads' battle
waged for sake of Dionysus.
Corybantes charged to battle,
boldly met the Indian army;
Melisseus broke and left them,

ran in the reverse direction:
Erythraean spear impaled him,
jutting through his hairy sternum.
Grim cyclopes, reckless, hurried;
Faunus fled with them, unruffled
by the Indian battle's clamor;
One Parrhasian Pan, deserter,
led the capric troop of runners
prancing quietly to forests
so that always-moving Echo
couldn't hear them hurrying rearward,
wouldn't call them skulking cowards.

Scene IV. The Nymphs Are Departed

Thus they all stole away from the front—
except Aeacus, who chose to fight on
alone, without unvanquished Dionysus at his side.
In spite of that, he stood his ground.
Elsewhere,
mountain-nymphs, the Oreads, slipped into the sea,
hid beneath the waves in the grotto of a naiad. Others
joined their comrades in the River Hydaspes; some
fled to nearby Indus, to dwell in its stream;
still others flowed together to the Sydrus; to Ganges
others journeyed, to cleanse themselves of dried blood.
Many in those watery companies went to lodge
with silver-footed Thetis, welcomer of refugees,
defender of virgins, who at her courtyard gate
awaited them, far beneath the billowing waves.
Others concealed themselves in the shade beneath the fruit
of a hamadryad's tree, or in the knothole of an oak.
The many Bassarids' fresh fountains of tears
mixed with clear water, flowed over stones,
and darkened the melancholy aspect of the spring,
as she deeply mourned unmourning Dionysus.

Book 33

Adrienne Atkins

Eros becomes bellicose in chapter thirty-three
and sets Morrheus burning for lovely Chalcomedê.

As for Dionysus, he tore off like a horned bull
to nowhere in particular, bucking as he went,
snorting out toxic breath as his madness surged.

Now sprightly Pasithea, one of the Graces, happened to be
in Erythraea, collecting cuttings from scented reeds.
She planned to brew perfume for lady Aphrodite
in the red-hot cauldrons of Paphos, the goddess's city,
by mixing the Indian blossoms with Assyrian oil.
After she had gathered all the dewy shoots,
she took a look around, and that was when she spied
her father, Dionysus, off in a thicket, all in a frenzy.
She wept in distress and with filial fervor,
dragging her nails on her cheeks, marking her grief.
Then she saw the satyrs trembling before Enyo,
goddess of war, and she saw Codone and Gigarto,
the young dead; the dust where they lay was their grave.
She ached for Chalcomedê, who at galeforce pace
was fleeing the blade of maddened Morrheus—
but she also felt a pang of envy that rosy Chalcomedê
might well be the favorite girl of shining Aphrodite.

So she sailed up to Olympus, suffering in silence,
concealing her grief for her father Dionysus.
Her blooming cheeks turned pale,
her sparkling features lost their luster.
She kept quiet, but Aphrodite noted her low spirits;
Pasithea's pained expression outed her.
The Cyprian goddess, lover of Adonis, offered comfort:

"My dear, what's wrong? Why the long face?
What happened to your blushing cheeks,
and all their springtime gleam? Who dulled them?
Your skin has lost its normal silver shine,
your eyes aren't laughing like they used to do.
So what's the matter? Is my Eros up to trouble?
Are you lovesick for some mountain herdsman,
the way Selene was? Or did Eros enchant you
with my magic lingerie?! He did that to Dawn once.
Wait, I know why you're all off color. That loner Sleep
is playing suitor! He's a real shady character.
Well if you don't want him, I won't force it. I'd never
match a bright girl like you with such a gloomy guy."

To this Pasithea responded through tears:
"Mother of Desires, sower of the seeds of life,
no! No herdsman's after me, Sleep's not out of line.
I'm no Selene, not unlucky like Dawn.
Dionysus is lost and suffering, that's why I'm upset!
The Furies are terrorizing him! My own father,
and your brother! Help him, if it's possible!"

Then she told the goddess all about her father's torment,
the endless lines of maenads that Morrheus slaughtered,
and the sorry state of the army of satyrs. She described
an oppression of unearthly origin rocking Dionysus,
and Gigarto wailing on the ground, gasping for air,
and Codone, too young to die. She stammered
recalling the suffering of sweet Chalchomedê.

The smile fell from Aphrodite's face,
normally bright and rosy, full of laugh-lines.
She ordered her assistant, the Grace Aglaea,
to call her son Eros, who travels high heaven
overseeing humanity's proliferation.

Aglaea set off to track down flighty Eros,
craning her neck to scan earth, sea, and sky,
since there's nowhere his wings do not take him
through all the four realms of the cosmos.
She found him on the peak of bright Olympus
playing a game, shooting dregs of nectar from a cup.
His competitor was standing at his side,
graceful Hymenaeus, hair tumbling loose like a mane.
Hymenaeus had offered as a prize a clever device
built by his mother Urania, the Muse of astronomy:
it was a globe, star-studded, like a head with a hundred eyes.
Winged Eros had matched the bet with a gold pendant
stolen from his mother Aphrodite, daughter of the sea,
as a dazzling reward for the winner. A silver vessel
marked out the goal, and as the target in the middle
they set up a statue of Hebe pouring wine. Ganymede,
Zeus' personal wine-boy, was on hand to referee,
with victory garlands ready. To decide who shot first,
they played a game of chance with their hands:
they opened their fists and showed a number of fingers
while guessing how many they both had flashed in total.
The rousing match went back and forth,
till Hymenaeus and his lovely locks won the face-off.
He took the cup and whipped it, sending a glob of nectar
high over the vessel. But he failed to pray to his mother,
the Muse, and after the dollop zoomed from the cup,
striking the air, flying at an even height,
it then changed course; it wobbled and danced,
and though some fell on the statue's face,
it didn't make a splat, so they didn't count it as a hit.

Now Eros was next for a turn with the cup.
He held it masterfully, and prayed to Aphrodite
in his heart, silently. He fixed his eyes on the mark,
then he fired off the sticky missile.
The drop of nectar hurtled through the air,
whirling straight and true, and smacked the statue
right between the eyes; it gave a mighty sound,
as if the figurine cried out, and the vessel's echo
sounded victory for Aphrodite's golden boy.
Ganymede, laughing, presented Eros with the garland,
and Eros scooped up the pendant and the globe.
Holding the two prizes from the nectar-drop game,
he went skipping around, full of himself,
dancing with pride, doing flips, trying and trying
to pry Hymenaeus' hands from his weeping face.
Aglaea approached the lord of happy hearts
and took the prizes from his hands. Pulling him aside,
with silence as her only witness, she whispered in his ear
a lie that cunning Aphrodite had concocted:

"Unconquered conqueror! Primordial giver of life!
Come quick! Aphrodite's in trouble, and her assistants
have abandoned her! Charis fled, Peitho is gone!
Pothos deserted! I was the only one left
for her to send! She needs your invincible bow!"

Eros wanted to know everything;
when you tell a young person the start of a story,
they are always impatient to get to the end.
A rush of words came spewing from his mouth:

"Who hurt Aphrodite?! I'll get my weapons!
I'll fight everyone! If my mother's in danger,
I'll aim my unstoppable bow at Zeus if I have to!
I'll turn him back into a sex-crazed eagle or a bull,
like I did when he wanted to get with Aegina and Pasiphaë!
Or if Athena has upset her, or Hephaestus hurt her—

maybe he attacked her with a torch from his festival!
I'll fight them both! Hephaestus and Athena!
Or if it's the archer Artemis that made her mad,
I'll pull Orion's sword out from the stars
and stab her! I'll run her out of high heaven!
Same for Hermes, I'll use my wings and carry him off
while he calls for his worthless wife Peitho to help him!
If it's Apollo, then screw my bow and quiver,
I'll whip him with his own laurel! He'll like that.
I'll tie him up with hyacinth, his dead lover's flower!
I'm not afraid of Enyalius, either! And Ares, he's easy!
I'll use Aphrodite's lingerie to bind him up! How sweet.
Hell, I'll drag down the heavenly bodies
to serve Aphrodite in Paphos! All second to my mom:
the Sun and his lover Clymenê, plus the Moon and Endymion!
Then everyone will know not to mess with me!"

At that he whirled around and shot into the air,
straight to the emergency at Aphrodite's house,
leaving Aglaea far behind thanks to his speedy wings.
Aphrodite received him with a carefree face,
spread out a happy hand for an embrace,
and hoisted him onto her lap—a heavy load, but a dear one.
He sat there while she kissed his lips and eyes
and inspected his heart-bending bow and quiver.
She huffed as if in anger, feigning an outburst, and said:

"My dear, you're neglecting your duty to me!
You're supposed to be making Pasiphaë hot for the bull.
Now her father, the Sun, is mocking me with impunity!
He's even arming his grandson, the warrior Deriades,
to slaughter the Bassarid followers of Dionysus
and drive off his satyrs, a randy bunch just like their leader.
What's worse, Ares has taken a mortal form
and he's stoking the battle together with Enyo!
He's completely forgotten his love for me.
He's taking orders from Hera and arming himself

against Dionysus, alongside the Indian king! Well,
if Ares fights for Deriades, then you must fight for Lyaeus.
He has a spear, but your bow is stronger; all kneel to it,
even lord Zeus and furious Ares and lawgiving Hermes.
Even Apollo fears it, the eminent archer himself!
My son, my dear, if you love me at all,
fight for the Bacchants and our Dionysus.
Go to the east as fast as you can, to the Indian land.
There's a girl there who serves Dionysus,
one of the Bacchants, unparalleled among her peers.
Her name is Chalcomedê. She clings to her virginity,
but my son, if you put her in a room with me,
you can't tell the one from the other.
Go and shoot Morrheus so he goes crazy for her;
it'll help while Dionysus is off wandering the wilderness.
I'll reward you accordingly for your archery
with a crown made by Hephaestus himself,
that glistens like sunbeams. So shoot your sweet arrow;
it will be a favor to us both, me and Dionysus.
Honor the bird of love, your symbol and mine,
the herald of happy and lifelong unions!"

No sooner had she spoken than Eros excitedly
sprung from his mother's lap, grabbed his bow,
and slung his mighty quiver on his little shoulder.
He shot through the air on his wings, and near Cernê
he pivoted nimbly to face into Dawn's rays.
He snickered as he sailed, recalling how he once set
the driver of heaven's chariot burning with his little arrows;
the fire of love had conquered the fire of the Sun.
Soon he was in the thick of the Indian troops,
he was bracing his bow along Chalcomedê's neck,
he was aiming an arrow around her pink cheek.
He let it fly into Morrheus' heart. Then he sailed off,
wings beating in unison like rowing oars,
and soared up to his father's domain in the stars,
leaving his fiery arrow fixed in the Indian prince.

The arrow of desire drove Morrheus here and there;
wherever Chalcomedê went, the sorry man went too.
His sword turned gentle, his spear hung idle in his grasp.
The spell of love had tamed his reckless mind,
and everywhere he passed his maddened eyes,
he only saw what Aphrodite wanted him to see.
Chalcomedê responded with a calculated lie:
she let the Indian leader think the desire was mutual,
but the love she performed was a sham.
Morrheus was riding high on empty hope,
fully convinced that Eros had struck her, too.
His mind was gone; he forgot about his looks,
thinking he could charm a modest girl with his dark body.
Chalcomedê reveled in the lie, treating it like a game.
She told her enemy about the swift feet of Daphne,
how she sped like the North wind while fleeing Apollo;
how she ran along the stream of a winding river,
the wide Orontes, and she was still a virgin;
how at the mouth of that river the Earth opened up
and took the child into her fold, saving her from the hunt.
When she told this story, Morrheus danced in delight.
But one thing bothered him: that in the hunt for Daphne,
the god never caught her. Apollo never violated her.
He called Apollo slow and secretly blamed the Earth
for hiding her away before she had her wedding night.
Passion's sweet fire set him trembling with fear
that Chalcomedê was like Daphne, devoted to her virginity,
that he would see her fleeing and follow on an endless chase,
that he was like Apollo, suffering for love he'd never make.

When evening came to still the squall of battle,
Chalcomedê went deep into the empty woods
in search of signs of Dionysus in his demented state.
She brought no drums or sacred cymbals
to perform rites for the sleepless god,
but held off from dancing and kept her head down,

confining her talkative lips to an uncommon silence.
She understood the pain of her protector Dionysus.

Slowly, gingerly, on tiptoes, Morrheus followed,
stealing glance after glance to watch Chalcomedê.
He cursed the Sun for setting so soon, but didn't let that
distract his mind from her. The arrow in his heart
kindled night's desire, and he grew so distressed
that an unmanly, love-induced cry burst from his throat:

"To hell with Ares' bow and arrow! Now a better one,
desire's arrow, drives me. Screw his quiver, too,
since now I wear the belt of Aphrodite on my body!
Never again will I take up arms against the Bassarids.
I'll leave behind Water and Earth, the gods of my people.
I'll set up an altar to Aphrodite and Dionysus.
I'll drop the bronze javelin of Enyalius and Athena.
I'll never take up torches into battle, now that
the fire of Eros has snuffed Enyalius' feeble flame.
The fire thrust on me is hotter! And I wish, I wish
I were a satyr. They're expected to be crazed for women.
I could join the Bacchant dances, touch Chalcomedê's arm,
and tighten the chain of my desire on her neck.
Let Dionysus drag me to Phrygia, let me go
from Deriades' righthand man to slave. Instead of my home,
let wealthy Maeonia accept me as one of its people.
After Mount Caucasus in India, I wish to live on Tmolus,
and to be called Lydian instead of Indian,
offering my life to Dionysus as a slave of Eros.
Let the river Pactolus carry me; what use is the Hydaspes?
The sweet home of Chalcomedê can claim me.
In this war, the men of Deriades fell to the weapons
of Aphrodite and Bacchus both, you could say:
her belt lashed me, and his thyrsus conquered our Orontes!"

So he cried, his anxiety a roaring sea,
and he crumbled at the thought of Chalcomedê.

It is at night, after all, that the sparks of desire grow hotter
and now the curving cover of a cloudless night
had begun to dart from the earth in a murky surge,
quietly deepening, pressing all things into a single fearful silence:
no traveler left a footprint in the Indian city,
no craftswoman laid a hand on her usual work,
nor did the spindle float in her practiced palms,
twirling itself under the familiar lamp,
dangling restless from a dancing thread.
Instead the working woman slept, head sunk low,
as her lamp kept vigil. A gentle snake crept inside
and lay where it fell, resting on its belly,
sleepy body in a coil, tail doubled under head.
Near the wall an elephant slumbered
upright on sky-high legs, bracing its frame on a tree.

That night, Morrheus alone was sleepless. He stole away
and paced feverishly, tracing odysseys with his feet
while Chirobië slept in their bedroom, companionless.
He recalled the lore he had heard from a wise old man
while at war in Cilicia near the Taurus Mountains
about the constellations' bitter liaisons, all divinely devised.
So when he gazed across the halls of heaven spread above,
he landed on Europa's mate, the Bull, an Olympian disguise.
Then he drifted his eyes to the north stretch of sky
where he spotted Callisto's stars, including the roving Plow.
She as a woman, he knew, had taken a female lover
who offered a false embrace; the Artemis lookalike was Zeus,
his body unrecognizable. And rising above the Bull
he spied the bright-shining Charioteer, Myrtilus,
who orchestrated a marriage; at the chariot race
for Hippodameia's hand, he replaced a wheel-peg with wax
so Pelops wound up with a wedding. Then near Cassiopeia
he saw the Eagle, wings wide, the mate of Aegina,
and he wished that he, too, had such a cunning device
so he might strip Chalcomedê of her virginity.
Then he, with bloodshot eyes, began to speak:

"I heard Zeus once turned into a satyr—the spitting image—
and by that wily disguise he bedded Antiope, then still a virgin.
He tricked her into sex at a wedding celebration.
That's the masquerade I want! Then all unnoticed
I could dance into the army of satyrs with their fancy horns
and score Chalcomedê's bed while she's drunk on strong wine.
Aphrodite, you resent us Indian men, and I know why:
your arrows target us just because we live near the Sun,
who exposed your affair with Ares; you were chained and shamed.
But I'm no kin to the Sun through Phaëthon. So why me, Aphrodite?
It's not like his bull-loving daughter Pasiphaë birthed me,
or Ariadne is my sister. Do you hear me, rocks? Raise your stony voice!
I want Chalcomedê. And she won't have me. Screw you, quiver,
and screw you, too, deadly-quick bow and arrows.
Ares didn't save me when Aphrodite dressed for war.
Haughty Bacchus couldn't kill Eros. And little Eros has beaten me, too."

So spoke Morrheus, wretched with lust. But to no avail.

Nor did the sweet distraction of fluttering sleep
lull Chalcomedê. She pined not for marriage, but death,
so terrified was she that in his hysteria Morrheus would take her,
an inferno of a man, and shackle her into forced union
while Bacchus was away. So she took a night walk
to the Erythraean Sea and called to unlistening waves:

"Melis, you had it good, never knowing the ways of Eros.
You cast your body into the whirling sea on your own terms
to avoid the bed of Damnameneus, who raged for women—
a happy death, devoted to a free life. Bitter Aphrodite,
born of salty sea, set him upon you as a groom-to-be
but the sea saved you from its own daughter;
you died in the waves a virgin still. I wish the water
would cover me, Chalcomedê, too. I'd go willingly
if it meant avoiding the bed of covetous Morrheus.
Or I could be a new Britomartis, who also shunned marriage:
when she spurned the lewd advances of King Minos,

the sea received her, then delivered her to friendlier land.
I have no reason to fear Poseidon's mad appetite
like Asteria did when he pursued her, still unwed:
she wandered back and forth across the sea,
riding restlessly, following the changing wind
till Apollo pinned her in the waves, transformed into an island.
So take me, sea. Take me in your welcoming lap.
Take Chalcomedê as you took Melis.
Take me unmarried like a second Britomartis.
Let me escape Morrheus and your daughter Aphrodite.
Oh defender of girls, pity Chalocomedê."

So her thoughts raced on the brink of the sea
and she would have plunged in the surf then and there
had Thetis not stopped her, doing Dionysus a favor.
The goddess came to stand by Chalcomedê in disguise,
sporting the form and comforting tone of a Bacchant woman.

"Be brave, Chalcomedê!" she said. "Don't fear Morrheus' bed.
Consider me an omen of chastity unbroken;
I swear your bed will never see a man.
I am Thetis. I, too, refuse marriage. I am like you,
Chalcomedê, in love with my independence. Yes,
Zeus once drove me from heaven, wishing to marry me
but old Prometheus curbed his lust with a prophesy
that I'd have a son with unmatchable strength;
Zeus was afraid that the son I bore him would conquer
and dethrone him, as he had done to his own father.
So be smart and keep your life. There is a way
to cheat your wedding night. Besides, if you kill yourself
then what's to stop Morrheus from slaughtering the Bacchants?
No, you must trick him. Then you will save your army,
which is cowering now that Dionysus' wits are whipped.
Act like you want him, even though you don't,
and if Morrheus tries to drag you to his bed,
you are not defenseless against his attempts. You have a guard;
a massive snake will emerge to ensure your belt stays fastened.

Then after the war in India, Dionysus will take your snake
and place it in the star-splendored sky to create
a constellation in celebration of your unbroken innocence.
It will sit near the god's own stars, the Crown,
that he will make to honor his beloved Ariadne,
and your snake will rival the Serpent in the northern sky
as it shines down on mortals with bright Ophiuchus.
Then you will praise me, Thetis, goddess of the sea,
when you spy your stars blazing beside Selene.
So face your wedding night undaunted;
your innocence will not become undone by any man.
I swear it by Dionysus, whom I have fed as my guest,
I swear it by your thyrsus, and even by sea-born Aphrodite."

With Chalcomedê thus consoled, Thetis shrouded her in clouds
so no guards would spot her, or lookouts
who were stealing about, tiptoeing a midnight route,
or goatherds, overbold and crazed for women,
who might drag the twilit girl to a wayside wedding.

Book 34

Anna Mayersohn

In the thirty-fourth book,
Deriades arms himself against the Bacchants
And kills them inside the ramparts.

The maiden, roaming the mountains on her fast-whirling soles,
Carried her noiseless footsteps and made her way to the wooded ridge.
Nor did Thetis tarry on the seashore, but she entered the seaweed hall of her father Nereus.
By now, Morrheus had his fill of straining his eyesight through the cloudless air
And watching the orbits of the stars. He spoke, smiting his heart with cares:

"My mind vacillates here and there. No one plan, no one intention comes to me.
A wide range of desires circle around me,
And I don't know how to accomplish any one of them. Should I kill lovely Chalcomedê?
What should I do so that she doesn't kill me with desire from beyond the grave?
But then, should I leave her alive and unhurt and publicly claim the maiden in marriage?
In my heart I tremble in fear of Deriades and I pity Chirobië.
I will never kill the maiden. If I lay her low, how can I live,
When I no longer see my girl?
I suffer when I am bereft of Chalcomedê for an hour."

Thus Morrheus went on, speaking fruitlessly,
Sputtering with distress caused by his desire-stricken thoughts.

As he wandered whirling round round again on the high riverbank,
Having abandoned the bed of his lonely, forgotten bride,
The bold, watchful Hyssacus spotted him;
Cleverly that most trustworthy of attendants perceived the private sting of hidden love.
He inquired with sly words, and this wily speech poured from his lips:

"Why do you leave your bed and your sleeping bride
And wander here and there in the twilight, dauntless Morrheus?
Perhaps Deriades scared you with threats?
Is Chirobië jealous and angry with you, believing that you are in love
With some Bacchant you won with your spear?
When women see their bedmates crazy with love,
They become jealous of some secret doing of Aphrodite.
Perhaps bold Desire, tamer of all, is arming himself against you with sparks of romance
From his tireless quiver? Do you yearn for some one of the Bassarids?
I hear that there are three Graces who dance at Orchomenus, attendants of Phoebus?
But the Graces of dance-weaving Lyaeus number three hundred in their ranks,
Of whom one shines alone, surpassing all,
Just as Selene herself obscures the light of the stars with her brighter rays,
Emitting her orbiting gleam. She arms herself with two weapons at once,
Shooting beauty and hurling iron. She is Pasithea in a flashing helmet,
And the Bacchae call her Chalcomedê;
I myself, however, will call her Artemis of the silver feet or Athena of the golden shield."

So he spoke and fell silent, and Morreus, sick with desire,
Drawing the points of his eyebrows together, spoke from his shamed mouth:

"Certainly Dionysus immersed himself in the sea's swell out of fear of Lycurgus
And armed the nereids who dwell in the deep sea's bosom,
And out of the sea he came bringing Ares' own sister, Aphrodite of the sea, against him.
Instead of a fragrant bridal gown he gave her a corselet of iron to wear,
And instead of an embroidered girdle he gifted her a bronze spear.
Changing the old name of the helmeted Aphrodite, he called her Chalcomedê.
She is a companion to the Bassarids.
I unwittingly fight against two gods at once: Cypris and Dionysus.
Why do I raise an impetuous spear in vain? Yield, spear-point.
If the Paphian conquered the thrower of lightning,
If with her spark she subdues him who bears the scepter of battle,
If she burned up blazing Phaëthon with her mightier torch
And agitates one who is already aflame, what could I accomplish with steel?
Tell me of some helpful trick to use against Cyprogeneia.
Shall I hurt Eros? How can I get to him, when he has wings?
Shall I raise my spear? He fights fire with fire!
Shall I draw my sword? He has a bow, a bow which has lit a fire in my soul.
Often have I been wounded amidst the din of battle,
But a doctor saved me from my suffering with his life-defending skill,
Wrapping a pain-killing flower around the wounded body part.
Hyssacus, don't keep this from me: what drugs should lay upon my heart
To heal the wound Eros caused? I am always strong against my enemies;
But when I see Chalcomedê near me, my spear goes limp.
I'm not afraid of Dionysus, but I cower before a woman,
Because she prods me with her beauty, emitting the light of her love-striking visage,
And I can no longer stretch my bow. Thus I have gazed at one of the nereids.
If it is not blasphemy to say so, either Thetis or Galatea fights alongside Dionysus."

He spoke, and returned to his bedroom,
Walking slowly and painstakingly on tiptoe,
Lest he wake his bedmate, who was passing the night in sleep.
He cast his eyes far from his dark-skinned bride

And wished that shining Chalcomedê might appear, along with early-born dawn.
Distressed by Eros, he fell down onto his sad bed.
His vigilant attendant Hyssacus, yearning for sweet slumber,
Once again fell asleep on top of his oxhide shield.

A vision of a dream cajoled Morrheus as he slept,
Springing from the mind-tricking gates of ivory,
And spoke a delightful, deceptive speech:

"Welcome me, your compliant Chalcomedê, bridegroom Morrheus!
Receive your bride in your bed after battle!
By day, you have gladdened your sight by looking at me;
At night, lie beside your beloved Chalcomedê. There is delight in marriage
During sleep, too, and the sweet, charming sting of bridal dreams.
I'd like to take you in my arms, and Dawn is near."

So it spoke, and flew away, and Morrheus jumped awake,
Realizing that the light of Dawn who parts lovers had arrived,
He thought Chalcomedê longed for him.
Immediately, feeding a deceptive hope of love, he spoke silently to himself:

"First light of Dawn, you bring a triple light,
For you bring Chalcomedê, and you bring sunlight,
And you send night running. May you also come, Chalcomedê,
Rosier than rose-crowned Dawn, to bring solace to wakeful Morrheus.
Never do the Seasons bring such a rose to the meadow.
Graceful girl, your cheeks are like a meadow in spring
That time does not know how to ruin.

"Your flowers flourish in the fruit-killing autumn season;
Your lilies shine even in winter; your body is a blushing white flower,
Never waning, tended by the Graces and unharmed by the gales.
You have graced your name with your triumphs in arms.
Your name is linked to your prowess: not in vain were you named after bronze,

For bronze Ares sired you when he danced in the bed of Aphrodite Cypris,
Who engenders love. Everyone else calls you Chalcomedê,
But I alone call you golden Chrysomedê, for you have the beauty of golden Aphrodite.
I believe you are of Spartan stock,
For I think Aphrodite of the iron tunic bore Chalcomedê."

So he spoke upon his wakeful bed.
But when far-shooting Dawn who brings battle in her wake
Sprang up and sent forth light from her blushing face,
Ares who rouses nations armed the sons of India.
Then the corseted Indians rushed from the quick caravans where they slept
Alongside the chariot of Deriades.

Although unconquerable Dionysus was nowhere to be seen,
The Bacchi came onto the plain downcast.
Though no confidence was left in their hearts,
They marched into the din of battle, trembling with fear.
By now, the frenzied women in their bronze tunics
Were no longer reveling with madness that breaks the ranks of men.
Foam did not spray from deep-bellowing throats,
But the untanned faces of their rattling oxhide shields stood still in undisturbed silence.
Pinewood torches of Enyalius did not shine with flame, belching deadly smoke;
But the warriors grew soft as women under the stinging divine scourge.
The satyrs did not shout, nor did the war-stirring flute make its customary sound.
The sileni waged a clear-headed war without a Bacchic hubbub.
They did not touch crimson ochre to their faces
Or turn their fair bodies the dark red color of blood as a frightening façade,
Nor did they sprinkle white gypsum to dye their brows as they used to.
The Pans' mouths did not drink the fresh blood of a wild-dwelling lioness
And revel like a whirlwind in the frenzy of battle, but became soft with fear.
Timidly they struck the ground with careful, noiseless hooves,
Suppressing the fearsome leaps of their mountain dance.

But arrogant Deriades fought the manly fight,
Shaking the points of his horns like the crest of a helmet,
And Morrheus leapt and raged madly against the female ranks,
For Chalcomedê did not stand with the Bacchae and disgrace him,
Stopping the spearpoint red with blood that rushed against the women,
But went with the champions on the frontline and took up the fight:
A lovely young girl, an Amazon winning fame with her bow,
Wearing a light cloak and a brilliant tunic on the plain.
In this way wise Thetis had told her to save the whole army,
Struggling as they were with Dionysus being shaken.

Then, having parted from a face resembling those of the Graces,
Morrheus captured eleven weak Bassarids,
Whom he judged to be inferior to Chalcomedê.
He pulled the Maenalids' hands behind their backs
And bound them tightly with knots that could not be loosened,
And, dragging their loose-haired ranks under the yoke of slavery, he brought them,
His spoils, to his father-in-law Deriades as servants: a second bride price for his wife.
For the sake of that marriage he fought a battle beside lofty Taurus,
When he joined himself tightly to Deriades' daughter, the young princess,
His agemate Chirobië, in a marital bond.
The chief of the Indians did not receive a gift for his daughter's marriage,
No delightful gold, no gleaming stone from the sea.
Deriades refused herds of cattle and flocks of sheep,
But yoked his daughters to strife-stirring warriors in giftless marriages
And then took Morrheus as a son-in law, as well as Orontes, nine cubits wide.
He gave his offspring to the two champions as brides:
To Morrheus, Chirobië, and Protonoea to Orontes.
Morrheus was not like other mortals,
But recalled the ancestral might of the earthborn Indians
In the towering form of his Giant-like limbs
(Being born of the Earth like lofty Typhon)
When by the neighboring rock of fire-nurturing Arima
He showed his race's strength to the witness Cydnus
And brought a bride price for his marriage, the sweat of Cilician work.

He was a groom without possessions, but he won a bride with his prowess.
So Assyria once bent the knee to the iron that sought a marriage for
Morrheus,
And Cilician Taurus bowed its rocky neck under the yoke of Deriades,
And bold Cydnus sank down, which is why in the land of the Cilicians
Morrheus is still called Heracles Sandes.
That all happened in earlier times.
In this later battle, Morrheus took Bacchants captive with his merciless spear;
Exulting, he let out an unbridled shout:

"First, sceptered lord, I bring to you Bacchae, treasures for your daughter.
Afterwards, I will give you Bacchus."

So Morrheus spoke, and the king of the Indians replied:

"You had Chirobië without payment, flashing-helmeted Morrheus.
You brought me a worthy bride price for your wedding
When you enslaved the cities of the Cilicians in a victory that exalted you.
Now, again, you favor me with new gifts.
If you wish, seize some Bassarids and fill Chirobië's whole house with
handmaids.
But when it comes to Bacchus, I have no need of Morrheus,
I shall fetter Dionysus myself and drag him under the yoke of slavery.
But you, just guard against any desire for a bedmate won by the spear,
Lest I view you as the same as these other woman-crazy Indians.
Don't gaze at the eyes and white neck of a Bacchant,
Lest your yearning make my daughter jealous.
But when I have slaughtered the whole army of Bromius,
I will set out for the land of Maeonia,
Whence I will bring back untold Lydian wealth, as much as Pactolus yields.
I will go to Phrygia, land of the fine vines,
Where Rhea lives, who cherished Bromius as a child,
And I will destroy the rich earth of silver Alybe nearby,
So that I may carry back bright, snow-white sheets of metal
From the mines that flow with riches.
And I will sack the land they call seven-gated Thebes,
And I will burn the flaming house of Semele,

Where the bedchambers bear the smoldering remains of the wedding turned to embers."

The lawless king spoke. Deriades then received the whole array of handmaids,
A gift from battle from his son-in-law, a man like Ares,
And offered the Bacchants, dragged by their hair, to Phlogius and Argius.
They were all tied up together; unbreakable straps bound their hands.

Phlogius led them bound in a procession through the city
As an announcement of the king's victory.
Some then hung up on high by the gate of the well-carved hall,
Their necks tied, ensnared in the strangling noose.
To others he gave the hot doom of a fiery death,
While others were buried in the flowing water of a well,
A hole dug in the earth, where from the deep hollow
Water is drawn forcefully by one hand, then another.
Then within the deep-dug pit, half-seen, unshaken,
One of them after another spoke:

"I've been told that Earth and Water are god to the Indians,
Nor was that a false report, for both have joined as one against me.
I am between an earthly death and a watery destruction,
And I have a twofold doom close by.
A strange muddy bond holds me, and I can no longer lift a foot.
I stand here, rooted and unshakeable,
My wet knees fixed in the clay, ready for the Fates.
A river pursued me, too, and I did not tremble before the streaming water.
I wish this were also a roaring stream,
So that I might row the oars of my hands
And break through the black water."

Each spoke, and, receiving the rushing stream into her open throat,
Little by little she died a tombless death.

Morrheus was in thrall to the sweet pang he felt for Chalcomedê.
He drove the whole weaponless army of the Maenalids
Into the beetling city on the ridge,

Poking at them from behind with his spear.
As when a herder drives the wandering ranks of sheep
Into the recess of a capacious pen in one mass,
Quickly guiding the flocks of wooly beasts with his staff,
And many other herdsmen fall in line,
Encircling the animals with their joined hands,
Driving the lines of sheep headlong,
Lest a wayward group of the enclosed flock should stray—
So storm-footed Morrheus drove the female throng into the high-built city
And barred the ranks of Bacchants inside the gates, cut off from the battle.
He toiled at this scheme, but it was all in vain.
If only he might leave the beautiful female spoils of battle
And drag Chalcomedê, his elusive prey, under the yoke of slavery
Together with the other women, so that she might be his servant by day
And by night his bedmate, alternately completing the work of two goddesses:
The deeds of Cypris in private, the weaving of Athena in public.

[There is a substantial lacuna here. When the text resumes the battle lines have shifted.]

Lance-shaking Morrheus acted with care.
He let Deriades, who was fighting nearby, take up the cowardly war against women
And assaulted the male fighters in Bacchus' army,
Aiming to surround the men as well.
They were driven to flight in the middle of the battle.
And the stormy girl stood armed before the city,
Right near the tower, an unveiled maiden. With phony nods and rolling eyes
The girl performed an impression of love-mad women,
And her white chiton, free from her usual girdle, was colored by her reddening breast.
Morrheus thrilled to look at her, and observed the full curve of her breast
Through her delicate mantle.

Then the maiden grabbed a well-made stone as round as a wheel,
A mighty burden for a wagon to bear, and hurled it with expert skill

At fine-crested Morrheus. The stone, borne along through the air
With a sharp whistling sound, smashed into the surface of the shield,
Where an image in beaten gold showed a counterfeit likeness of Chirobië,
False in its beauty. It cut off her wrought head,
Chiseled her face with its flying, flashing point,
And pulverized the round portrait that imitated her form.
Congratulating his shield, Morrheus danced to and fro,
And laughing in his heart he secretly said to himself:

"Dauntless Chalcomedê! A new Peitho of the rosy fingers!
Pretty likeness of Cypris and well-corseted Athena!
A Bacchic early-born Dawn and an unsetting Selene!
You have scraped off the carven impression of my wife;
I wish you might also have cut the throat of my real bride, Chirobië herself."

So saying, he chased the unmarried girl before the city.
His tongue held threats, but his hand held no weapon.
He hurled words but did not pierce the maiden with his spear.
He lifted a merciful spear in his gentle palm.
With guile he let out the sound of a rough shout,
As if this kindly enemy were truly angry.
In his mind he was laughing, while he showed anger on his face.
Gently he brandished a dubious spear and deliberately launched it at a useless target.
The swift-kneed lady fled, running with the misty breezes.
As she exerted herself on knees fast as the wind,
The gales disheveled her clustered curls,
Exposing her neck which rivaled Selene's.
Morrheus deliberately ran on sparing feet,
Now looking at the soles of her feet,
Bare of well-stitched sandals, and her rosy ankles,
Now watching the locks of hair flowing behind her as she moved,
He pursued Chalcomedê. And he shouted sweetly,
Letting gentle words flow softly from his mouth:

"Wait for me, Chalcomedê, wait for your lovesick warrior!
You are protected by your beauty, not by your running!

Spears cannot smite a man as well as the sparks of love can.
I am not your enemy, do not fear.
Your beauty has defeated my bronze point in combat.
You need neither lance nor shield. The brightness of your face is like a sword,
Like a hurtling shaft, and your cheeks triumph by far over an ashen spear.
My hand is sapped of its awesome strength.

"It is no cause for anger if my shaft is conquered,
For even savage Ares grows soft as a woman when Cypris stands before him.
Receive me amongst your satyrs. The Indians will be the best at war
As long as my hands are equipped with weapons,
But if you wish, I will act as a servant to Dionysus.
If you wish, overpower me by my neck or flank.
I don't care about dying cloven by your spear.
Just grieve for me once I have fallen; Chalcomedê shedding tears will
bring me back
Even from Hades. My girl, why do you quiver when I lift a kind spear?
I saw your curly locks upon your shoulders
And I removed my helmet, leaving my own hair uncovered.
One glance at your deerskin, and I hate wearing my corselet."

So he spoke, and the woman turned aside and joined the Bacchants.
Heading away from the path of the killer Morrheus,
She took up the fight bravely, vying with men in battle.

Then, leaving the chaos and cacophony of the battle behind,
The Bacchic army took a respite while Morrheus retreated.

But Deriades pursued the lines of the Bassarids before the city,
Striking at them with his sword, until he drove them close to the ramparts,
Trapping the whole host within the open gates of the towering wall.
Chased into the city by iron, they were cut off from their woodland haunts.
Unsteadily the ranks roamed here and there along the unfamiliar curves of the
road—
Some toward the wing of Eurus,
Some toward the shore of Zephyrus on the western side of the land,
While some wandered along the coast of Notus

And other Bassarids rushed to Boreas' lands.
The maenads freed themselves from their manly dispositions
And became women again.
They rejected battle, remembering their fondness for the arts
Of weaving and basket-making, and wished once more to busy themselves
With the spindle of Athena, not the equipment of Lyaeus.
The dark men had the din of battle in their city as they destroyed the snow-white host.

Book 35

Maryrose Larkin

In the thirty-fifth, look for Morrheus seduced
and the Bassarids shedding blood in battle.

Deriades, outside
the city walls his pike blitz lust steeped His stump
sword & sierra stones   the mad battle

Throes & arrows stones & arrows
battling chaste girls within the city where
the streets chaos paved & Bacchante blood runs

On the wall above the city
old men sit above as old men do: watching war
maidens wept as their sister-selves died below

While into the battle, she carried a thyrsus
& she fell

    to the foot soldier
    her broken body
    a charm
    & her dress his blade his eyes   his fingers in
                                                      her wounds
    in death

he branded her
as a white & rosy bow

& he fell
besotted with beauty
love soaked in bloodied death

hidden as he fights on

While Protonoë
Deriades' daughter
who still mourned Orontes
rose up to avenge him

Her sister Chirobië
stolen spear & shield amok

Orisboë, wife, fights beside Deriades.

What are daughters & wives

as the spears of others
as the shield of others
as the wars of others

While the women of the city are shut up & screaming in courtyards
some enter the fight

Alone before city walls
stepped back from the war
Chalcomedeia waits for Morrheus

Eros struck, he sees her
as she bolts
& he follows
her nakedness under her fluttering robe

& he fell
deeper & charmed

Chalcomedeia coaxing & modest:

if you wish to be my bridegroom
know my bed is not a battlefield

for even Ares shed war at weddings
& danced in finery white

as you are love struck, brave soldier
so we are bound together by Desire

I will not marry a one bronzed
in war's blood splatter & dust

Pull your helmet from your hair
Your armor from your flesh

Let me see you washed clean before me.
Let your body kindle my desire.

A modest maiden does not show her love
but I too was spellbound by Eros' double arrows

Chalcomedeia, all in deceit, a warrior playing a maiden.

Morrheus, falling deeper

Should I keep my spear to embrace you?
No, I will reject my spear, my armor

Let me bathe myself of war
Let me love you with unbloodied hands

For love, I will abandon my wife & country
I will abandon Deriades & his fight

If you wish I will fight besides you
Until the all the Indians are dead

& we will be as Aphrodite & Ares
Naked & embracing on the spent battlefield

Morrheus armor down spear & oxhide abandoned

steps into the Red Sea the wave wash wars' dust & blood but leave a brown
body brown

Aphrodite mocks how love has conquered Ares

Chalcomedeia schemes maiden modest
& clad white

while his love insists & claws
& guardian asps rise from her breast

they cradle her in coils
they multiply poisons &
their hissing shakes the sea

Calamitous mouths & serpent tails tighten around Morrheus' throat
Within city walls, within war

Deriades' army
slays Bacchantes
on slick red streets

Winged Hermes

Protector of heralds
Cloaked as Bromius

divine summoner
he guides the girl soldiers through alleys

At the wall,

Hermes charms leaves India's warriors in darkness

the women run free
through city gates
Under Hermes' sun

Deriades, sleepless in the deceitful night

the girls are also lost wandering the cloistered city easy prey

shadow victory then
the false dusk breaks

Maenalids have fled outside the walls

Deriades curses the sleeping Zeus,
the Pantheon, the lost Dionysus
& gathers his army to hunt

Zeus, Waking:

Hera, can you ever be sated?

My son, Dionysus is insane

his abandoned warrior nymphs
flee outside the city walls

India's king & army amok
They revel in slaughter

As you, Hera, revel in jealousy

Dionysus is half mad as a   circle center
half dead   & dying women surround him

Haven't you been cruel enough?
His mother is long dead

Remember   I tied
stones to your body
& dangled you
in the clouds
while your children
stood helpless below?

Should I now tie Ares to a breaking wheel
until Dionysus slays each son of India?

Instead make my son whole & sane
let his rich wine frenzy prevail

Heal Dionysus & welcome him home
as your child of your sweet breast
as a god among us on the mountain

& I will spread your milky stardust
across the night sky

Hera's shame & jealousy collide

she anoints Dionysus
her body's ambrosia
erases the madness

Hera suckles him beautiful again
mothers him into a god

fleeing away to Olympus
Hera wonders if any child
was perfect as Dionysus whole

Shining Dionysus cloaked in Zeus' favor

his votaries gathered

As my father slew the Titans
with a vineyard noose I will conquer
Deriades & his Indian kingdom

He arms them with ivy

I am no longer mad, and lost, and blind
But Deriades is still alive
and Ur-warrior Opheltes unburied

We shall take vengeance for our fallen sisters

They will swallow silt and blood
while we float my wine-running river

He arms them with thyrsus

For how can I
tell Arestor of his son's
forsaken death?

Or Agelaus with
Antheus unavenged?

How can I face Minos
while his son suffers and bleeds?

Come with your maiden ecstasy to the battle, again.

Book 36

Rebekah Curry

In the thirty-sixth, when Bacchus' delirium ends,
He shifts shape and attacks; Deriades defends.

So he stirred up their hearts. And Deriades armed his soldiers.
The gods were taking sides, some for Deriades
and some for Lyaeus, and they drew up battle ranks,
and Zeus, who reigns on high, held the balances of war
as he always must. It was blue-haired Poseidon
versus Helios, Ares versus bright-eyed Athena,
Hephaestus versus Hydaspes the river god,
mountain-dwelling Artemis versus Hera,
and Hermes the staff-bearer versus Leto.

Ares made his move. He hurled a spear at Athena,
but it missed the mark, and only struck the aegis.
The point stuck in the coils of snaky hair that wreathe
the Gorgoneion on her breast. Then Athena
threw her own spear, the very one that she was holding
when she sprang out from Zeus' head already dressed
for battle. Her trusted weapon hit its target,
and Ares sank down on his knees in pain.
But he was unhurt, and Athena helped him up
and sent her brother back to his mother Hera.

Meanwhile, Artemis made ready and aimed her bow
at Hera, who seized on one of Zeus' clouds
and wrapped it around her shoulders to use as a shield.
Artemis filled the cloud full of arrows like cranes
wheeling in the sky, but still it held fast.
Then Hera took up a mass of hail and flung it
at Artemis, and broke her curved bow, and struck her
on the breast. Artemis dropped her quiver,
and Hera mocked her:
"Go shoot at wild beasts instead!
What do you care about war? Let Athena
be the fighter—go look to your hunting and tend
to your stags! What is this son of Zeus to you?
Be a midwife and work together with Eros
and Paphian Aphrodite—go to the chambers
of the woman in labor and be with her like a lion.
And, for that matter, stop guarding your chastity—
by now, you must have heard how Zeus puts on your shape
to seduce unwedded virgins. The mountains
and woods of Arcadia still mourn for Callisto,
whom Zeus brought to bed by usurping your form.
Now leave off fighting with those who are stronger than you!
If you like, fight Cytherea—you, the goddess
who brings birth to completion, against the one
who brings marriages to pass."
So Hera left her
stricken with fear. But Phoebus came and gathered her
into his arms. He took her from the battlefield
to set her down in a quiet grove, then returned
to the fray.
Now Phoebus faced off with Poseidon.
He wielded his bow against the sea god's trident,
and, in either hand, ambidextrous, brandished
torches against the swelling waters.
Thunder crashed in the heavens, his home,
and in answer the sea roared in his ears
like a war-trumpet. Triton rose up from the waves,

half man above, half green-scaled fish below,
and blew a booming blast on a conch shell.
The nereids shouted a war-cry, and Nereus
emerged from the depths and bellowed.
Underworld Zeus heard
their tumult and feared that the Earthshaker's pounding waves
might shift the whole world out of place and uncover
the realm of the dead, a sight forbidden
to those above, and pour down his waters
to flood the rotting gates of Tartarus.

But Hermes came then to be a peacemaker:
"Both of you, brother and son of Zeus, lay down
your arms! Stop fighting among yourselves, or the Titans
will laugh to see it! Let there not be war in heaven
as there was when Cronus was thrown down from Olympus.
Let Zeus not rage for the sake of late-born Bacchus
as he did for Zagreus, and assault the whole world
once more with fire and rain; do not let his showers
drench Selene's chariot and quench Phaëthon's flame!
You who are younger should yield to the elder,
who has power over the sea. Extend this grace
to your father's brother; Poseidon honors your island,
Delos in the midst of its waters. And you,
Earthshaker, should not stir up strife, as when
you and Hera contested over Argos.
Why are you fighting with Apollo as well
as Athena, and why seek out another conflict?
And you, horned Hydaspes, father of Deriades,
beware Hephaestus' fire after Bacchus' torch,
lest it consume you."
The gods listened to him
and ceased their warfare. And Deriades burned
with fury when he saw Bacchus and the Bacchants
alive and unharmed. He rallied his commanders
and roared out barbaric threats to his soldiers:

"Either I will drag Dionysus away
by the hair, or he will destroy our nation!
Attack the satyrs, burn Bacchus' vines and all his trappings!
Carry off the Maenalids as slaves, burn the thyrsi!
Reap a crop of heads with your blades, from the sSileni
and the satyrs, and place their skulls around our houses
for decoration! I will not let Phaëthon turn to sunset
before I lead the satyrs and Bacchus off in chains!
Burn the women's vine-wreathed locks to ashes!
Be fierce! Sing of Deriades' glorious victory,
so that, even when generations have passed,
other nations will live in fear of the Indians."

He spurred on the elephant drivers and set
the commanders to lead the foot soldiers on
in tight formation. With equal zeal for battle,
Bacchus drove his host of beasts into combat.
There were serpents spitting jets of poison from their fangs,
strangling the Indians in their coils. The Bacchants,
war-maddened, imitated Phidaleia,
who showed what a woman can be in battle,
hurling snakes as missiles at her foes.

One caught Deriades with a spike of poison
like a spear and spattered his breastplate
with the drops. Nearby lay the corpse of a man
that venom had killed. Then a panther leapt on
an elephant to bring it down, and many more
fell when they heard the lions' fearsome roar.
One trembled at the bellow of a bull and the sight
of his horn stabbing at the air; another fled
from the dreadful maw of a bear. The hounds
of unconquerable Pan barked in chorus
with the roaring beasts and terrified the Indians.

Both sides fought fiercely. The thirsty earth
was soaked with blood, and the black river Lethe

was choked with scattered bodies, and Hades threw
the gates of the underworld wide to admit
the dead crowded there. As they descended,
never more to see the light, the riverbanks
echoed with the rumblings of Tartarus.

So many men fell in the battle-stirring clamor.
One, struck in the throat, slipped down from his horse;
one was skewered through the chest; one fell
from a chariot, his belly ripped open.
Another, with an arrow fixed in his chest,
rolled over and died; one was struck in the girth,
one through the shoulder, and one, who left
his stricken horse and tried to flee on foot,
was pierced through the spine by a lance. Another,
no more than a boy, his face smooth and beardless,
mourned for his friend, who was the same age.
Another, with an arrow in his liver,
fell off his elephant; his head sank down
on the ground, and in despair he clawed at
the blood-drenched earth.
One man had filled the hollow
of his shield with dust and lay in wait
as a horseman approached, then leaped out and choked
the horse with sand. It reared and tossed its head
to shake the dust from its mane and spat out
the jeweled bit. It foamed at the mouth
and rose up on its hind legs trembling, pawing
the dust, then flung its rider to the ground.
The other man rushed on him and slashed his throat
as he lay there stunned.
Another horse heard the crack
of some nearby driver's whip and bolted
in fright, trampling its rider, who lay there
wounded and dying, gasping in the dust.

Elsewhere, Colletes, a man to be reckoned with,
nine cubits tall, rampaged through Bacchus' hosts.
He intended to win a troop of Bassarids
to drag into his bed after the battle,
paying no bride-price for them. But he fought
for a lost cause, like Otus, who trespassed
on the forbidden ground of heaven
in his lust for Artemis; like Ephialtes,
who wanted to make Athena his bride,
when he mounted an attack on Olympus.
That was Colletes, heaven-high; in his veins
ran the blood of his ancestor, the giant who founded
the Indian race. He was so great
that, like those sons of Iphimedeia,
he could have imprisoned Ares. And yet,
impressive as he was, he fell down dead
when Charopeia, a leader of the Bacchic dance,
struck him with a sharp stone.
One who looked on
at this scene spoke out in a trembling voice,
half in wonder, half in anger:
"Ares, Ares!
Put aside your bow and your shield and spear!
Ares, you are conquered! Leave the Caucasus,
for Dionysus brings his own brand of Amazons
to dispatch the men. They have no weapons,
and yet they defeat armed soldiers. I have seen
a sight almost too strange for believing:
these Amazons carry no shields, no spears,
but the well-armored women of the Caucasus
do no such feats as they do. The Bacchants
have no need for cold steel—they cast bunches of leaves
as darts! I pity mad Deriades!
These women rip coats of mail apart
with their fingernails!"
So he spoke, marveling
at how the girl had taken the huge man down

with that rough missile.
Deriades, untouched
by any weapon, ran at the Bacchants
in their frenzy and went in pursuit of Charopeia,
but she escaped him and took her stand with Dionysus,
boldly wielding her flowering thyrsus.
Then, with his spear, Deriades killed
Orithallus, one of the Curetian tribe
who dwell in the land of the Abantes.
To avenge his death, their chief Melisseus
struck down Cyllarus, king of the Carminians,
and cut his throat with his sword, and also
Logasides, who, for his prowess in war,
was of more value to Deriades than any
of the Indian spearmen; second only
to Morrheus, he was the king's favorite.
He had often eaten at his table and had lived
as a son alongside his daughters,
for he surpassed all his peers, both with his spear
and with his brains. Then one commander
fought against another: quick-footed Halimedes
versus Peucetius, Maron versus Phlogius,
Leneus versus Thureus.
Cronion shifted
the balance of the battle to his son.
Dionysus attacked Deriades, bringing
thyrsus against spear. As the king tried to stab him,
he shapeshifted into a multitude of forms.
Sometimes he was a wildfire with tongues of flame
shooting out, sometimes water with rolling waves.
Or he became a lion and, lifting his head,
let out a terrible roar, like his father's
loud, crashing thunder. Then he became a tree
stretching toward the sky, a pine or a plane tree;
his locks were leaves, his torso the trunk,
his arms were branches, his clothing bark,
and his feet were rooted in the earth, and he whispered

in Deriades' ear. Then he put on a dappled
coat and, as a panther, leapt in the air
and fell upon an elephant's neck.
It lunged sideways, smashed the chariot, and threw
the driver down. In spite of this, the warrior
fought with Lyaeus and wounded the panther
with a spear thrust. But the god changed again
and rose as a moving fire, and shot
a blazing bolt at Deriades' breast.
His coat of mail was blackened, his crest was withered
by the flame, and his helmet scorched him.
Then Dionysus became a lion,
then a wild boar, opening his jaws wide to show
his gaping throat, rearing up on his hind legs
and tearing at Deriades with his hooves.

Proud Deriades went on fighting these mirages
and tried to seize the intangible shapes.
At last he thrust his spear in the lion's face
and cried out, threatening many-formed Dionysus:

"Dionysus, why hide and resort to tricks
instead of fighting? Are you afraid of Deriades?
I have no fear of Dionysus' panther—
I will shoot his bear, chop down his tree,
slash his false lion across the flank!
I will muster my brahmins against you! They walk
unarmed and naked, but their incantations
have often caught Selene in their spell
and brought her down from heaven, and halted Phaëthon
as he hurried on his course."
So he spoke,
still unbelieving, hoping to contrive
some magic to defeat Dionysus.

Deriades mounted his chariot, but the god,
in answer to his impious folly,

made a vine spring up to attack him. The plant
sent tendrils around the silver wheels
and twined itself around him, dangling clusters
of new grapes before his face and enveloping him.
Deriades was drunk on the sweet-smelling fruit
as the vine grew fetters around his feet
and rooted the elephants' legs to the ground,
so that the driver lashed them in vain.
The glorious prince of the Indians,
who had faced countless blades and come out on top,
was defeated by a plant! Deriades struggled,
choked by the tendrils that entangled him.
No matter how hard he tried, he could not move,
so he let out a stifled cry and with gestures
and tears sent up a prayer of supplication,
holding out a hand that spoke in silence,
and his tears were a voice.
Then Dionysus
broke his green chains and undid the vines that wreathed
the elephants' necks. But Deriades, freed
from the bonds that grew around him, resumed his threats
and boasts. Once more he defied the gods;
the only question in his mind was whether
Bacchus should be killed or enslaved instead.

But darkness fell upon both the armies
and put an end to that day's fighting. When the night
was past and all had awoken, the dawn
armed them again.
Battle had not yet ended
for Dionysus; first many cycles of years
must pass while the war-trumpet sounded in vain.
But after the turn of strife-stirring years,
the Bacchic battle raged all the more.

Meanwhile, the Rhadamenes of Dicte remembered
Dionysus' command to them; they worked together

to build warships for Lyaeus. One was turning pegs,
one worked on the keel, one was fitting planks
over the ribs and fastening them.
Others raised the mast that would carry
the billowing sail and rounded the yard-arm at the top.
So they made ships for Bacchus, with the skill
that only they had. Amid fears of war,
he remembered Rhea's prophecy: the end
of the war would be in sight when Bacchants fought
the Indians at sea. Lycus, whom the god
had appointed as commander of his navy,
drove his sea-chariot over the waves to Dicte.

When time circled around into the sixth year,
Deriades the king summoned the nation
of India to an assembly; his herald
called all the peoples in their own languages.
Many tribes gathered, and Morrheus addressed them:

"My friends, you all know how I had my work
cut out for me, until the Cilicians and Assyrians
submitted to Deriades' yoke. You know
what I have done against Dionysus
and the satyrs, and how I hand-delivered
a horde of Bassarids to Deriades in chains
as prizes of war. The city streets ran red
with their blood when they were slaughtered, while others
were hanged, and others were buried in a pit.
But again I have better ideas for the people.
I hear that those woodcutters the Rhadamenes
have built ships for war-fleeing Dionysus.
I have no fear of their sea-fighting trees!
When have women throwing leaves killed men on shipboard
equipped with shields? When will mad high-horned
hill-haunting Pan tear our ships apart?
Silenus cannot travel over the waves
and sink a warship, leaping in a bloody dance,

striking up a death-bringing ode—on the sea
he can never gore a man with his horns.
No, one blow will bring him down, and he will lie unburied
in the waters! The Bacchants, struck by spears,
will sink into the deep, stained with their own blood.
And I will smash Dionysus' ships by putting
a twenty-cubit sea-fighting spear straight through them!
Fight, friends, and know victory is ours! Let no one
retreat when he sees Bacchus' ships arrayed
against us, for we Indians are better fighters
on sea than on land. I will not capture many satyrs—
instead of two hundred warriors, I will drag
girl-crazy Dionysus away by the hair,
to be Deriades' attendant."
So speaking,
Morrheus, full of schemes, persuaded
Deriades. The people all cheered
with one voice, like the crash of waves. The king dismissed
the assembly, and sent his herald on
to declare war by sea against Bromius.

But both sides agreed to hold off from fighting
for three cycles of the moon, until they could
perform burial rites for the many fallen.
There was a short-lived peace, never far from war,
a stillness in labor to give birth to battle.

Book 37

Jonathan Mayhew

As we turn the page to Book 37,
there are games around the funeral pyre,
men competing for prizes.

Now the Indians, coming to their senses,
devote themselves to comradery
and release to the winds the war against Bacchus.
With dry eyes they bury their dead, who are like
prisoners escaping from the earthly bonds
of human life
in which the soul, in a circular chain,
has been sent back to where it came from:
the beginning of the cycle.
The army of Bacchus rests.

And Dionysus, seeing the calm of the truce
at the heart of war,
in the early morning
sends out mules and muleteers
for dry wood from the mountain
to burn the lifeless corpse of Opheltes.
(Their guide through the pine groves is Faunus,
seasoned in the secrets of the forest,
at home in the wild haunts of his mother, Circe.)

And row by row trees are felled
by the iron of axes:
how many elms succumb to the metal,
how many swaying oak canopies
come crashing, pines and firs with dead needles,
a landscape of stone:
tree nymphs abandon their homes
moving in with naiads in
alien streams.

Men coming up and down cross on
winding mountain paths,
a tangle of feet in every direction:
up, down, across—with logs
in rope-bound bundles hung from
mules' backs.
In single file they hurry loudly down the trails,
the logs digging ruts
in the sandy soil.
Pan and his satyrs work tirelessly, chopping
with blades, pulling down limbs,
lifting trunks, dancing over rocks.
The woodcutters lay the fuel out
on the ground, where Euios has marked
the pyre of Opheltes.
Numerous is the crowd, from multiple cities.
Sobbing, they cut
garlands of their hair.
one by one,
for the funeral wreath,
covering his body.
Bacchus, dry-eyed, stoic,
cuts one hair from his mane,
his gift to the fallen Opheltes.
The Idaian comrades of Dionysus build a pyre
a thousand square feet,
the body of Opheltes in the middle.

Asterion of Dicte unsheathes his sword
and slits twelve Indian throats,
encircling Opheltes' corpse,
then lays down jars of oil and honey,
butchering sheep and oxen
for the pyre.
He lays out in a circle,
around the cadaver, the bodies
of the slaughtered cattle
with rows of newly killed horses,
taking out the fat
to lay around the body.
Now they need to light the fire, so Faunus,
son of Circe the rock-dweller,
at home in the wilderness,
schooled by his mother,
native of the Tyrensian lands,
brings flintstone known to mountain men;
from a place where lightning had struck
he finds remnants of the bolts
to light a fire for the dead.
He smears sulfur on the two flintstones
and strikes them against each other,
male against female,
drawing newborn sparks out of the rock
and lighting the pyre
of the mountain wood.
But the fire, once lit, fails to spread;
so the god, his eyes fixed
on Phaëthon, calls on Eurus
(the East Wind)
to fan the flames.
As Bromius calls,
the Morning Star, close by, hears his plea
and sends her brother to Lyaeus,
so that his powerful breath can make the wood burn.
And, leaving the rosy realm of his mother,

Aurora, the wind bellows the flames all night
tending the fire nourished by his breath.
And the wild winds, neighbors of Helios,
send the flames high into the air.
With grief-struck Lyaeus, Asterion of Dicte,
also of his clan, makes the dust drunk
with sweet wine spilled from a two handled cup
to honor the wind-borne soul of his comrade.

But when Aurora, announced by dawn's rosy chariot,
pierces the night
with her rose-colored flames
all arise and douse the flames
one by one
with cups of Bacchus' wine.
Now the fiery wind goes back
to the radiant house of Helios
on fast wings.
Asterion, collecting the bones,
envelopes them in layers of fat
in an urn of gold.
Then the whirling Corybants,
since Ida is their homeland,
trace the circle of the tomb.
They dig its foundation and
in a hole dug in the ground
inter the body,
a native of their own isle, the true lineage
of Crete. And they scatter on Opheltes
the final dust of a foreign land,
and they erect his monument
with tall stones, etching these lines
as token
of their newfound sorrow:

"Here lies the Cnossian Opheltes, son of Arestor,
too quickly fallen,

scourge of the Indians
and comrade of Bromius."

Now the god of the vine brings out the prizes
for the funeral games,
retaining the army there
in a vast assembly—
having marked out the course
for the chariot race.
On the ground is a stone the length of an arm,
in the shape of a half-moon, polished
on its two sides
as though, sculpting it with skillful hands,
an old craftsman had rounded its forms
to create a divine image.
Raising it in his arms, a monstrous Cyclops
places it on the ground to mark the turn
and another for the opposite end.
The prizes are varied: cauldrons, tripods,
shields, horses, silver, Indian metal,
cattle, Pactolian gold.
And the god lays out the prizes for the charioteers:
for first place is an Amazonian bow and quiver,
a half-moon shield,
an Indian warrior woman
he had snatched when he saw her bathing
on the banks of Thermedon.
For second place, he offers a mare
as fast the north wind
with long mane
and pregnant, her belly swollen
with the foal a stallion
had given her.
And for third place, a corselet, and fourth a shield:
this was a work of art from a Lemnian anvil
with gold patterns,

silver adornments,
For the fifth, two ingots
from the banks of Pactolus.

Now he stands up to exhort the charioteers:

"My friends, to whom Ares
taught the art of war
that destroys cities,
you to whom the art of chariot driving was given
by the God of the dark hair,
you are not soft men, but battle-hardened.
Our warriors have a taste for manly contests of all sorts:
one of Lydian birth, from Tmolus,
will match Pelops' racing crown.
A man from Pisa, cradle of horses,
a man from Elis with its magnificent chariots,
a countryman of Oenomaus,
he knows the reward
of wild Olympian olives:

but this is not the race of Oenomaus:
our drivers do not seek marriage
that causes the death of a stranger—
this is a race for honor, not love.
A man from Aonia, or one with the blood of Phocis,
he knows the Pythian contest honored by Apollo.
If he has as his birthplace Marathon,
rich in olives, the land of wisdom,
he knows the jar with the fragrant oil.
If he is from the fertile land of Achaea,
he has learnt of Pellene, where
shivering from cold
the men compete for the prize
of a woolen coat to keep their limbs warm
through winter.

If he has grown up Corinth,
he knows the Isthmian contest
of my dear Palaemon."
He speaks, and the drivers rush forward
to mount their chariots,
one after the other.
First Erechtheus harnesses his swift stallion Xanthê
and beside him the mare, Podargê:
both sired by Boreas
when he ravaged a Sithonian Harpy—and the North Wind gave them
to Erechtheus when he took
Orithyia as his bride.
Second, Actaeon
cracks his Ismenian whip.
And the third
is the son of the master
of the waves
and shaker of earth, Scelmis
of the swift horses, who used to
cut through the sea driving
the chariot of his father, Poseidon.
Fourth, Phaenus jumps up, coming up alone
through the sand, looking like his mother's father
with four horses, like those
of the chariot of the sun god.
The fifth, Achates, rides in
on his Sicilian chariot, always eager
for a race. In him flows the river
that waters the olive groves of Pisa: he lives in the land
of the nymph dear to Alpheus,
river of sorrows in love
who brings to Arethusa
as gift of love, his fragrant, unsalted waters.
The father of the presumptuous Actaeon
draws him aside from the crowd
giving tender advice to his impatient son:

“Son of Aristaeus,
son of a father of superior skill,
I know
you are strong enough, you have the flower
of youth with bravery. In you
flows the blood of my father Apollo. I know too
our Arcadian horses are the best
when the race is to be run.
But all is in vain! Neither the strength nor speed wins races
but the astuteness of the driver.
What you need is nuanced
technique, for driving a chariot
requires of a driver
wisdom and skill.
Hear from me, your father,
the countless subtleties of the equestrian art,
all that time has taught me
I’ll teach you now. Make haste
to honor me with your victory. A race
is as glorious as war:
you’ve been victorious
on the battlefield,
now do the same
on the racecourse
so I can call you a champion in games
as well as a warrior.
My son, may your acts be worthy
of your cousin Dionysus, worthy at once
of Phoebus and
strong-handed Cyrene.
May your deeds surpass those
of your father Aristaeus.
Show that you have the art of driving, proving that
your subtle wit can lead you
to victory.
An ignorant man, in the middle of the arena,
letting his chariot stray far from the others
goes from side to side;

in their uncertain course, the restive horses
no longer obey the constraints of the whip
nor the bit. The driver
missing the turn, loses
control, and the horses drag him
where they want.
But the driver who is a master of his *métier*,
if he is very smart, can triumph
even with inferior horses.
He keeps them going forward, their eyes
fixed on the chariot in front
and follows the course always near
to the post. He drives his chariot around the stone
without touching it. Look:
pull on the reins to steer
and make the horse on the left turn
in one movement, making it
clear the post, leaning
to the side to almost touch
the wheel to the post
with subtle measure.
But be careful of the stone:
take care not to touch it with your axle
ruining both chariot and team.
And when, in one direction
and then the other,
you drive your chariot
behave exactly like a helmsman,
your chariot on the course
without straying.
With his skillful directions
the intelligence of the driver
is the rudder of the chariot."

He speaks, then steps aside,
having taught to his son the art
of his family trade, chariot driving.

Inside their helmets, as was their custom,
each places an unseeing hand,
turning the head the other way for luck—
like one who blows on his hand
throwing the dice.
The drivers
draws lots for position. Horse-crazy Faunus
is first, of the lineage of Phaëthon,
then Achates;
next the brother of Damnamenes, then Actaeon.
Last—though the best driver—is
Erechtheus, whipper of horses.
Now the charioteers raise their leather whips,
each on his throne
lined up for the start.
The judge is the honorable Aeacus, his charge
to watch the drivers greedy for the crown
as they round the corners.
He is there as witness to the truth,
judging with infallible eyes
the horses' movements, resolving disputes.
The race begins at the starting line:
one jumps ahead, another
tries to catch up, another
jockeying for position; another in last place
trying to catch these other two.
As the race goes on
they switch positions, bumping against each other,
with hands shaking the reins,
the bridle bits coming out of the horses' mouths.
Another, staying in line with the other
bearing down on him, wages
an indecisive battle, an equal contest.
He leans to the side, strains forward, then
falls back with slack reins, and
driving his docile team with

with capable hand, he whips them softly, looking
out of the corner of his eye
at the driver pursuing him.
Time and again he looks back
apprehensive of the driver behind him.
Speeding ahead, the horses
would have flipped over
if the driver had not pulled up
to block the chariot from passing him:
a driver in front will move back
and forth erratically
so the other cannot pass him.
And Scelmis, son of the earthshaking god,
cracks Poseidon's whip
and drives his father's team, raised in the sea;
Pegasus, flying through the sky,
never so swiftly sliced through the air
with long wings,
as the feet of these ocean horses
run over the racetrack
on unfamiliar soil.
The spectators watch the race from a bluff
glimpsing from afar
the course of the galloping horses.
One paces nervously, one scolds a driver
with wagging finger,
another's heart beats in synch to the
horses' hooves. Another, a fervent fan
of horse racing, has so much passion
in his blood for the ponies
that he undergoes in his own spirit
a race identical to that
of his favorite chariot driver.
Another, seeing his driver
is at the head of course, claps his hands
and cries out

deliriously,
cheering, trembling,
yelling at him.
The sturdy cars, faster than swift winds,
now fly through the air,
now come back to earth
hardly touching the dust.
And in the rapid turning of their wheels,
the chariots racing forward in a straight line
do nothing but scratch the sand
in their vagabond course.
The fight is on:
the kicked-up dust rises chest-high, the horses' manes
shake in the wind,
the agitated drivers
yell all at once,
drowning out the sounds
of their own whips.

As they start back, Scelmis forces the issue;
He's in first place: the driver
of the chariot of the sea. After him
Erectheus whips his team, his chariot
almost climbing on top
of the sea god's car,
for the eager horse of Erechtheus
is in the air,
panting and snorting
breathing down the neck of Scelmis.
Scelmis turns and
almost grabs Erechtheus' horse by the mane:
the foaming steed would have tossed his head
and shaken off the bit;
but Erechtheus
pulls up short
and swerves to the other side
with a strong jerk of the reins.

Now he follows close again,
having courted disaster—
almost losing control of his team.
And Scelmis, on his chariot, seeing his rival
bear down on him, utters
these menacing words:

"Basta! Against the horses of the sea,
nobody can compete. Long ago
Pelops, in my father's chariot,
beat the undefeated horses of Oenamaus.
For equine inspiration I call on
the Great Horseman of the sea.
My friend, whipper of horses,
pray only to wise Athena.
I don't care for olives. I'll win a different garland:
a crown of grapevines."
Erectheus was rash,
and Scelmis' boast made him madder.

His crafty mind began plotting
while his hands drove the car,
his heart directing a please to Athena:
"Lady of Cecropia, mistress of horses,
motherless Pallas:
just as you won a contest against Poseidon
so let Erechtheus
an Athenian citizen with a horse from Marathon,
beat Poseidon's son!"

With this plea he beats the flanks of his team
and pulls up beside him.
With left hand he grabs the mouth
of his rival's horse and
yanks out the bit. With the right he whips
his own team.

In this way he switches places with Scelmis,
now in second. He looks back laughing at the son of Poseidon,
mocking with clever banter.
the words streaming over his back:

"Scelmis, you have lost.
Erechtheus has whipped you
with his swift old mare. She beat your horse,
son of the West Wind, young and vigorous,
who can swim the seven seas without getting wet.
If you are so boastful
of Pelops' skill, remember
it was Myrtilis who cheated then,
making a wax simulacrum
of the axle, to fool his master.
If you are proud of your father,
shaker of the earth and god of the Horse
as you name him, riding
the oceanic chariot,
lord of sea and wielder
of the trident, remember that Athena,
a goddess, beat him in a race."

As he speaks, the Athenian
runs past him. Next comes Faunus
beating his four horses.
Fourth was Actaeon,
an astute driver, who hasn't forgotten
his father's lessons.
In last place is Achates.
Now bold Actaeon devises a clever strategy:
on Faunus' tail
with sharp crack of the whip,
he turns his horses straight-head
just passing his rival
then leaning his knee into the rail
he scrapes the other chariot
with his wheel:

the other car tumbles over
with its driver; three horses
lay on the ground
lying on side, belly, and neck.
One stays up, shaking his mane,
holding up another horse's leg
he lifts up the whole chariot
by the yoke.
They were in a pile in the dirt.
The driver tumbles in the mud
by the wheel, his head and chin
soiled, his arm stretched out
and his elbow torn open.
He jumps up quickly
standing before his wreck,
pulling up the second horse
and whipping him with angry lash.
Haughty Actaeon sees Faunus' plight
and jeers at him:

"That's enough: it's useless
to whip your sad beasts.
I'll come in first, and tell
Dionysus to let all the others pass you.
He'll drag your car past the line.
Have pity on your team: it hurts me
to see their backs torn up
by your cruel whip."

Faunus is irate at the words, at the driver
races past him with active whip.
He pulls at the horses' tails
and with great efforts makes them
rise from the mud.
One, who had escaped the harness
he refastened to the bridle. He arranges
the horses' feet on both sides
and gets back in the driver's seat,

resuming the race with determination,
whipping the team with fearsome blows.
Harder than ever Faunus drives
urging on his valiant steeds,
quicker than ever
he sets sights on the driver before him.
He catches the next chariot, for Earthshaker,
the god of horses,
invests the team with vigor
to honor his brave son. Seeing a narrow pass
he quickly hatches a tricky plot
to catch up with Achates
with canny driving.
We see a deep gorge
that a wanton storm
of rainwater had carved from the side
of the course—the winter
ravages of Zeus. There,
the floodwaters cut away
a gash in the earth,
forming a narrow ridge.
Achates, when he sees this,
has to brake, against his will,
to avoid a collision.
As Faunus drives up behind him
he yells out with quivering voice:

"Your clothes are filthy,
stupid Faunus; you haven't cleaned
your harness or your muddy horses.
What's the point of driving now?
I'm afraid you'll fall again! Watch bold Actaeon,
he'll catch you and
whip you into the mud again.
Your face is still torn up. Why are you still raging,
disgracing your father Poseidon
and Helios as well?

Heed the mockery of the satyrs,
Of the sileni and Dionysus' retinue.
They will laugh at your wreck of a chariot.
Where are your medicinal plants now?
Circe's potions? It's all deserted you
once you began this race."

This is the jeering speech of Achates,
as recorded by Nemesis.
Now Faunus comes beside him;
car hits car; his axle breaks the other's
turning wheel, it breaks off
and falls twisted in the dirt—
just as with the chariot of Oenamaus,
when the fake wax axle melted
in the sun's rays
and ended that race.
Achates stays on the narrow ridge,
while Faunus,
leaning over, overtakes him
with eager whip
ignoring the speech.
He beats the necks of horses
with renewed vigor,
now behind Actaeon
by the length of the throw of a quoit
launched by a strong youth.
The assemblage
are frenzied,
bickering and placing bets
on the uncertain outcome.
They place money on the storm-footed horses:
tripod, cauldron, sword and shield.
Countryman fight with countryman,
friend with friend,
old with old, young with young,
man against man.

Everyone takes sides,
yelling confusedly: one lauds Achates,
another condemns Faunus
for taking a spill; a third claims
that Erechtheus is second
behind Telchis, driver from the ocean.
Another claims to see
the astute Athenian.
They are still arguing when Erechtheus
wins the race by nose, beating
his horses on left
and right, swinging his shoulders.
Sweat poured down in streams
on the horses' hairy necks and flanks,
their driver covered with dust;
the chariot follows close on the horses'
hooves in rising
swirls of dust,
and the placid surface of the ground
was roiled up
by the spinning wheels.
After this raucous race, he comes up among
the spectators, wiping with his sleeve
the sweat pouring from his forehead.
He quickly jumps out, resting his fierce whip
on the yoke, and his groom Amphidamas
unties the team.
Then with happy hand he lifts the first prize,
bow, quiver, and helmeted woman,
shaking the flat half shield.
Scelmis comes in second, in his sea-chariot—
for his car is Poseidon's—as
far behind the other
as the wheel is behind the running horse,
the hairy tail
just grazing it.

He takes the second prize,
the pregnant mare, and gives her
to Damnamenes.
In third place is Actaeon: he lifts his prize,
the corselet of brilliant gold,
superb handiwork of Olympus.
Next is Faunus. He stops his chariot,
lifting the round shield of silver,
still with dust on his face and body.
When Achates comes up despondent
in the slowest car, a Sicilian groom
gave him two gold ingots:
a consolation prize from his kind friend, Dionysus.

Now the god announces the boxing match,
a harsh contest. The winner gets a bull
from Indian stables.
Second prize,
for the loser,
a shield with layers of hide.
Now, standing up, he exhorts the boxers
two men
to step forward to box.
When Bromius finishes, battle-worn Melisseus
stands up, a skilled and practice pugilist.
Grabbing the bull by its horns
he yells to the crowd these boastful words:
"Come forward anyone who wants
this painted shield.
For I won't let anyone else have the fat bull
as long as I can keep my hands up."
Silence gripped the crowd.

Eurymedon alone rose to face the challenge,
bestowed with fighting skill by Hermes.
A son of Hephaestus, he had grown up

at the god's furnace beating
strips of metal on the anvil.
His brother Alcon
dresses him excitedly, placing his body belt there
and fitting the harness to his loins,
coiling strips of dry leather
around his brother's hands.
Now the champion steps into the ring
holding his left hand up for defense,
and the leather straps on his right
serve as jabbing spear.
Constantly he keeps
his guard up before the lethal attack
of his enemy, so as not to be punched
on brow or face, drawing blood
or smashing temple
with wayward blow, tearing into
the brain, or with hook
tearing eyes out of blinded face, or break
his jaw, shattering
a row of his teeth.
But now, rushed by Eurymedon, Melisseus
lands a punch to the chest; he counterpunches
with a blow to the head
but misses, fanning the air.
Trembling in eagerness, he steps around
and land a right below the nipple.
Now they clinch, jockeying for position,
in short steps, hands blocking hands.
The punches come quick,
the leather straps on their fingers
makes fearsome sounds. Cheeks
are ripped open,
blood on the straps, jaws cracking
under the battering, cheeks swollen
in puffy faces,

sunken eyes.
    Eurymedon is stunned by Melisseus
        and his bobbing and weaving.
He has to face the harsh sun
    shining in his eyes and blinding him.
        Melliseus rushes in,
dancing with quick feints and dodges,
    landing a punch below the ear.
        Eurymedon falls
on his back and rolls in the dust, helpless,
    reeling like a drunk. He rolls his head
        to the side
and spits out foamy blood.
    His brother Alcon picks him up
        and carries him out of the ring,
knocked out by the blow,
    and quickly lifts up
        the great Indian shield.

Next Dionysus calls for two wrestlers to step forward,
    announcing the prizes for the contest:
        a sacrificial tripod of twenty pounds
for the victor; a cauldron decorated with flowers
    for the losing man.
        He rises and with commanding voice
says "Come here, comrades, for fine sport."
    At the words of the prize-loving god
        Aristaeus arises first, then Aeacus,
well versed in the art of burly wrestling.
    The fighters are naked except for their loincloths.
        They grab each other's wrists,
pulling this way and that
    over the scattered dust, grabbing
        arms with tight fingers.
It is an even contest, man pulling man
    with balanced moves, pushing and shoving.
        They embrace

with both arms,
bending their necks,
pressing their foreheads,
bearing down. Sweat runs
from their brows as testament
to the battle. Both backs are bent
by the pressure, the force
of two pairs of interlaced hands.
Both wrestlers are bruised,
with purple welts of blood, marking both
bodies. Thus they demonstrate
all the ruses of the wrestler's craft.
Now Aristaeus encircles his opponent and throws
him to the grounds. But Aeacus,
an cxpert grappler
does not forget his moves:
with sudden leg sweep
he catches the left knee
of Aristaeus, rolling
him over, defenseless on his back
on the ground
like a fallen cliff. The spectators are astonished,
seeing the son of Phoebus, so magnificent,
so renowned, so haughty,
fallen to the floor. Now Aeacus easily lifts
the giant son of Cyrene above the ground
an exemplar of courage
for his sons, Peleus the tireless and mighty Telamon.
He holds him in his arms,
not bending in either direction,
carrying him around the middle.
They resembled two cross beams
a carpenter might build
to protect a building from stormy winds.

Aeacus throws him down at full length
and gets his back, thrusting both legs
under his stomach,

interlocking knees and elbows.
He reaches over and chokes him
with two hands on his throat
like a necklace, with interlaced fingers,
like a shackle for his neck.
Sweat pours and makes mud
of the dust,
but he wipes away the drops
so his opponent cannot escape,
using his own sweat to slip away.
As he lies dying in this tight hold, the heralds
rush forward, the men chosen
as the referees,
to stop the match before the victor
choked him to death.
For there was no law
as later was devised, allowing a man
to tap on the body of the one
strangling him, to put a nonlethal end to the match.
Now the Myrmidons pick up the tripod,
servants of the winning king;
And Actaeon grabs the cauldron,
the second prize,
and carries it off
with rueful hand.

Now Bacchus announces the footrace:
for the fastest runner, a silver mixing bowl
and a captive woman.
Second prize is a Thessalian horse
with dappled neck. Third,
a sword with silver strap.
He arises and announces the contest
calling for the swift-footed runners.
"These will be the prizes for the sprinters."
At these words Ocythoös of Dicte steps forward,
shaking out his agile knees.
Next speedy Erechtheus runs up, a favorite of

Pallas Athena, goddess of victory;
then Priasus
of the fertile Island of Cybele.
Off they go, Ocythoös taking the early lead
light as the wind running straight
before the others.
Erectheus is in second place, breathing down
the leader's neck, warming his nape.
As near as the spindle
to the breast of the girl who loves
to spin, when she holds it
with capable hand
at just the right distance,
such is the distance between them,
as the steps in the footprints
before the dust settles.
It's a dead heat, but Octhyoös senses his rival
at his back and picks up the pace
increasing his lead. Then Erechtheus wanting to win
lifts up a cry to Boreas:
"Help your own Erechtheus
and your tender bride, if you still love her. Lend me your
velocity for an hour
so I can overtake the speedy Ocythoös running up ahead."

Boreas hears this supplication, giving him
the speed of a hurricane. All three
run like the wind,
but the contest is not an equal one:
Erechtheus is beating Ocythoös,
and Ocythoös leads Priasus,
proud denizen of Phyrgia,
by the same length. On they run.
But close to the finish line.
Ocythoös slips in the mud,
in the huge heap of dung from the cattle
slaughtered by Dionysus with Mygdonian dagger.

He steps back, springs forward and
almost catches his nearest rival;
with a little more time
he would have surpassed the Athenian
or at least tie him for second.
Agile-footed Erechtheus lifts up the Sidonian bowl,
with well-crafted design; Ocythoös wins
the horse of Thessaly; Priasus modestly
takes the third prize,
the silver-strapped saber.
The satyrs jeer at the Corybant
covered in filth
spitting the dung
he had caught in his throat.

Now Dionysus brings out a crude lump of metal
and lays it on the ground,
calling for the shot-putters.
First prize is two spears and a helmet
with a crest of horsehair.
Second,
Melisseus takes up the weight, swings it around
and threw:
the sileni jeer at his feeble attempt.
Next, Eurymedon picks up the weight
and makes his attempt; highborn Acmon now
takes it, swings it around
with strong wrist, and casts it
through the air, swift as the wind.
beating Eurymedon's mark.
Halimedes, standing upright, sends the weight
whistling through the storm winds
launched by a strong hand like an arrow
from bow; flying through volatile air
it descends to the earth and keeps
rolling, retaining momentum

from the skillful hand,
seeming to move of its own accord
until it surpasses the other marks.
The assembly crowd around and cheer, awed
by the free movement of the shotput
with forceful momentum.
Halimedes haughtily picks up the double prize
going off with plumed helmet, shaking
the two spears in two hands.
Acmon steps forward for the gold-plated belt; Eurymedon,
in third place, takes
the two-handled bowl.
Melisseus, hanging his head,
Carries off
the mottled skin.

Now Dionysus brings out the prizes
for the best archers, a sturdy mule,
seven years old,
he displays before the crowd
and an ornate goblet
for the second-best shot.
Euryalus embeds a ship's mast
in the sand, tying a pigeon
to the top with twine.
The god calls for archers
among those gathered,
to bring down the flying target.

"The one who pierces the pigeon's skin
will get the sturdy mule as testament to his victory.
The one who draws his bow and misses,
letting the bird fly off unharmed, hitting only the string,
will be the worse archer, deserving of the worse prize.
Instead of the mule he'll get the goblet,
to drink a libation to Winged Apollo and the God of Wine."
So says the rich Lyaeus, and Hymenaeus
whose arrows travel far steps up.

First, though, Asterion aims at the mast with Cnossian bow,
with his first shot hitting the string.
The bird flies up
as the string falls. Hymenaeus the archer
follows the bird's flight
into the clouds; with bow taut
he releases a quick shot
at the soaring target. Apollo holds the shot
steady, in sympathy with his brother,
Bacchus. The shaft pierces
the flying pigeon's breast,
and it plunges to earth
flapping its wings in agony
around the dust at the feet
of dancing Dionysus.
Now the god
jumps up to congratulate the winner.
The whole crowd is amazed at Hymenaeus'
cloud-high shot. The laughing god brings out
the mule for the archer, while Asterion's friends
lift up the goblet for him.

Now Bacchus makes a call for a friendly contest
of javelin throwing—the prizes
a pair of greaves and a stone
from the Indian Sea. Standing up, he calls
for two warriors to engage in harmless sport,
tossing the metal in fictive war.

"Only gentle Ares and serene Enyo
will preside over the contest," says Bromius.
And Asterion steps forward shaking
his iron weapons, and Aeacus too
with bronze spear and fancy shield,
like a lion in the jungle ready to kill

a bull or savage boar.
Both spearmen strut out, covered in steel
mesh. Asterion throws an angry javelin
with the strength of his father, Minos, wounding
his foe's right arm. Aeacus aims for the throat,
with spirit worthy of his father Zeus.
But Bacchus catches the spear in mid-flight,
so no harm is done.
Then he stops them both, calling with raucous voice:
"Drop your weapons! This is a friendly match, a
bloodless battle," he cries, and Aeacus proudly takes
the prize of victory, the gold-plated greaves.
Asterion accepts the second prize:
the Indian stone,
won in hard combat with the enemy.

Book 38

Denise Low

I

A (Fortuitous) Omen

Dionysus searches the heights, sights an eagle.
It clutches an asp. The raptor soars to the river.
The snake frees itself, falls into the Hydaspes.

On the banks all Greeks wait in silence as even
the water trembles. Dionysus holds his breath.
Idmon the seer smiles. He recalls omens—

Urania's Zodiac and comets, solar eclipses,
thunderclaps, strikes of flaming meteors.
Idmon, master of occult teachings, speaks:

"No cause to fear, Greek soldiers. The Eagle
drowned the serpent. Punjab will fall."
In vision he sees a blood-choked river.

II

A (Shaman's) Prophecy

Idmon grasps his fennel staff. He nears
Erectheus the Athenian king, the querent,
a man who studies prophesies like eclipses,

spirals of comet tails, red moons—
omens of chaos. Now eerie gloaming
obscures the crowd as shadow douses sun.

Idmon the seer shakes his staff, speaks:
"I give voice to the mountain spirits.
Fear not the smoldering meteors that fall."

The king's breath quickens. Idmon trembles,
"Here is the interpretation. The Greek Eagle
killed the Horned Snake of India. It drowned.

"So the Hydaspes River will swallow Deriades,
prince of the Indian armies. He will die.
The river god Hydaspes will kill his own son."

The seer falls silent in the unnatural night.
The Athenian king holds the quivering prophet
until he calms. Lightning crackles in the distance.

III

(Hermes/Mercury's) (Re/) Interpretation

Now to Dionysus, alone among barren rocks,
comes his brother the glistening traveler Hermes
silvery from sky's cirrus frost. "Zeus sends me,"

he says. "Let me interpret your father's augury."
As he speaks Dionysus recalls the eclipse—
shining day blotted the color of blackest caverns.

Hermes holds the shaken man's shoulders a moment,
says, "You will win the Indian War." And again,
"You will win. You are the rising sun who returns.

Not the tragic child Phaëthon, who flogged horses
across the heavens so fast the firmament capsized
and the boy, like your omen's snake, fell into water."

Dionysus replies, "Say more about Phaëthon
whose sisters still line the riverbanks and weep,
turned into bowed-down willows with teardrop leaves."

IV

Hermes Tells the Story (Within a Story) of Phaëthon

"Phaëthon's story explains the omen," says Hermes,
"and I will continue the tale, the romance, for you,
how Sun's fires flamed for the beautiful Clymenê,

daughter of Oceanus. This virgin swam mornings
in ruddy-tinted waves, nude and lovely.
When hot-rayed Sun saw her, he burned with lust.

Their love child was Phaëthon, a boy marked
by Sun's round face and curling yellow flares,
also loved by his grandfather Oceanus.

V

Phaëthon (the Boy) Tangles in Moira's Net

Too soon the baby's grim fate appeared
to Grandfather Oceanus as he tossed the child
high over swells, tumbling him in play.

An omen: Phaëthon plummeted into riptides,
rehearsing his final plunge and drowning—saved
now by Oceanus from being swept under.

Grasping, the grandsire protected Phaëthon
from gravity's law, although he grieved to see
foreshadowing of Phaëthon's prophesized death.

Phaëthon's mother watched the boy's splashes,
happy with his exuberance, not knowing
a knife too soon would pierce her heart in grief.

The willful boy explored his mother's household.
When still a child he traveled to Sicily
to visit vineyards and cattle of his sun god father.

There the boy made a horsewhip of willows,
crafted a garland star, and carved a toy chariot.
He fastened torches to his head in play.

When barely a man he pined for a man's power.
He handled his father's horses and the whip.
He beggéd his sun god father, cajoled, and wept.

VI

Helios (the Sun God) Restrains the (Flawed) Son

Helios tried to calm his half-Titan son,
child of the Stars but also an Ocean spirit,
handsome and restless, nowhere at peace.

Eloquent Phaëthon was, as he demanded
his patrimony—his place in Sun's orbit.
The father tried to reason with examples:

"Ares, son of Zeus, holds a soldier's bugle,
not his father's thunderbolts and lightning.

"Hephaestus the Blacksmith hammers iron
without demanding his father's rumbles and claps.

"Hermes the Messenger carries a staff
not his father's shield draped with Medusa's head.

"Yes, Zagreus, favored by Zeus, held lightning—
but Titans envied him and killed him.

"He committed the sin of selfish hubris.
Zagreus' body was chopped into bloody pieces."

Helios, weeping, kissed his son and turned.
Higher than all gods, even Zeus, is Fate
who spins the length of every person's life.

VII

Helios Gives His Son an (Unheeded) Star Map

"If you must drive my fiery chariot," said Helios,
"here is what to expect: a circling zodiac
of constellations, divided into twelve parts.

Around this circuit meander planets
each a god, each with its own cycle—
Cronus the slowest, moving thirty degrees

in two-plus years. Moon takes one month
to go the same distance. Cronus is outermost,
then Zeus circles the Zodiac in a long year.

Red-burning Ares strides through the houses.
Next I, Sun, like a planet, course the skies
never backwards, only forward like time.

Each quarter of the Zodiac is a season,
each in turn, spring to winter, invariable.
Moon measures months, I the Earth's year.

Most perilous is the tipping point,
the shadowy nadir of the year, solstice.
Most distracting are inner planets.

Hold steady through the Zodiac's road.
Stay in place, no matter the comets and flares.
Don't rush. Finish each house's degrees."

VIII

Helios Explains (Sequential) Time

Helios continued his advice, "Phaëthon,
listen. Begin in Aries, the Ram. Zephyrs
christen land with warm winds and rain.

Fork-tailed swallows mate. Days stretch
longer. My beams of light strike wet fields
with life's fire. Grapes and barley swell.

At summer's height, Cancer the Crab reddens.
Then comes lesser light and the leaves shake.
Libra's scale of light and dark hangs balanced.

Winter comes last, with Capricorn, a mermaid-goat
creature of dark months. Storms rinse sins
of the year away. Midnight lasts for hours."

Phaëthon kept quiet but gazed away, starward.
"The year must follow this sequence," Helios said.
"Each day I cross the Zodiac in this order

or chaos would arise." But he saw the boy only
desired the golden helmet with seven rays.
He only desired the blazing horses of ecstasy.

IX

The (Tragic) Story
Unfolds

Helios said nothing. His face hardened
to stone as he handed a webwork of reins
to Phaëthon—guides of the chariot.

Helios trembled as Phaëthon grabbed the whip
while Clymenê, his water nymph mother,
splashed in the blue ocean, proud and unaware.

Morning Star blazed eastward. So it began.
A long moment, Phaëthon surveyed his range:
Earth, Moon, orbiting planets, and comets.

As he gazed at his new domain, horses trod
through the Zodiac's arc, as was their habit.
Phaëthon's sight finally settled on distant stars.

X

The (Vainglorious) Son
Proceeds

Phaëthon's eyes blazed. He flailed the whip
across the horses' necks, maddening them
out of their usual course, the Zodiac's path.

Boundaries of north and south broke apart.
Hot and cold winds tangled into whirlwinds.
The goaded horses ran wildly in all directions.

"Stop this," Morning Star warned Phaëthon.
"Quit lashing the Sun's steeds. Beware
the constellations' killing powers unleashed.

"Orion the Hunter's knife can slash you.
Boötes' oxen team can trample you.
Archer's fire-tipped arrow can pierce you."

Yet as the Morning Star spoke, Phaëthon
pushed his team faster and faster until finally
the very center axle of Heaven cracked.

XI

The (Chaotic) Constellations and (Chaotic) Planets Devolve

~ ~Serpens joins its head to its tail ~ ~ escapes Asclepius the Healer ~
~ hisses at Taurus the Bull ~ ~ ~ slithers to the Equator

Lion roars flames at *Canis* the Dog ^ ^ ^ swipes at the Crab's claws ^
^ ^ ^

switches his tail like a whip \ \ \ \ \ flogs Virgo the
Maiden \ \ \ \ \

Virgo darts out of her place in the Zodiac circle * * * * * *
past Boötes the Herdsman
to his wagon near the North Pole.
She shivers alone in the cold polar night. | *

Morning Star bullies past the Evening Star in the west and takes its place.
\+ + +

Eos the Dawn walks deep space ☼

The blue-hot star Sirius leaps at the Big Bear, *Ursa Major*, scorching its
fur. ++ /\/\ ++

The two fishes of Pisces < / >
one headed north
the other south

break apart.
</ />

Dolphin splashes into Capricorn's place and tumbles with the monster goat
with a fish's tail.
^^^ ^^^ ^^^ ^^^ ^^^ ^^^ ^^^ ^^^ ^^^ ^^^ ^^^

Moon carouses midday sky O
fades without the torch of the Sun's rays. o

Scorpio -^ wakens from its trance
scuttles after Orion, raising its stinger at the giant. -^ -^ -^ -^ -^

Chorus of the seven Pleiades resonates among the planets
a cacophony
interrupting the seven spheres in their celestial song. o o o o
o o o

The planets jostle out of position
Venus challenging Zeus ♀ ♀

Mars pushing aside Father Cronus. ♀♂ ♀♂ ♀♂ ♀♂

Faithful Hermes son of Zeus
abandons the careening chariot
no longer keeping
steady course
through
Chaos.

XII

Zeus (Re-) Orders The Firmament

Phaëthon barely hung onto the shredded reins
as Sky's menagerie threatened. The Olympian Bull
raised shining horns and stomped the stardust.

Orion drew his sword. Boötes raised his cudgel.
Pegasus the Horse strafed the ground and charged.
Bears of the North Pole prowled to the southern void.

Into the starry chaos at last came Zeus.
With a thunderbolt he struck Phaëthon dead
and dropped him into the river below, Eridanus.

The river turned to flames and rose into the sky,
a meandering path of lights, the Milky Way.
Zeus restored Hours, Days, Months, Years.

He positioned Phaëthon in a constellation,
The Charioteer—with arms raised, always ready
for a fool's race against the gods' god—Fate.

Book 39

Anthony Corbeill

In thirty-nine, after the deluge we can watch Deriades
fleeing with his fleet of fire-gleaming Indians.

The latest myth recounted, Hermes flew up untouched,
leaving his brother Dionysus in joy and wonder.

As Bacchus kept marveling at the uncosmetic array of stars,
at the thud of Phaëthon gliding down,
scorched, to the Celts in the western ocean,
ships arrived in formation from afar.
The Rhadamanes steered toward battle-ready
Ares on a waveless sea, alternating
their thrusts to stir up the waters.
A whistling wind propelled Lyaeus
on anxious barges while Lycus
led, his chariot skimming the waves,
unmarked by hooves.

Meanwhile, enormous Deriades, up high in his tower,
was eying angrily the speedy ships'
cloudish canvases. When this monster learned
an Arabian artisan had lathed these combative keels
he swore: "I'll fell those Arab lumberjacks,

disappear Lycurgus' city,
and thresh the Rhadamanes with iron flails!"
Still, his fearless Indians feared; they saw
the fleet and the war god slapping the sea,
which made even Deriades the bold, Indian king,
weak in the knees. Feigning laughter on a calm face,
he ordered three hundred islands, with their foothills
difficult to pass and rich in elephants,
to levy an army. So his messenger swiftly cut a path,
limbs constantly twisting from one land to another,
until the fleet arrived from these widespread isles
promptly at the royal bidding. Craning his neck, the king
dragged into the sea of war these caparisoned tugs
and bucked up all the sailors with these high-minded words:

"Men! My father Hydaspes, lustful of battle, has reared you,
so do battle once again with a cool head. Add to the war
gleaming fire, light it up with endless firebrands.
so that I can torch those ships, newly arrived
with spears, armor, boats—and Dionysus!—,
and overwhelm in the sea this wet-wandering navy.
Bacchus a god? Then Bacchus will perish in my flames.
It's enough that he has reddened beloved Hydaspes by sprinkling
his stream with psychotropic drugs culled from
Thessalian blossoms. I watched in silence, enduring
the sight of a flowing river gone mad.
If that flow arose from any river but Hydaspes,
my father, sacred to Indians and Ares,
I would have cloaked with floods of dust
Bacchus' grapey stench and my father,
a streaming drunk, I'd have used as a doormat
for my dusty feet—without getting them wet!
As at that time in Argos you've heard about,
when Poseidon blew the river dry and you could see
hoofprints in the sunburnt dust of the Inachos.
A god? He is no god, his origins are a myth.
He can't shake Zeus' aegis on Olympus, or possess

a splinter of the lightning that knocks people down.
No banging and crashing in the skies for him.
Does Zeus himself arm for war with a cabernet vine?
Jingle-jangle tambourines sound nothing like rolling thunder,
and impaled pine cones can't compare with a divine scepter.
A breastplate of fruit is nothing next to heavenly clouds?
What is a spotted fawnskin next to a starry night?
You will say that Zeus, who helps everything
grow, gave him grapes and wine-sap? Well, once
there was this Trojan boy, a rube of a shepherd,
and Zeus gave him the nectar of Olympus.
Ganymede's nectar versus wine—no comparison. Give up, bearers
of pine cones! Bacchus feasts on earth with goat-men,
while Ganymede feasts with the deathless sky-dwellers.
If he really is the son of god,
he'd share a table with Zeus and the blessed ones.
Once upon a time, they say, the original Dionysus—
Zagreus—received the scepter of Olympus.
Lightning for Zagreus, a vine-tendril for Bacchus."

He rushed to the noise of battle, with army,
swords, and shields, and transferred
any hope for victory from land to sea.
In turn, Dionysus addressed his leaders with a maenad's frenzy:

"Children of Ares and of warrior Athena, courageously
you hope and pray for the noisy clashing of war.
So hurry! Deliver the Indians to maritime genocide;
you've won on land, get a second by sea.
Send an oceanic message of battle by assembling
your compound spears with their double weld,
bonding hard bronze at their tips,
and letting loose on the foe fearful sea-Furies.
Faster! before my fire-gleaming torch
hits your ships and arsons your asses!
Be true god-crazed revelers and fight fearlessly
against these hopeless water-warring wranglers!

Try as he might, sitting astride his lofty elephants,
head in the clouds, touching the ether but untouchable
by us, the Indian chief couldn't finish battle on land.
As for me, I've got plenty of allies.
My father is Zeus, who reigns over sea and sky.
Or I will call my uncle Poseidon to arms,
to crush the Asian squadrons with his trident.
And Glaucus, from Poseidon's seed, lives near my home,
under the water off the mainland of Aonia.
Also from the sea comes Phorcys, and Melicertes,
who'll bury Deriades' fleet as it flounders on the main.
He delights in honoring Bacchus: his mother,
Ino, nursed me as an infant, and we two babies,
Dionysus and Melicertes, shared one milk.
The Old Mantic of the sea, dear Proteus,
foretold our naval victory from depths
most profound. Beloved Thetis will give
arms to the nereids and my nursemaid
Ino will fight beside our Thracian girls.
Aeolos too will hand out weapons, javelins
to the East Wind and spears to the North
(who took the daughter of Erechtheus),
and the Ethiopian South Wind will fight too,
while the West destroys the enemy fleet
with winds of war, the more so since he sleeps
with Iris, Father Zeus' messenger. On second thought:
Aeolos should stay far from the contest
between India and thyrsus. Let him do his duty
in peace, keeping tightly sealed his sack of winds
and not let them lord over slaughtered Indians.
I'll destroy the ships with a shake of my thyrsus."

That said, he armed his trusty leaders.
The bugle stood ready to call the charge,
the shrill shriek of the war pipes gathered
the troops, shields clanged together—
the noise of bronze rattling across the waters—

and the various pan pipes summoned the assembly.
And yet the cliffs did not echo this cacophony:
only vibrations filled the sea, whispering war.

And then! The fighters confusedly clash amidst
a clamorous roar. The Bacchic fleet matches
expectations, encircling in tight formation
the whole Indian navy, cinching the enemy
like fish in a silken net. Then for the Aeacides
Aeacus himself, foreseeing Salamis' sea-fight,
initiates battle with this god-driven voice:

"Here's to you, Zeus of the Rains. In the past
you heard my suppliant voice, and eased drought
by sending moisture to revive parched earth.
Now give the same gift before it is too late,
People will sing out
when they hear of our victory: 'Both on land
and on sea Zeus honors his son!' Maybe
some Achaean will announce: 'With the same hand
Aeacus slays Indians and produces life. He harvests
heads and plants seed, thereby giving Demeter
joy and Dionysus a merry heart.' Oh God,
protect our fleet! Just as I gave to the parched
hollows of earth the waters that revive life,
I call up fatal tsunamis from the hollows
to oppose the sea forces of Deriades.
My father, who art leader of life and battle,
prove your paternity by sending your eagle,
an auspicious sign for our fighters and your dear Dionysus,
and let inauspicious birds fly in the enemy's face.
To each his own, maybe, but to us the better:
I'll watch as our eagle plays the thief, lifting
with sharp talons an immeasurable snake,
carving its flesh as it dies from needlelike piercings:
that's how we foresee the foe in our grip.
But our enemy's avian visitor looms dark,

prophesying slaughter with its inky wings,
and prompting to mass suicide. But Father,
if you'd prefer, use rolling thunder to signal victory,
or the bolts that illuminated Bacchus' birthday—
honor your son with fire once again. Your lightning
can pierce enemy hulls, no matter how well protected.
You preyed on the virgin Aegina as an eagle—
so don't bring shame on such a fitting love-bird!"

He spoke, and starts fighting. Now Erechtheus
began. Eyeing the path of the boustrophedon
Great Bear, he starts with a prayer to Boreas:

"Arm yourself, North Wind, and help out your father-in-law
through guided gusting, gifting me a sea victory
in exchange for bedding my daughter.
One favorable wind for Bacchus' fleet secures
gratitude from two—Erechtheus and Dionysus.
As for Deriades, whip the waters into a frenzy,
weaponizing your whirlwinds on the waves.
You're a veteran at fighting—is it your Thracian blood?—
yes, you're as much a veteran as Ares himself,
so let your ill winds blow some good. Pierce
this hostile navy with icicle spears, hurl hailstones
as swift as bullets, send Furies in the guise of
hurricanes! Zeus, Athena,
Dionysus, they'll all love you for it.
Remember your wedding day? The women of Athens
weave the story of your shared love, honoring the river
who arranged it all when your bride, snatched up
by lusty breezes on his banks, was placed
on your firm shoulders.

"I've also learned that the East Wind,
since he lives nearby, will help the Indians. But no need
to fear him in battle, bold as he is:
all winged winds are Boreas' subordinates.

And may the South Wind never again warm the plowlands
of Corymbasus, Ethiopian leader. No,
let his soul recall those warm winds as he imbibes
the cold waters that carry across the dead.
The West Wind?—who cares, when Boreas is weaponized.
Show that you're as Athenian as I am; then Poseidon
will use his trident to help you battle for the
Dionysians side by side with Athena,
she for her people, he for me, his nephew.
On our side too Hephaestus, honoring
Erechtheus' line, burns for a furious water fight,
randomly swinging his torch at their wooden ships.
Please, let me win too, and afterward
Erechtheus will lead home his people in one piece
so the Athenians can hymn Boreas and his bride."

After this epic plea, Erechtheus casts his well-turned
spear over the sea-tossed combatants, a Marathon
infantryman lusting for water. In the same way Ares,
in love with rowing, became the perfect sailor,
with Panic at the stern and the admiral,
shearing Terror, snipping at the moorings.

Companies of cyclopes sail in their own fashion,
picking off boats with crags torn from the shore—
there's Euryalus, screaming, and there's Halimedes,
like a tidal wave towering to the clouds.
Battle repeatedly echoes against the armies
on water as it had on land—with indecipherable
sea-yells, Indians swamp Bacchants.
Slaughter is everywhere, gore floods the waves
as fighters fall from ships; the crests of the sea,
once blue, redden with bloodbath.
On both sides, while sailing this swollen sea,
one after one falls into liquid death,
the Winds ferrying crowded corpses
in vicious circles. They show no pity.

The dizzying turmoil of battle also claims
victims; cast overboard and forced to swallow
brine, sinking with their armor, they face Fate,
who snips her threads underwater. Wine-dark, the sea
renders blacker still the swollen corpses, sunk
deep in muck; both armor and owners
ooze slime and mud, lying buried in
Davy Jones' Locker. Several are entombed,
but in Leviathan's jaws, while the swift seal's
throat, vomiting streams of tawny gore, becomes
the fish-reeking coffin for others. Arms
of the dead fill the sea: a crested helmet bobs
alone, ripped from its owner, now fresh meat.
In the storm-tossed current circular shields
swim out in all directions, their straps
having a life of their own, while beneath the surface
roils saltwater foaming grey and red,
its once whiteness inked by crimson coils.

In the sea below, these blood libations redden Melicertes,
while Leucothea, Bacchus' wet-nurse, crows
joyously, the slain Indians prompting her
to crown herself with blossoming seaweed.
Atop the sea, Thetis' bare head ups periscope,
the goddess propped on Doris and Panopea as she gazes
with pleasure at Dionysus and his lovely shaft of thyrsus.

Galatea, floating up from the depths into Poseidon's
lap, scratches the surface imperceptibly, but
the sea-fearing fury of the blood-stained cyclopes
sends her spinning and flushes her cheeks with fear
as she thinks she sees Polyphemus fighting
beside Bacchus, facing Deriades' screaming Indians.
Frightened, she begs first seaborn Aphrodite
to save the best of Poseidon's sons and then
the blue-maned god himself, praying
that Polyphemus be shielded from battle pain.
But Poseidon, encircled by fifty sea nymphs,

already sees all. Leaning on his trident, the god
who shakes the earth feels all around the conflict
from Dionysus' well-equipped forces. Jealous
at the heroism of cyclopes who are not his own,
he blasts Bacchus for warring where he doesn't belong:

"Grape-god, you've gathered so many cyclopes, but
what about that one there, all alone, nowhere near the fighting?
Your brawl has cycled through some seven years,
Endlessly feeding hope after hope. Just forget
your mighty warrior ranks; all you need
is one of them, Polyphemus the invincible.
Let that son of mine go where the fighting is,
swinging my own trident
and as your true ally he'll scrunch his way clean
through the chest of that cow Deriades;
in fact, he'll slice open the entire dreaded opposition—
Indian genocide in a single day! Once upon a time,
another son of mine, the polydextrous Aegaeon,
helped Zeus, your father, defeat the Titans.
You'll remember Cronus fleeing in fear when Aegaeon,
locks flowing, stretched high his several
wingspans and left the sun in the shade.
Result? the burly Titans sneaked out of Olympus,
cowering before each of Aegaeon's hundred hands."

So Poseidon, in righteous rage.
And Thoösa looked down in shame
since her love-crazed son was not in the fight.
Once the noisy labor of battle had died down,
and Nereus saw his dear sea flowing blood.
Poseidon too marveled at the gory expanse, where
fish preyed on men and heaping corpses
created a bone-dry bridge over the waters,
as the Dionysiac troops swarmed over the Indians.

Countless enemy squadrons lie dying,
pierced through by blades and arrows.

Over here a sling-bullet blends the bowels,
over there a bronze spear—smack in the middle
of the forehead—rifles a deep gash in a skull.
All around, countless Indians pull oars,
the dark sea yielding to stroke after stroke
as it whitens from the constant upchurning.
All that work in vain—give up, rowers!
Too late. The admiral slices through the tow-ropes
and cuts off all connections, all hope.

Both armies fight in the shade as a whooshing
thundercloud fills the air—arrows, unerring.
One strikes the mizzenmast, one, going like the wind,
pierces through a sail, now well-trimmed;
a third slices the forestays just as two more hit target;
the first fast in the mastbox, the second veering
through the breeze to hit the yardarm's crested tip.
The rowing benches are hit, and the steersman
nearly, arrows just scraping past and boring
through the tip of his wildly-moving rudder.
Even famed Phlogius, sending his dart into the wind,
could only hit the deck—at Bacchus' feet.
And look at that arrow! Winging aimlessly over the waves,
it becomes entwined in a squid's tentacle tips.
No one hits targets—though one arrow, tipped with
Red Sea steel and aiming for Bacchus, slices a porpoise.
Corymbasus launches his spear toward a satyr's tail.
Another miss: he lances a fish, still
underwater, and shaves off its forked tail
with a razor's edge. And Deriades—
he tried for Dionysus the invincible when
thwack!—his lance's deadly
point burrows into the spine of a dolphin right
where the dorsal fin starts to curve.
The fish, flip-flopping in a circle,
leaps half-alive in a gay dance of death.
In like fashion, on all sides other fish, backs
spiked, jump, spin, and tumble from life.

Here come the cyclopes! Steropes leads,
and Halimedes the highstepper hurls
a sea crag at the foe, the jagged edge
of the spinning stone sinking a straying ship.
Then a spear follows close upon, skimming
the sea, and yokes one ship to its neighbor,
fastening the two tight in a single bond,
all clouded together, clashes reverberating over and over.

Both navies form a quadripart formation,
one side at the spine of the fiery-faced East Wind,
another along the dewy wing of the Southwest, plus
Boreas, with South along the furthest end. Speedy Morrheus,
traversing ships with spears in each hand,
startles the forces of the Bassarids—jittery gulls.
He prevails at sea, until Bacchus thwacks
him with his thyrsus, a debilitating gash that
sends him home, licking his wounds.

How to heal a god-given injury? Try the divine
hand of a Brahman, whose Apolline arts ease pain
by intoning an endless angelic song.
Meanwhile,
the Ares that is Bacchus continues his assault,
and the enemy fleet recharges, the war Fury
putting wind in their sails. But the two sides,
while churning water equally, differ in success.
Jagged stones, slung sickle-blades,
and spears and knives cast Indians overboard.
The sea swallows them as they haplessly dog-paddle
in the black water, arms and feet flailing.
But when a wine god warrior is knocked off ship,
he propels his body smoothly through the water,
arms equal to its undertow, human opponents
now replaced by the surging enemy sea.

At last, Zeus decides to tip the scales
to give Dionysus a watery triumph. Blue-haired

Poseidon lends him his deep-sea trident
along with a chariot, which Melicertes
drives like a drunk over the crests of the waves.
The four Winds too gust down over the sea
as if on horseback, rousing a towering tsunami
designed to annihilate the enemy convoys—
that of Deriades for some, for others, those of Bacchus.
Even winds fight: Zephyrus crests a wave as Notus
hisses at Eurus, and Boreas whips the back
of the angry sea with savage counterblasts.
Strife herself commandeers Deriades'
fierce fleet, but billowing the sails for Dionysus
is Victory, Indians choked in her deadly grip.
With embouchure locked to conch,
Nereus blares out the call to attack,
and in defense of Bacchus Thetis' war-cry
reverberates against the waves of her father.

Eurymedon the mystery-god, predictably,
raises a torch, but it's a trick: he ignites
his own longship, and the flames cooperate.
Set afloat, the boat rams the opposing fleet,
dancing about at the whim of Dionysus.
Bouncing from ship to ship with random spins
it eddies chaotically but not aimlessly,
kindling everywhere all it touches.
The bareheaded nereids feel the gleaming
sea in flames and plunge into the depths,
descending through watery Greek fire.

The Indians, recoiling, beach their entire fleet and
Phaëthon laughs brightly at Ares: he narrowly
escaped not bed-chains this time, but Hephaestus' fire.
Deriades, out of reach, flies like the wind to beat
the flames to shore, knees pumping, leaving
the water world to Dionysus, sea-warrior.

Book 40

Deborah H. Roberts

Book 40, where the Indians' leader gets a wound
And Dionysus enters Cadmus' native Tyre.

He could not steer clear of panoptic Justice
nor of Fate's spindle with its never-broken threads.
Pallas Athena spied him as he ran away:
she sat, seaside, upon a rugged promontory,
watching the crested Indians battle in their ships,
then leapt up from this lookout, shaped herself as male,
and with mind-thieving talk deceived Deriades.
Disguised as Morrheus she stopped him in his tracks
to make the wine god happy, putting on concern
about the conflict, strident in her fear and blame.

"Running away, Deriades? And who is left
To lead the fight among the ships? How does this look?
How will you face Orsiboë, who stands and meets
her enemies, if once she hears you have run off
and will not meet these women? You should be ashamed
to let Chirobië—wrecker of men—catch sight
of how you cower, afraid of unarmed combat
with Dionysus, while *she* grasps her eager spear,
and hoists her shield to fight against the Bassarids
beside her husband. You have left the field, so leave

the war to me. And if you like, I will display
my bravery in arms and kill that coward Bacchus.
You are no father-in-law of mine. You ran away.
Your girl Chirobië can find another husband.
Shame will drive me from your city. I will travel
among the Medes or else to Scythia: some place
where no one will address me as your son-in-law.
You say my wife is well-armed and has studied war?
Well, but the Amazons live near Mount Caucasus—
with many finer fighters than Chirobië—
and if I want to I can capture one at spearpoint,
marry her and acquire a good strong bride for free.
I will not share my bedroom with your daughter:
The daughter of a man who runs away from war."

Athena's words persuaded proud Deriades;
and gave his courage back—all so he might be beaten,
struck down by Dionysus and his deadly wand.
Not knowing that he faced the goddess in disguise,
he confidently answered pseudo-Morrheus
and his attacks with words a bit embarrassed
but reassuring:
"Spare your words, brave Morrheus:
why do you blame me? This man is no fighter,
no ordinary fighter: he keeps changing shape.
I have no means of knowing my opponent,
or who my target is. If I try eagerly
to hit this Dionysus with a feathered arrow
or take my sword and strike his neck, or throw my spear
to wound him in the belly, in his place I find
a spotted leopard rushing to attack me.
I fight a lion; struggling to cut his throat,
I see instead a bold and terrifying snake.
And when I go for that, a bear's back meets my eyes.
I throw my spear in fury at his curving shoulders:
No use. He seems a flame that flutters through the air,
untouched. I see a boar attack, but hear a bull's

loud bellowing; I look around and find no boar.
Instead a bull sideswipes and spears our elephants
with deadly horns. I whirl my sword around at beasts
of many kinds, and cannot overcome one beast.
Suppose that I observe a tree; when I take aim,
there goes a geyser, racing towards its airy goal!
So, yes, I am afraid of these charm-laden marvels
and run from Dionysus' changeful battle-cry.
But I will arm myself again, till I unmask
the artful magic he so treacherously weaves."

With these words he put on the old familiar rage.
And when the fight among the ships came to an end
and uproar filled the plain he battled Bromius.
He had forgotten how the god had conquered him,
when branches manacled his neck and he had begged
and begged again as Dionysus watched him beg.
So now he made a comeback: more theomachy!
He had two plans in mind: should he kill Bromius
or take him as a slave? He threw his spear three times,
and missed, striking the air; then for the fourth time,
too confident, Deriades rushed up to meet
the wine-bright Bacchus, raised his spear and threw it—
useless against its mark. He called on Morrheus,
his son-in-law, but found him gone. Athena
had changed her trickster shape and stood beside the god
of grapevines. When Deriades caught sight of her;
he felt his knees grow weak with more than mortal fear.
Clever Athena's trickery was clear to him.
But Dionysus was delighted when he saw her,
and knew her for his ally in her lying.
The grapevine god grew frenzied in his anger,
towering high, and vast, like Mount Parnassus,
he chased Deriades, and that fast runner fled,
sped lightly, stretched out in the slipstream of the winds.
But when they reached the place where old Hydaspes
sends surging forth a rabid flood to breed fresh war,

Deriades stood tall beside the river banks,
sure that his father, roaring, would be on his side,
and drive his water spear at armored Dionysus.
The god of vines let fly his wounding thyrsus,
and though it just inscribed the surface of the skin,
its deadly ivy bunch struck down Deriades.
Headfirst, he slid into his father's stream; his height
made him a natural bridge across the whole expanse.

After their lengthy war against the Indians,
the gods went home, with Zeus who governs everything,
back to Olympus. And the Bacchants yelled in triumph:
"Hurrah for Dionysus! Who can beat him?"
And many of them, crowding round Deriades,
stabbed at his skin all over with their spearpoints.
Up on the city walls, a site of lamentation,
Orsiboë was wailing, mourning for her husband,
carved as he lay there, and with grieving nails she marked
her cheeks, tore out an unkempt lock of tangled hair
and poured down on her head smoke-blackened ashes.
Chirobië screamed out in lamentation
for her dead father as she beat her blue-black arms,
ripped in two her white tunic, and exposed her breast.
Protonoë, with shoes off, scratched her cheeks, and fouled
her face with dust: she wept for both of them, her husband
and father, doubled grief. She cried out loud in sorrow:

"You died so young, and left at home a widow
who never went through childbirth, never had the comfort
a baby son would be. I never saw my husband
come home again victorious. He killed himself
with his own steel, and perished among strangers,
giving a stream his name. And now I call that stream
my seedless, suicidal, straying spouse, Orontes.
I cry for both: Orontes and Deriades,
who died a like and liquid death. Floodwaters hid
Deriades, killer of men; the current covered

Orontes. But my loss is much worse than my mother's.
Orsiboë could sing her daughters' wedding song:
she saw me married, met her son-in-law, Orontes,
and yoked Chirobië with an unconquered partner
whom even the great Bacchus fears. Chirobië
enjoys her husband still: he is alive, capsized
by neither stream nor thyrsus—while I suffer twice:
for my departed husband and my father, lost.
Nurse, will you stop this pointless consolation?
Give me my husband, and I won't lament my father.
Show me a child to soothe my sorrow for my spouse.
Oh, who will bring me where the broad Hydaspes flows
to kiss that honeysuckle river's darling crest?
And who will take me down to Daphne's sacred valley
to hold Orontes even as he tumbles forth?
I wish I were a stream, desired and longed for.
I wish I were a spring, rained on by my own tears,
where my dead husband's lovely waters crest and roll:
his riverbed-mate. I'll be like Comaetho,
who fancied a fine river once, and even now
gladly keeps Cydnus in her arms and in her bed.
According to my sister's husband Morrheus
they like that sort of story in Cilicia.

"Pass by my sweet Orontes, whom I long for,
Like Periboia, as she ran away? No, never.
I will not ever draw aside my waters
as they meander, to ward off my fluid spouse.
If I'm not meant to die with Daphne as my neighbor,
hide me, granddad Hydaspes, in your billows.
Don't make me spend the night in bed with satyrs
or join a Phrygian spree and shake my cymbals
to take my playful part. Don't make me travel
to Tmolus or Maeonia; don't make me live
in Bacchus' house beneath the heavy harness
of slavery, and have to hear such talk as this:
'The daughter of Deriades the daring king
serves Dionysus now, his after-battle booty.'"

The women joined her in their pitiful lament:
their sons or brothers had been killed, their fathers,
their husbands, barely bearded, dead before their prime.
Chirobië tore out her hair and scratched her cheeks,
lashed by a double agony. Grief for her father
was nothing to her wifely indignation.

She knew her husband was compelled by crazy love
and caught by Chalcomedê's cheating chastity.
She tore her tunic and declared:
"Morrheus' failure
to fight has killed my father, who goes unavenged.
Because he wanted Chalcomedê—how I hate her!—
he would not drive away those warlike women
but caters to the Bacchants still. So tell me, Fates:
what divine grudge destroyed our Indian city
and set upon the daughters of Deriades?
Orontes, dead in battle, left Protonoë
to mourn in solitude; my husband Morrheus,
although I am still living, has rejected me.
My suffering is more pernicious than my sister's.
Her husband helped the country that had nurtured him.
My husband was his fatherland's destroyer:
a fighter useless to his own; Love's brave attendant;
now one thing, now another; Bacchus' true believer.
Even my marriage took up arms against me:
my city fell because of Morrheus' desire.
I lost my father for my husband's sake. Once proud,
mistress of India and daughter of a king,
I will become a serving girl, and—misery!—
call Chalcomedê, once a slave, my mistress.
You cheater, Morrheus! Now India's your home;
Tomorrow, by your choice, you'll leave for Lydia
compelled by Chalcomedê's beauty to serve Bacchus.
Make her bed public knowledge, bridegroom Morrheus!
No need to fear Deriades' severity.
The snake whose sibilance kept safe a bridal bed
and guarded it from plunder summons you. Get out!"

Such were the grieving wife's words, weighted with her tears.
Protonoë cried out again. Both women felt
their downcast mother's arms around them as she shouted,
"Our fatherland and all its hopes have fallen!
Husband and son-in-law: I will no longer see them.
Deriades is dead, our city has been plundered.
The walls no one could break have fallen. How I wish
Bacchus would kill me with the husband he has killed,
take me and throw me in Hydaspes' rushing river.
No earth for me! My husband's father's waters
will take me in, with him. I never want to see
Protonoë compelled to follow Dionysus,
or hear Chirobië cry out again, dragged off
to do her captor's will: a spearpoint wedding.
I want no second spouse after Deriades.
I'd rather join the naiads, like Leucothoë.
I'll be a nereid: not white, not silver-footed:
My feet will gleam blue-black among the waves."

So, that was how these long-robed women carried on,
lined up along the wall in teichoscopic grief.
But Bacchus' followers dispensed with battle
and clashed their cymbals as they shouted with one voice:
"Kudos for us! We killed the Indians' leader."
And Dionysus laughed and shook with glee: he'd won!
Now for a break from hard and bloody struggle,
to honor, first, the rows of still unburied dead.
He built around the pyre one common tomb, immense:
a generous width, one hundred feet in length. Among
the bodies, panpipes tremulously trilled a dirge
while Phrygian flutists wove their manly melodies
with mournful mouths, and maenads danced. Ganyctor sang
his pretty arias in Bacchic tones. Cleochus
took up the double flute, which bawled and bellowed
a frightful Libyan lament, the very one
Medusa's sisters sang! One sound from many throats
came whistling as they wept the just-beheaded Gorgon,

while their two hundred snakes, those hissing tresses,
expressed their grief in polyphonic part song—
the mode known as "Medusa's many-headed dirge."

Now Bacchus left his labors, purified his body,
and chose Modaeus, a godfearing man, to rule
the Indians—who joined the Bacchant banquet,
ate from a single table, shared a drinking cup
of pale gold liquid from the stream that flowed with wine.
They danced and danced. The Bacchants' crazy feet
tapped out the rhythm while the satyrs, tumbling, drummed
their feet against the sounding floor, and put their arms
around the necks of far-from-sober Bacchant women.
Bromius' soldiers danced around with oxhide shields,
in maddened circles, mimicking the Corybants.
The cavalry stood up to dance, with waving plumes,
to hail the conquering hero, Dionysus.
No tongue was silent; all together now they shouted.
The zodiac re-echoed with "euoi" and "alalei."

Their revels now were ended: no more holiday.
Bacchus packed up the loot won from the Indians
and once more called to mind his ancient fatherland,
having "resolved" the cause of seven years of war.
His fighters got the spoils, the enemy's whole wealth:
an Indian jasper, or a hyacinthine stone
engraved like Phoebus' flower, and an emerald.
One soldier took straight home through Himalayan heights
his captured elephants, while by the mountains' deep
romantic chasms another proudly drove a team
of migrant lions. And a third had tightened
the harness on a panther's neck and hustled him
down to the shores of Macedon. There went a satyr,
festively whipping with his tipsy-turvy leaves
a tiger who stalked stripily in front. Another
was coming home with presents for his Phrygian bride:
the sea's sweet-smelling reeds, the sea's soft-gleaming pearls.

And many black-skinned brides, asleep beside their husbands,
were taken captive, dragged off by their hair, and forced
to bend their neck and wear the yoke of slavery.
The Bacchants, god-sped, went their way to Tmolus' peaks,
letting their hands grow lighter as their wealth dispersed
and singing songs to celebrate their god's return.

So Dionysus shared the spoils among the fighters
and sent the army home. The war was over.
His people hurried off, with shining pearls held high
(gifts of the eastern seas), and bright shape-shifting birds.
They journeyed back, all singing songs to celebrate
unbeaten Dionysus and his Bacchic rites,
and left behind all memory of war's hard work,
gone with the North Wind, dissipated by his breath.
And so each one came home at last, victorious.
Except Asterius: instead of Crete he chose
to settle down beneath the Bears that never set
foot in the ocean, in a land that lacks all warmth,
beside the Phasis river and the Caspian sea.
Grandfather Taurus, ankle-deep in snow but still
somehow transported to the stars, shone down on him.
He stayed away from Cnossus and his family,
hating his father Minos and Pasiphaë.
Scythia suited him.
And meanwhile, Dionysus
was on his own with no one but his satyrs
and Indian-killing maenads. After fighting
beside a river in the Caucausus, now toured
Arabia a second time. They knew him not,
and so he taught them how to lift the thyrsus,
and garlanded their hills with dense and fruitful vines,
then left Arabia's dark-shaded forests
and took on foot a shortcut to Assyria,
thinking he might go visit Cadmus' fatherland.
So, off to Tyre he went, and on the way observed
Assyria's extensive fabric works—amazing!

What craftsmanship, what colors! And Arachne
of Babylon: he gazed upon her silver web,
He viewed cloth they dyed with murex shells from Tyre:
it seemed to give off purple sparks like sea-spray.
How was the dye discovered? Well, one day a dog
down by the seaside, foraging, was feeding on
that subtle fish sublime with glaring jaws, and found
his snowy jowls dyed purple with the creature's blood,
lips reddened with a liquid fire, once the sole source
of crimson dye that colored the bright cloaks of kings.
The sight of Tyre delighted Dionysus.
Poseidon had encircled it, but not completely.
The city's sash of sea had given it the shape
the moon weaves when just one iota short of full:
a gibbous grace. And when he saw the land and sea
conjoined, the wine god felt a twinned astonishment,
since Tyre's salt-water site means the three-sided belt
of channels round her land is buckled by the sea.
It is as if a swimming girl were standing,
solidly planted, with her feet on mother earth,
with head, and neck, and breast above the water,
her arms stretched out below, her body white with foam.
Poseidon holds the city tightly in his grip,
Swimming around her like a water-bridegroom
who splashes as he holds his bride in his embrace.
Bacchus gave way to greater wonder. Only here
could cowherds travel side by side with sailors
as they walked piping by the shore, and goatherds
accompany the fisher as he spreads his nets.
Plows cut the earth; in parallel, oars plowed the sea.
In coastal copses shepherds gathered gossiping
with boatmen, fishermen with lumberjacks. One place
resounded with the roaring of the sea, the moos
of cattle, and the whispering of leaves; ship's cables,
trees, voyages, groves, water; ships and barges, plows,
sheep, reeds, and sickles, sailcloth, skiffs, and armor.
And as he gazed, the god expressed amazement.

"An island on the mainland? Am I seeing straight?
I've never seen—can it be right to say?—such beauty!
The tall trees rustle by the waves, the sea nymph speaks
and from the woods nearby a dryad listens in.
A southern breeze from Lebanon blows gently
on Tyrian waters and on croplands by the shore,
a breath that nurtures fruit and sends ships safely off
cools down the farmer, takes the sailor voyaging.
Demeter, harvest goddess, sets her sickle near
Poseidon's trident, calling on the water king,
who drives across calm, silent seas with wheels still dry,
to set on that same course her eager chariot,
while she whips on her airborne team of dragons.
O well-known city, earth's stamp, image of the sky,
With three-side seaside belted into unity!"

So saying, Dionysus strolled around the city
gawking at all he saw: the streets that gleamed with gold
inset with fine-cut stones! His own ancestral home!
He gazed at Cadmus' courts and women's quarters,
and went into the unprotected rooms where once
Europa lived until Zeus seized her as his bride.
(This made the god recall his bull-horned father.)
The ancient springs impressed him even more: a stream
comes pouring through the earth; then, one hour later,
nurturing water bubbles up and freely flows.
He saw three streams named after nymphs: Abarbarea
the fruitful; Callirhoë, that charming eponym;
Drosera's waters, delicate as any bride.
But when his pleasure-loving soul had seen it all,
he led a Bacchic party to the temple
of Star-Coat Melkart, also known as Heracles
and Helios the Sun, and with these mystic words
called on the stars' commander:
"Star-Coat Heracles,
Fire-lord and leader of the universe, O Sun,
shepherd of mortal life, long shadow maker,

you drive your horses, and your fiery discus whirls
all round the sky; you turn the twelve-month year, time's son,
in circle after circle. From your chariot flows
our life, transmogrified by youth and by old age.
A midwife wise in labor pains, you bring to birth
the trifold image of the unmothered moon:
Selena, fresh as dew, who milks reflected light
from your birth-giving rays to fill her crescent horn.
Heaven's bright eye, your chariot brings us winter
as autumn fails, then turns the spring to summer.
And when you whip your silver-harnessed horses
to run straight out, the night flees from day's hurtling torch.
When your light shines it scatters into flight
the stars before it from the field of night.
Cool after bathing in the eastern ocean's waves
you shake life-giving water from your dampened hair
to bring the rain, with mellow fruitfulness, and drop
the early morning dew from sky on fertile earth.
The wheat fields labor; you bring forth the harvest,
watering crops that crowd life-giving furrows.

"By the Euphrates, Belus; Apis by the Nile;
Libya calls you Ammon; you are known as Cronus
among the Arabs, Zeus among Assyrians.
And every thousand years, the subtle Phoenix
brings incense-wood with crooked claw, constructs a nest
upon your fragrant altar and begets his end
and his beginning. He is born again, the image
of duplicated time, since on the pyre he burns
old age, and on the pyre exchanges it for youth.
Be Sarapis, that cloudless Zeus of Egypt;
Cronus, or Phaëthon of many names, or Mithras,
Delphic Apollo, Helios of Babylon,
Gamos the marriage-god, whom Eros shadow-sired
in dreams, when he fulfilled a specious craving
for counterfeit connubiality. (Zeus slept,
his self-sufficient swordpoint scratched the fertile ground,

spreading his moist seed, and the craggy cliffs gave birth!)
Painkiller Paean! Changeful Sky! (We call you Star-Coat,
because at night your constellations cloak the heavens
in light.) Your ears should give my voice a friendly welcome."

This was the kind of thing he tossed out. All at once,
and right there in the shrine, shaped by divinity,
Star-Coat cast lightning. From his fiery eyes he sent
a glancing rosy gleam. The radiant god, with robe
of many colors, changeful as the sky, world-icon,
stars sparkling from his golden beard and mustache,
held out his hand to Bacchus and invited him
to join him for a friendly meal. It was a pleasure:
a meal for which no animals were slaughtered.
You can't find fault with nectar and ambrosia;
Heracles drank sweet nectar after Hera's milk.

Now Dionysus poured out eager questions:
"This city, model mainland, island's pattern:
Say what immortal hand or eye could frame
this fearful symmetry? Who hoisted up these rocks
to plant them in the sea? Who was the craftsman here?
Where did these springs all get their names? And who combined
mainland and island, joining them with mother sea?"

Heracles calmed his questioner with friendly words.
"Bacchus, just listen, and I'll tell you everything.
Time's siblings lived here, sole contemporaries
and comrades of the ever-living cosmos,
the pure descendants of the unwed mother earth;
It was the mud, unseeded and unplowed, that bore
their shapes, spontaneously generated.
Their native ingenuity sufficed to raise the city
from stone foundations on a likewise stony soil.
And once upon a time they drowsed together
in low beds by the lovely springs, just tugging
at sleep's contentment and his winged forgetfulness

as earth lay steaming, beaten by the fiery sun.
I loved that city with a frenzied passion,
and so I stopped beside these earthborn sleepers,
and hanging over them with mortal shadow-face
sent them an oracle from my prophetic mouth.

'Not working? Shed this sleep, you children of the earth!
Make me a novel chariot to walk the waves.
Take your sharp axes, fell the pine trees on the ridge,
and build me something clever. Setting up stout ribs
in sequence, nail the planks on, fasten them to fit
together tightly, making an unshakeable
brine-chariot, first ship to voyage forth and lift you
over the sea! Give it a long, curved beam, placed first
to span the whole from prow to stern and bear the weight.
Then fasten planking to the ribs that circle round
to form a close-packed wooden wall. And in the center
set up a post: high, straight, attached by cables.
Mid-post, attach a broad expanse of linen cloth
with ropes on either side to keep the cloth spread out
and let it grow big-bellied with the wanton wind,
patron of ships. If new-joined timbers show their seams,
use slender dowels to make them tight, and all around
cover the sides with thickly layered wicker mats
to keep the sea from secret seepage where a hole
gapes in the hollow ship. To guide your vessel,
provide a tiller that can steer you safely through
the sea-road's twists and turns, and spin now here, now there,
as your mind takes you. With your wooden vessel
carve the sea's back, until you reach the destined place
where twin rocks drift unmoored and wander through the sea.
Nature has named them: the Ambrosials.
                                        On one,
born with, joined with, self-rooted in and centered on
this rock that roams the sea, an olive sapling grows.
Upon its topmost treetop you will gaze upon
an eagle, seated, and a finely crafted bowl.

The tree, in flames, ablaze by no one's hand, shoots forth
amazing sparks; fire's brightness feeds upon but never
burns up the olive sapling, through whose lofty leaves
a snake performs its spiral dances: added wonder
for eyes and ears alike. And no, the snake does not
go creeping up without a sound and sideways cast
its coils to threaten that high-flying eagle.
It does not spit death-dealing venom from its teeth
and then devour the bird. As for the eagle: no,
he does not clasp the creeping coiling creature
with crooked claws, and fly high, cutting through the air;
nor does he lacerate it with his tooth-sharp beak.
Fire does not spread from branch to branch of that tall tree
and feed upon it; no, the olive stays unharmed.
Fire does not shrivel up the serpent's scales that coil
along a nearby pathway, nor leap up to catch
even the woven feathers of the bird. Instead,
at the tree's heart it gleams and gives off friendly smoke.
The bowl, high up but still unshaken, never slips
and falls, although the treetop's shaken by the winds.

'Hunt down this clever eagle, twin-born with the olive,
and sacrifice him to Poseidon. On the rock
that roams the seas, pour out his blood: an offering
to Zeus and all the gods. Result: the restless rock
no longer wanders, water-borne, but freely fixed
on firm foundations joins itself with unbound rock.
Plant on both rocks a city, situated
by double waterfronts, a sea on either side.'

"That was my oracle. The Earthborn people woke,
and shivered, as this word a god had sent them
in dreams that never err kept ringing in their ears.
The dreams flew off; I bothered them with one more sign,
to show I love to build up cities and to guard them:
a little octopus that uses arms as sails
poked up its head and showed its likeness to a ship,

a shape just made for self-taught voyaging.
Once they had gazed upon this shipshape fish,
it wasn't hard to learn the art of sailing,
and build a ship just like the fish, to imitate
its archetypal traveling across the sea.
Then they set sail, their cargo a quartet of stones
that weighed the same, to balance out their sailing,
and trusted to the sea—in imitation of
the crane, who carries in her mouth a heavy stone
to help her keep the wind from whipping her light wings
off course. And so they traveled till they spied the place
where rocks go voyaging, gale-guided, on their own.
They stopped the ship beside the sea-wreathed island
and climbed the bluffs on which Athena's tree was growing.
And when they sought the eagle by the olive's hearth,
the bird that treads the sky stopped willingly for death.
The Earthborn seized their prey, well-plumed and god-possessed,
pulled and bent back his head and bared his stretched-out neck,
then sacrificed the eagle (by a path he chose)
to Zeus and to the sea-god. When the knowing bird
was killed, the god-sent blood came flowing from his throat,
and with daemonic drops made the sea-roaming rocks
take sea floor root near old Tyre's city on the shore.
There on that solid stone the Earthborn built a city,
New Tyre, to nurture them from its unfailing breasts.

"I've told you this, Lord Dionysus—all about
the race of Giants, self-engendered, from the soil,
Olympian—so you might understand the origins
of your own ancestors, indigenous to Tyre.
And now, about those springs: they were in olden times
young women with more sense than sensibility.
Eros grew heated, irked by their virginity;
he took an arrow of desire, and to the nymphs
who had so far avoided marriage made this speech:

'Abarbarea, although you love the single life
you too will feel, with every living thing, my arrow.
Here I will build Callirhoë a bridal bower
and sing Drosera's wedding song. Oh, you may say,
"My water-family suits me; I was born a naiad,
all self-sufficient, from the streams; it was a spring
that nursed me." Well, and Clymenê? A naiad too,
and Ocean's daughter, still, she let herself be married
once she had seen the stalwart sea god as Love's slave,
shaken, not stirred, by Aphrodite's frenzy.
Ancestral Ocean, who commands the rivers, fell
in love with Tethys and enjoyed a water wedding.
Put up with it, like Tethys. Then there's Galatea:
descended from a great sea, not a little spring,
she longs for Polyphemus and his singing.
Sea-deep, she has a dry-land spouse, and charmed by his
sweet pipes she keeps commuting from the sea to land.
Springs know my arrow too, and I will not instruct you
in watery desire. You've heard the story
of Arethusa, spring fatale from Syracuse,
and of her fluid love; you've heard of Alpheus,
who hugs that nymph with liquid hands in their damp bed.
You are descended from a spring, so why enjoy
The company of Artemis? She wasn't born
from water, Aphrodite was! Callirhoë
should hear this, so should Drosera: don't hide it!
It's Aphrodite you should please, since she herself—
although she nurtures all the loves—submits to Love.
Desire stings. Take it in. And I will summon you
to love, to join a water-dwelling family
as Aphrodite's sister.'
Drawing back his bow,
he shot three arrows; in that bridal bedroom,
beautifully be-watered, Love united
the arable earth's sons with these three naiads,
and sowed the seed of Tyre's own god-begotten folk."

That was the story Heracles the chief of heaven
told Dionysus as they had their pleasant chat.
The wine god relished it, and gave a golden bowl
for mixing wine (crafted in heaven) to Heracles,
who fitted Dionysus with a starry coat.

Goodbye, Tyre's guardian, with spangled mantle blue;
Bacchus is off to fresh Assyrian fields and regions new.

Book 41

Diane Arnson Svarlien

Here, you shall see, in the forty-first book, Aphrodite the golden
bears a new Cypris to Myrrha's son: she is called Amymonê.

Once he had planted his vine—overseen by the Lebanese cliffscape—
late-summer's luminous fruit—he then bestowed intoxication
all through the wine-growing lands, throughout every arable valley.

Then he laid eyes on the site of the Paphian goddess's wedding:
sheathing the deep-shaded grove in newly-sprung shoots of the grapevine,
he made a gift of this bower to Adonis and fair Cytherea.

Graces danced in attendance. From the exuberant thicket
high-flying ivy, girt all around with green tendrils of grapevine,
making a vigorous leap, ascended, encircling the cypress.

Muses of Lebanon, now, on the neighboring shore of Beroë
bringer of laws, give voice to the hymn of divine Amymonê.
Tell of the war between Zeus of the Ocean and well-hymned Lyaeus:
Ares staged on the waves! Rampaging through vineyards, Enyo!

There is a city, Beirut: the keel of existence, Loves' harbor.
Sea-swept, islanded, green-spaced: this is no ridge, with an isthmus
narrow and long, a neck rising out of the rough, salty water,
lashed on both sides by the waves of the twofold oceans that flank it—

No! This city, beneath the deep-wooded ridge of the blazing
East Wind, stretches alongside Assyrian Lebanon, channels
whistling breezes that make life bearable, bringing the people
cool, fragrant air when the winds come and shake the cypress's branches.

Here is the home of farmers, where often, alongside the brambles,
Deo, with sickle in hand, would meet the god Pan making music.
There, with his neck to the plough-tree, the husbandman scattered his seed corn,
flinging it out behind him, into the freshly-cut furrow;
halting his team of bulls, he would pause, hunched over, alongside
wooded pastureland, there to speak with a shepherd, his neighbor.

There, on the other side, by the sea, stands the city: she stretches,
offers her breast to Poseidon; her liquid husband extends his
watery arm, enfolding the teeming neck of his sweetheart,
sending seawater kisses to reach the lips of his young bride.
She, in her welcoming bosom, accustomed to gifts from Poseidon,
gathers the presents he scoops from the deep: all the flocks of the ocean,
fishes, many-hued gifts for his bride, adorning her table,
fishes that twitch on the undersea table of Nereus, there where,
on the northern bank, the deep waves wash the long channel.

At the southern neck of this land that delights the affections,
by the southernmost ridge, there are sandy paths leading out to
Sidon, land of multiform trees, growing amply in orchards,
grapes with long, flowing tresses, and there, beneath shady branches
lies an unmistakable road, stretching out for all travelers.

Slanting waves of the sea strike hard on the dark western coastline;
Zephyrus, sure on his mount, heels fluttering, makes for his western
haunts, and the Libyan coastline is brushed by his dew-laden whistling,
there where, alongside the sea, a flowering place, filled with gardens,
flourishes: trees form a welcome canopy; breezes make music,
rattle the thriving leaves as the forest inhales and exhales.
There the shepherd—the fisherman's elderly neighbor—made music.

Here dwelt a race just as ancient as early-born Dawn; fruitful Nature
acting alone, unwed, begat them without copulation;
Nature (herself unbirthed; she has no father or mother),
when the atoms were mixing together with four types of bonding,
brought them forth, blending water with air's fiery breath; seedless childbed
gave them shape—an intelligent race, engendered in fertile
clay, and given the gift of life: inhaling, exhaling.

Nature gave to this race perfect form. Unlike primitive Cecrops
they did not bear a freakish stamp: half a man, half a serpent,
Cecrops scraped the earth—reptilian, feet shooting poison,
crawling—a dragon below, and from the waist up his appearance
manly, but bizarre and imperfect, a twin-natured monster.
Nor did they bear the wild stamp of Erechtheus, born from a furrow
when Hephaestus sowed the earth with his conjugal dewfall.

This race, first to appear, autochthonous—rooted in home soil—
looked like gods, this first, gleaming crop of mankind—they were golden.
Here they dwelt in Beirut, the original, first-founded city,
seat established by Cronus, when he, at the bidding of clever
Rhea, introduced to his ravenous gullet a jagged
banquet: one great stone played the part of a midwife, propelling
by its impressive weight, the child-crammed mass of his offspring;
gaping wide, he sucked up the stream of a river: a cloudburst
in one gulp—the water would help with the birth pangs that roiled his
chest full of turbulence—thus he relieved the strain of his swollen
belly. One by one, his pregnant gullet eructed
twice-born sons; his mouth played the part of the channel of childbirth.

Zeus was young then; truth be told, still a baby. In those days
lightning strikes did not yet split the hot clouds with their dancing
flashes, bursting in spates; not yet did the thunderbolts fly from
Zeus' helping hand in the thick of the war with the Titans,
nor did the bellowing heavens resound with a raucous explosion,
rain cascading in sheets as the clouds massed, roaring and squalling.

Long before this came Beroë—Beirut, our city. The first-born,
Time himself, her coeval, together with Earth, gazed upon her.
Tarsus (delight of mankind) did not exist then, nor did Thebes,
nor did Sardis (as old as the Sun), where the opulent mudbanks
sparkle beside the Pactolus, the river whose backwash is golden.
Then, the race of mankind did not yet exist, nor did any
city in Achaea; Arcadia, even—that region
older than the moon, did not yet exist. For Beroë
grew all alone; she was older than Phaëthon, source of Selene's
gleam; she preceded all lands, and to her all-mothering bosom
she gathered light: the Sun's bright beam, newly created;
the just-perfected glow gracing unsleeping Selene.
She, Beirut, was the first to shake off the cone of the misty
darkness, to tear from her face the shadowing veil of chaos.

She was the first, in her welcoming port, to receive Aphrodite—
long before Cyprus!—newly birthed from the sea, and Beroë
greeted the goddess, preceding the Isthmian city of Corinth.
This came to pass when the pregnant wave brought forth Aphrodite,
ocean-born, from the furrow where Uranus sowed with his virile
fluid the water's current; there was no rite of marriage;
this procreation, complete in itself, gave shape to a daughter
fashioned of foam, and Nature herself was the midwife presiding.
With the goddess arose her embroidered girdle, encircling,
like a garland, her hips—a spontaneous sash for our lady.

She, the divine one, in search of a beach that was noiseless, went swimming
past Paphos and past Byblos; she avoided the breakers
along the shore of Colias; speedily circling,
even from Cythera's town the goddess stayed at a distance.
She used clusters of seaweed to give her body a rubdown
till her skin glowed purple. She rowed with her hands through the waveless
deep; she clove the water that birthed her godhead; in silence,
swimming, her breasts arrayed on the ocean's surface, she paddled,
made her mark on the brine with each stroke of her foot, staying buoyant
through the calm, as the gentle waters parted around her,
keeping both feet in motion, creating a wake with her kicking,

she emerged at Beirut. The Cypriots claim that the goddess
made first landfall there, and they point to her footprints. They're liars.

First was Beroë. She was the one who gave welcome to Cypris,
at whose approach the harbor was crowned with self-burgeoning meadows;
seaweed erupted as grass, and bloomed here and there. In the sandy
bay, the beaches were crimsoned with clusters of blossoming roses;
the foam-flecked stone, pregnant with fragrant wine, on her rocky
bosom furrowed by surf, gave birth to a bright purple offspring.
Milky streams burbled forth, a dewfall of white, overshaded
by the gushing flow of the winepress; fragrant effusions
whirled up into the air a cloud of spontaneous perfume,
making the breezes drunk. Then, at her approach to the harbor,
once she appeared, she gave birth to furious Eros, the primal,
first-sowing source of all generation, the chariot driver
holding the reins of cosmic harmony, the life-giver.
He, the swift-footed boy, was able to hasten the birth pangs
of that womb that had known no midwife; he kicked with his feet then,
bringing about his male birth; he battered the sealed enclosure
of his mother's body—she who had not known a bridegroom.
Even before he was born, he was fiery. Flipping his light wings
he made an acrobat's move, pushing open the portals of childbirth.
Then, right away, restless Eros sought out the embrace of his mother,
leaping onto her shining arm, going after her upright
breasts, and reclining there in her bosom, sustenance-giving
nurturing mammaries! His desire for food was instinctive,
self-taught. He latched on to the tip of her untested nipple
and, insatiable, drained every drop of the milk in his mother's
swollen breasts, that were full to bursting with life-giving liquid.

Taproot of life, Beirut: O nurse of civilization,
boast of rulers, the Firstborn, Time himself her twin brother,
agemate of the cosmos, seat of Hermes, where Justice
strides the land, O city of laws, where Happiness sojourns,
dwelling place of the Paphian goddess, home of Erotes,
charming precinct of Bacchus, place of the Archeress, jewel
of nereids, abode of Zeus, courtyard of Ares,

Orchomenus of the Graces, star of the Lebanese landscape,
as ancient as Tethys; a running partner of Ocean,
who, in his watery bedroom, planted the seed of his daughter,
mingled in liquidy wedlock with Tethys; she brought forth Beroë,
whom they called "Amymonê" when she was born under the sea waves.

There is another story, though, a more recent one: some say
Cytherea herself, who pilots all human existence,
conceived her all-white offspring with Assyrian Adonis.
Nine times Selene ran her course; bearing her burden,
the goddess waited; arriving in anticipation
came the swift-footed god; he held a tablet, in Latin—
herald of things to come!—Hermes was there as assistant
to Cypris' birth pangs, and Themis was her Eileithyia;
she unfolded the veil, and lightened the pain—the sharp arrow
piercing the mother—as the fully ripe birth made its progress
through the swollen womb and the narrow passage, emerging
there where Themis held the laws of Solon, while Cypris,
feeling the press, leaned back in the arms of the birth-aiding goddess,
and there she bore her child, a wise daughter, upon that
ancient Athenian tome, just as Spartan mothers deliver
their sons on round oxhide shields. From her female belly
she ejected her newborn babe—with a masculine midwife:
Hermes, the Judge, son of Maia. Thus the child came to the light.

The girl was washed by four winds, the ones that go riding
through the world's cities, filling the world with the laws of Beroë.
While the child was still being born, the Ocean announced her
laws—their first proclaimer!—and provided the natal
bath; he poured his waters around the loins of the cosmos,
circling the world with a liquid belt that flows on forever.

Time himself, the coeval of Ocean, extended his wizened
hands, and swaddled the newborn girl in the vestments of Justice—
prophet of things to come, he'd be free of the burden of aging—
just like a snake, who shakes off the coil of his old, useless squamae—
he would again be young, when he'd bathed in the laws' cleansing waters.

Arm in arm, the four Seasons joined their musical voices,
struck up a song for the marvelous child of divine Aphrodite.

When the wild beasts learned of the Paphian goddess's childbirth,
Bacchic abandon possessed them. Softly and gently, a lion
planted a playful kiss on the neck of a bull, with a friendly
mooing kind of sound, through pursed lips. And the horse,
with his pounding
hooves, went galloping over the resonant plain, with a rhythm
fit for a birthday hymn. The dappled panther then gamboled,
making a vigorous leap with his paws, and played tag with the rabbit.
The wolf, from his jocular throat, howled joyfully, kissing
the sheep with harmless jaws. Meanwhile, deep in the thicket,
the hunting dog, stung by a sweet new impulsion, abandoned
his quest for deer, and capered, a rival in rhythm
with the wild boar, his fellow dancer. Then, standing upright
on her hind legs, the bear embraced the heifer by wrapping
paws round her neck in a nonlethal clasp, an innocuous bond.
Bobbing her playful, round head up and down, the calf gamboled over,
licked the lioness' body, and sent forth an inchoate
lowing from her young throat; the elephant's affable ivory
tusks were touched by the snake, and the trees spoke!
Lover of laughter,
Aphrodite looked on with a gentle expression, and chuckled
as she always does, to see the wild beasts so delighted,
playing their games for her birth celebration. Joyfully gazing
on all, letting her eyes range in every direction, her glance fell
on all alike, except the wild boars; she did not want
to see them in their merriment: she was a prophet
and knew that sharp-toothed Ares, in the shape of a wild boar,
shooting a death-dealing venom, would weave doom for Adonis,
crazed by jealous rage.
Astraea, the nurse of the cosmos,
virgin who nurtured the Generation of Gold, held her arms out,
took the tiny laughing baby girl from her mother—
even then she was babbling precepts of law, as she suckled
Astraea's learnèd breast, from which flowed, intermingled

with her virginal milk, jurisprudence, to moisten the babe's lips.
Into the young child's mouth she poured the sweet Attic honey,
the bee's intricate labor, sugary progeny, born in
myriad indentations, eloquent honeycomb, which she
mixed in her wise cup. If the girl ever said she was thirsty,
she offered her the articulate water of Pytho,
water kept under special guard and reserved for Apollo.
Or, she would give her a drink from the streams of Ilissus, inspired
by the Athenian Muse, when Pierian breezes of Phoebus
rustle its banks. For her delicate baths, the Paphian's handmaids,
dancers of Orchomenus, drew the intelligent waters
from the spring of the horse hoof, which the nine Muses cherish.
From the sky she drew starry Spica, twisting a golden
necklace for the girl.

And so she flourished, Beroë,
hunting with her running partner, the Archeress, hoisting
her hunter-father's nets. She looked just like her mother
the Paphian, and her feet were dazzling—Thetis,
bobbing up out of the waves, a dancer, her snowy feet flashing,
gazed on a second Thetis, silvery-footed. She shrank back
mortified, fearing again the comments of Cassiopeia.
Zeus, when he looked upon her—another young girl of Phoenicia!—
felt his heart leap once again, and wanted to change his appearance;
he would have taken the form of a bull, and carried Love's burden
over the sea as he plied his path, barely skimming the surface,
keeping the woman aloft on his back, untouched by the salt waves,
but his memory stopped him: his Sidonian wedding
crowned with bull's horns; and a jealous throat bellowed down from the heavens
an astral tune. It was the bridegroom of Europa,
Bull of Olympus, objecting, lest there be in the night sky
a second starry bull, icon of seafaring Eros.
So Zeus refrained, and left Beroë for his brother—
she had watery wedlock in store for her, with Poseidon;
Zeus was unwilling to fight with the Earthshaker over a mortal.

Such was Beroë, the Graces' sapling. If ever she sent forth
her honeyed voice, the bees' envy, sweet-spoken Persuasion
perched, insatiable, there on her lips, impelling the wisest
minds, the most resistant to charm, with her spur. And the glances
shot by her laughing eyes, shafts of Eros, with their dazzling
grace, outshone all the girls of Assyria, all of her agemates,
just as Selene, shooting her cloudless beams, when she's shining
at her fullest, will hide every star in the sky. So empurpled
with healthy glow were the legs of Beroë, their rosy
hue shone through the white robes that fell to her ankles. No wonder
she had more than her share, for her age, of beauty: both parents'
radiant looks were sparkling in her face; she was gorgeous.

Then Aphrodite, pregnant with prophetic prediction,
gravid with foreknowing voice, unleashed her keen aspiration,
sent her swift mind whirling and galloping, wandering freely
through every land; she surveyed the radiant groundwork
of ancient cities: Mycene, girt round with a garland
of walls, the construction of Cyclopes, named for the lovely
nymph Mycene, whose eyes were spirited; and, on the southern
Nile, the city of Thebes, which was named for primeval Thebê.
Cypris had the desire to inscribe a new city, and name it
after Beroë, impelled by her own, equal passion for cities.
Thinking of Solon's laws in their orderly columns, those guardians
warding off harm, Cypris cast a sideways glance to the city
of Athens with its broad streets. She envied her sister,
the Judge. Donning her sandals, traversing the vault of the heavens,
whistling like an arrow, she sped to Harmonia's dwelling,
Mother of All Things; the nymph had a house that resembled the cosmos,
self-formed, in four quadrants; four gates shielded that fortress
from the four winds, and around that circular home (little model
of the universe) there were handmaids, duly positioned.
The servant Oriens guarded the gate of the East Wind;
Occidens, the nurse of Selene, guarded the western
gate of Zephyrus; and the fiery bolt of the south gate
was held by Mesembrias. Arctus the Bear was the keeper
of the North Wind's gate, snow-beaten and hammered by hailstones.

Charis, fellow traveler of foam-born Cypris, went running
on ahead to that place, and she knocked on the dawn-gate of Eurus.
Astynomeia, at her post inside, when the saffron
eastern portal resounded, ran to see, and beheld there
Cypris, standing by the entranceway. She reversed course,
followed her footsteps back, to bring advance word to her mistress,
who was plying Athena's loom, the workshop of marvels,
back and forth with her shuttle, weaving a robe: she depicted
Gaea, earth, in the center, the navel. Then, around Gaea,
she wove the sky, circling around and imprinted with starlight;
she wove the rivers, too, each green image with bull's horns
on a human brow. On the outermost edge of the garment
Ocean flowed all around, the rim of the cosmos.

The servant approached the female loom of her mistress
to tell her that Aphrodite was standing and waiting
outside the gate. When Harmonia heard this announcement
she let go of the threads of the garment, abandoned her shuttle—
implement divine, cast down by her loom-working fingers.
Swiftly she wrapped herself in a snow-white robe; she was shining
more brightly than gold, and she took her place, as accustomed,
in her throne, to await Cytherea. Then, at a distance,
Aphrodite approached, and Harmonia leapt up to honor
and welcome the Paphian. Eurynome in her long robes
seated the goddess alongside her mistress. Harmonia noticed
the demeanor and downcast eyes of the Cyprian, hinting
at some grief, and so Harmonia, Nurse of Existence,
addressed her with these words—friendly, sweet, and consoling:

"Taproot of life, Cytherea seed-sower, midwife of being,
hope of all the cosmos, when you give your sign of approval
the unwavering Fates spin the threads that spell out our adventures . . ."

[There is a lacuna here. The text resumes with Aphrodite's reply.]

"Share with me, please, your prophetic voice—as a nurse of all living,
nurturer of immortals, as agemate of the cosmos,

speak to me, I am asking. Can you say for which city
the means of royal speech are reserved and protected,
the unshakeable reins of the Laws that free us from struggles?
I helped Zeus, you see, when the spur of desire impelled him:
he was driven by love for his sister Hera, and wanted
wedlock—this went on for three hundred years!—and I joined them
as man and wife. Zeus, as a worthy exchange for this favor,
fair payment for his bedchamber, nodded approval
with his prophetic brow that to one of the cities
that fell to my lot he'd hand over the precepts of Justice.
I'd like to know now: is it Cyprus? Or Paphos? Or Corinth?
For what land is this gift reserved? Could it be Sparta,
Lycurgus' land? Or could it be the land of Beroë,
land of good men, my own daughter's city? Take heed now of justice,
and bring harmony to the cosmos—you, the preserver
of nature, Harmonia. For, indeed, I was sent here
hurrying to see you, by the Virgin of Starlight,
nurse of law-bringing men. And furthermore, I have been given
this honor by Hermes, the keeper of laws; it is only
I who preserve the men I myself have sown, by upholding
marriage law, using force if I must. In this way I save them."

To this speech the goddess gave an encouraging answer:

"Be of good cheer; do not fear, o mother of Loves. There are seven
oracular tablets in my possession, containing
predictions for the cosmos, and each one is named for
a planet, one of the seven. First is Selene,
in her lovely roundness. And the second, gold, tablet—
Hermes' tablet—is called "The Gleaming One." On it are written
all the Laws' mysteries. Tablet number three is rose-colored
and named after you, for it bears the stamp of your Eastern
Star. The fourth is Helios, the center and navel
of the seven planets. The fifth one is reddish and fiery,
named for Ares. The sixth is called Phaëthon, named for
the son of Cronus' planet. And the name of the seventh
is "The Shining One"—for Cronus, whose course is the highest.

Upon these tablets the elder Ophion has graven,
in bright red letters, pronouncements decreed for the cosmos—
all of them, divinely ordained, multitudinous, varied.
But, since you ask of the Laws which direct men's minds, I will tell you:
this is an honor I reserve for the eldest of cities.
Which is it? Was Arcadia first, or the city of Hera?
Sardis perhaps is older; Tarsus is hymned by the poets
who call her "Protóptolis"; maybe there is another—
I have not learned this. Cronus' tablet answers these questions:
which arose first, which city is the agemate of Eos."

She spoke, and led her to the wall's luminous answers.

Aphrodite she made out (just barely) the passage Ophion
had written, with great art, upon Cronus' tablet
in wine-dark ochre letters, concerning Beroë—
the prediction, late in fulfillment, concerning her country:
"First to appear was Beroë, the agemate of the cosmos,
bearing the name of the nymph born later; immigrant people,
sons of the Ausonians, Rome's supreme shining beacons,
will call her Beirut, since she is Lebanon's neighbor."

Such was the oracular tale that she learned. When the goddess
had studied fully the seventh tablet's beginning,
she spied, there on the opposite wall, the second great tablet,
where the various intricate works of artistry's brilliance
were inscribed for every craft, in prophetic pronouncements:
how Pan would be the first to discover the syrinx;
the lyre's inventor would be Heliconian Hermes;
luxury-loving Hyagnis would find, on the perforate aulos,
the double melody. Orpheus would be the maker
of divine streams of music and mystical dancing;
Linus, son of Apollo, would discover the epic;
and Arcas the wanderer would account for the twelve months'
measures, and the path of the Sun, whose chariot brings forth
the cycle of years; and wise Endymion, crooking
his fingers with skill, would know recurrent Selene's

three changing phases; Cadmus would bring together the vowels,
join them with consonants, and teach the world eloquent speaking;
Solon would be the inventor of impeccable statutes;
Cecrops would find the way to form indissoluble unions,
lawfully joining pairs by the light of the pine torch of Athens.

The Paphian, when she had surveyed all the Muse's
intricate future adventures, studied fully the many
deeds of the widespread cities. She beheld on the central
orb of the cosmos' tablet a wise utterance, written
in verses inspired by the Muses of Hellas, declaring:

"When Augustus holds the whole world's reins, and its scepter,
Zeus of Ausonia will give divine Rome power to govern;
to Beroë he will hand the reins of the laws, when,
girded by shield-bearing ships, she has lulled to its end Cleopatra's
sea-battling tumult. Before that day, violence will be persistent;
city-sacking aggression will beset city-saving
peace, until Beirut, the nurse of gentler living,
dispenses justice on land and upon the salt ocean,
fortifying towns with a wall that cannot be shaken,
the wall of Law, one city for all the world's cities."

When the goddess had learned the whole of Ophion's prediction
she retraced her steps and went home, positioned her golden
throne beside her son, sat beside him, embraced him, and drew him
onto her lap—her arms were open, her countenance gentle—
balancing the weight of her son on her knees: a beloved,
effortless burden. Kissing the mouth and the eyes of her dear son,
touching the bow with which he charms minds, and caressing the quiver,
feigning pique, she spoke these words of pretended annoyance:

"Hope of all life, who beguiles the foam-born goddess! Cronion
singles out my children for pitiless treatment! Consider:
I fulfilled nine of Selene's cycles, awaiting the piercing
dart of birth pangs, pain of labor; I brought forth a daughter,
and now she, Harmonia, suffers a whole range of hardships,

grievously vexed. But Leto bore a helper for birth pangs,
Artemis Eileithyia, the assistant of women.
Child of my womb, Amymonê's brother, you know already:
my blood was born from the salt wave and the aether. I'm longing
to accomplish a worthy deed: I was born from the heavens;
beside the sea, my mother, I'll establish a heaven
on earth. But now, for your sister's beauty, I ask you:
draw your bow to charm the gods—in particular, one shaft
must strike two at once: both Poseidon and vine-clad Lyaeus,
both of them blessèd gods. In exchange for your toil I shall give you
a worthy gift, suitable wage for your shooting: the golden
nuptial tortoise-shell harp that Harmonia took from Apollo
beside her bridal chamber. I will place it in *your* hands,
souvenir of a future city; then, like Apollo,
you will be both an archer and a musician, a lyrist."

Book 42

Charles-Elizabeth Boyles

This is the forty-second book, in which I sing
Bacchus' tender love and the Earthshaker's longing.

She said it convincingly, and at time's own pace
warm, unattainable Eros shook his wind-lifted feet,
the cloud-dweller carving the air with feathered soles,
bearing a flashing bow, and on his shoulder
the quiver fell into place, full as it was of fire.

And just as

that keen traveler through the cloudless ether,
the shooting star, shakes forth scattered sparks,
bearing a sign of war to an army, or some sailor,
written on the back of the sky with its yoked trail of fire—

so too impetuous Eros shot across the sky,
fanning his wings furiously as he hissed through the air.
Landing on the rocky coast of Assyria,
he notched two flaming darts onto his bowstring
to wound two suitors into one yearning
for the beloved maiden, instilling the same zeal to wed her
into the Grape-Bearer and the Charioteer of the Sea.

Poseidon in a whelming wave left the sea-bordering harbor,
while Dionysus leapt the Tyrian frontier to the Lebanese heights,
and they met face to face. Maron let loose
the sweating leopard from the bristling chariot,
shook off the dust, and with water from the cool stream
washed away the heat that etched the neck of the beast.
There inexorable Eros came close to the girl
in order to strike both gods with two arrows,
driving Bacchus mad to give the girl precious gifts—
the good cheer of life and the oxblood grapes of late summer—
and goading into love the Lord of the Trident
to double love's dowry to the girl by the sea:
Ares' sea-sprayed battles and glimmering meals at the table.
And Eros burned the more into Bacchus, as wine awakened
his mind to Desire, by whose senseless dart younger men
gain the spirit and freedom to be wholly enchanted.
Eros struck Bacchus, the whole arrow penetrated his heart,
and so he was burning, all the more enchanted by sweet persuasion.

Eros stung both of them. A spurious bird
along the heavenly road,
he circled into the howling gale
raised by wingèd sandals,
and he jeered these words:
                                        "If it's by wine
that Dionysus drives men, I drive Bacchus by fire!"

And the vine-clad god, stretching out his gaze,
measured out the nymph's grace and her curling locks,
wonderment giving rise to longing. And as he looked,
his eye became the passageway of desire.

Having secretly turned his gaze on Beroë,
Dionysus entered the forest's sweet enchantment
and went along a little behind the path of the girl,
unable to find surcease in beholding,
and no matter how long he watched her,

he wanted to look so much the more.
Then, mentioning the friendship of Clymenê,
he entreated the first among the stars,
Helios, the Sun—perched on his chariot-board
in the heavens, his horses bridled with bits—
to prolong the sweet light: that slow should come the sunset,
that he should spare the whip to lengthen the day.
And, planting step on deliberate step in Beroë's tracks,
he flitted around her, pretending not to see her.

Meanwhile, the Earthshaker
was stealing away from Lebanon, his footsteps
retiring reluctantly to the slow-churning sea.
His mind was as unsettled as its surface,
his roaring thoughts boiling like the waves.

And, insatiable, in the sweet woods of Lebanon,
Dionysus was forsaken, alone beside the nymph,
Dionysus was forsaken.

Mountain nymphs, tell me,
could he have wished for anything lovelier
than to be alone and see the girl's body
free from the Earthshaker's dark desire?

And so, crawling stealthily, he pressed numberless kisses
on the ground where her foot touched, for wherever
the girl trod the dust was marked by her rosy sandals.
Bacchus gazed at the girl's sweet neck, gazed at her ankles
as she walked, admiring the beauty nature had given her.
Beroë had not dusted her rosy face with rouge:
her cheeks beguiled through no cosmetic trick.
No glancing at the copper mirror's witness for her.
She did not laugh at her mimicked face's unbreathing form
to gauge how beautiful she was, and no technical rule
balanced her hair above her brows,
nor set the stray hairs into a clustered bun.

But to one well and truly girl-crazed,
unkempt good looks goad with sharp pangs:
mussed curls of a tousled head
are all the prettier in their disheveled wandering
around a snowy face.

And when she got thirsty,
stricken down by the Dog Star's fiery breath,
she sought a nearby spring
for her crackling lips. Drawing down her head,
she bent down, and with her hands cupped deeply,
the girl drew her birthright water into her mouth.
Her thirst slaked, she left the creek, and when she left,
Dionysus bent his knee down into the lovely stream.
Hunched over, he cupped his hands as the beloved girl had,
and the water tasted sweeter than free-flowing nectar.
And whenever she noticed him twitching with lust,
the deep-breasted, barefoot girl would call out:

"You drank that sweet water in vain, Dionysus:
not even the whole flow of the Ocean could quench love's thirst
Ask your own father. Europa's bridegroom went through
the same waves and couldn't quench that fire,
but was even worse off in the water.
Look how Alpheus, vagabond servant of water-crossing Eros,
though dragged through wave on rushing wave,
did not escape searing love,
even if he did become a water-soaked traveler."

So saying, she sank into the spring,
the unattached naiad exulting over Lyaeus himself.
And the god, righteously indignant at the Lord of the Sea,
shook with fear and jealousy, because the girl had chosen
water over wine. And Bacchus, in the dull air,
as if he had her there, already convinced, said:

"Maiden, take the nectar! Water, leave my beloved girl!
Flee spring-water carousal, so the dark-haired Water God
doesn't carry your maidenhood into the sea.
He's become girl-crazed and wily. You know about
his love of Thessalian Tyro, and their seafaring wedding.
Watch out for his free-flowing wiles,
so that false-dealer doesn't untie your belt,
adulterous just as Enipeus was!
Oh, I wish I were a flood like the Earthshaker,
and, roaring by the lovestruck stream,
thirsty and unguarded, could take my Lebanese Tyro
into my arms!"

The god spoke, and transforming himself,
he entered the thick shaded woods where the girl was.
Euios was now in all ways like to a hunter.
Unrecognizable, he approached
the untrammeled curl-crowned maiden
in the guise of a young man, and on his face
he wore a steadfast and chaste expression.
He looked first at the peak of a lonely cliff, and then
into the long-branched shadowed trunks of the forest,
and then turned his striving eye through pines and elms,
until he glimpsed with furtive glance the girl nearby,
but avoided turning towards her. For a youth,
simply gazing at the beauty of a girl the same age
is small comfort for what Eros does to him.

He came near to Beroë and wanted to say a word to her,
but he was bound up by fear.

Beloved Wine God, where is your man-slaying
thyrsus? Where your fearful horns? Where the
gleam of earth-fattened, coiling snakes in your loosened hair?
Where the baritone roar of your mouth?

O, a great wonder: Bacchus trembled
before a girl—he who made tremble the race of Giants.
Fearsome Love destroyed the destroyer of the Earthborn,
he who struck down the berserkers of India—
and he feared this one, weak, handsome girl,
he feared a soft-fleshed woman.
In the hills with his beast-taming fennel
he silenced the frightening roar of the lions,
yet now he quivered at the thought of making offers to the lady.
In his despairing mouth, the vagabond word
stretched out on the tip of his tongue, right up to his lips,
shooting from his heart and to his heart creeping back,
bittersweet fear holding him in bashful silence.
He drew breath to speak into the light once and for all,
but when words finally formed upon his lips,
he broke his silence, asking Beroë
these pretended questions:

"Artemis, where is your bow?
Who snatched away your quiver?
Where did you leave it, the chiton you wear so short on your thigh?
Where are your sandals, swifter than the circling breeze?
Where your attendant chorus? Your hunting net? Your sleek hounds?
You aren't equipped to chase the fawn—you don't want
to hunt where Cypris and Adonis sleep together."

He said this with astonishing guile, and the girl smiled
in her heart. Knowing nothing of evil, she wanted
to lift her haughty neck and exult in her youthful grace
since she, a mortal, was being compared to a goddess.
She perceived no trick from mind-boggling Dionysus.
Bacchus was pained all the more, since the girl
in her naiveté, understood nothing of desire,
and he wanted her to see the depths of his distress.
After all, when a girl notices, there is hope for love,
hope that she will return his affections.

When a woman is totally unaware
a man's longing is completely hopeless.

And so day by day, there in the pine woods,
noon and afternoon and in the creeping evening,
Euios lingered, resolved to wait for the girl.
Though a man be fully content, with pleasant dreams
and tuneful song, and a turn in a whirling dance,
for the lonesome, love-crazed man there is no end
to his desire, in spite of what Homer said.

Suffering, Dionysus groaned in silence,
beaten by daemonic whips, eaten alive
by the hidden heart wounds of sleepless Eros.
As when

> a sacred bull runs into the lonesome plain,
> picked out from among the herd of other bulls
> by the stinging gadfly
> in the leafy thicket, its stylets sharpened to a point,
> the animal is stricken in the flank
> by the little pest—
> so badly bitten that up over his back
> again and again he curls his tail,
> and inflamed and hunched-up over the ridge of the hill
> he swipes his sharp horns, striking only thin air—

so too Dionysus, whom Victory so often wreathes,
was driven mad by a hex from little Eros' goad.

Finally, seeking a soothing cure to counter Aphrodite,
he bewailed his love to shaggy-breasted Pan,
displaying Cypris' unsleeping demands
and asking counsel for defense against Eros.
And hearing Bacchus breathe fire over his torment,
hornèd Pan laughed—jaded, but impassioned still,
the lovelorn pitying the lovesick,

and he spoke of Cypris' will, and took comfort in knowing
that another was burned by a spark from Eros' quiver.

"We suffer together, dear Bacchus.
I pity your toil at our common suffering.
So bold Eros was victorious over you too? Well,
Eros emptied his quiver into you and me both.
Still, I'll tell you all about the pitfalls of painful longing.

"Every woman wants more than any man, but ashamed
and lovesick herself, she conceals the arrows of Eros,
and so suffers the more from love's hot spark.
Women conceal in their hearts the arrows of Love,
and so out of necessity, they tell their desires
to one another, and with labor-lightening talk,
they sneak away from the cares of Cypris.
You too, Bacchus, should further your love
with the mimicked blush of false shame.
Assume a solemn appearance, and stand near Beroë
as if by accident. Holding your linen nets, pretend
that you just noticed the rosy girl, and start praising
her beauty. Say that Hera can't measure up,
that the Graces are her inferiors, criticize
both Artemis and Athena, tell Beroë
that she is more beautiful even than Aphrodite.
The girl, eating up your fulsome praise,
will love it, and she'll be set up. She won't care about
all the happiness gold can bring. All she'll want
will be to hear about her delicate rosy form,
her beauty surpassing all the others girls'.
Then seduce her through thoughtful silence,
sending signs with your eyelids, winking at her;
smack your brow with a flat, unsparing hand.
Pretend to be amazed, signal your honesty
with prudent silence, and then go ahead and say
that you fear being close to such a sensible maiden.
But tell me, what can one girl alone do to you?

She's not brandishing a spear, her rosy hand
draws no bow. No, her darting eyes are Eros' spears,
the javelins are in the maiden's roseate cheeks.

"When it comes to tokens of your longing,
do not lay out either Indian gems or pearls
like some girl-crazed fool. For Love to succeed,
your own lovely form is sufficient, your beautiful
body is what women desire, not gold.
I don't need more evidence than this: what gifts
did Selene accept from silken-haired Endymion?
What gifts of love did Adonis give Cypris?
Orion didn't give silver to the early-born Dawn;
Cephalus didn't give her delightful riches. Only lonesome,
lame Hephaestus, because of his less than enchanting looks
sent sparkling gifts, and still couldn't win over Athena,
in spite of his midwifing ax. No, he lost the goddess
he desired.

"If you want, there's a much stronger spell
for weddings that I can teach you. Pluck
the strings of the lyre, consecrated to your Rhea, with your hand,
that delicate adornment by Cypris' wine-cup.
Let your song pour out in harmony with the lyre.
Daphne hymn first, and the course of unsteady Echo,
the responsive din of that unsilent goddess,
both of whom abhorred the gods' passions.
But also hymn Pitys herself, who hated marriage, and who flew
like the mountain breeze from Pan's luckless, lawless wooing—
sing her fated disappearance into the ground—blame Earth herself—
and right away she'll weep at the pangs of the nymph,
pitying her fate. Keep your glee quiet
when you see the girl's honeyed tears flowing down.
Laughter never did the trick. No, women are more desirable
when they are flushed with wine and start to sigh.
Praise Selene, love-mad for Endymion;
hymn the wedding of Adonis, and even the goddess

Aphrodite, shoeless and road-dusted,
tracking her mountain-roaming betrothed. She will not flee you
when she hears your sweet, erotic elegies.

"And I've said all these things to you, downhearted Bacchus,
but you'd have to teach me the spell for my own Echo."

And with that, he sent away Thyonê's reassured son.
Dionysus, putting on a straight face, asked the maiden
about Adonis, her father, as if he were a dear friend of his,
as another hunter in the hills. She stopped, and he
put a desire-wracked hand to her breast, straightening her sash
almost absently. But when he touched that breast,
the right hand of love-mad Dionysus went numb.
Then, in the foolishness of her youth, the girl asked
the son of Zeus who bore him, who he was.
At Aphrodite's very gates, he found inspiration
in the vine-clad orchard, the nourishing fruits of the earth,
the dewy meadow, and the flickering trees in sight
and, full of guile, as if he were a lonesome farmer,
made up some nonsense:

"I am a farmer from your native Lebanon. If you want,
I'll irrigate your land; I myself will husband your fruits.
I know the ways of the four seasons. When I see
the olives about to ripen, I'd say something like,
'Scorpio rises, bestowing life—the herald
of fruitful furrows! Let's yoke our oxen up to the plough.
The Pleiades are sinking; when will we sow our fields?
The furrows bear fruit when the dew splashes onto the land
dried out by Phaëthon.' When the Heavenly Bear
nears Arcturus, foreseeing cold rains, I'll call out,
'When the land thirsts, Zeus weds her with rain.'
In the morning, when spring first rises, I will cry out,
'Your flowers blossom! When should I pick the lilies and roses?
See how the hyacinth overruns the adjoining myrtle,
how the laughing narcissus overcome the anemones!'

And when I see the harvest grapes arriving, I'll tell you,
'The grapevine has ripened, unpruned and flourishing.
Maiden, Virgo has risen: when do we gather our fruits?
Your grains have ripened and need harvesting—
I'll reap your wheat crop, and instead of to Deo
I'll make offerings to your Cyprus-born mother.'
Take me as a helpful laborer in your garden,
a vine-dresser who'll care for your Foam-born child,
so that I can put in your life-bearing plants,
and know the unripe grapes of your vines,
feeling the fresh buds in my hand.
I know how the apples ripen; I know to plant
the broad-leafed elm so it leans on the cypress;
I'll mate the joyful male palm with the female
and husband pretty saffron—if you want—beside bindweed.
But don't give me gold for my keep; I don't need it.
I'll have two apples as wages, and a bunch of grapes at harvest."

He said all this in vain. The girl didn't reply at all,
didn't understand Bacchus' girl-mad banter.

Dionysus showed her one trick after another,
taking the hunting net from Beroë's hands,
feigning astonishment at her art, shaking it
and whirling it around, as he incessantly questioned her:

"What god made this gear, what divine skill wrought it?
Who made it? I can't believe it—to think that
maddened, jealous Hephaestus wrought this,
a hunting kit for Adonis!"
He said all these things,
trying to enchant the heart of the artless girl.

And once, atop the spread-out leaves of some anemones,
sweetly asleep, he was stricken by a dream of the maiden
clad in a bridal garment.

The image of what a man does
in the day, he sees by night;
the cowherd dreaming drags
a hornèd bull into a field,
nets appear in hunters' dreams,
the sleeping farmer plows the land
and sows the furrows to bear corn; parched
in the midday sun, the man possessed of fiery thirst
wily Hypnos drives to the flowing river.

In just this way Dionysus revisited his travails,
bringing his winged mind to mimetic dreams,
and attended his shadow wedding. But when he woke,
he didn't find the maiden, and wanted to sleep again.
He made up the empty, makeshift bed gracefully,
resting in the leaves of the swiftly decaying poppies.
He complained to the spread of voiceless leaves, imploring
Sleep and Eros and twilight Aphrodite,
begging them for a return to his dream's vision,
longing for even a false share of marriage.
Bacchus slept near the myrtle again and again
but there came no wedded sleep. Instead,
he suffered sweet travail, and by lovestruck care
limb-loosening Dionysus' own limbs were loosened.

Then, going to Beroë's father, the son of Myrrha,
he demonstrated his hunting prowess. Brandishing his thyrsus,
he draped himself in the skins of fresh-slain fawns,
all the while secretly looking at Beroë. She was wary
of the unchecked eye of Dionysus as he stood by,
hiding her flushed cheek in her mantle.
This heightened Bacchus' passion, since Eros' subjects
stare harder at modest women, longing all the more
for a full view of the hidden face.

Once, when her father left the unwed girl alone,
Bacchus was nearby, gazing, and shed his human form,

standing as a god before her. He told her
his lineage and name, about the slaughter of the Indians,
the vine-clad dance, and the outpour of sweet wine
that he discovered for men. Striving for her affection,
he blended his courage with the opposite of modesty,
and fawned over her with this spangled speech:

"Maiden, for your love I have moved out of the heavens.
The caves of your father are better than Olympus.
I love your home more than those airy peaks,
nor do I desire the scepter of my father Zeus
as much as wedding you, Beroë.
Your beauty triumphs over ambrosia,
and your garments breathe out
the fragrant nectar of the heavens.
Maiden, I was astonished to hear that your mother
is Cypris. How did her charmed cestus
leave you unenchanted? How did you alone
have kinship with Eros, and yet not know Love's gadfly?
Of course, you might say that bright-eyed Athena
knows nothing of marriage, since she was born out of wedlock.
But neither she nor Artemis conceived you: you, girl,
are the blood of Cypris—why do you flee Cypris' rites?
You shouldn't shame your mother's line.
If you are truly of graceful Assyrian Adonis' blood,
learn the gentle laws of marriage from your father,
honor the Paphian's embroidered cestus
and beware the wrath of the nuptial Loves
who punish women for passion unrequited.
You know of Syrinx, who dishonored fiery Cythera:
she paid for her arrogance and virginal pride
and became a reedy plant, transformed as she tried
to escape Pan's love—and she still sings Pan's yearning.
Then there's the daughter of Ladon, that honored river—
the nymph who hated her husband's body and became a tree
rustling with wisdom. She fled Phoebus' bed
but wreathed his head with prophecies.

Beware divine anger. Don't let hot Eros smite you
with the weight of his wrath. Be lavish with your girdle,
and wait on Bacchus, companion and bed-mate both.
I myself, taking up the nets of your father Adonis,
will make the bed of my sister Aphrodite.

"What notable gifts could the Earthshaker give you?
Wouldn't he choose saltwater for your wedding present,
and lay out sealskins, breathing deep marine stench,
Poseidon's sea-blankets? Don't take his sealskins.
I will present you with bacchants as handmaids
and satyrs as servants to attend your bridal chambers.
Accept my wedding gift of vine-clad summer.
If you want a fearsome scepter, sole daughter of Adonis,
you'll have my spear, the thyrsus—reject the trident's tooth.
Flee, dear girl, the wicked sound of the unsilenced sea,
flee maddened Poseidon and his ill-intended love!
Once dark-haired Poseidon lay beside Amymonê,
but the girl, coming to bed, became a stream of tears.
He slept by Scylla, and set her up as a stone in the water;
he moved on Asterië, and made her a solitary island;
the virgin Euboia he interred in the sea. He courted
Amymonê, who ended up petrified in his bed.
These are the wedding gifts he will offer you:
a little stream of water, or briny seaweed,
or a conch shell from seabed. As for myself,
standing before you, undone by your beauty,
what gifts shall I give you?
The child of golden Aphrodite has no need for gold.
Should I give you many treasures from Alybe?
A silver arm has no need silver.
Brilliant gifts from light-bringing Eridanus?
Your beauty, your bright light blushing, would shame
the Heliades' treasure; Beroë's neck glitters
with flashing rays of amber that rival Dawn.
The sheen of your skin puts to shame
the most prized marble. I would not send you gemstones

glowing like a lamp—your eyes send me light.
I would not send you a beautiful bouquet
of roses—roses are there in your cheeks."

Bacchus said all this, but the girl had put both her hands
over her ears to keep from hearing it.
She didn't want any more talk of love:
everything to do with wedding was hateful to her.
And so she created hardship and deep dismay
for the love-blighted Loosener. What is more shameless
than Love, when women cut men loose who are
mad about them, or when their modesty
drives them fully mad? The love in a man's heart
is doubled when a woman keeps her distance.

And so Dionysus, whipped by desire's stinging cestus,
withdrew from her, but wracked by bittersweet pangs
he fantasized that he and the loosely girt maiden
wandered together, hunting in the hills.
Then out of the sea,
his wet footprints shaking the thirsting hills,
Poseidon came questing for the maiden,
his dripping feet treading on the dry land.
As he sped along the thriving woodland slopes,
the highest peaks of the mountain trembled under his tread.
He saw Beroë, and from her feet to the top of her head,
he measured her up as she stood there—a godlike girl.
With his steady eyes, he took stock of the girl
mirrored before him, peering through her delicate garments,
taking in her sparkling breasts as if she were naked
while cursing the spangled bands that hid her chest.
Rolling his love-crazed eyes, he looked unguardedly at her face,
at her whole body. Driven to distraction, the Earthshaker,
ruler of the sea, beseeched maritime Cytherea,
and as the maiden stood by the field-dwelling flocks,
he propitiated her with loving words:

"You're the one girl who puts to shame
all the most beautiful women of Hellas;
not Paphos, not even Lesbos can be praised—
not even Cyprus can be called the mother of beautiful children.
I wouldn't sing praise to the women of Naxos,
and you outshine Sparta's birth pangs and children.
No, not Paphos, not even Lesbos, Amymonê's eastern nurse,
which carried off the whole glory of Orchomenus
for one single Grace. Indeed Beroë, younger
than all three, will blossom into the fourth.
Maiden, come away from this land. Your mother,
Aphrodite, daughter of the sea, didn't grow from any soil.
The sea is yours, my endless bride price, greater than any land.
Prepare to challenge Zeus' wife, so all will say
the wife of Cronides and the Earthshaker's
lovely companion rule everywhere. On snowy Olympus
Hera holds the scepter, but Beroë has the might of the sea.
I won't put you in the hands of mad-eyed Bassarids,
I won't send you with a frolicking satyr or silenus.
For your marriage bed, I'll present you with Proteus
as attendant and Glaucus as your minion—
have Nereus and Melicerte, too, if you want.
From the broad border of the ever-flowing world,
I would summon the sounding Ocean as your attendant,
and I'll send you all the rivers at once as a wedding gift.
And if you'd like handmaidens, I'll put you
in the care of the nereids. And even if she refuses, I'll make
Ino, the nurse of Dionysus, your handmaid."

So he spoke. The maiden, unconvinced, was now enraged,
and he left her, pouring forth these vain words into the air:

"Oh, happy son of Myrrha, your family is blessed
with a beautiful daughter. You alone have doubled your honor,
renowned as Beroë's father and bridegroom of the Foamborn!"

The Earthshaker was stricken by the enchanted kyrtle,
and he dedicated many gifts to Adonis and Cytherea,
the bride price of the girl he loved. Wounded by the same arrow,
Dionysus brought out his treasures, all the gold the Ganges' rich vein
could bear for him, but in vain he entreated foamborn Aphrodite.

The Paphian was shaken, afraid of both the girl's suitors.
Seeing that the two of them were equally stricken
with Love's zeal, she called for a martial conflict
for the hand of Beroë—both a battle for a wedding and
a war for love. And then, when the girl was groomed
and dressed in gracious attire, Cypris set up her child
on top of a hill—a graceful prize for the contest—
and to both of them together she spoke, saying:

"I wish that I had been lucky enough to have two daughters.
I could have married one, rightly, to the Earthshaker
and the other to Lyaeus. But since I am not the mother of twins,
the sacred laws of marriage do not permit that one girl
should be yoked to two lovers, redistributed and dealt out.
For one wife alone, let battle-din be the bride-escort, since
not without toil will Beroë be in your bed. To win her hand,
both of you must be willing to conduct a battle,
and whichever is victor will have Beroë without bride price.
Both of you must abide by my dearest oath: I fear for my daughter's
nearby city, since I, that city's patroness, fear
that by Beroë's beauty I may lose Beroë's city.
Make a treaty before the marriage, so that neither
will the Earthshaker, bereft of victory, lay waste to the land
by lashing out with his trident, nor will Dionysus,
angered by Amymonê's marriage, destroy the vine-clad town.
Be gracious after the turmoil. Both of you,
jealous in your single-minded passion,
must agree to a common resolution:
to grace the nymph's fatherland with brighter beauty."

Aphrodite spoke, the suitors assented. Both swore
a firm oath on Cronides and Gaea, on Aether and
the Stygian rapids, and the Moirae were witnesses.
Strife and Turmoil loomed large as the Loves' referees,
and Persuasion, who attends on weddings,
armed both the combatants. And down from Olympus
came all who dwelt there, waiting with Zeus
to watch the fight from Lebanon's rocky cliffs.

But then an ominous portent appeared for lovesick Dionysus.
A hawk was swooping down on a ground-feeding pigeon,
when suddenly an osprey snatched the bird up and flew
off to the sea, clutching its prey lightly in merciful talons.
Seeing this, Dionysus cast off all hope of victory
but still went off to do battle. And his father,
the son of Cronus, looking down from on high,
smiled at the contest between his brother and son.

Book 43

Bethany Christiansen

Look hard at this forty-third book of mine
In which I sing of Water's war with Wine.

Ares, war-monger of epic proportions,
announced the battle:
"Prepare for the fight!
Earthshaker Poseidon vs. Dionysus Satyr King."

Enyo, goddess of war, who inflicted terror at Troy,
and Hymenaeus, marriage god, were there too,
promenading and chanting battle hymns.
The prize: a young woman. She stood silent,
facing a foreign wedding with the violent god
of the surging sea. Her preference was for Dionysus,
just as Deïaneira once favored Heracles
over that fickle bullhorn of a river god.

A spinning mass of clouds whirled overhead,
clearing the sky as the Blue-Maned One shook
his Assyrian trident and bellowed furiously.
Opposite him, Dionysus, draped in vine leaves
hung with clusters of grapes, wielded his thyrsus
as he sat in his mountain-ranging mother's chariot,
ringed by a vine that encircles Bacchus' body

and pulled by a lion whose claws scratched the earth
as he let out a roar from his snarling lips.
An elephant slowly plodded to a nearby spring
planting his tree-trunk legs on its banks and lapping
the rainwater with parched lips until he drained the pool,
driving out the naked and thirsty resident nymph.

Meanwhile the sea god readied himself for war.
nereids, small water deities, jumbled themselves
into straggling battle lines in the offshore shallows.
The seawater, Poseidon's home, is beaten into a frenzy,
the god's trident shattered mountaintop caverns,
shaking distant trees from their rooted foundations
and uprooting all the cedars of Lebanon.
Bacchus' allies, the Thyiades, made a mad dash
at Poseidon's precious, glossy black cattle
who were grazing at the edge of the sea. In a show
of causal cruelty they cornered a bull,
one of them cutting through along his spine,
another shearing the horns from his head.
The beast's belly was skewered on a sharpened stick
and its other side sliced from shoulder to haunch.
Half-dead, he fell, helpless in the dust,
rolling on the ground, eyes wide, as one rager
ripped a hind leg off: another, his forelegs.

Dionysus called five captains for his five contingents.
First came Cilician and his corps; second, one led
by rosy Helicaon with his long mane.
Next came Oenopion, then Staphylos, brothers both.
The fifth was Melantheus, son of a nymph.
These were the leaders of Bacchus' host,
furnished with vine-wrapped arrows.

Bacchus called to his army in a strident voice,
stirring up their hearts with a long-winded speech.

"Fight, Bassarids! Let the horns of war sound a battle cry,
the drums beat in time with the conch-song
Bind up the sea gods with ivy—tie up Proteus' hair,
make him bow to me; teach old Phorcys to tend vineyards,
not beds of seaweed! Drive Nereus out of the sea,
press Palaemon into servitude on my mother's chariot,
goading her lions with a whip!
"No longer will my family
linger in the deep. I will see the brine-soaked army
defeated and draped in fawnskin. Come, nereids,
here with hydriads and Bacchants. Only spare
Thetis and her house, though she comes from the sea.
Give Leucothea shoes, and have Doris carry the torch,
alongside my Bacchants. Have Panopeia throw some snakes
into her hair and get her out of the seaweed.
Let Eidothea rattle that warlike tambourine, whether
she wants to or not. As for Galatea, what's wrong
with her serving Dionysus? She's as passionate as he,
mad like his own mad love, a skilled weaver of robes.
Only let alone Nereus' brood—no handmaidens
from the sea for me, or Beroë might be jealous.

"Let proud Pan, that old hill-climber, unarmed but adorned
with curving horns, strike Poseidon full in the chest
with his prongs, break Triton's backbone with his hooves,
or a great rock, and split the man where his two natures meet!
And let Triton's servant Glaucus attend to Bacchus now,
give a shake to the cymbals tied around his neck.

"You think I fight only for beautiful Beroë?
Not so! I fight too for her hometown, fair Berytus,
that the Earthbreaker not shatter it with his trident.
Though Berytus stands in the sea, Triton
has no special claim to her; for she has ten thousand
vines of mine. May my plants, like the olive trees,
be celebrated as city-sustainers. I will not leave

Berytus to the waves, but wall her off with sharp hills,
cage her with stony dams, make smooth her roads.

"Take heart and fight, my faithful followers!
My fawnskin is red with blood shed by Giants
freshly killed, and the east quivers in fear of me."

When Dionysus finished, Seabluehair mocked him, saying,
"You fled from Lycurgus' poleax, and yet you dare
confront me, great trident-swinger? I am almost ashamed
to face you. Look, Thetis, at reprobate Dionysus,
who scorns the life-giving sea, and bites the hand that feeds.
You don't surprise me, Torchbearer: fire took your mother
when she birthed you, and now you're like fire yourself.

Rise, Tritons—tie the Bacchants up and see if they can swim!
May Silenus' cymbals be swallowed by the sea,
may the satyr, dragged by the wave, float on the flood,
his Euian pipe swept away by roiling waters.
May Bassarids make my bed in underwater halls.
—No, I don't want any satyrs, nor do I draw
Maenads to the depths. I'd rather have the nereids.
As for the Mimallones, let them gulp salty seawater
rather than rivers of sweet red wine.
May the Bassarids, driven by Proteus' pike into the sea,
drift in a death dance between crashing waves.
Into these depths let Ethiopians and Indians be drawn,
the nereid's reward; drag Cassiopeia's daughters
down to become Doris' slaves. Let Oceanus
cast Sirius, dancer of the winepress, from Olympus
and wash Maera's star in its never-ceasing flood.

"Hey, Bacchus—pick a weapon other than the thyrsus,
take off your pretty fawnskin, and get ready.
Zeus' flame was your midwife, wasn't it? So fight!
Let flame be your weapon, fireborn, and a thunderbolt
from your father be your left hand. Throw lightning
at the trident-bearer, and brandish your father's aegis.

"This is no minor contest with little Lycurgus
or damp-rag Deriades, or an unworthy Arabian.
No, your rival is the death-dealing sea, a mighty foe.
Heaven knows that a battle with the sea is deadly,
and Heaven itself shivers in dread of my spear!
Even Phaëthon, in his course across the sky, felt
my spear's jab in that war waged in the stars for Corinth.
The seas rose from their beds and climbed into the sky,
bathing constellations. Maera's dog cooled his heels
in that salt water. Waves lifted like a feather duvet
from the ocean's bed, high over the heavens, while
sea-dolphins and sky-dolphins frolicked through the waves."

Thus the sea god spoke, shaking his trident, stirring
the sea's secret depths, foaming the surf with rage,
bashing the sky with water torrents and frenzied floods.
Taking up their shields, his brine-soaked army readied
themselves beneath the sea. Beside cold Cronion,
Melicertes brandished his spear and yoked the team,
setting the sea king's spear at the chariot's side.
The horses' neighing blended with the lions' roars.

He urged the team on their watery way, the car
speeding along the surface, untouched by the wet.
Triton calls out for battle, his body visible:
he shows off his two kinds of limbs, one set
humanish, one set of a different type, green.
From groin to crown, he bears a man's torso and arms,
but dangling from his loins is a forked fishtail.

Beside their sea manger, Glaucus yoked his team,
sent them galloping with his water-soaked whip
to chase the satyrs. Pan delicately tread water,
his goat's feet dry over the tumultuous ocean
as he skipped and whipped the sea with his staff,
a battle-tune piping from his well-known pipes.
He heard an unexpected echo borne on the wind

so he dashed across the flood, his hill-treading feet
chasing a new sound; in turn, his pipe's tune
was itself chased. Someone destroyed an island cliff
and heaved it at the hydriads. Missing the nereids,
the boulder shook the foundation of Palaemon's hall.

Gliding out of the Isthmian sea of Pallene,
Proteus took up a sealskin, the ocean's breastplate.
The dark-skinned Indi rushed at him,
surrounding him, urged on by Bacchus.
They had curly hair like sheep, and they held on hard
to the polymorph, like ugly jewelry on age-spotted limbs
as the seal-shepherd went through form after form.

Proteus made his arms and legs like warm wax
pressed into a mold, or pulled taffy, always changing,
stretched out only to be doubled back on itself
writhing first into the shape of a spangled leopard, then
slithering into a dendrite form
planted in the earth like a tower swaying in a sandstorm.

On his back he inscribed slick painted scales,
reared up as a dragon, coiled and flexed his muscles.
With a mighty pulse of his tail-tip, he whirled,
threw his head up, mouth gaping wide
he hissed and spat a torrent of poison.
So from one obscure form to the next he blurred his body—
a shaggy lion, a bristling boar, flowing water.
The Indi struggled to grip his volatile flood
as the counterfeit water, which spasmed,
expanded and contracted, slipped between their hands.

Clever old Proteus! He could take on as many shapes
as those of Periclymenus, the one Heracles killed
when he gripped the false bee between finger and thumb.
Sea monsters surrounded the old man as he struck out
for dry land, seals screaming from the shallows.

Old Nereus took up a spear and led his daughters
into the skirmish. Spearpoint flashing, he leapt
at elephants, the cliffs around him tumbled
at the strike of his salt-drenched trident.
Barefoot nereids scream in triumph and rush
forward as a raging horde, eager for combat.
Fleet-foot Ino strides unarmed into the fight
with satyrs, foam flecking her red lips.
Panopeia, terrible to behold, slashes her way
bestride a sea lioness, alight with rage.
Sea nymph Galatea lifts a club, gift from lovelorn
Polyphemus, and bashes a Bacchant's head.
On a great Pilot fish's back rides bold Eido,
cresting the tumult of the waves, undampened, fierce.

As in a circus, when the driver brings her team around
the post, tugging the near horse in, letting the far horse
out on a looser rein, shouting incitement and threats,
she crouches, leans to one side, gives a little whip
when the horse needs it, keeping an eye to the back
at the driver behind—so the nereids, who drove
their fish like race horses to the watery battle.
Not only fish but dolphins too bore the seamaids,
fighting the reins, leaping over one another, eager
to pursue their sea courses, half-visible in the spray.

On Dionysus' side came the mighty Rivers,
with roars of encouragement for their lord;
Oceanus opened that great maw of his and bellowed
while Poseidon's horn rang out the battle-cry.
Ocean's depths boomed with support for the sea god.
The Myrtoan Sea hastened to the Icarian in preparation
and Sardinian Sea rushed toward the Hesperian,
while the swelling Iberian rolled to the Celtic,
the stormy Ionian Sea crashed into the Aegean tides
and the Adriatic climbed into the sky and fell
onto Sicily's feet. Libyan Nereus took up

his conch from Syrtis' waters and blew a mighty note.
From the surge rose one who stood his left foot
on a sea boulder, and with his right broke
a clifftop, hurling it at the head of a maenad.
Mad Melicertes, so like his mother, lunged
with his brine-soaked trident at Dionysus.

Bassarids too marched to battle. One shakes
the filthy tendrils of her hair, armed with rage
for the water conflict, dancing with restless feet.
Another, from the Cabiric cavern of Samothrace,
calls out a primitive Corybantian tune.
Yet another, from Tmolus, rides a young lioness
snakes wreathed through her hair; and unveiled,
a Mimallon bellows, her mouth a cavern
flecked with sea foam, foot outstretched on the slope.
On Mygdonian lions ride the sileni, drops of wine
moistening their mouths, straining against the sea crowd,
brandishing vine-wrapped poles over their lions' necks,
gripping the manes as if they were rough bridles.
One silenus attacked Palaemon with a rock, and forced
relentless Ino back into the waves with his ivy spear.

Trident fought against thyrsus; Sea-spear against ivy-spear.
Defending the sea, foam-speckled Nereus came ashore
to fight mountain-ranging Pan. A landborn Bacchant
chased Poseidon with bloody ivy, to no avail.
Glaucus attacked Dionysus, but Maron his charioteer
threw his thyrsus and drove Glaucus off.
An earth-breaking, sky-scraping elephant
lumbered, his huge unbending limbs stamp,
his trunk upending a shore-bedding seal.
Satyrs in their frenzied dance rely on the strength
of their thick-horned heads, their long tails out straight
as they dash into the fray. Hordes of sileni
charge along; one straddled a bull, his pipe
bleating a simple tune. Another Bacchant

shook her cymbals, hair a chaotic banner in the wind.
She goaded her mount, a wild bear, urging it
against the sea monsters; likewise, a mountain panther
is goaded by a thyrsus into the tumultuous waves.
Locked in madness, one of the Bassarids leapt
over the sea, untouched by water, as if she danced
on Poseidon's crown. She trod the churning sea,
threatened the silent water, dashed her rod against the foam,
unsinking. More wondrous still, her hair burned in flames
but burnt her not.
On the beach, sad Psamanthe
watched the battle blaze between Dionysus and his foes,
and wretched words sprang from her heart to her lips:

"Ah, Zeus! Aren't you grateful for Thetis and Briareus?
Have you forgotten Aegaeon, the shield of your laws?
Then help us! Save us from mad Bacchus and his brood.
Don't let me see a dead Glaucus, or an enslaved Nereus.
Don't let sobbing Thetis become Bacchus' servant,
or Bromius' slave; she would look on the land
from the ocean depths and lament in a single cry
Achilles, Peleus and Pyrrhus, grandson, spouse, and son.
Take pity on Leucothea in her agony, whose husband
butchered their child with a knife!"
As Psamanthe spoke,
Zeus in heaven heard her prayer. To the Earthshaker
he gave Beroë's hand and calmed the quarrel.
He sent thunderbolts to threaten and surround Dionysus,
pausing the battle for Beroë and the undecided betrothal.
Stinging from love's arrow, the wine god still desired
the beautiful girl; but Father Zeus let sound a trumpet
of thunder, warning Bacchus to stay his hand.
Convinced but still reluctant, Bacchus set off,
stepping slowly, giving a last glance at his beloved.
Jealous tears clouded his vision.
The bridal songs
of Amymonê sounded, and from the sea, pan-pipes sang

that the bridal rites were half complete already.
Nereus, acting as chamberlain to Amymonê,
displayed the bridal bed and waved the wedding torch
that water cannot quench. Phorcys sang, and Glaucus
danced with Melicertes. Galatea swept through a marriage jig,
leapt and capered, twirled and spun, singing the marriage verses,
aptly taught by Polyphemus on his shepherd's pipes.

Poseidon Earthshaker was friendly to Beroë's native land
after his joyful wedding in the sea. In return for his bride,
he gave them the promise of victory in sea-wars.
What a splendid wedding! To the underwater bridechamber
Nereus brought a worthy present, forged by Hephaestus
for the bride: earrings and bracelets and necklace
he brought, made for the nereids with utmost skill;
there in the salty depths he struck his anvil, blew
his ersatz winds into the bellows, stoked the furnace
until it blazed, unquenched. These gifts Nereus brought
in various forms. Then Persian Euphrates came,
gave the girl gifts embroidered by webspinners.
Gold was the gift offered by Iberian Rhine,
while Pactylus brought offerings from his rich mines
(though carefully, since he feared Bacchus his king,
and his neighbor Rhea, who held his land Mygdonia).
Eridanus offered opulent amber from the Heliad trees
that drip wealth; and Seabluehair gave all the metals
of Strymon and the riches of Geudis to Amymonê
as a worthy wedding gift.
When the dances ended,
happy Poseidon went to his watery bridal bed.
But Bacchus' face was grim, and his brother Eros
came to console him.
"Why bear a grudge, dear brother,
against the fates who brought this marriage about?
Beroë was not a proper mate for you, but this
sea marriage was appropriate. I married seaborn
Aphrodite's daughter to a sea-dwelling husband,

after all. And anyway, I kept the sweeter one for you,
Ariadne of the Minos clan, and of your kin.
Let worthless Amymonê stay in the sea, for she
came from the sea to begin with. Go to Phrygia,
leave mountainous Lebanon and Adonis' waters.
That is where all the beautiful women are.
A better woman, not salt-stained, is waiting there,
Aura, from Titan's line. Thrace will receive you
with a victory wreathe and a bridal chamber.
Pallas summons you there, too, and next to her
I will award you the wedding wreath for your strength
when you win that wrestling match of Aphrodite's."

So spoke Eros to broken-hearted Bacchus.
Then he flapped his wings, and like an artificial bird
swept through the skies to the home of Zeus.
Dionysus himself swept from the Assyrian gulf
to Lydia, where rich lime reddens the mud.
He came to Maeonia and offered worthy gifts
to Rhea his mother. Then, departing the rich river
and the Phrygian plain, that land of easy living,
he established his vine on the northern plain
and passed from Asia's villages to Europe's cities.

Book 44

Tessa Cavagnero

And now I weave the forty-fourth, with women running mad
and Pentheus' self-important threats on full display.

Already he had passed Illyria
and the Daulantians, the peak of Pelion, the steppe
of Thessaly—already he had Hellas in his sights.
His troupe assembled on Aonian plains, the trumpet boomed;
the country folk began the rites of Tanagraian Pan.
The Horse-Spring chattered on the spot where Pegasus' hoof
had grazed the earth and hollowed out the source that bears his name.
The nearby waters danced: the river Asopos exhaled
a jet of fire and twirled his currents; Dirce's spring poured forth
its streams in spirals, dancing with her father Ismenus.
And every now and then a hamadryad darted forth,
half-visible among the lofty oaks' abundant leaves,
and harmonizing with the barefoot nymph who guards the spring
she cried aloud, exulting grape-crowned Dionysus' name.

The thunder of the untanned oxhide drums
resounded from the mountain-tops and reached the hostile ears
of Pentheus, a lawless and incorrigible king
who hated Bacchus, Lord of Wine. He armed a warlike band
and called his men to fortify the seven gates of Thebes.
They closed them tightly, locked them one by one. But suddenly

the bars sprung free; the doors swung open of their own accord,
and when the servants strove to set the long bars back in place
they found their efforts foiled by high-blown gusts of wind.
No sentry, once he saw the Bacchants, tried to ward them off;
no serviceman with shield and spear would stand his ground for long
before the old, unarmed sileni. With one joyful voice
the soldiery cried out, cast down its weapons, joined the dance,
and shirked the orders of the raging king. They circled up,
they leapt around and round with well-wrought oxhide shields still on
their arms, the spitting image of the boisterous Corybants,
and meanwhile on the mountains bristling she-bears cried aloud,
beset by mania; the leopard bared his teeth and made
a soaring leap into the air; the playful lion gave
his mate, the lioness, a gentle, unassuming roar.

At once the hall of Pentheus shuddered free
from its till-now secure foundation, shifting on all sides;
the gates flew open and the thresholds shook with earthquake force—
an omen of calamities to come. Athena's shrine
by the Oncaean Gate convulsed as if alive (the shrine
that Cadmus built, where cautiously the mantic heifer's hoof
broke ground, and marked the future site of tower-girded Thebes).
Upon the city-guarding goddess's holy effigy
a sheen of sweat appeared, poured out in drops by heaven's will
to terrify the populace. And Ares' statue, wet
from head to toe with gore, prognosticated future woe.

Throughout the streets of Thebes the panic spread,
and boastful Pentheus' mother trembled, terrified
and nearly mad with dread, remembering a prophecy
of awful things, a dream of butchery she once had had
when Pentheus first seized the crown his grandfather had worn.
A lifelike dream, a phantom, leapt out from the Gate of Horn
whence only honest visions come, and haunted her all night
with drowsy whispers, striking fear into her sleeping mind.
The nightmare showed her son dolled up and dancing in the streets,
adorning his male body with a *peplos*—women's clothes.

His kingly purple mantle lay forsaken on the ground;
his right hand bore no scepter, but the Bacchic pilgrim's wand.
The scene transformed; this time she seemed to see him seated far
above her in a tree whose branches blocked the sun. The top
was lofty, and he sat there unafraid. But round the base
a savage throng of beasts was circling, rushing wildly from all sides
and threatening with jagged fangs and vicious jaws
to tear the tree up by its roots. They shook the great tree's trunk,
and spinning, twisting, tumbling headlong, Pentheus came down.
A heavy thud. Then frenzied she-bears mauled his fallen form;
a lioness, a beast insatiable in madness, ripped
his arm out of its socket. Feral, lunging at his face,
she planted a bloodthirsty foot upon his mangled throat;
with razor claws she tore straight through the neck and snatched the head.
She lifted it, smeared red with blood and pitiably torn,
in one rapacious paw and brandished it in Cadmus' face.
He could not look away. She spoke to him with human voice:

"I am your daughter, scourge of vicious beasts,
Agavê, who bore Pentheus, the luckiest of men.
Accept the vanquished lion's head, the spoils of victory
by which I prove my strength. How massive was the beast I slew—
my sister Ino never killed a monster so immense,
nor Autonoë. Come: this trophy of your dauntless child
Agavê's love is yours. Display it proudly in your hall."

So ended the princess's awful dream.
Then terrified Agavê thrust away the sleep god's wing.
At dawn she summoned forth the mantic son of Chariclo,
Tiresias, for he was learned in the ways of gods.
She told him of her blood-soaked vision. He instructed her
to sacrifice a bull before the altar where men praise
the name of Zeus who wards off ills, beneath the tall fir's shade
where high-peaked Cithaeron spreads out its ridge; and in the copse
where dwell the nymphs called hamadryads, she should kill a ewe.
The offerings, he said, would keep her fears from coming true.
The prophet knew the beasts she'd seen had human souls; he saw

Agavê on the prowl, her prey the child of her own womb,
a filicidal fight, and Pentheus' head—but fear
made him conceal the vision's false-depicted victory
in voiceless silence, lest the king's fierce temper be provoked.
She, loving mother that she was, obeyed the wise old man
and went out to the high-peaked mountain. Cadmus walked in front,
and Pentheus brought up the rear. And at the horned shrine
that stands by Zeus' sacred grove, where mountain trees grow thick,
the son of Agenor ignited fire to please the gods
and offered up a ewe together with a horned bull,
female with male, a single sacrificial rite for Zeus
and hamadryads both. But when the sacred flames were lit
and fragrant smoke went swimming through the air in spirals, sweet
with fat that sizzled on the altar, and the bull's broad neck
was cut, a spurt of bloody dew shot straight up from the throat
to paint Agavê's hands bright red with gore.

[There is a short lacuna in the text here.]

A circling serpent, tame and gentle, wrapped its swollen coils
around the sinewed throat of Cadmus like a necklace, arched
in crooked orbit, winding upward toward his head to form
a twisting turban, and with trailing tail it crowned the king,
and meekly, like a pet, it swept its tongue across his chin
and spat forth friendly venom from its docile open maw.
A female serpent, meanwhile, crowned his wife Harmonia
and garlanded her forehead, twining through her yellow curls.
But Zeus the son of Cronus petrified the pair of snakes
to signify the fates of Cadmus and Harmonia:
how, by the mouth of the Illyrian Sea, where vipers feed,
one day their forms would change to those of serpents carved from stone.
With this new terror following the terror of her dream
Agavê headed home, beside her father and her son.

So went the vision and its aftermath;
recalling this, Agavê, loving mother, shook with dread.

Now rumors flew within the seven gates,
announcing chorus-weaving Dionysus' secret rites
and prompting every citizen to dance. The rustics flocked
to town and garlanded the streets with springtime greenery,
and grapevines growing of their own accord cast pleasant shade,
intoxicating with sweet-smelling fruit the bedchamber
of Semele, still smoky from the bridal thunderbolt.
Surveying Dionysus' varied awe-inspiring deeds
King Pentheus' narcissistic fury reared its head,
and pouring out a heavy-handed stream of empty threats
the haughty Pentheus spat out a lecture to his slaves:

"Escort the girlish Lydian stranger here
to be my slave and serve in Pentheus' dining room,
to pour some other beverage in the goblets meant for wine,
sweet water, milk, or something else. And I will thrash my aunt,
my mother's sister Autonoë, with vindictive blows,
and we will cut off unshorn Dionysus' pretty locks.
So throw the ringing cymbals to the winds, the clattering
of Berecyntian Cybele, and Rhea's Bacchic drums;
bring in the maddened Bassarids, arrest the revelers,
the Bacchae, handmaids always at the side of Bromius,
and hurl them into Theban Ismenus' liquid bed.
As naiads let them mingle with Aonian river nymphs,
or let old Cithaeron receive them, Bacchus' followers
no longer, but companions for the hamadryads there.
Attendants, bring your torches, for by retribution's law
I will deliver Bacchus to the fire from which he came.
As Zeus killed Semele, so too will Dionysus die.
And if he wants to test his strength against my thunderbolts,
then he will learn to fear the fire that earthborn mortals wield,
which burns with hotter sparks than heaven's fire, its opposite.
Today I'll finish him, and clothe the vine-clad god with ash.
And if he shakes his thyrsus violently and calls for war,
then he will learn to fear the spears of earthborn men when I
destroy him—not by wounding him in foot or flank or chest
or stomach, nor by taking up an axe and hacking off

the twin curved horns that grow upon his forehead, like a bull's,
nor slicing cleanly through his neck, but rather, I will pierce
straight through his meaty thigh with my bronze spear, and drag him down
because the liar says he came from mighty Zeus' thigh
and claims that heaven is his home. But he will never reach
the gates of Zeus, for I will send him down to Hades' depths
in death, or drown him in the undertow of Ismenus
though tumbling headlong in his hasty flight he seeks the sea.

"I will not worship him, a mortal man,
a fraud. Like Dionysus, I can lie about my birth:
I do not trace my line from earthly Cadmus; Helios,
my father, king of stars, begat me; sown man Echion
contributed no seed; Agavê did not bear me, but
Selene. I am the child of Cronides, a citizen
of heaven; I dwell in the starry sky—farewell to Thebes!
Athena is my consort, Hebe my immortal wife.
I suckled, after Ares, at Queen Hera's holy breast;
I issued, after Phoebus did, from sacred Leto's womb.
I am engaged to eager Artemis, who does not flee
from me, as once she fled when Phoebus sought her maidenhood,
avoiding incest and the shame of marriage to her twin.
Enough of this—no flames from heaven burned your Semele,
but Cadmus, to protect his daughter's reputation, set
the fire in his own house, and claimed it was the lightning's work,
and called the sparks thrown off by earthly torches thunderbolts."

Thus spoke the king. The soldiers fell in line
and took up arms to fight against the insubstantial winds.
An army of innumerable henchmen filled the woods
and searched among the pine trees for unseen Lyaeus' tracks.
While Pentheus was giving orders to his underlings,
his rival Dionysus waited for concealing night,
and looking toward Olympus, called out to the circling moon:

"O child of Helios, unstinting Moon
of many forms, Selene who steers the silver chariot:

If you are Hecate with many titles, if by night
you wield the ceremonial pine-torch in your fiery hand,
Night-Haunter, Nurse of Puppies, whom the nightly howling hounds
salute with echoes of their whimpering groans, be present now.
If you are Artemis, Deer-Slayer, who hunts zealously
upon the hills with Dionysus, Slaughterer of Fawns,
come, be your brother's helper, for although I am the flesh
and blood of ancient Cadmus, I am driven out of Thebes,
my mother Semele's ancestral land—a mortal man,
an enemy of gods, expels me. Goddess of the night,
defend your Dionysus, persecuted in the night.
And if you are Persephone who wakes the dead, and if
the souls that serve the throne of Tartarus belong to you,
let me see Pentheus in his grave; let Hermes who escorts
the souls to you lay grieving Dionysus' tears to rest;
and with the Tartarean lash of your Tisiphone,
or mad Megaera's whip, make earthborn Pentheus desist
from foolish threats, since Hera, mastermind of wicked plots,
has placed him, like a late-born Titan, squarely in my way.
But you, O Moon, subdue the lawless creature; elevate
the name that Dionysus took from ancient Zagreus.
And you, Lord Zeus, observe the madman's boastful arrogance,
hear, Father, Mother: he disgraces your Lyaeus. Let
the bridal lightning seek revenge on Semele's behalf."

He finished, and the horned Moon replied:

"O Dionysus, comrade to the Moon,
Night-Shining One who tends the vines, your grapes are your concern,
but Bacchic rites concern me too, since Gaea feeds your fruits
with gleaming dew Selene disperses while the world's asleep.
You, Bacchus, with your ivy wand, whose dancing shakes the ground,
see to the grapes, your offspring; have no fear of feeble men,
a race whose minds are always empty, and whose boasts and threats
the whips of the Eumenides stave off with brutal force.
Beside you I will arm myself against your enemies.
For wild insanity is my domain as well as yours;

I am the Bacchic Moon, who whirls the months around the sky
and rules and rouses rage and mania and lunacy.
I will not let this earthly insolence against you stand.
Look: King Lycurgus, he who doubted Dionysus' might
and viciously attacked the maenads, once was swift of knee,
but now he wanders as a blind man, now he needs a guide.
And here and there throughout the Erythraian swamp, among
the clustered reeds, a crowd of Indian cadavers lies,
a monument and witness to your strength. Reluctantly
Hydaspes covers up impetuous Deriades,
his son, who, fleeing, smitten by an ivy-covered spear,
plunged down into his grieving father's melancholy stream.
Tyrsenian pirates, too, learned of your valor, when their ship
transformed: the mast held up by ropes stood on its own and grew
into a living tree wrapped up in vines; the sail fanned out
beneath the shadowed canopy and formed a veil of vines
replete with grapes; the forestays, newly poisoned, hissed with knots
of squirming snakes. Your enemies' appearances were changed:
they left behind their mortal forms, the light drained from their eyes;
as dolphins, lacking human minds, they dove into the sea,
and still they mark the rites of Dionysus in the waves,
and skip across calm seas as gracefully as acrobats.
The corpse of Indian Orontes lies inert beneath
Assyrian waters, felled by your sharp thyrsus' stroke, and still
he dreads the name of Bacchus, even in the river's depths."

Thus spoke the goddess with the gilded reins.
While Bacchus was conspiring with the all-encircling moon,
Persephone was arming her Erinyes. She had heard
the prayers of Dionysus Zagreus, and pitying
her younger brother's situation, rushed to his defense.
And at Cthonian Zeus' signal, the Eumenides
prepared for war against the citadel of Pentheus.
One, leaping from the shadowy abyss of Hades, held
aloft her serpentine Tartarean lash and drew a draft
of water from Cocytus and the River Styx, and strewed
Agavê's house with hellish drops.

[There is a short lacuna in the text here.]

so great the lamentation and prophetic tears for Thebes.
The goddess bore an old Actaean knife from Attica
still stained with blood from Itylus' murder long ago,
which lionhearted Procne used to dice his precious meat
for Tereus' child-devouring feast, when she had slain
her darling son with steel and help from fierce Philomela.
The Fury, carrying that tool of slaughter in her hand
and digging in the dust with wicked claws, concealed the knife
among the roots of the enormous silver firs that grew
upon the mountainside, the haunt of maenads and the place
where Pentheus was doomed to die beheaded. She had scraped
Medusa's blood into a spiral shell when it was fresh,
the Gorgon newly slain, and now she smeared a tree with drops
of Libyan red. And so the mad Erinys worked her spell.

Night-Shining Dionysus crept unseen
into the house of Cadmus, shape transformed into a bull's,
and wielding Pan's insanity-inducing Cronian whip
he visited the wife of Aristaeus, rousing her
to Bacchic mania, and spoke bewitching words to her:

"O Autonoë, happier than Semele!
Your son's new marriage puts you on a level with the gods;
your prayers are answered; Artemis is joined with Actaeon,
a splendid husband, and Selene has wed Endymion.
Your Actaeon still lives. He did not change into a beast;
the spotted stag's long antlers never sprouted from his head;
he did not take a hybrid form, did not distort his shape,
did not look back to see his own dogs on their master's trail.
With idle gossip in their heads and on their evil tongues
the countryfolk made up the story of your son's demise
because of their resentment for the virgin goddess's groom.
The falsehood came from envy: other people's wedding-songs
make women hate the Paphian goddess and her marriage rites.
Awake! and hurry! Hasten with your storm-swift sandaled feet

into the mountains, where you won't be found, and there you'll see
your Actaeon beside Lyaeus, partners in the hunt,
his feet laced up in racing boots, his quiver in his hand,
with shining hunting-nets in tow, and Artemis nearby.
O Autonoë, happier by far than Semele,
because the arrow-pouring goddess has become your child
by marriage; happier than Ino with her handsome sons,
because your son now shares a marriage-bed with Artemis
where haughty Otus and Orion, daring suitors, failed.
Your father Cadmus, young again, rejoices on the hills
beside the bridal chamber; and delighted by the bride,
he shakes his snowy hair out in the gusty mountain air.
Awake! and plan the wedding, midwife, mother of the groom.
This love is fitting; holy Artemis takes as her spouse
no stranger, but she sleeps beside the grandson of her twin.
And one day when the marriage-shunning goddess births a child
and when you rock the Arrow-Pourer's offspring in your arms,
a proud grandmother, show Agavê, make her envy you.
Why shouldn't the Houndmistress wish to bear a son conceived
in wedlock in her bed, a son to hunt and shoot at hares
just like Cyrene, who hunted on the cliffs, or Actaeon,
a son to ride the chariot pulled by his mother's deer?"

Book 45

Anna Mayersohn

Look also to the forty-fifth book,
where Pentheus binds the bull fast,
instead of the strong-horned Lyaeus.

Bromius spoke, and the nymph ran out of the house,
Possessed with a mad delight, to see
The bridegroom Actaeon sitting beside Artemis of the pouring arrows;
And as she rushed to the mountain on staggering feet,
Raving Agavê, without her headband,
Ran right alongside her, running with the breezes,
And as the pangs of the Cronian whip scourged her mind
She let thoughtless words rush from her raging lips:

"I am armed against worthless Pentheus, so that he may learn
That Cadmus fathered a brave Amazon, Agavê.
I too am full of manly might. If I should so wish,
I would wholly subdue Pentheus with my bare hands
And smite his well-armed soldiers
Without a weapon of my own to hold. I have my thyrsus;
I do not need a spear of ash, I brandish no shaft;
I hit the spear-wielding man with my vine-covered lance.
Though I wear none myself, I will overpower the man
Who wears a good breastplate.

Shaking the cymbals and striking my oxhide drum on both sides,
I glorify the son of Zeus, and I do not honor Pentheus.
Give me the Lydian tambourines! Why do you delay, time of frenzy?
I will go to the peaks, where the maenads, where women, peers,
Become hunters alongside the hunter Lyaeus.
I am jealous, Dionysus, of lion-killing Cyrene.
Spare Bromius for me, oh you who fight against the gods,
Spare him, Pentheus! I am inexorable.
I will come to the mountain peaks, so that I myself,
Singing of Evius, may twirl and beat my feet upon the ground.
No more do I reject the rites of Bacchus of the grapes,
No more do I hate the dance of the Bassarids.
Rather, I fear Dionysus, whom an immortal marriage bed begot,
Whom the thunderbolts of Zeus, ruler on high, anointed.
I will be swift of foot, a companion to the goddess of pouring arrows,
Bearing her nets, and not the spindles of Athena."

She spoke, and off she flew, a new prancing Mimallon,
Shouting "Evoe!" and following the leaping steps of the dance
Of the winepress, crying out to Bacchus and singing of Thyonê.
And she also called out to Semele, wife of highest Zeus,
And sang of the blaze of the bright nuptial lightning.

And there was much dancing in the mountains:
All around, the rocks resounded, and varied sounds
Rushed around the land of seven-gated Thebes.
Deep-sounding Cithaeron echoed with the harmonious cries
Of the dancers. The sea sounded with a dewy roar.
You could see trees reveling, hear crags calling.
A maiden ran dancing from her bedroom
When the pipe of horn sounded through its holes,
And the striking of the untanned oxhide, sounding all around,
Drove the girls into a frenzy, drove them all alone
From their well-wrought halls toward the high-peaked mountain.
Another girl, goaded to madness, her hair loose,
Darted on stormy sandals from her maiden chambers,

Leaving behind the shuttle and Athena, goddess of the loom,
And casting aside the disheveled veil from her hair,
She mixed with the Bassarids, and an Aonian became a Bacchant.

Tiresias had set up an altar to Dionysus who wards off evil
And was sacrificing, so that he might curb the hubris of Pentheus
And diffuse the implacable anger of Lyaeus.
But he sacrificed in vain, for the thread of Fate had arrived.
The prudent seer also summoned Semele's father,
So that they might partake in the dance of Dionysus.
Old Cadmus danced with heavy feet,
Having crowned his snow-white hair with Aonian ivy.
Beside him, Tiresias, twirling his sluggish foot,
Striking up a jovial Phrygian dance for Mygdonian Dionysus,
Went as Cadmus' partner as he rushed into the dance
And he propped his aged arm up on a god-fearing wand of fennel.
Looking askance at the old companions Tiresias and Cadmus,
Arrogant Pentheus shouted:

"Why do you rage so madly, Cadmus?
For which god do you stir up this revelry?
Remove the ivy from your polluted hair, put down the fennel wand
Of Dionysus, who drives the mind off course.
Pick up the sober bronze of Athena Oncaea.
And Tiresias, silly as a child with your garland,
Take those leaves from your hair and throw them to the wind,
That counterfeit crown. Instead of a thyrsus,
Pick up rather the Ismenian laurel of Phoebus Apollo.
I respect your age, I honor your gray hair,
Witness to the immense length of your years and of their own.
If that old age of yours and your locks didn't stop me,
I would have twisted your hands with chains
And sealed you up, bound, in a dark room.
Your thoughts do not elude me. You have a grudge against Pentheus.
You fashion a man into a false god through deceptive divination.
You've accepted gifts from a cozening Lydian man,
Gifts from the renowned golden river.

But you will say, 'Bacchus discovered the fruit of the bacchanal!'
Wine always drags the drunken one to Aphrodite,
Wine stirs the unstable man's mind toward murder.
'But he has the form, the garments of Father Zeus!'
Zeus who rules on high wears golden robes, not a fawnskin,
When he hurls lightning among the blessed. Ares, too,
Fights against men holding a bronze spear;
He doesn't raise a wine-red thyrsus.
Apollo doesn't wear the horns of a bull.
Did a river marry Semele, and as a bride did she give birth
To a horned bastard son for her ox-horned bed-mate?
But you will say, 'Pallas Athena of the gleaming silver eyes
Goes into battle alongside men, holding her native spear and shield.'
Lift you too the aegis of the son of Cronus."

Pentheus spoke, and the wise seer responded:

"Why do you harass Dionysus, whom Zeus who rules on high begot,
Whom his father, the son of Cronus, bore from his pregnant thigh,
Whom Rhea, mother of gods, nourished with her cherishing milk,
Whom previously, half-formed, still smelling of his mother,
Sparks of lightning bathed but did not burn?
He alone is rival to Demeter, bringer of sheaves,
With his summer rich with grapes opposed to her corn.
Rather, beware the anger of Bromius.
If you like, I will tell you, child, a Sicilian tale.

"Some sons of the Tyrsenians were once sailing on the sea—
Killers of strangers, roving sailors, plunderers of wealth,
Snatching flocks of sheep from everywhere along the shore—
And here and there many an old sailor
Was rolled half-dead from the spear-won ship to a watery fate,
While another man, a bulky herder, held his shield in front of his flock
And reddened his grey hair with his blood.
If a trader then sailed on the sea, if ever a Phoenician
Had purple robes from Sidonian waters for sale,
A Tyrsenian pirate would take him unexpectedly upon the sea

And set upon his ships abounding in riches. Many men
Lost immeasurable cargo without compensation
And the Phoenician man was brought as a captive
To Sicilian Arethusa, with no share in the captured wealth
And with his city left behind.
But with a trick Dionysus took on a deceptive appearance
And cheated the Tyrsenians. He put on a false shape
Like a young, pretty boy with a hairless upper lip,
Wearing gold jewelry on his neck; around his head
Was the darting radiance of shining ribbons,
Of inextinguishable ruby and the green surfaces of emerald,
And the Indian stone, the sparkling of the bright sea.
Upon his frame he wore robes more splendid than the cycling
Of the newly-formed Dawn, sprinkled with dye of Tyrian snails.
He stood at the edge of the beach, as if he himself desired
To board the ship. They leapt at Thyonê's splendid wile-weaving son
And carried him off, stripping away his possessions.
The rope ran around Dionysus and bound his hands, drawn back behind him.
Suddenly the young man became huge with wondrous beauty,
Like a man in shape, but horned, and rising as high as Olympus,
Touching the airy clouds above him. Like an army nine thousand strong
He bellowed melodiously through his throat.
The long ropes became trailing serpents,
Changed into the living, winding bodies of snakes.
The forestays were hissing, a horned serpent rose
And ran, its coils trailing, up to the mast's sailyard.
The mast was a towering cypress, shaded by green leaves,
Neighboring the high air. On the tie-beam, high-soaring ivy sprouted up,
bordering the ether, wreathing a spiraling cord around the cypress.
Around the rudder, the Bacchic vine-pole, stooping over the sea,
Grew heavy with the fruit of the vine.
Up from the heavy stern a fountain of drunkenness danced like a Bacchant,
Spouting the wine of Dionysus, sweet to drink.
Climbing over the prow and around all the benches wild beasts spread out;
Bulls bellowed, and a lion roared a grim sound from its throat.
The Tyrsenians cried out, and they raved with madness,

Being spurred into fear. The furrows of water
Gave forth the wave-born flowers of the plant-bearing sea.
Even the rose sprouted, and below it, as if in a garden,
The foaming hollows of the sea turned red,
And the lily, too, shone among the rushing waves.

"As they gazed upon the false meadows, madness struck their power of sight,
And a deep-wooded mountain appeared before them,
And the pasturage of the forest, and a band of country dwellers,
And the flocks of the shepherds, and they thought they perceived
The sound of a clear-voiced herdsman playing a herder's pipe,
And hearing the tune from the shrill pipe with its many holes,
As they sailed aloft in the middle of the endless sea
They thought they saw land. Under the sway of mind-stealing madness
They rushed into the deep and danced in the stillness of the sea
As ocean-faring dolphins; their appearance had changed
And their humanity gave way to an ichthyic shape.

"You too, child, beware the cunning anger of Lyaeus.
But you will say, 'I am strong of body, I am full of the terrible blood
Of the Giants who created themselves, with teeth as their seeds.'
Then flee from the divine hand of Dionysus, killer of Giants,
Who once, beside the foundation of Tyrsenian Pelorus,
Crushed Alpus, the god-fighting son of Plowland Earth,
As he used crags as weapons and threw hills like spears.
At that time, a traveler, fearing the mad Giant's row of gullets,
Would not approach that rocky peak.
And if someone traveled that forbidden path unawares,
Driving a strong horse with his whip,
The son of Plowland Earth would notice him,
And, entangling the driver and the foal in his wide hands,
He would bury them in his throat. Often an old herder,
Bringing his flocks over the wooded mountain
Toward the pasture at noon, was chopped to pieces.
Nor, at that time, did Pan, servant of the Muses,
Join reeds and make music sitting beside goat pastures or cattle folds;
Nor did Echo, sounding after him, respond

With the sound of the pipe, but, talkative though she was,
And wont to resound with the flute music of never-silent Pan,
Silence shut her up, for the Giant then beset all.
Nor, at that time, was any cowherd there,
Nor did any band of woodcutters bother the young nymphs
As they cut wood for ships, and no wise carpenter
Put together a trading vessel with compact beams,
A wayfaring chariot of the sea, until Bacchus traveled there
And went past that peak, brandishing the Evian thyrsus.
As Lyaeus was passing by, the huge son of Plowland Earth, tall as the clouds,
Beset him, heaving a shield of stone onto his shoulders,
Took a cliff as a javelin, and leapt upon Bacchus,
Holding a nearby tall tree as a spear,
Hurling pine or plane at Dionysus.
He held the pine like a club and lifted an olive tree,
Swinging it like a sword, torn from the ground roots and all.
But when he had emptied the mountain of hilltops to throw far,
And the deep-wooded ridge was stripped of its shady forest,
Bacchus who raves with the thyrsus hurled his missile
To the target with its customary whistling sound
And hit tall Alpus in his broad chin,
And the sharp green Bacchic spear flew into the middle of his throat.
Then the Giant, pierced with the small, sharp thyrsus,
Rolled over, half dead, and fell into the nearby sea,
Filling the whole deep hollow of the sea.
Raising a torrent against the Typhaonian rock,
He inundated the warm surface of his brother's bed,
Cooling his fiery body with a rush of water.
But take care, child, that you don't also see something similar,
Like what the sons of the Tyrsenians saw, like the strong son of Plowland Earth."

He spoke and did not persuade.
Then, rushing together with Cadmus, he went fearlessly in his sandals
Towards the high-peaked mountain to reach the dance.
But Pentheus with his flashing helmet, lifting his shield,
Cried out to his iron-wielding warriors:

"My servants, go into the city and the middle of the woods
And bring me this feeble vagabond, weighed down with chains,
So that he may be struck with Pentheus' whips of retribution
And no longer beguile women with drugged drinks,
But he will bend his knee. And my insane mother herself,
Who loves her son, remove her from the mountains
And the sleepless madness of the dance,
Dragging her by handfuls of her frenzied hair, free of its headband."

Thus Pentheus spoke, and his followers ran on swift feet
To the ridge, rough to walk on, of the towering wood,
Searching for the footprints of Dionysus, wanderer in the mountains.
They just barely spotted Dionysus, who raves with the thyrsus,
Near an isolated rock, and the warriors rushed at him.
They tied leather straps around Bromius' hands
And they meant to throw chains upon unconquerable Dionysus.
He, however, became invisible and rushed away, not to be found,
With his winged sandals. In speechless silence the servants were overcome
By divine force, shrinking in fear from the wrath of the unseen Lyaeus,
And in the form of a shield-bearing warrior
Bacchus took hold of an unyoked bull,
Grasping it by the horn with his hand,
As if he were a servant of Pentheus warding off Dionysus
In a horned disguise, and, putting on an angry face, came near mad Pentheus.
Somberly he mocked the manly boasts of the mad king sitting there
And shouted a dreadful, deceptive speech:

"This man, O holder of the scepter, drove your Agavê to madness;
This man desires the royal throne of Pentheus.
Seize the horned one, the wily vagabond Bacchus,
And with unbreakable bonds bind him who pursues your throne,
And beware the head of ox-horned Dionysus
Lest he take you and stab you with his long-pointed horn."

Thus Bromius spoke, and Pentheus, battler of the gods,
In the grip of the madness in his mind,
Cried out a threatening speech:

"Bind him, bind this man who would plunder my throne!
He comes here armed against my scepter,
Desiring the throne of Semele and her father Cadmus.
What a noble thing for me to have as a partner in my royal honors
Dionysus, begotten in a secret marriage bed, a bull in the form of a man,
His ox-horned face displaying a false guise,
Him whom Semele perhaps, following Pasiphaë's example,
Bore to a bull, having joined herself to a horned grazer as bedfellows!"

He spoke, and, restraining the feet of the wild bull,
He bound them with unbreakable bonds.
Seizing him instead of Lyaeus, he led him in chains near the horses' trough
Thinking he was imprisoning the son of Semele and not some bull.
The captive battle line of Bassarids, bound with knots around their hands,
He sealed up in a dank room—a hollow house of unhappy constraint,
Impossible to escape, so dark it seemed to imitate the Cimmerians' land,
A room where Dawn has no place—he sealed up Bromius' festive servants,
Around whose hands, chafing under constraint, leather straps were bound,
And bronze chains pressed upon their feet.

But when the time came to run in the fast-turning dance,
The maenads cavorted. Like a whirlwind, never standing still,
Each Bacchant pushed off the loosened coils of the unbroken straps,
Twirling with the dancing motions of their feet,
And with their hands they rattled out a free song of Evius
By clapping the rhythm; the strong, heavy bronze bonds on their ankles
Broke apart, split by the whirling of their feet.
Then a godsent radiance surrounded the gloomy building,
Pouring into the dark room of the Bassarids.
The gates of the dark pit unfolded on their own,
And the guards, stunned by the quivering leaps of the Bassarids' feet
And their roaring and the savage foam upon their teeth,
Were driven to flee. The women, meanwhile, escaped
And turned their tracks back whence they came,
To the ridge with its lonely wood.
One hacked a herd of cattle to pieces with her skin-piercing thyrsus
And defiled her hands with blood, tearing the bulls' rough skin

With her nails. Another cut up sturdy flocks of wooly sheep
With a bloody stick, and another killed goats.
They turned themselves red with bloody streams of gore
From the slaughtered flock. Another seized a three-year-old child
From his father and stood him—unafraid, unshaken, unrestrained—
Upon her shoulders, lifting the boy, putting him at the winds' mercy
As he sat there, laughing, not falling in the dust.
The boy begged the Bacchant for milk as if she were his mother,
Pawing at her chest, and the unmarried maiden's breasts
Spontaneously gushed with milky moisture.
Unfolding her wooly tunic for the hungry boy,
She extended her nipple, newly flowing, to his young lips,
And a virgin satiated a child with unusual liquid drops.
Many women hoisted away the babies of a shaggy-chested lioness,
Who had just given birth, and nursed them.
Another, striking the dry earth with her sharp thyrsus,
Smote the top of the mountain, splitting it in two.
Rough rock turned red as it gushed wine all by itself,
Or from smitten stone white fountains of milk
Flowed on their own in streams.
Another woman threw a snake against an oak.
The snake twisted its coils around the tree and became wandering ivy,
Which girded the trunk with its winding, bending curves,
Just like the coils of spiraling serpents.
A satyr, too, went around carrying a beast with its teeth bared,
A menacing tiger lying aloft on his back,
Fierce in disposition, yet not touching its bearer.
An old Silenus, too, dragged a boar by the tip of its chin
And playfully hurled the jagged-toothed pig into the air.
Another with springing, whirlwind-like movements of his feet
Threw himself swiftly onto a camel's bristling back,
And another leapt and flung himself onto a bull's back.

So it went among the crags. But in Thebes, built by the lyre,
Bacchus displayed a variety of wonders to all the citizens.
There, too, women danced in a Bacchic frenzy
With reeling feet and foaming lips. All of Thebes trembled,

And the streets spat flaming sparks.
The foundations shook, and the unbending gates of the halls
Bellowed like the throats of cattle. Even the unshaken house roared,
A voice letting loose on its own with a din like a trumpet of stone.

Dionysus did not cease from his anger.
He raged like a bull and from his throat roared his divine voice,
Which wandered through the air to the wheel of the seven-pathed stars.
As he assailed the maddened Pentheus with a torch, his witness,
He filled the whole house with flashing light.
A branching, dancing fire threw light round the walls on all sides
And rained down burning sparks,
And all around the crimson robes on the chest of the purple-clad king
A fiery spiral extended, all without burning his clothing.
Beams ran in distinct flashes,
Jumping hotly from Pentheus' foot to the middle of his back
Over his waist to the top of his back
And traveling around the tendons of his neck.
Often in the dancing motion of the self-moving fire
The wondrous blaze spat unburning sparks onto the fine blankets
Of the bed of the earthborn king.
Seeing the spiraling flames, Pentheus let out a cry
And called upon his slaves to bring water as a remedy
And to quench the fire's flames,
Dousing the house streams to ward off the evil.
Hollow vessels were emptied of water
And the flowing stream dried up, though great,
As countless vessels drew from the river.
Their labor was vain, the water useless.
The fire only increased in the streams of water
And its tongues only became hotter.
Under the roof, there was a sound
Like the ringing bellow of many bulls,
And the house of Pentheus sounded with thunder from deep within.

Book 46

Melina McClure

Here is the forty-sixth, which will provide
Pentheus' high head and Agavê filicide.

And when Pentheus grasped with hand and mind
the chains which slipped from wrists unaided
and saw the maenads free to frolic
swept away to mountain glades and ranges,
he sensed the giddy ploys of a lurking Dionysus.

And he paced and cursed and rage spilled off him
till the god appeared, all gleaming tresses,
loose curls that drip in winding tendril,
ill-wrangled by a circlet of ivy.
And from a throat made hoarse from wrath raves Pentheus:

"I should thank you for sending Tiresias.
I hear none of your words and I have seen past your seer.
For how could Rhea give sweet milk and warmth
to the son of Thyonê but keep
at bay from bosom her own suckling Zeus?
"If lips of stone were free to speak, the cave
on Dicte might tell you, and Corybants corroborate,
where wee Zeus stretched and flushed in boyhood
without once a pearly bead from his mother,

yet plump on the milk of Amalthea.
And you too hold the stamp of treacherous mother,
for Cronides lit lying Semele with bolt torch.
Beware that he not tame you the same.
"Neither do I follow in barbarous blood.
Primordial Ismenus poured me out,
no ripple of coursing Hydaspes.
I know no Deriades, nor answer to Lycurgus.
"So now with your satyrs at hand
and your shuddering, feverish Bacchants, abandon
the river Dirce, dredge up another Orontes
from the vast host of Assyrians,
and slaughter the fresher one with your thyrsus.
You are no Olympian son of Cronion.
For the lightning howls down the guilt
of your mother undone and departed,
and the thunder bears witness to her secret bed.
Rain-bearing Zeus did not consume in flames
Danaë after he came to her as golden rain,
did not submerge Europa in the yawning sea,
sister of my Cadmus, but rather carried her across
steady and unshaken, though trembling with fear.
I know that the celestial flame licked
at babe along with blazing mother
and delivered from this withering birth
a bastard child unfinished, crude, and raw.
But if he was not overcome by searing glow—
since you can inherit no blame from the secret affairs
of your mother in an earthbound bed—
unwillingly I yield to your claims
and call you not child burnt by lightning
but child of lofty, sky-brimming Zeus.
"Reveal to me this with a true word as witness:
Did Zeus mother Phoebus or Ares from his thigh?
If the blood of the god pounds through your heart,
embrace the towering vaults of Olympus,
take your home in heaven, and leave Thebes to Pentheus.

Sprinkle a bit of mind-charm Persuasion
into that sweet, sweet guile,
and chase down a more feasible origin:
perhaps that you crowned from that childbearing temple
already acquainted with the births of gods.
Surely this is not as suspect a tale:
that you followed Athena from Cronides' skull.
  "If only you had an Olympian birth,
if only it were Cronion who'd sown you,
I would yearn to pluck up a godly stalk
and rid the lands of Dionysus, son of Zeus."
And these words crawled beneath the god's skin,
kindling rage, but he buried the prick
of deadly menace in his chest and said:

"Happy is the land of Celts to obey barbarous law,
where the Rhine can smell the strange blood of a bastard child
and, judge of parentage and purity, appraise
babies still sticky from the womb.
  "I am not judged by the whims of a river,
but by far more reliable heralds.
Look up, Pentheus, look no further than the lightning.
Let the Gaul be persuaded by water,
but you by the proof in heat and choke of torch.
I do not need this hut of yours, tethered to the sand;
the home of Dionysus is in his father's heaven!
But tell me, which would you be more likely to choose,
If you were to weigh the earth against sparkling, astral blue?
Seven zones or seven gates? High heaven or earthly Thebes?
No, I do not need this hut of yours, tethered to the sand.
  "Just do not abuse those ripe-month blooms,
over-dripped with deep treacle honey.
Do not profane the drink pulled from the Dionysian vine
and wage no war with Bromius, Indian-killer.
But now, if you are able, face one single woman
from the man-rending order of Bacchants.
It seems that the Fates gave you a fitting name,

prophetic harbingers of your death.
It is no fault that the Pentheus who harbors
the earthborn blood of his forefather
harbors too an imitation of the Giants' woes.
Neither is it a fault that Olympian Bacchus
should have both the blood and imitation
of his own Giant-slaying father, Zeus.
"If you wish to ask about the Teiresias
who vexes you, then ask Pytho who slept with Semele,
who fathered the child of Thyonê.
But if you want to learn the secret rites
of that Bacchus who revels in dance,
Pentheus, shed your royal costume,
submit to wearing a lady's cloth,
and become the woman Agavê,
for fear the others may rush upon you hunting them.
If you should stretch beast-killing bowstring in your hand,
Cadmus would praise you for joining your mother in the chase.
All alone, grapple with Bacchus, and if it is ordained,
by Artemis, I will call you Lion-Slayer
and you will follow in Actaeon's footsteps.
"Lay down these weapons; you will have no need of them.
My women, ever untouched by cold armor,
kill ironclad soldiers with only their hands.
If they should conquer you in an unarmed, female charge
while you yourself are all arrayed in dazzling armor,
who among your subjects would speak of a man
whose breath was stolen on a woman's battlefield?
A Bassarid does not flinch before winged arrows,
she does not flee the spear. But wrap yourself up
in trickery, take up an unknown face,
and you may behold all the secrets of Dionysus."

With these words the god succeeded in his persuasion,
since he whipped the man's mind red, shook him,
bound him tightly to the pulse of ranging madness . . .
The Moon descended, in league with Bromius,

and she too licked at Pentheus with her divine lashings.
the rabid bite of mind-depriving Selene took form,
and to the roiling eyes of Pentheus
he brought to light all manner of dread phantom,
spiraling Echionides deep into nightmare
and far, far away from any former longings.
And she echoed in the ear of Pentheus,
distorted, unbalanced, again and again,
and battered out reverberate din
from the mouth of her avenging trumpet.
And the man was afraid.

Pentheus found himself stepping into the palace,
stung by swarming madness and brimmed with yearning
for those untold rites of the Bacchic flock.
Tossing the lids from sweet-smelling chests
he felt women's robes between his fingers,
threads cast in the form of Sidonian Sea,
a gaping, salt-rich purple of the deep.
And he slipped himself into the robe of Agavê,
woven in all iridescent, sun-dapple splendor,
hid his hair beneath the veil of Autonoë,
encircled his kingly breast in finely bordered cloth,
and bound his feet in women's sandals.
In his hand he took up a thyrsus,
and as he joined the crowd of Bacchants,
brilliant, multicolored cloth lapped at his pounding feet,
feet that learned to echo the rhythm around him
and pulled his body into the twist and writhe of the dance.
And bathed in the sweetness of frenzy,
Pentheus shuddered from toe to toe
and rattled the ground with tilting, dipping sandal.

Softening both his hands he waved them loose and aloft,
one after the other in rapid, double pulses,
just like a woman who delights to strike the ground with dance,
and just like a woman shaking the twin coppers

of the tambourine in its rattling, twofold frame
he let loose his wild curls to the wind
and struck up an Euian song from Lydia.
You might well say that you saw a true Bacchant
reveling in feral release from her mind.
And with such clarity he saw the sun doubling before him,
twin suns suspended above twin Thebes,
and he wished to pry up the entrance to seven-mouthed Thebes
and lay it down upon his unwavering shoulders.

His subjects encircled him like jewels in a crown
one on a rounded hilltop, one on a high rock,
one braced against a friend's shoulder with heels lifted high,
straining to see, toes fixed to the dust,
some man found a jagged crest of earth,
another sat upon a jutting parapet,
one stretched his eye to watch from the high-crested towers,
and one scaled a pillar with toes gripping the stone,
hands wound round its trunk, and he gawked with all the rest
at Pentheus shivering in the pulse of madness,
lifting the thyrsus, setting his woman's veil to trembling.
Already he had rounded the walls of seven-mouthed Thebes
while the gates twisted open and closed of their own accord.
Already he was outside the city,
already he passed by the graceful waters of Dirce,
where the dragon used to bathe and slake his thirst,
and on frenzied feet he turned out the steps of the dance
and trailed the vine god in gait and gesture.

But when he came to the place of trees and dance, the place
which harbors the riotous rites of Bromius,
and where Bassarids stalk deer in bare feet,
then the vine god spotted an ancient fir
through the tangled knots of thicket, a giantess
that stretched to the breathless heights of flanking crag
and with broad matted green threw cloud-scrape hills into blue shade.
And with a callous hand he gripped the highest bough

and bent the entire spine to the ground, to the ground
as it creaked and cried to face the soil
and lay splayed for but a moment beside Pentheus,
until man and tree lost their tether and found flight.
Pentheus gripped madly at the fir that bore him aloft,
clawing at those spindle sparse branches at its crown,
and as though in some erratic, windswept dance
swiveled round and round the trunk with fluttering feet.

And then it was time for the Bassarids to dance;
hitching up their skirts, tossing fawn skin about their bodies,
they spurred one another into movement.
And with hot froth coloring her lips stark and pale,
Agavê, haunt of the hills, showed her teeth and shrieked:

"Autonoë, let us hurry to that place
where a dance is danced for Lyaeus,
where there is heard a mountain-wandering shrill
from that ever-so familiar pipe
and where I might stitch a sweet and worthy melody,
learn who first will rouse the Dionysian chorus,
and who eclipses whom in sacrifice.
You've dallied behind, you prancing truant,
and now Ino has shown her face before we have.
No longer is she turned away from her homeland,
wandering across the sea, but has surfaced from the brine
beside wave-splitting Melicertes,
has surfaced to offer up a shield
between Dionysus and the shadow pursuing him;
that profane Pentheus must not be allowed
to crash and swell against our lord Lyaeus.
Come to your posts, to the heights, Initiates,
and come, all Ismenian Bacchants.
Let us now set about our sacred rites,
and in leaping fervor for the dance
contend with the Bassarids of Lydia,
and they will say that the Mygdonian Mimallon
has been mastered by maenad Agavê."

As these final words left her wet and feverish lip,
movement caught the corner of Agavê's eye
and she blinked to see against dazzling sky
some violent silhouette perched high in a fir tree.
And she looked straight at her own blaspheming son,
straight at the face come from between her own thighs,
at the shining eyes opened first at the warmth of her chest
and saw not her child but a savage, bristling lion.

And she turned towards him the licking flame
of the entire collective gaze of Bacchants
and in a voice clipped in rabid madness
assigned to her son, a man with mind and sense of presence,
the name of beast: blank, numb, coarse, and carnal.
And the women encircled the one crouched amongst the leaves,
took the trunk into merciless embrace, a choke of hands,
wanting to fell tree along with clinging fruit, Pentheus.
And then Agavê joining the swarm
splintered ancient bark between her palms
and the tree gave out an earth-writhing shiver
as its roots were torn from fertile soil and blanched at the open air.
And the entire weight fell to the ground and Cithaeron was stripped bare
and the bold lord Pentheus like a dancer
curled in on himself as he tumbled from the air
rolling over and over and over until *smack*.
And it was then that the mind-warping madness
of Dionysus abandoned the man,
and his former thoughts resurfaced from their hidden keep
and on the ground he watched as fate crept towards him
from every direction and he let slip a desperate grief:

"Conceal me, help me, hamadryad nymphs!
Do not let me be destroyed by the mother who loves me,
by kin-murdering, child-murdering hands.
Mother! Mother, and yet no mother,
unknot yourself from this madness unfeeling, untender.
How can you call me a beast, me, your son?

Is there fur on my chest? Are my words only roars?
Do you not know me, whom you raised, do you not see me?
Who has stolen from you your thoughts and your eyes
Goodnight, Cithaeron, goodnight trees and rock.
Keep me with you, Thebes, and keep me with you, mother,
cherished, beloved, child-killing mother Agavê.
Look at this young man's beard. You look at a human being.
I am not a lion. Look! Look at me! I am no beast.
Spare the pains of my birth, relentless woman, spare your breasts
and look at me, at Pentheus, whom you raised . . .
But . . . dear tongue, I think it is time for stillness.
Lock up your stories, for Agavê is not listening.
Mother. Mother who will howl and scream.
If you kill me now at the will of Dionysus,
do not let another Bassarid touch me, hurt me
with those hands of theirs so foreign to my skin, so strange,
but kill me on your own, your son, please just your hands, just you."

With these words he pleaded, but Agavê did not hear him.
The women washed over him in a wave of fervent hands:
one yanked at his feet as he twisted in the dust,
one took up his right arm and tore it from its socket,
and then Autonoë in balanced violence did his left.
And the wandering mother so far away from herself
pressed her heel into her fading son's chest
and with her sharp thyrsus cut through his throat.

In mad joy of blood she ran about on quick-crook knees
and presented to unhappy Cadmus
the head that dripped glistening ruby droplets in the sand.
She beamed at the fruit of her hunt in her hand,
the lion she held up by his scruff—
a false lion, yes, but how real to her then—
and screeched out these words from mad, burning throat:

"Blessed Cadmus, I say that you are even more blessed,
for Artemis has just watched Agavê in the heights

snatching up greatness with naked hands,
and even if that goddess was crowned once king of the hunt,
it is now with underpinnings of jealousy
for your own great, lion-slaying daughter.
Even the dryads marveled at my good work,
and our Harmonia's father Ares
watching from behind his thick helmet
nearly dropped his spear in shock when your child
took deadly aim at lions without iron
but only a thresher. He was so proud.
Cadmus, call here the man who rides the throne,
so that Pentheus can swallow an envious sight,
the still exalting sweat of a woman-made kill.
O slaves! Come, fasten this head above the gates of Cadmus
as an ornament to my victory.
Little sister Ino never killed such a well-ripened beast.
Autonoë, behold and give a bow before me,
for such delights only visit you in daydreams and prayers.
I have displaced the fame of your mother-in-law
Cyrene, lion-killing mother of Aristaeus,
and I banish all this prattling over her minor triumph."

She spoke these words with her prize, the dear weight,
held aloft in her hand. And before her was Cadmus
hardly restraining himself from weeping
as he absorbed the sight and mad ramblings of his daughter,
glowing all peachy pride and not yet sensing the dark.
Tears and words dropped from him inseparable,
the heaving ripple of a man's voice drowning:

"What beast have you caught, Agavê, sentient, sapient,
what beast have you caught, which you grew in your own belly,
what beast have you caught, the seed which Echion planted?
Look again at your lion, which as a cub I lifted
in my palm, blessed in my duty to cherish him.
Look again at your lion. Your mother Harmonia
used to lift him to your breast and help him latch.

And now you ask for your son, ask me for your son,
so that he too may admire your labors,
but how am I to call him when you hold him in your hands?
You kill . . . I know you did not know . . . but how can I call him?
How? Look closely at your beast and recognize your child.
Dionysus, what lovely gifts for your caring Cadmus.
What a lovely marriage Cronion gave to me,
gifts worthy of Ares and divine Aphrodite.
Ino's lungs are filled with salt water, Semele's with smoke,
Autonoë's with sharp tears for her son of crescent horns,
and now this wretch has killed the only child she ever had,
ending the boy blindly and before his time.
And my Polydorus wanders and suffers
so far away now from father and fatherland.
With Pentheus dead and Polydorus gone,
to whom can I turn? I am left but a corpse that breathes.
What distant city will welcome me within their walls?
To hell, Cithaeron. You have ripped from Cadmus
anyone who would nurse him through his final years.
You have claimed Pentheus for your own
and you conceal Actaeon from my sight."

Then Cadmus fell silent but Cithaeron himself
cried out, an old man pouring out a surge of groans
and flood-tears. The trees shrieked and keened, and naiad nymphs
lay shrill dirges upon the mountain air.
The greying head and wailing tongue of Cadmus
demanded respect even from Dionysus
and extracted from the god a tear, out of place
on a face otherwise unmoved but for laughter,
and he allowed the mind of Agavê to fly home
and lucid reason to light upon her
so that she might cry for her Pentheus.
The mother, twisted back into mind and honest eyes,
stood for a time without voice, bracing and rerooting . . .

She blinked once at the head of dead Pentheus.

She fell in a ball to the floor rolling.
Rolling in loose dust and tangled her hair in tight knots.
She threw the wooly cloak from her chest
and the bowls for Bromius' revelry.
She made her pale breast red with the blood she drew in long tracts.
She kissed the eyes of her son and the cheeks once pink now waxen
and the graceful locks now crimson matted.
And in shattering, splinter voice at last she spoke:

"Dionysus the Cruel, quenchless thirst for his own family,
give back to me the madness, for in my knowing mind
I have a madness even worse than I did before.
Give back to me that safe and balmy vacuity
and again I will call my son a beast.
I thought I struck a beast, but instead of the freshly hewn head
of a lion, I hold up the brow of my Pentheus.
Autonoë is blessed to cry for Actaeon,
blissful life of a mother who has not killed her own son.
Only I have become a child-killer.
My dear wandering Ino did not kill Melicertes,
not Learchus, but it was the father who destroyed
that which he himself had created.
How wretched am I, wretched, wretched.
Zeus lay with Semele and now I weep for Pentheus.
Zeus, father, author, birthed Dionysus from his thigh
and put to blank waste the entire legacy of Cadmus.
Oh have clemency, Dionysus, it's done,
all collapsed, you've leveled the bloodline.
But as he did once between the tables of singing gods,
of marriage feast, by the bed of Harmonia
and in the bridal chamber of my Cadmus,
may Apollo again move the lyre
and sting us all with a dirge, a single dirge
for Autonoë and Agavê, and cry hell
for their Pentheus and Actaeon dead so soon.

"My boy, what drug can lull my pain?
The skittering light of your bridal torches
has not yet touched my face, nor have the hymns
touched my ears with testament to your love and union.
Where is your son whose face and little fists
would radiate flickering solace?
If only you had been mauled by another,
any other, but not your own sorry Agavê.
But please, Pentheus so damned, do not blame your mother
for the things she did as a puppet of madness.
Point your blame at Bacchus. Mommy is innocent.
"Sweet boy, my hands drip with dew from your open neck,
from your head drained of color, this blood which dyes my robes red.
Yes, yes, give me the cup of Bromius, I beg you,
for I wish to pour for Dionysus
a libation not of wine but of Pentheus' blood.
For you, son stolen from full life and full age,
will my own hands pile high your tomb,
filthy hands chafed raw from wiping tears,
and tuck you into the earth, dear headless trunk,
and carve these words upon the mark of your grave:
'Visitor, I am the body whose name was once Pentheus.
I was given to light by Agavê's child-loving womb
and her child-killing hand took me away.'"

And though she was barely out of reach of madness,
barely on this side, she spoke with a clear mind.
And Autonoë's tears carved sparkling lines down her cheeks
and she let out her own sob, the closest thing to comfort:

"Agavê, I envy you and plead for your misfortunes,
since you are at liberty to hold Pentheus in your sight
and touch his mouth and his beloved eyes
and twirl your fingers in that cowlick he could never tame.
Yes, yes, I say that you are lucky,
even if you must live a filicide.
For instead of weeping over Actaeon, I wept

over the carcass of a fawn, my son's form warped and stretched,
those alien eyes like saucers and hard hoof for hand,
and instead of the head of my son, I lowered into the ground
some deer's long face and antlers, a stranger to womb and eye.
This may be but a small consolation, or none at all,
but you have not seen your son with his face
molded into the outline of something else,
the bristling fur, cloven hoof with no opposable thumb
by which to create or hold, and oh those horns.
Only I have seen the anonymous corpse of my son.
I did my shrieking over a form all dappled and mute,
and now they say I am a fawn's mother and not a boy's.
But, Artemis, chaste daughter of prurient Zeus,
honor your kindling, coruscant twin,
father to my husband Aristaeus,
and rid me of this human form. I would rather be a deer.
Give grace to Apollo. Although those fabled hounds
are still sated from Actaeon's blood, give me as dessert,
or, if not to them, then to your own bitches.
Let Cithaeron look on as mother follows son
against the teeth and tear of hound. But! When I am a doe,
and my face at last again reflects my boy,
do not chase me and whip me and yoke me, mossy antlers,
to your cart, wilding against the bit and cracking my lips.
Goodbye, Pentheus tree, goodbye, Cithaeron,
you glutton of havoc and ruin.
Goodbye, fennels of mind-depriving Dionysus,
keep me with you, Phaëthon, delight for all mankind,
paint your light over the hills and lay it thick
upon Leto's daughter and Dionysus.
But if you know how to end mortal life in blinding rays,
then do catch Autonoë and Agavê in clear flame.
Be Pasiphaë's avenger so that you may aim
cutting laughs at Harmonia's mother Aphrodite."

She finished speaking and Agavê wept even harder.
Dear mother buried the body she had deprived of life
and her face eroded in gulf of teary churn.

Her citizens fashioned a handsome tomb.
Not an eye was lifted from the ground as they wept
and the lord Bacchus harbored pity
as he went down the line and touched to the lips of each
a drug rich in oblivion, a drop of Lethe
palate-hidden in wine behind honey-sweet vibrancy.
Like a nurse he eased the cries of Cadmus with words as salve.
He tucked Autonoë and Agavê into bed
and showed to them bright harbingers of fated hope.
Across Illyria to the land of evening sea
he escorted Harmonia away from her homeland
with Cadmus by her side, two alike in age and exile,
for whom crawling time bestowed the form of stone serpents.

And Bacchus, graceful sight, swept up his satyrs and Pans
and away in lark traced his lynxes with the whip
and lollied off to Athens, a city never silent.

Book 47

Cyrus Console

Wherein Perseus, the death of Icarius, and splendid Ariadne.

Rumor already was noising abroad Dionysus, the tippler's
Figurehead, lord of the vineyard, had come into Attica. Athens
Broke out in revelry, dancing, abandon. The Giver of License
Elicited multitudes, forests of scintillant hands filled the cobbles
Fluttering undulant colorful banners. Bacchus' fine tendrils
Mantled the fixtures of Athens. With flowers lithe women adorned them,
Garlanded ivy in ebony locks. The Ilissos to worship
Great Dionysus its spirited water unfurled on the creekbed.
Reed-banked Cephisus reprised a euphonious general music.

Up sprang green vines from between mounded loam warmed in
sunshine and birdsong.
Olive groves blushed with the juice-swollen undergrowth suddenly ripened.
Trees woke and whispered, aroused to their tenderly tingling leaf tips.
Seasonal meadows unfolded the rivalrous banners of rosebud.
Strove from the hillsides autonomous lilies. Athenian woodwind
Instruments chorused with Phrygian. Delicate quick-study fingers
Coaxed from the vents of Acharnian reeds their ambivalent ditty.
Celebrant slipping her arm around celebrant lofted this descant
Over the throaty Mygdonian clef, the divided flame surging
Night after night from twin torches ignited in Zagreus' honor
Long ago won, Dionysus' come lately. The nightingale warbled

Infinite notes to commemorate Philomel, Itylus, sadly
Weaving together their melodies. Up in the eaves twittered swallows
Making no mention of Tereus.

None in the city stood motionless; Bacchus, exuberant, grandly
Called at the house of Icarius, first in the region for planting
Introduced species of trees. When the weather-worn gardener noticed
There in his door, Dionysus, he kicked up his clodhoppers, dancing.
Then his good daughter, Erigone, rose to bring goats' milk. Bacchus
Stayed her. The god interposed skins of palliative liquor; his right hand
Reaching a tumbler of redolent wine to the farmer.
"The boon grape,
Heretofore unknown to Athens, I offer you, fortunate pair, whose
Countrymen celebrate you from today to eternity, singing
'Not even Celeus rivals the fame of Icarius; far, far
Brighter Erigone's glory is than Metaneira's.' Resembling
Ancient Demeter come bearing a gift for Triptolemus, I stand
Laden with goods for this husbandman who works the soil. As Demeter
Introduced harvest-corn; I bring the wine-suffused grape. But to rival
Heavenly Ganymede, only Icarius answers, renowned
Honored and blessed even more than Triptolemus, given that corn can't
Soften the sorrow that gnaws at the heart of your kind, whereas wine-grapes
Solve human pain."
So he handed a handsome cup brimful with bracing
Drink to the welcoming gardener, who took a sip, and again, and
Drank yet again, by the end of his working day thirsty and tired out
Craving the trickling drops. Then Erigone poured no more goats' milk.
Cup after winecup she reached him until he was drunken in good time.
Up from the humble board littered with cups he arose, lurching, staggered
Bandy-legged into the trees with a chant for the god Dionysus.
Later some slips of the vine Dionysus presented him, showed him
Delving and grafting and bending the shoots in rich earth.
Then the plowman
Taught his companions in turn how to foster the grape, intermingling
Bottomless fountains of wine in his homely thrown crater. Together
Throwing their hearts in their cups did his banqueters praise him, the genius
Pouring out hyacinth-scented ambrosia from bristling wineskins:

"Say, boss, describe how you happened to find out the nectar of gods was
Freely available here in our sublunar vale. From Cephisus
Flows no elixir like this one. The naiads bestow no intoxicant
Lethal as your stuff. Ilissus, not even at sunset, might ripple
Colors majestic as this limpid indigo. Not from the panniered
Honeybee nor from the olive derives equal remedy. Brother!
What is this drink nonpareil, like sweet milk with indefinite shelf life,
Heady as jasmine and lilac? If all of the seasons' alembics
Stilled in one vessel the odors of every blossom, a vernal
Beverage befitting Adonis, your wine would excel it. Goodness
Gracious, it's strange how my former anxieties dissipate. Heaven
Airily wafts them aside, insubstantial and vaporous. Maybe
Hebe the goddess of youth, or Athena your patroness—is it
Possible Ganymede's jigger was swiped from the cabinet night? Whereby
President over immortals the almighty Zeus waxes jocund?
Or—can it be?—you yourself entertained an immortal here? Some god
Gave you this benison for your hospitable service, like Ceres?

So he spoke, watching the wine catch the torchlight and loosen his speech.
So they drank under the zodiac, reflex diminishing, second-
Order cognition and sense of propriety weakening, until
Rolling their eyes and distending the veins on their temples, the liquor
Reddened their countenance, heating the bodily argument. Coursing
Lavishly over their faces and into their ungathered tunics
Wine overwhelmed them. It felled them in various attitudes. Spinning
Ceaselessly now the horizon seemed mocking their innocence.
Then
No one could say how it started but they were upon him, the drinkers
One with a poleaxe, a shovel, a sickle, those implements handy
One with a big hunk of limestone, another a cudgel, a cattle
Prod whose keen end the responsible gardener felt as it traveled
Into his torso. Icarius dropped to the ground. With his elbows
Shielding his forehead, he doubled his person first this way—as if
Hopeful to work himself into some sheltering crevice while awful
Blows fell around him—now that way, upsetting the wine-bowl, the red
Posseting streaks of his blood where it splashed on his agonized body.
"Wine brings sweet pleasure to all, but to me it brings bitter repentance.

Sorry! Erigone! Sorry! No comfort in drink shall be yours, no,
Gay Dionysus has served you this evening with tears. I salute you."

Scarce had he spoken these words when he opened his eyes somewhat wider
Blinking no more, the original vintner's career interrupted.
Meanwhile his murderers snored intermittently, supine on bare earth,
Blotto. With daylight came sickening groans as the company scoped out
Yesterday's recklessness. Upland they shouldered Icarius, gaining
Mountainous country, there washing his gashes in ice melt. His killers
Buried the man they had brutalized. Culpable hands sprinkled topsoil
Over his disjointed bulk.
                    But the ghost of Icarius hastened
Furtive and vague to Erigone's bedside, like smoke in a corpse shape
Beckoning her to acknowledge the unexplained holes in his garment
Sodden with blood and distressed by the hastily improvised weapons.
Supplicant trembling hands made to reach for his daughter but faltered.
Screams bulged her throat, where they shuddered to trespass her motionless features.
"Rise!" he called, "Wake! Oh my daughter, your father is mutilated, killed.
Riot and wine made his menials pierce him with iron and offend him.
Fortunate girl, to be sleeping insensate while visitors brained me.
Hammer blows splintered my bones and disfigured me far from your earshot.
Darkness custodial warded your sight from the havoc of spilt gore.
Echo alone was responsible when I cried "mercy!" and "Succor";
Echo commemorates my dying words with their effigy. Succor!
Mercy! And where will you find them, unhusbanded, fatherless? Never
Now will you dibble good seed into welcoming furrow, no helpmeet
Chaperone you and your flock through the wildflower pastures. But mark me:
Leave wine alone, though it promises honeyed oblivion. Grieve me
Under earth's mantle, despondent, who suffers the plight of his orphan"

Phantasm spoke, and then vanished. The girl bolted upright and wailed, scored
Trenches from cheekbone to abdomen, raking her fingernails, gasped,
Ripped out thick swatches of hair, leaving pale pinkish channels of raw scalp.
"Where is Icarius' body," she cried to the cattle who stood still
"Where has my father gone? Where are his murderers? Speak to me, dumb things

Bystanders, innocent animals, knowing him better, perhaps—
Isn't he dead? Might he wander these meadows distributing priceless
Knowledge and skill among dutiful neighbors and countrymen, still? Speak!
Tell me his business—so long as he lives, I'll abide his removal.
I'll join him again, then, to work in the garden and water the vineyard.
So help me, gods, is he dead? If he's dead, I will hazard a like death."

Into the forested mountains she ran, but no trace of her father appeared there.
Shepherd and huntsman alike answered none of her desperate pleading.
Pallid and thin, she was wandering still when a gardener touched her,
Quietly gave her the terrible news and escorted her, mute,
Up to the place where the body was buried, the covering branches
Some of them still with their leaves. There he left her, disconsolate, sober.
Plucking a hair, now another, to lay on the gravesite, the barefoot
Woman stood facing it, wetting her tunic with tears. For a long time
Nothing was said. While Erigone stared, her companion, a pet dog
Shared in her misery, whining and tilting his head. But unfit to
Follow her clambering hand over hand through the branches he stayed down
Running tight circles and yelping incessantly. She made a collar
High in the canopy, tethered herself to the branch, and then let go.

Quietly now, he approached, sniffing twice as her heels beat the fresh air.
Later, protecting the single cadaver from scavengers, this dog
Wordlessly pointed the suicide out to some passersby, who cut
Down the cadaver and hollowed a grave near the tree. He seemed almost
Cognizant of their intention and bowed to encourage them, barking
Stretched out his forelegs, and scrabbled the dust with his toenails. Their grim task
Finished, the travelers went on their way. But the animal lingered.
Nothing could move him now, steadfast and vigilant mourner. He lay down
There to endure his remainder and die where Erigone left him.
Zeus took compassion, installing Erigone's form near the three stars
Hindmost in Leo. Her portrait was wanting some property, bunched grapes
Offered the god, but she waved him away. He depicted her father,
"Boötes," he called him. The dog appears, too, he is happily chasing
Rabbits, they say, in a firmament image of nightfall upstate.

Bacchus departed Ilissus' mellifluous waters to visit
Naxos, an area shaded with vines. Aphrodite and Eros
Led him. The bridegroom pushed onward, for Theseus' ship had sailed,
Stranding deceived Ariadne, whatever his promises. Wonder
Grappling with love in his voice, Dionysus admonished the maenads:
"Quiet your timbrels and pipes. That's enough with the dancing.
Allow her—
Cypris? Pasithea? Hebe? Selene? Athena? Or Thetis?
Artemis? Quiet, you satyrs! Whoever she is, let her sleep on."
It was too late, though. The grass widow rose and, beholding no fleet,
Nor even tracks in the sand where her suitor had ghosted her, wept
Raucous as kingfishers' laughter. The seashore was smoothed by a smooth sea.
"Theseus! Theseus!" Calling this name, the forsaken young woman
Bent her disorganized steps up and down in the dunes, hoarse
Obloquies tattered to shreds in the breeze. She condemned jealous sleep first,
Bargaining next with the several winds, as if they could be held
Liable for the catastrophe, bearing her lover away, or
Ordered to change, to repair him to her under sail. In the meantime
Eros mistakenly thought he beheld Aphrodite there, gorgeous
Weeping resplendent in Naxos where none should feel sadness.

Sadness became Ariadne, whose beauty surpassed Aphrodite's,
Charactered only with joy, Aphrodite's expression was lifeless
Viewed against lineaments drawn in the chiaroscuro of true grief.
Sorrow the catchlight made even a goddess's eyes seem the less deep:
"Merciful sleep soothed my head after Theseus vanished—if only
Sleep might stay faithful to me. In my dream I saw Attica stirring,
Theseus' place all commotion, the servants and caterers set out
New wine and delicacies. Was the wedding my own, I wondered
Touching the wreath in my hair as if I had been given a blow there.
Dancers assembled; musicians sat up; but a quiet persisted.
Laid on the altar beside me, this hand looked familiar, as if mine—
Pardon me, Charity! Conjured in darkness, this elegant tableau
Envious glances of daylight dart in now to perforate.
Come back,
Charming and vacuous sleep! How religiously Theseus made love—
How like a beast he concludes it! He wasn't like this when he gathered

Up in both trembling hands the continuous thread that his partner
Skeined him, that time in the labyrinth. Why did the minotaur not kill
Theseus then, who returns all my love with a token of salt sea?
Whom can I turn to? My husband and father are lost to me. What god
Pities me or can convey me to Marathon? I've lost the thread now!
I would crawl back to you, Theseus, even as charwoman, making
Beds in your suite, or whatever capacity, hefting the strange jug
Only to be near your side, as your prisoner, even a dumb cow
Such as my mother was once. For a drover she buckled her spine, lowed
Nothings and nuzzled the ear of that obstinate bullock who got fresh
Cattle upon her. For pastoral instruments she could care less, but
Bullroaring moved her. For my part, I leave off the crook;
    oaken stanchions
Hold no dominion where I am concerned. By my queen I stand ready, though,
Theseus' voice like a bellows that stokes me, intoning cheesy
Nuptial melodies when they are wedded, and bite back the bitter
Jealousy, palpable down to the roots of my molars, their union
Starts in my ruminant gut. I would do this for him. But hello,
Sailor!"
        Delighted to hear her complaint, Dionysus, godlike,
Comforted her. Meanwhile, Eros invisibly whipped Ariadne's
Flesh into frenzy. Hypnotic, the low voice of Bacchus suggested:
Why waste your tears on duplicitous playboys? Relax, look:
This is the face of a god, his dexterity, suavity. You see?
What could he possibly do to compete with a specimen like me?
Killing a fictional monster barehanded somewhere in a dirt maze?
Maybe he gratified you with his rigor and stamina, mortal
Though they were?
                    None could refuse such a glorious ask. Ariadne
Entered in marriage, engendering numerous children. But midlife
Turmoil and fondness of memory working together led Bacchus
Back to the mainland of Hellas, a pleasant diversion until proud
Townspeople spurned him in Argos, where Hera preeminent lorded.
Stung, Dionysus sent madness among the Inachian women
Causing atrocities. Mothers first whetted long knives and then, rabid,
Spitted their infants upon them. The times looked increasingly like war.
One gave her babe to the falchion; another her toddler rended;

One plucked her child from the nipple and lofted him bodily, loosing
Pitiless laughter to see how the little form somersaulted, mouth
Noiseless and terrified working incessantly over jejune air
Inachos ran with the blood of infanticide tinging its bad spate.
Dead-eyed, the mother did not recollect either childbirth or labor
Youths, by long usage, on coming of age, had made offerings: shorn locks
Draped on Asterion's hyaline flank, but Asterion, this time,
Swallowed the young ones themselves and ran burbling in tribute amok.

Up came a man and began to harangue Bacchus' entourage: Hey, you
Spindly varietal! Argos has Perseus, worthy of Hera!
Here is no need of a wine god who minces the grapes with his left foot.
Perseus, winged at the ankle, can tread silver clouds in the moonlight!
Faced with his sickle, your ivy-strewn fennel staves droop and are mown
down!
Three cheers for Perseus, scourge of the Gorgons. And who cares for Bacchus?
If on the occident waters this libertine petrified one ship,
Perseus mineralized the impressive leviathan wholly!
If on a beach somewhere, Bacchus picked up Ariadne, clueless,
Perseus airborne unshackled Andromeda, and for a bridal
Token offhandedly managed to execute Cetus in marble.
Perseus, furthermore, bearing out motives immaculately pure
Wed Ariadne, and not on the rebound from Theseus merely.
Though curiosity cremated Semele, Danaë stood by.
Perseus' father conceived him in showers of opulent gold then.
Look at the champion here with his licorice implement, hang on
Perseus, don't condescend to hew ivy with Gorgon-quenched blue steel!
Wait now, don't stoop to these open-toed heels worn by women and actors;
Hold off the Lord of the Underworld's invisibility headgear;
Form not your glorious weapons against the sad parvenue Bacchus.
Or, if you like, you can mobilize doughty Andromeda against
Louche and defenseless Lyaeus. Be gone, Dionysus, I say
Quit this equestrian city, go back to deranging poor Theban
Women or murder yourself one more weak, randy Pentheus. What beef
Has Dionysus with Perseus? Leave off disturbing the limpid
Inachos! Crawl back to Thebes with its indolent waterways reeking.
Lightning has once before struck the Asopus and boiled it, remember?

Thus the derision that Bacchus endured from the locals, while Hera
Taking the shape of the seer Melampus, and rendering warlike
Music in Perseus' ear:
"Son of Zeus, interpose your keen falx!
Suffer not women with thyrsi to pester our city of Argos!
Be not afraid of one snake in the hair when your sickle has done for
Venomous adders as rank as the hairs on my head! To the breach! Fight!
Picture your mother prostrating herself at the feet of this playboy.
Demonstrate now that you come of that rainmaking provenance, bellow
'Mine is the jouissant profusion of gold in the bower, birthright!'
Harry the satyrs! Devolve upon insolent Bacchus the Gorgon;
Bring me this libertine after the manner of Seriphus made stone!
Hera, invincible, Bromius' stepmother, marches beside you!
Rally Mycene and brandish your sickle! Parade Ariadne
Nude through the city, crestfallen, at spearpoint before you, abject!
Murder the rabble of horn-headed satyrs, transfix in the cold-eyed
Stare of Medusa unfortunate Bassarids, turning them marble!
Deck every alleyway out with their stony facsimiles frozen
Diffident, as they beheld you advance with the Gorgon's fell dreadlocks
Snaked through your resolute fingers; wherefore do you tremble now, scion?
Bacchus sprang not from a gold-seamed marriage bed. Impotent, is he
Not? Can he so much as touch you, this half-assed pedestrian loser?"

Perseus, heartened by Hera's incitement, strode into the fray, broad
Horn-blasts assembling belligerents over the battlefield, spearmen
Lynceus, then Phoroneus, renewed in their time-honored weapons
So too Pelasgus; the oxhide of Abas again into battle
Rode on the arm of a partisan; old Proetus' quarterstaff also,
Hewn of stout ash, and Acrisius' quiver, and Danaus' bronze sword
Long ago hefted aloft at a festive mariticide; broadaxe
Inachus wielded to shatter the brows of a sacrifice, back when
Priest and enthusiast chosen he stood to great Hera and city.

Chariots took to the field; the proud cavalcade lifted its bright hooves
Perseus rallied before them and rasped out the battle-cry, nocking
Shaft to taut bowstring; the Argives' defender then readied his sickle,
Laced up the thongs of his high-stepping sandals and hoisted on high that

Dire Gorgoneion no bodily eye might behold and remain flesh.
Bacchus convened the horned satyrs and flowing-haired women about him
Perseus ran through the dustup; the sight provoked Bacchus to frenzy.
Thyrsus before him, he carried a crystalline amulet, knowing
Zeus-seeded diamonds were proof against baleful Medusa's cold stare.
Perseus stifled a laugh when he saw these accoutrements. He said:
"Look at you, girded for battle with jewels and nosegays, pretending!
Now let us see what you're made of! If yours is that watery mettle
Licking the banks of the Pactolus, mine is the golden deluge! Mine,
Danaë's bedchamber, carbuncles laid in its mortar, resplendent
Witness to Zeus' brisk chrysopoetic largesse! Better go now,
Son of Persephone. Hera is landlord in Argos; we'd all die
Laughing if she set the bringer of freedom at liberty." He spoke,
Striding the blast.
The Bacchantes omnipotent Hera dispersed. Like
Lightning, she burst on them. Laying about her the scimitar that put
Paid to Medusa, she routed the Bacchants, her weapons all gleaming,
Sky-splitting lances she darted at Bromius bullroarer. But he,
Chuckling, retorted:
"That fulminant sword doesn't frighten me, Hera,
Foibled with corposants! I was inchoate, an infant, when lightnings
Tickled my chin and made over me, lightsome and anodyne. You there,
Perseus, waving your reaper, just give it a rest. In this hubbub
Stakes are a bit more than Gorgons, or damsels in chains. Bacchus
Menaces you. Sired by Zeus, he was suckled by Rhea, by thunder!
Born in a house fire and raised in a leg! All Deriades' armies
Yielded to him; his one tendril of ivy dilacerated
Even Orontes' bronze thorax and drove him to suicide two ways.
Bacchus! Before whom brave Alpus went down on one knee, that huge
Titan whose shoulders were shrouded in cumulonimbus. Before brave
Bacchus whole nations kneel down! The Sicilian adventurers' shanties
Tell how I turned the Tyrrhenian pirates to pilotfish. No doubt
Seven-gate Thebes echoes yet with the maddening cry wherewith
Pentheus, rent limb from limb by the maenads, and by his own mother
Agavê he was paraded back into the town on a pikestaff!
Suffer me not to remind you how Argos has weathered my onslaught
Mothers and wives mourning still for their brutalized children, but go on

Perseus, fight me and find out what happens. And when my green arms
Finally close up the wings of your sandals, my maenads triumphant,
Thyrsus in hand, I will persecute you and your host until Argos
Watches me skewer your throat on this lancet of vines while your sickle
Rusts on a carpet of leaves. There is no one can save you, not Zeus;
Neither can owl-eyed Athena see other than darkness before you
Hera, her hatred for me notwithstanding, can aid you but nothing.
Blowhard Mycenae the head of Medusa's beheader will watch
Horrified, jogging its way into town on the point of a spear.
Maybe I'll batten the slats of a sea chest about you and lightly
Cast you adrift on those waters familiar to you. If you like, take
Gold Aphrodite as well, since you never shut up with your precious
Gold."
    Dionysus stopped talking and bent to the fight then in progress.
Bacchant and satyr alike made their way into battle. Aloft
Perseus skimmed over Bromius, beating his winglets, but Bacchus
Vaulted himself into heaven and strode with huge limbs over airborne
Perseus. Then through the sky Dionysus conducted his dread hand
Touching Olympus and crushing the velvety clouds so that winged
Perseus trembled with fear. Dionysus continued his hand's sweep
Brushing the sun and encompassing all of the moon so that, quaking,
Perseus turned with the head of Medusa and met the bacchantes,
Shaking the serpentine locks. It was thus Ariadne became stone.

Into an access of fury this sent Dionysus. Mycene,
Argos, Danaans, the lot of them—Bacchus would level their cities
Visiting death and destruction on everything, Hera included
Veiled though she was in the guise of a typical mortal, and even
Perseus would have been slaughtered, regardless of destiny, had not
Merciful Hermes restrained him by grasping his hair and remarking:
"Offspring of Zeus! (if but natural son to snide Hera), remember
Fire fell from heaven the day that I gave your safekeeping to Lamus'
Beautiful daughters, those nymphs, and yourself still a child; how again
Bundling you into my arms I betook you to Ino your wet nurse!
If you remember these favors, I beg you to leave off the bloodshed
Think of how Bacchus and Perseus meditate fratricide, since both
Spring from the same mighty sire. Therefore humor the people of Argos;

Look on the sickle of Perseus with equanimity! White-armed
Hera incites him to this, puts the falx in his hand, and she fights, too
Openly, there on the field in the shape of Melampus. So stand down,
Bacchus, lest Hera the juggernaut trundle you to smithereens. Rage
Not at the death of your partner the fair Ariadne, who has
Died in the glorious manner of heroes in battle, and was slain
Worthier still, by the hallowed immortal who vanquished Medusa!
Destiny will not be reasoned with, much less commanded. Electra
Made it with Zeus and she perished. Europa and even your mother
Suffered this fate, after all.
"Ariadne will rise into heaven
Shedding benevolent starlight on meadow and dale and the townsfolk,
Citizens, oceans, is there a more pleasant eternity? Gently
Put down the thyrsus and breathe, Dionysus, a draught of the cool air.
Smile on this city of mothers and sons, stay your hand, and some day
They will raise altars to honor both Hera and her whom you loved."

Hermes ascended a column of air, having fomented friendship.
Hera relinquished his form to the seer and returned to Olympus
Once more himself, old Melampus addressed the Icarian army:
"Follow your soothsayer; rattle your tambourines, honor him: wine-face
Bacchus! Rejoice and make noise with the clashing of cymbals and bronze shields,
Sound for the mother of god, and appease Dionysus, lest he
Murder the lot of you, killing men, women, and children, and end
Inachus totally. Sacrifice, dance, and be merry, before Gods!"

Everyone gathered together and struck up a chant in the darkness,
Dancing for Bacchus and beating their drums under flickering torchlight,
Whiting their faces with sanctified chalk for the holy procedures.
Kettledrums thundered; the double-tap registered deftly on bronze sheets;
Fountains of oxblood and muttonfat colored the hecatomb altars;
Women and men made their peace with the god at this ledge, singing
Songs of salvation. Inachian women and maenads alike let
Go of the madness as if it were smoke on the wind.

Book 48

Stanley Lombardo

In the forty-eighth find the Giants undone,
Pallene, and slumbering Aura's son.

SO:

Bacchus behind the rail of his panther-drawn chariot
rolled out of the horse-breeding fields of mythic Phoroneus
and was pomping his way through Thrace.
Inachian Hera though
had not softened her rancor over the gadflying of Argus,
and remembering the frenzy of the Achaean women
she breastplated herself again against Dionysus.
Lying through her teeth, she prayed to all-mothering Earth,
bawling about what Zeus had done, about Bacchus' boldness,
how he blotted out that nebula of Indic Giants.
And when the nourishing Mother heard how Semele's son
had obliterated and short-fated the offspring of India
she groaned all the more for her brood. Then she armed a ring
of earth-sprung mountainous Giants around Bacchus
and goaded on her high-crested children to din of battle:

"Attack, my boys! Attack ivy-crested Dionysus. Go at him
with cliff-high rocks, catch this Indian-slayer son of Zeus
who has destroyed my family. Don't let me see him

co-reign with Zeus as a bastard lord of Olympus!
Bind him, bind Bacchus and bring him to the bridal hall
when I bless Porphyrion with Hebe as his bride,
give Cytherea to Chthonius, sing Greyeyes to bed
with Enceladus, and Artemis with Alcyoneus.
Bring me Dionysus so I can make Zeus suffer
when he sees a captive and enslaved Lyaeus.
Or slice him to ribbons and kill him for me
just like Zagreus, so that gods and mortals may say
that Earth in her fury armed her assassins twice,
the elder Titans against the earlier Dionysus
and the younger Giants against this later version."

These words pumped up the entire Giant army
and the earthborn battalions marched off to war,
one of them wielding a mountain from Nysa,
another a cloud-high peak lopped off with steel,
and each armed with jagged rocks against Dionysus.
Here comes one with a promontory torn from the sea,
another with a reef wrenched from an isthmus.
Pelorius' innumerable arms hefted Pelion's summit
ready to hurl, baring Philyra's cave when its roof
was torn off, and her husband trembled, old Chiron,
that unfinished human form melded with a horse.
Bacchus though, holding a bunch of vine lethal to Giants,
charged Alcyoneus as he held a mountain overhead.
The god wielded no thrusting spear, no blood-stained sword—
just a bunch of tendrils that sheared off the Giants'
multitudinous hands, tendrils that sheared away the swarming,
scaly, ground-bred serpents, lopped off the Giants'
snake-haired heads, and left severed necks to dance in the dust.
Countless tribes were destroyed. Rivers of blood flowed endlessly
from the slain Giants, and crimson torrents stained their gorges red.
Swarms of earthborn snakes slithered away in panic
before the curled, viperous tresses of the god Dionysus.

The god fought with fire too, hurling a torch through the air
to destroy his enemies. Arcing high overhead
the Bacchic flame spiraled in flight and spat down
flesh-eating sparks on the limbs of the Giants,
then reformed into a dragon, hissing flares of heat
from its scorched throat and spewing out smoke
in lieu of venom from its menacing lips.
The tumult was unquenchable.
Then Bacchus stretched up
and raised his battle flare over his enemies' heads, roasting
the Giants' carcasses with a supreme conflagration,
a spitting image of a Zeus-hurled thunderbolt.
Torches blazed; encircling fire licked Enceladus' head,
heating the air but not vanquishing the Giant:
Enceladus did not bend his knee in the chthonic steam,
reserved as he was for a bolt of lightning.
Monstrous Alcyoneus, armed with Thracian crags,
leapt upon Lyaeus and lifted a cloud-high peak
of blizzardy Haemus—a futile weapon
against his target, the invulnerable Dionysus.
He hurled the cliff, but when the craggy stones touched
Lyaeus' impenetrable fawnskin they splintered apart.
Typhoeus the Younger—very much like the Elder,
who himself had hoisted many rugged strips of his Mother Earth—
ripped up Emathia's mountains and hurled them hard
against Dionysus, who ignored the attack as he unsheathed
the sword of someone gasping on the ground and with it
attacked the Giants, pruning from their heads snaky crops
of poison-spewing hair. Even without a weapon in hand
he destroyed their leaderless forces, fighting furiously,
javelining Giants with longleaf tendrils of ivy.
He would have killed them all with his crippling thyrsus,
if he had not withdrawn of his own volition
to leave enemies alive for his Father to kill.

And he would have sped off to Phrygia then,

but another labor detained him: to kill,
after so many had already died, a lone murderer,
Pallene's death-mongering father, Sithon of Thrace.
Possessed of an unholy passion for his daughter,
he thwarted her engagements, hindered her marrying,
killing legions of wooers, cutting them down
as if he were harvesting wheat. The wrestling grounds
groaned with their murders and ran red with blood.
Until Bacchus came, that is, Justice's champion.

Approaching the dyserotic father of Pallene,
and poised as ever to marry, Bacchus proposed,
offering Sithon lavish gifts for a mad marriage
with his frightful daughter. Her bristly father
responded to Lyaeus' request by demanding
he win the bride in a wrestling match,
and led him to the inhospitable arena
where the bold girl stood, armed with a spear,
her oxhide bridal shield slung over one shoulder.

The Cyprian goddess refereed. In the middle
her naked son Eros held out to Bacchus a bridal wreath.
Wrestling would win the bride, but Peitho already
was draping her delicate body in a silvery robe,
foretelling success for Lyaeus' courtship.
The girl stripped the fabric from her strapping limbs,
then laid down the wedding spear, and there she stood,
Sithon's daughter, more delicate now, barefoot,
unveiled, revealed as a woman, weaponless.
A crimson band caressed the curve of her breasts.
Her torso was otherwise covered only by the tresses
that curled round her neck. Her legs were exposed
to well above the knees, with a white cloth around
her upper thighs and hips to cover her private parts.
All her skin, and especially her arms, had been rubbed
with rich oil so that she could slip out easily
from a wrestling hold too strong to break.

She faced off with her Dionysiac wooer, spat out
some threats, and gripping a chain in both hands
flung it around the neck of the god. Bacchus merely
shrugged the chain off, dislodging at the same time
the girl's delicate fingers. Then he encircled
Pallene's waist with both his arms and shook her
from side to side with pulsating dance steps.
He took erotic comfort in holding her rose-pink hand,
wanting not so much to throw the girl to the ground
as to touch her soft flesh, thoroughly enjoying
the sweet chore at hand. He feigned breathlessness,
as if he were a mortal, and deliberately
postponed victory. Lovely Pallene tried to lift
Lyaeus' body with a wrestling move,
but her woman's arms were unable to heft
the great weight of the god. She wore out and let go
the masculine limbs of immovable Bacchus,
who then took a similar hold on the lovely girl,
taking her in his two arms and lifting her as lightly
as if she were his thyrsus. He slung her body
over his shoulder, and then with a solicitous hand
swung the strong girl back off and gently laid her body
full length on the ground. His eyes moved furtively,
gliding over the limbs of the girl, her fine hair unkempt
and coated with dust as it fanned out in the dirt.

And then she rose from the dust and was up
on her feet again, steady as ever. Dionysus
planted a relentless knee in Pallene's belly
and tried to roll her over onto the ground,
then switched to a hold around her waist,
his fingers gripping the small of her back,
and hooking an ankle behind one of her knees
the god rolled over backwards onto the ground
and let himself be conquered by her delicate hand,
an exquisite cure for his passion as he lay supine,
beautiful in the lovely dust and bearing on his belly

the full weight of Love. He lay still and did not
throw the girl off but held her close in soul-soothing
bonds of desire. She finally extricated herself
from the grip of love-mad Lyaeus and got to her feet
with a lithe kip-up, but the god effortlessly rolled over
and laid the roseate girl flat on the ground.
So there she lay, arms outspread, as the deity
wrapped his arms dexterously around her neck.

Her father hustled over and intervened.
The girl wanted another bout, but Sithon
restrained her, and awarded the victory
to Dionysus, fearing that his might might be her death.
Eros crowned his brother with a wedding wreath
for polishing off this sweet nuptial tussle.
It had been the sort of contest that Hippomenes won
when he rolled golden apples past Atalanta's feet.

Then Bacchus, still dripping with sweat
from his marital match, struck down Sithon,
murderer of suitors, with a thrust of his thyrsus;
and, while her father was rolling in the dust, gave the girl
the murder instrument as a token of his love.

The wedding brimmed with song, the hall never silent.
sileni chanted, Bacchants danced, drunken satyrs
wove a love song hymning the athletic marriage.
Nereids from the neighboring Pallenic peninsula
encircled Dionysus with wedding ballets,
singing melodies as they danced. Old Nereus,
once Bromius' host, danced beside the Thracian Sea;
Galatea skipped over the wedlock water and caroled
Pallene's union with Bacchus. Thetis gamboled,
though herself still innocent of love. Melicertes
crowned the isthmus' bridal reef, chanting "Euoi!"
for Pallene's nuptials. Hordes of hamadryads
lit Thracian torches on Athos for the wedding

in nearby volcanic Lemnos.
Meanwhile the bride,
mourning her father's death, was being comforted
by the Euian bridegroom with these tender words:

"Don't mourn for your father, sweetheart. He was
a mean man and just wanted to get into bed with you.
What kind of father wants to marry his own daughter?
Don't feel sorry for him. Now that Sithon is slain,
Justice dances and laughs and lights a wedding torch
with her virgin hands. She's never been married,
but she's singing at your wedding because she sees
another Oenomaus dead. When he died, his daughter,
Hippodameia, was only too glad to make love
with her new husband. You too should throw your grief
for your father to the winds and take joy in uniting
with your vine god lover, free from your father's shame.
I'll not remind you of Sithon's odious love for you,
or of your postponed marriage, or of the suitor-slaying blade
in his murderous hand, or how he let you grow old,
unmarried and loveless and alone in bed.
Look at the rotting remnants of your suitors' bodies,
whom the Paphian adorned and a Fury killed;
and those heads hanging by your doors like gourds,
still dripping with gore from inhospitable weddings.
But you are no mortal seed of Sithon. No, you are divine,
sprung, I believe, from your own Thracian Ares
and brought into this world by Cytherea herself.
You bear the marks of both your parents:
the fighting spirit of Ares and Aphrodite's glow.
No, I believe Lord Hermes fathered you when he entered
Peitho's delicate bed. She brings marriages about,
and he taught you the wrestling that leads to Love."

With words such as these he soothed her sorrow
and laid the mourning maiden's lovely tears to rest.
He remained with his wedded bride for some time,
delighting in the love of this newly joined marriage.

Then, leaving the halls of Pallene and Thracian Boreas
he went to Rhea's domain, where, on Phrygian soil,
stood the temple of the fertile goddess Cybele.
It was in the foothills of Dindymon there that Aura,
a virgin mountain girl, grew up hunting,
a young lass not yet acquainted with love,
a cohort of the Archeress. She kept her distance
from unwarlike young ladies, and was herself,
this daughter of Lelantus, a younger Artemis.
The Titan Lelantus, who had wedded Periboia,
a daughter of Ocean, had in fact fathered
the storm-footed girl, who could have passed for a man
and knew nothing of Aphrodite. This rosy-armed,
lovely being had a growth spurt that left her
tall for her age. She found joy hunting in the hills,
where she would run down wild bears, send her spear
hurtling into a cougar. She never hunted small game—
fawns or hares—no, she bore her tawny quiver
to shoot down prides of ravenous mountain lions,
her shafts bringing certain death to such beasts.
And her name matched her action: Aura could run
as swiftly as air can swoop down a mountain.

Once, during the sweltering summer heat,
the lass took a nap, resting from the labors of the hunt.
Stretching out on Cybele's grass and propping her head
on a bush of chaste laurel, she lay asleep at high noon
and saw in her dreams a vision that foreshadowed
the pangs of a coming marriage—how the fiery god,
impetuous Eros, notched shafts to burning bowstring
and shot hares deep in the woods, his trifling arrows
mowing game down in rows. Cypris was there too,
laughing, wandering with Adonis as he hunted.
And Aura herself was there, carrying Eros' quiver
on her shoulder that until then had borne Artemis' bow.
Eros went on killing beasts until he wearied

of shooting arrows into a panther's scowl or a bear's snout.
Then he caught a lioness alive with his bewitching cestus
and dragged her off to show her fettered to his fun-loving mother.
And Aura saw in the gloom how impish Eros teased herself too
as she leaned her arm on Cytherea and Adonis
while he made the proud lioness genuflect to Aphrodite
as he shouted,
"Garlanded mother of the Loves, I lead to you
Aura, fond of her virginity, and she bows her neck.
And now you Graces, dancers of besotted Orchomenos,
crown this cestus, this strap that attends on marriage,
because it has subdued this stubborn, invincible lioness!"

Such was the prophesy mountain-bred Aura witnessed.
It was a dream come true for the Erotes, the Loves
who ensnare men and go hunting for women.

Aura awoke, and raged against the prudent laurel,
cursed out Eros and his Paphian mother,
but saved her best reproaches for nervy Sleep
and issued threats at the Dream. She was furious
with the laurel leaves as she sputtered these words:

"Daphne, why do you persecute me? What does your tree
have to do with Cypris? I was crazy to sleep
under your neighboring branches, hoping your plant
was friendly to virgins. Your reputation failed me!
So what was it, Daphne? Did your metamorphosis
transform your morals too? Did you become a servant
of conjugal Aphrodite after your death?
This isn't the tree of a decent girl but of a new bride.
You'd expect dreams like this if you slept under a myrtle.
This is a whore's dream! Did Peitho plant you,
or did your laureled Apollo, with his own hand?"

She was angry at the plant, Sleep, and Eros all at once.

Not long after this, Artemis, queen of the hunt,
was roaming the hills in the middle of summer,
when Helios flogs Leo's back with his whistling whip;
and, her skin getting sunburnt, she readied her chariot
to drive to a pool in the hills so she could cool off
with her naiad nymphs. The hill-ranging goddess
yoked up her prickets, and virginal Aura
mounted the car, took the reins and whip in hand,
and drove the horned team like a hurricane.
Artemis' handmaids, the unveiled daughters
of ever-flowing Ocean, attended the Archeress,
one sprinting in front of her queen's chariot,
while another tucked up her tunic and ran abreast,
and a third ran alongside with a hand on the car
as it sped along. The face of the arrowy goddess
glowed with light, shedding radiance from above
on her attendants.
Think of Selene the Moon
in her heavenly chariot, showering cloudless beams
as she rises full, refulgent among the fire-fed stars
and dimming all of heaven's lights with her face.

So too the effulgence of the Archeress
traversing the woodland, until she reached
a murmuring brook fed by the waters
of the heaven-fed Sangarius River.

There Aura stopped swinging her whip and reined in
the golden-bridled prickets, bringing her mistress's
radiant car to a stop by the banks of the stream.
The goddess quickly dismounted. Upis took the bow
from her shoulders, and Hecaërge the quiver.
The daughters of Ocean unloaded the hunting nets
and took care of the hounds. Then Loxo
unbound the boots from the goddess's feet.
As the water rippled around her in the midday heat
the goddess guarded her maiden modesty,

edging through the water with sparing steps
and lifting her tunic little by little from foot to head,
just its hem getting wet, and keeping her feet and thighs
close together as she gradually bathed her whole body.
Looking sideways at her across the water,
her sharp eyes bold and unashamed, Aura scanned
the holy body of the Maiden who is not to be seen,
gazing at her chaste mistress's divine beauty.
Then virgin Aura stretched out her hands and feet
and swam alongside of the now swimming divinity.
When the goddess emerged and was standing
half visible on the stream's bank, wringing out her hair.
Aura stood beside her and, fondling her breasts,
provoked the goddess with these impious words:

"Artemis, you're a virgin in name only,
because your breasts are soft and round
like Aphrodite's, and not manly like Athena's,
and your rosy cheeks are just glowing with light.
So, since your body is like the love goddess's,
you should reign over marriage along with her,
the Cytherean with her elegant hair, and welcome
a bridegroom into your chamber. Or if you want,
leave Athena and sleep with Hermes and Ares.
Or take up the bow and arrows of the Loves,
if a quiver full of arrows is all your passion.
With all due respect, my body is much better.
Just look at my physique. Your Aura's body
is quite masculine, and she can outrun the wind.
Look at my arms. See these muscles? And my breasts
are firm and unripe, not like a woman's at all.
Yours are practically oozing with drops of milk.
How do you keep your hands so soft?
Why aren't your breasts round disks like Aura's,
announcing to all unsullied virginity?"

She was mocking the goddess, who listened,
her head bowed in ominous silence,
anger swelling within her and her eyes flashing death.
She leapt up from the stream, put her tunic back on,
and tied the sash around her pure loins again,
deeply aggrieved. She went off in search of Nemesis,
and found her high in the clouds near Taurus,
close to Cydnus, where she had put an end
to the haughty boasts and threats of Typhoon.
A wheel rotated before the queen's feet,
symbol of the avenging wheel of Justice
the all-conquering deity who turns the path of life—
the wheel that rolls the proud to the ground.
Around her throne flew a bird of vengeance,
a winged griffin that can also go on all fours
before the flying goddess, this to demonstrate
that she travels to all four quarters of the world,
bridling high-crested men with her ineluctable bit:
such is the symbolism of that image, and indeed,
she rolls the proud man around as if with a whip.
When Nemesis saw Artemis' pallid face
she knew she was offended and threatened murder,
and so questioned her gently with these friendly words:

"Your looks, Artemis, shout out your anger.
What impious son of Earth torments you?
What new Typhoeus has sprouted up from the ground?
Has Tityus risen again to ogle your mother Leto
and touched the robe of the untouchable goddess?
Where is your bow, Artemis, and Apollo's arrows?
What Orion is forcing himself on you again?
Well, the wretch who touched your dress still lies
in his mother's flanks, a lifeless corpse; and if any man
clutches at your clothes with lascivious hands,
just grow another scorpion to avenge your maidenhood.
If bold Otos or boastful Ephialtes has panted
after your love, so out of their reach, just slay

the wooer of your unwedded virginity.
If some mother with a lot of kids aggrieves
your mother Leto, make her weep for her children,
another stone Niobe. So what if I make
another rock formation on Sipylus? Don't tell me
your almighty father is pestering you to marry,
as he did Athena, or that he's promised you to Hermes
as he promised Hephaestus to the same chaste Athena!
But, if it's some woman who is harassing you,
as one did your mother Leto, I myself
will avenge the goddess who showers arrows."

The avenging goddess had not finished speaking,
when the puppy-breeding maiden cried out, saying:

"All-vanquishing Virgin, Creation's Pilot,
it's not Zeus, not Niobe, not bold Otos either
who's persecuting me; no Tityus has tugged
at my mother Leto's long robes. No new Orion
born of the Earth forces himself upon me.
No, it's that loudmouth virgin daughter of Lelantus,
Aura, who mocks me, offends me with abusive speech.
How can I tell you what she said? I'm too embarrassed—
her calumny of my limbs, her abuse of my breasts!
But yes, mine and my mother's pain are alike.
Niobe offended Leto in Phrygia,
and in Phrygia Aura offended me.
But Niobe paid for it, Tantalus' daughter
who still weeps for her children with stony eyes.
I am the only insulted one who bears her disgrace
without vengeance. Aura, proud of her virginity,
washes no stone with her tears, has seen no spring
broadcasting the faults of her unsparing tongue.
Honor your Titan birth and honor me as you did my mother,
so I may see Aura's body metamorphosed into stone.
Don't leave a girl of your own race in grief
and having to watch Aura laugh at me again—
or just use your bronze sickle to drive her mad!"

Thus Artemis, and the goddess, reassuring her:

"Daughter of Leto, virgin huntress, sister of Phoebus,
I will not punish a Titan girl with my sickle,
or transform a maiden into Phrygian stone,
for I myself am of ancient Titan blood,
and her father Lelantus would blame me when he heard.
But I will do this for you, Archer Goddess: Aura
has slandered your virginity, and so she will be
a virgin no longer. You shall see her lapped
in a mountain stream, weeping a fountain of tears
for the sash she wore when she was a maiden."

After Nemesis consoled her, Artemis mounted
her deer-drawn chariot, and leaving the mountain
headed back to Phrygia. And with speed to match,
the avenging goddess left in pursuit of Aura,
her chariot drawn by harnessed aerial griffins
coursing swiftly through air until she drew on the bits
of her four-footed birds and landed on Sipylos' peak,
right in front of Niobe's stone-eyeballed face.
Then she went up to proud Aura and lashed her neck
with her snaky whip, struck the poor girl
with the round wheel of justice, and bent her foolish,
unbending mind. The viperous Adrasteian lash
curled around Aura's maiden sash, pleasing Artemis
and her brooding brother Dionysus as well.
And even though she knew nothing of love
she prepared for him another love, a love after Pallene
and after the loss of Ariadne—the former left
in her own country, the latter a stone in a foreign land,
a stone like Hera's statue—and most of all
for his lack of success in bedding Beroë.

Then Nemesis flew back to snow-beaten Taurus
until she came to Cydnus again. And Eros
wounded Dionysus with a sweet arrowshot
and flew lightly to Olympus on swooping wings.

The hill-roaming god was now scourged with a greater fire
and without the slightest relief, with no hope
of Aura's love and no cure for his passion. Eros inflamed him
more and more with a soul-hexing fixation
to mate with the obstinate Aura no matter how long it took.
He struggled to keep his desire hidden, used no sweet-talk
with Aura in the woods for fear she might avoid him.
Is there anything more shameless than men desiring
what women do not? Wandering Bacchus
felt Love's arrow fixed in his heart whenever the maiden
was driving her pack of dogs in the woods. If he glimpsed
just a thigh when a venereal breeze lifted her tunic,
he melted like a woman. At last, battered by his desperate
desire for Aura he cried out in a deranged voice:

"I'm the spitting image of lovesick Pan whenever that girl
runs from me like a wind-gypsy, wandering the wild
with sandals more agile than invisible Echo's.
You are lucky, Pan, much more than I, for you found
in your roaming a drug for your love: a mind-soothing voice.
Unstatic Echo follows your beat and returns your sounds
in tune with your voice. If only virginal Aura
had done the same and let a single word slip from her lips!
This love of mine is unlike all others, for the girl herself
has a nature unlike all the rest of the girls.
What cure is there for my pain? Charm her
with a nod and a lover's wink? Ha! When could
Aura ever be charmed by an eyelid flickering?
Who could seduce a she-bear with love-mad looks,
woo one with whispers? Has anyone ever beguiled
a pine tree? Persuaded a dogwood? Wedded a rock?
What man could charm the mind of love-proof Aura?
What man could charm her? Who would mention marriage,
mention aphrodisiacal girdles to this unbelted girl?
Mention the sweet sting of love or Aphrodite's name?
Athena would be persuaded sooner. Unflutterable Artemis
avoids me as much as virginal Aura does.

If she would at least say to me with her dear lips,
'Bacchus, stop pining, forget about Aura.'"

Bacchus said these things to the vernal breezes
as he made his way through meadows in flower.
At noon he stopped to rest beside a fragrant myrtle,
leaning against the tree's trunk and listening
to the West Wind's whispers, overcome with fatigue
and with Eros. As he sat there a hamadryad nymph,
huddled within her native tree, peeked out through her veil
and, out of loyalty both to the Cyprian goddess
and to lovelorn Lyaeus, spoke these words:

"Bacchus can never lead Aura to bed
unless he binds her first in heavy chains,
winding her hands and feet in Cyprian bondage;
or else yokes her in marriage while she is asleep,
stealing her maidenhood without paying a bride price."

Then the hamadryad hid again in her coeval tree,
reentering the timber that was her home.
But Bacchus,
beset with love-breeding dreams, put his mind on parade.
The soul of dead Ariadne came, borne on the wind,
and stood beside the sleeping Dionysus,
jealous after death, and spoke as a dream speaks:

"You have forgotten your former bride, Dionysus.
You yearn for Aura and no longer care for Ariadne.
O my dear Theseus, whom a bitter wind stole.
O my own Theseus, whom Phaedra got as husband.
It was my fate that a perjured husband desert me
if the sweet lad left me while I was asleep, and instead
I was married to Lyaeus, a fickle husband and cheat.
I should have wed a mortal, one who would die soon,
or armed myself against love-crazed Dionysus
like a Lemnian woman. But now, after Theseus,

I'll have to call you too a perjured bridegroom
who climbs into multiple marriage beds!
If your new bride wants a gift, here, take this distaff,
my friendly donation to her dowry, so you can give
your mountaineering bride a little something
from your Minoan wife, and so people can say,
'She gave Theseus a thread, a distaff to Dionysus.'
You are just like Zeus, exchanging bed for bed,
just like Cronus, his lecherous father,
with an insatiable itch for playing musical beds!
O yes, I know all about your recent marriage
to Sithonian Pallene, and to Althaea as well.
I won't even mention your affair with Coronis
from whose bed the triplet Graces were born,
joined at the hip. But O Mycenae, shout out my fate
from the rooftops, and the savage glare of Medusa!
Shores of Naxos, cry aloud Ariadne's bondage
to a despicable love, and say 'O bridegroom Theseus,
Minos' daughter calls you out against Dionysus!'
But why do I think of Cecropian Athens?
It is with Paphian Aphrodite I lodge my complaint
against them both, Theseus and Dionysus as well!"

And her shade flew away like shadowy smoke.

Bold Bacchus awoke and shook off hovering Sleep.
He pitied Ariadne for her sorrow in his dream,
then tried to dream up some scam that would lead him to Love.
First off he recalled how he had bedded the Astacid nymph
long ago, how he had wooed her with a sly potion
and made sleep an ingress to intoxicated nuptials.

While Bacchus was planning how to trick her into bed
Lelantus' daughter was wandering in search
of a fountain or spring to quench her parching thirst.
The god couldn't help but see her running through the hills,

thirsty Aura. He leapt up quickly and with his thyrsus
started to dig at the foot of a cliff. The hill split open,
and from its scented bosom out gushed a purple stream of wine.
And to please Lyaeus, the Seasons, Helios' handmaids,
painted the spring's margins with flowers, and fragrances
from a fresh meadow wafted through the soft air.
Clustered there were the blossoms named for Narcissus,
the beautiful boy begotten by Endymion upon Selene
on leafy Latmos—Narcissus, who long ago gazed
at his reflection in the water, mute visage
of a lovely deceiver, and died as he stared
at his shape's shadowy image. Growing there also
was the Amyclaian iris (another Hyacinthus)
and flocking above the burgeoning meadow
nightingales sang over the springtime blossoms.

It was noontime there when Aura ran up
in her quest for water—raindrops from Zeus,
a fountain, a stream cascading down from the hills—
but Eros had shed a mist over her eyelids.
As soon as she faced the treacherous fountain
Peitho dispersed the fog shading her eyes
and called to Aura like a herald at a wedding:

"This way, maiden! Take a sip from this nuptial fountain
and then receive your lover into your bosom."

The maiden saw it with joy, and falling to her knees
gulped through open lips the Dionysiac liquid.
And when she had drunk, virgin Aura exclaimed:

"Naiads, what is this miracle? Where does this soothing water
come from? Who bubbled this drink? What heavenly womb
bore him? I certainly can't walk after drinking this. No,
my feet are heavy, I'm in the spell of sweet sleep,
my speech is slurred and all I can do is stammer."

She spoke, and then staggered along, stumbling
and swerving this way and that as she went her way,
her brow quivering and her temples throbbing.
Her head sagged and tilted down to her shoulder
as she collapsed on the ground beside a tall tree,
commending to Earth her unguarded virginity.

When fiery Eros saw Aura's knees buckle
he leapt down from heaven with a peaceful smile
and in accord with the wine god said to him:

"In the hunt, Dionysus? Virgin Aura awaits."

And he was off to Olympus, flapping his wings,
bur before he left he inscribed on the springtime petals:

Bridegroom, complete your nuptials while the bride still sleeps,
and let us be silent lest sleep abandon the bride.

And Bacchus, seeing her on the unblanketed ground
plucking the Lethaean feather of nuptial Sleep,
crept up barefoot and on tiptoe without a sound
and approached the mute bed of voiceless Aura.
With a sparing hand he put away the girl's quiver
and hid her bow in a hollow of a boulder
so she couldn't shoot him if she shook off Sleep's wing.
Then he tied her feet together with unloosable knots
and spiraled a cord round about her wrists
so she couldn't escape. Then he laid her in the dust,
a virgin heavy with sleep readied for Aphrodite,
and stole the bridal fruit from slumbering Aura.
This husband left no gift. The poor girl, drunk with wine,
immobile on the ground, was wedded to Dionysus.
Aura's body was wrapped in Sleep, who with shadowy wings
was Bacchus' wedding marshal, for he too had experience
with the Paphian, and was yoked with the Moon,
and accompanies the Loves in nocturnal caressing.

So the wedding was like a dream, and instead of folk
frolicking in dances, the hill itself leapt and skipped,
the half-visible hamadryad shook her agemate fir,
and only virginal Echo did not dance in the mountains,
but blushing with shame hid herself beneath the rock,
unwilling to witness woman-mad Bacchus' wedding.

When the vine god groom had consummated his marriage
on that soundless bed, he lifted his feet cautiously,
kissed the bride's lovely lips, untied her feet and hands,
retrieved the quiver and bow from the boulder
and laid them beside her. Then he went back
to his satyrs, a whiff of wedlock still about him,
leaving to the winds Aura still asleep on the ground.

After this affection the bride lurched up, shaking off
the limb-slackening sleep that testified to lovemaking—
and was shocked to see her breasts bereft of modest bodice,
the cleft between her thighs exposed, and her dress spotted
with the drops of wedlock that were witness
to a maidenhood ravished without bridal dowry.
She was maddened at the sight, then somberly bound
her bodice around her chest, and tied (in vain now)
her maidenly band over her rounded breast. And then,
she shrieked in anguish, and in the grip of madness
she chased the countrymen, slaughtered shepherds
on the leafy slopes to punish her treacherous husband
with avenging justice, cut down oxherds with savage steel,
for she knew all about the charming Tithonus, Dawn's lover,
the lovelorn oxherd; knew also that Selene drove cattle
as did her Latmian lover Endymion; and she had heard
of Phrygian Hymnus too, unlucky in love, a herdsman
whom another maiden slew. Then she went after goatherds,
killing them and their flocks of goats whole, for she had seen
Pan, the distempered lover with a shaggy goatface,
and was convinced that Pan, tormented with desire for Echo,
had violated the nymph in her sleep. She was even harder

on the farmers, mowing them down as being slaves to Cypris,
since Iasion after all had tilled the soil and had been
a bedmate of Demeter, mother of sheaves. As for the hunters,
she killed them believing an old story, that Cephalus,
a hunter from the country of unmothered Athena,
was also the husband of rose-garlanded Dawn.
Then there were the vintners, workmen of Bacchus.
She killed them too because they are Lyaeus' servants
who squeeze out his dewy, intoxicating juice,
and, always being drunk, are dangerous lovers.
She had not yet come to grips with Dionysus' cunning,
or the seductive potion that the Cytherean serves up.
But she did make the herdsmen's mountain huts empty,
and she drenched all the hills with scarlet blood.

Deeply disturbed, quivering with madness,
she came to the temple of Cypris. Untying the belt
that cinched her newspun tunic, she began to flog
the invincible goddess's delicate statue,
then took it to the banks of the Sangarius
and sent Aphrodite rolling into the stream,
naked among the naked naiads, with the whip
twisted around it; and throwing the temple's
delicate image of Eros into the dirt, she left
the foamborn goddess's shrine deserted.
Then, wandering out of sight, she plunged into her familiar,
forested haunts, set out net-stakes and remembered the hunt,
her eyes filled with tears as she lamented her maidenhood:

"What god has undone my virginity's bond?
If it was scheming Zeus in some disguise
who forced me as I lay alone on my bed,
if he did not respect our neighbor Rhea,
I will leave the wild woods and shoot the starry sky!
If Phoebus Apollo lay with me as I slept
I will destroy Pytho stone by sacred stone!
If Cyllenian Hermes has defiled my bed,

my arrows will annihilate all Arcadia
and I will make gold-chapleted Peitho my slave!
If Dionysus came unseen and raped me in a dream,
I will go to Cybele's high hall and chase
the lust-mad god from Tmolus' high ridges!
Quiver of death on my shoulders, I will attack Paphos,
Phrygia, draw my bow on both Dionysus and Cypris!
And you, Archeress, you have enraged me most,
because you, a virgin yourself, did not kill me
as I slept still a virgin, and did not defend me
against my bedfellow with your pure shafts!"

Overcome with tears, she checked her trembling voice.
And then poor Aura, bearing the burgeoning seed
of child-begetting Bacchus, bore a double weight,
cursing as a maddened wife her embryonic burden
and as Aura lamenting her lost maidenhood,
not knowing whether it was a virgin conception
or the work of some scheming human or god.
She remembered Zeus' bride Bercyntian Plouto,
so unhappy in bearing her son Tantalus.
In her senseless fury she wanted to cut herself open,
tear open her womb so that the half-formed baby
would not survive and have to be reared.
She even picked up a sword and considered
driving it through her bare chest with unsparing hand.
And she would often go to the cave of a lioness
with newborn cubs, hoping to be ensnared by Fate,
but the dread beast would run out to the mountainside
in mortal fear and hide in the rocks, leaving her cubs behind.
She often thought of piercing her swelling womb
and by committing suicide escape from shame itself
and the taunts that would issue from Artemis' mouth.
And she longed to know her husband, so she could
serve up her son in a dish to the loathsome bastard
and be a child-slaying mate, so that men might say,
"Aura, grim bride and infanticide, is a second Procne."

And then Artemis, seeing her great with child,
came up to her with a smirk on her face
and began to tease the poor girl mercilessly:

"I saw it all, saw Sleep, Aphrodite's chambermaid,
saw the deceptive, beige bridal fountain
where young girls drink treacherous potions
and loosen the undies they have worn all their lives
in a dream of maidenhood-stealing marriage.
O yes, I have seen the slope where a woman
is made a bride unforeseen, in deceitful sleep,
beside a mating rock. I have seen Aphrodite's
mountain of love where paramours steal
women's virginity and run away to hide.
Tell me, you little prig, why are you walking
so slowly today? You used to be as quick
as the wind, so why are you plodding along like this?
You were wooed unwilling and don't know your lover!
You can't hide your sneaky wedding, because your breasts,
newly swollen with milk, announce a husband.
Tell me, heavy sleeper, pig-butcher, virgin, bride,
why is your once ruddy complexion so pale?
Who defiled your bed? Who stole your virginity?
Blond naiads, do not hide Aura's bridegroom!
I know your furtive husband, you heavyweight woman.
No matter how much you want to you can't hide
your wedding from me. I saw your husband, O yes.
You were lying down, your body heavy with sleep,
and didn't budge when you were wedded by Bacchus.
Alright then, leave your bow, renounce your quiver,
and take up the mystic rites of woman-mad Bacchus,
tambourine and trilling hornpipes in hand.
But one more thing. What kind of wedding gifts
were you given by your new husband Bacchus?
A fawnskin to show you're a married woman?
Bronze rattles for your kids to play with?
Well, a thyrsus for sure, so you can spear lions.

Or maybe the cymbals that nurses shake
to soothe little children when they scream in pain."

Having mocked Aura, the divinity went off
to shoot arrows at her wild beasts again,
letting her anger dissolve in the aerial winds.

The girl disappeared into the mountain's high rocks,
and when she felt the sharp pangs of childbirth begin
she roared like a lioness in labor, and the cliffs resounded
as mournful Echo answered her shrieks and moans.
Aura pressed her hands on her belly as if to seal off
the delivery of her ripening child, and she did delay
the now perfected foetus, for she hated Artemis
and would not beseech her in her pain. Nor would she pray
to the Eileithyiae, goddesses of childbirth,
fearing that as daughters of Bacchus' stepmother Hera
they might oppress her delivery with even more pain.
At last the girl cried out with the agony of one
who had never been in the grip of Necessity:

"May I see the Archeress and the warrior Athena
just as I am now, see both of them pregnant!
Give Artemis a hard time in labor,
O midwife Seasons! Be there at her delivery
and say to Tritogeneia, 'Well, greyeyed virgin,
the motherless has now become a new mother!'
And may I see Echo, who loves virginity so much,
suffer as I do after she has slept with Pan
or with Dionysus, who started all my trouble.
And if you gave birth, Artemis, it would comfort Aura
to see you ooze milk from your masculine breast!"

So she spoke, lamenting her heavy birth pangs.
And Artemis delayed the birth, giving the bride
the added pain of retarded delivery.
But Nicaea, who led the mystic rites of Lyaeus,

saw Aura's pain and her distraught sense of shame,
and spoke to her secretly in tones of pity:

"Aura, I know what you're going through,
grieving for your lost virginity. But since you do
carry in your womb pregnancy's painful burden,
endure for me now the pangs of delivery,
endure giving your untaught breast to an infant.
Oh, why did you drink wine, that robbed me
of my chastity too? Why did you drink wine, Aura,
to the point you were pregnant? You too suffered
what I suffered, and you an enemy of marriage!
And you also have to blame a treacherous sleep
sent by the Loves, who are friendly to marriage.
The selfsame fraud forced marriage on us both.
A single husband for Aura and virgin Nicaea,
the mother of children! I no longer possess
a hunting bow, no longer draw, as once I did,
my arrow-notched bowstring. I am a female drudge
working the loom, a wild Amazon no more."

She spoke in pity of Aura's birth pangs
and as one who had felt those pangs herself.
But Artemis, hearing Aura's echoing cries
came again to the bride and triumphantly
taunted the miserable girl with stinging words:

"Well, virgin, who has made you a pregnant mother?
How did this milk form in your breast if you knew
nothing of marriage? I've never heard of a virgin
bearing a child. Has my father altered nature?
Do unmarried women now bear children?
You're a virginal girl, but you're having babies
even though you despise Aphrodite. Do women in labor
no longer call on Artemis for help, or do you alone
not want the Archeress, goddess of the wild?
You know, Eileithyia, who guides your birthing,

didn't see your Dionysus either when he emerged
from his mother's womb. No, thunderbolts
were his midwives, and he was only half-formed!
And don't be upset that you are delivering
among these crags, where Rhea too has borne children.
It's no great matter, you bearing children in the mountains,
mountaineering dame of mountain-ranging Dionysus!"

She spoke, and though the nymph was indignant
and laboring, she still was ashamed before Artemis.
The poor girl still wanted her maidenhood
though she was about to give birth. One baby
quickly came into the light, for as soon as Artemis
spoke the word that triggered delivery
Aura's womb opened, and then a second babe came—
a set of twins. It was after these twins
that Dindymon, Rhea's twin peaks, were named.
And Artemis, seeing how beautiful
these boys were, changed her tune and said:

"Wetnurse, lone woman, twin-bearer, ill-married bride,
offer your callow breast to your sons, virgin mother.
Your boys are calling papa, asking for their father.
Tell your children the name of your covert lover
Artemis knows nothing of marriage, she's never nursed
a son at her breast. These mountains were your bed,
and dappled fawnskins will swaddle your babies. "

She spoke, and plunged swiftly into the woods' shade.
Then Dionysus called Nicaea, his own Cybeleïd nymph,
and smiling pointed to Aura still berating her childbed.
Proud of his late marriage to the bereft girl, he said:

"At last, Nicaea, you have consolation for your love.
Your Dionysus has stolen a marriage bed again
and forcibly mated with another virgin, one who
once shrank from the mere name of Love but now has seen

a marriage modelled on yours, Aura of the mountains.
You are not alone in having sweet sleep guide you to love,
not alone in drinking deceptive wine that stole your virginity.
Once more a spring of nuptial wine has burst from a rock,
and, not knowing what it was, Aura drank deep.
You have learnt childbirth's throes the hard way,
and so, by Teletê, your dance-weaving daughter,
I beg you, hurry and lift up my son, before Aura,
my desperate Aura, strangles him. I know she will kill
one of the two baby boys in her madness,
but you must save Iacchus, the better of the two,
and your Teletê will serve son and father both."

Having said this Bacchus departed in triumph,
proud of both of his Phrygian marriages,
one with an older wife, one with a younger bride,
who meanwhile was in deep distress beside the rock
where her twins had been born. Still in childbed
she held up the two boys and cried aloud:

"From the sky came this marriage, I will throw my offspring
back into the sky! I was wed by the wind
and saw no mortal's bed. My namesake winds
came down to the marriage of Aura the Windmaid,
so let the breezes carry off my womb's offspring.
Off with you, accursed children of a treacherous father!
I never bore you. What are women's sorrows to me?
Come out in the open now, you lions, and hunt unafraid
in the woods. Aura is no longer your enemy.
Dancing-eyed hares, you are better than hounds!
Come play with me, jackals! I will watch the leopard
cavorting fearlessly beside my bed. Bring your friend,
the bear! Don't be afraid. Now that Aura has children
her bronze-tipped arrows have become womanish.
A virgin once, I am ashamed to be called a bride,
which would mean offering my strong breast to infants,

pressing out sham milk with my hand, or being called
'mother dear' in the woods where I killed wild beasts!"

So she took her babies and laid them in a cave
as a meal for a lioness. But a thoughtful leopard
nuzzled their bodies with her jowls and nursed
Dionysus' beautiful boys at her wise breast.
Astonished serpents with venomous mouths
surrounded the nursery, for Aura's bridegroom
had made even the beasts gentle in guarding his newborns.

Then Lelantus' daughter leapt up like a lioness,
tore one child from the leopard's muzzle and hurled it
high into the stormy atmosphere. The newborn baby
fell from the sky headlong onto the ground's whirling dust,
and she snatched him up and entombed his body
in her own maw, a dear dinner indeed. Artemis
was terrified of this heartless mother, and seizing
Aura's other child she hurried off through the woods,
cradling an unfamiliar burden in the crook of her arm.

After her Bacchic mating and childbirth's delirium,
Aura was anxious to escape her besmirched reputation.
She still held sacred her sense of maidenly shame.
So she went to the banks of the Sangarius, threw
her recurve bow and quiver into the water,
and plunged headfirst into the river's depths,
too mortified to let her eyes look on the light of Dawn.
The river water covered her, and Zeus son of Cronus
turned her into a wellspring. Her breasts became spouts
of cascading water, the stream was her body,
her hair turned into flowers, her bow became the horns
of the bull-like horned river, the bowstring became a rush,
and the whistling arrows turned into vocal reeds.
Her quiver sank to the river's muddy bed and changed
into a hollow channel that poured out babbling water.

Then the Archeress laid her anger to rest. She scoured
the forest, looking for traces of Lyaeus
in the mountains he loved, with Aura's newborn babe
still in her arms, still bearing another's burden,
until she delivered with all due respect
the son that was his to her brother Dionysus.

The father entrusted his son to Nicaea to nurse.
She took him and, pressing out milk from her breasts
nursed the baby boy. When he was still quite young
Bacchus took little Bacchus into his chariot
and presented him to Athena as she celebrated
her Attic mysteries. The boy babbled "Euoi"
in her temple, and the goddess received him
into her maiden, god-welcoming bosom
and nursed the child with the breast that until then
only Erectheus had sucked, and let the ersatz milk
trickle unbidden from her unripe breast.
The goddess entrusted him to the Bacchants of Eleusis,
and these wives of Marathon, decked in ivy,
circled the boy Iacchus in nightly dances,
lifting the Attic torch to honor this lateborn deity.
They honored him as a god, second only to the son
of Persephone, and to Semele's son himself.
And they established sacrifices to honor
Dionysus lateborn and firstborn Dionysus,
and thirdly they chanted a new hymn for Iacchus.
Athens reveled in these three celebrations,
and in the latest dance the Athenians still honor
Zagreus, Bromius, and Iacchus together.

Nor had Bacchus forgotten his beloved Cydonian,
no, he still remembered the bride that was his,
and he placed in the Olympian sky the tiara
of deceased Ariadne as a witness of his love,
an eternal sign marking a garlanded wedding.

And then

the vine god ascended to his ancestral heaven
and at table with the father who had given him birth,
after all the mortals' banquets, after all the wine poured out,
he drank celestial nectar from nobler goblets,
and sat with his brothers,
Leto's son Apollo,
and Hermes, son of Maia.

On Translating Nonnus

We asked a cross-section of our translators from different backgrounds to set down their thoughts on Nonnus, on translation, and on their experience of both. Here are their responses.

Frederick Ahl

You won't find my name, or that of many contributors here, in Nonnus bibliographies. Most of us aren't Nonnus scholars. Neither was Douglass Parker. Nonnus isn't even mentioned on his Wikipedia page. But Doug found Nonnus frolicsome, frolicked with him, and let us in on the frolics through recitations from his unpublished translations of the first two books of the *Dionysiaca*, circulated privately among colleagues and students. It was ancient Greek poetry for the sheer fun of it, an extravaganza of interplay between ourselves, the poet of Panopolis, Egypt, and the poet of LaPorte, Indiana. Some colleagues or fellow students reckoned it scholarly energy dissipated on a long and inconsequential ancient epicist. Yet Doug and Nonnus awakened a little of the poet and translator in us all. That's why this unique volume finally publishes not only his wonderful versions which might otherwise have been lost, but what may prove to be a Parkerian reading of this whole unique poem. Few scholars have devoted the years necessary to grasp, much less wrestle into another language, the rhetorical brilliance of the *Dionysiaca* in its entirety—not even Doug, who, as a translator, could outmatch Aristophanes in wordplay, or those listed in every Nonnus bibliography: the amazing Francis Vian and W. H. D. Rouse, whose Loeb first made Nonnus accessible in English.

My tiny fragment of this vast work was many months in the making. I've tried to retain Nonnus' frolicsome tone and complex wordplay, while staying close to his grammar and syntax. I've kept Nonnus' hexameter metrical format (though I use more spondees) because I want to sustain his traditionally epic rhythm without imparting to him the distinctly Elizabethan or Victorian overtones that Derek Walcott finds in the commonly used iambic pentameters. I have also not "antiqued" my usage. English, like Latin, doesn't need archaizing language to sustain Homeric hexameters, as Nonnus does within the tradition of Alexandrian and Byzantine Greek verse, where poetic usage is far distant from contemporary vernaculars. I have occasionally expanded the original slightly when most readers will need more detail than he supplies to catch his point.

Catherine Anderson

Ancient Wars, Modern Memories

I celebrate
the first fruits of war and how the honey-trickled river
waters turn to wine.

When I came to Book 17, our country was in the nineteenth year of the war in Afghanistan, the longest in our modern history. The descriptive heading at the beginning of Nonnus' seventeenth book, a celebration of the "first fruits of war" posed a challenge to a person of my time, skeptical of all wars, fearful of their infinite propensity to keep expanding. The aftermath of the long war of my childhood, the war in Vietnam, can still be felt in our global policies and how we care for our veterans. The war of my father and uncles, World War II, though viewed by many as an honorable war, still took its toll on the capacity of our fathers to feel and express emotions or dissent. Whatever skepticism our fathers may have harbored as our country entered into a future conflict with Southeast Asia, they held back. They did not want to seem unpatriotic and by their silent approval, the Vietnam War continued. One war shadows another war. All shadows are alike.

With much humility, as I am a poet and not a scholar of ancient Greek, I wanted to convey a slice of this startling epic as felt by a modern reader. Such an interpretation requires looking through a long telescope of history, to see the tumultuous present layered by a vivid past. In any war, an enemy is constructed, given character and imbued with a personality sometimes malevolent, stupid, or cunning. Yet both sides know little or nothing about each other. An honest reckoning of World War II takes into account the Japanese side, and the killing of hundreds of thousands of Japanese civilians in the bombing of Hiroshima and Nagasaki, where no resemblance to honor remains. If Book 17 is a "celebration" of a battle, however mythological, the first thing I wanted to do was level the killing field. To give the opposing side, Bacchus' enemy, a name worthy of its intention to confront power, I called these fighting men, with roots in ancient geography, "Warriors of the River Indus." By offering a bit of equality on the mythical field of the imagination, I thought we could better understand the poem in modern terms, that is, heavy with loss on both sides.

Such a choice infers a narrator steering the direction of these mythological adventures of the god of wine. Was there a narrator? Who is the "I" of the verse heading to Book 17? Could it be Nonnus, carrying on the bardic tradition of Homer? If so, it was important to reflect a witness to these horrors, and so I included a narrator's voice, the "I" behind the subtitle. Taking liberty, I inserted a few lines not found in the original, ones I thought were implied by the verse. Often these were questions probing the actions just narrated, such as at the conclusion of a series of brutal battles when Aristaeus moves among the Bassarids offering healing unguents and for a moment, unsteady calm. As a counterpoint, the conjured narrator asks: "But when does war truly end, wounds / healed, men and women recovered?" These narrations were offset in italics, implying a quiet, embedded speaker. The point was for the modern reader to be made clear of the paradox of loss felt in wars that obliterate everything human.

If the poet Nonnus was writing as a descendant of Homer, then this book carries some of the characteristics of the *Iliad*, a "poem of force," as Simone Weil so justly described it. Like the *Iliad*, Book 17 is about retribution, and as Weil reminds us, all epic is retribution. Weil states that the Greeks were "endowed with spiritual force that allowed them to avoid self-deception." To the Greeks, she tells us, force was a hero, a force not ignored, covered up, or avoided. As modern readers of this kaleidoscopic epic, we yearn to feel that heroic force transcending time to better understand our own experience—without self-deception—of too many wars lasting too many years.

Adrienne Atkins

Although the two books that I translated, 29 and 33, both center on the war in India, they differ dramatically in their tone, style, pace, and content. Book 29 is battle-focused, low on direct speech, and largely catalogic. The conflict of Book 33, meanwhile, is emotional and psychological rather than physical, with narrative structures and characters familiar from the Greek novel and Christian martyr stories (see Hadjittofi, "Erotic Fiction and Christian Sexual Ethics"). One of my greatest challenges—and I'm sure other translators on this project agree—was to develop a translation style capable of encompassing the variety present in my sections of the poem.

Given this need for flexibility, I opted for a free-verse translation. Rhythm and rhyme are excellent ways to ensure that narrative poetry feels like poetry without compromising the clarity of the story, and I made frequent use of these; however, I found it useful to adapt them to suit the needs of the passage. In addition, this approach allowed me to manipulate line length here and there for emphasis or emotional effect (e.g., the diminishing lines in 33.48–54). More broadly, I also committed to shorter lines in Book 29 to maintain momentum in the battle narrative, and gave myself greater leeway in Book 33, where it was often necessary to unpack obscure mythological references.

This raises the issue of glossing. Given the length of the poem, it seems likely that many readers will drop in for specific books or episodes rather than reading straight through. With this in mind, I adopted a policy of glossing names and references liberally, even in the case of recurring characters like Morrheus and Deriades, and recurring mythological references like the story of Hyacinthus. I frequently added titles (e.g., "*King* Deriades") or clarified relationships (e.g., "*Apollo's lover* Hyacinthus"). This approach was also useful in the case of Nonnus' more obscure references, which were especially concentrated in the second half of Book 33. The storyline here centers on the difficult themes of sexual assault and suicide, and Nonnus develops these themes through a whirlwind of mythological allusion, culminating in juxtaposed speeches by the aggressor and the victim. Here especially, it seemed important to explicate Nonnus' allusions freely so that they didn't act as a barrier between the readers and the characters.

One of my favorite aspects of the *Dionysiaca* is the vividness of its characters, and developing their voices was a high priority for me. Nonnus packs a lot of personality into direct speeches, even those by side characters, like the dream that visits Ares (29.328–61). As such, I often manipulated the tone of speeches to convey the personalities I saw represented. Nonnus also sometimes develops his characters through striking imagery, and I tried to flag these moments; so, for instance, πολυφλοίσβῳ δὲ μερίμνῃ (33.263) became "his anxiety a roaring sea" to highlight Nonnus' psychological use of an epic auditory adjective that is typically applied to the sea. These are some of the most rewarding features of the *Dionysiaca*'s poetics, and I hope readers will enjoy experiencing them in this translation.

Gordon Braden

Being only one of forty-two translators of Nonnus' epic is a blessing, and not only because of the poem's length. Short of some kind of miracle (though those can happen), the poem's baffling aesthetic—unified by an obsessive verbal style but weirdly diverse in its tone and action—defies any attempt at imagining an inclusive equivalent in English. Freed from the obligation to come up with anything like that, the individual translator can concentrate on getting some one thing right, or nearly right. With my own assignment, Book 24—the poem's halfway point, preceding a kind of intermission and a six-year break in the action—I took my cue from the poet's repeatedly demonstrated self-consciousness about the tradition, a self-consciousness which by its very nature brings with it an often inscrutable sense of detachment from that tradition. To catch that note, I had the idea of using *ottava rima*, a prosodic form associated in European poetry since the Renaissance with a similar sense of epic operating at a certain distance from itself. It is the form used in Italian by Lodovico Ariosto for his *Orlando furioso*, the great and immensely influential sixteenth-century poem inflecting chivalric legend with contemporary knowingness; the form was memorably anglicized by John Harington (queen Elizabeth's godson, remembered as the inventor of the flush toilet and more recently as an ancestor of Kit Harington) to translate Ariosto's poem into English. Three centuries later, Byron made it the vehicle of his greatest contribution to the language, his disillusioned but undaunted *Don Juan*. It is also, as it happens, the form of Giambattista Marino's *L'Adone*, the poem that shows more than any other literary work of its time the effect of the early modern rediscovery of Nonnus' epic. From this formal choice on my part I found the actual translating followed with surprising ease.

A major part of the effect of ottava rima in English has to do with the feminine rhymes. In Italian the rhymes are all feminine—that comes with the hendecasyllabic line—but in English feminine rhymes are more difficult to sustain, and have tended to be used for special effect, usually comic. I opted for the discipline of alternating masculine and feminine rhymes in the first six lines of the stanza, a pattern Byron often adopts; doing so I thought might induce under everything a tone in which seriousness and frivolity are constantly and rapidly juxtaposed. (Such a juxtaposition is writ large in the action of the poem as a whole, and specifically in the second half of Book 24, split between the lamentations of the defeated Indians and the hard-partying and joking of the victorious Dionysians.) The strain of finding so many feminine rhymes itself has a way of generating silliness. Byron famously embraced that result in his first stanza, where he rhymed "new one" and "true one" with "Juan" (in the process making a joke about anglophone mangling of foreign names). I was happy to welcome similar outcomes—most shamelessly, and with conspicuous strain, "lick in / stick in / obstetrician." I also welcomed the opportunity presented by the strict form (my stresses can wander around a bit, but the syllable count is rigorous) for antic enjambments to jolt the tone of things (the first of these between stanzas 3 and 4), and found they kept happening almost on their own. I am aware that I was effectively writing off a major dimension of Nonnus' style, the thunderous way his mannered hexameters incorporate a fair amount of the epic grandiloquence they simultaneously disorder. But grandiloquence isn't very accessible in contemporary American English, except as a third-rate joke; I leave that challenge to other translators, and concentrate on amplifying the playfulness and skepticism inside all the racket.

I have made some brief subtractions and additions. The former are signaled in the text, and the reason for them should be obvious. The signals themselves constitute additions, making explicit the kind of literary self-reference everywhere operating in the Greek though mostly now visible only to scholars; my intruded suggestion in stanza 6 that readers think back to Books 1 and 2 is in the same general category. In a similar spirit, I have occasionally supplemented Nonnus' carpet of literary allusions with quotations from my own more recent cultural memory; readers who think they detect the presence of Leonard Cohen, Frank Sinatra ("unhand the threads"), and Walter Cronkite (!) will not be mistaken. (I realize that these now date me, but they were too handy to pass up.) More seriously, in places I add a word or two to impart what seems to me a relevant spin to the action. The first of these comes at the very start and indeed gave me my sense of direction for the rest. Nonnus tells us that Father Zeus gathered his clouds and sent out a thunderbolt; it occurred to me that the right note to sound would be a slightly detached awareness of playing a role: "My cue to intervene, thought Zeus the father." In this saturated tradition, even the king of the gods knows he's working from a script. At the end of the book a less ironic inflection seemed in order, as things quiet down and the epic as a whole reaches its midpoint and a pause. Nonnus ends with a closing look, after the god himself has withdrawn and most of the celebrants have drunk and danced themselves into unconsciousness, at a contingent of women continuing by torchlight up on the mountain. I enhanced this, without, I hope, distorting it: "the endless light / Of Bacchants dancing all the blessed night." It is a distant, eerie vision of the "indestructible life" (*unzerstörbar Leben*) that the Hungarian scholar Karl Kerényi saw as the core of the original Dionysiac cultus. My contribution is "blessed": an enigmatic sanctity glowing out there in the dark in the wake of triumphant violence.

Anne Carson

Book 23 is a wordy, violent book; not my style, so far as poetry goes. But in the struggle to capture his battering chunky hexametric grace, I came to admire Nonnus. Who knows what it was like trying to make a name as a poet in the hectic fifth century CE? His fascination for everything Dionysiac is apparent in Book 23, yet he seems also to have been a convert to Christianity, or at least at some point in his life wrote a paraphrase of the *Gospel of John*, which still exists and is lightly admired by theologians. That's a serious aesthetic point-spread, Homer to St. John. No one is sure which came first, the gospel paraphrase or the epic poem. Personally, I like to work on several projects at once; I wonder if Nonnus did. It would be nice to know if he kept his rough drafts in separate notebooks, or made some days of the week pagan, some Christian, or had trouble preventing Homeric adjectives from seeping into his *koine*. There is some evidence of seepage in the opposite direction: the very Christian concept of "witness" and "witnessing" turns up in passages of the *Dionysiaca* that are hard to translate because the μάρτυς-word doesn't seem to fit. It would be helpful to know how devout Nonnus was and when that started. It would be helpful to know if he had a sense of humor—I couldn't help a sort of high-styled archness pervading the language of my translation and am still not sure whether this came more from me or from him. Certainly Nonnus is no Homer and certainly he is telling you he knows that with every line of the *Dionysiaca*. But he's keen to give you a good time anyway. That became my aim too as I worked through Book 23. A default flamboyance took over, despite which there were a few locutions I didn't find a way to use. I list them here, blaming no one. Together they almost make what in Icelandic is called a *drápustúfr* ("poem stump").

Abrim,
oversalted,
transpicuous,
big knotty penis
and gold all up your grill.
What would the fox say?

Cyrus Console

The epic meter made famous by Homer uses a six-foot line based on the dactyl, which in Greek means "finger": the three bones of that digit correspond to the three syllables of the metrical foot. As with the bones, the first syllable is long and the second two short. The first four feet of the hexameter freely substitute spondees (two long syllables); the sixth foot is a spondee or trochee (long followed by short). Transposed into English, which marks accent rather than vowel length, the dactyl comprises one stressed followed by two unstressed syllables: "This is the forest primeval, the murmuring pines and the hemlocks."

Longfellow's holodactylic line represents the classic pattern down to the placement of the caesura in the third foot. In this highly formalized tradition, Nonnus' main technical innovations were to increase the regularity of the line by reducing both the amount and variety of substitution, and, more importantly, to reconcile the ancient quantitative verse with the increasingly stress-accented language of the time (I gathered this from Magnelli's "The Nonnian Hexameter"). Rouse (whose translation was my source text) says the *Dionysiaca* interests us chiefly because it represents "the longest and most elaborate example we have of the Greek myths in their final stage of degeneracy." Nonnus arranged this troubled content in a compromised medium, "the musical accent having already given way to stress, long and short vowels having become confused in speech, and their sounds being confused also."

English's (it seems to me) increasingly dactylic character tracks the arc of another mythos, where a drive to learn about the object world turned into a drive to manipulate it, and ended in a drive to profit by it. The "inkhorn terms" of the Renaissance (organize, interest, abdomen, generate, analyze, national) gave way to an influx of jargon from science and industry (armament, surgical, galvanize, nuclear, photograph, therapy). Suffixes dressed out this idiom: -ivity, -ality, -ectomy, -ational, -ology, -anity; then gasoline, bakelite, Microsoft, Nutrasweet, Sertraline, Infowars. Each wave of coinages aspired to the same linguistic superstratum, but with less and less discernment, worse and worse faith, beginning with loanwords and ending with chimeras.

Trying to find sympathy with Nonnus in this experience of prosody and meaning shifting together beneath the feet, I focused on translating the book into dactylic English hexameters, continuing his project by making them as regular as possible, with minimal substitution. I also tried to evoke what Rouse calls "his Niagara of words" by selecting from a wide gamut of speech registers and choosing language that stood out as arresting or unpredictable. For example, here is Rouse's death of Icarius, followed by my own version:

> Before he could finish his words, fate came first and stayed his voice: there he lay dead with eyes wide open, far from his modest daughter. His murderers heavy with wine slumbered careless on the bare ground like dead men. When they awoke, they mourned aloud for him they had unwittingly slain, and in their right mind now they carried his body on their shoulders up to a woody ridge, and washed his wounds in the abundant waters of a mountain brook.

> Scarce had he spoken these words when he opened his eyes somewhat wider
> Blinking no more, the original vintner's career interrupted.
> Meanwhile, his murderers snored intermittently, supine on bare earth,
> Blotto. With daylight came sickening groans as the company scoped out
> Yesterday's recklessness. Upland they shouldered Icarius, gaining
> Mountainous country, there washing his gashes in icemelt.

The meter enforces a front-stressed line with a driving rhythm that has no time for preliminary prepositions or articles, a verse ripe for enjambment. I tried to exploit this by breaking lines at moments of word choice that highlighted the lexical exuberance of the poem and/or where the break enacted the content, as in the backward glance of "scoped out / Yesterday's recklessness." I tried also to reproduce my sense of periodic lapses in discipline, like the contemporary formulas intruding on phrases like "original vintner's career interrupted," or the too-stately procession of "upland they shouldered," or the bathos of "blotto."

John L. Gronbeck-Tedesco

The initial stimulus towards the eventual translations of Books 12 and 15 was the recognition that the Greek I had studied in a Catholic seminary had faded, which required me to shuttle back and forth between Nonnus' Greek and W. D. F. Rouse's English. The frustration was provocative for it stirred recognitions of what Rouse was up to and up against—recognitions that helped me to understand the challenges and the possibilities more clearly.

I was struck by Nonnus' descriptions. The tone was one of intensity brought on by a sense of immediacy. Nonnus created an author who had been present at the events he was narrating. I wanted to keep the connection between the intensity of tone and the sense of immediacy. I located that connection in the way Nonnus piled up modifiers. The density of adjectives and adverbs made for very specific descriptions that also conveyed the sense of a narrator whose emotions were stirred mightily by what he had witnessed. I discovered one way to recreate the tone was by using hyphens to conjoin words so as to extend the number and increase the specificity of the modifiers. This became a stylistic strategy to which I kept returning in both books. For example, "young-blooded, sky-prancing, light-bearing charioteer, / golden-skinned Helios" (12.6–8).

Book 12 showed me the intensity had to be controlled. Chapman's fourteeners were inviting. What could offer more fitting control than a verse pattern used in a neoclassical translation of Homer's *Iliad*? But the seven iambs per line suffocated the intensity; so, I decided to retain the fourteen syllables but let the feet vary randomly. This proved a copout. I needed a more deliberate technique. First, I decided to give precedent to stress rather than the short or long value of a syllable. Second, I discovered the power of the Greco-Roman Aeolic colon, made up of one dactyl and one trochee. I must admit to betting on a certain amount of inevitability. Dactyls, trochees (and iambs too) have a way of showing up, given that in English conjunctions and prepositions sometimes come with articles and sometimes not; for example, "young *and* playful" (and "*from a* lofty tree" (12.133). I admit that the process was altogether messier and more serendipitous than it sounds. All of these choices showed up more through error than trial and were eventual rather than predetermined. (Memory has a way of cleaning things up.)

The comic antics of the drunken Indian troops in the first three-fourths of Book 15 triggered three associations. The first was the memory of the topsy-turvy, calamitous physicality of Mack Sennett's Keystone Kops. Second, tracing a line vertically from top to bottom and from one punctuation mark to another on a page of an early draft produced a busy zigzag. The third association came from the way actors (the contemporary progeny of rhapsodes and *hypocrites*) learn to speak by "riding the breath." This involves imagining a word or line as a ping-pong ball, while the breath is imagined as a vertical column of air that keeps the ball floating at exactly the same height throughout an utterance. But comedy, by way of frequent exception more often than other genres, requires moments when the breathing is short and puffy, so the ball (i.e., the utterance) bounces up and down. These three images prompted me to use short phrases and frequent changes in the syllabic count of the verse in the first part of Book 15 before the story of Nicaea and Hymnus.

Thomas Hart Benton's "Ballad of the Jealous Lover of Lone Green Valley," Uncle Walt's Band, one of the most popular groups in the Austin scene of the late 1970s and 1980s, and "Don't Forsake Me, Oh My Darlin'," evoked the diction and pace of the "Sad Romance of Hymnus and Nicaea"—my title for the end of Book 15. Country Americana seemed the right stuff for the tale about two characters from separate worlds: a superhuman naiad, committed to chastity, and a hormone-driven shepherd boy who could not bear to let his passionate desire go unrequited.

The murder of Hymnus reintroduces the violence that is continual throughout the *Dionysiaca* from which the comic wonder later in Book 12 and the physical comedy early in Book 15 are respites. And so, a last image, one version of the classical comic vision: a man steps off a street corner with his eyes on the stars; slips on a banana peel and falls on his face just in time to be missed by a low flying spear launched from an unknown source. Like no other creature, human beings kill one another nonstop. We murder ourselves not by dint of an unconscious reflex that comes unbidden from nature but consciously and voluntarily—aided and abetted by even more murderous gods. Yet, like the man who falls on his face, the species continues to survive. Is it in spite of or because of our deadly flaws or both? Is it by the will of some deity outside the classical pantheon, or simply a mysterious and fortunate accident?

Rachel Hadas

The *Dionysiaca,* a poem of whose existence I'd managed to remain ignorant for seventy years, is a long—a very long—poem that first struck me, when I recently made its acquaintance, by its lavishness. Bubbling with irrepressible energy, it features violence and sex, mythological riffs and learned digressions, and rhetorical set-pieces. The dactylic hexameter and Homeric diction Nonnus chooses to employ do not detract from the poem's luxuriance; on the contrary. But neither do they endow the poem with a Homeric simplicity of style. Rather, the poet's technical mastery of this meter is one feature of a brimmingly baroque quality.

My decision to render my chosen book, 16, into rhymed fourteeners was swift and instinctive. If I try to retrace my thought process, I don't find any linear sequence. But a few factors stand out. I wanted a long line to accommodate the overflowingly full feeling of the long lines in the Greek. As for rhyme, that part of my decision felt equally intuitive, but it also has a precedent in my other translations of ancient poetry, notably Tibullus' elegies, a tragedy of Seneca, and three plays of Euripides. Rhyme activates my inventiveness, keeps me on my toes. For a poem as long as the *Dionysiaca,* rhyme provides pace and snap.

And since rhyme minus meter is doggerel, the decision to rhyme is always linked to a decision about meter. But what meter? Blank verse seems alien to the decorative mode of Nonnus; in addition, blank verse translations can be very dull. Rhymed couplets: too aphoristic, self-enclosed, end-stopped, logical. If rhyme is ornamental and pleasurable, conveying the colorfully embroidered quality of Nonnus' language, then a long, bouncy line, it seemed to me, might best suggest the ramifying, teeming quality of the Greek.

Again, I didn't set out with these considerations exactly; the rationale came after the fact. But neither, as I recall, did I hesitate for very long before plunging into the waters of those fourteeners. Only well after I was launched on the project of translating Nonnus did it occur to me that I was following in the footsteps of two translations I'd long admired: Alicia Stallings's's brilliant rendering of Lucretius' *De Rerum Natura* into rhymed fourteeners, and Kenneth Koch's use of the same metrical and rhyme scheme for the episode from Ovid's *Metamorphoses* which Koch translated in Michael Hofmann and James Lasdun's *After Ovid.* I don't have *After Ovid* in front of me—it's quarantined in my office in Newark. But I can well remember Koch's delicious couplet: "The king of gods, espying her with her bodacious tresses, / Desired for to fuck with her among the water cresses." This kind of randy Ovidian voyeurism, whose gusto Koch captures with such panache, is much closer to the spirit of Nonnus' poem than it is to the magisterial mode of *De Rerum Natura*. And yet both Koch's and Stallings's choices of rhymed fourteeners for to render these respective master works into English strike me as inspired.

Lucretius, Ovid, Nonnus: three very different poets, none of whom wrote in rhymed fourteeners. Doesn't the very disparateness of such a troika go to show how flexible an instrument this vigorous, speedy meter can be for the translator, and, when spiced with rhyme, how elegant and witty? That's how it felt for me, as January 2020 gave way to February: the meter and rhyme were the reliable engines that kept me moving. Marianne Moore, thinking of other poetic dilemmas and decisions, put it memorably: "Ecstasy affords the occasion, and expediency determines the form."

Joseph Harrington

1. The Immortal Panopolitan

As far as I can tell, Nonnus is the Ed Wood of ancient epic writers. The effects are obviously fake: you can see the line holding up the spaceship. The boom mic and grips are in the shot. The editing is sloppy. The storytelling is sometimes incoherent. The lines are wooden, and the acting is beyond bad. And yet, it's so bad it's good—or funny, fascinating, oneiric. People still watch Ed Wood. People still read Nonnus.

Reading him myself for the first time reminded me of nothing so much as the experience of browsing through an eighteenth-century anthology of English poetry, filled with fourth- and fifth-string imitators of Pope: lots of stylized, stock analogies and conventional topoi; verbose ornamentation; lengthy sentences with inverted syntax; narrative digressions; feeble attempts at wit; and an endless expanse of heroic couplets, as far as the eye could see.

This is how I "discovered" Scilly Cobber, a deservedly little-known and long-forgotten poet of that era (who may or may not have existed, in actuality), who produced a deservedly little-known and long-forgotten partial translation of Book 3 of the *Dionysiaca*. I incorporated some of these fragments into my translation, along with a biographical footnote of my composition. Cobber's assistance proved invaluable: I dragooned him into the role of sous chef, and he obligingly whipped up those frothy confections which so proliferate in Nonnus, when he kicks into descriptive mode and can't get out. Thus I was left free to tell the story. Stor*ies*, rather: Homer had his extended similes, Nonnus, his digressions.

2. I Can Read Greek, I Just Don't Understand It

Like some of my colleagues in this project, I have little Latin and less Greek, which can make for problems. But knowing the alphabet, sounding out the words, and looking some of them up in the lexicon came in handy—in tandem with a couple of fine editors who know the language very well indeed. "A little learning is a dangerous thing," as Scilly Cobber's model once said, "but it can provide a wealth of false cognates." These produced some interesting misprisions, off-rhymes, and implicitly metaphorical language that suggested approaches to rendering certain words and phrases; and one needs that sort of thing to make a poem that's livelier than cardboard.

In "my" sections of Book 3 (the non-Cobber stuff), my default mode was . . . well, not exactly hexameter, but rather a loosey-goosey accentual meter with kinda-sorta six stresses per line, depending on how you read. And I tried to stick as much as I could to plain American that cats and dogs can read (and crows can speak, apparently). As with any narrative work, one wants to make sure the story gets told and to try not to be boring in the process. In this, I hope I have succeeded as far as one can, with the material at hand.

3. Hiawatha vs. Godzilla

I also had a go at Book 32, which presented a different challenge. For one thing, there was no Scilly Cobber to fall back on. For another, the narrative style differed from Book 3. If the *Dionysiaca* really were a movie (gods help us), Book 3 would be a continuous narrative with flashbacks. But Book 23 contains several jump cuts between very different scenes. So, I divided it into scenes and used a style that seemed most appropriate to each. For scene 1, the pillow-talk of Zeus and Hera, I used the six-beats-a-line approach I'd used in Book 3. In scene 2, Dionysius goes mad under the harrying of the Fury Megaera; here, a more open-field, fragmentary, discontinuous form felt right.

Scene 4 is the battle scene. At first, I considered doing real sho-nuff Anglo-Saxon accentual meter, but a) it seemed too obvious, since other translators had done it, and b) if you really do it right, it's super-hard—it's not just the four-stress line, caesurae, alliteration and kennings—there are a *lot* of rules. So, I turned to a meter I knew less about: trochaic tetrameter. Readers of English-language poetry know this meter from Longfellow's *The Song of Hiawatha* ("By the shores of Gitche Gumee / Of the shining Big-Sea-Water," etc., etc.). But Longfellow got it from an antique epic, the *Kalevala*. Turns out trochaic tetrameter works a lot better in Finnish than in English. But it has that kind of rough-hewn, laconic, emphatic quality to it that seemed right for battle scenes. And if you can hear the Kalevala behind Hiawatha, you can certainly hear Homer (and Homer imitators) behind the *Dionysiaca*.

Moreover, the whole thing is, Ed-Wood-wise, Over the Top. So, if you hear Hiawatha at the same time that all these satyrs, maenads, and monsters are carrying on . . . well, it seems to me to be in keeping with the spirit of the work. But really (spoiler alert), the battle scene is not much of a battle: it's more of a chase scene. The final section zooms in on the nymphs among Dionysus' disorderly-retreating band. This scene is less frenetic, more elegiac; here, I returned to the six-stress line.

Hopefully, the reader of this sprawling work (or even part of it), will appreciate the psychedelic, variform phantasmagoria that is the *Dionysiaca*, even if a boom mic occasionally drops into a shot.

Mike Lala

Two and a half centuries before Nonnus of Panopolis was born, an unknown sculptor (a Roman) carved forty figures—animals, gods, and people—into a slab of white marble roughly three by three by seven feet wide, which, in the unknown 1,500 years between its completion and purchase by the Dukes of Beaufort in 1733, served as a sarcophagus. For whom, we don't know.

The piece now sits in Gallery 162 of The Metropolitan Museum of Art of New York City (Fifth Avenue), the city in which I live, in the country to which I was born, and remain, a citizen. Gallery 162 and its surrounding rooms contain dozens of Greek and Roman objects from antiquity, including the more impressive and more sumptuous "Fragmentary colossal head of a youth," whose lips have hung open for four-thousand years, and whose image adorns a countless number of my contemporaries' arms, legs, and torsos as a popular tattoo.

"Marble sarcophagus with the Triumph of Dionysus and the Seasons," however, emits an altogether quieter pull, the tangle of life on its three finished sides grotesque in density, like insects, like a swarm. It depicts Dionysus, seated with his thyrsus on a panther rendered something like a dog with a beard (the sculptor certainly never encountered a panther), while around him, the Seasons bear gifts and look out toward the viewer, or viewers, contrapposto. Behind and below and around them, dozens of women, men, putti, and animals teem with purpose, carrying fruit, emboldened with wine.

It's this swarm, this unruly assembly, that draws me to the *Dionysiaca's* Book 13, to public speech, and to poetry. And it is a fact of language across eras, the transhistorical ur-translative pull of words in excess of literal meaning that makes such a swarm possible. What else could draw these people together, to leave their homes, their families, their parents and lovers and children, their communities, and to form, ill-equipped, the regiments of fighters that would travel, mostly by foot, nearly four-thousand miles to invade a country that by any account but Zeus and Iris' doubtful assertion that its people, in plainly racist terms, were unjust, had little to take from, or offer to, them?

Nothing but language, that ancient technology our culture today has largely left in service to the image as it and we regress into a new dark age. "Fragmentary colossal head of a youth" then, in his de facto incompleteness, his perfect, slack-jawed mindlessness, this half-boy who whispers, or speaks, or shows the tongue, but whose mind is elsewhere, in a cloud of dust, the silt in a river or at the bottom of the sea, speaks a common language to those of us who are, or are soon to be, lost.

And it is, perhaps, there, in that space, in the expectancy of loss, where people are in need of meaning, which language purports to convey. Thus powerful men make appeals to greater purposes here and again, and the power of language is deployed, and a mass is composed and rallied.

There is little evidence of Nonnus' life, says the semi-democratic, mostly open, and thus always shifting informational front of Wikipedia. There is, obviously, also no evidence for Dionysus, but it's not difficult to understand Nonnus' purpose in composing his epic of military and erotic conquest that itself composes a long, dying breath of Greek myth and culture, at the advent of the Christians.

Two centuries before, Alexander of Macedon invaded India in an imperial campaign that ended with his troops in mutiny, their refusal to forge on delivered in an eloquent speech by Alexander's most successful general, Coenus. Nonnus, despite his ignorance about the subcontinent, drew a number of details directly from Alexander's route and major battles, ascribing them to the god and rewriting Alexander's semi-retreat into a triumph.

This act—the revision of history—and myth, or religion's, role in that revision, hardly needs translation. What is untranslatable in Book 13, and in the larger campaign of Dionysus is that which needs no translation because it perseveres across time: the composition of nationhood and purpose, the power of rhetoric to do the composing, and the machinations of power translated into purpose for the rest of us via silver tongue.

Deep in the grip of the pandemic in 2020, in the midst of the ongoing global civil war, after five days in which a million of my fellow citizens became infected with an illness that stems from the folly of power, I needed to hear a voice across time. I scanned my bookshelves and came across two translations of Sappho, whose voice only partly perseveres.

I read:

Some say an army on horseback, some say on foot,
and some say ships are the most beautiful things
on this black earth, but I say
it is whatever you love. (tr. Lombardo)

and

Some men say an army of horse and some men say an army on foot
and some men say an army of ships is the most beautiful thing
on the black earth. But I say it is
what you love. (tr. Carson)

Beside the revisionists, the speechwriters, the colossal talking heads, we work in loss's dark inheritance. This incomplete sarcophagus bears us to another time and place, still subject to men who love horses, and their aims.

Maryrose Larkin

Book 35 is Nonnus' relentless and blood-struck *now*, full of tangled desire, chaste yet bold Bacchantes, a scrim of proto-Christianity mixed with Indian kings, half-mad gods, and war.

The gods and kings battle, while daughters, wives, and the young are fodder. Chaste girl soldiers, bleeding in the streets, are objects of desire. Dionysus lies insane in a pile of death, helpless until suckled and adopted by a longtime enemy. He then rises and conquers.

I had no idea how to approach translating a piece of Nonnus' poem. So much action! So much happening! So much blind desire! So many descriptions! So many words that say so very little! Tricky too that the events of Book 35 closely resemble the aggressive grandiosity of our own bloodthirsty, celebrity-obsessed era.

Florid language and hazy details are suspect, both in the poem and in the real. I thought of *Lolita*'s Dolores Haze, wholly obscured by the narrator's desire just as Nonnus reduces girl soldiers to desired (but dead) objects.

My friend, the poet David Weiss, suggested that Book 35 and the rest of the poem are the ancient Greek equivalent of *Bill and Ted's Excellent Adventure*, where the heroes are thrust into time and have one adventure after another with little plot and lots of guest characters. This idea allowed me to be less seamless in my translation, to allow Nonnus' jerky transitions to remain with the poem.

I pushed against the continual love of battle, the foot soldiers besotted with a dead girl's beauty, decisions made in rage or desire, young soldiers' facelessness on both sides of the battle, the crazed behavior of Zeus and Hera, and the florid and bombastic language and proto-Christian morality.

I stripped the text down to a series of events and sentences. I would read a section and translate it with the fewest and most true words I could find. I distilled the story out and poured it back in, attempting to humanize the wives, the daughters, and the dead.

Nonnus wrote a glorification of battle, and I translated a critique of the same. I hope thyrsus bearers have faces now.

William Levitan

Ancient epic poets developed the habit of beginning their works at the very top of their rhetorical range. Not only could they then open with a flourish but they put their readers on notice that, whatever subtle beauties and terrors might later unfold, this beginning would mark the furthest extent of their upward verbal reach. In some ways, Douglass Parker's version of the first book-and-a-bit of Nonnus plays a similar role for this volume as a whole. Not through any design, of course (Parker's translation dates from 1970) but his Nonnus bursts onto the scene in explosions of language, style, genre, literary history, and even typeface—Nonnus writ large, literally as well as figuratively, a restless, assertive, imprudent poet, always flogging the extremes. And strictly in sheer size and verbal chutzpah, nothing later in the volume does surpass it.

Parker translated only through Book 2, line 162 of the Greek text. My own continuation of the book is very plainly in a different key. It presents a poet more concerned with limit than expansion, more Olympian, I might be tempted to say in other circumstances, than Titanic. Its lines are shorter, with clipped phrases and a scarcity of syntax; its lexicon is restricted, its tone flattened out. At one point the translation shifts into prose, and I can't say the change is dramatic. I pulled back from the humor in the text, from its hijinks, bling, and dazzle, curtailed its performative swagger, and did what I could to lower its temperature, if not always its intensity—Nonnus writ small, figuratively as well as literally. My thought was to lay down a rhetorical floor far enough below Parker's de facto ceiling to open the most capacious space for the full cavalcade of translations to come.

The "fifes," "shawms," and "tumult" of lines 18 and 19 are from Chapman's Homer, by the way. Nonnus glances at *Iliad* 10 at this point in the poem, and I did not think I could do better.

Stanley Lombardo

In Book 48, Nonnus, the latest born son of Homer on record, brings his sprawling epic to a close with four main scenes, each reprising the poem's hero: (1) a last, brief battle with Giants, apparently simply for old times' sake; (2) a pornographic wrestling match culminating in a marriage; (3) a seven-hundred-plus line epyllion starring Aura, a virginal huntress who, after being verbally assaulted by Artemis, goes berserk, is raped by Bacchus, and gives birth to two sons, one of whom she eats before she drowns herself in a river and is transformed into a fountain; and (4) a brief coda in which the god's surviving son, Iacchus (Dionysus' so-called "third birth"), is entrusted to Athena, who will prep him to lead Dionysiac rites while the wine-god himself sits in Zeus' heaven drinking nectar.

All of this violence and sex and divine shenanigans ramble on in a very refined but vigorous variant of Homeric dactylic hexameter, the adjustments in the metrics having been motivated by earlier Greek's tone accent having morphed into a stress accent by Nonnus' time. Though he lived in an era when silent reading was still, as Augustine reminds us, an anomaly, Nonnus was no oral poet in the sense that Homer was. Still, his verse reads beautifully out loud and registers as compelling performance. In this respect I want to applaud Rob Turner, one of our translators, who tells us that he recorded Book 5 in Greek and listened to it as he worked out his translation.

My own serious practice as a translator began thirty years ago when I was working on Hesiod's *Works and Days*, listening to his Greek and trying to capture his voice as dirt farmer and poet while crafting verse for public performance. A decade or so later I approached Homer's *Iliad* and *Odyssey* in the same way, recalling from my graduate school days Gareth Morgan's magnificent recitations of Homer's Greek and developing my own voice as I worked to compose verse that was as much a script for performance as a translation. I was so invested in the performative nature of my translations of *Iliad* and *Odyssey* that I did not feel publication was complete until I had recorded audio books of both.

It has been much the same way with Nonnus. While I don't imagine I would ever actually produce a recording of Book 48, it has been my aim to produce a translation that could come alive as a script for performance as well as succeed as a poem on the page. Both modes are well served, I hope, by my efforts to stay true to the dominant practice of Anglo-American poetry in the last century, which is to say drawing the language and rhythms of the translation from idiomatic, natural speech as much as possible.

Denise Low

My translations of the *Dionysiaca*, two books of the total forty-eight, are faithful to the original plotline. In each book, six-beat lines predominate and I parse the whole into sections with subtitles. My rendition, however, also compresses the original content of the epic, subtracting from the original Greek. Book 28 depicts a battle between the armies of India and the Greeks. Wounded and dead soldiers litter the field. The translator's page is another kind of battlefield, with losses suggested by open spaces—omissions of lines. In finding the lyric nugget within a scene, I cut much away, in a series of erasures.

Book 38 is Phaëthon's story of usurping his father Helios' chariot, the vehicle that hitches the Sun across the sky each day. My account leapfrogs some of the background to focus on action. At the climax of Phaëthon's prideful journey, he overturns the order of the sky. Here, I break with the orderly hexameter lines to approximate chaos on the page, using jumbled typology and keyboard characters. At first, I tried using astrological glyphs, but these did not reproduce consistently in print media, so I turned to carets, parentheses, and tildes. Ovid describes Chaos as the confusion of elements, and I include words and letters. My alphabetic representation of words is interrupted by special characters used out of context. I had hoped to make spirals of individual lines on the page, but chose instead a more stable linear format, but erratic, which still replicates the idea of chaos in broken lines. Ptolemy's astrology, which antecedes the contemporary practice, informs this section; I have practiced astrology over fifty years.

Most of all, my goal was for the verse to sing, to have lyric qualities equal to or greater than the narration. Compression, focus on dramatic moments, highlighting of imagery—these were ways to shift focus from head to heart. Set rhymes are replaced with repetitions of sounds within sections.

One of the revelations of this project was the importance of dance. In Book 28 as Greek soldiers prepare to engage the Indian army, they rehearse with war music and rhythmic movement. A review of the Pyrrhic war dance (https://www.youtube.com/watch?v=cYelSpTWVUw) shows the tradition continues among cadets of the Hellenic Army Academy, for example: quick footwork, swordsmanship, and mock duels. Drums, stringed instruments, and flutes of the present day suggest the spectacle of the original. This dance music played in the background as I worked on the translation. The description of the military parade to battle, then, gained more dimensions as I worked on my own recomposition process, even if that music does not sound overtly. My own translator's dance is solitary; yet it combines with the chorus of other translators in the project.

In an effort to shift from my own point of view, with Book 28 I invited the writer Eileen R. Tabios to co-create a response to Nonnus' epic. She composed a counterpoint that expands on my response to the original. The eighth of nine sections, with Tabios's part in italics, reads:

Warcries of the Cyclopes resounded to heavens
of Mount Olympus. Battle dancers joined
Bacchant women in feints, quick steps,

ecstatic twirls for Dionysus. Voices
and drums beat rhythms for deft footwork.
The runner Ocythoös sounded his rush of wind.

Giant Mimas wove measured leaps and stamps
into his fighting stance as he slew soldiers.
Their heads were blood sacrifice to Dionysus.

Of course this drunken
god chooses the heads of men,
not hands which wielded
swords for battle. Heads contain
the mouths which, once, imbibed wine.

The counter-text creates a duet not unlike the mano-a-mano movements of the dance and of the battlefield. My gratitude to Tabios for her insights and for the second voice as we engage with the text together. Poetry, from Homer to the present, is a shared genre, incomplete without a reader and at least one responder if a chorus is not available.

This translation is a patchwork process, developed from Rouse's translation; my rudimentary Greek (I had one inglorious semester); consultation with handbooks of mythology; and a lifetime's study of verse. With any success, I might be able to convince you that this is Nonnus rendered into twenty-first century American English. The study of ancient epic in its earliest form has revealed the connection between performance and the creation of verse: "composition and performance in oral poetry are aspects of the same process, in that each performance is an act of recomposition" (in Gregory Nagy's phrase). This translation, too, both reprises and recomposes.

Jonathan Mayhew

A lot of contemporary translation of poetry, to my taste, is bland and colorless, aiming for a kind of unobjectionable literalism—at best. In approaching Nonnus, I had two principles in mind: (1) Every text requires a unique approach from the translator, based on its unique qualities. I would not render Nonnus in the same style I would use for Lorca. (2) A translation of a poem is a poem: it must give pleasure in its own right, without spurious appeals to the virtues of the original. Although we tend to judge translations by comparing them to the original texts, their intended reader is normally someone who does not know the original and thus cannot perform this comparison. (3) A verse translation must have a distinctive prosody, a rhythmic shape. It should not be a prose crib divided into lines.

With these principles in mind, my version of Book 37 attempts to harness the dynamic exuberance of Nonnus' verse through a variation on Williams Carlos Williams's indented tripartite line, which he developed in poems like "Of Asphodel, That Greeny Flower" in the later part of his career. I came upon this solution almost immediately as I began work, and I was pleased even with my very first attempts. I did not try to imitate Williams's prosody with any exactitude, but instead sought to exploit the elasticity implicit in his concept of the "variable foot." This allows both for short and relatively long phrases rather than a more uniform movement that might become tedious. Later, I remembered that Williams had used this form for a translation of an idyll by Theocritus, and that my first published article was on Williams's prosody.

Nonnus is especially skilled at describing physical movement, as in his quite lengthy, exuberant, and virtuosic accounts of the chariot race and other athletic contests in Book 37. A literal line-by-line rendering, I thought, would make him sound too clunky, failing to do justice to his gift for conveying kinetic energy through the movement of his verse. The elasticity of the tripartite line also afforded me a great deal of leeway. I could fit a lot of words into some lines, or set apart a very short phrase for emphasis. I deliberately did not make my line divisions correspond to those of the original text.

It is quite evident that his epic poetry does not conform to our contemporary aesthetic ideals of concision and narrative economy. In conversations with some other translators in this project, I often heard his work described as simply "bad." (I'm sure I expressed this opinion myself as well.) Coincidentally, I have been interested in bad poetry for quite some time, writing two unpublished books of deliberately inept poems. This experience came in handy as I was translating Nonnus, because it allowed me a certain freedom from prejudgment. I could allow the poetry to be what it was without trying to improve it or apologize for it. What some might see as the excesses of the Greek original, such as its redundancy and its long-winded, hyperbolic, and seemingly gratuitous descriptions, provide an opportunity for a loose and playful approach to translation. If I have done my job well, Book 37 should be a lot of fun to read in English.

Melina McClure

"This Greek is not kosher," was the first thought I had while reading the *Dionysiaca*. And herein lies the first difficulty in translating Nonnus: he makes you doubt your own knowledge of Greek. He writes Homeric dialect in tight hexameters, but at the same time, he stretches the Greek language like a body on the rack. In addition to dredging up words from the depths of obscurity and bending syntax, Nonnus also constructs many of his own words and new compounds (several that appear in his work only and nowhere else), a little bit like a tamer, fifth century, Egyptian Joyce. Thus to render into English this work, this combination of archaism and innovation, is to produce some very wacky English indeed. To keep up with this Nonnian spirit of verbal creation and recreation, I have offered some funky English fusions of my own, which I hope you will either enjoy or forgive.

Despite how bloody he is, how violent, Nonnus remains very playful, in part through the cleverness of his language, almost saucy at times, almost ironical. The gore is broken apart by moments so saccharine that they nearly feel like parody, such as the opening lines of Book 27, which I translated. However, despite the lingering notes of irony, the *Dionysiaca* is not at all unfeeling, but rather, in the midst of these long episodes of battle and battle lust, Nonnus hits high emotional extremes with scenes such as that of Pentheus begging his own mother, Agavê, to spare his life in Book 46. Scenes such as this one are powerful in part because of the hurtling breathlessness and pointed repetition with which Nonnus endows them, and I have tried to mimic this effect with a raw, desperate rush of English.

Whoever reads this translation alongside the original Greek will surely notice several places where I have made expansions upon that Greek. At certain times, these expansions have been made where I have decided that a modern reader would benefit from further context, but, perhaps more often, admittedly, these expansions have been made upon my own poetic kick, in faith to the Nonnian spirit of wily verbal antics, whim and rollick. Where there was the opportunity, I have chosen to focus on bodies, and particularly the bodies of women.

Judith Roitman

You don't have to read Greek to realize that Nonnus is at best a mediocre writer. Pathetic fallacies abound, and he doesn't use one word when fifty will do; cf.,

Aphrodite/Peisinoë's monologue—anyone would agree to anything just to shut her up. Inconsistencies (not all of them excused by their origin in myth) pop up; didn't Athena tell him to let five giants live? but they all seem to get killed. (Note the lower case *giant*; these are Very Large Men, not members of the separate species Giant who attack Dionysus in Book 48.)

Nonnus' mediocrity is a gift to those tasked to bring him into contemporary English, freeing us to find the shape beneath the sludge, even while following him closely. Book 4 essentially (and almost exactly) splits in half, encouraging two distinct rhetorical modes. We begin with a long scene in the women's quarters as Electra unsuccessfully and Aphrodite/Peisinoë successfully (see the above paragraph) convince Harmonia to leave everything behind and follow Cadmus. I imagine Electra as a Real Housewife of Beverly Hills (Nonnus describes clothing and interior decoration in unwarranted detail), Aphrodite/Peisinoë as a vacuous sex-obsessed daughter of that culture, and Harmonia the ingenue too innocent to realize she is being played. Then we focus on Cadmus, a man among men, so to speak—there's nothing he can't do!—and the rhetoric (mine, not Nonnus') tightens up, including bullet points to organize lists, even in moments of intense violence.

In places I throw in bracketed remarks, to inform the reader about things Nonnus assumed his readers would know, or because I can't resist making (at times snarky) editorial comments. Full disclosure: I don't read Greek. But I did have access to an expert when I had questions, which I frequently did. Finally, a tip of the hat to Dr. Google, who generously filled in the details of obscure references to myths, including those that contradicted each other.

Christian Teresi

An American Modernist Translates Nonnus

It is not lack of originality that links the themes of the *Dionysiaca* with modernity, but rather that the biggest philosophical questions have changed little over time. Book 7 of the *Dionysiaca* details how human misery and hardship made *Aiōn* ("Eternity" in this translation) plead with Zeus to create wine to ease suffering. Translating Book 7 while millions die from a pandemic made it hard not to think how true in our imaginations this may be. Because all things of value and comfort need to have an origin story, Nonnus writes how Zeus creates Dionysus to "give mankind a defense for grief / whose taste flows sweetly" (7.76–77).

It is an act of kindness and concern that begins Book 7, and this continues as Nonnus describes the highly ritualized courtship of Zeus and the human Semele that leads to Dionysus' conception. It is idealized human love and longing Nonnus conjures, where water is a symbol of renewal and purification, where after sacrificing a bull to her god, Semele "waded into the Asopos River where she was born / To wash her mottled dress in the water's current" (7.172–73). This is the preparation for a kind of love that is endemic to poetry and no less romantically hyperbolized than Emily Dickinson's

Wild Nights—Wild Nights!
Were I with thee
Wild Nights should be
Our luxury!

And Nonnus builds the tension of Zeus' passion for Semele until it is uncontrollable:

His vast power was everywhere and without bounds,
Yet her eyes baited him with their ornamentation.
He knew the truth only when near the unmarried girl. (7.219–21).

The *Dionysiaca* is a poem where language signifies human hopes and desires in all their complications. This sentiment is at the heart of *nostalgia*, that word of Greek origin that arrived to English from *nostos* meaning homecoming and *algos* or suffering. From his hometown in Hellenized Egypt, Nonnus pondered these things while Germanic tribes moved south through a frightened Europe and future Christian saints and martyrs spread the gospel in the waning days of the Roman Empire. Columbus was a thousand years away from reaching Caribbean shores. At that time there was still the need to express longings as fundamental to Nonnus as any to contemporary poet. It is an essential part of living to express human wonder. To turn our back on the fraction of ancient Greek poems that exist would be anathema to our past and what it means to be alive.

Rob Turner

In the twelfth book of his vast poem, Nonnus staggers—at last—onto the subject of wine, a drink that he sees as containing all plants, and tasting of everything all at once. The same is true of the epic itself, with its hyper-digressive structure, and cosmic polyphonic style. His lines often seem stuffed with the voices of others, swallowing Homer, Apollonius, and (presumably) many other long-lost cyclical poets, before barfing them out in a stew of hexameters. To steal a line from Edmund Spenser, his "vomit full of bookes and papers was."

Approaching such a mad, intertextual work, I started by forcefully decentering the English rendering I was already familiar with (Rouse's 1940 prose version), drowning it out with other voices. At the center of the book I was translating lay Nonnus' spin on the Actaeon story, so I started listening to Charpentier (Op. H481) and Purcell (Z. 626), picking at snippets of translations of Callimachus and Euripides, and—in particular—wandering the Theban sections of Arthur Golding's *Metamorphoses*, looking for tips from the text that Ezra Pound saw as "the most beautiful book in the English language."

Getting away from Rouse also meant crawling towards the Greek, something that called for the use of dictionaries and colleagues (thanks and apologies to Henry Power). I recorded my own wobbly recitation of the original, penciled out a verbatim gloss of its 621 lines, and then sat listening to my tongue-tied Greek while leafing through eighteen pages of mangled English. The experiment taught me a few things: firstly, that it would be a nightmare to obey the strict rules that shaped the poet's Callimachean hexameters. Secondly, I found that Nonnus filled his lines with inventive sonic details: puns, echoes, and alliterative effects. In 5.49–50, for instance, there's a startling blur of the monarch's name with the uproar surrounding his conquest ("*kudoimou / Kadmos*"), a ripple I copied with "clamorous Cadmus." In general, my approach has been to prioritize such local effects above metrical regularity, while working with a loose four-beat line.

Dragging Nonnus away from hexameters and into Anglo-American free verse—and thereby making the fifth-century poet of Panopolis seem more like one of us—raises one final obstacle to translating him. Unlike so many of his epic predecessors (a tradition for which his book is, in part, a funeral pyre), Nonnus is often cruel. Where Homer could stand with Helen on the walls of a city at war, gazing upon all with care and sympathy, the *Dionysiaca* can come across as racist, proto-colonial, and misogynistic. Speaking these passages today, in a contemporary idiom, raises the question of how to deal with the ugliness that lurks beneath.

In his fifth book, Nonnus shows us his grotesque side with repeated scenes of sexual control and assault, foreshadowing the rapes of Nicaea and Aura later in the poem. The text cannot—perhaps *should* not—be forced to condemn or even lament these crimes, but it does seem possible to unpick and deconstruct it from within: in other words, to amplify the muted echoes and dissonances that run through the original. Working through the text I hunted for ways to do this, teasing out small connections, creating feedback loops of violence.

A few examples will illustrate the covert strategy. By gendering the sacrificial animal in the opening lines as female, for instance, I found that it became possible to hint at a parallel between this early slaughter and the division of land in Thebes. That pairing soon echoed onward, sounding beneath the uneasy subdivision of four daughters to husbands. Elsewhere, spots of direct verbal repetition (not explicitly present in the Greek) could be smuggled in, drawing out parallels between Actaeon's erotic hunger and Artemis' canine revenge, say, or between Actaeon's voyeurism and the more frightening gaze of Zeus in the fifth book's closing lines. These tiny resemblances and reverberations combine—I hope—to trouble, and quietly threaten, Nonnus' rapist gods. As the book draws to an end, we might even catch a flickering glimpse of some dim, future revenge: a doomed tyrant "burning for Persephone."

Notes on Contributors

Frederick Ahl is a professor of classics and the Stephen H. Weiss Presidential Fellow at Cornell University, as well as the author of many books and articles on ancient drama and the literature of the Roman Empire. As a translator, he has published versions of Seneca, Sophocles, and Virgil. His recorded greetings in Greek, Latin, and Welsh are currently aboard the Voyager 1 and 2 space probes launched in 1977.

Catherine Anderson is an American poet and the author of several books, including *In the Mother Tongue* and, most recently, *The Work of Hands* (Perugia Press, 2000). She has published poems in *Harvard Review*, *The Journal*, *The Women's Review of Books*, the anthologies *Working Classics: Poems on Industrial Life* (University of Illinois Press, 1990) and *Poetry 180* (Random House, 2003), as well as in other journals. She lives in Kansas City, Missouri, and is the director of development at the Kansas City Zoo.

Diane Arnson Svarlien has published three volumes of verse translations of the plays of Euripides with Hackett Publishing. Her current project is the translation of Aristophanes' *Lysistrata*, *Women at the Thesmophoria*, and *Frogs*. She lives in Lexington, Kentucky.

Adrienne Atkins is a PhD candidate in classical studies at the University of Pennsylvania. Her interests include epic poetry and its reception, literary translation, and the history of classics in the United States. She is currently completing a dissertation on epic parody during the classical period.

Andrew Barrett is a poet and musician living in Detroit, Michigan. He translates from ancient and modern Greek and from Latin and teaches mythology and ancient Greek literature at Wayne State University. He has held residencies at both the Bread Loaf Translators' Conference and the Banff Literary Translation Centre. His earlier translations from Nonnus have been published by Anomalous Press (2011) and Aldus (2013).

Charles-Elizabeth Boyles holds a BA in classical languages from the University of Kansas and works at the Nelson Museum of Art in Kansas City. They are a contributing editor at Broken Hands Media, and are currently working on a literary translation of Tibullus.

Gordon Braden is John C. Coleman Professor of English Emeritus at the University of Virginia and the author of many books and articles on Renaissance literature and the reception of classical poetry, recently including *The Oxford History of Literary Translation in English: 1550–1660* with Robert Cummings and Stuart Gillespie (Oxford University Press, 2010), and *Petrarch's English Laurels, 1475–1700*, with Jackson Campbell (Boswell, 2012).

Anne Carson is a widely acclaimed Canadian poet, essayist, translator, and classical scholar, author of over two dozen books, and recipient of many distinguished literary prizes, including Guggenheim and MacArthur Fellowships, the Lannan Literary Award, Pushcart Prize, Griffin Poetry Prize, T. S. Eliot Prize, Princess of Asturias Award, and PEN Award for Poetry in Translation. As a translator, she has published versions of Sappho, Euripides, Aeschylus, Sophocles, Catullus, Steisichorus, Mimnermus, Simonides, Alcman, Ibycus, and Plato, among others.

Tessa Cavagnero holds a BA in classics from Knox College and MA degrees in classical antiquity from the University of Kansas and comparative literary studies from Northwestern. She is currently a PhD student in classics at the University of Wisconsin.

Bethany Christiansen holds degrees from the Universities of Kansas and Cambridge, as well as a PhD (2020) from Ohio State University. Her academic work largely treats philological topics, with publications on Old English and Latin lexicography. She is currently working on a graphic novel on soteriology.

Cyrus Console is the author of *Brief Under Water* (Burning Deck, 2008), *The Odicy* (Omnidawn, 2011), and *Romanian Notebook* (Farrar, Straus and Giroux, 2017). His recent poetry has appeared in *Brick*, *Harper's*, and *The Paris Review*. He is a professor of creative writing at the Kansas City Art Institute.

Anthony Corbeill is Basil L. Gildersleeve Professor of Classics at the University of Virginia and the author of many books and articles on the literature and culture of the Roman world, most recently *Sexing the World: Grammatical Gender and Biological Sex in Ancient Rome* (Princeton University Press, 2015), which was awarded the Goodwin Award of Merit from the Society for Classical Studies.

Rebekah Curry is a writer and professional archivist educated at the University of Kansas and the University of Texas at Austin. She is a recipient of the Willis Barnstone Translation Prize, and her translations appear in journals including *The Evansville Review*, *Pusteblume*, and *Ezra*. Her original poetry has been featured in journals such as *Mezzo Cammin*. She lives and works in the Flint Hills region of Kansas.

Alex Dressler is an associate professor of classics at the University of Wisconsin and the author of many studies of the literature and culture of the later Roman world. As a translator, he has published versions of Seneca, Ausonius, and Paulinus of Nola.

David Fredrick is an associate professor of classics and the director of humanities at the J. William Fulbright College of Arts and Sciences of the University of Arkansas. He has published on Roman architecture, painting, and poetry, and is the editor of *The Roman Gaze: Vision, Power, and the Body* (Arethusa, 2002).

John L. Gronbeck-Tedesco is professor emeritus in the Department of Theatre at the University of Kansas and cofounder and first editor of the *Journal of Dramatic Theory and Criticism*. His poetry, translations, and plays have appeared in a variety of publications and venues, including *Tuck Magazine*, *Outsider Poetry*, *Madness Muse Magazine*, the Cleveland Public Theatre, the Kansas City Fringe, and Karamu House Theatre.

Rachel Hadas is the author of more than twenty books of poetry, essays, and translations, most recently including *Piece by Piece* (Paul Dry Books, 2021), *Questions in the Vestibule* (Northwestern University Press, 2016), *Talking to the Dead* (Spuyten Duyvil Press, 2015), and *The Golden Road* (Northwestern University Press, 2012). She coedited *The Greek Poets: Homer to the Present*, with Peter Constantine, Edmund Keeley, and Karen Van Dyck (W. W. Norton, 2010). She is Board of Governors Professor of English at Rutgers University—Newark and lives in New York City.

Joseph Harrington is a professor of English at the University of Kansas and the author, most recently, of the poetry books *Of Some Sky* (BlazeVOX, 2018), *Things Come On (an amneoir)* (Wesleyan University Press, 2011), and *Goodnight Whoever's Listening* (Essay Press, 2015). He has been named a Millay Colony resident fellow, a Fulbright Distinguished Chair, and is a three-time Pushcart Prize nominee.

Richard Jenkyns is an emeritus professor of the classical tradition and the Public Orator at Oxford University, and the author and editor of numerous, acclaimed books on classical literature and its reception, including *The Victorians and Ancient Greece* (Harvard University Press, 1980), *Virgil's Experience* (Oxford University Press, 1998), and *Classical Literature: An Epic Journey from Homer to Virgil and Beyond* (Basic Books, 2016).

Mike Lala is an American poet, lyricist, translator, and sound artist living in Brooklyn, New York. He is the author of the drama *Twenty-Four Exits—A Closet Drama* (Present Tense Pamphlets, 2016) and the prizewinning collection *Exit Theater* (University Press of Colorado, 2016). His work has also appeared in *Boston Review*, *Fence*, *Denver Quarterly*, *The Brooklyn Rail*, *BOMB*, and *VOLT*, among other journals.

Maryrose Larkin is the author of several books of verse, most recently *The Name of This Intersection is Frost* (Shearsman Books, 2010), *Marrowing* (Airfoil, 2011), and *The Identification of Ghosts* (Chax, 2013). Her work has been included in the anthologies *I'll Drown My Book: Conceptual Writing by Women* (Les Figues, 2011) and *The Arcadia Project: North American Postmodern Pastoral* (Ashata Press, 2012). She lives in Tucson, Arizona.

William Levitan, one of the editors of this volume, has taught at the University of Southern California, Princeton, Bryn Mawr, Middlebury, and Grand Valley State University in Michigan, where he was founding chair of the Department of Classics and is now Professor Emeritus. His translation of the letters of Abelard and Heloise was published in 2007. He lives in Mount Freedom, New Jersey.

Michael B. Lippman is an associate professor of practice in the Department of Classics and Religious Studies at the University of Nebraska—Lincoln. His main interest has been in ancient theater, especially comedy, and he is at work on translations of Aristophanes.

Stanley Lombardo, one of the editors of this volume, is a professor emeritus of classics at the University of Kansas. He is best known for his translations of Greek and Latin poetry, including Homer's *Iliad* and *Odyssey* (a *New York Times* Book of the Year). He has recorded audiobooks of his translations of Homer and performed dramatic readings from them across the country. His other translations include the poems of Hesiod, Callimachus, and Sappho, Virgil's *Aeneid*, Ovid's *Metamorphoses*, the *Odes* of Horace, Statius' *Achilleid*, Dante's *Divine Comedy*, the *Epic of Gilgamesh*, and the *Bhagavad Gita*.

Denise Low is a former Kansas Poet Laureate, who has won awards and recognition for her verse from Red Mountain Press, Kansas Notable Books, Pushcart Prize (6 nominations), Best of the Net, Poetry Society of America, and others. She has recent verse in *The Sun*, *New Letters*, *Chariton Review*, *Numéro Cinq*, *Virginia Quarterly*, *Yellow Medicine Review*, *Apogee*, and numerous anthologies. Low teaches in Baker University's School of Professional and Graduate Studies.

Anna Mayersohn has a BA degree from Haverford College with a major in English and a minor in classics, and an MA in classics from the University of Kansas. She is currently working towards an MS in information science at the University of Michigan.

Jonathan Mayhew is a professor of Spanish at the University of Kansas. A poet and translator, he is the author of five books on Spanish poetry and on Federico Garcia Lorca, most recently *Lorca's Legacy: Essays in Interpretation* (Routledge,

2018). Currently, he is working on a book on musical adaptations of Lorca's work.

Melina McClure studies classics at the University of Southern California. Her primary areas of interest are currently Roman tragedy and the reception of Seneca in English Renaissance drama; she describes herself as "a massive fan of Kyd and Marlowe." She is also at work on a translation of Ovid's *Heroides*.

Darwin Michener-Rutledge is a member of Mount Holyoke College's class of 2024. She is devoted to storytelling, through both words and movement. Her language studies include French, Italian, Latin, and Greek; and she has been dancing pre-professionally for fifteen years.

Sheila H. Murnaghan is the Alfred Reginald Allen Memorial Professor of Greek at the University of Pennsylvania, and the author of many books and articles on ancient Greek literature and its reception, especially in the genres of epic and tragedy. These include *Disguise and Recognition in the Odyssey* (Princeton University Press, 1987) and, with Deborah H. Roberts, *Childhood and the Classics: Britain and America, 1850–1965* (Oxford University Press, 2018). She was President of the Society for Classical Studies in 2020.

Rachel Murray received her BA in classical studies *summa cum laude* in 2017. She is currently pursuing an MA in comparative literature and cultural studies, with a focus on translation, at the University of Arkansas.

Alison R. Parker holds degrees in classics from Princeton and the University of North Carolina and has pursued a career as a newspaper journalist and editor of Latin law maxims and romance novels. She lives in Springfield, Missouri.

Douglass Parker was an American classicist, poet, and groundbreaking translator, best known for his versions of ancient comedy, Aristophanes in particular, for which he became a National Book Award finalist. Professor of classics at the University of Texas for forty years, Parker died in 2011.

Zachary Puckett received his BA and MA in classics from the University of Kansas. He teaches Latin at Lawrence High School and Lawrence Freestate High School.

Deborah H. Roberts is the William R. Kenan Jr. Professor of Classics and Comparative Literature at Haverford College. Her recent publications include articles on the reception and translation of ancient literature, translations of Aeschylus' *Prometheus Bound* and Euripides' *Andromache*, and, with Sheila H. Murnaghan, *Childhood and the Classics: Britain and America, 1850–1965* (Oxford University Press, 2018).

Judith Roitman's most recent book of poems is *Roswell* (theenk Books, 2018); her most recent chapbook is *Provisional* (Dancing Girl Press, 2019). Her poems have appeared most recently in *Equalizer, the tiny, December, Rogue Agent, Galatea Ressurects, E.ratio, Writing Disorder, Futures Trading, YEW, Eleven Eleven*, and *Otoliths*. Her book *No Face* (First Intensity Press) appeared in 2008. She lives in Lawrence, Kansas.

Anne Shaw has undergraduate degrees from the University of the Witwatersrand and the University of Exeter, and a PhD in classics from the University of Texas, where her teachers included Douglass Parker. She has taught Latin at both the secondary and university level for many years in Lawrence, Kansas, and was a member of the revision team for the fourth edition of the Cambridge Latin Course.

Michael Shaw was a member of the Classics Department at the University of Kansas for over forty years, where he taught Greek at all levels and was active in both the Women's Studies and Western Civilization Programs. He is the author of studies of ancient drama and of Thucydides.

Eileen R. Tabios has released over sixty collections of poetry, fiction, essays, and experimental biographies from publishers in ten countries. Most recently, she has published a short story collection, *PAGPAG: The Dictator's Aftermath in the Diaspora* (Paloma Press, 2020) and a poetry collection, *The In(ter)vention of the Hay(na)ku: Selected Tercets 1996–2019* (Marsh Hawk Press, 2019). Her first book, *Beyond Life Sentences* (Anvil Publishing, 1998), received the Philippines' National Book Award for Poetry. Translated into ten languages, she has also edited, coedited, or conceptualized fifteen anthologies of poetry, fiction, and essays.

Christian Teresi's poems and translations have appeared in *American Poetry Review*, *Blackbird*, *Crab Orchard Review*, *The Kenyon Review*, *Literary Hub*, *The Literary Review*, *Narrative*, and *Subtropics*, among others. He lives in Washington, D. C.

Rob Turner is a Lecturer in English at the University of Exeter, specializing in twentieth- to twenty-first-century literature. His book, *Counterfeit Culture* (Cambridge University Press, 2019), examines the epic tradition in American literature since 1960. He is currently editing a collection of essays tracing the relationship between hip-hop and oral poetry.

Brian Walters is an associate professor of classics and translation studies at the University of Illinois at Urbana-Champaign, and specializes in Latin literature and the reception of classical texts. His translation of Lucan's *Civil War* was published by Hackett in 2015.

Suggestions for Further Reading

Although English has not at all been the primary language of modern writings on Nonnus, we have privileged works in English in the list below for the sake of its usefulness to our readers. An extensive bibliography is provided in *Companion to Nonnos*. We regret that *Nonnus in Context III* appeared too late for us to take detailed account of its contents.

Modern Bilingual Editions

Nonno di Panopoli. *Le Dionisiache*. 4 vols. General ed.: D. Gigli Piccardi. Milan: Biblioteca universale Rizzoli, 2003–4.

Nonnos de Panopolis. *Les Dionysiaques*. 19 vols. General ed.: Francis Vian. Paris: Société Les Belles Lettres, 1976–2006.

Nonnos. *Dionysiaca: With an English Translation by W. H. D. Rouse; Mythological Introduction and Notes by H. J. Rose; and Notes on Text Criticism by L. R. Lind*. 3 vols. Loeb Classical Library. London: Heinemann, 1940.

Multiauthor Collections

Companion to Nonnus — Accorinti, Domenico, ed. *Brill's Companion to Nonnus of Panopolis*. Leiden: Brill, 2016.

Homère revisité — Acosta-Hughes, Benjamin, Christopher Cusset, Yannick Durbeck, and Diduer Pralon. *Homère revisité: parodie et humour dans les réécritures*. Besançon: Presses universaires de Franche-Comté, 2011. https://www.persee.fr/issue/ista_0000-0000_2011_act_1200_1

Nonnus in Context I	Spanoudakis, Konstantinos, ed. *Nonnus of Panopolis in Context: Poetry and Cultural Milieu in Late Antiquity with a Section on Nonnus and the Modern World.* Trends in Classics 24. Berlin: De Gruyter, 2014. https://doi.org/10.1515/9783110339420
Nonnus in Context II	Bannert, Herbert, and Nicole Kröll, eds. *Nonnus of Panopolis in Context II: Poetry, Religion, and Society.* Proceedings of the International Conference on Nonnus of Panopolis, 2013, University of Vienna. Leiden: Brill, 2017.
Nonnus in Context III	Doroszewsky, Filip, and Katarzyna Jazdzewska, eds. *Nonnus of Panopolis in Context III: Old Questions and New Perspectives.* Proceedings of the International Conference on Nonnus of Panopolis, 2015, Cardinal Stefan Wyszynski University, Warsaw. Leiden: Brill, 2020.
Studies in the Dionysiaca	Hopkinson, Neil, ed. *Studies in the* Dionysiaca *of Nonnus.* Cambridge Philological Society, Supplementary Volume 17, 1994.
Le Voyage des légendes	Lauritzen, Delphine, and Michel Tardieu, eds. *Le Voyage des légendes: hommages à Pierre Chuvin.* Paris: CNRS editions, 2013. https://books.openedition.org/editionscnrs/23840

Nonnus In His Time, Before His Time, and Thereafter

Accorinti, Domenico. "Naming the God of Metamorphosis: The Ever-Changing Shape of the Infant Dionysus in Nonnus' *Dionysiaca.*" In *The Gods of Greek Hexameter Poetry: From the Archaic Age to Late Antiquity and Beyond*, edited by James J. Clauss, Matine Cuypers, and Ahuvi Kahane, 256–67. Stuttgart: Steiner, 2016.

Accorinti, Domenico. "The Poet from Panopolis: An Obscure Biography and a Controversial Figure." In *Companion to Nonnus*, 11–53.

Acosta-Hughes, Benjamin. "Composing the Masters: An Essay on Nonnus and Hellenistic Poetry." In *Companion to Nonnus*, 481–506.

Agosti, Gianfranco. "Contextualizing Nonnus' Visual World." In *Nonnus in Context I*, 141–74.

Agosti, Gianfranco. "L'epillio nelle Dionisiache? Strutture dell'epica nonniana e contesto culturale." *Aitia: Regards sur la culture hellénistique au XXIe siècle* 6 (2006). https://doi.org/10.4000/aitia.1579

Agosti, Gianfranco. "La letteratura agiografica e le *Dionisiache* di Nonno: note di lettura." In *Le Voyage des légendes*, 83–94.

Agosti, Gianfranco. "Nonnus in Late Antique Society." In *Companion to Nonnus*, 644–68.

Agosti, Gianfranco. "Usurper, imiter, communiquer: le dialogue interculturel dans la poésie grecque chrétienne de l'Antiquité tardive." In *L'oiseau et le poisson: cohabitations religieuses dans les mondes grec et romain*, edited by Nicole Belayche and Jean-Daniel Dubois, 275–99. Paris: Presses de l'Université Paris-Sorbonne, 2011.

Bannert, Herbert, and Nicole Kröll. "Nonnus and the Homeric Poems." In *Companion to Nonnus*, 481–506.

Bernabé, Alberto, and Rosa García Gasco. "Dionysus and Dionysiac-Orphic Religion." In *Companion to Nonnus*, 91–110.

Bowersock, G. W. "Dionysus as an Epic Hero." In *Studies in the* Dionysiaca, 156–66.

Braden, Gordon. *The Classics and English Renaissance Poetry: Three Case Studies.* Yale Studies in English 187. New Haven: Yale, 1978.

Braden, Gordon. "Nonnos' Typhoon: *Dionysiaca*, Books I and II." *Texas Studies in Literature and Language* 15 (1974): 851–79. https://www.jstor.org/stable/40754300

Calasso, Roberto. *The Marriage of Cadmus and Harmony.* Translated from the Italian by Tim Parks. New York: Knopf, 1993.

Cameron, Alan. "The Poet, the Bishop, and the Harlot." *Greek, Roman and Byzantine Studies* 41 (2000): 173–88. https://grbs.library.duke.edu/article/view/2131/3591

Carvounis, Katerina. "Dionysus, Ampelus, and Mythological Examples in Nonnus' *Dionysiaca*." In *Nonnus in Context II*, 33–51.

Carvounis, Katerina. "*Peitho* in Nonnus' *Dionysiaca*: The Case of Cadmus and Harmonia." In *Nonnus in Context I*, 21–38.

Chuvin, Pierre. "Local Traditions and Classical Mythology in the *Dionysiaca*." In *Studies in the* Dionysiaca, 167–76.

Chuvin, Pierre. "Nonnos de Panopolis et la 'déconstruction' de l'épopée." *Entretiens sur l'Antiquité classique* 52 (2006): 249–66.

Chuvin, Pierre. "Revisiting Old Problems: Literature and Religion in the *Dionysiaca*." In *Nonnus in Context I*, 3–18.

De Stefani, Claudio. "Homeric Parody in Nonnus." In *Homère revisité*, 65–79.

Dijkstra, Jitse H. F. "The Religious Background of Nonnus." In *Companion to Nonnus*, 75–88.

D'Ippolito, Gennaro. "Nonnus' Conventional Formulaic Style." In *Companion to Nonnus*, 372–401.

Duc, Thierry. "La question de la cohérence dans les *Dionysiaques* de Nonnos de Panopolis." *Revue de Philologie, de Littérature et d'Histoire Anciennes* 64 (1990): 181–91.

Faber, Riemer A. "Nonnus and the Poetry of Ekphrasis in the *Dionysiaca*." In *Companion to Nonnus*, 443–59.

Faulkner, Andrew. "Nonnus' 'Younger Legend': The Birth of Beroë and the Didactic Tradition." *Greece & Rome*, second series, 62 (2017): 103–14. https://doi.org/10.1017/S0017383517000031

Fincher, Joshua. "The Tablets of Harmonia and the Role of Poet and Reader in the *Dionysiaca*." In *Nonnus in Context II*, 120–37.

Frangoulis, Hélène. "Annonces et présages chez Nonnos ou le destin annoncé de Cadmos." In *Le Voyage des légendes*, 179–89.

Frangoulis, Hélène. "Des procédés romanesques dans l'épopée de Nonnos." In *Roman grec et poésie: dialogue des genres et nouveaux enjeux du poétique*, edited by Michèle Biraud and Michel Briand, 311–32. Lyon: Maison de l'Orient et de la Méditerranée-Jean Pouilloux Éditions, 2017. https://books.openedition.org/momeditions/2339?lang=en

Frangoulis, Hélène. *Du roman à l'épopée: influence du roman grec sur les 'Dionysiaques' de Nonnos de Panopolis*. Collection ISTA. Besançon: Presses universitaires de Franche-Compté, 2014. https://doi.org/10.3406/ista.2014.2958

Frangoulis, Hélène. "Réécritures parodiques et humoristiques d'Homère chez Nonnos de Panopolis." In *Homère revisité*, 95–106.

Geisz, Camille. "Narrative and Digression in the *Dionysiaca*." In *Companion to Nonnus*, 173–92.

Geisz, Camille. *A Study of the Narrator in Nonnus of Panopolis'* Dionysiaca*: Storytelling in Late Antique Epic*. Leiden: Brill, 2018.

Gigante Lanzara, Valeria. "Il gioco dei contrari." In *Homère revisité*, 123–32. www.persee.fr/doc/ista_0000-0000_2011_act_1200_1_2936

Gigli Piccardi, Daria. "Nonnus and Pindar." In *Nonnus in Context II*, 255–70.

Gigli Piccardi, Daria. "Nonnus' Poetics." In *Companion to Nonnus*, 422–42.

Giraudet, Vincent. "Les Dionysiaques de Nonnos de Panopolis: un poème sous le signe de Protée." *Bulletin de l'Association Guillaume Budé* 2 (2005): 75–98. https://doi.org/10.3406/bude.2005.3646

Goldhill, Simon. "Preposterous Poetics and the Erotics of Death." *Eugesta: Revue sur le Genre dans l'Antiquité* 5 (2015): 154–77.

Hadjitoffi, Fotini. "The Death of Love in Nonnus' *Dionysiaca*: The Rapes of Nicaea and Aura. *Ramus: Critical Studies in Greek and Roman Literature* 37 (2008): 114–35. https://doi.org/10.1017/S0048671X00004938

Hadjitoffi, Fotini. "Erotic Fiction and Christian Sexual Ethics in Nonnus' Episode of Morrheus and Chalcomede." *The Ancient Novel and the Frontiers of Genre*, edited by Marília Pulquério Futre Pinheiro, Gareth L. Schmeling, and Edmund Paul Cueva. Eelde: Barkhuis, 2014: 187–204.

Hadjitoffi, Fotini. "Major Themes and Motifs in the *Dionysiaca*." In *Companion to Nonnus*, 125–51.

Harries, Byron. "The Pastoral Mode in the *Dionysiaca*." In *Studies in the* Dionysiaca, 63–85.

Hernández de la Fuente, David. "The Influence of Nonnus on Baroque and Modern Literature." In *Companion to Nonnus*, 714–54.

Hernández de la Fuente, David. "Neoplatonic Form and Content in Nonnus: Towards a New Reading of Nonnian Poetics." In *Nonnus in Context I*, 229–50.

Hernández de la Fuente, David. "Nonnus, Peacock and Shelley: A Note on the First

English Translations of the *Dionysiaca*, " *Res Publica Litterarum: Studies in the Classical Tradition* 10 (2007): 188–98.

Hernández de la Fuente, David. "Parallels between Dionysos and Christ in Late Antiquity: Miraculous Healings in Nonnus' *Dionysiaca*." In *Redefining Dionysos*, edited by Alberto Bernabé, Ana Isabel Jiménez San Cristóbal, and Raquel Martín, 464–87, plus plates. Berlin: De Gruyter, 2013.

Hernández de la Fuente, David. "Poetry and Philosophy at the Boundaries of Byzantium (5th–7th Centuries): Some Methodological Remarks." In *New Perspectives on Late Antiquity in the Eastern Roman Empire*, edited by Ana de Francisco Heredero, Sergio González Sánchez, and David Hernández de la Fuente, 81–100. Newcastle upon Tyne: Cambridge Scholars Publishing, 2014.

Hernández de la Fuente, David. "The Quest for Nonnus' Life. From Scholarship to Fiction." In *Nonnus in Context II*, 355–73.

Hollis, Adrian S. "The Hellenistic Epyllion and Its Descendants." In *Greek Literature in Late Antiquity: Dynamism, Didacticism, Classicism*, edited by Scott Fitzgerald Johnson, 141–57. Aldershot: Ashgate, 2006. https://chs.harvard.edu/CHS/article/display/3261.adrian-hollis-the-hellenistic-epyllion-and-its-descendants

Hollis, Adrian S. "Nonnus and Hellenistic Poetry." In *Studies in the* Dionysiaca, 43–62.

Hopkinson, Neil. "Nonnus and Homer." In *Studies in the* Dionysiaca, 9–42.

Knox, Peter E. "Phaethon in Ovid and Nonnus." *Classical Quarterly* 38 (1988): 536–51. https://www.jstor.org/stable/638998

Kröll, Nicole. *Die Jugend des Dionysos: Die Ampelos-Episode in den* Dionysiaka *des Nonnos von Panopolis*. Millennium-Studien 62. Berlin: De Gruyter, 2016. https://doi.org/10.1515/9783110419207

Kuhlmann, Peter Alois. "The Motif of the Rape of Europa: Intertextuality and Absurdity of the Myth in Epyllion and Epic Insets." In *Brill's Companion to Greek and Latin Epyllion and Its Reception*, edited by Manuel Baumbach and Silvio Bär, 473–90. Leiden: Brill, 2012.

Lasek, Anna Maria. "Nonnus and the Play of Genres." In *Companion to Nonnus*, 402–21.

Lasky, E. D. "Encomiastic Elements in the *Dionysiaca* of Nonnus." *Hermes: Zeitschrift für Klassische Philologie* 105 (1978): 357–76. www.jstor.org/stable/4476066

Lefteratou, Anna. "Dionysus' 'Catabasis' to India: Christian Echoes in Nonnus' Indiad." In *Reading the Way to the Netherworld: Education and the Representations of the Beyond in Later Antiquity*, edited by Ilinca Tanaseanu-Döbler, Gabriela Ryser, Anna Lefteratou, and Konstantinos Stamatopoulos, 164–88. Göttingen: Vandenhoeck & Ruprecht, 2014.

Lightfoot, Jane. "The Bonds of Cypris: Nonnus' Aura." *Greek, Roman and Byzantine Studies* 39 (1998): 293–306. https://grbs.library.duke.edu/article/view/2411/5933

Lightfoot, Jane. "Oracles in the *Dionysiaca*." In *Nonnus in Context I*, 39–54.

Lindsay, Jack. *Leisure and Pleasure in Roman Egypt*. Frederick Muller, 1965. First U.S. edition, New York: Barnes & Noble, 1966.

Maciver, Calum Alisdair. "Nonnus and Imperial Greek Poetry." In *Companion to Nonnus*, 529–48.

Middleton, Fran. "The Poetics of Later Greek Ecphrasis: Christodorus Coptus, The Palatine Anthology, and the Periochae of Nonnus' *Dionysiaca*." *Ramus: Critical Studies in Greek and Roman Literature* 47 (2018): 216–38. https://doi.org/10.1017/rmu.2019.1

Miguélez Cavero, Laura. "The Appearance of the Gods in the *Dionysiaca* of Nonnus." *Greek, Roman and Byzantine Studies* 49 (2009): 557–83. https://grbs.library.duke.edu/article/view/1281/1361

Miguélez-Cavero, Laura. "Cosmic and Terrestrial Personifications in Nonnus' *Dionysiaca*." *Greek, Roman and Byzantine Studies* 53 (2013): 350–78. https://grbs.library.duke.edu/article/view/14711/3861

Miguélez-Cavero, Laura. "Gesture and Gesturality in the *Dionysiaca* of Nonnus." *Journal of Late Antiquity* 2 (2009): 251–73. https://doi.org/10.1353/jla.0.0041

Miguélez-Cavero, Laura. "Harmonia's Necklace (Nonn. *D.* 5.135–189): A Set of Jewellery, *ekphrasis* and a Narrative Node." In *Rhetorical Strategies in Late Antique Literature: Images, Metatexts and Interpretation*, edited by Alberto J. Quiroga Puertas, 165–97. Leiden: Brill, 2017.

Miguélez-Cavero, Laura. "Invective at the Service of Encomium in the *Dionysiaca* of Nonnus of Panopolis." *Mnemosyne* 63 (2010): 23–42. https://doi.org/10.1163/002670710X12603307970513

Miguélez-Cavero, Laura. "Nonnus and the Novel." In *Companion to Nonnus*, 549–73.

Miguélez-Cavero, Laura. "Nonnus' Natural Histories: Anything to Do with Dionysus?" In *The Alexandrian Tradition: Interactions between Science, Religion, and Literature*, edited by Luis Arturo Guichard, Juan Luis García Alonso, and María Paz de Hoz, 245–86. New York: Peter Lang, 2014.

Miguélez-Cavero, Laura. "Personifications at the Service of Dionysus: The Bacchic Court." In *Nonnus in Context I*, 175–92.

Miguélez Cavero, Laura. *Poems in Context: Greek Poetry in the Egyptian Thebaid 200–600 AD*. Berlin: De Gruyter, 2008.

Miguélez-Cavero, Laura. "Rhetoric of Novelty in the *Dionysiaca* of Nonnus of Panopolis." In *The Theodosian Age (A.D. 379–455): Power, Place, Belief and Learning at the End of the Western Empire*, edited by Rosa García Gasco, Sergio González Sánchez, and David Hernández de la Fuente, 191–95. Oxford: Archaeopress, 2013. https://doi.org/10.30861/9781407311074

Minuto, Cristiano. "Nonnus of Panopolis and Technical Poetry: Astronomic Upheaval in the Episode of Phaethon." Κοινωνία 39 (2015): 223–32.

Newbold, Ronald F. "Mimesis and Illusion in Nonnus: Deceit, Distrust, and the Search for Meaning." *Helios* 37 (2010): 81–106.

Newbold, Ronald F. "The Psychology in the *Dionysiaca*." In *Companion to Nonnus*, 193–212.

Newbold, Ronald F. "Some Problems of Creativity in Nonnus's *Dionysiaca*." *Classical Antiquity* 12 (1993): 89–110. https://doi.org/10.2307/25010985

Paschalis, Michael. "Ovidian Metamorphosis and Nonnian *poikilon eidos*." In *Nonnus in Context I*, 97–122.

Schmiel, Robert. "Composition and Structure: The Battle at the Hydaspes (Nonnos' *Dionysiaca* 21.303–24.178)." In *Des géants à Dionysos: mélanges de mythologie et de poésie grecques offerts à Francis Vian*, edited by Domenico Accorinti and Pierre Chuvin, 469–81. Alessandria: Edizioni dell'Orso, 2003.

Schmiel, Robert. "Nonnus' Typhonomachy: An Analysis of the Structure of *Dionysiaca* II." *Rheinisches Museum für Philologie* 135 (1992): 369–75. https://rhm.phil-fak.uni-koeln.de/inhaltsverzeichnisse/rhm-1990-1999#135

Schmiel, Robert. "The Story of Aura: (Nonnos, *Dionysiaca* 48.238–978)." *Zeitschrift für Klassische Philologie* 121 (1993): 470–83. http://www.jstor.org/stable/4476984

Schmiel, Robert. "The Style of Nonnos' *Dionysiaca*: The Rape of Europa (1.45–136) and the Battle at the Hydaspes (22.1–24.143)." *Rheinisches Museum für Philologie* 141 (1998): 393–406. https://rhm.phil-fak.uni-koeln.de/inhaltsverzeichnisse/rhm-1990-1999#141

Shorrock, Robert. *The Challenge of Epic: Allusive Engagement in the* Dionysiaca *of Nonnus*. Mnemosyne Supplements 210. Leiden: Brill, 2001.

Shorrock, Robert. "Christian Themes in the *Dionysiaca*." In *Companion to Nonnus*, 577–600.

Shorrock, Robert. "A Classical Myth in a Christian World: Nonnus' Ariadne Episode (Dion. 47.265–475)." In *Nonnus in Context I*, 313–32.

Shorrock, Robert. *The Myth of Paganism: Nonnus, Dionysus and the World of Late Antiquity*. Classical Literature and Society. London: Bristol Classical Press, 2011.

Shorrock, Robert. "*Ut poesis pictura*: Nonnus' Europa Episode as Poetry and Painting." In *Nonnus in Context II*, 374–92.

Spanoudakis, Konstantinos. "The Resurrections of Tylus and Lazarus in Nonnus of Panopolis (*Dion*. XXV, 451–552 and *Par*. Λ)." In *Le Voyage des légendes*, 191–208.

Spanoudakis, Konstantinos. "The Shield of Salvation: Dionysus' Shield in Nonnus *Dionysiaca* 25.380–572." In *Nonnus in Context I*, 333–72.

Van Minnen, Peter. "Nonnus' Panopolis." In *Companion to Nonnus*, 54–74.

Van Opstall, Emilie M. "The Golden Flower of Youth: Baroque Metaphors in Nonnus and Marino." *Classical Receptions Journal* 6 (2014): 446–70. https://doi.org/10.1093/crj/clt029

Verhelst, Berenice. *Direct Speech in Nonnus'* Dionysiaca: *Narrative and Rhetorical Functions of the Characters' 'varied' and 'many-faceted' Words*. Leiden: Brill, 2016.

Verhelst, Berenice. "Minor Characters in the *Dionysiaca*." In *Companion to Nonnus*, 152–72.

Vian, Francis. "Dionysus in the Indian War: A Contribution to a Study of the Structure of the *Dionysiaca*." In *Studies in the* Dionysiaca, 86–98.

Vian, Francis. "Mythologie scolaire et mythologie érudite dans les *Dionysiaques* de Nonnos." *Prometheus* 4 (1978): 157–72.

Vian, Francis. "Théogamies et sotériologie dans les *Dionysiaques* de Nonnos." *Journal des Savants* 2 (1994): 197–233. https://doi.org/10.3406/jds.1994.1579

Whitby, M. "From Moschus to Nonnus: The Evolution of the Nonnian Style." In *Studies in the* Dionysiaca, 99–155.

Winkler, John Joseph. "In Pursuit of Nymphs: Comedy and Sex in Nonnos' *Tales of Dionysos*." PhD diss., University of Texas at Austin, 1974.

Glossary of Personal Names

Personal names in *Tales of Dionysus* are difficult and fluid things, owing to the poem's programmatic use of multiple names and variant spellings for single individuals, its allegorization of abstract entities as persons, and its free but inconsistent personification of places, geographical features, as well as atmospheric and celestial phenomena. We have included below those personal names whose identification we believe will be most useful to readers, omitting persons mentioned only in passing and without consequence to the narrative, but including referenced mythical and historical figures assumed to be familiar to the poem's original readership. As a general rule, we have followed spelling conventions derived from Latin rather than Greek throughout the text; hence, "Bacchus" rather than "Bakkhos." Exceptions are chiefly for names whose Greek forms have already been naturalized in English (e.g., "Nike") and for Greek words turned into names strictly for the purposes of the poem (e.g., "Ampelos," "Cissos," and "Staphylos").

Abarbarea (1): A virgin nymph of the area around Troy, mentioned in the *Iliad* as the mother of two warriors. See Book 15.

Abarbarea (2): A naiad turned into a fountain. See Book 40.

Abaris: Legendary priest of Apollo, said to fly throughout Greece carried on an arrow of the god. See Book 11.

Achilles: Son of Peleus and the sea goddess Thetis, grandson of Aeacus, greatest of the Greek warriors at Troy and central figure of Homer's *Iliad*.

Acrisius: Father of Danaë, hence grandfather of the hero Perseus. See especially Books 8 and 47.

Actaeon: Son of Aristaeus and Autonoë, one of the daughters of Cadmus and Harmonia; while he was hunting, he came across Artemis nude and was transformed into a stag, then attacked and killed by his own pack of hounds. See especially Books 5, 13, and 46.

Admetus: Beneficent king of Pherae in Thessaly, whom Apollo served as herdsman for a year during a term of exile from Olympus.

Adonis: Beautiful mortal from Cyprus (or Assyria) loved by Aphrodite but killed while hunting by a boar sent by Ares (or by Ares in the shape of a boar); from his blood (or from Aphrodite's tears) sprang flowers, and Adonis became the focus of a long-lived cult involving ceremonies of lamentation and rebirth. See especially Books 31, 41, 42, and 48.

Adrasteia: Allegorical figure of retribution; the name means "inescapable."

Aeacus: Son of Zeus and the nymph Aegina, father of Peleus, hence grandfather of Achilles; his exploits in the army of Dionysus, especially in Books 22 and 23, parallel those of his grandson as recounted in the *Iliad.*

Aegaeon: Hundred-armed son of Poseidon, who aided Zeus in his war with the Titans.

Aegina: Nymph, daughter of the river-god Asopus, loved by Zeus in the form of an eagle, mother of Aeacus.

Aegyptus: Eponym of Egypt, whose fifty sons married the fifty daughters of his brother Danaus, all but one of whom murdered their husbands on their joint wedding night. See especially Book 3.

Aeolus: God and governor of the winds.

Agamemnon: King of Mycene and commander of the Greek armies in their war at Troy, who was prepared to sacrifice his daughter Iphigeneia at Aulis in return for favorable winds for his fleet.

Agenor: King of Tyre, father of Cadmus, Europa, et al. See especially Books 3 and 4.

Agavê (1): One of the four daughters of Cadmus and Harmonia, wife of Echion, mother of Pentheus, whom she killed and beheaded in a Bacchic frenzy. See especially Books 5, 44, 45, and 46.

Agavê (2): One of the nereids. See Book 6.

Agraeus: Indian warrior, son of Eulaeus and brother of Phlogius. See Book 26.

Ajax: Greek fighter in the war against Troy, considered second only to Achilles, committed suicide during a bout of madness.

Alcimacheia: Mountain nymph from Lemnos fighting in Dionysus' army, killed by Morrheus. See Book 30.

Alcmene: Mother of Heracles by Zeus, who came to her in the guise of her husband Amphitryon through a night which he stretched to three times its natural span. See especially Books 7, 23, 31.

Alcon: Son of Hephaestus and Cabiro of Samothrace, brother of Eurymedon, Greek warrior in the army of Dionysus. See especially Books 29, 30. and 37.

Alcyone: One of the Pleiades, seven daughters of Pleione and the Titan Atlas, who were pursued by the hunter Orion, then transformed into a constellation along with their pursuer and his hound.

Alcyoneus: Earthborn Giant at war with the forces of Dionysus.

Alpheus: River god of Elis in the Peloponnesus, who loved the nymph Arethusa and pursued her under the sea to Sicily. See especially Books 6, 13, and 42.

Alpus: Giant, monstrous son of Earth, enlisted in the Indian war against Dionysus. See especially Books 5 and 45.

Althaea: Mother by Dionysus (or her husband Oeneus) of the Argonaut Meleagrus; the story of her fatal quarrel with her son plays no role in Nonnus' narrative. See Book 48.

Amalthea: She-goat who gave milk to the infant Zeus and was set among the stars.

Ambrosia: Nymph in the army of Dionysus, who was transformed into a vine rather than be carried off by the Indian soldier Lycurgus; her name means "immortal." See Book 21.

Ammon: Major Egyptian deity identified by the Greeks with Zeus; the oracle of Zeus-Ammon in Libya was renowned in the ancient world.

Ampelos: Satyr youth, favorite of Dionysus, tempted to pride by Atê and killed, transformed after death into a vine; the name itself means "grapevine." See especially Books 10, 11, and 12.

Amphiaraus: Theban seer in the generation after Oedipus, whose wife, bribed with the necklace of Harmonia, persuaded him to military expedition against the city, even though he foresaw that he would not survive the attack.

Amphion: Musician, son of Zeus and Antiope, whose lyre-playing enchanted stones to rise from the earth of their own accord and form the walls of Thebes.

Amphitrite: Consort of the sea god Poseidon.

Amphitryon: Theban military commander whose wife, Alcmene, became the mother of Heracles by Zeus.

Amymonê (1): Daughter of Danaus, loved by Poseidon, who created a fountain in Lerna named for her. See Book 8.

Amymonê (2): A name for the nymph Beroë. See especially Books 41, 42, and 43.

Androgeneia: Mother of Asterion of Dicte.

Andromeda: Daughter of Cepheus, son of Agenor and king among the Ethiopians, and Cassiopeia; chained to a rock as a sacrifice to a sea monster but rescued by and married to the hero Perseus. Like all the other figures in the story, she is raised to the skies as a constellation. See especially Books 18, 25, and 49.

Antiope: Mother of the twins Amphion and Zetus by Zeus, who came to her in the guise of a satyr. See especially Book 33.

Aphrodite, also Citherea, Cypris, the Paphian: Goddess of sexuality; in the more common story, she is born from the foam resulting when the severed testicles of Uranus/Sky fell into the sea, coming to shore first on the island of Cyprus; otherwise, she is the daughter of Zeus and Dione.

Apis: Egyptian diety identified by the Greeks with Dionysus.

Apollo, also Phoebus: Son of Zeus and Leto, born on the island of Delos, twin of Artemis; an archer god, bringer of both plague and healing, a musician associated particularly with the lyre; god, too, of prophecy, especially at his oracular seat at Delphi; as Phoebus, often identified with the sun.

Arachne: An expert weaver who challenged Athena and was transformed into a spider for her presumption; her name became a metonym for weaving.

Arcas: Son of Zeus and Callisto, eponymous founder of Arcadia; as a constellation, also Boötes or Arctophylax; rationalized as an astronomer in Book 41.

Ares: God of war, son of Zeus and Hera, sometime lover of Aphrodite; a fragmentary story from the *Iliad* mentions his year-long captivity in a bronze jar at the hands of the giants Otos and Ephialtes until he was released by the god Hermes. For Ares as an ally of the Indians, see especially Books 27 and 32.

Arestor: Father of Greek warrior Opheltes, who was slain by Deriades.

Arethusa: Nymph pursued underground by the river god Alpheus from Greece to Sicily, where she emerged in Syracuse as a freshwater fountain very near to the sea, which flows still today. See especially Books 6, 37, 40, and 45.

Argus: Creature with multiple, unsleeping eyes set by Hera to watch over her rival Io after she was transformed into a heifer; he was lulled to sleep by Hermes, then beheaded, his eyes becoming ornaments on the tail of the peacock, Hera's bird..

Ariadne: Daughter of Minos of Crete, granddaughter of Zeus and Europa; eloped with Theseus of Athens but is abandoned on the island of Naxos; discovered by Dionysus and married to him; accidentally turned to stone by Perseus wielding the head of Medusa. After her death, Dionysus raises her wedding crown to the sky as a constellation. See especially Book 47.

Aristaeus: Son of Apollo and the hunter nymph Cyrene; inventor of beekeeping, olive cultivation, and other rustic pursuits; married to Cadmus' daughter Autonoë and father of Actaeon; a member of the army of Dionysus in India. See especially Books 5, 13, 17, 29, and 37.

Artemis, also Hecaërge: Virgin goddess, hunter and protector of childbirth, daughter of Zeus and Leto, twin sister of Apollo; often identified with the Moon. See especially Books 5 and 48.

Asopus: River god, father of the nymph Aegina, hence grandfather of Aeacus.

Aspetus: Leader of the Uatocoetae, or "Ear-sleepers," allies of the Indians in the war with Dionysus.

Asterië (1): Nymph of the island of Delos, who escaped the aggression of Zeus by leaping into the sea, where she was then pursued by Poseidon. See Books 2 and 42.

Asterië (2), also Astris: Granddaughter of Oceanus, daughter of Helios, married to the river Hydaspes, mother of the Indian king Deriades. See Book 23.

Asterion, also Asterius: King of Dicte in Crete, married to Europa, leader among the troops of Dionysus in India; after the war, he settled in Colchis rather than return home. See especially Books 2 and 37.

Asteropaeus: A Trojan victim of Achilles, described in Homer's *Iliad.*

Astraea: The personified constellation Virgo, identified with Justice, who lived among men during the Golden Age and was among the last divinities to leave the earth when that era came to an end. See Book 41.

Astraëis: Indian prince, son of Brongus (2), warrior enspirited by Hera to fight against Dionysus. See especially Books 17 and 26.

Astraeus (1): Titan, seer and spirit of prophecy, husband of Eos, the Dawn, and father of the winds; the name means "starry." See Book 6.

Astraeus (2): Satyr in the army of Dionysus. See especially Books 12 and 48.

Atalanta: Athletic virgin who would not marry any man who could not beat her in a foot race; beaten by (and then wed to) Hippomenes, who rolled golden apples in her path and sped by her as she would slow to pick them up. See especially Books 12 and 48.

Atê: Personified spirit of mental blindness or delusion.

Athamas: Husband, first, of Nephelê, who bore him Helle and Phrixus, then of Ino, daughter of Cadmus, who bore him the sons Learchus and Melicertes; driven mad, he killed Learchus while Ino and Melicertes escaped by leaping into the sea. See especially Books 5, 9, and 10.

Athena, also Pallas, Tritogeneia, the Tritonian: Virgin warrior goddess, clad in armor, born without mother from Zeus' head; patroness also of women's crafts, weaving in particular. See especially Books 4, 5, 26, 27, 30, 36, 40, and 48.

Atlas: Titan of prodigious strength, condemned by Zeus to support the sky.

Atropos: One of the personified Fates; the name means "unbending."

Attis: Self-castrated Lydian devotee and cult-companion of Cybele, paradigm of gender indeterminacy in classical literature, functions as messenger of Cybele-Rhea in Book 25.

Atymnius: Cretan boy, beloved of Apollo; after his death, Apollo transformed him into a flower and adopted his name for occasional cult purposes.

Augustus: Historical first emperor of Rome, 63 BCE—14 CE. See reference in Book 41.

Aura: Virgin hunter and comrade of Artemis, daughter of the Titan Lelantus; raped and impregnated by Dionysus; mother of twins, one of whom she kills at birth, the other of whom, Iacchus, is delivered safely to his father; her name means "wind." See especially Book 48.

Autonoë: One of the four daughters of Cadmus and Harmonia, married to Aristaeus, mother of Actaeon. See especially Books 5, 44, 45, and 46.

Bacchae/Bacchi: Bacchants; general name for the female and male followers of Dionysus in their frenzy.

Bacchus: Frequent name for Dionysus.

Bassarid: Bacchant, once considered specifically from Thrace and clad in fox skins but by Nonnus' time no longer with any geographical reference.

Bellerophon, Bellerophontes: Corinthian hero, sometimes said to be the son of Poseidon; slayer of the monstrous Chimaera, tamer (with Athena's guidance) of the winged horse Pegasus, from whose back he was thrown as he attempted to ascend to the heavens. See Book 11.

Belus: Hellenization of the Semitic god Baal; in Nonnus' narration, great-grandson of Zeus and Io, father of many children, including Aegyptus, Danaus, and Agenor, father of Cadmus; identified with Zeus-Ammon in Libya and with a divinized Heracles in Assyria. See Books 3 and 40.

Beroë, also Amymonê: Nymph, daughter of Aphrodite and Adonis, eponym of the city of Beirut, beloved both of Dionysus and Poseidon; as Beirut, the site of a school of law renowned in the Roman era. See especially Books 41, 42, and 43.

Blemys: Indian war leader who submits to Dionysus and is dispatched to settle Ethiopia. See Book 17.

Boötes: Constellation, the Plowman or the Oxherd, identified with the rustic Icarius set in the skies as an honor after his death.

Boreas: Personification of the north wind, abducted and married Oreithyia, daughter of the early Athenian king, Erechtheus.

Botrys: Son of King Staphylos and Queen Methê of Assyria, who entertained Dionysus on his march to India; the name means "grape cluster" and is from the verbal root meaning "twisted" or "curly," as a lock of hair. See Books 18, 19, and 20.

Britomartis: Cretan nymph devoted to chastity, who leaped into the sea to escape King Minos, became entangled in fishermen's nets, and was returned to land; according to some stories, she made her way to the island of Aegina, where she encountered Minos again and again escaped him.

Bromius: Frequent name for Dionysus; the name means "roaring" or "boisterous."

Brongus (1): Upland shepherd who entertains Dionysus along his march to India. See Book 17.

Brongus (2): Indian, father of troop leaders Cyllaris and Astraëis. See Book 26.

Brontes: Cyclops in the army of Dionysus; the name means "thunderer."

Byzas: Migrant from Egypt and eponymous founder of Byzantium, son of Poseidon, grandson of Zeus and Io. See Book 3.

Cabiro: Nymph of Lemnos, mother of Hephaestus' sons Alcon and Eurymedon, warriors in Dionysus' army. See especially Books 14 and 27.

Cabiri: The sons of Cabiro and Hephaestus, Alcon and Eurymedon.

Cadmilus: In the present work, equivalent of Hermes. See Book 4.

Cadmus: Europa's brother, Harmonia's husband, founder and first king of Thebes, and grandfather of Dionysus through his daughter Semele, whose sisters Antinoë, Agavê, and Ino were equally ill-fated. In the present work, Cadmus in shepherd's guise conspires with Zeus in the struggle with Typhoeus. See especially Books 1–5, 13, 45, and 46.

Calamos: Lovely boy, son of the river Maeandrus, who drowns himself after the death of his friend Carpos and was transformed into river reeds; the name itself means "reed." See especially Book 11.

Calliope: One of the Muses, mother of Orpheus. See especially Book 22.

Callisto: Nymph favored by Artemis, seduced by Zeus and turned first into a bear, then into the constellation Ursa Major.

Calycê: Bacchante in army of Dionysus. See Books 14 and 29.

Camandrus, also Scamander and Scamandrus: The river god Scamander, ally of the Trojans in Homer's *Iliad.*

Campê: Female monster, Zeus slew her to release the Cyclopes for his war with the Titans. See Book 18.

Carpos: Lovely boy, friend of Calamos, who drowned pathetically and was transformed into fruit; the name itself means "fruit." See especially Book 11.

Cassiopeia: Queen in Ethiopia, wife of Cepheus: her vanity angered Poseidon, who sent the sea-monster Cetis to ravage the land until her daughter, Andromeda was offered as a sacrifice. Perseus rescued Andromeda, but Poseidon placed her mother on a throne upside-down in the heavens.

Caunus: The incestuous advances of his sister Byblis drove him from his home into Caria, where he became a king. Byblis, inconsolable, turned into a spring.

Cecrops: Legendary founder of Athens, which is sometimes called "Cecropia." A later Cecrops was king of Athens during the earthly careers of both Dionysus and Perseus. See especially Book 41.

Celaeno: One of the Pleiades.

Cephalus: A mortal so handsome that Dawn (Eos) took him as her lover. See especially Books 4, 11, and 48.

Cepheus: Son of Agenor, hence brother of Cadmus and Europa; king of Ethiopia, husband of Cassiopeia, and father of Andromeda; after death he was placed near his wife among the stars. See especially Books 2, 25, and 30.

Ceroëssa: Daughter of Zeus and Io; her son by Poseidon, Byzas, founded Byzantium.

Chalcomedê, Chalcomedeia: Bacchante in Dionysus' army so hotly desired by the Indian hero Morrheus that he temporarily abandons the fighting. She both dreads and exploits his passion, eventually tricking him into a deadly embrace. See especially Books 33, 34, 35, and 40.

Chariclo: Nymph and mother of the Theban seer Teiresias.

Charis: Any of the Charites or Graces, who in the present work are daughters of Dionysus. The name becomes a catch-all for feminine beauty.

Charopeia: Bacchante in Dionysus' army, she slew the Indian hero Colletes.

Chirobië: Wife of the Indian hero Morrheus. See especially Book 40.

Chiron: Immortal and erudite centaur whose famous pupils included both Jason and Achilles. See especially Book 13.

Chthonius: One of the Giants.

Circe: Immortal sorceress featured in the *Odyssey*, who usually turned visitors to her island into beasts. This was the fate of Odysseus' crew, but she fell in love with their captain, detaining him for ten years. Mother of the woodland god Faunus. See especially Book 37.

Cissos: Satyr playfellow of Dionysus and Ampelos. When Ampelos is transformed into the first grapevine, Cissos becomes ivy. The name itself means "ivy." See especially Book 12.

Cleopatra (1): Daughter of Boreas, the North Wind, and Orithyia, princess of Thrace, married to Phineus, brother of Cadmus. See Book 2.

Cleopatra (2): Historical queen of Egypt and last ruler of its Ptolemaic dynasty. With her suicide in 30 BCE, Egypt came under Roman control. See Book 41.

Clymenê: Consort or lover of Helios the Sun, mother of Phaëthon. See especially Books 8, 33, 38, and 40.

Clytius: Phrygian warrior in Dionysus' army, slain by the Indian hero Corymbasus. See Book 28.

Codone: Maenad slain by Morrheus. See Books 30 and 33.

Combê: Mother of the Corybantes.

Comus: Divine personification of festivity.

Corybantes: Warrior cult devoted to Rhea/Cybele, their ecstatic worship features frenzied drumming and dancing. In the present work they are mostly interchangeable with the Curetes and Dactyli.

Corymbasus: Prominent warrior in the Indian army, referred to as "chief of the Ethiopians." See especially Book 28.

Cronides, Cronion, Cronius: Son of Cronus, regularly Zeus, but occasionally referring to Zeus' brother Poseidon.

Cronus: Titan, son of Earth and Sky, castrated his father to assume control of the universe; father of Zeus, Poseidon, Hera, et al., but swallowed his children just after their birth. When the youngest, Zeus, was born, his mother substituted a stone in his place, which Cronus swallowed. In time Zeus overthrew his father and forced him to disgorge his other children.

Curetes: Caretakers of the infant Zeus, identified in *Tales of Dionysus* with the Corybantes.

Cybele: An ancient Anatolian mother goddess, focus of an ecstatic cult. In *Tales of Dionysus*, Cybele is another name of Rhea, the mother of Zeus, and foster mother to Dionysus. See especially Books 9, 10, 25, 44, and 48.

Cydnus: Anatolian river god and father of naiads.

Cyprian, Cypris, Cytherea: Aphrodite.

Cyrene: Eponym of the city in N. Africa; huntress and companion of Artemis, she was beloved by Apollo. Their children included Aristaeus, father of Actaeon.

Dactyli: Cretan devotees of Rhea associated with ironworking, often identified with the Corybantes; the name means "fingers."

Damasen: Serpent-killing son of Earth, depicted on the shield of Dionysus described in Book 25.

Damnameneus (1): One of the Cretan Dactyli. See Book 23.

Damnameneus (2): Unwelcome suitor of the nymph Melis, otherwise unknown. See Book 33.

Damneus: One of the Corybantes.

Danaë: Imprisoned by her father King Acrisius of Argos, whose death at the hands of a grandson had been foretold, she nonetheless bore a son, Perseus, after Zeus visited her in the form of a shower of gold. Set adrift with her son in a wooden chest, they both came to shore on the island of Seriphos. See especially Book 25.

Danaus: Fled to Argos from Egypt with his fifty daughters, after his brother, Aegyptus, demanded they wed his own fifty sons. Pursued to Argos, Danaus capitulated but secretly instructed his daughters to murder their new husbands on their wedding night. Credited with numerous inventions. See especially Book 4.

Daphne: Naiad pursued by Apollo, she escaped by becoming a laurel. See especially Books 2, 15, and 33.

Dardanus: Son of Electra by Zeus, he left his home in Samothrace for Asia Minor and founded a city bearing his name. The Trojan royal line were his descendants. See especially Book 3.

Deïaneira: Wife of Heracles, she was also an accomplished warrior. Tricked by the dying centaur Nessus into using his poisonous blood as a love potion, she inadvertently caused her husband's death. See Book 43.

Demeter, also Deo: Fertility goddess whose sorrowing during her daughter Persephone's extended annual visits to the underworld brings winter. She is hostile to Dionysus, whom she views as a rival. See especially Books 5, 6, 19, and 27.

Deriades: Son of the river Hydaspes, king of the Indians and Dionysus' principal adversary in the Indian War, he has the support of Dionysus' enemies Hera, Ares, and Demeter. His death in single combat with Dionysus shadows the death of Hector at the hands of Achilles in the *Iliad.* See especially Books 23–30 and 34–40.

Deucalion: Forewarned by his father, Prometheus, of Zeus' cosmic flood, he built a chest in which he survived with his wife, Pyrrha, repopulating the world afterward. His son Hellen was ancestor to the Hellenes (Greeks).

Dia: Nymph impregnated by Zeus in the form of a stallion, she was the mother of Perithous, companion of Theseus.

Didnasus: Father of the Indian warriors Orontes and Mor.

Diomedes: King of the Argives; one of the most formidable Greek warriors at Troy, he is a major figure in the *Iliad.*

Dione: Titan and, in some versions of the myth, mother of Zeus' daughter Aphrodite.

Dionysus, also Bacchus, Bromius, Eiraphiotes, Euios/Evius, Iobacchus/Yobacchus, Lyaeus: God of viticulture and wine-making, irrationality, and madness (and, later, theater), his orgiastic rites involved dancing, drunkenness, and animal sacrifice. His rampaging female devotees, maenads, brandished the thyrsus, a pinecone-tipped wand of giant fennel wound with ivy or grape-leaves. Dionysus was presented as a latecomer and outsider among the gods, bitterly resented by Hera, Demeter, and Ares. Though a son of Zeus, his mother, Semele, was human and did not survive his birth, so the divine child was raised by various caregivers, lastly Zeus' own mother, the Phrygian earth-goddess Rhea. Zeus assigned Dionysus a twofold task: the conquest of India and the dissemination of the grape. Thus the new divinity ascended to heaven only after lengthy adventures as he spread his worship, often by force of arms, from India to Greece. In *Tales of Dionysus,* Dionysus is understood to be one incarnation of a trinity of gods, the first being Zagreus, son of Zeus and Persephone, who was ripped apart by Titans soon after his birth, the third being Iacchus, Dionysus' own child by the nymph Aura.

For his conception, see Book 7, for his birth Book 8, for his infancy and upbringing Book 9, for his discovery of wine Book 12, for his war against the Indians Books 13-40, for his return to his birthplace in Thebes Books 44–46, for his ascension to Olympus Book 48.

Doris: One of the Oceanid sea nymphs, wife of Nereus, mother of the fifty nereids.

Earthshaker: Frequent epithet of Poseidon.

Echidna: Half-woman, half-snake consort of Typhoeus and the mother of many noted monsters, among them Scylla, Cerberus, the Chimera, the Hydra, and the Sphinx.

Echion: One of the surviving Sparti (warriors sprung from the furrow when Cadmus sowed the dragon's teeth), husband of Cadmus' daughter Agavê, and father of Theban king Pentheus. See especially Book 5.

Echo: As punishment for distracting Hera from Zeus' infidelities, she was limited to repeating the last words spoken by others, dooming her love for Narcissus. See especially Books 6 and 48.

Eërië: When her father, Tectaphus, lay starving in Deriades' dungeon, she tricked the guards into letting her in, then nourished him with her own breast milk. In admiration, Deriades freed the prisoner. See Book 30.

Eido, also Eidothea: Sea nymph and daughter of Proteus; in the *Odyssey* she advises Menelaus how to hold fast to her father amid all his changes.

Eileithyia: Goddess of childbirth and midwifery, sometimes to be identified with Artemis.

Eiraphiotes: An alternate name for Dionysus. Its meaning is unknown.

Electra: One of the seven star-nymphs known as the Pleiades, queen of Samothrace, and foster-mother of Aphrodite's daughter Harmonia. See especially Books 3 and 4.

Emathion: Son of Electra and king of Samothrace, in whose palace Cadmus encounters Harmonia. See especially Book 3.

Enceladus: One of the Giants, son of Earth and Uranus/Sky, ultimately crushed under the island of Sicily.

Endymion: Handsome shepherd, beloved of Selene, the moon goddess.

Enipeus: River god of Thessaly who rejected the advances of a mortal woman, Tyro. Lustful Poseidon visited her in Enipeus' form. See especially Books 1 and 42.

Enyalios: In the present work, a synonym for Ares.

Enyo: Goddess of war, female counterpart of Ares. See especially Book 2

Eos: Divine personification of dawn.

Epaphus: Son of Zeus and Io, an ancestor of Cadmus. See especially Book 3.

Ephialtes: Giant, son of Iphimedeia, who with his brother, Otos, assaulted Olympus, attempted the abduction of Hera and Athena, and imprisoned Ares in a bronze jar. See especially Book 2.

Erechtheus: A king of Athens. See especially Book 37.

Erigone: Daughter of the shepherd Icarius, who shared Dionysus' gift of wine with his neighbors, who then killed him in drunken rage. She hanged herself and became the constellation Virgo. See especially Book 47.

Eros: Son of Aphrodite and her frequent collaborator. His arrows instill uncontrollable desire. See especially Book 7.

Europa: Daughter of Phoenician king Agenor and sister of Cadmus. Zeus in the form of a bull abducted her and swam with her on his back to Crete, where she bore him sons, including Minos, before marrying the Cretan king, Asterion. See especially Book 1.

Eurymedon: Son of Hephaestus in Dionysus' army, one of the Cabiri. See especially Books 30 and 37.

Eurynome: Titan queen who once ruled Olympus with her consort, Ophion, until Cronus and Rhea overthrew them.

Faunus: Italian woodland god, identified as a son of Circe. See especially Book 37.

Gaea: Earth personified as a goddess, mother by Uranus/Sky of the Titans and of many monstrous figures.

Galatea: Nereid of Sicily loved by the jealous Cyclops Polyphemus, who crushed her lover Acis with a boulder. See especially Books 6, 14, 39, 40, and 43.

Ganymede, Ganymedes: Trojan prince famed for beauty. Zeus, infatuated, took the form of an eagle and abducted him to Olympus, where he became cup-bearer to the gods. See especially Books 8, 23, 25, and 33.

Geryones: Three-headed giant. In the tenth of his Labors, Heracles slew Geryones and stole his cattle.

Gigarto: Maenad featured in the fight with Lycurgus, later wounded by Morrheus, and eventually slain in battle. See especially Books 21, 30, and 33.

Glaucus (1): Lycian ally of the Trojans in Homer's *Iliad*. Discovering their grandfathers had been friends, he and his Greek adversary, Diomedes, swore friendship and exchanged armor, Glaucus giving up his own gold armor for Diomedes' bronze. See Book 22.

Glaucus (2): Originally a mortal fisherman, he ate an enchanted herb and became a fishtailed sea god with the gift of prophecy. See especially Book 1.

Glaucus (3): One of several offspring of Pan who joined the forces of Dionysus in the Indian war. See Book 14.

Glaucus (4): Corinthian son of Sisyphus killed by his horses during funeral games. See book 11.

Hades: Son of Cronus, brother to Zeus and Poseidon, Hades' portion of the cosmos was the underworld, making him god of the dead. His abduction of Demeter's daughter, Persephone, brought about the annual cycle of the seasons.

Harmonia: Daughter of Ares and Aphrodite, foster-daughter of the Pleiad Electra, and foundress with her husband, Cadmus, of the House of Thebes. Her renowned and ill-starred daughters included Dionysus' mother, Semele, as well as Ino, Agavê, and Antinoë. With her divine pedigree, Harmonia was also a goddess of marital and social concord. See especially Books 3, 4, 5, and 12.

Hebe: Ganymede's predecessor as cup-bearer to the gods, she later married Heracles. See especially Books 2, 4, 19, and 33.

Hecaërge: Epithet of Artemis, "the far-worker," from her involvement in archery.

Hecate: Goddess of night and witchcraft, occasionally identified with Selene the Moon.

Hector: Son of Priam, King of Troy, and foremost of the Trojan heroes in the *Iliad*. He was killed by Achilles.

Helios: Titan who, as the personified sun, daily drives his chariot across the heavens. Sometimes conflated with his own son, Phaëthon, or with Apollo. See especially Books 2, 12, and 38.

Helle: Daughter of Ino's husband, Athamas, from a previous marriage. She and her twin, Phrixus, fled Ino's enmity on a flying golden ram, but Helle plummeted into the waters known thereafter as the Hellespont. See especially Books 9 and 10.

Hephaestus: Son of Hera, lame god of metalworking and craftsmanship, responsible for countless marvels, including the chariot of Helios, Achilles' armor, and the magic girdle of Aphrodite, his serially unfaithful wife. See especially Books 5, 25, 26, 29, and 30.

Hera: Queen of heaven, daughter of Cronus, sister and consort of Zeus, and enemy of Dionysus. Hera's vengeful schemes are a driving force in many myths, including those of Heracles, Io, the Golden Fleece, and the Trojan War. In *Tales of Dionysus* she consistently plays the role of antagonist, working against Europa in Book 1, Zagreus in Book 6, Semele in Book 8, Dionysus in Book 9, and throughout the rest of the poem; see especially Books 14, 20, 21, 27, 31, and 32.

Heracles, Hercules: Mortal son of Zeus and Alcmene (thus half-brother of Dionysus), greatest of Greek champions, and the hero of innumerable adventures, among them his famous Twelve Labors. At his death, he was elevated to a place among the stars. See especially Books 25 and 40.

Hermes: Son of Zeus and Maia, god of travelers and thieves, with a talent for dissimulation. His winged helmet and sandals allow lightning-fast travel, and he is frequently employed by his fellow Olympians as a go-between or as an emissary to mortals. In the poem, he is a consistent champion and protector of his younger half-brother Dionysus. See especially Books 3, 8, 9, 35, 38, and 47.

Hippodameia: Her father, Oenomaus, slew any suitor unable to beat him in a chariot race. Pelops borrowed a chariot from Poseidon and suborned Oenomaus' charioteer, Myrtilus, winning the race and Hippodameia's hand. See especially Books 20 and 33.

Hippolyta: Queen of the Amazons, whom Heracles killed and stripped of a famous belt.

Hippomenes: Won in marriage the man-shy huntress Atalanta, whom no suitor could outrace, by dropping in her path three irresistible golden apples. See especially Books 12 and 48.

Hyacinthus: Spartan prince beloved of the god Apollo, who killed him inadvertently with the throw of a discus; transformed after death into the flower that bears his name. See especially Books 3, 10, and 11.

Hyagnis: Legendary inventor of the *aulos,* a double-reeded wind instrument sometimes associated with frenzied Dionysiac or Corybantic rites.

Hydaspes: Eponymous Indian river god and father of the Indian king, Deriades. The river joined the fight against the Dionysian forces. See especially Books 22–24.

Hylas: Heracles' youthful arms-bearer and fellow Argonaut, abducted by nymphs when the ship stopped at an island for water. While Heracles vainly sought him, the Argo sailed without them.

Hymenaeus: Archer in Dionysus' army and object of the god's passion; the name means "wedding hymn." See especially Books 29, 32, and 37.

Hymnus: Young shepherd whose desire for the celibate nymph Nicaea so angered her that she killed him. See Book 15.

Hyperion: Titan whose children were Helios, the Sun; Selene, the Moon; and Eos, the Dawn. See especially Book 12.

Hypermnestra: Only one of Danaus' fifty daughters to refuse his command to murder their husbands the night of their mass wedding. See Book 3.

Iacchus: In the present work, the third divine incarnation of Dionysus, son of the god and the nymph Aura; also occasionally, another name for Dionysus himself. See especially Book 48.

Iapetus: Titan son of Uranus and Gaea and father of Prometheus and Atlas, among others. After the war between the gods and the Titans, Zeus sent him to Tartarus.

Iasion: Demeter spied this handsome youth at Cadmus and Harmonia's wedding and seduced him in a nearby field.

Icarius: Hospitable Athenian gardener to whom Dionysus taught winemaking. His neighbors came, drank, and, believing themselves poisoned, slew him. See especially Book 47.

Idmon: Seer who sailed with the Argonauts despite foreseeing his own death in the adventure. See especially Book 38.

Ino, also Leucothea: Daughter of Cadmus and Harmonia, Dionysus' aunt, and, briefly, his foster mother (incurring Hera's wrath). Surprising her maddened husband, Athamas, in the act of boiling their son Melicertes, she seized the child and leapt into the sea. The two became marine divinities. See especially Books 5, 9, 10, and 21.

Io: Argive princess and object of Zeus' desires, she was transformed into a white heifer. Hera sent a gadfly, which drove her in torment across the known world. Eventually she regained human form and became an ancestress of the royal houses of Thebes and Argos. See especially Books 1, 3, and 31.

Iobacchus, Yobacchus: A name for Dionysus, derived from a ritual cry.

Iolaus: Nephew and companion of Heracles. As Heracles cut off the Hydra's many heads, Iolaus cauterized the wounds, preventing new ones from sprouting.

Iphigeneia: Her father, Agamemnon, attempted to sacrifice her to Artemis. The goddess whisked Iphigeneia to the land of her devotees, the savage Taurians. Iphigeneia became their priestess, and when her brother Orestes appeared there, saved his life. See Books 13 and 15.

Iphimedeia: Mortal mother of the preternaturally large and violent twins, Otos and Ephialtes, who assaulted Olympus and imprisoned Ares in a bronze jar. See Book 2.

Itylus, Itys: Son of Procne, who served him in a stew to her husband, who had cut out her sister Philomela's tongue after raping her. See especially Books 44 and 47.

Ixion: Thessalian king who tried to rape Hera. Zeus bound him to a burning wheel which revolves forever in the underworld.

Lacedaemon: Legendary founder of Sparta, son of Zeus and the Pleiad Taÿgetê.

Ladon: God of the eponymous Arcadian river, father of Daphne. See Book 42.

Lamos: Anatolian river god whose daughters were the nursemaids of Dionysus. See Book 9.

Laodameia: Daughter of Bellerophon and mother, by Zeus, of the formidable Trojan ally Sarpedon. See Book 7.

Learchus: Elder son of Athamas and Ino. Athamas in his madness took him for a stag and slew him. See especially Book 10.

Leneus: Satyr companion of Dionysus' youth, who later took part in the Indian war. See especially Books 10 and 36.

Leto: Titan and mother, by Zeus, of Apollo and Artemis. Hera persecuted her relentlessly. See especially Books 2, 4, 27, and 48.

Lyaeus: A name for Dionysus; it means "loosener," "liberator," or "deliverer."

Lycaon (1): Arcadian king who brought doom on himself by feeding human flesh to a mysterious guest who was Zeus in disguise. See Book 18.

Lycaon (2): Son of Priam killed by Achilles in the *Iliad*. See Book 22.

Lycurgus (1): Thracian bandit-king whose ferocious attack drives Dionysus into the sea, throwing the Bacchic forces into disarray. See especially Books 20 and 21.

Lycurgus (2): Semi-legendary Spartan ruler and lawgiver who forged that city's militaristic society. See book 41.

Macris: Daughter of Aristaeus and Autonoë and early caregiver of Dionysus. See Book 21.

Maia: Eldest of the Pleiades and mother by Zeus of Hermes.

Maron: Dancing satyr, son of Silenus, and Dionysus' charioteer. See especially Books 18 and 19.

Marsyas: A satyr who challenged Apollo to a contest on the *aulos*. Apollo won, then flayed Marsyas.

Medusa: Snake-haired Gorgon. Since the sight of her turned one to stone, Perseus beheaded her using his shield as a mirror. The winged horse Perseus sprang from her blood, and her severed head became a weapon Perseus wielded. See especially Books 25 and 47.

Megaera: One of the Furies.

Melampus: Celebrated seer, conversant in the speech of animals, who came to rule in Argos. See Book 47.

Melaneus: Archer in the Indian army who wounded Dionysus' lover Hymenaeus. See Book 29.

Melicertes: Younger son of Ino, thus Dionysus' cousin and foster-brother. When Melicertes' father tried to boil him, Ino leapt into the sea with her child in her arms. Both became marine divinities, Melicertes' name becoming Palaemon. See Books 5 and 39.

Melisseus: One of the Curetes (Cretan devotees of Rhea, guards of the infant Zeus) who joined Dionysus' army. The name means "bee-man." See especially Books 13 and 37.

Mene: Selene, the Moon.

Menelaus: King of Sparta, brother to Agamemnon, and husband of Helen, whose abduction by the Trojan Paris began the war with Troy.

Merope: One of the Pleiades.

Methê: Wife of Assyrian king Staphylos, who plays host to Dionysus; the name means "drunkenness." See especially Books 18, 19, and 20.

Miletus: son of Asterius and founder of the city of Miletos.

Mimas: Corybant fighting in Dionysus' army. See Books 13 and 28.

Minos: Son of Zeus and Europa, king of Crete, and keeper of the Minotaur in its labyrinth. Father of Ariadne. After death he became a judge in the underworld. See especially Book 25.

Mnemosyne: Titan, mother by Zeus of the nine muses; her name means "memory."

Modaeus: Hero in Dionysus' army, later made governor of the defeated Indians. See especially Book 32.

Moira: Any of the three Fates.

Morrheus: Foremost Indian hero and son-in-law of Deriades, wracked by passion for the maenad Chalcomedê. See especially Books 30, 32–36, and 39–40.

Myrrha: Tricked her father into a sexual union, then fled his wrath, finally becoming a myrrh tree before bearing a son, Adonis. See especially Book 2.

Myrtilus: Charioteer of King Oenomaus, whom he betrayed in the king's chariot race with Pelops for the hand of Hippodameia. See especially Books 20 and 33.

Mystis: Handmaid to Ino and devoted nurse of the infant Dionysus, first employer of the paraphernalia that later became part of Dionysian initiation rituals; her name means "initiate." See especially Books 9 and 10.

Narcissus: Known for his beauty, he fell in love with his own reflection in a pool and wasted away with longing, becoming the flower that bears his name. See Books 10, 11, 15, and 48.

Nemesis: Divine personification of vengeance, punisher of pride.

Nephelê: First wife of Ino's husband, Athamas. When Ino persecuted Nephelê's children, Phrixus and Helle, she sent a flying golden ram to rescue them, with mixed results; the name means "cloud."

Nereus: Sea god and father of the fifty sea nymphs known as the nereids. See Books 1, 2, 6, 9, 10, and 13.

Nicaea: Virgin huntress who spurns the advances of herdsman Hymnus, whom she eventually slays. She is raped by Dionysus in her sleep and gives birth to a daughter, Teletê. See Books 15 and 48.

Nike: Divine personification of victory, daughter of Zeus and sometimes driver of his chariot. See especially Books 2, 4, and 5.

Niobe (1): Boasted of her fourteen children to the goddess Leto, who had only two, Artemis and Apollo. Artemis killed Niobe's seven daughters; Apollo, her seven sons. Niobe, in her grief, turned to stone. See Books 2 and 12.

Niobe (2): Mortal daughter of Phoroneus of Argos, very early love of Zeus. See Book 32.

Oceanus, Ocean: Child of Earth and Sky, god of the earth-encircling river of the same name and ranking deity of all waters. See especially Books 1, 2, and 23.

Oeagrus: Father of Orpheus by the muse Calliope and himself a musician as well as a formidable warrior in Dionysus' army in India. See Books 13 and 22.

Oenomaus: Father of Hippodamia, who forced his daughter's suitors to compete in a chariot race against him. When they lost, he had them beheaded. The nineteenth suitor, Pelops, won the race and married Hippodamia. See especially Books 20 and 33.

Oenone: Maenad in Dionysus' army. See Books 13, 29, and 43.

Opheltes (1): Son of King Lycurgus of Nemea and killed as an infant by a serpent. See Book 35.

Opheltes (2): A warrior killed by Deriades and for whom Dionysus builds an elaborate funeral pyre. See Book 32.

Ophion: Titan who ruled Olympus with his consort Eurynome until deposed by Cronus and Rhea. See especially Books 2, 12, and 41.

Orestes: His mother, Clytemnestra, murdered his father, Agamemnon, upon his return from Troy. Orestes avenged his father by killing his mother and was hounded thereafter by the Furies for the crime of matricide. See Books 13 and 14.

Orontes: Indian commander and hero who wrought havoc among Dionysus' army, then engaged the god in single combat. Defeated by the thyrsus, he fell upon his own sword. See Books 17 and 40.

Orpheus: Preeminent musician and poet trained by Apollo, his music charmed even animals, rocks, and trees. See Books 13, 19, and 41.

Orsiboë: Wife of the Indian king Deriades. See especially Books 30 and 40.

Otos: Giant son of Iphimedeia, who with his brother, Ephialtes, assaulted Olympus, attempted the abduction of Hera and Artemis, and imprisoned Ares in a bronze jar. See especially Books 2, 5, and 36.

Palaemon: Divine name of Ino's son Melicertes. See Books 5 and 39.

Pallas: Frequent name for Athena.

Pallene: Her suitors must wrestle her, but her father murders every one. Dionysus pins her, wins her, and slays the father. See Books 43 and 48.

Pan: Half-goat god of flocks, shepherds, and the wilderness, associated with sexuality and fertility. His riotous followers of similar shape are also known as "Pans." See especially Books 14, 16, and 42.

Panopeia: A sea nymph, daughter of Nereus. See Books 39 and 43.

Pasiphaë: Queen of Crete, and wife of Minos. Poseidon cursed her with lust for a bull; their union produced the Minotaur. Mother also of Phaedra and Ariadne. See Book 33.

Pasithea: One of the Charites, or Graces, consort of Hypnos (Sleep). See especially Books 31 and 33.

Pegasus: Divine winged horse born from the blood of the beheaded Medusa; ridden by Bellerophon to defeat the Chimera, among other adventures. See Books 7, 11, 25, 28, 37, and 38.

Peitho: Divine personification of persuasion and seduction. As an attendant of Aphrodite, in mortal guise she guided Cadmus into Samothrace. See Book 3.

Pelasgus: Mythical ancestor of the Pelasgians (ancient forerunners of the Greeks). See Book 47.

Peleus: Mortal son of Aeacus, married to the sea nymph Thetis; their son is Achilles. See Books 22, 37, and 43.

Pelops: Eponym of the Peloponnesus. His father, Tantalus, served him in pieces to the gods at a banquet, hoping to fool them. Undeceived, the gods reassembled and resurrected him. Pelops went on to win and wed Hippodamia, becoming ancestor to the House of Atreus. See Books 18, 33, and 37.

Penthesilea: Amazon warrior and daughter of Ares who fought on the side of the Trojans in the Trojan War. She was killed by Achilles. See Book 35.

Pentheus: Theban king, grandson of Cadmus, and cousin of Dionysus, whose worship he resisted, angering the god. In a Bacchic frenzy, Pentheus' mother, Agavê, and the other Theban women mistook him for a lion and tore him limb from limb. See Books 44, 45, and 46.

Persephone: Daughter of Demeter and mother by Zeus of Zagreus. Queen of the underworld following her abduction by Hades, she spent half the year above ground, where she was a goddess of spring, fertility, and renewal. See especially Books 5, 6, 30, 31 andd 44.

Perseus: Mortal son of Zeus and Danaë who beheaded Medusa and rescued Andromeda from the sea monster Cetus. Thanks to winged sandals borrowed from Hermes, he was able to fly. When Dionysus arrived at Argos to propagate his cult, Perseus resisted ferociously until Hermes reconciled the half-brothers. See especially Book 25 and also Books 13, 18, and 47.

Phaëthon: Son of the sun god, Helios. Allowed to drive his father's chariot across the sky, he lost control of the horses, fell to the earth, and died. His name is sometimes used for Helios himself. See especially Book 38 and also Books 15 and 30.

Phaedra: Cretan princess, wife of Theseus, daughter of Pasiphaë and Minos. See Book 48.

Phanes (1): Primeval deity of light, a "first-born" god hatched from the world-egg of Cronus. See Books 9, 12, and 19.

Phanes (2): One of the Pans in the army of Dionysus. See Book 14.

Philomel, Philomela, Philomena: Her sister's husband, Tereus, raped her and cut out her tongue. Afterward, she was turned into a nightingale. See Books 2, 4, 44, and 47.

Phlogius (1): Indian soldier in the army of Deriades; the name means "fiery." See Book 26.

Phlogius (2): Soldier in army of Dionysus killed by Morrheus. See Book 35.

Phobos (1): Divine personification of fear, son of Ares. See Books 20 and 39.

Phobos (2): A son of Pan. See Book 14.

Phoebus: Frequent name for Apollo; the name means "radiant." See Book 36.

Phosphoros: "Light-bearer," the Morning or Evening Star.

Phryxus: Son of Athamas and his first wife Nephelê; he escaped a mysterious doom by fleeing through the air on a golden-fleeced ram.

Pierides: Nine sisters who lost to the Muses in a singing contest; they were then turned into birds. See Books 1, 2, 19, and 41.

Pithos: Greybeard tippler and servant at Staphylos' palace, later a member of Dionysus' army; the name means "winejar." See Books 18, 19, 20, and 30.

Pitys: A nymph pursued by Pan who turned into a pine tree to escape him. See Books 2, 16, and 42.

Pleiades: Seven sisters, daughters of Atlas and the sea nymph Pleione, who were transformed into stars, giving their name to the Pleiades star-cluster. Electra, step-mother of Harmonia, is one of the Pleiades, and recounts to Cadmus her sorrows in being separated from them. See Books 1, 2, 3, 13, 38, and 42.

Plouto: Nymph loved by Zeus and mother of his son Tantalus. See Books 1, 7, and 48.

Polydectes: Enamoured of Danaë, he dispatched her inconvenient son, Perseus, on an impossible mission to slay a Gorgon. Perseus returned with the head of Medusa, the sight of which turned Polydectes to stone. See Books 25 and 47.

Polydorus: Eldest son of Cadmus and Harmonia. See Books 5, 8, and 46.

Polyphemus: Cyclops, son of Poseidon, in love with the sea nymph Galatea, blinded by Odysseus as described in the *Odyssey*. See Books 6, 14, and 39.

Poseidon, also Earthshaker, Seabluehair: Son of Cronus and Rhea, brother of Zeus and Hades, and god of the sea, earthquakes, storms, and horses. See Books 1, 3, 8, 40, and 42.

Procne: Wife of King Tereus, who raped and mutilated her sister Philomela. In revenge, Procne killed her son by Tereus, forcing Tereus to eat him. She then turned into a swallow. See Books 2, 4, 44, and 48.

Prometheus: Titan and benefactor of humankind through the gift of fire. Zeus chained him to a rock and sent an eagle each day to eat his liver, which grew back each night. See especially Book 2 and Book 33.

Proteus: Shapeshifting sea god, whose prolonged wrestling match with Menelaus is described in the *Odyssey*. See Books 1, 3, 21, 39, 42, and 43.

Protonoë, Protonoeia: A daughter of the Indian king Deriades. See Book 34 and especially 35.

Pyramus: Eponymous river diety and lover of Thisbe. See Books 6 and 12.

Pyrrha: Wife of Deucalion, who with him survived the great flood caused by Zeus and regenerated the human race. See Books 3 and 19.

Rhadamanthys: Son of Zeus and Europa, brother of Minos, known as a lawgiver in Crete and, later, a judge of the dead. See Book 19.

Rhea: Wife and sister of Cronus and mother of Zeus, Poseidon, Hera, and other gods. Cronus swallowed her children at birth until she tricked him substituting a stone for her youngest child, Zeus, who was then raised in a cave on Crete. Sometimes identified with Cybele, she is Dionysus' grandmother and the young god's final and only successful caregiver. See Books 8, 9, 10, 12, and 13.

Scylla (1): Famed six-headed monster, belted with dogs' heads, who seized and devoured many sailors from ships passing through the Straits of Messina. See Book 42.

Scylla (2): Daughter of Nisus whose purple lock of hair magically protected the city of Megara. Out of love for Minos, who was besieging the city, Scylla cut off her father's lock while he slept, causing the city's fall. Disgusted by this faithlessness, Minos spurned Scylla and she leaped into the sea in despair. See Book 25.

Selene, also Selena: Divine personification of the Moon.

Semele: Daughter of Cadmus, beloved of Zeus, and mother of Dionysus. At Hera's urging, she asked Zeus to reveal himself in his true form; when he did so, she could not abide the sight and died as struck by lightning. Deified after her death, she became known also as Thyonê. See Books 5, 7, and especially 8.

Silenus: An older satyr, and companion of Dionysus. In the plural, sileni, the group of satyrs collectively. See especially Book 10.

Solon: Athenian statesman of the sixth–seventh centuries BCE, lawmaker, and poet, whose reforms laid the groundwork for Athenian democracy. See Book 41.

Staphylos: Assyrian king who hosts a drunken party for Dionysus and his entourage, then dies the following day. Dionysus consoles the family with more wine, and they depart with him for the Indian war. The root of the name means "bunch of grapes." See Book 18.

Steropes: Cyclops in the army of Dionysus; the name means "lightning."

Syrinx: An Arcadian nymph, beloved of Pan. When she fled his advances, she was turned into a clump of reeds. The name means "reed" or "pan-pipe." See Book 2.

Tantalus: When the gods visited him, he fed them his son, Pelops as a test; Pelops was resurrected, but Tantalus was punished in Hades, placed in water up to his neck, which he could not drink, and with fruit low over his head, which he could not eat; father also of Niobe. See Books 1, 10, 18, 35, and 48.

Taÿgetê: One of the Pleiades and special companion to Artemis, eponymous nymph of Mt. Taygetus near Sparta. See Book 3.

Tectaphus: An Indian archer who was saved from starvation in prison by suckling from the breasts of his daughter Eërië. See Book 26.

Teiresias: In Nonnus' version of the story, blinded by Athena for seeing her naked, he was compensated with the gifts of prophecy and longevity, serving seven generations of the royal house of Thebes. See Books 5, 7, 20, 45, and 46.

Telamon: King of Salamis, brother of Peleus, and father of Ajax and Teucer, he was also an Argonaut and friend of Heracles. See Books 13 and 37.

Teletê: Daughter of Nicaea, who bore her after being assaulted by Dionysus, noted for her dancing; the name means "initiate into the mysteries." See Books 16 and 48.

Tereus: Husband of Procne and rapist of Philomela; all three were eventually turned into birds. See Books 2 and 4.

Terpsichore (1): One of the nine Muses, associated with lyric poetry and dance. See Book 13.

Terpsichore (2): Maenad in the army of Dionysus. See Book 29.

Tethys: Titan, wife of Oceanus. See Books 8, 38, 40, and 41.

Teucer: Famed as an archer, he was a son of Telamon and brother to Ajax, for whose fate at Troy his father blamed him. See Books 13 and 28.

Thasos: Son of Agenor who sailed with his brother Cadmus to search for Europa, eponymous king of the Aegan island of Thasos. See Book 2.

Thaumas: A Titan, and the father of both Iris and the Harpies; the root of the name means "amazement." See Book 26.

Themis: Titan and goddess of natural law and divine order.

Themisto: Third wife to Athamas. Attempting to murder the children of her predecessor, Ino, she inadvertently killed her own. See Books 9 and 10.

Theseus: Athenian hero who slew the Cretan Minotaur with the help of princess Ariadne. On the voyage home, he abandoned her on Naxos, where Dionysus encountered and wed her. See Books 47 and 48.

Thetis: A nereid sea nymph, wife of Peleus, and mother of Achilles.

Thisbe: Eponymous river nymph and star-crossed lover of Pyramus. See Books 6 and 12.

Thoösa: Daughter of Phorcys and mother by Poseidon of Polyphemus. See Book 39.

Thyonê: Dionysus' mother, Semele, after her apotheosis; the root of the name means "incense," "smoke," and "sacrifice." See Book 1.

Tisiphone: One of the Furies. See Books 10, 12, and 44.

Tithonus: Bridegroom of Eos, Dawn. who obtained for him the gift of immortality but failed to ask for eternal youth. See Books 15 and 48.

Tityus: Giant who attempted to rape Leto and was slain by her son, Apollo. Each day in the underworld, where he was staked to the ground, vultures ate his liver. See Books 2, 4, and 20.

Triptolemus: A prince of Eleusis, charioteer of the goddess Demeter and associate of her rites. See Book 13.

Tritogeneia: Athena. See Books 13 and 28.

Tros: Mythical ancient king of Troy.

Tylus: Eponymous ancestor of the Lydian clan of Tylonians, in legend killed by a poisonous snake. See Book 25.

Typho/Typhoeus/Typhon/Typhoon: Colossal, hundred-headed, two hundred-armed monster, son of Earth, who nearly overcame Zeus in an epic battle for cosmic supremacy. See Books 1 and 2.

Tyro: She fell in love with the river Enipeus; Poseidon visited her in Enipeus' shape, fathering Pelias and Nereus. See Books 1, 8, and 42.

Urania: One of the nine Muses, particularly associated with astronomy. See Books 24, 33, and 38.

Uranus: Primordial sky god and father of the Titans, who was castrated by his son Cronus. From his severed genitals flung into the sea rose Aphrodite. See Books 2, 13, and 41.

Zagreus: Infant son of Zeus and Persephone, cut to pieces by the Titans at Hera's insistence, and sometimes referred to as the first Dionysus. Zeus in his grief hatched a plan for a second Zagreus: Dionysus. See Books 5, 6, 10, 24, 36, 39, 47, and 48.

Zeus: Supreme Olympian god, ruler of the cosmos, father of Dionysus, and husband of Hera. His philandering and her ire are the mainsprings of innumerable myths. His father was the Titan Cronus, hence the epithets Cronides and Cronion. See especially Books 1, 8, 24, 31, and 36.

Geographical Index

In the following pages we have included places and geographical features we believe will be of greatest interest to readers. We have not distinguished between real and mythical or fanciful places, although we have not included the frequent instances in which a place or feature is fully personified as a god or nymph; when in Book 23, for example, the army crosses the river Hydaspes on inflated bladders, we cite the occurrence of the name in the index below, but when the river-god Hydaspes begins to speak a few lines later, we do not. We also have silently folded in adjectival forms of a place along with the proper noun, "the Spartan land," for example, along with "Sparta."